Integrated Marketing Communications

Integrated Marketing Communications

FIFTH EDITION **STRATEGIC PLANNING PERSPECTIVES** KEITH J. TUCKWELL

St. Lawrence College

 Pearson

EDITORIAL DIRECTOR: Claudine O'Donnell
ACQUISITIONS EDITOR: Darcey Pepper
MARKETING MANAGER: Leigh-Anne Graham
PROGRAM MANAGER: John Polanszky
PROJECT MANAGER: Susan Johnson
MANAGER OF CONTENT DEVELOPMENT: Suzanne Schaan
DEVELOPMENTAL EDITOR: Christine Langone
PRODUCTION SERVICES: Rajiv Sharma, iEnergizer Aptara, Inc.
PERMISSIONS PROJECT MANAGER: Shruti Jamadagni

PHOTO PERMISSIONS RESEARCH: Monika Schurmann
c/o Red Packet Productions
TEXT PERMISSIONS RESEARCH: Monika Schurmann
c/o Red Packet Productions
INTERIOR DESIGNER: Anthony Leung
COVER DESIGNER: Anthony Leung
COVER IMAGE: Bloomua/Fotolia
VICE-PRESIDENT, CROSS MEDIA AND
PUBLISHING SERVICES: Gary Bennett

Pearson Canada Inc., 26 Prince Andrew Place, Don Mills, Ontario M3C 2T8.

ISBN 13: 978-0-13-427037-1

1   16

Library and Archives Canada Cataloguing in Publication

Tuckwell, Keith J. (Keith John), 1950-, author
      Integrated marketing communications : strategic planning
perspectives / Keith J. Tuckwell, St. Lawrence College.—Fifth edition.

Includes bibliographical references and index.
ISBN 978-0-13-427037-1 (paperback)

      1. Communication in marketing—Textbooks. I. Title.

HF5415.123.T82 2017   658.8'02   C2016-904842-X

To Esther ... for your patience, understanding, love, and support over the years

Brief Contents

Contents

PART 2   PLANNING FOR INTEGRATED MEDIA   93

Preface

Teachers face many challenges in the classroom. It is difficult to get students to read a textbook; multicultural classrooms present language problems; and it is often hard to cover course material in the time allotted. This textbook is designed to conquer these problems. My primary goal is to present essential elements of integrated marketing communications in a clear, concise, and informative manner. Many students who have read previous editions comment that this is an "enjoyable" text to read!

Keeping content current in such a rapidly changing environment is a constant challenge. The impact of new technologies makes it difficult for educators and practitioners to keep pace. The ongoing shift to digital communications presents both challenges and opportunities for advertisers and their marketing communications agencies. Striking the right balance among the communications options is the primary task of the marketing communications agencies responsible for making recommendations to their clients. In such a rapidly changing environment, teachers and students must recognize that presenting the latest information in a text is difficult. I have done my very best to ensure that the content presented here is as up to date as possible. The core content and the strategic planning principles included reflect contemporary practice.

From a teaching perspective, textbook readability has always been an issue with me. Readability is a primary strength of *Integrated Marketing Communications: Strategic Planning Perspectives*. The text is written in a straightforward, easy-to-understand manner and is full of examples and illustrations that students will quickly identify with. If you accept the notion that being familiar with something makes it easier to understand and apply, then your students will be better equipped to develop a marketing communications plan once they have read this text.

Most courses in marketing communications are one semester (14 to 15 weeks) in length with only 45 to 60 course hours available for teaching. You will find the format of this text ideal for such a course. Its *primary strength* is that it is truly a marketing communications text. It is not an advertising text with additional chapters devoted to integrated marketing communications (IMC) content. This text offers balance across the various components of marketing communications. Current users have identified *other strengths*, which are:

- It is the only Canadian IMC text available, and features a Canadian perspective on media and marketing communications practice instead of an American one.

- There is an emphasis on strategic planning, with a separate chapter devoted to the subject as well as discussion of it throughout the text. The concept of "integration" is stressed and demonstrated continually.

- The lead-in chapter on branding is a natural starting point for marketing communications planning, since all plans start with a sound understanding of the brand.

- There is ample discussion of recent trends and issues facing the industry, identifying the challenges faced by practitioners.

- It is the only text on the market offering an illustration of a strategic plan, which demonstrates how an organization applies planning principles and concepts.

- Material is presented in an "easy-to-understand" writing style—practical, friendly, and student-oriented.

The textbook includes four parts and 12 core chapters that cover all aspects of integrated marketing communications. A common planning model is presented in relevant chapters to demonstrate how the various components of marketing communications work together to achieve objectives. Each chapter includes two **IMC Highlight boxes** that show how organizations apply marketing communications concepts. Approximately 70 percent of these boxes are new.

Appendix 1 offers information about how to plan and buy media time, and is an ideal supplement to all media-related chapters. **Appendix 2** presents an integrated marketing communications plan, something you will not find in any other text.

Some of the key issues and trends addressed in this edition of the text include:

- The integration of long-term strategic plans (all primary forms of media and marketing communications) with short-term tactical plans (experiential, event, and public relations tactics).

- The constantly changing consumers' media habits, which create a dynamic situation that presents new challenges and opportunities for reaching target markets.

- The impact of new technologies, which are changing the communications playing field and producing new opportunities for reaching consumers more directly through mobile devices, social media, and video games.

- The influence of database management techniques and customer relationship management programs on the direction of marketing communications strategies, moving them away from macro-based (mass appeal or traditional forms of targeting) toward micro-based (individual targeting).

- The impact of technology on media planning and media buying

- The expanding role of experiential marketing, public relations, mobile communications, and social media communications, and the presentation of new insights into this trend.

The impact of technology on media planning and media buying is presented in more detail. New concepts, such as programmatic media buying and real time bidding, are included in Appendix 2 as both concepts directly affect the buying process for interactive media.

Organization of the Text

The book is divided into four essential parts.

PART 1: UNDERSTANDING INTEGRATED MARKETING COMMUNICATIONS

This section presents an overview of essential inputs that a manager would consider when developing a marketing communications plan. The content included in Chapter 1, Integrated Marketing Communications: An Overview, introduces the various components of the marketing communications mix and summarizes the essential concepts dealing with consumer and organizational behaviour. This edition includes additional discussion on the shift to digital communications and its prominence in the marketing communications mix. The chapter also discusses many of the ethical issues associated with the practice of marketing communications.

Chapter 2, Strategic Planning Principles, shifts the focus to strategic planning. Relationships are drawn between plans and planning at various levels of an organization and how they are integrated. The structure and content of a marketing plan and a marketing communications plan are examined in order to show how plans work together to resolve marketing problems.

Chapter 3, Branding Strategy, introduces the concept of branding and branding strategy. Discussion about branding is strategically located to precede detailed coverage of the components of the marketing communications mix. Branding strategies and brand positioning strategies are the foundation upon which marketing communications strategies are devised. New insights into the importance of brand trust and brand loyalty and the need for a strong positioning strategy have been added.

PART 2: PLANNING FOR INTEGRATED MEDIA

This section examines planning considerations for all primary media choices. Chapter 4, Advertising Planning: Creative, introduces the communications process and the various planning concepts that are considered when briefing an agency about message requirements. The role of strategies and tactics—and the distinctions between them and creative objectives—is considered.

Chapter 5, Advertising Planning: Broadcast, Print, and Out-of-Home Media, presents the media planning process and stresses the importance of creating an effective yet efficient media plan. The various strategic decisions that apply to using broadcast, print, and out-of-home media alternatives are presented in detail.

Chapter 6, Planning for Direct Response Communications, introduces the rapidly expanding field of direct response communications. Since direct response relies on database management techniques, there is considerable emphasis on customer relationship management practices and the crucial role played by individualized marketing communications strategies in fostering solid customer relationships.

Chapter 7, Planning for Online and Interactive Communications, examines the expanding role of web-based communications, mobile communications, and social media communications in the marketing communications mix. The chapter offers expanded coverage of all forms of interactive communications. There is an emphasis on technology and how it affects consumers' media consumption patterns, and ultimately, media planning decisions.

PART 3: PLANNING FOR INTEGRATED MARKETING

Because organizations look for synergy, the objective is to integrate related marketing and marketing communications practices with the media strategies already presented in the text. Chapter 8, Sales Promotion, introduces the various sales promotion alternatives that are frequently employed in integrated marketing communications plans. The roles of consumer promotions and trade promotions are examined in detail.

Chapter 9, Public Relations, examines the role of public relations in communications. The content focuses on the various strategies and tactics that are available, planning procedures, and measurement techniques. A new section on media relations has been added to show the importance of building effective relations with the press. A new section on internal public relations has also been added to this chapter.

Chapter 10, Experiential Marketing, Events, and Sponsorships, examines the expanding role of experiential marketing, event marketing, and sponsorships in contemporary marketing. It introduces the criteria for participating in events, and the steps and procedures for planning an event.

Chapter 11, Personal Selling, covers the role of personal selling in a variety of business settings. Personal selling adds a human component to the integrated marketing communications mix, and for this reason plays a very important role in establishing and building solid customer relationships.

PART 4: MEASURING PLAN PERFORMANCE

This section examines the role of various research procedures for evaluating the effectiveness of marketing communications programs. Chapter 12, Evaluating Marketing Communications Programs, introduces some fundamental methodologies for collecting and analyzing primary research data, and distinguishes between qualitative and quantitative data. The role and influence of collecting and interpreting information on the development of marketing communications strategies are considered. New content on various social media measurement techniques have been added to this chapter.

Appendix 1, Media Buying Principles and Media Information Resources, is a supplement that provides additional media details and shows students some fundamental procedures for estimating costs and buying media time and space in a variety of media and other components of the marketing communications mix. Students can quickly refer to media-buying information in this specific section. Review questions will challenge the students to understand and apply rate card information.

Appendix 2, Integrated Marketing Communications Plan: Mr. Sub, provides an example of a marketing communications plan so that students can quickly see the relationship between various planning principles such as objectives, strategies, and execution, and between the various components of the marketing communications mix with respect to how each contributes to achieving objectives. The integrated marketing communications plan has been revised to include a social media component. No other text offers an illustrative marketing communications plan.

Success Stories Dramatize Integrated Marketing Communications Practice

Each chapter includes at least two **IMC Highlight boxes.** These inserts reflect important aspects of marketing communications planning or provide actual illustrations of how organizations apply marketing communications concepts. By way of example, students will learn how

- Boston Pizza planned and implemented a new campaign to attract a "family" target market.

- ING DIRECT transformed and rebranded itself to Tangerine with the help of an intensive and carefully phased-in communications campaign.

- Axe personal care products repositioned its brand portfolio to appeal to an older target market.

- The Stratford Festival effectively used a social media campaign to boost ticket sales.

- McDonald's effectively uses sales promotion techniques to build its market share in the restaurant coffee market.

- Nike effectively uses ambush marketing techniques to gain a presence in elite events it does not sponsor.

- Harry Rosen, a prominent men's fashion retailer, effectively uses personal selling, interaction, and service to build long-term relationships with customers.

Other companies and brands that appear in feature stories include General Motors, MEC (formerly Mountain Equipment Co-op), Scotiabank, Budweiser, Honda Canada, Apple, and TD CanadaTrust.

Pedagogy

Learning Objectives. Each chapter starts with a list of learning objectives directly related to the key concepts contained in the chapter.

Advertisements, Figures, and Charts. Throughout each chapter, key concepts and applications are illustrated with strong visual material. Sample advertisements and other forms of marketing communications augment the Canadian perspective and demonstrate important aspects of marketing communications strategy and execution.

Key Terms. Key terms are highlighted in boldface in the text and in colour in page margins, where they are accompanied by definitions. Students also have quick access to key terms and definitions in the glossary.

Chapter Summaries. The summary at the end of each chapter reinforces major points and concepts.

Review Questions, and Discussion and Application Questions. Both sets of questions allow students to review material and apply concepts learned in the chapter.

Appendix 1, Media Buying Principles and Media Information Resources. The essentials of buying media time and space in various media outlets are covered in this section. Review questions that test students' understanding of and ability to apply rate card information are included.

Appendix 2, Integrated Marketing Communications Plan: Mr. Sub. This plan shows how various elements of marketing communications combine to form an integrated marketing communications plan. A variety of charts and figures are included to show how media and marketing communications budget allocations are presented in a plan.

Glossary. A glossary of all key terms and definitions appears at the end of the textbook.

Supplements

The following instructor supplements are available for download from a password-protected section of Pearson Education Canada's online catalogue (www.pearsoned.ca/highered). Navigate to your text's catalogue page to view a list of available supplements. See your local sales representative for details and access.

INSTRUCTOR'S RESOURCE MANUAL

The Instructor's Resource Manual includes learning objectives, chapter highlights that can act as lecture outlines, additional illustrations of key concepts that can be built into lectures, and answers to review and discussion questions.

TEST ITEM FILE

This test bank in Microsoft Word format contains over 1000 questions in multiple choice, true/false, short answer, and essay formats.

POWERPOINT® SLIDES

A complete set of slides that are specifically designed or culled from the text is available electronically. Full-colour versions of ads, photos, and figures from the text, found in the Image Library, can be inserted into your presentations.

IMAGE LIBRARY

The Image Library contains various full-colour images from the text such as photos, ads, and figures. Instructors can integrate these images into their own presentations.

Acknowledgments

Many companies, organizations, and associations contributed visual material for this book. Each contributor is acknowledged on the figures and charts appearing throughout the book. I would like to sincerely thank all of these suppliers for their cooperation and contribution.

For undertaking the task of reviewing the text I would like to thank Hilary Sadler, McMaster University Downtown Centre for Continuing Education.

From Pearson Canada Inc. and its suppliers I would like to thank Darcey Pepper, Karen Townsend, Christine Langone, and Susan Johnson. Special thanks to Monika Schurmann and Sarah Ellen Horsfall for their hard work on securing permissions. I would also thank copy editor Ruth Chernia, proofreader Sally Glover, and production editor Rajiv Sharma for their diligent work on this project.

A very special thank you to my wife, Esther, for her patience, understanding, and unwavering support. Another one is done!

Keith J. Tuckwell
2016

Understanding Integrated Marketing Communications

Part 1 focuses on several introductory issues that are associated with the development of integrated marketing communications programs.

Chapter 1 introduces the components of the integrated marketing communications mix and the factors that encourage their use. The latter part of the chapter introduces the reader to a variety of ethical issues that confront marketing communications practitioners.

Chapter 2 introduces the student to essential strategic planning principles while drawing relationships between the planning that occurs at various levels of an organization. The various inputs for marketing and marketing communications planning are presented along with the content of typical marketing and marketing communications plans. The intent is to show how integrated planning provides solutions to marketing problems.

Chapter 3 concentrates on issues related to branding strategy. Marketing communications strategies are the primary vehicle for building the image of a brand or company. Since brand positioning is the focal point of most marketing communications strategies, the role that positioning strategy statements play in the development of communications campaigns is examined in detail. The role and influence of packaging and product design strategies and their impact on brand image are also examined.

CHAPTER 1

Integrated Marketing Communications: An Overview

Learning Objectives

After studying this chapter, you will be able to

1. Appreciate the role of integrated marketing communications planning in business today

2. Identify the components of the integrated marketing communications mix

3. Identify the conditions that have led to the emergence of integrated marketing communications

4. Explain how consumer behaviour and organizational buying behaviour influence marketing communications

5. Identify basic ethical issues confronting marketing communications practice

6. Describe the role that laws and regulations play in guiding marketing communications in Canada

Organizations today are searching for complete solutions to their communications needs and are calling upon experts in various marketing communications areas to get the job done. The challenge for organizations is to successfully combine various communications disciplines into an effective marketing communications strategy and plan. This often requires specialists from various external agencies to collaborate on projects—that too is a challenge for organizations to coordinate.

The environment that businesses presently operate in continues to change rapidly. The influence of technology alone has forced business organizations to examine how they deliver messages to their target markets. Generally speaking, there has been a movement toward targeted media and away from mass media. People's media habits have changed. The average consumer relies less on newspapers and television, and more on computers and smart phones for receiving news and commercial messages. Consequently, marketing organizations are shifting their spending to digital media options and are experimenting with other, more personalized activities, such as social media and experiential marketing. Going beyond traditional forms of communications helps create "buzz" for products.

How people consume media is changing. Wise marketing organizations keep track of that change. There are only so many hours in a day, and people are spending more time than ever online with digital and social media. Advertisers, therefore, are placing more ads on the Internet and are looking at innovative ways to deliver advertising messages via social media outlets such as Facebook, Twitter, YouTube, Pinterest, and Instagram. Their objective is to deliver messages to where their customers are.

The nature of marketing communications planning has changed dramatically. No longer do companies rely on disjointed strategies from a variety of sources, even though those sources are experts at what they do. The overall goal of communications now is to deliver the same message through a variety of media in order to have a synergistic impact on the target. Furthermore, the development of message strategy is now in the hands of fewer external suppliers. Many traditional advertising agencies have evolved into full-fledged marketing communications agencies and offer services in areas such as public relations, sales promotion, direct response, and online communications. The range of services is greater, and the level of specialization that agencies provide is more concentrated than before. In effect, these agencies are changing with their clients' needs and are providing integrated marketing communications solutions.

The Integrated Marketing Communications Mix

integrated marketing communications The coordination of all marketing communications in a unified program that maximizes the impact on the intended target audience.

Integrated marketing communications involves the coordination of all forms of marketing communications in a unified program that maximizes the impact on consumers and other types of customers. It embraces many unique yet complementary forms of communication: media advertising (a focus on message strategies and media strategies in a mass media environment); direct response communications (communications that encourage immediate action); digital communications (including social media, mobile, and video game communications); sales promotion (both consumer and trade promotions); public relations; experiential marketing; and personal selling (see Figure 1.1). The growth of social media is a factor that an organization must consider. Given the media behaviour of today's consumers, it is essential that an effective and well-planned social media strategy be integrated into the communications mix.

Effective communications integration also considers the role of packaging and its impact on consumers at point of purchase, and the role that all employees of an organization play in communicating a positive attitude about a company to its various publics. Any customer touch-point is part of integrated marketing communications.

How an organization plans and manages the various components of the mix is important. An organization rarely employs all components at one time, but rather selects and uses those components that are deemed appropriate for the situation at hand. Clients look for a "total solutions" communications approach to resolve their business problems. As a result, they seek comprehensively planned, seamless campaigns from their communications agencies. Integration of message strategy, regardless of the medium, is crucial to generating maximum impact on the target audience.

Let's start the discussion about integrated marketing communications by clearly explaining the fundamental nature of each form of marketing communications. Refer to Figure 1.1 for a visual image of the marketing communications mix.

ADVERTISING

advertising A paid, media-delivered message by an identified sponsor designed to stimulate a positive response from a target audience.

Advertising is the placement of persuasive messages in time or space purchased in any of the mass media by organizations that seek to inform and persuade members of a target

FIGURE
1.1

The Integrated Marketing Communications Mix

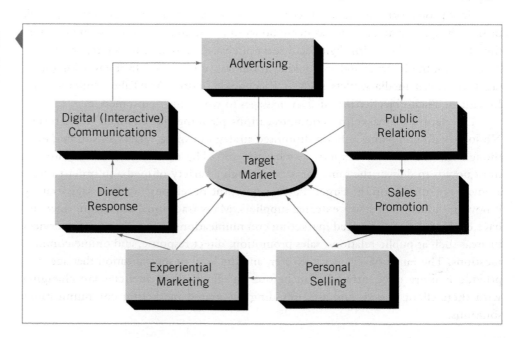

market about their products, services, organization, or ideas. In the context of the integrated marketing communications mix, good advertising (advertising that has an impact on the audience) will influence the behaviour of that audience—that is its primary function. Once a positive attitude toward a specific product or company is created in the customer's mind, that customer may be motivated to purchase the product or look favourably upon it.

Advertising can be either product oriented or promotion oriented. **Product advertising** provides information and helps build an image for the product, whether it's a brand or a company, by presenting the features, attributes, and benefits of the product in a persuasive manner. An ad for GREEN WORKS® cleaning products stresses essential benefits that consumers are looking for—a powerful cleaner without harsh chemical fumes. GREEN WORKS® cleaning products appeal to consumers who are concerned about the harm cleaning products can have on the environment. Refer to the illustration in Figure 1.2.

Promotional advertising is designed to accomplish a specific task—usually to communicate a specific offer in order to elicit some type of immediate response from the customer. Including a coupon or contest promotion with a print advertisement, for example, is a form of promotional advertising. The content of the ad presents the features and primary benefits to help build the image, and the coupon provides an incentive for customers to buy. Automobile manufacturers, for example, are well known for their

product advertising Advertising that provides information about a branded product to help build its image in the minds of customers.

promotional advertising Advertising that communicates a specific offer to encourage an immediate response from the target audience.

FIGURE
1.2

A Benefit-oriented Advertisement for GREEN WORKS® Cleaning Products

Source: GREEN WORKS ®. GREEN WORKS is a registered trademark of The Clorox Comopany and is used with permission.

rebate and low-cost financing programs, both of which are advertised heavily to attract customers. Packaged goods manufacturers use coupons and other incentives to encourage more immediate action by consumers. Offering a promotional incentive could be the entire focus of an integrated marketing communications campaign.

DIRECT RESPONSE COMMUNICATIONS

direct response communications   The delivery of a message to a target audience of one; the message can be distributed by direct mail, direct response television, or telemarketing.

Direct response communications involves the delivery of a message to a target audience of one. As the term implies, "direct" means directly from the marketing company to a specific or prospective user of a company's product. Direct mail is a common form of direct response communications. Other forms of direct response include direct response television (DRTV), telemarketing, and mobile communications. This segment of the communications industry is growing at a much faster pace than traditional forms of advertising. Time-pressed consumers, for example, find the convenience of direct response appealing. They can learn about the benefits of a product and actually buy it, if they so desire, all in one stage.

Figure 1.3 shows the content of a direct mail leaflet for the Subaru Legacy. This attractive leaflet effectively displays the design of the automobile and offers an incentive (a $500 gift card) to encourage prospects to lease the automobile. More details about the incentive are available from a quick response (QR) code. Subaru also does a lot of television and print advertising to generate awareness and interest in the brand: another example of effective integration.

DIGITAL (INTERACTIVE) COMMUNICATIONS

In an integrated marketing communications context, **digital (interactive) communications** are commercial messages for an organization placed on the Internet, a cell phone, or other personal electronic device. Technology is changing so rapidly that there is little doubt that communication by way of electronic devices is the future of marketing communications. In fact, investment in online communications by Canadian advertisers is growing at a pace much faster than any other form of advertising. In 2014 (the latest year available), investment in online advertising in Canada was $3.8 billion, overtaking television ($3.4 billion) for the largest share of ad spending.[1]

"The growth of online advertising in Canada speaks volumes about the importance of the medium to marketers in terms of its ability to reach, target, engage, and dialogue with consumers," says Paula Gignac, former president, IAB Canada.[2] Currently, the Internet is the number-one medium among Canadians 18 to 34 years old in time spent with a medium. This age group spends 33 hours a week online, compared to 15.5 hours a week with television. Canadians 25 to 54 years old currently spend slightly more time online than they do with television.[3]

The new emphasis that business organizations place on **customer relationship management (CRM)**, combined with their ability to manage internal databases, is forcing them to move toward direct response and interactive communications. At present, organizations communicate through their own websites and through various forms of online advertising such as search advertising, display ads, and video ads. The addition of advertising on social media sites will play an increasing role in the communications mix in the future.

SALES PROMOTION

Sales promotion involves special incentives to stimulate an immediate reaction from consumers and distributors. An organization's promotion expenditures tend to be divided between consumers and distributors. Strategies that include coupons, free samples, contests, and cash refunds are classified as consumer promotions. The on-pack sales incentive shown in Figure 1.4 is a good example of how sales promotions are integrated with

digital (interactive) communications   The placement of an advertising message on a website, or an ad delivered by email or through mobile communications devices.

customer relationship management (CRM)   A process that enables an organization to develop an ongoing relationship with valued customers; the organization captures and uses information about its customers to its advantage in developing the relationship.

sales promotion   An activity that provides incentives to bring about immediate response from customers, distributors, and an organization's sales force.

FIGURE
1.4

Sales Incentives Are Designed to Encourage Immediate Purchases by Consumers

Source: © Keith Tuckwell

media advertising. On-pack sales incentives encourage immediate purchases while media advertising builds brand image. Offering price discounts to distributors for purchasing goods in large quantities or for performing some kind of marketing or merchandising task on behalf of a marketing organization is classified as a trade promotion.

The marketing organization is constantly challenged by how to divide the sales promotion budget between consumers and trade customers. Regardless of how the budget is allocated, it is imperative that consumer promotion strategies are aligned effectively with advertising programs (to pull the product through the channel of distribution) and that trade promotions are aligned effectively with personal selling programs (to push the product through the channel of distribution). In business, it is the integration of various marketing communications programs that pays off for the organization.

PUBLIC RELATIONS

public relations　A form of communications designed to gain public understanding and acceptance.

Public relations communications are primarily directed toward gaining public understanding and acceptance. Public relations (PR) messages influence the attitudes toward and opinions interest groups have about an organization. Consequently, progressive-minded marketing organizations fully appreciate the role that public relations campaigns can play in generating positive attitudes toward products.

Public relations involve placing messages in the media without having to pay for them. In effect, they can generate "free" exposure. For example, a company issues a press release announcing a new product. The release includes all the virtues of the product, where it will be available, and how it will be advertised. Stories about the new product will appear on television newscasts, newspaper and magazine articles, and online blogs. Such exposure offers a legitimacy that advertising does not have.

Public relations also play a major role when a company finds itself in a crisis. Senior managers of an organization must be prepared to deal with the media and to issue effective communications when unpleasant circumstances arise. Financial guru Warren Buffet once said, "It takes 20 years to build a reputation and 5 minutes to ruin it."[4] In 2012, Korean automakers Hyundai and Kia were fined a record $100 million by the U.S. Environmental Protection Agency for overstating fuel economy figures on new models. With that fine, a main pillar of both brands was undermined. During fuel economy tests, Hyundai engineers allegedly chose favourable results rather than average results from a large number of tests.[5] Since consumers compare average results across comparable vehicles, this is a big issue—one in which Hyundai and Kia had to act upon in order to restore consumer confidence.

Traditional public relations are changing rapidly due to the popularity of social media. Communications tools such as Facebook and Twitter get regular people communicating information (positive and negative) about products and companies. Consequently, company-sourced social media communications are now part of an effective public relations strategy.

EXPERIENTIAL MARKETING

experiential marketing　A form of marketing that creates an emotional connection with the consumer in personally relevant and memorable ways.

Experiential marketing is a blend of marketing communications disciplines that engage people with a brand in a more personal way. For example, when Colgate-Palmolive launched Speed Stick GEAR men's deodorant it was entering a crowded market so getting noticed was a priority. An experiential marketing campaign was devised that involved building a 20-metre ice wall in downtown Toronto. The brand was targeting active, adventurous, millennial males in their 20s and early 30s. The brand's street team encouraged young males passing by to try climbing the wall. It was a great way to engage the target market with the new brand. Anomoly Toronto developed the creative for the campaign

FIGURE
1.5

**Experiential Marketing
Programs Are Personal in
Nature and Engage Consumers
with a Brand**

Source: Courtesy of Anomaly Toronto and
Free For All Marketing

and Free For All Marketing managed the construction and operation of the ice wall.[6] Refer to the image in Figure 1.5. This type of promotion engages consumers with the brand.

Event marketing and sponsorships fall under the umbrella of experiential marketing. A well-planned event will engage consumers with a brand experience; once involved, they may perceive the brand in a more positive light. The experience could be anything from attending an event where a sponsor's product is freely distributed to devising a specific branded event that becomes the focal point of an entire integrated marketing communications campaign. **Event marketing**, therefore, involves planning, organizing, and marketing an event, whether it is an event for a company or a brand.

Sponsorship simply means that a company provides money for an event in return for specified marketing privileges, granted because the company is associated with the event. Rogers, for example, is involved in event marketing as the title sponsor of the men's and women's Rogers Cup, a major tennis championship held annually in Toronto and Montreal. Rogers defrays the cost of holding such events by selling sponsorships to other companies. The presenting sponsor of the Rogers Cup is the National Bank of Canada.

event marketing   The process, planned by a sponsoring organization, of integrating a variety of communications elements behind a single event theme.

sponsorship   The act of financially supporting an event in return for certain advertising rights and privileges.

> **FIGURE 1.6** **Marketers Are Attracted to Events and Sponsorships Because They Reach a Target Market Directly**

Source: Courtesy of Tennis Canada

Those companies have advertising and on-site signage privileges at the event and can use the event logo to help market their product to the public. Refer to the image in Figure 1.6.

Marketers are attracted to events because they reach their target market directly and improve brand awareness when associated with the right event. At events, people expect to see branded content; they are generally more receptive to brand messages and therefore more engaged with the experience.

PERSONAL SELLING

personal selling Face-to-face communication involving the presentation of features and benefits of a product or service to a buyer; the objective is to make a sale.

As the term implies, **personal selling** involves the delivery of a personalized message from a seller to a buyer. The message presents the features, attributes, and benefits of a product or service. Personal selling is important in many situations, whether the seller is a car salesperson in a Toyota showroom, a store clerk in Best Buy, or the Pepsi-Cola sales representative presenting a new product to a buyer at the head office of Loblaws.

Compelling advertising campaigns for new automobiles encourage consumers to visit dealer showrooms. That money could go to waste if the salesperson in the dealership is unprepared to handle customer inquiries effectively. Equally, if Unilever's Dove brand is launching a new line of skin care products with a big advertising campaign, and the salesperson does not successfully sell the new product to head office buyers at major chains like Shoppers Drug Mart, Rexall Drugs, Loblaws, and others, Unilever could face a significant setback. No amount of advertising will help sell the product—it simply will not be available in these stores. The job of the sales representative is to secure distribution of the product in a timely manner. The availability of the product in stores must coincide with the scheduling of media advertising. If that does not happen, a lot of advertising money could be wasted.

In summary, contemporary organizations realize there are significant benefits to be achieved if all forms of marketing communications they choose to use are integrated successfully. Integration fosters a cooperative approach to communications planning, presents a unified message, and creates a higher level of impact on the target audience.

Factors Encouraging Integrated Marketing Communications

Selecting the right combination of marketing communications alternatives to solve unique business problems is the key to success. That is a difficult challenge. Contemporary thinking suggests a cooperative approach to communications problem solving and planning—an approach in which each communications alternative is an equal partner; an approach where there is media neutrality; an approach in which creative solutions are recommended to solve business problems. This way of thinking is the foundation on which integrated marketing communications strategies are built.

Several key issues and trends continue to affect marketing and marketing communications practice. Among these issues and trends are:

- Consumers' media habits are shifting toward digital media alternatives.
- The popularity of social media networks presents challenges and opportunities for organizations.
- Mobile communications are positioned to become the next "big thing" in marketing communications.
- The role of database marketing and direct forms of communications to reach individuals is expanding.
- The demand for efficiency and accountability in organizations is increasing.

MEDIA CONSUMPTION TRENDS AND THE SHIFT TO DIGITAL MEDIA

There is definitely a trend toward newer, electronic forms of communication and away from traditional forms of communication. Canadian consumers are spending less time with print and broadcast media each week and more time with the Internet (see Figure 1.7 for details). Readers of newspapers and magazines are migrating to online or tablet versions of their favourite read; television viewers are going "on demand" and are streaming their favourite

FIGURE 1.7   Media Consumption in Canada: Time Spent with the Media

The figures are the average per capita weekly number of hours spent with each medium.

Medium	Adults 18+	Adults 18–34	Adults 25–34	Adults 55+
Television	24.0	15.3	20.3	33.4
Radio	17.3	13.3	17.3	19.3
Internet	21.4	33.0	24.3	12.0
Print	2.2	0.8	1.4	4.2

Source: Based on data from Numeris RTS Canada, Fall 2014.

shows to their computers or televisions at a time convenient for them. With so many Canadian households having access to high-speed Internet service, the demand for streaming of shows has skyrocketed. The streaming of video content presents new advertising opportunities.

With eyeballs shifting to digital formats, advertisers have to reconsider how and where they place their advertising dollars. As well, media outlets such as CTV, *The Globe and Mail, Chatelaine* magazine, and others have to encourage advertisers to move their dollars from their traditional format to their digital format or to place a portion of their budgets in both formats.

Consumer behaviour while using social media is another factor that marketers must consider. Content is being consumed across multiple devices. While television remains a very popular medium, 20.8 percent of viewers use their smartphones at the same time and 35.5 percent use their tablets.[7] The consumer's attention is constantly shifting from one platform to another, making it more difficult to reach people with advertising messages. Grabbing a consumer's attention with an advertisement in such an environment is a challenge for those who create the message (creative planners) and those who plan the delivery of it (media planners). The situations described in the previous paragraph illustrate the need for a well-planned and integrated marketing communications strategy.

SOCIAL MEDIA PENETRATION AND POPULARITY

The most recent data available reveal that Canada has the highest social media penetration in the world. Eighty-two percent of Canadians use a social network. By comparison, U.S penetration is 75 percent. Further, 55 percent of online Canadians, or 19 000 000 people, are active on a social network. The most popular social networks are Facebook (16 000 000 users) followed by Twitter, Google+, Linkedin, and Pinterest.[8] Canadians spend 2 hours, 20 minutes each day on social media, leaving less direct time for conventional media such as television, radio, and print.

From a marketer's point of view and to use Facebook as an example, the sheer size of the audience seems overwhelming to many marketers, and they remain uncertain about the benefits that their investment in social media will generate. While all kinds of analytical information is available to measure the success of a social media campaign, marketers remain skeptical—they need to see the impact social media have on sales revenue and market share. Regardless, all age groups are now online, so social media advertising is a logical extension of a brand's marketing communications strategy. The most popular sites have advertising models in place, but they are constantly experimenting with new techniques (for example, sponsored posts on Facebook) to find a model that is financially prosperous for advertisers and themselves.

Internally, there is an urgent need for an organization to change how it approaches social media. Rather than looking at hard-core metrics such as sales and market share, it should adjust its thinking and see the value in the dialogue-style of marketing present in social media. Social media is more about the conversation between a company and the consumer; it is a means of engagement. Effective two-way communications between customers and an organization can produce positive word of mouth—an intangible that can't be underestimated in buying decisions.

MOBILE COMMUNICATIONS: THE NEXT BIG THING

Mobile communication devices are becoming a vital means for communicating information about goods and services, and conducting business transactions with customers. Currently, there are 27.9 million cell phone subscribers in Canada, and 68 percent of them have a smartphone. Further, there is a definite trend to cell phone usage only: in one in five households, cell phones are the only form of telephone service. Exclusive use of cell phones is pronounced in households where members are under 35 years of age.[9] This trend will have a significant impact on future marketing communications.

With consumers' eyeballs shifting from the "big screen" (television) to the "small screen" (tablets and mobile devices), companies are reacting by experimenting with new media communications mixes to more effectively reach and have an impact on their target audiences. While all ages use cell phones, younger consumers spend much more time with their phones than older consumers. Younger consumers' mobile activities include using downloaded applications, emailing, and accessing social networks and blogs.

If the under-35 age group is a primary target, marketers have to give mobile communications due consideration. That group will carry their media behaviour forward as they age. Therefore, with each passing year, mobile communication will become a more prominent component of an integrated marketing communications strategy. There is one key benefit for advertisers moving in this direction—they will have a personal link to consumers at any time, wherever they are.

There is no doubting the shift away from traditional media and toward digital media, social media, and mobile communications. Strategically thinking managers now realize that online and other forms of interactive communications complement traditional media. The challenge for all organizations is striking the right balance among all forms of media.

DATABASE MANAGEMENT TECHNIQUES AND CUSTOMER RELATIONSHIP MARKETING

Database management systems continuously collect and analyze information about customers. Companies that embrace database management can predict how likely it is that the customer will buy and can then develop a message precisely designed to meet that customer's unique needs. Technological advances allow a company to zero in on extremely small segments of the population, often referred to as niches. The ultimate goal is to aim directly at the smallest segment: the individual. The database is the internal vehicle that facilitates implementation of customer relationship management programs.

database management system   A system that collects information about customers for analysis by managers to facilitate sound business decisions.

Business today is all about relationships—the relationships that an organization has with its customers, distributors, and suppliers. Customer relationship marketing may involve numerous companies working together to achieve common goals, or it may involve only one company trying to build a meaningful relationship with its consumers. Customer relationship management (CRM) programs are concerned with establishing, maintaining, and enhancing long-term relationships. These programs call for marketing and marketing communications programs that are designed to approach customer groups (targets) collectively and each customer individually, when applicable.

To demonstrate CRM, let's examine the marketing communications used by Shoppers Drug Mart. Shoppers Drug Mart has amassed information about its customer demographics and shopping patterns in order to identify items customers are "likely" to buy. The Optimum Rewards program has one of the largest customer databases in Canada. It provides a means to communicate information and offers directly to loyal customers. Consequently, Shoppers now spends much less on traditional media, such as television and weekly flyers (formerly a staple means of communication in its mix), and more on mail and email. Shoppers can mail free samples of branded items that their customers are likely to be interested in. Refer to the illustration in Figure 1.8.

In today's very competitive business environment, equal consideration must be given to attracting new customers and to retaining existing customers. Typically, the more traditional means of communications are used to pursue new customers, and non-traditional media, such as online communications, social networks, and loyalty programs, are used to retain and enhance the customer relationship.

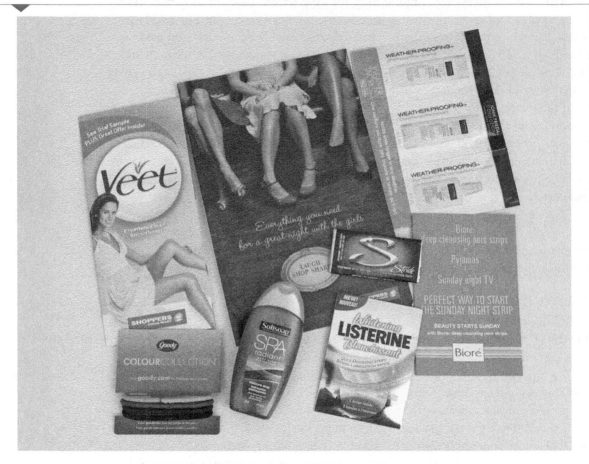

Source: © Keith Tuckwell

THE DEMAND FOR EFFICIENCY AND ACCOUNTABILITY

Organizations now understand that scarce resources can be put to better use if the efforts of individual activities are coordinated. A coordinated effort encourages synergy, which in turn should have a stronger impact on the target audience. Managers today are under intense pressure to be more accountable for producing tangible results with their marketing communications investment. Therefore, efficient communications strategies are popular, as are strategies that can be measured easily in terms of return on investment. Such a demand is fuelling interest in digital communications because consumer responses to the communications can be tracked electronically and without cost. Similar measurements are not possible when traditional forms of communications are employed.

Toyota Canada was quick to recognize how integrated media and marketing strategies produce efficient communications. At Toyota, all communications departments now work together in one integrated group. "We combined all departments in order to ensure that we were speaking with a consistent voice and were sending out a consistent message all the time. It's given us an opportunity to think more 'out of the box' in terms of ideas. With all disciplines working together there are tremendous efficiencies," says Peter Renz, national director of public relations and advertising at Toyota Canada.[10]

Input for Marketing Communications Planning: Consumer Behaviour Essentials

A basic understanding of some important behavioural concepts is essential because such knowledge is applied directly in the development of marketing communications strategies. Knowledge in the areas of needs and motives, personality and self-concept, attitudes and perceptions, reference groups, and families is considered when an organization plans its marketing communications strategies.

Consumer behaviour is the study of how people buy, what they buy, when they buy, and why they buy. In the context of marketing and marketing communications, it is imperative that organizations understand what influences consumers' behaviour. Consequently, organizations invest considerable sums of money in marketing research to understand consumers better. Information is power, as the saying goes.

consumer behaviour The combined acts carried out by individuals choosing and using goods and services, including the decision-making processes that determine these acts.

NEEDS AND MOTIVES

There is a direct link between needs and motives. Individuals have a **need** when they perceive the absence of something that is useful to them. A **motive** is a condition that prompts the individual to take action to satisfy the need. Consumers are motivated by friends and family members (word of mouth), or they can be influenced by what they see and read in the media or by broadcast messages on radio and television. An appealing presentation of a product's features and benefits as they relate to a target's needs is often good enough to stimulate action—a purchase decision. For example, you might say to yourself, "I need (want) a fresh meat sandwich for lunch, so I'm going to a Subway restaurant. 'Subway . . . Eat Fresh!'" That's the power of advertising!

need The perception of the absence of some necessity.

motive A condition that prompts an individual to take action to satisfy a need.

Maslow's *hierarchy of needs* and *theory of motivation* have had a significant impact on marketing and marketing communications strategies. Maslow classified needs from lower level to higher level. His theory is based on two assumptions. First, when lower-level needs are satisfied, a person moves up to higher-level needs. Second, satisfied needs do not motivate; behaviour is influenced by needs yet to be satisfied.

Maslow states that individuals move through five levels of needs, as shown in Figure 1.9. Numerous advertising examples can be cited to show how needs theory is applied.

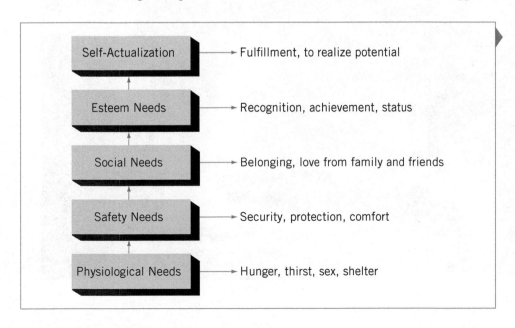

FIGURE

1.9

The Hierarchy of Needs

Source: Based on Maslow, A., Frager, R., Fadiman, J., *Motivation and Personality*, 3/E, © 1987.

For example, safety needs are used to motivate people to buy life insurance and retirement plans. A tagline such as "You're in good hands with Allstate" captures the message of protection and security.

The manufacturers of beauty merchandise, personal care products, and automobiles are famous for appealing to the social and esteem needs of both men and women. How a person's face and body look has an impact on social acceptance. What about the car you drive? Doesn't that say something about you to others? As seen in Figure 1.10, Cadillac presents itself as a brand that will help satisfy the esteem needs of a car buyer—someone seeking prestige and status in their ride.

PERSONALITY AND SELF-CONCEPT

personality   A person's distinguishing psychological characteristics that lead to relatively consistent and enduring responses to the environment in which that person lives.

Personality refers to the individual's distinguishing psychological characteristics that lead to relatively consistent and enduring responses to the environment in which that person lives. Personality is influenced by self-perceptions, which in turn are influenced by family, reference groups, and culture. An understanding of that self-concept provides clues as to how to communicate with consumers. The self-concept goes beyond needs and focuses on our desires.

According to self-concept theory, the self has four components: real self, self-image, looking-glass self, and ideal self.[11]

1. **Real Self:** An objective evaluation of one's self. You as you really are.
2. **Self-Image:** How you see yourself. It may not be your real self, but a role you play with yourself.

FIGURE 1.10   A Luxury Car Brand Such As Cadillac Appeals to the Esteem Needs of an Upscale Group of Car Buyers

Source: Courtesy of Cadillac

3. **Looking-Glass Self:** How you think others see you. This can be quite different from how they actually see you.
4. **Ideal Self:** How you would like to be. It is what you aspire to.

Based on these descriptions, the real self and self-image are less significant. In contrast, the looking-glass self and ideal self appear dynamic—they focus more on desires, the way in which we would like to be perceived. Consequently, many communications campaigns revolve around the looking-glass self and the ideal self. Marketing communicators know that consumers buy on emotion, so they present messages for goods and services that make consumers feel and look better. Marketers know that the next level of fulfillment is attractive to consumers.

People buy grooming products to satisfy social and esteem needs. Such behaviour is also influenced by people's desire to achieve their ideal self—how they would like to be. Women, for example are influenced by body images presented in magazines such as *Cosmopolitan* and *Vogue*, and men are influenced by images presented in *Maxim* and *Men's Health*. Marketers of popular brands such as L'Oreal and Biotherm have responded by marketing scrubs, moisturizers, cleansing products, and body sprays for both genders. Refer to the image in Figure 1.11.

FIGURE 1.11   A Message Directed at Men for a Product That Will Help Them Feel Good about Themselves

Source: © Neilson Barnard/Getty Images for L'Oreal Professionnel

ATTITUDES AND PERCEPTIONS

attitudes An individual's feelings, favourable or unfavourable, toward an idea or object.

Attitudes are an individual's feelings, favourable or unfavourable, toward an idea or object. People form attitudes based on what they hear, read, and see about a product, as well as from the opinions of others they trust. Friends, for example, have a dramatic impact on the attitudes held by youth. Trendsetters and opinion leaders who embrace new products also help to shape consumer attitudes.

As a rule, organizations present their product in accordance with attitudes held strongly by their target audience. It makes little sense to go against the grain; many an organization has discovered it is very expensive to try to change an attitude. For example, if teens see themselves on the edge of what the rest of the world considers normal, they will be attracted to products where the advertising message pushes the boundaries. Apple, for example, has been successful with products such as the iPhone and iPad—its products are positioned as sleek and sexy, and relevant to the lifestyles of all ages.

Attitudes do change, and marketers must keep track of the changes. To demonstrate, the change toward a more health-conscious lifestyle has spurred food manufacturers to create many new products. Consumers are demanding products that are easier on the waistline. Kellogg's Special K has always been positioned as a "good for you" product. There are now many new healthier lifestyle products in the Special K product line. See Figure 1.12 for details.

perception The manner in which individuals receive and interpret messages.

Perception refers to the manner in which individuals receive and interpret messages. Given the prevailing model of human behaviour, it is safe to say that consumers accept messages that are in line with their needs, personality, self-concept, and attitudes,

FIGURE
1.12

Special K Granola Bars are a Good Fit for Canadians' Trend Toward Healthier Living

Source: © Education Images/UIG via Getty Images

and ignore or reject messages that are not. Theory states that we are selective about the messages we receive and that there are three levels of selectivity:

1. **Selective Exposure:** Our eyes and minds notice only information that interests us.
2. **Selective Perception:** We screen out messages that conflict with our attitudes.
3. **Selective Retention:** We remember only what we want to remember.

To demonstrate how perception works, consider a situation that Toyota recently faced. Toyota is a company built on a strong reputation for quality. Some years ago, Toyota surpassed General Motors and became the world's largest automobile company. The public believed in the company. That feeling changed in 2010 when Toyota suffered backlash from massive recalls, the result of sticky gas pedals and braking problems. While Toyota was dealing with the problems, the public's perceptions of Toyota changed. In Canada, the company suffered a 20 percent decrease in sales. A common phrase applies here: "Perception is reality." It is the perceptions held by consumers that advertisers must deal with.

In contrast, consumers will quickly tune into messages for products and brands they are contemplating purchasing. As discussed earlier, consumers who are interested in healthier food products will tune in to advertising messages that include expressions such as "lighter," "less," "all natural," "no additives and preservatives," and so on. Relevant messages get noticed!

REFERENCE GROUPS

A **reference group**, or **peer group**, is a group of people with common interests that influence the attitudes and behaviour of its members. Reference groups include schoolmates, sports teams, fraternities and sororities, and hobby clubs. There is considerable pressure on members to conform to the standards of the group—a desire to "fit in." Take, for example, the mild hazing that occurs among rookies of a college or university sports team, or the rituals associated with joining a fraternity.

The influence of reference groups is quite strong among younger people. For example, teens share a desire to have the latest gadgets, shop at the trendiest stores, or have parts of their body tattooed. It's all part of their social scene and their desire to satisfy social needs. They turn to their peers for information on what behaviour is desirable. With the right strategy, a marketer need only associate its brand with a certain situation, and the target will become interested in the brand. Brands such as Burton (snowboards) and DC (skateboard shoes and clothing) have carved out a significant niche with the youth market. Refer to the image in Figure 1.13.

Advertisers have to be very careful when approaching the youth market. Too much advertising and the target sees the practice for what it is: a disingenuous attempt to attract youth consumers without having a clue about their actual tastes.[12] Reaching youth works if the message is authentic. If a brand "goes underground" (the place where most pop culture originates) or uses some kind of viral marketing technique such as a video on YouTube, it has a better chance of connecting with the youth target.

FAMILY INFLUENCES

Family and friends are the number-one influences on women's decision making, according to a recent study. The study revealed that family (70 percent), friends (67 percent), and trusted experts (34 percent) have the greatest influence on female consumers' decisions to try a new product.[13] Marketers look to media and social media to tap into influencers, but apparently they should also be looking at the old-fashioned way of doing things: the lost art of tapping into family and friends.

Within a family, each member has some influence on the behaviour of other family members and thus an influence on buying decisions. Such behaviour today relates to the

reference group (peer group) A group of people who share common interests that influence the attitudes and behaviour of its members.

changing roles and *responsibilities* of family members. Traditional attitudes, roles, and responsibilities are out—things are no longer what they were. Households are also different. There are same-sex households, lone-parent households, and dual-income (two-worker) households. In the dual-income but traditional household, much of the decision making is shared between partners. No longer can the maker of a household product assume the woman is the primary buyer, and a financial advisor cannot assume that the man makes all the investment decisions. In fact, men are handling grocery shopping more than ever before, either on their own or shared with a spouse. Supermarkets and grocery product manufacturers are adjusting their merchandising and advertising strategies accordingly.

On the female side of things, financial progression has had an impact on household decision making. Currently, 31 percent of wives earn more than their husbands, and 20 percent earn about the same. Further, 92 percent of Canadian women are solely or jointly in control of family finances, and 55 percent say they make the daily financial decisions.[14] Marketers can no longer make assumptions about who the primary buyer is. They must consider both buyers and influencers and the fact that major decisions are often shared by people who live together in any type of household formation.

double targeting   Marketing strategies that reach both genders effectively.

Companies that are in tune with these types of changes are **double targeting**—they are devising marketing strategies that reach both genders effectively.

Financial companies, automobile manufacturers, and retailers recognize these changes and are devising new campaigns that take advantage of such knowledge. Retailers like Mark's and Canadian Tire have redesigned store layouts, created a better shopping environment, and implemented a new marketing communications strategy aimed directly at women. See the Mark's ad in Figure 1.14.

Source: Courtesy of Canadian Tire Corporation, Limited.

Boston Pizza Goes Family

For years Boston Pizza positioned itself as a sports bar—a place where men could hang out and watch games with friends. Large screen TVs, great-tasting food, beer, and a casual environment were conducive to the "sports" pitch. In the very competitive casual dining restaurant market, there were many other establishments appealing to the same customer. A change in direction was necessary.

Boston Pizza kept the focus on males but did so in a different manner—it focused on dads with family responsibilities who had other reasons to visit a restaurant. What emerged was a "Here to Make You Happy" campaign that presented dads as responsible individuals—family leaders and engaged parents in the household. The initial television commercial, called "Finger Cooking," took a humorous approach; it promoted a delivery service for men who didn't really like to cook.

The new approach worked. Prior to the campaign, sales revenue was declining marginally across the chain. During the campaign, sales revenue increased annually for three straight years. It proved that good advertising works!

Sensing a need for change again, Boston Pizza decided to become more inclusive in its approach. Rather than just focusing on dads, moms and children were added to the mix—dining there would become more of a family affair. Boston Pizza brought back its connection to sports but in a different way. Television commercials embraced images of kid's sports teams and included both male and female athletes. The campaign theme and tagline for the campaign was "We'll Make You a Fan." The tagline offered a double meaning—it alluded to Boston Pizza's sports connections and its promise to deliver a high-quality dining experience. From consumer research, Boston Pizza knew that 85 percent of Canadians watch sports and 47 percent of the audience is female. Further, both moms and dads share responsibilities of getting their kids to the soccer pitch, baseball diamond, or hockey arena.

The sports and family message will continue to play a greater role in Boston Pizza advertising. Beyond advertising, Boston Pizza sponsors several teams and organizations including Hockey Canada, the Vancouver Canucks, Calgary Flames, Winnipeg Jets, and more. Sponsoring teams has been part of Boston Pizza's marketing strategy from its very beginnings. The new advertising campaign and sponsorship activities continue to impact sales in a positive manner. This particular campaign and the activation of it helped get Boston Pizza nominated for Marketer of the Year for 2015.

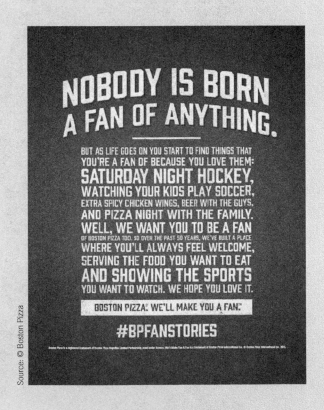

Source: © Boston Pizza

Based on Susan Krashinski, "Boston Pizza Ads Take a Slice out of Life," *The Globe and Mail*, February 27, 2015, p. B5.

Today's children (commonly referred to as generation Z) also have considerable influence on family buying decisions. They don't necessarily make requests, but parents actively seek their input on anything from clothing to cars to family vacations. "Their influence on family spending is that they essentially are co-purchasers," says Kelly Mooney, president of Resources Interactive.[15] Children are technologically savvy and are helping their parents research products and make online buying decisions—a real shift in power! Through social media, children access the opinions of their network of friends whom they communicate with regularly.

For more insight into family influences, changing roles and their impact on marketing communications, read the IMC Highlight: **Boston Pizza Goes Family**.

Inputs for Marketing Communications Planning: Business and Organizational Buyer Behaviour

The buying process of organizations is very different from consumer buying. In a nutshell, organizations exhibit more rational behaviour than consumers: consumers do a lot of buying based on emotion. The **business-to-business (B2B) market** is managed by individuals in an organization responsible for purchasing goods and services needed to produce a product or service or promote an idea. This market includes business and industry, governments, institutions, wholesalers and retailers, and professionals.

business-to-business (B2B) market   A market of goods and services needed to produce a product or service, promote an idea, or operate a business.

The business market has several characteristics that distinguish it from consumer markets. Business markets have fewer buyers, and those buyers tend to be concentrated in industrial areas in and near large cities. The buying criteria are very practical, with decisions based on the best buy according to predetermined requirements. There is usually a formal buying process for evaluating product and service alternatives. Business buying processes have changed dramatically because of advancing technology and the benefits derived from buying goods online.

The key factors that a business organization must address when marketing to other businesses are the criteria established by the buying organization. In most situations, those requirements are established in advance, and companies can compete with each other by submitting bids. The buyer customarily chooses the bid with the lowest price, assuming the criteria have been met. What are those requirements?

- **Quality:** Buyers want consistent quality on every order. What they buy could have a direct impact on the quality of goods they, in turn, produce and market.

- **Service:** Buyers want reputable suppliers who provide prompt service and believe that the initial order is simply the start of a business relationship.

- **Continuity of Supply:** Buyers want suppliers who can provide goods over the long term. A steady source of supply ensures consistent production scheduling.

- **Price:** Buyers evaluate price in conjunction with the other criteria. The lowest price is not always accepted. Potential long-term savings could outweigh an initial low price.

To ensure that the right buying decision is made, organizations employ a formal or informal approach. A formal approach involves a **buying committee**. The committee is made up of key representatives from various functional areas of the company, such as finance, marketing, manufacturing, purchasing, and so on. A committee takes a very rational approach when evaluating alternatives, and participants need to know that costly decisions are shared decisions.

buying committee   A formal buying structure in an organization that brings together expertise from the various functional areas to share in the buying decision process.

A **buying centre** is an informal purchasing process with individuals in an organization involved in the purchasing process, but not necessarily having direct responsibility for the actual decision. These roles are summarized in Figure 1.15.

In terms of marketing or marketing communications, the seller must know who on the committee or within the buying centre has the most influence. It could be one person

buying centre   An informal purchasing process in which individuals in an organization perform particular roles but may not have direct responsibility for the actual decision.

FIGURE
1.15 **The Buying Centre**

Role	Description	Example
Users	Those in the organization who use the product directly.	If the product is a personal computer, any end-user in the organization.
Influencers	Those who define the product specifications.	An engineer.
Buyers	Those with the authority to buy.	A purchasing manager.
Deciders	Those with the power to finalize the purchase.	Where high-cost decisions are involved, the CEO may be the decider.
Gatekeepers	Those who control the flow of information to the members of the buying centre.	A purchasing manager may also fulfill the role of gatekeeper.

or several people. Once that is known, the best means of communicating can be determined. Based on the nature of business buying, it becomes clear that personal selling and direct forms of communications are vital components when trying to influence the decisions of business buyers.

INTEGRATION AND PARTNERING INFLUENCES B2B COMMUNICATIONS STRATEGIES

Business markets have embraced customer relationship management in an attempt to establish efficient business systems. CRM promotes the seamless transfer of information throughout the channels to ensure the efficient and continuous flow of goods. Forming partnerships with suppliers implies a long-term relationship. Therefore, to be part of a CRM system, the marketer must be more familiar than ever with the role the product plays in the customer's operations. Collecting information about customers and their operations is crucial.

The strategies employed to reach business customers are also evolving. Yet, in spite of all the technological advances and the direct nature of the buying and selling process, customers must still be made aware of the product alternatives that are available. Creating awareness is always the first step. Therefore, the need for print advertising directed at business customers will continue, along with the need for strong personal sales contacts. The inclusion of sales promotion programs to assist salespeople is also important. Event marketing in the form of trade show participation will help keep marketing organizations on a buyer's radar screen, and direct marketing techniques, such as direct mail and Internet-based communications, will become more of a priority. A website containing essential product information is indispensable in B2B marketing situations. The same tools are employed in consumer marketing; they are just given different priority.

Ethical Issues in Marketing Communications Practice

The way an organization communicates is always under review by the public and critics of the marketing communications industry. Rightly or wrongly, planned or unplanned, advertisers sometimes deliver messages that spark controversy. Many organizations tolerate the controversy as long as the campaign is delivering sales, while others bow to public pressure and remove offending messages. Some of the key issues that make the headlines are discussed in this section.

PRIVACY ISSUES IN AN ONLINE WORLD

An ongoing and rather hot issue revolves around the collection of information about people's behaviour when using the Internet. What do marketers know about people, and how do they use this information? Consumers must recognize (many do) that every online activity is tracked and logged, and has potential value for marketers. For many people, this is a frightening thought, and it should be if the information is not used for legitimate purposes.

Data is king in marketing today, and marketers are good at collecting and interpreting data. Marketers have always done this, but in the age of technology, the data is available in a fast and furious manner. The collection of online data provides marketers with an opportunity to devise unique advertising messages based on personal interests (as expressed by online surfing behaviour) that can be delivered directly to your mobile device in real time.

So what do consumers fear? One recent survey found that 64 percent of respondents viewed targeted advertising as invasive, with 40 percent saying they would change their online behaviour if advertisers were collecting data. Such feelings can vary by age category. For example, 47 percent of 55- to 64-year-olds were concerned about access to behavioural data. Among 18- to 24-year-olds, only 33 percent were concerned.[16] Marketers like data, and if they use the data legitimately, it will help their business grow.

There are regulations in place to ensure consumers are aware of their rights with regard to how information is used. Various opt-in and opt-out clauses are found in agreements people sign when dealing with online organizations, but there is a fear that marketers disregard the regulations. Privacy law does exist in Canada through the *Personal Information Protection and Electronic Documents Act* (PIPEDA). The Act does not offer rules but does offer a list of guiding principles for businesses to follow. For example, an organization must obtain consent for the use or disclosure at the time of collection, and purposes for the collection of information must be limited and well defined, and stated in a clear and understandable manner. The degree to which organizations abide by these principles fuels the ongoing debate with consumers.

SEX IN ADVERTISING

A common complaint about advertising revolves around the use of sex to sell something. As an old saying goes: "Sex sells!" So what's the beef among members of contemporary Canadian society? Using sex appeal in an appropriate manner and for appropriate products seems natural, but gratuitous sex is something consumers shouldn't have to tolerate.

Is it pornography or simply provocative advertising? American Apparel, a very popular brand, is known for controversial advertising. An outdoor ad that once appeared in downtown Toronto showed a woman from behind leaning forward in a provocative pose. It sparked controversy but passersby certainly noticed it—the intention of any advertisement. The ad raised the ire of many women who suggested it objectified women. Marsha Brady, creative director of the company at the time, defended the ad, saying, "When there's a group of people attempting to shame female creativity, female beauty, female pride under the auspices of protecting women, it's really, really scary."[17] A sample of American Apparel advertising appears in Figure 1.16. You can judge for yourself if the ad is too "sexy" or not.

DANGEROUS OR DISTURBING ADVERTISING

The extent to which advertisers will go with their message in order to have an impact on their audience can sometimes be an issue. For example, the strategy of depicting

dangerous or disturbing situations in advertising has come under much scrutiny in recent years. Automakers are under the gun for showing unsafe driving practices in ads. In some cases, dangerous driving practices are glamourized. A Corvette spot entitled "A Boy's Dream" depicted an enraged driver racing wildly in the sports car. Many critics believe an ad like this helps encourage young people to get involved in risky activities such as street racing.

ING DIRECT (now Tangerine) was forced to pull an ad called "Are You Suffering" (part of an RSP campaign) that showed an image of a forlorn man sitting on a couch. The man was cured of whatever ailed him when his wife took him to ING DIRECT. The image combined with the dim lighting in the room did not paint a pleasant picture. The ad garnered negative response from many mental health professionals who accused ING DIRECT of reinforcing negative stereotypes about mental illness. Marketers want people to take notice of their brands, but sometimes they cross a line they did not anticipate. ING DIRECT ultimately made the right decision about the advertisement.[18]

MISLEADING ADVERTISING

Sometimes ads can mislead the public or simply misrepresent the brand. Sometimes the public misinterprets the advertiser's message and the campaign backfires. The control of misleading advertising is the responsibility of Advertising Standards Canada. (More information about its role in the advertising industry appears later in this chapter.) Some of the more interesting examples involve green marketing claims, ads targeting children, and cultural diversity.

EXAGGERATED GREEN CLAIMS   Given the rate at which organizations are making claims about how green they are and what they are doing to protect the environment, this category of misleading advertising is worthy of special attention. Manufacturers of bottled water, for example, claim they are offering a better product than the water that municipalities offer, forgetting that a large portion of the plastic bottles wind up in landfill sites, which ultimately harms the environment.

A recent survey about environmental claims shows that 75 percent of Canadians take into account the environmental impact of an organization's actions when they buy a product. As well, 75 percent of respondents firmly believe that most environmental claims are just marketing ploys. Phrases such as "green," "organic," or "low emissions" suggest all is good, but where's the proof?[19] Consumers want to ensure that companies are not getting away with "greenwashing," a term associated with the exploitation of environmental ideas to make a company look good.

TARGETING CHILDREN   Advertising messages directed at children often bypass parents. As a result, parents are concerned about the content of these messages, which have a powerful influence on the child's behaviour. Children may start demanding higher-priced "in" goods, while parents prefer to buy less expensive alternatives. In other words, at what age do children become "brand conscious"?

Companies such as McDonald's, Kellogg's, PepsiCo, and Nestlé, among many others, are frequently targetted by critics who suggest the consumption of their products and the ads that encourage their consumption have contributed to the rise in childhood obesity. In fact, a panel appointed by the Chronic Disease Prevention Alliance of Canada called for a ban on all junk food advertising that targets children—a move the federal government has promised to consider. In the wake of the criticism, many food companies have committed to an industry-sponsored Children's Food and Beverage Advertising Initiative that encourages responsible marketing to children. Some companies are eliminating ads targeted to children altogether, while others are promising healthier products for children.[20]

CULTURAL DIVERSITY   Currently, Canada's foreign-born population represents 19.8 percent (about one in five Canadians) of the total population and is expected to rise to as high as 23 percent by 2017.[21] The largest visible minorities are South Asians, Chinese, and Blacks. These people tend to live in large cities. In Toronto, visible minorities comprise 47 percent of the population.

Given this data, advertisers are often criticized for not reflecting the diversity of Canada's population in commercial messages. Critics claim that advertising remains too targeted on white consumers, and they may be right. Marketers must consider the size and profit potential of an ethnic marketing campaign. Multinational companies consider Canada to be a small market; to break down the market further and absorb the costs of a definitive marketing campaign for various ethnic groups may not be profitable.

Many advertisers are adopting multicultural marketing communications strategies and are including ethnic populations in their ads. Some of the leaders in ethnic-oriented

Smaller Target, Bigger Opportunity

The ethnic market is actually a big market in Canada. Statistics Canada reports that a vast majority of Canadians belonging to a visible minority group live in major cities. In Toronto they represent 47 percent of the population, in Vancouver 59 percent, and in Montreal 31 percent. Those numbers are significant! The largest visible minority group are people of South Asian descent, followed by Chinese, Black, Filipino, and Latin American.

According to Emma Fox, senior vice-president of marketing at Walmart Canada, it is absolutely vital that her company pursue the ethnic market. "It's really important that we win our share of that market. It's a necessity because all the future market growth in terms of spending is coming from new population growth." She's right. The new Canadian population is growing at five times the rate of the overall population.

Walmart Canada has been a leader in ethnic marketing and marketing communications. The company is moving forward with a "store of the community" concept that caters to local needs and tastes. Simply put, a

store in the east end of a city might carry different merchandise than one in the west end. The location of various ethnic groups in a city will be a determining factor influencing what merchandise a store carries. Walmart uses one of its supercentres in Toronto as a laboratory for tailoring offerings to the large surrounding Asian population.

Scotiabank holds similar views and is pursuing niche markets that competitors may be neglecting. Scotiabank recently focused on the Latin American market in Toronto and Montreal. According to Fabiola Sicard, director of Latin American markets at Scotiabank, "They are a smaller market than other immigrant communities, they are fragmented geographically, and no significant research has been done on their needs." Despite this, the bank sees great opportunity, as the Hispanic population in Canada numbers over 600 000. Scotiabank sees Hispanic Canadians as a growth market for its StartRight bank accounts, which are tailored to the needs of newcomers.

Scotiabank stays away from mainstream media in its marketing communications, preferring a more grassroots approach. The bank targets professional associations, street festivals, and blogs aimed at people living in Latin American countries who are mulling a move north. To reach recent arrivals, the bank gives seminars in Spanish; often as many as 150 people show up. Similar strategies are in place to reach the Filipino community. Scotiabank does not neglect the larger Chinese and South Asian communities, but the other banks are aggressively targeting them as well. Scotiabank is going into areas nobody else is targeting—a wise move on their part.

Source: © Steve White

Sources: Marina Strauss, "Walmart Aims to Cater to a More Diverse Palate," *The Globe and Mail*, April 17, 2012, p. B7; and Simon Houpt, "Unknown, Ignored and Invisible," *The Globe and Mail*, November 18, 2011, p. B7.

advertising include Walmart, Shopper's Drug Mart, McDonald's, TD CanadaTrust, and RBC Financial, among many others. These companies recognize the importance of appealing to the widest possible audience. It's only a matter of time before other organizations get on board.

For more insight into ethnic-oriented marketing communications, read the IMC Highlight: **Smaller Target, Bigger Opportunity**.

Laws and Regulations Governing Marketing Communications

The marketing communications industry in Canada is highly regulated. Regulation and control come from Advertising Standards Canada (ASC), which administers regulations based on codes of practice that are voluntarily established; and the Competition Bureau (a federal agency) through the *Competition Act*, which established laws and regulations for all marketing activity in Canada.

ADVERTISING STANDARDS CANADA

Advertising Standards Canada is the industry body committed to creating and maintaining community confidence in advertising. Its mission is to ensure the integrity and viability of advertising through industry self-regulation. ASC members include advertisers, agencies, media organizations, and suppliers to the advertising sector.

ASC operates two divisions. The Standards Division administers the industry's self-regulating code, the *Canadian Code of Advertising Standards*; handles complaints from consumers regarding advertising; and administers the industry's *Trade Dispute Procedure*. The Advertising Clearance Division previews advertisements in five categories, helping advertisers adhere to applicable legislation, regulatory codes, and industry standards.[22]

The *Canadian Code of Advertising Standards* (Code) is the principal instrument of self-regulation. The Code was developed to promote the professional practice of advertising and forms the basis upon which advertising is evaluated in response to consumer complaints. The Code is supplemented by other codes and guidelines, including gender portrayal guidelines, which are intended to help advertising practitioners develop positive images of women and men in their commercial messages. The Code also addresses concerns about advertising, including the accuracy and clarity of messages, disguised advertising techniques, price claims, bait and switch tactics, comparative advertising claims, unacceptable depictions, scientific claims, and advertising to children.

Advertising Standards Canada rules against advertisers when necessary and makes suggestions for changes in message delivery. Copywriters and art directors are frustrated by such responses from the public or regulating bodies. It's no wonder there's so much dull advertising that simply blends together. Being cautioned to stay away from the creative edge is not good for the future of advertising. In the unregulated online world, user-generated content of a risky nature is quite common. The playing field doesn't seem as level as it once was.

For more insight into the role of Advertising Standards Canada, visit the ASC website at www.adstandards.com.

COMPETITION BUREAU

The Competition Bureau is responsible for the administration and enforcement of the *Competition Act*, a law that governs business conduct and marketing practices in Canada. The *Competition Act* contains criminal and civil provisions to address false, misleading, and deceptive marketing practices. Among the practices that come under scrutiny are deceptive telemarketing, deceptive notices of winning prizes, and pyramid selling schemes. Other provisions prohibit representations not based on adequate and proper tests, misleading warranties and guarantees, false or misleading price representation, and untrue testimonials.

Organizations that violate these laws and regulations are subject to financial penalties and other actions. To demonstrate, the Competition Bureau determined that Bell Canada misled consumers about the prices it offered for its services. Bell's website had been advertising a bundle of home phone, Internet, and television services starting as low as $69.90

per month. However, it was impossible for customers to buy the bundle at that price. The lowest possible price, including mandatory fees, was $80.27 (15 percent higher). Mandatory fees were hidden from consumers in the fine-print disclaimers. Bell agreed to pay an administrative penalty of $10 million, the maximum allowable under the *Competition Act*.[23]

For more insight into the Competition Bureau visit its website at www.competitionbureau.gc.ca.

SUMMARY

The rapid pace of change in business today has forced organizations to re-examine and change the way they communicate with customers. More than ever before, organizations are demanding integrated marketing strategies to help resolve marketing problems and to take advantage of new opportunities.

The integrated marketing communications mix is composed of seven unique yet complementary components: advertising, direct response communications, interactive communications, sales promotion, personal selling, public relations, and experiential marketing. The organization evaluates marketing situations and employs the components of the mix that will effectively and efficiently reach its target market.

Several key issues and trends have led to the emergence of integrated marketing communications. Among them are consumers' changing media habits and their shift to digital media consumption; the penetration and popularity of social media networks and the challenges and opportunities they present to organizations; the potential growth of mobile communications; the expanding role of database marketing and its impact on direct forms of marketing communications; and the greater demand for efficiency and accountability in organizations.

In the process of developing marketing communications strategies, an organization must understand and apply various consumer behaviour concepts. Among these concepts are needs and motives, personality and self-concept, attitudes and perceptions, reference groups, and family. Research into these factors provides clues about what forms of marketing communications to employ to deliver a more effective message.

Marketing communications strategies must also consider business buying behaviour. While consumers tend to be swayed by emotion, business buyers maintain a rational approach when making buying decisions. Business buying is based on predetermined criteria such as quality, service, continuity of supply, and price. Decisions are made formally by a buying committee or informally by a buying centre. Technology and relationship marketing practices have taken hold in B2B marketing. Companies must adapt to this way of doing business or perish. Tools such as personal selling, direct response communications, and interactive communications are effective in reaching business customers.

Marketing communications practitioners must contend with ethical issues when devising message strategies. Some of the more contentious issues today include consumers' concern for privacy in the online world, the use of sex in advertising, and the depiction of dangerous and disturbing images in advertisements. Advertisers are also under the gun for making exaggerated green claims, targeting children with ads, and not portraying Canada's cultural diversity in advertising.

Regulation and control of the marketing communications industry is the jurisdiction of the federal government and Advertising Standards Canada. Laws and regulations are enforced by the Competition Bureau, and voluntary regulations are administered by Advertising Standards Canada.

KEY TERMS

advertising   4

attitudes   18

business-to-business (B2B) market   23

buying centre   23

buying committee   23

consumer behaviour   15

customer relationship management (CRM)   7

database management system   13

digital (interactive) communications   7

direct response communications   6

double targeting   20

event marketing   9

experiential marketing   8

integrated marketing communications   4

motive   15

need   15

peer group   19

perception   18

personal selling   10

personality   16

product advertising   5

promotional advertising   5

public relations   8

reference group   19

sales promotion   7

sponsorship   9

REVIEW QUESTIONS

1. Identify and briefly explain the components of the integrated marketing communications mix.
2. Explain the difference between product advertising and promotional advertising.
3. Briefly describe the key issues and trends that have led to the emergence of integrated marketing communications.
4. "An understanding of Maslow's hierarchy of needs and theory of motivation has a direct influence on advertising strategy." Explain.
5. According to the self-concept theory, the self has four components. Identify and briefly describe each component.
6. How important is assessing customer attitudes when developing an advertising campaign? Explain.
7. What role and influence do reference groups have when a consumer is deciding what products to buy?
8. Explain the term "double targeting," and provide a new example of a company or brand that is applying this concept.
9. What essential criteria do organizational buyers consider when making buying decisions?
10. What is the difference between a buying committee and a buying centre?
11. What roles do the Competition Bureau and Advertising Standards Canada play in the marketing communications industry?

DISCUSSION AND APPLICATION QUESTIONS

1. How significant will digital communications be in future marketing communications strategies? Will advertisers continue to shift their dollars to digital communications? Conduct some secondary research to offer new information that will justify your opinion.
2. Experiential marketing is growing in popularity. Will this trend continue, and will experiential marketing play a more dominant role in future marketing communications strategies? Conduct some research on this topic and present an opinion on it.
3. "Relationship marketing practices will dramatically alter marketing communications strategies in the future." Is this statement true or false? Conduct some online secondary research and form an opinion on this statement.
4. Cite some examples and provide actual illustrations of companies or brands that use the following consumer behaviour theories when developing communications strategies. Provide a description that relates the theory to the practice.

   a) hierarchy of needs and theory of motivation
   b) personality and self-concept
   c) reference groups
   d) family influences

5. From the following list of goods and services, identify what you think is the most important marketing communications tool for building and sustaining the brand. Provide some justification for your choices.

   a) Coors Light
   b) BMW automobiles
   c) Shoppers Drug Mart
   d) RBC Financial Group

6. Are advertising laws and regulations in Canada too conservative? Should riskier or more controversial advertising messages be allowed? Refer to the ethical issues section of the chapter for some background information before responding to this question.

ENDNOTES

1. Canadian Media Directors' Council *Media Digest*, 2015–2016, p. 28.
2. Paula Gignac, "2007 Canadian Online Revenue Climbs to $1.2 Billion," press release, IAB Canada, July 3, 2008, www.newswire.ca/en/story/290659/2007-canadian-online-advertising-revenue-climbsto-1-2-billion.
3. "Where is the time spent?" *TV Basics 2015–2015*, Numeris RTS Canada, Fall 2014.
4. Angela Scardillo, "Old Spice Guys Lesson in Crisis Management," *Marketing*, August 30, 2010, p. 27.
5. Jeremy Cato, "Hyundai and Kia's big black eye," *The Globe and Mail*, November 8, 2012, p. D10.
6. "Colgate-Palmolive takes deodorant marketing to new heights," *Marketing*, March 18, 2014, www.marketingmag.ca.
7. "Canada Digital Future in Focus," study comScore, 2014.
8. "Canadian Digital, Social and Mobile Statistics on a Global Scale," *Canadian's Internet.com Business*, http://canadiansinternet.com/canadian-digital-social-mobile-statistics-on-a-global-scale.

9. "Facts & Figures: The Canadian Marketplace," *Canadian Wireless Telecommunications Association*, 2014, www.cwta.ca.

10. Richard Rotman, "When World's Combine," *Marketing*, September 29, 2003, p. 8.

11. John Douglas, George Field, and Lawrence Tarpay, *Human Behavior in Marketing*, (Columbus, OH: Charles E. Merrill Publishing, 1987), p. 5.

12. Sam Grewal, "Manufactured Cool," *Toronto Star*, February 22, 2005, p. C4.

13. Rebecca Harris, "Friends and Family Still Top Influencers: Veritas Study," *Marketing*, June 10, 2014, www.marketingmag.ca.

14. Karen Mazurkewicj, "The Pink Purse Strings," *Financial Post*, September 15, 2007, www.canada.com.

15. Jennifer Watters, "Young, with Tons of Purchasing Power," *Market Watch*, October 11, 2006, www.marketwatch.com.

16. Josh Bernoff, "Does Data Collection Affect Consumer Behaviour?" *Marketing*, January 25, 2012, www.arketingmag.ca.

17. Dakshana Bascaramurty, "American Apparel is at it again," *The Globe and Mail*, August 23, 2008, p. M3.

18. Chris Powell, "ING Direct Pulls RSP 'Suffering' Ad over Complaints," *Marketing*, January 22, 2013, www.marketingmag.ca.

19. Richard Blackwell, "Eco-friendly? Canadians Want to See the Proof," *The Globe and Mail*, July, 2008, pp. B1, B3.

20. Megan Harman, "Sprouts with That?" *Canadian Business*, April 14, 2008, p. 23.

21. "Study: Canada's Visible Minority Population in 2017," Statistics Canada, www.statcan.gc.ca/daily-quotidien/050322/dq050322b-eng.html.

22. Advertising Standards Canada, www.adstandards.com.

23. "Competition Bureau Agreement with Bell Canada Requiring Bell to Pay $10 million for Misleading Advertising," Competition Bureau Canada, press release, June 28, 2011, www.competitionbureau.gc.ca/eic/site/cb-bc.nsf/eng/03388.html.

Strategic Planning Principles

Learning Objectives

After studying this chapter, you will be able to

1. Identify essential external trends and conditions that influence organizational planning

2. Describe the steps in the strategic planning process

3. Identify the distinctions and relationships among the various types of plans

4. Characterize the essential elements of a corporate plan

5. Outline the structure and content of a marketing plan

6. Outline the structure and content of a marketing communications plan

7. Show how integrated marketing planning provides solutions to marketing problems

All business planning is an integrated process that involves planning at three levels of an organization: corporate planning (planning conducted by senior executives), marketing planning (planning conducted by brand and marketing managers), and marketing communications planning (plans designed by communications specialists based on guidelines provided by brand and marketing managers). When a planning system works properly, each level of planning is linked to the other levels. Corporate plans provide guidance and direction for marketing plans, and marketing plans provide direction for marketing communications plans.

How plans are struck varies considerably from company to company. There is no perfect model to follow. Some organizations produce very detailed plans, while others take a more action-oriented approach. The common factor among all companies should be integration, meaning integrating one plan with another and integrating all the pieces of a plan together so that a consistent strategic direction is followed when the plans are implemented. This chapter presents a potential model for preparing strategic plans. Students should recognize that the model can be altered to fit the specific needs of an organization.

Factors Influencing Strategic Planning

strategic planning (corporate strategy) The process of determining objectives (setting goals) and identifying strategies (ways to achieve the goals) and tactics (specific action plans) to help achieve objectives.

objectives Statements of what is to be accomplished in terms of sales, profit, market share, or other measures.

strategies Statements that outline how the objectives will be achieved, such as the direction to be taken and the allocation of resources needed to proceed.

tactics (execution) Action-oriented details that outline how a strategic plan will be implemented.

Strategic planning, or the **corporate strategy**, is the process of determining objectives (setting goals) and identifying strategies (ways to achieve the goals) and tactics (specific action plans) to help achieve objectives. Based on this definition, a strategic plan includes three common variables:

- **Objectives:** Statements of what is to be accomplished in terms of sales, profit, market share, or other measures.

- **Strategies:** Statements that outline how the objectives will be achieved, such as the direction to be taken and the allocation of resources needed to proceed.

- **Tactics (execution):** Action-oriented details, including precise details about the cost and timing of specific activities.

Strategic planning is a cyclical process in most organizations and typically occurs on an annual basis. A company's strategic plan is influenced by changes in the economy, among consumers, in technology, in laws and regulations governing business practices, in competitor activities, and in environmental issues. This section briefly discusses the nature and implications of these influences (see Figure 2.1).

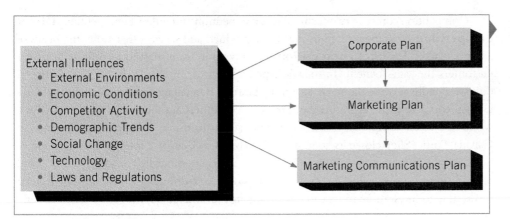

FIGURE
2.1

**External Influences Affect
All Levels of Planning in an
Organization**

ECONOMIC INFLUENCES

The general state of the economy has a direct impact on how aggressive or conservative a company is with its business plans. Should it be investing in marketing and marketing communications to expand its business, or should it conserve funds to protect profit margins? The general state of the economy is determined by growth rates in the gross domestic product, inflation rates, levels of employment, the value of the Canadian dollar in relation to foreign currencies, and income distribution among consumers. The relationship among these variables is dynamic. For example and in very general terms, if the value of the gross domestic product has dropped for a few consecutive years, if levels of employment have been dropping, and if real income has been dropping marginally from year to year, the economy could be in recession. If consumers aren't spending, marketing organizations might adopt a conservative approach and control investment in marketing and marketing communications. In contrast, if an economy is expanding, employment is plentiful and incomes are growing, it would be a time for an organization to invest more funds in marketing and marketing communications.

The relationship among these economic variables is dynamic and wise marketing managers stay abreast of changes and adjust their strategies appropriately. Dollarama, for example, Canada's largest operator of dollar stores, continues to expand, saying it has been benefitting from consumers' concern about household debt and the weak economy. The company's low price strategy is timely; in 2014 annual sales reached $2.3 billion with an operating income of $422 million.[1] At the same time, other retailers suffered during that time and ceased operations. Among the casualties were Target, Mexx, Smart Set, and Jacob stores.

Smart marketing organizations find solutions to poor economic situations. Recession-weary consumers seeking a cheap meal have flocked to McDonald's in recent years. McDonald's value menu has been a hit with consumers. McDonald's uses the value menu as a traffic builder, knowing that consumers will trade up to a higher price point on the menu in better economic times.

COMPETITOR INFLUENCES

Assessing the activities of competitors is probably the most thoroughly analyzed aspect of marketing planning. Such analysis provides input into how one brand can differentiate itself from others and perhaps stand out more in the eyes of consumers. Most Canadian markets are very competitive and are described as an **oligopoly** (a market with a few major brands) or as being **monopolistically competitive** (a market with all kinds of brands). In either case, the consumer has a choice of what brand to buy, and the effectiveness of the marketing and marketing communications strategies will influence the decision.

oligopoly   A market situation in which only a few brands control the market.

monopolistic competition   A market in which there are many competitors, each offering a unique marketing mix; consumers can assess these choices prior to making a buying decision.

direct competition   Competition from alternative products and services that satisfy the needs of a target market.

indirect competition   Competition from substitute products that offer the same benefit as another type of product.

Competition comes in two forms: direct competition and indirect competition. **Direct competition** is competition from alternative products and services that satisfy the needs of a target market. **Indirect competition** is competition from substitute products that offer customers the same benefit. In today's hypercompetitive marketplace, the lines between direct and indirect competition are becoming blurred. In retail marketing, for example, stores used to compete with each other, but now that consumers are shopping online, the virtual world is the real competitor. How a company adapts to online competition is crucial. In Canada, Future Shop closed its doors in 2015. Owned by Best Buy, the two-banner arrangement caught up with the company. Two brands offering essentially the same products and services increased costs while customer visits to stores were dropping. The company decided it was time to invest more money in developing its ecommerce business under one banner.[2]

DEMOGRAPHIC INFLUENCES

For the purpose of devising a profile of potential customers, commonly referred to as a target market profile (see the discussion on this topic that appears later in this chapter), an organization must stay abreast of Canadian demographic and lifestyle trends. This section highlights several of these trends.

THE POPULATION IS AGING   As of 2015, Canada's population was 35.8 million, and the annual growth rate is averaging about a 1 percent a year increase. Two-thirds of population growth comes from immigration—a factor that will play an important role in the future. Within this framework, the population of Canada is aging. As Figure 2.2 shows,

FIGURE 2.2   Canada's Population by Age

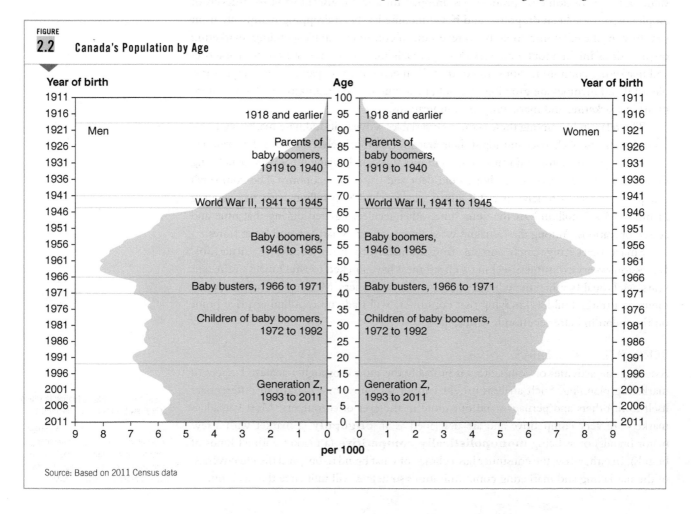

Source: Based on 2011 Census data

middle-aged Canadians (a group commonly called baby boomers) comprise the largest portion of the population. The baby boom generation (born between 1946 and 1965) was followed by a "baby bust" in the late 1960s and early 1970s; a mini boom occurred in the 1980s. The latter group is commonly called generation Y or millennials (the video generation or digital natives). Generation Y, a tech-savvy group, is a primary target for marketers now and in the future.

It is predicted that by 2020, 30 percent of all retail sales will be to millennials. Many brands already target them. McDonald's markets the McWrap, a healthier offering for calorie-conscious millennials; General Mills changed the name of Hamburger Helper to "Helper" as part of a strategy to attract men between the ages of 18 and 30. It uses the slogan "Need a dinner idea, we're here to help."[3]

Baby boomers are also a primary target. It is estimated that by 2021 baby boomers will comprise 40 percent of the population. Further, many will have retired, placing a burden on Canada's social programs and health care systems. Brands that focus on this target market now will have to adjust their marketing strategies to stay in tune with their changing needs. As mentioned, these brands must also attract younger consumers if they are to experience growth in sales. This poses a challenge for many existing and popular brands. A brand like Nike, for example, is popular with older customers, but generation Y is beyond such a brand. They are more interested in Skechers or Vans that present a style and image more suited to them. The two generations are miles apart in age and attitude.

URBAN POPULATION   The trend toward urbanization continues in Canada. According to the 2011 Census, 80.3 percent of the population lives in urban areas, and that figure will continue to grow by the time the next census data [2016] are available. Further, six metropolitan areas account for 46 percent of Canada's population: Toronto, Montreal, Vancouver, Calgary, Ottawa-Gatineau, and Edmonton. Edmonton and Calgary are the fastest growing cities in Canada; much of their growth is attributed to international migration, inter-provincial migration, and the formerly flourishing oil and oil-based industries.[4]

Keeping track of where Canadians live is an important consideration when developing marketing strategies and marketing communications strategies. With the population so clustered, companies now devise plans that are regional in nature or dwell specifically on key urban areas. Such a trend also helps explain the popularity of regional brands. In Atlantic Canada, for example, Alexander Keith's beer is a leading brand of beer. A national brand like Molson Canadian or Labatt Blue must adapt its national strategy to suit the needs of Atlantic beer drinkers if it is to make headway in that region.

CHANGING HOUSEHOLD FORMATIONS   There was a time when the traditional family was described as a married couple with children. The father worked full time, and the mother stayed at home to raise the children (a family structure reflected in the popular TV drama about advertising, *Mad Men*). Trends such as the postponement of marriage, the pursuit of careers by women, increases in divorce rates, and same-sex partnerships are producing new households in Canada. Now, married couples comprise only 67 percent of households.[5]

Today, modern households are described as lone-parent families (either from divorce or the absence of a partner), same-sex families (openness and acceptance of gay and lesbian lifestyles), and blended families (families that bring together children from previous marriages). Canadian households are also shrinking. Presently, the average size is 2.5 people, a reflection of these trends.[6]

Products and services must explore the unique opportunities these trends present. For example, companies in the packaged foods or household goods businesses must offer a variety of sizes to meet the needs of such household variation. As described in Chapter 1 (in the consumer behaviour section), the companies must also be aware of who is making the buying decisions or influencing the decisions. To present a brand improperly or in an old-fashioned manner could be harmful to the brand's development.

ETHNIC DIVERSITY　Canada is a culturally diverse country, a situation that presents unique challenges and opportunities for marketing organizations. The population is quickly changing from a predominantly European background to an Asian background. Existing within Canada are many diverse **subcultures**—subgroups within the larger cultural context that have distinctive lifestyles based on religious, racial, and geographical differences.

> **subcultures**　Subgroups within the larger cultural context that have distinctive lifestyles based on religious, racial, and geographical differences.

Canada's foreign-born population represents 20.6 percent of the population and is expected to rise to 23 percent by 2017.[7] Asian immigration has increased over the past two decades. At present almost half of the visible minority population is immigrants from South Asia and China. Most Asian Canadians reside in the urban areas of southern Ontario, the Greater Vancouver area, and Montreal. In Toronto, visible minorities comprise 49.1 percent of the population. In the communities surrounding Toronto (part of the GTA) the figure is even higher: in Markham visible minorities comprise 72 percent of the population and in Brampton, it's 66.4 percent, illustrating the fact that new immigrants tend to migrate to the suburbs of large cities.[8]

Companies that embrace marketing to various ethnic groups will profit the most in the future. The sheer size of this developing market and the fact that unique groups tend to cluster in urban areas make them a reachable target for Canadian brands. The key to an organization's success is to spend time learning more about the target—their customs, beliefs, mores, and so on—and then formulate appropriate communications strategies. Walmart is a leader in this area; the retailer adjusts its merchandising strategies to meet culture-based local market conditions and runs television ads featuring different ethnic groups.

SPENDING POWER AND WEALTH　How much people earn has an impact on their spending patterns. The trend in recent years is for Canadians' disposable income (after-tax income) to grow at a lower rate than the cost of basic necessities required in a household (food, shelter, transportation, clothing, household supplies, and so on). Canadians are working harder than ever, but there is less available for optional purchases such as vacations, sports, and recreational activities. Lower- and middle-income Canadians (the masses) are more cautious about how and on what they spend their money.

Another income trend in Canada is the concentration of wealth among upper-income groups. The old expression "the rich are getting richer and the poor are getting poorer" applies here. Census data from Statistics Canada verify a polarization of incomes at the upper and lower ends of the spectrum. The 2011 census data, which measured income change between 1995 and 2011, revealed that average after-tax incomes increased by 12.7 percent among families with incomes in the bottom 20 percent; for families with incomes in the middle 60 percent, it rose by 23.2 percent. However, in the top 20 percent income group, after-tax incomes rose by 37.2 percent. The average after tax income for the lower income group of families is $16 000; for middle income families $39 800; and for top income families $87 100. Income disparity is becoming an issue in Canada.[9]

How people spend their disposable income varies with the state of the economy (as discussed earlier in the chapter). With the present economy growing only at a modest rate, consumers are more cautious about parting with their money. Therefore, marketers

FIGURE
2.3

Walmart's Marketing Strategy Has Always Placed an Emphasis on Price

Source: © Kristoffer Tripplaar/Alamy Stock Photo

who stress value in their marketing strategies will be successful. There's no doubting Walmart's success. Walmart has always tapped into the consumers' appreciation for good prices for the quality of merchandise it sells. Walmart emphasizes price and value in its marketing communications. The current slogan, "Save Money. Live Better" and its former slogan "Always low prices" aptly summarize the company's marketing strategy. Refer to the image in Figure 2.3.

SOCIAL INFLUENCES

Marketers and marketing communicators must also stay in touch with social change. For a variety of reasons, the lifestyles of Canadians are always changing, and generally speaking, Canadians are very concerned about the natural environment and what companies are doing to preserve and protect it.

LIFESTYLES   There are two key issues affecting lifestyle: Canadians are living hectic lives while trying to live healthier. We are now a society that places greater emphasis on quality of life than on work, but we need to work to sustain the type of life we desire. The mythical "40-hour" work week doesn't exist for many Canadians. People choose to work longer hours to get ahead. Being pressed for time suggests a need for convenience. Is it any wonder that 50 percent of revenues at fast food restaurants such as McDonald's, Wendy's, and KFC comes from the drive-through? It's all about satisfying the "on-the-go" consumer.

Canadians are also expressing more concern for their health and welfare. Issues such as obesity and the aging process are causing consumers to make wiser choices. Marketers are responding to these demands by marketing healthier foods. Kraft Foods, one of the largest food companies, has announced an "obesity initiative"—proposing healthful changes to its products and marketing strategies. Ultima Foods also places an emphasis on health with many of its product offerings, including its highly successful IÖGO yogurt product lines. See the image in Figure 2.4.

NATURAL ENVIRONMENT   Today's consumers show serious concern for the natural environment and tend to favour companies that have a strong reputation for protecting our

natural resources and for contributing to worthy causes. This notion is particularly true of millennials, the next big generation of consumers. Essentially, companies with a strong social conscience stand to benefit now and in the future. Companies that are perceived as showing only tokenism toward such a serious issue can be quickly punished when consumers resist buying their products.

To demonstrate, Naya Spring Water was the first bottled water company to use 100 percent recycled plastic in its bottles. Recycled plastic is reprocessed to create new bottles. Naya's 1.5 litre bottle represents a carbon footprint reduction of 30 percent of the same bottle made with virgin plastic. Nature Valley reduced the size of its packaging without reducing the size of the granola bars it contained—an estimated savings of 2.8 million kilos of paperboard per year.[10] Marketing decisions like these are good for the environment.

TECHNOLOGY INFLUENCES

Several factors are combining to make an impact on how we learn about products and buy products. These factors include the availability of information through the Internet and our obsession with electronic devices such as smartphones and tablets. Canadians are a connected society; 86 percent of Canadians are Internet users (29.7 million people).[11] Monthly Canadians spend 33 hours online and 49 percent of that time is tied to mobile devices. Currently, 68 percent of Canadians own a smartphone.[12] Collectively, this data show the impact that technology will have on marketing communications strategies.

Canadians have also integrated social media such as Facebook, Twitter, Instagram, and YouTube into their daily routines to the extent that ordinary people are producing video content for the brands they like, a phenomenon referred to as **consumer-generated content**. Once apprehensive about this practice, marketers seem to have embraced the idea of consumers actively engaging with their brands; some marketing organizations run promotions to actively seek video content they may actually use.

consumer-generated content   Online content, often brand oriented, that is created by consumers for consumers.

Advancing technologies are causing marketing organizations to re-examine their marketing communications mix. Given the shift in media consumption toward digital media and away from print and broadcast media, media planners are moving away from mass reach and frequency campaigns toward strategies that stress selective reach and engagement with the target audience. The Internet, mobile devices, and social media will play a larger role in the communications mix in the future.

LEGAL AND REGULATORY INFLUENCES

Strategic plans are affected by new developments in the political and legal arenas. Most laws and regulations governing business practices are created by federal and provincial legislation. As well, many industries establish and abide by their own self-regulating policies and practices. In some cases, the self-regulation guidelines are more stringent than the government ones. Industry Canada regulates Canadian businesses through the *Competition Act*. As discussed in Chapter 1, sometimes an organization disregards the law and finds itself in court for marketing issues related to exaggerated product claims or misleading advertising.

Advertisers should follow the *Canadian Code of Advertising Standards*. The Code contains regulations about gender portrayal, product claims, price claims, advertising involving product comparisons, and advertising to children. The Code is administered by Advertising Standards Canada, a group representing advertisers and advertising agencies.

Canadians are also protected by various privacy laws, the *Privacy Act* and the *Personal Information Protection and Electronic Documents Act* (PIPEDA). The *Privacy Act* places limits on the collection, use, and disclosure of personal information and gives Canadians the right to access and correct any information about them held by government organizations. It also sets rules for how private organizations collect, use, and disclose personal information.

Self-regulation is an alternative to government regulation. The Canadian Marketing Association (CMA) has established policies and guidelines that all member organizations agree to follow. The CMA's *Code of Ethics and Standards of Practice* is a document covering issues such as protection of personal privacy, protecting the environment, and media-specific standards of practice. The CMA also established a Privacy Policy that identifies policies regarding the protection of information collected by CMA members. For more insight into CMA regulations and policies, visit its website at www.the-cma.org.

Mountain Equipment Co-op, or MEC as it is now known, carefully assessed market trends, its position in the sporting goods market, and opportunities for future growth when it decided to implement a new marketing campaign to pursue an urban target market. For insight into this campaign read the IMC Highlight: **Mountain Equipment Co-op Rebrands**.

Mountain Equipment Co-op Rebrands

"Stand still and you're dead" say many marketing experts. Survival in the business jungle today largely depends on an organization's ability to adapt to change, and change is occurring at breakneck speed.

Mountain Equipment Co-op is a successful sporting goods company. Its roots are firmly entrenched in outdoor sports such as mountain climbing and hiking. If you enjoy being outdoors, chances are you've shopped in one of their stores. The company has 3.5 million members across Canada who generate over $300 million in revenue annually.

Being so successful, why would MEC rebrand itself and adopt a new direction? After assessing its position in the market, the company realized its core customer (the outdoor adventurer) was getting older. They were transitioning to other less taxing sports for recreation; they were also spending more time in the city. The company decided it needed a new strategy for growth. It would have to dwell less on its past reputation as a niche marketer of backcountry supplies and find a way to get urban outdoor enthusiasts into their stores.

The first step in the rebranding was a new logo. Gone was the familiar mountain, replaced by a very simple design featuring MEC in bold white type on a green background. All marketing strategy starts with the brand! The new logo gave the company a new look as well as a contemporary urban feeling. The decision to go urban was sound. Some 70 percent of members live in cities and are active where they live as well as in the backcountry. Your current customers are always your best customers.

New product lines and more fashionable apparel were needed to appeal to urbanites. The company didn't give up on backcountry supplies—these items would simply play less of a role in the product mix. New products included running, cycling, walking, and yoga gear, along with essential apparel items associated with these sports. A service shop for bike repairs was also added.

To attract more members and make customers aware of the changes, MEC launched a marketing communications campaign featuring the tagline "We Are All Outsiders." That message was a clear attempt to attract younger urban shoppers who are more inclined to run or take yoga classes. Ads were placed in appropriate sports and fitness magazines, on outdoor posters, and through digital media. The company's website was redesigned integrating social, video, and editorial content. The stores were completely redesigned to carefully integrate the new product lines while still emphasizing traditional products.

The rebrand has been successful. With the addition of the new product lines, sales volume jumped 12 percent in the first year. Almost 70 percent of the revenue increase was attributed to the new products. MEC's future looks bright. "Change is good" say many marketing experts.

© Felix Choo/Alamy Stock Photo

Adapted from Wing Sze Tang, "Mountain Equipment Co-op Launches New Campaign with New Branding," *Marketing*, September 18, 2013, www.marketingmag.ca/ and Ashante Infantry, "Retailer's MEC-over Complete," *The Toronto Star*, September 18, 2013, pp. B1, B7.

Strategic Planning Process

A fairly common approach used by many organizations to develop their strategic plans is to start the process at the top or senior level of the organization and work downward. In other words, the strategic plan, or corporate plan, devised by senior executives will influence the nature of the various brand marketing plans developed by middle managers, and the brand marketing plans will influence the nature of the marketing communications plan.

In the **corporate plan** developed by senior executives, most objectives are financial in nature and become the goals that must be shared by all of the company's divisions or products. Typically, the corporate plan is not an exhaustive document. Once the corporate plan has been struck, the various functional areas, including marketing, start their planning process. See Figure 2.5 for a illustration.

A **marketing plan** is developed for each one of a company's products and sets out the objectives for all brands. The plan determines how the various elements of the marketing mix will be employed so that they have the desired impact on the target market. The target market is identified through some combination of demographic, psychographic, and geographic variables; a positioning strategy statement guides the development of the plan.

Once the role of marketing communications has been determined, specific plans are then developed for the various components of the marketing communications mix. At this stage, the goal is to develop a synergistic communications plan that will improve the success of the product or service. Decisions are made on what components of the marketing communications mix to employ—advertising, interactive communications including social media, direct response communications, sales promotions, public relations, and experiential marketing.

The integration of all relevant components in a strategic plan will help achieve objectives. The saying "A chain is only as strong as its weakest link" appropriately describes the relationships among various components of the marketing communications mix. As in war, a unified attack has a better chance of success!

The corporate plan provides guidance for the marketing plan, and the marketing plan provides guidance for the marketing communications plan. All plans are based on the same background information and any analysis stemming from that information. Corporate plans are strategic in nature. Marketing plans and marketing communications plans are both strategic and tactical in nature.

corporate plan A strategic plan formulated at the executive level of an organization to guide the development of functional plans in the organization.

marketing plan A short-term, specific plan of action that combines strategy and tactics.

The corporate plan provides guidance for the marketing plan, and the marketing plan provides guidance for the marketing communications plan. All plans are based on the same background information and any analysis stemming from that information.

FIGURE
2.5

Strategic Planning: Links among Various Organizational Plans

The Corporate Plan

mission statement   A statement of an organization's purpose and operating philosophy; provides guidance and direction for the operations of the company.

The mission statement is the guiding light for all forms of strategic planning. A **mission statement** is a statement of an organization's purpose and an indicator of the operating philosophy the organization follows. A good mission statement is customer and marketing oriented, considers the competition, and looks toward the long term. In other words, once a company establishes its mission, it must provide adequate time and resources to carry through with it. Tim Hortons mission statement is brief: "Our guiding mission is to deliver superior quality products and services for our guests and communities through leadership, innovation and partnerships." An organization might also develop a **vision statement**, which is a statement of what an organization would like to be. Tim Hortons has one: "Our vision is to be the quality leader in everything we do."[13] There's no disputing the success of Tim Hortons in Canada—they do live up to these statements based on the quality of products offered, convenience, and service provided. They are also actively involved in the community with programs such as food drives, Timbits hockey, and opportunities for free skating and swimming.

corporate objective   A statement of a company's overall goal; used to evaluate the effectiveness or ineffectiveness of a company's strategic plan.

With the mission confirmed, executive attention turns to setting corporate objectives, determining strategic direction, and allocating resources. **Corporate objectives** are statements of a company's overall goals. These objectives are usually financial in nature and are used to evaluate the effectiveness or ineffectiveness of a company's strategic plan and the people who manage the organization. At the end of the year, actual financial results are compared to the objectives. The degree of success is there for all concerned to see. Here are a few examples of corporate objectives, both quantitative and qualitative:

- To increase company sales revenue from $50 000 000 to $60 000 000 in 20XX.

- To increase category market share (share in a market for all company brands) from 25 percent to 30 percent in 20XX.

- To increase return on investment from 10 percent to 15 percent in 20XX.

- To exhibit constructive social responsibility by investing in research and development to discover environmentally friendly new products.

The last objective on the list above is qualitative. At the end of the year, however, the organization will evaluate in some way its investment in social responsibility programs. The first three objectives on the list are quantitative in nature. Objective statements like these have a direct impact on the development of marketing objectives and strategies. All company brands must contribute to achieving the company's goals. It is the total sales revenue of various brands that constitutes overall company sales revenue. For example, General Mills Canada divides its brands into separate categories such as baking products, cooking products, cereal products, yogurt products, and snack products. Some of their popular brand name logos from these product categories appear in Figure 2.6.

When an organization determines its corporate strategy, it considers several factors: marketing strength, degree of competition in current or new markets under consideration, financial resources, research and development capabilities, and management commitment to particular goals. It is common for a company to follow numerous strategic directions at the same time, largely due to the dynamic nature of the marketplace. To follow one direction and fail could have a long-term negative effect on the company.

To grow and be profitable, a company will give due consideration to a variety of strategic options. Among the options are a penetration strategy, an acquisition strategy, a new product development strategy, and a strategic alliance strategy. All these strategies

Source: © General Mills Canada

imply a desire for growth. In some cases, a company may decide to get smaller. While that may seem odd, many companies find that too much expansion can have disastrous results on profits. Growing at the expense of profit doesn't make sense!

In such cases, a company may decide on a **divestment strategy** and sell off various divisions or products. Such a course may also have to do with how well a product or division of a company "fits" with the direction the company is heading in. In 2012 Procter & Gamble sold off Pringles, the fourth-largest brand of sweet and savoury snacks in the world, to Kellogg Co. Over a period of time, Procter & Gamble had been weaning itself of food products, preferring to increase its presence in personal care and household goods categories.

For Kellogg's the transaction was part of its **acquisition strategy**. Kellogg's bought a product of interest, a product that fit well with the direction the company was heading. For a price tag of $2.7 billion, Kellogg's became the second-largest snack company in the world (behind Pepsi-Co's Frito Lay division).[14]

A **penetration strategy** involves aggressive marketing of a company's existing products. The goal is to build the business by taking customers from the competition or by expanding the entire market. Coca-Cola invests considerable sums of money into key brands such as Coca-Cola, Diet Coke, Minute Maid, Powerade, and Dasani to retain its overall leadership in the beverage industry. Arch-rival PepsiCo also invests considerable sums of money in Pepsi-Cola, Diet Pepsi, Tropicana, Gatorade, and Aquafina to build its market share in the industry. Advertising and marketing communications play key roles for all the brands owned by these companies in the battle between two giants for market share.

divestment strategy   Selling off divisions or product lines that no longer fit the strategic direction an organization is taking.

acquisition strategy   A plan of action for acquiring companies that represent attractive financial opportunities.

penetration strategy   A plan of action for aggressive marketing of a company's existing products.

new product development strategy
A marketing strategy that calls for significant investment in research and development to develop innovative products.

New products, the result of a **new product development strategy**, offer another option for growth-minded companies. New products create new revenue streams at a much greater rate than simply trying to expand existing products. Think of all the new products that have contributed to Apple's success: iPod, iTunes, iPhone, iPad, and so on. Apple's roots are in computers, but they are only a fraction of Apple's overall business today.

Molson Coors Canada expanded beyond beer when it launched a new product in Ontario and Quebec in 2014: Mad Jack Apple Lager. The new beverage was aimed at consumers who don't like the bitterness of traditional beers. They're looking for a sweeter taste, something different than a standard lager and traditional coolers and ciders. The marketing communications strategy, aimed at adults aged 25 to 34, utilized out-of-home media, social media, and in-store sampling.[15] The initial launch for Mad Jack saw one of the highest ever conversion rates from trial to purchase for a new Molson Coors product. It was rolled out nationally in 2015. Refer to Figure 2.7.

strategic alliance A relationship between two companies where the resources of those companies are combined in a marketing venture for the purpose of satisfying the customers they share.

Strategic alliances occur when separate companies with complementary strengths join forces to satisfy their shared customers. Alliances are now very popular among companies searching for ways to reduce costs or improve operating efficiency. Apple and IBM would seem to be strange bedfellows given the nature of the competition between the two, but in 2014 they formed a strategic alliance. The two technology companies are working together to develop mobile applications for a wide range of industries. CEO Tim Cook of Apple said his company doesn't understand corporate customers like IBM does. Apple leans heavily on consumer marketing. IBM CEO Ginni Rometty said the alliance will help her company widen the audience for its technology tools. It's about two powerhouses working together to maximize the potential of mobility for businesses. Both companies will benefit financially in this arrangement.[16]

FIGURE
2.7

New Products Meeting New Needs Increase a Company's Sales Revenue

Source: Courtesy of Molson Coors Canada

Marketing Planning

With the details of the corporate plan determined, the marketing department starts the process of marketing planning. **Marketing planning** involves analyzing, planning, implementing, and controlling marketing initiatives to satisfy target market needs and achieve organizational objectives. Marketing plans are short term in nature (one year), specific in scope (they involve precise actions for one product), and combine both strategy and tactics (they are action oriented). The marketing plan should also include a **contingency plan** to provide alternative courses of action in the event that new circumstances arise.

The marketing plan revolves around the customer, specifically the knowledge an organization has about its customers. An essential ingredient in the development of a marketing plan is a precise description of the target market. The **target market** is the group of persons for whom a firm creates and markets a product that specifically meets the needs and preferences of that group. A target market is described in terms of demographic, psychographic, geographic, and behaviour response characteristics.

DEMOGRAPHIC CHARACTERISTICS   Demographics describe a customer group in terms of age, gender, income, occupation, education, marital status, household formation, and ethnic background. Depending on the nature of the product, some characteristics may be more important than others. Some may not be important at all. Given the role changes among males and females in Canadian households, many brands and products that used to be gender-specific are rethinking their target market description. Also, given the growing diversity of Canada's population, strategies that target ethnic groups are now more common than ever before.

PSYCHOGRAPHIC CHARACTERISTICS   Psychographics describe a customer group in terms of attitudes, interests, opinions, and activities. The focus is on the "lifestyle" of the members in the group. It is quite common in marketing and marketing communications to appeal to consumers based on their current lifestyle or the lifestyle they would like to have. It's not so much *what* is said in a message but *how* it is said or portrayed visually. Psychographic knowledge can directly influence message and media strategy. For example, if the target market spends more time online and less time watching television than it used to, such knowledge will influence media selection strategy.

GEOGRAPHIC CHARACTERISTICS   Where a person lives (for example, a certain region of the country or large cities across the country) has an impact on marketing communications strategy. According to Statistics Canada, some 80 percent of the population lives in an urban area. More to the point, Canada's top three cities (and surrounding areas) comprise about one-third of the population. Marketers, therefore, have the option of marketing nationally, regionally, or in designated urban areas, all of which influences decisions on how to allocate a budget and what media to employ.

BEHAVIOUR RESPONSE   The behaviour of group members rounds out a target market description. For example, many products (suntan products, skis, flowers, and toys) are seasonal in nature, and consumers concentrate their purchases over short periods of time. Certain members may consume a product more quickly than others. Such users are described as "heavy users" and may have a slightly different profile than other users. Some members may also demonstrate more loyalty than others. Perhaps the profile of a truly loyal user is somewhat different from that of the average user. Can information

marketing planning   The analysis, planning, implementing, and controlling of marketing initiatives to satisfy target market needs and achieve organizational objectives.

contingency plan   The identification of alternative courses of action that can be used to modify an original plan if and when new circumstances arise.

target market   The group of persons for whom a firm creates and markets a product.

about heavy users and loyal users be used to advantage? While usage and loyalty can never be taken for granted, it does give marketers an opportunity to develop strategies aimed at the less loyal users who could switch to competitive brands if enticed the right way. As is often said, "Knowledge is power!"

There is no perfect format for a marketing plan, although Figure 2.8 offers an illustration. Marketing plans vary considerably from one organization to another in length, detail, and content. This section will examine the content of a marketing plan, but readers must realize that the content of a plan is modified to suit the needs of each specific organization. Essentially, a marketing plan is divided into two major sections. The first section is a compilation of background information about the market, target market, competition, and product. The second section is the plan itself; it contains the objectives, strategies, and tactics for the product for the year ahead, and provides specific details about how the budget is allocated and the timing of all activities.

FIGURE 2.8   An Illustration of a Marketing Plan Model

Marketing Background	Marketing Plan
External Influences • Economic trends • Social and demographic trends • Technology trends • Regulatory trends	**Positioning Strategy** • Positioning strategy statement
	Target Market Profile • Demographic • Psychographic • Geographic
Market Analysis • Market size and growth • Regional market size and growth • Market segment analysis • Seasonal analysis	**Marketing Objectives** • Sales volume • Market share • Profit • Other
Competitor Analysis • Market share trends • Marketing strategy assessment	**Marketing Strategies** • Product • Price • Marketing communications • Distribution
Target Market Analysis • Consumer data • Consumer behaviour	**Marketing Execution (Tactics)** • Product • Price • Marketing communications • Distribution • New products • Marketing research • Service • Partnerships and alliances
Product (Brand) Analysis • Sales volume trends • Market share trends • Distribution • Marketing communications • New product activity	
SWOT Analysis* • Strengths • Weaknesses • Opportunities • Threats	**Budget and Financial Summary** • Budget allocations (by activity, by time of year) • Brand financial statement **Timeline or Calendar** • Activity schedule

Corporate Plan

Marketing Plan
• Marketing Background (SWOT Analysis)
• Marketing Plan

Marketing Communications Plan

*Note: Including a SWOT analysis is optional. Some planners believe that the SWOT analysis occurs when the information is compiled in the preceding sections of the plan. Other planners believe that such information must be analyzed further to determine priorities. The latter is the intention of a SWOT analysis.

MARKET BACKGROUND

The direction a marketing plan takes is directly influenced by internal conditions (strengths and weaknesses) and external conditions (opportunities and threats). The first step in planning is analysis. In marketing terms, such an analysis is referred to as a **SWOT analysis**. The acronym SWOT stands for strengths, weaknesses, opportunities, and threats.

STRENGTHS AND WEAKNESSES   The internal capabilities and resources are reviewed to determine the relative condition of a brand and its capability to pursue new directions. The review considers a variety of controllable marketing factors and may extend to the areas of manufacturing, finance, human resources, and technology. Any limits on current strengths may justify developing new strengths.

OPPORTUNITIES AND THREATS   The manager reviews relevant external data that may affect the direction of the marketing plan. Such a review may include economic trends, demographic trends, social trends, legal and regulatory influences, competitive activity, and technology influences. Opportunities are prioritized, and threats are classified according to their seriousness and probability of occurrence. The absence of marketing action in either area could hinder the development of a brand.

A variety of information is collected and analyzed. The goals of a SWOT analysis are to capitalize on strengths while minimizing weaknesses and to take advantage of opportunities while fending off threats. Typically, a SWOT analysis should review the following information (refer to Figure 2.8 for an illustration of a marketing plan model).

SWOT analysis   An analysis procedure that involves an assessment of an organization's strengths, weaknesses, opportunities, and threats; strengths and weaknesses are internal variables, whereas opportunities and threats are external variables.

EXTERNAL INFLUENCES

- **Economic Trends:** The current and predicted states of the economy are considered. Is the economy growing (recovery or prosperity) or is it sputtering (recession)? Appropriate statistical information is evaluated in this section of the plan.

- **Social and Demographic Trends:** Basic trends in age, income, household formation, immigration, migration, and lifestyles are evaluated to identify potential target markets. For example, the aging of Canada's population, the attitudes of millennials, the migration of the population to urban areas, or concern for the environment will be factors influencing future marketing strategies.

- **Technology Trends:** The rapid pace of change and its impact on behaviour must be considered. Technology quickens the speed with which new products come to market and the way companies deliver messages about products to customers.

- **Regulatory Trends:** A company should always stay abreast of changes to any laws and regulations affecting the marketing of its products. For example, privacy laws have been introduced in Canada to protect consumers and regulate companies engaged in emarketing practices.

MARKET ANALYSIS

- **Market Size and Growth:** A review of trends over several years is considered for the purpose of making sales projections for the year ahead. Is the market growing or declining, and how fast?

- **Regional Markets:** Sales trends by region are analyzed to determine what areas need more or less attention in the year ahead. Some markets may be growing while others are not. A regional analysis helps determine priorities.

- **Market Segment Analysis:** There could be numerous product segments in a market. For example, in the hotel industry there are budget hotels, mid-priced hotels, and luxury hotels. Are all segments growing at the same rate, or are some segments doing better than others? Interpretive comments about the various segments should be included.

- **Seasonal Analysis:** Seasonal or cyclical trends over the course of a year are examined. For example, volume trends for beer and barbecue-related items would be much higher in the spring and summer seasons. The timing of proposed marketing activities needs to consider such trends.

TARGET MARKET ANALYSIS

- **Consumer Data:** The profile of primary users (and secondary users, if necessary) is reviewed for any changes during the past few years. The aging population and lifestyle changes could be affecting the profile of product users.

- **Consumer Behaviour:** The degree of customer loyalty to the market and products within a market is assessed. Are customers loyal to the brand or do they switch brands? Knowledge of such behaviour has a direct influence on advertising and promotion strategies. Should the plan attract new customers, prevent existing customers from departing, or do both?

PRODUCT (BRAND) ANALYSIS

An assessment of a brand's past performance is included in this section of the plan. An attempt is made to link past marketing activities to the performance of the brand. Have previous strategies been successful, and will changes be needed in the year ahead?

- **Sales Volume Trends:** Historical volume trends are plotted to forecast sales for the year ahead.

- **Market Share Trends:** Market share is a clear indicator of brand performance. Market share trends are examined nationally and regionally, and by key markets to determine areas of strengths and weaknesses. Is the brand's market share growing faster or slower than competitors' shares? Where are the priorities for improving market share?

- **Distribution:** The availability of the product nationally and regionally is reviewed. Regional availability will affect how much marketing support a brand will receive. Should the new plan focus on areas where distribution is high or low?

- **Marketing Communications:** Current activities are assessed to determine if strategies need to be retained or changed. A review of expenditures by medium, sales promotions, experiential marketing activities, and social media is necessary to assess the impact of such spending on brand performance.

- **New Product Activity:** Sales performance of recently implemented initiatives is evaluated. For example, the performance of new product formats, sizes, flavours, and so on is scrutinized to determine the impact of those factors on sales and market share.

COMPETITOR ANALYSIS

In order to plan effectively, a manager should know competitors' products as well as his or her own product. A review of marketing mix activities for key competitors provides essential input on how to revise marketing strategies. A brand must react to the actions of another brand or suffer the consequences of lack of action.

- **Market Share Trends:** It is common to plot and review the market share trends of all brands from year to year. Such analysis provides insight into which brands are moving forward and which brands are moving backward.

- **Marketing Strategy Assessment:** An attempt is made to link known marketing strategies to competitor brand performance. What is the nature of the competition's advertising, sales promotions, experiential marketing, and social media effort? Have they launched any new products or implemented any new distribution, pricing, or communications strategies? What changes are anticipated in the year ahead?

MARKETING PLAN

The market background analysis leads directly into the development of the action plan. The plan section clarifies the positioning strategy of the company's brands, establishes objectives for the year, determines how the various elements of the marketing mix will be employed, and outlines the investment and timing of all activities that are recommended.

POSITIONING STRATEGY   **Positioning** refers to the selling concept that motivates purchase or the image that marketers desire a brand to have in the minds of customers. The **positioning strategy statement** has a direct impact on the nature of the message that must be communicated to consumers. To illustrate, consider the positioning statement that has guided Visa Canada recently:

> Visa gives you confidence that you are able to do anything.

The positioning statement clearly identifies where the company wants the product to be in the consumer's mind. In Visa's case, it is a currency that enables people to fulfill their needs. The positioning statement guides the direction of the message that will ultimately be communicated to customers. Furthermore, it serves as the standard for considering what strategies to use and not use. For example, if a marketing communications agency presents a new creative strategy for the brand, the client will evaluate it against the positioning strategy statement to see whether the new creative idea fits with the strategy.

In the case of Visa, the benefits of having and using a Visa card are portrayed in ads that say: "More people go with Visa." This slogan aptly reflects Visa's positioning strategy and brand platform. 'Go' is the active word in the new slogan—Visa is a brand of action. It encourages consumers to take advantage of the superior value that Visa offers. Refer to the illustration in Figure 2.9.

TARGET MARKET PROFILE   At this stage, the manager identifies or targets a group of customers that represents the greatest profit potential. As discussed earlier in the chapter, a target market is defined in terms of similar needs and common characteristics based on demographic, psychographic, geographic, and behaviour response variables.

To demonstrate, the following profile might represent a target market for an upscale automobile or watch:

Age: 25 to 49 years old

Gender: Male or female

Income: $100 000+ annually

Occupation: Business managers, owners of companies, and professionals

Education: College or university graduate

Location: Cities with 500 000+ population

Lifestyle: Risk takers who like to experiment with new products, adventure seekers interested in outdoor recreational pursuits, jet-setters who travel extensively, and art lovers interested in the arts and entertainment

positioning   The selling concept that motivates purchase or the image that marketers desire a brand to have in the minds of consumers.

positioning strategy statement A summary of the character and personality of a brand and the benefits it offers customers.

The advertisement that appears in Figure 2.10 shows how Mercedes–Benz appeals to the upscale target market just described.

marketing objective A statement that identifies what a product will accomplish in a one-year period, usually expressed in terms of sales, market share, and profit.

MARKETING OBJECTIVES **Marketing objectives** are statements that identify what a product will accomplish in a one-year period. Similar to corporate objectives, they tend to focus on financial measures, such as sales and profits, or other quantitative yardsticks. Objectives may also be qualitative in nature and include new product introductions, product line extensions, launching of new packaging, and so on. Here, the objective may be to simply get the new activity into the market at the planned time. Objectives do not always have to be measured in terms of dollars or market share.

To illustrate how marketing objectives are written, let's assume you are the brand manager for Mountain Dew (a brand marketed by PepsiCo.). You are developing your objectives for the next year based on your present market share of 5 percent. Mountain Dew is the third most popular soft drink in Canada. The soft drink market in Canada is estimated to be worth $2 billion and annual growth is flat.

You might set out the marketing objectives for Mountain Dew for the year ahead like this:

- To increase market share from 5.0 percent to 5.2 percent (reflecting a desire to grow marginally in a very competitive market by taking market share from other brands).

- To increase dollar sales from $100 000 000 to $104 000 000 (assumes flat market growth and achievement of market share objective).

- To successfully introduce a new flavour (a product line extension) to extend Mountain Dew's presence in the market.

- To secure 75 percent distribution (in stores selling soft drinks) for the new flavour.

FIGURE 2.10   Mercedes-Benz Targets an Upscale Market with Its M-Class

Source: Courtesy of Mercedes-Benz Canada Inc.

Objectives are written so they can be measured to facilitate evaluation at the end of the plan period. Were the objectives achieved or not? Was the plan too aggressive or not aggressive enough? It will depend on the dynamics of the marketplace over the next 12 months.

MARKETING STRATEGIES   **Marketing strategies** are the master plans for achieving the objectives. The importance of having a good strategy must be emphasized. There is a saying that "Good strategy with weak execution can produce reasonable results." Likewise, another saying states, "Poor strategy with good execution produces terrible results." The reason these sayings have become so common is that they are true. The goal should be to have the right strategy and then simply to work on better execution as time goes on. Most professional hockey or football coaches would agree with this principle.

In the development of the marketing strategy, the role and contribution of each component of the marketing mix are identified. Priority may be given to certain components depending on the nature of the market. For example, the success of a brand of beer

marketing strategy   A plan of action that shows how the various elements of the marketing mix will be used to satisfy a target market's needs.

as measured by market share depends largely on the impact of advertising on the target market. In the transportation market, the product environment (a combination of product and additional services) is an important consideration among travellers. VIA Rail, for example, stresses the benefit of staying connected with Wi-Fi service on select rail cars and calls their railway "a more human way to travel." See the illustration in Figure 2.11.

The budget allocated to the product will be identified in the strategy section of the plan. There are various methods for arriving at a budget. Some methods estimate sales first and then base the marketing or marketing communications budget on sales. Other methods develop the budget first, a method based on the premise that investing in marketing communications creates sales, so the budget is not the outcome of sales. Regardless of the method used, the budget must be carefully calculated and defended when the plan is presented to senior level executives. See Figure 2.12 for details about budget methodologies.

MARKETING EXECUTION (TACTICS)   The tactics (execution) outlined in the plan are program details drawn directly from the strategy section of the plan. Such details will identify what programs are to be implemented, how much they will cost, what the timing will be, and who will be responsible for implementation. The unique action plan provides specific details regarding how the various elements of the marketing mix will be used to achieve the marketing objectives. This section of the plan may also include a description of activities in areas such as marketing research, service programs, and potential partnerships and alliances.

Typically, only the key elements of various marketing communications plans (advertising, sales promotion, public relations, direct response, interactive communications, and so on) are included in the marketing plan. Specific and lengthier information about marketing communications strategies and tactics is presented in their respective plans or in a marketing communications plan.

BUDGET AND FINANCIAL SUMMARY   In order for a marketing plan to be improved, it is crucial to show the financial implications of the activities to be undertaken. Senior executives like to know how the company's money will be spent and how profitable the investment will be. Therefore, the budget section will itemize all activities and indicate the associated cost. Major areas such as media, consumer promotion, trade promotion, and marketing research are often subdivided into more specific activities.

FIGURE
2.12   Methods for Determining a Marketing Budget

Method	Procedure
Percentage of Sales	A predetermined percentage of forecasted sales is allocated to marketing or marketing communications.
Fixed Sum/Unit	A predetermined dollar amount per unit sold is allocated to marketing or marketing communications.
Industry Average	The average amount (current or forecasted) spent on marketing or marketing communications by all brands in a market is allocated to marketing.
Advertising Share/Market Share	Invest at a level to retain share (ad share equals market share); invest at a level to build market share (ad share is greater than market share).
Task (Objective)	Define the task, determine the activities to achieve the task, and associate a cost to the activities.

In many companies, the brand managers and marketing managers are responsible for bottom-line profitability for their brands. If so, a financial statement for the brand is included. Such a statement should provide some financial history for the previous year, current year, and a forecast for the plan year. Senior executives are interested in seeing progress in marketing and financial terms. The financial statement will include such measures as sales, market share, cost of goods sold, gross profit, marketing expenses, and net profit before taxes.

EVALUATION AND CONTROL It is quite common for an organization to plan for semi-annual or quarterly reviews to assess its financial position. Marketing and marketing communications managers often fear such reviews, because that is often when budgets are given the axe. Nonetheless, evaluation of activities is essential because changes will likely be necessary while a plan is in midstream. **Marketing control** is the process of measuring and evaluating the results of marketing strategies and plans, and then taking corrective action to ensure the marketing objectives are attained.

> **marketing control** The process of measuring and evaluating the results of marketing strategies and plans, and of taking corrective action to ensure marketing objectives are achieved.

The evaluation process also provides an opportunity to change marketing strategies if necessary. If financial obligations are not being achieved, then new strategies must be explored. Furthermore, it is an opportunity to review key financials, such as sales, costs, and profits, and to reforecast the figures for the balance of the year. If the original objectives are not achievable, they should be modified, as should the marketing activities and expenditures that support the product.

Marketing Communications Planning

Since plans have to be struck well in advance of their implementation date, the marketing communications plan is developed simultaneously with the marketing plan so that its key components can be integrated into the marketing plan. The various components of marketing communications rely on the same input (background information, target market profiles, and positioning strategy statements) that are in the marketing plan. A marketing communications plan model is included in Figure 2.13.

> **marketing communications plan** A plan that identifies how the various elements of marketing communications will be integrated into a cohesive and coordinated plan.

A **marketing communications plan** is usually prepared by an outside organization. Depending on the nature of the plan, it could be an advertising agency, a public relations company, an experiential marketing agency, or any combination thereof. At some point, all the agencies working on the same plan must compare notes to ensure that their strategies are synchronized. Each aspect of the marketing communications plan has its own objectives, strategies, and tactical plans. In fact, it is crucial that the role and contribution of each component—advertising, sales promotion, public relations, direct response, interactive communications, experiential marketing, and personal selling—be identified.

The role of the marketing communications components will vary depending on the nature of the product and the target market. The key to success is the integration of the various components to produce a unified approach to building the brand (or company). Selecting the right communications components is essential.

MARKETING COMMUNICATIONS OBJECTIVES

Marketing communications objectives are very diverse and could involve any of the following:

- Building awareness, interest, and trial purchases for a product.
- Changing perceptions of the product held by consumers.

- Differentiating the product from others by presenting unique features and benefits.
- Attracting new target markets to the product.
- Engaging consumers with the brand or brand experience.
- Offering incentives to get people to buy the product.
- Creating goodwill and fostering a positive public image (usually for a company).
- Motivating distributors to carry the product.

To demonstrate communications objectives, let's continue with the Mountain Dew example initially presented in the "Marketing Objectives" section. Mountain Dew is a firmly established and well-known brand, so awareness objectives are not relevant.

FIGURE
2.13   A Marketing Communications Plan Model

Marketing Communications Objectives
- Identify what is to be accomplished

Marketing Communications Strategies
- Identify the role/importance of mix components
- Budget available

Creative Plan
- Objectives (what to say)
- Strategies (how to say it)
- Execution (specific details)

Media Plan
- Objectives
- Strategies
- Criteria for reaching target
- Rationale for media selection
- Execution (cost, coverage, and timing details)

Direct Response Plan
- Objectives
- Strategies
- Tactics
- Budget

Interactive Plan
- Objectives
- Strategies
- Tactics
- Budget

Sales Promotion Plan
- Objectives
- Strategies
- Tactics
- Budget

Public Relations Plan
- Objectives
- Strategies
- Tactics
- Budget

Experiential Marketing Plan
- Objectives
- Strategies
- Tactics
- Budget

Personal Selling Plan
- Objectives
- Strategies
- Tactics
- Budget

Calendar of Events
- Week
- Month

Budget Summary
- Total and allocation by various plans

Corporate Plan

Marketing Plan

Marketing Communications Plan
- Advertising Plan
- Direct Response Plan
- Interactive Plan
- Sales Promotion Plan
- Public Relations Plan
- Experiential Marketing Plan
- Personal Selling Plan

Note: These plans assume adequate input is provided from the background section of the marketing plan. See Figure 2.8 for details.

However, here are some examples of other marketing communications objectives Mountain Dew might identify:

- To firmly position Mountain Dew as an "on-the-edge" brand in the minds of the primary target market.
- To achieve a brand preference score of 40 percent among primary buyers (12- to 19-year-old males).
- To achieve a trial purchase rate of 25 percent for the new flavour among members of the primary target market.

These objectives imply that marketing communications will be an integrated effort including activities beyond advertising. Certainly the company will employ sales promotions (both consumer and trade) and interactive communications, including social media. There is also room for experiential marketing, as Mountain Dew likes to participate in extreme sporting events. Such a marketing communications mix will help solidify the Mountain Dew brand image in the primary target's mind. Refer to the Mountain Dew image in Figure 2.14.

General Motors' brand Buick is has been associated with an older male target market. After an assessment of the brand's position in the market and various social and demographic trends, the company realized that the path to future success lay with the brand's ability to attract new, younger consumers. Buick targeted younger females with a new model and new image in 2013. For insight into that campaign read the IMC Highlight: **Buick: Going Younger**.

FIGURE
2.14 **Mountain Dew Is an Active Participant in Experiential Marketing Activities**

Source: Photo by Matt Forsythe/Push.ca.

Buick: Going Younger

When a brand is facing declining sales and its primary target market is aging, what must it do to get things back on track? Many marketers try to reposition their brand so that it appeals to a younger target market. That said, can the same product appeal to diverse age groups? Making it happen is more difficult than it sounds.

Buick, a product line marketed by General Motors, faced this very situation. The brand had always been popular with older men and its image had become rather stale. While Buick cannot ignore its primary target, future success depends on attracting new, younger customers. The product and the marketing behind it had to change.

The solution was Melina, the internal name GM gave to the new target market Buick would pursue. Melina is

© Car Collection/Alamy Stock Photo

a tech-savvy urbanite making a good salary who likes to treat herself to nice things—spa treatments, nice clothes, and nights out with the girls.

Buick launched a completely new vehicle called the Verano for Melina. A new style of advertising featured young women enjoying fine coffee; relaxing in beach settings; and driving the new compact, fuel-efficient vehicle. A well-balanced traditional media campaign combined with a new social media and experiential marketing campaign introduced the vehicle to the market. Buick actually lent the Verano to young people who had influence on social media. The goal was to get the influencers to spread the word via Facebook, Instagram, and Twitter.

General Motors is happy with the results. Buick sales are trending upward with the increase fully attributed to the launch of the Verano. As well, the buyers are younger, and non-GM buyers—a sure sign that the advertising campaign had an impact on the new target market.

GM now has its eye on younger targets for future sales. Rob Assimakopoulous, director of marketing and communications for Buick says, "The products we're building for Buick today reinforce the needs of a modern consumer; in many cases a younger consumer."

Adapted from Susan Krashinsky, "There's Something about Melina," *The Globe and Mail*, November 23, 2012, p. 5.

MARKETING COMMUNICATIONS STRATEGIES

The marketing communications strategy provides a basic outline of how the various components of the mix will be used. As indicated by the Mountain Dew example, all components may not be used, but those that are used are often ranked in terms of priority and what they are able to achieve.

This section of the strategy also identifies the budget allocated to marketing communications and how funds will be allocated to the various activities. What percentage of the budget will be allocated to advertising, to sales promotions, to experiential marketing, and so on?

ADVERTISING PLAN The **advertising plan** is divided into two primary areas: creative (message) and media. The **creative plan** is concerned with what message will be communicated and how it will be communicated to the target market. The message usually stresses the most important attribute of the product—that which is most important to the

advertising plan A plan that includes creative and media components.

creative plan A plan that outlines the nature of the message to be communicated to the target audience; involves the development of creative objectives, creative strategies, and creative execution.

customer. Agencies draw on such techniques as humour, sex, emotions, and even facts to tempt us to buy something. To illustrate, consider the ad for JM that appears in Figure 2.15. A sexual appeal technique certainly draws attention to the ad and the brand name. JM markets underwear and swimwear. Complete details about creative planning are presented in Chapter 4.

media plan A strategy that outlines the relevant details about how a client's budget will be spent; involves decisions about what media to use and how much money to invest in the media chosen to reach the target audience effectively and efficiently.

The **media plan** involves strategic decisions about what media to use and how much money to invest in the media that are chosen. The overall goal of any media plan is efficiency: The plan must effectively reach the target audience at the lowest possible

FIGURE 2.15 A Sexual Appeal Technique Grabs the Reader's Attention Quickly

Source: JM Intimode Canada

cost. Since a company invests considerable sums in media advertising, wise decisions about usage are critical. Other media decisions involve timing, what markets to advertise in, how much money to allocate to regional markets and to key markets (cities), how long the campaign should last, and so on. Developing a media plan is complicated and best left to media specialists. More details about media planning for mass media options are presented in Chapter 5.

DIRECT RESPONSE PLAN   Direct response communications have a significant advantage over traditional mass media advertising: The direct results of the investment can be determined. Because direct response techniques can be accurately measured for success or failure, they are attractive to companies that stress accountability in their operations. Advancing technology, database marketing practices, and customer relationship management programs have fostered interest in marketing and communicating directly to individuals. More details about direct response communications are included in Chapter 6.

INTERACTIVE COMMUNICATIONS PLAN   The Internet is a fast-growing medium for placing advertising messages. What about a video on YouTube? If it goes viral, millions of views are a possibility, though that is the exception, not the rule. What about a brand page on Facebook? How about a Twitter feed? Engaging consumers in conversation with a brand is now an integral aspect of an interactive communications strategy. The Internet and its advertising opportunities, social media networks, and mobile communications are fast becoming key components of a brand's marketing communications strategy. Online advertising is now the leading form of advertising, in dollars spent, in Canada. Interactive communications strategies are discussed in more detail in Chapter 7.

SALES PROMOTION PLAN   Sales promotions concentrate on reaching and influencing consumers, trade customers (distributors), and a company's sales force. Funds allocated to promotion strategies are traditionally divided between consumer promotions and trade promotions. Consumer promotions focus on objectives such as encouraging trial purchase, repeat purchase, or simply getting customers to buy a product in greater quantity.

Trade promotions are designed to encourage merchandising and marketing support among distributors. Getting a product listed and on the store shelves of major supermarkets, for example, requires offering financial incentives to retailers such as Safeway, Sobeys, Loblaws, Shoppers Drug Mart, and others. In Canada, prominent retailers have significant clout with manufacturers, and as a result, considerable sums are spent on trade promotions each year. Sales promotion planning is discussed in detail in Chapter 8.

PUBLIC RELATIONS PLAN   Public relations involve communicating with various groups beyond customers. For example, companies communicate with governments, prospective shareholders, the financial community, the media, and community groups. Typically, the goal of such communications is to enhance the company's public image. Public relations can be used to tell the public about the positive things a company is doing, for example, creating awareness of its environmental programs.

In a product sense, public relations play a role in generating interest in new products or spreading "news" about an existing product. Such communications are designed to secure media support for newsworthy information. The nature of public relations is such that written or broadcast news about a company or its products can be of more value. A third-party endorsement through public relations can have greater impact on consumers than advertising. Unlike advertising, public relations are an unpaid form of communications for the most part. For that reason alone, public relations' usefulness must be exploited. The role and impact of public relations are presented in detail in Chapter 9.

EXPERIENTIAL MARKETING Engaging consumers in a brand experience is becoming a popular option for marketing and marketing communications managers. Participating in planned events hosted by others (say a sponsorship opportunity) or creating and implementing a unique branded event gets the target market more actively involved with a brand. Careful planning is needed if the organization is to achieve maximum value from the event. A variety of communications elements must be built into the plan to show how the event will be supported. All of this information is documented in the communications plan. Experiential marketing planning is presented in Chapter 10.

PERSONAL SELLING PLAN Personal selling plays a key role in marketing, especially in business-to-business market situations. As indicated earlier, personal selling techniques create desire and action. The role of a sales representative is to present the benefits of products and show how they resolve a customer's problem. The sales representative is also responsible for presenting the marketing and merchandising support plans to distributors who resell the company's products. Trade customers must be made aware of all activities that will potentially influence sales. Personal selling is discussed in more detail in Chapter 11.

MEASURING AND EVALUATING MARKETING COMMUNICATIONS

The final step in the marketing and marketing communications planning process involves measurement and evaluation. It is essential that an organization monitor all programs to distinguish effective activities from ineffective activities. There's a famous expression about marketing planning and budgeting: "50 percent of my budget works and 50 percent doesn't work. But I don't know which is which." Yes, a lot of marketing decisions are made on instinct, but many more are based on hard and fast measurements.

In marketing communications, some activities are difficult to measure, and very often too much burden is placed on communications. It is such a visible aspect of marketing that it is convenient for senior managers to be critical of it. Each element of marketing communications should be accountable for what it can accomplish. If it is advertising, awareness scores can be measured; if sales promotion, the number of entries in a contest may be a useful measure; if social media, the number of views of a YouTube video may serve as evaluation. Each component can be measured and evaluated in unique and different ways. This topic is discussed in detail in Chapter 12.

>> SUMMARY

Strategic planning is an integrated process that involves developing plans at three levels of an organization. The planning process is cyclical and is subject to constant change based on conditions in the marketplace. To stay on top of things, an organization monitors the economy, competitive activity, social and demographic changes, technology, and laws and regulations.

A marketing communications plan (its direction and content) is influenced by a marketing plan and a corporate plan. When one plan is complete, it provides direction to the next plan. Planning usually starts with the corporate plan, a document prepared by senior executives. Corporate planning starts with the development of a mission statement, followed by corporate objectives and strategies. When deciding upon a strategy, the organization evaluates its marketing strength, degree of competition, financial resources, research and development capabilities, and management expertise.

Marketing planning involves analyzing, planning, implementing, and controlling marketing initiatives. The plan revolves around the customer and includes a precise description of the target based on demographic, psychographic, and geographic characteristics; a sound positioning strategy statement; and clearly worded objectives, strategies, and tactics.

The marketing communications plan identifies the various communications objectives for the year and the strategies that will be employed to achieve them. The plan is subdivided into specific areas, depending on which components of the mix will be employed. The advertising plan focuses on creative and media decisions. In the creative plan, objectives and strategies

(what to say and how to say it) are identified. The media plan states the media objectives by identifying the target market, how often its members should be reached, and when they should be reached. The media strategies rationalize the use of media alternatives and provide detailed information about how the budget is allocated.

If the plan is an integrated plan, other components of the mix are included. Depending on the situation a brand or company faces, the plan could include sales promotion, public relations, experiential marketing, direct response communications, interactive communications, and personal selling. Objectives, strategies, and tactics for each are included in the plan. The goal is to have a unified plan—all forms of marketing communications delivering a unified message to a target market in a convincing manner.

KEY TERMS

acquisition strategy   45

advertising plan   59

consumer-generated content   41

contingency plan   47

corporate objective   44

corporate plan   43

corporate strategy   34

creative plan   59

direct competition   36

divestment strategy   45

execution   00

indirect competition   36

marketing communications plan   56

marketing control   56

marketing objective   52

marketing plan   43

marketing planning   47

marketing strategy   54

media plan   60

mission statement   44

monopolistic competition   35

new product development

strategy   46

objectives   34

oligopoly   35

penetration strategy   45

positioning   51

positioning strategy statement   51

strategic alliance   46

strategic planning   34

strategies   34

subcultures   38

SWOT analysis   49

tactics (execution)   34

target market   47

vision statement   44

REVIEW QUESTIONS

1. What are the external trends and conditions that should be considered when commencing a new planning cycle?
2. What are the key components of a corporate plan? What guidelines does the corporate plan provide to operational plans such as marketing and marketing communications?
3. What is a mission statement, and what role does it play in planning?
4. Identify and briefly explain the four variables or characteristics for describing a target market.
5. What role does a positioning strategy statement play in developing a marketing strategy?

6. "Marketing strategies are the master plans for achieving objectives." What does this statement mean?
7. What is the difference between marketing strategy and marketing execution?
8. What is meant by marketing control, and how does it influence marketing planning?
9. What are the essential decision areas for a creative plan and a media plan?
10. What is the relationship between the various components of an integrated marketing communications plan?

DISCUSSION AND APPLICATION QUESTIONS

1. "Marketing communications objectives are diverse by nature, but a good campaign must have a specific focus." What does this mean?

2. Evaluate the marketing situation for the following companies. What makes them unique, and what is/are their differential advantage(s) compared to their primary competitors? Develop a positioning strategy statement for each company based on your assessment of the situation.
   a) Canadian Tire
   b) Special K
   c) Maxwell House
   d) Dairy Queen

3. Using a variety of online sources, conduct a market analysis for a branded product of your choosing. The market analysis should include the following information:
   a) market size and growth
   b) importance of regional markets
   c) market segment analysis (which segments are growing, declining, and so on)
   d) seasonal analysis

   What conclusions can you draw from your analysis?

4. Compare and contrast the marketing communications strategies of two competing brands (a brand leader and a brand challenger). Do these brands use all elements of the marketing communications mix or do they selectively use only certain elements? What conclusions can you draw based on your analysis of each brand? Some brands to consider might be
   a) Coca-Cola and Pepsi-Cola
   b) Nike and Adidas
   c) Dove soap and Olay soap
   d) Crest and Colgate toothpaste
   e) Canadian Tire and The Home Depot

5. Analyze the marketing communications strategies for an automobile (car or truck) of your choosing. Based on the images portrayed in any and all forms of marketing communications, describe in detail the target market that the automobile is pursuing and the positioning strategy of the brand. Provide a profile based on demographic, psychographic, and geographic characteristics.

ENDNOTES

1. www.dollarama.com.

2. Marina Strauss, "No Place for Future Shop as Shopping's Future Shifts," *The Globe and Mail*, March 30, 2015, p. B1.

3. M. Thrasher, "11 Ways Big Brands Are Chasing Millennials," *Business Insider*, August 2, 2013, www.businessinsider.com.

4. "The Canadian Population in 2011: Population Counts and Growth." Statistics Canada, www.12.statcan.ca/census-recensement/2011/as-sa/98-310-x/98-310-x2011001-eng.cfm.

5. http://www12.statcan.gc.ca/census-recensement/2011.

6. http://statcan.gc.ca/tables-tableaux/sum-som/101/cst01/famil53a-eng.htm

7. "Young, suburban and mostly Asian: Canada's immigrant population surges," *National Post*, May 8, 2013, www.nationalpost.com.

8. "National Household Survey: Immigration Dramatically Changing Makeup of Toronto and Canada," *Toronto Star*, May 8, 2013, www.thestar.com.

9. "Indicators of Well-being in Canada," Employment and Social Development Canada, http://www4.hrsdc.gc.ca.

10. Doug Picklyk, "Are Packages Sustainable?" *Marketing*, April 2012, p. 54.

11. "Canadian Digital, Social, and Mobile Statistics on a Global Scale," Canadian's Internet.com Business, January 23, 2014, www.canadiansinternet.com.

12. Jordan Pinto, "Smartphone Penetration Reaches 68% in Canada," *Media in Canada*, March 27, 2015, www.mediaincanada.com.

13. "Company Facts," www.timhortons.com.

14. "Kellogg to Swallow P&G's Pringles for $2.7 billion," *The Globe and Mail*, February 16, 2012, p. B10.

15. Michelle Dipardo, "Molson Coors Introduces Mad Jack Apple Lager, " *Marketing*, June 6, 2014, www.marketingmag.ca.

16. "Apple Turns to IBM for Help in Selling Corporate Customers," *Marketing*, July 16, 2014, www.marketingmag.ca.

Branding Strategy

Learning Objectives

After studying this chapter, you will be able to

1. Describe the concept of branding and the role it plays in marketing communications and other business-building programs
2. Identify the various components of a brand
3. Describe the benefits of branding for organizations and consumers
4. Characterize the various stages of brand loyalty

5. Describe the role and importance of brand positioning and its relationship to marketing communications plans
6. Explain various brand positioning strategies commonly used in marketing communications
7. Describe the role and influence of packaging and product design in the brand-building process

Think of marketing and marketing communications as a loop. The loop starts somewhere and ends somewhere, but where exactly? Well, it starts with the brand and ends with the brand. Marketing and marketing communications programs create awareness for the brand (the start of the loop). All kinds of messages are sent to consumers through a variety of touch-points, such as packaging, personal selling, events, promotions, news articles, advertising, and social media. Collectively, these messages heighten interest and desire for the brand. While all this is happening, competing brands are doing the same thing. The goal for all brands is to get the consumer to buy their brand. The consumer is now standing in front of a store shelf looking at all the brands. Which one does he or she buy? The customer takes action and places one brand in the shopping cart. Which one? The loop just closed.

What this loop principle suggests is that every form of communication is going to have some kind of impact. The impact of the message and its ability to stimulate action are determined by what a brand has to offer (for example, a compelling reason why someone should buy it) and the convincing way in which the message is delivered to potential customers. Essentially, the brand offering and the message communicated to consumers form the backbone of brand strategy and positioning strategy. This chapter provides insights into how brand strategy and positioning strategy are developed and shows the influence of marketing communications in developing a relationship between the customer and the brand.

Defining the Brand

brand An identifying mark, symbol, word or words, or combination of mark and words that separates one product from another product; can also be defined as the sum of all tangible and intangible characteristics that make a unique offer to customers.

Just what is a brand? A **brand** is a name, term, design, symbol, or any other feature that identifies one seller's good or service as distinct from those of other sellers. The legal term for brand is trademark. A brand may identify one item, a family of items, or all items of that seller.[1]

In today's hypercompetitive marketing environment, branding is a hot button. Marketing executives are busy trying to find or build their brand essence, brand architecture, or brand DNA. Maybe that's a little overdone! However, brands and branding have been around for centuries; only recently has the concept worked its way into everyday conversation.

Marketing communications in any form have an impact on how customers perceive a brand. It seems that a brand is more than just a tangible product. It can embrace intangible characteristics as well. Customer perceptions of brands are largely based on the brand name and what it stands for. It is an image they hold of a brand over an extended period, and that image is based on what they have learned about the brand. For example, a brand such as Rolex suggests a certain quality or status. A potential buyer does not have to question the quality of the watch; he or she is buying the image and reputation of the watch, created by marketing communications over a long period. A packaged goods brand such as Cheerios cereal has a loyal customer following because it offers value beyond good taste—customers perceive Cheerios as a product that enhances their daily life (health) in some small way. Cheerios leads all adult cereal brands in brand loyalty rankings.[2] Refer to the image in Figure 3.1.

As indicated by the definition of a brand, there are elements beyond the name that contribute to a brand's image. These elements working together help differentiate one brand from the others that are available to customers. Let's take a closer look at the components of a brand.

The **brand name** is the part of the brand that can be spoken. It may consist of a word, letter, or group of words and letters. Nike, Gatorade, WD-40, Apple, Starbucks, and Google are all brand names. Brand names are usually presented with their own unique font. For example, Coca-Cola appears in a stylized font on all bottles, cans, and other forms of marketing communications. The presentation of the name is consistent at all times. Even in other languages and alphabets, you can recognize the brand.

brand name That part of a brand that can be spoken.

FIGURE
3.1   **Packaging and Other Forms of Messaging Play a Role in Communicating a Brand's Intrinsic Value, a Factor that Encourages Brand Loyalty**

Source: © Patti McConville/Alamy Stock Photo.

brand logo   A symbol that plays a key role in branding and creating an image.

Some kind of symbol, referred to as a **brand logo**, also plays a key role in branding and creating an image. When marketing communications work effectively, consumers can quickly identify a brand logo or associate a logo with a brand. With Apple, it's an apple with a bite taken out of it. With Nike it's a swoosh. The swoosh is so well known that it can stand alone in advertisements and communicate a message about the brand. When this happens the trademark holder is a victim of its own success because the trademark loses its distinct nature. Such is the case for famous brands like Band-Aid, Kleenex, and Xerox—names that have become synonymous with their product categories.

The design of the product or package, along with a colour scheme, also plays a role in creating brand image. Coca-Cola has a unique bottle design and a red cap. Its can is red. In contrast, the dominant colour for Pepsi-Cola is blue. Brands protect their properties by trademark. A **trademark** is that part of a brand that is granted legal protection so that only the owner can use it. The symbol ™ designates trademark claims. The ® symbol is used when the trademark has not only been claimed, but registered with the government trademarks office. Trademarks can include the brand names and symbols described above. Coke®, Coca-Cola®, the unique style in which these names are printed, and the bottle design are registered trademarks of the Coca-Cola Company. For a selection of famous brand logos refer to Figure 3.2.

trademark   The part of a brand that is granted legal protection so that only the owner can use it.

What to name a brand is a critical decision. Consequently, companies spend considerable amounts of time and money developing and testing brand names. When you think of it, virtually every marketing activity undertaken revolves around the brand name. It has to be distinctive and meaningful. It has to be the right name. What to name a product involves a creative decision and a strategic decision.

Brand names come in many forms. They can be based on people (Calvin Klein, Tommy Hilfiger, and Tim Hortons), places (Air France and Air Canada), animals (Grey Goose vodka and Dove personal care products), inherent product meaning (Ticketmaster and StubHub), product attributes (Bounty paper towels and Fibre One cereal), or they can be completely made up to simply sound scientific or attractive (Telus in telecommunications and Classico in sauces).

Brands are more than just a tangible product. A company adds other dimensions that differentiate it in some way from other products designed to meet the same need. These differences might be rational and tangible, or they might be emotional or intangible entities related to what the brand represents. Through marketing communications, the "personality" of a brand evolves, and the combination of brand attributes (tangibles) and

FIGURE 3.2   A Selection of Famous Brand Logos

Sources: © rvlsoft/Shutterstock.com, © Rose Carson/Shutterstock.com, © Karen Bleier/AFP/Getty Images/Newscom, © Rose Carson/Shutterstock

brand personality (intangibles) is what influences brand choices by consumers. The key for any brand is to be perceived as offering something unique.

Brand Image and Reputation

Brands are more than physical products and services. Whenever and wherever a consumer is choosing among alternatives, brands play a role in the decision-making process. While brands provide customers with an assurance of quality, they also express a set of values that customers can identify with. The Coca-Cola brand is more than just a sweet-tasting soft drink; it carries a set of American values that strike a chord with consumers around the world. Similarly, a brand like Virgin (Virgin Mobile, Virgin Atlantic Air, Virgin Radio, and so on) represents a youthful, rebellious attitude, much like that of Virgin's maverick founder, Richard Branson.[3]

Marketing communications play a key role in building a brand's image and reputation. A good reputation doesn't just happen—it is the end result of a consistent approach to marketing and marketing communications over an extended period. Year after year the same brands top the "best brands in Canada" list in Canada. In 2015, the top five brands were MEC, Cirque du Soleil, WestJet, Tim Hortons, and Roots. MEC's rise to the top of the reputation list is attributed to its transformation from a clearinghouse of mountaineer equipment to a national hub for outdoor lifestyle enthusiasts. MEC successfully targeted new, urban customers with new products that were needed for the company to grow.[4] Among international brands, Google, Heinz, and Kellogg's are the top three brands.[5]

Canadian Tire is a brand with a solid reputation among Canadian consumers. Canadian Tire has withstood incredible competitive pressure from big American retailers such as Home Depot and Walmart. It is an innovative company that experiments with new ways of providing value to its customers and as a result remains a leader in general merchandise and hardware retailing. For a list of the top brands in Canada by reputation, according to a study by Leger research, see Figure 3.3.

Companies like those in Figure 3.3 never lose sight of the brand and what it means to its customers. To many consumers, Shoppers Drug Mart means health, beauty, and convenience. Shoppers also has one of the most popular loyalty programs—Shoppers Optimum—in the country. The company loves the program too!. Beyond being a branding asset, the

FIGURE 3.3

Canada's Brand Leaders by Reputation 2016

Source: Based on the 2014 Leger Corporate Reputation Study, www.marketingmag.ca.

The net score for each brand is based on good and bad opinions expressed about the brands by respondents in the survey.

Rank	Company/Brand	% Good Opinion	% Bad Opinion	Net Score
1	Google	91	2	89
2	Heinz	84	5	79
3	Shoppers Drug Mart	83	5	78
4	Canadian Tire	85	8	77
5	Kellogg	83	7	76
6	Dollarama	81	6	75
7	Samsung	80	5	75
8	Kraft	83	9	74
9	Campbell	80	7	73
10	Tim Hortons	83	11	72

FIGURE
3.4

**Shoppers Loyalty Program Is
a Brand Asset That Is Very
Popular with Its Customers**

Source: © Deborah Baic/The Globe and
Mail/CP Images

information the program collects about consumer shopping behaviour is among the most extensive in Canada. Refer to the image in Figure 3.4.

BRAND LOYALTY

brand loyalty   The degree of attachment to a particular brand expressed by a consumer. There are three stages of brand loyalty: brand recognition, brand preference, and brand insistence.

Brand loyalty is defined as the degree of consumer attachment to a particular brand. Loyalty is influenced by such factors as marketing communications (what is said about a brand), family or peer pressure, friendship with a salesperson, and, ultimately, how satisfied a person is with the product. For example, someone intending to buy a new car might return to the same dealer and person he or she has bought from before. Satisfaction based on experience with that individual and product helps build loyalty.

Brand loyalty is measured in three distinct stages: brand recognition, brand preference, and brand insistence (see Figure 3.5).[6]

In the early stage of a brand's life, the marketing objective is to create **brand recognition**. It is imperative to communicate the brand name, the unique selling point, and what the product looks like (for example, the package if it is a consumer good, or the look and style if it is a shopping good, such as an automobile or appliance). A marketing communications campaign plays a key role here.

brand recognition   Customer awareness of the brand name and package.

brand preference   The situation where a brand is perceived as an acceptable alternative by a customer and will be purchased if it is available.

When a brand achieves the status of **brand preference**, it is on a short list of brand alternatives that the consumer will consider buying. Such a position is good, because

FIGURE
3.5   **The Stages of Brand Loyalty**

| **Brand Recognition** Consumer is aware of the name, benefit, and package. | **Brand Preference** Brand is top of mind and considered a good alternative. Consumer will buy if available. | **Brand Insistence** Consumer buys one brand only. If brand is not available, the purchase is postponed. |

consumers retain only a select group of brand names in their minds for any product category. Furthermore, it is an indication that the message strategies and other marketing strategies are working; the customer knows something about the brand, has evaluated it in relation to his or her needs, and will purchase it if available when it is needed.

At the **brand insistence** stage, a consumer will search the market extensively for a particular brand. No alternatives are acceptable, and if the brand is not available the consumer will likely postpone the purchase until it is. Such an enviable position shows the type of bond that can develop between a brand and a consumer.

As suggested earlier, consumers want consistent quality from their brands. The famous Coca-Cola marketing debacle of 1985 confirms how brand insistence works. Coca-Cola made the decision to replace Coca-Cola with a new formula. When the change was implemented, the backlash from customers was so swift and strong that the company had to bring back the original formula under the name Coca-Cola Classic. Some 22 years later (in 2007), the Classic name was dropped, and Coca-Cola returned to its original brand name. Some critics insist that Coca-Cola is a brand that has gone beyond brand insistence. So strong is the bond with consumers, the product cannot be changed—ever.

Since one of the tasks of marketing is to keep customers loyal, smart companies plan and implement loyalty programs. Loyalty programs range from the simple to the complex. McDonald's, for example, offers a coffee card program whereby a customer gets a free coffee (any type or size) after seven purchases. A program such as Shoppers Optimum (mentioned earlier) is more complex and is intended to gather data that will assist the company in developing better marketing programs. The Shoppers Optimum program has over 10 million members in Canada. Loyalty-oriented marketing programs are presented in Chapter 8.

Brand-insistent consumers often become advocates for the brand—they like the brand so much they will openly recommend it to others. As discussed in Chapter 1, a word-of-mouth network, particularly a social media environment, is a powerful communications tool that influences buying decisions. This phenomenon will be discussed further in Chapter 7.

For more insight into brand loyalty and how to achieve it, read the IMC Highlight: **Brand Loyalty: It's the Emotional Connection that Counts**.

brand insistence A situation where the consumer searches the market for the specific brand.

BRAND EQUITY

Brand equity is a confusing term that has been historically defined in different ways for different purposes. For our purposes, **brand equity** is defined as the value a consumer derives from a brand over and above the value derived from the physical attributes. Equity is influenced by several variables: brand name awareness, the degree of loyalty expressed by customers, perceived quality, and the brand's association with a certain attribute. Canadian brands that consistently rated high based on this definition of equity include Tim Hortons, Canadian Tire, CBC, and Air Canada.

Brand equity can also be expressed in monetary terms. A brand is an asset of an organization, and therefore has some tangible financial value. On a global scale, brands such as Apple, Google, Microsoft, IBM, and Visa lead the way. In 2015 Apple was the world's most valuable brand, estimated to be worth $246.9 billion.[7]

When Canadian brands are ranked on this basis, a different set of names emerge. Among the leaders are financial institutions such as Royal Bank of Canada and TD Canada Trust and telecommunications companies such as Bell and Rogers. A list of Canada's top 10 brands by brand value appears in Figure 3.6.

Effective marketing and marketing communications strategies play a key role in building a brand's equity. Scotiabank and RBC Financial invest heavily in advertising

brand equity The value (monetary or otherwise) of a brand to its owners; influenced by brand name awareness, degree of customer loyalty, perceived quality, and the brand's association with a certain attribute.

Brand Loyalty: It's the Emotional Connection that Counts

Some recent marketing research from the United States reveals that the core drivers of brand loyalty are emotional in nature rather than rational. The research produces a Customer Loyalty Engagement Index (CLEI) each year, and over the years emotional engagement factors have become more important. In the 2012 research, two specific components rose significantly: the brand's "values" and the consumer's brand "experience."

For the purposes of the research, brand value is defined as what a brand stands for or means to the consumer on an emotional level. Across 83 product categories studied, it became clear that consumer loyalty depends upon the degree to which a brand has established a clear core value proposition—something that goes beyond the tangible characteristics of the product. Typical rational characteristics such as quality and price will get people to knock the tires. For marketers, the challenge is to show how a brand enhances the consumer's daily life in some way.

To demonstrate, in the soft drink category the core drivers of loyalty are "refreshing taste" and "brand appropriate for entire family." Based on these criteria, Coca-Cola ranked first and Pepsi-Cola second. The research observed that Coca-Cola's "Open Happiness" brand positioning and tying its polar bear icon to social responsibility activities were emotionally connecting with consumers.

Among quick-serve restaurants, McDonald's and Subway tied for first place in the loyalty rankings. The top loyalty drivers in this category were "brand value" and "healthy choice." For certain, Subway's well-known slogan "Eat fresh," connects with consumers.

Among kids' cereals (your former favourites perhaps), Frosted Flakes and Lucky Charms lead the pack. In this category, loyalty used to be based on a good price/value proposition. The latest research shows that a brand family focus and taste are the leading drivers of loyalty.

Information of this nature, if known by brand marketers, will impact product and marketing communications decisions.

Adapted from Karlene Lukovitz, "Brand Experience, Values Increasingly Drive Loyalty," *Marketing Daily*, February 6, 2012. www.mediapost.com.

Source: © The Advertising Archives / Alamy Stock Photo

FIGURE
3.6

Canada's Leading Brands Ranked by Financial Value

Source: "The Country's Most Valuable Brands? Banks." *Linda Nguyen The Canadian Press*, Published on Fri Feb 27 2015

Rank 2015	Brand	Industry	Value (C$ Billion)
1	Royal Bank	Financial Services	12.5
2	TD Canada Trust	Financial Services	11.1
3	Bell	Telecommunications	7.6
4	Scotiabank	Financial Services	7.0
5	Bank of Montreal	Financial Services	6.9
6	Rogers Communications	Telecommunications	4.9
7	Telus	Telecommunications	4.8
8	Enbridge	Energy Resources	4.3
9	McCain Foods	Food Processing	3.9

It's not how much you make. It's how much you keep.

Investing outside a registered plan often comes with an unwelcome tax bill. **Scotia Corporate Class Funds** give you the freedom to adjust your investments as life changes, while keeping more of your wealth working for you.

Visit a branch today and ask a *Scotia*® advisor how **Scotia Corporate Class Funds** can work for you.

You're richer than you think.

scotiabank.com/corporateclass

® Registered trademarks of the Bank of Nova Scotia.
Scotiabank includes The Bank of Nova Scotia and its subsidiaries and affiliates, including Scotia Asset Management L.P., and Scotia Securities Inc. ScotiaFunds are available from Scotia Securities Inc. and from other dealers. ScotiaFunds are managed by Scotia Asset Management L.P. Commissions, trailing commissions, management fees and expenses may be associated with mutual fund investments. Please read the fund's simplified prospectus before investing. Mutual funds are not guaranteed or insured, their values change frequently and past performance may not be repeated.

FIGURE 3.7

Effective Marketing Communications Help Build a Brand's Image, Loyalty, and Equity

Source: Courtesy of Scotiabank.

media to build their respective images and to instill a feeling of trust among present customers and new customers. A sample of Scotiabank's advertising appears in Figure 3.7.

THE BENEFITS OF BRANDING

Based on the discussion of various branding issues in the preceding sections, it can be seen that consumers and organizations benefit from branding. Some of the benefits for consumers are as follows:

• Over time, the brand name suggests a certain level of quality. Consumers know what to expect; they trust and have confidence in the brand.

• There can be psychological rewards for possessing certain brands. For example, buying a brand new BMW automobile might suggest the owner has achieved some goal. The automobile says something about the driver; it expresses his or her self-image.

- Brands distinguish competitive offerings, allowing consumers to make informed decisions based on what a brand stands for. Marketing communications play a key role in differentiating one brand from another.

Over time, a relationship develops between a consumer and the brand; it's like a bond. Consumers offer their trust and loyalty in return for consistent product quality from the brand. Essentially, a brand is a promise delivered to a consumer. Consumers place their trust in brands and make ongoing buying decisions based on that trust.

So what are the most trusted brands in Canada? A survey of Canadian consumers by the Peter B. Gustavson School of Business at the University of Victoria ranked brands according to attributes such as quality, innovation, value, leadership, and social responsibility. The survey reveals that Tim Hortons is Canada's most trusted brand, followed closely by Presidents Choice (or PC). Other familiar names in the top 10 include Canadian Tire, Kraft, and Campbell Soup. Refer to Figure 3.8 for a sample list of the most trusted brands in various product categories.

Brands play a key role and offer numerous benefits to an organization as well. At the operational level, they help staff to plan production runs, maintain inventory counts, and facilitate order processing and delivery. In a marketing context, the key benefits are as follows:

unique selling point (USP) The primary benefit of a product or service that distinguishes it from its competitors.

- A good brand name communicates the point of difference, or **unique selling point (USP)**, and highlights the distinctive value added. A name such as Lean Cuisine, for example, addresses two benefits: "Lean" communicates low calories and "cuisine" implies it tastes good.

- Branding (and the marketing communications that promote a brand) allows for the creation and development of an image. For example, Nike suggests an independent spirit, Visa provides freedom for people to follow their passions, and Coca-Cola inspires moments of happiness. For these brands, extensive advertising campaigns have instilled such images in the customer's mind.

- Satisfied customers will make repeat purchases and, marketers hope, remain loyal to the brand. Such loyalty stabilizes market share and provides for certain efficiencies in production and marketing. Reliable estimates of future sales facilitate internal brand planning.

In summary, branding decisions are important decisions. A brand name stands for much more than simply differentiating one brand from another. Decisions about brand name, benefits offered, package design, and the desired image form the foundation for marketing and marketing communications strategies.

FIGURE 3.8

Canada's Most Trusted Brands in Various Product Categories

Source: http://notable.ca/these-are-the-most-trusted-brands-in-canada-by-industry

Product Category	Brand
Cars	Honda
Beer	Alexander Keith's
Confectionary	Cadbury
Travel	WestJet
Beverages	Coca-Cola
Dairy	Natrel
Energy	Shell
Media	CTV
Hotels	Holiday Inn
Technology	Google

Building the Brand

Building a brand (building brand image and equity) is the responsibility of the brand manager (or category manager or marketing manager, depending on a company's organizational structure). A **brand manager** develops and implements the marketing plans for the brands he or she is responsible for. The process of building a brand involves four essential steps (see Figure 3.9 for an illustration of the steps):

1. Identify and establish brand values and positioning strategy.
2. Plan and implement brand marketing programs.
3. Measure and interpret brand performance.
4. Grow and sustain brand equity (managing a brand through its life cycle).

Since the concept of brand equity has already been discussed, the remaining discussion in this chapter will focus on brand values and positioning, and the development of marketing programs.

ESTABLISHING CORE VALUES AND BRAND POSITIONING

What does a brand stand for? The answer to that question will relate to the core values of a brand. **Core values** are the primary attributes and benefits a brand delivers to the customer. An **attribute** is a descriptive feature; a **benefit** is the value consumers attach to a brand attribute. For example, Dove tells women to focus on internal beauty and the health of their skin; everyone should be happy with who they are (a self-esteem message). Dove emphasizes an attitude more than the product itself.

The smartphone market is large and very competitive, and all brands essentially perform the same tasks. Some brands will focus on product-specific attributes while others will focus on psychological benefits. Each brand will use a different angle on how to communicate a key benefit. Apple is the leader in the premium phone market and generally prefers the psychological benefit approach. Apple products (phones, laptops, music devices, and tablets) are technical in nature but are promoted as items that suit the lifestyle

brand manager   An individual assigned responsibility for the development and implementation of marketing programs for a specific product or group of products.

core values   The primary attributes and benefits a brand delivers to the customer.

attribute   A descriptive feature of a product.

benefit   The value a customer attaches to a brand attribute.

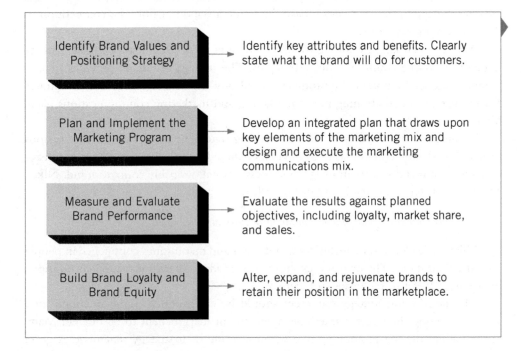

FIGURE
3.9

The Brand-building Process

Identify Brand Values and Positioning Strategy	Identify key attributes and benefits. Clearly state what the brand will do for customers.
Plan and Implement the Marketing Program	Develop an integrated plan that draws upon key elements of the marketing mix and design and execute the marketing communications mix.
Measure and Evaluate Brand Performance	Evaluate the results against planned objectives, including loyalty, market share, and sales.
Build Brand Loyalty and Brand Equity	Alter, expand, and rejuvenate brands to retain their position in the marketplace.

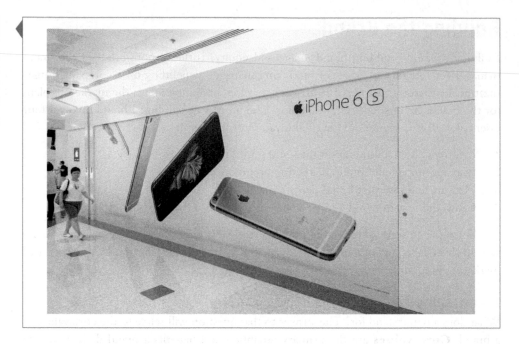

needs of consumers. The iPhone is perceived as simple, sleek, and sexy—very different from its competitors. Refer to the image in Figure 3.10.

Brand Positioning Concepts

positioning The selling concept that motivates purchase, or the image that marketers desire a brand to have in the minds of consumers.

As discussed in Chapter 2, **positioning** is the selling concept that motivates purchase, or the image that marketers desire a brand to have in the minds of customers. It is a strategy influenced by a brand's core values, attributes, and benefits. Simply stated, each brand wants to differentiate itself from competitive offerings. Therefore, positioning involves designing and marketing a product to meet the needs of a target market and creating the appropriate appeals to make the product stand out from the competition in the minds of the target market.

A clearly defined positioning strategy statement provides guidance for all marketing and marketing communications strategies. The strategy statement provides a compelling reason why potential customers should buy the brand. Figure 3.11 illustrates the importance of positioning in the marketing and marketing communications planning process.

To illustrate the importance of a positioning statement again, consider the various forms of marketing communications Nike has exposed you to over time. Nike is a heavily advertised brand so certain images and messages will probably come to mind. Nike's positioning statement could be written as follows:

Nike brings inspiration and innovation to every athlete.

Nike is a leader in shoe technology, and is a brand that inspires confidence in people who use their shoes. The images they show in their ads aptly demonstrate their positioning strategy. Refer to the image in Figure 3.12.

The positioning strategy statement should be clear, concise, and uncomplicated while addressing the target market's need and the primary benefit to be offered. Many experts adopt the 4D-positioning rule when devising their strategy statement. A good

A clearly worded positioning strategy statement provides guidance for developing all marketing and marketing communications strategies.

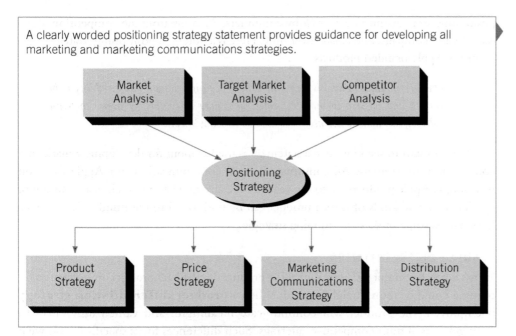

FIGURE
3.11

The Importance of Positioning

FIGURE
3.12

Nike's Positioning Strategy for Shoes Is Based on Innovation (Product) and Inspiration (People)

Source: © Eugene Gologursky/WireImage

positioning strategy must be *desirable* by consumers, *distinctive* from the competition, *deliverable* by the company, and *durable* over time. Here is a potential positioning strategy statement for Apple branded products.[8]

> *The core of Apple's brand is great innovation, beautiful design, and an ability to bring warmth and passion to those customers who may be completely averse to technical gadgetry, but nonetheless need it to survive in today's world.*

You can start to see how such a statement is used as input for developing a marketing communications strategy. All consumer-directed communications for Apple focus on how simple Apple products are to use yet offer the absolute latest in technical innovation.

There are all kinds of ways a product can be positioned in the minds of customers. Let's discuss some of these positioning strategies.

PRODUCT DIFFERENTIATION

product differentiation strategy A plan of action for communicating meaningful attributes and benefits of a product to a target market.

Here's what the product is! Here's what the product does! That's product differentiation—nothing could be more straightforward. When a **product differentiation strategy** is employed, the product will communicate meaningful and valued differences to distinguish itself from competitive offerings. Such differences focus specifically on what the product may offer and refer to the form of the product (size, shape, or physical structure), performance quality (it lasts longer), durability (ability to withstand stress), reliability (it won't break down), or style (the look and appearance of the product or package).

BAND-AID® brand adhesive bandages compete with many other brands. One of its unique attributes is a super-stick adhesive—it will stay on longer even in the toughest, wettest conditions, offering better protection. Another unique attribute is Quiltvent technology. As stated in the advertisement appearing in Figure 3.13, this technology wicks away fluids and offers superior breathability—benefits of interest to customers.

BRAND LEADERSHIP POSITIONING

leadership positioning A marketing strategy in which a product presents itself as a preferred choice among customers.

As the name suggests, **leadership positioning** is a strategy often employed by brand leaders. Good marketing and marketing strategies from the past have helped such a product achieve an enviable position in the marketplace and in the minds of customers. These brands have high brand equity. The message such a brand delivers is designed to reinforce its lofty position. Probably the best example of leadership positioning is Coca-Cola. In most North American markets, Coca-Cola is the number one brand with a legion of loyal brand users. In advertising, Coca-Cola struts its stuff. The brand has used catchy phrases such as "Coke is it," "Can't beat the real thing," and "Always Coca-Cola" to communicate its leadership position. More recently the brand has used the phrase "Open happiness." The brand exists to "inspire moments of happiness" among its users.

Brand leaders have characteristics in common that give them an advantage over competing brands: They have greater consumer awareness, are readily available, and have significant marketing budgets to protect their position.

HEAD-ON POSITIONING (COMPARATIVE POSITIONING)

head-on positioning A marketing strategy in which one product is presented as an equal or better alternative to a competing product.

Head-on positioning involves a comparison of one brand with another. Typically, the brand doing the advertising presents itself as being better than another brand. The message focuses on an attribute that is important to the target market. To dramatize the claim of superiority or whatever the claim may be, it is common to demonstrate how

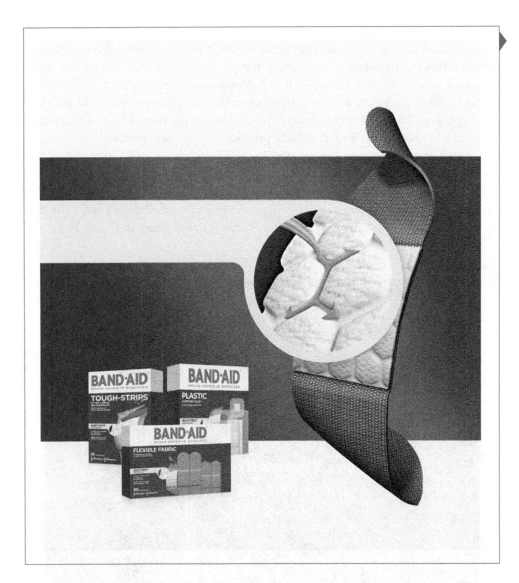

FIGURE
3.13

**Offering a Significant
Benefit to Consumers Helps
Differentiate BAND-AID® Brand
Bandages from Competitors**

Source: © Johnson & Johnson

both brands perform. For example, we often see popular brands of household products use head-on positioning strategies. Bounty, for example, shows how much water one of its towels can pick up, while a competing brand is shown to be incapable of picking up as much. The Bounty towel still looks partially dry; the competitor's looks saturated. Bounty is well positioned as "the quicker picker-upper."

The "Pepsi Challenge" is now the classic example of effective head-on positioning. Originally, television commercials showed people trying Pepsi and Coke in blind taste tests with Pepsi being the preferred choice—a hard-to-believe situation for those taking the taste test. In a recent television commercial, a Pepsi truck driver and a Coke truck driver are sitting at a diner counter. The Coke driver tries a sip of Pepsi, unaware that the Pepsi driver is taking his picture and uploading it to the Internet for the world to see. A fight ensues between the two. Pepsi effectively delivered its message in the commercial.

Challenger brands often adopt a head-on positioning strategy. Their mission is to instill "thought" leadership in the customer's mind. Such brands will spend considerable sums of money to deliver their message. Challengers must also be aware that a brand leader may retaliate, thus escalating the financial commitment required to maintain the challenge.

INNOVATION POSITIONING

An innovation is a product, service, or idea that is perceived by consumers as new. **Innovation positioning** is a marketing strategy that stresses newness as a way to differentiate a brand from the competition. Innovation may imply that the company or brand is "leading-edge" in the market it competes in. As mentioned earlier in the chapter, Apple is well known for its innovative yet easy-to-use products. It's not a coincidence that Apple is also the leader in all of these product or service categories.

In the razor and razor blade market, both Gillette and Schick Quattro duel with each other for innovation supremacy. Three blades, four blades, five blades—just how many blades are needed for a close shave? Gillette launched the new Fusion ProGlide razor with flexball technology, which promises men a smoother, closer shave. The flexball responds to every contour on a man's face. Refer to the image in Figure 3.14.

innovation positioning   A marketing strategy that stresses newness (based on a commitment to research and development) as a means of differentiating a company or a brand from competing companies and brands.

FIGURE
3.14

Innovations Such As New Flexball Technology Help Keep Gillette at the Forefront of the Male Grooming Market

Source: © 2014 P&G

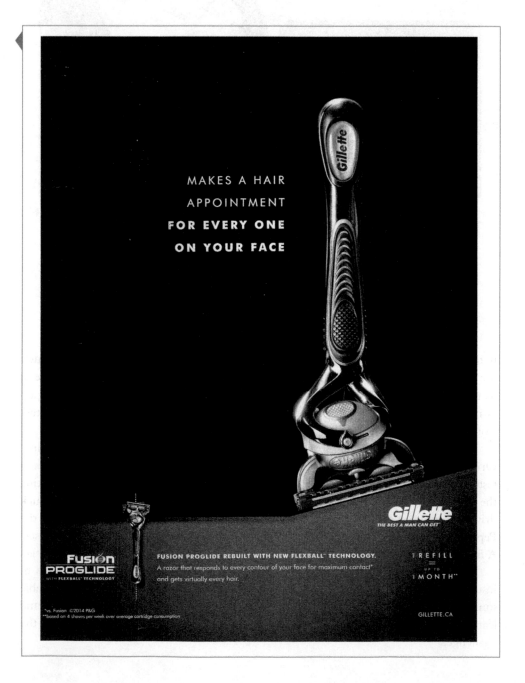

PRICE (VALUE) POSITIONING

A **price positioning** strategy is based on the premise that consumers search for the best possible value given their economic circumstances. Some consumers search for low prices, others are willing to pay more for something perceived as offering good value, and still others don't even look at price. Some people shop for high-end goods and services and expect to pay a lot for the products they buy.

Walmart seems to have a lock on the low-price positioning strategy in the North American retail marketplace. The store's image is firmly entrenched in the consumer's mind from ads showing prices always being slashed to save people money. It used the slogan "Always low prices" to communicate its positioning strategy. In recent years, Walmart has shifted its price position somewhat and begun using the phrase "Save Money. Live Better." Their promise to consumers: Saving money on little things adds up and helps families live better. Refer to the image in Figure 3.15.

Another retailing example shows how high-price positioning is an effective strategy. In men's fashion, Harry Rosen (an upscale men's clothier) comes to mind. The Harry Rosen image has been carefully cultivated over time so that customers know exactly what to expect when they shop there. Harry Rosen keeps its edge on the competition by carrying many exclusive products and by moving to customer relationship marketing and pitching wares directly to individual customers in mailings and through special events. According to Larry Rosen, current CEO and son of the founder, "A man looks powerful, authoritative, confident, and professional in a suit. To get the right suit that man knows where to shop—Harry Rosen." Refer to the image in Figure 3.16.

LIFESTYLE (IMAGE) POSITIONING

In very competitive markets where product attributes of so many brands are perceived to be equal by consumers, it is difficult to follow the positioning strategies outlined above. **Lifestyle positioning**, or **image positioning**, involves moving away from the tangible characteristics of the product toward the intangible characteristics (things that aren't there, for example). Products in categories such as beer, alcohol, perfume, automobiles, and travel frequently use this strategy, as do brands that wish to attract a youthful customer.

price positioning A marketing strategy based on the premise that consumers search for the best possible value given their economic circumstances.

lifestyle (image) positioning A marketing strategy based on intangible characteristics associated with a lifestyle instead of tangible characteristics.

FIGURE
3.15

Walmart's Price Proposition Is Firmly Entrenched in the Minds of North American Consumers

Source: Robyn Beck/AFP/Getty Images/Newscom.

FIGURE
3.16

A High-price, High-quality Positioning Strategy Works for Harry Rosen

Source: Jesse Johnston/CP Images.

The use of psychographic information allows companies to develop campaigns based on the lifestyle or desired lifestyle of the target market. Generally speaking, lifestyle positioning involves using emotional appeal techniques such as love, fear, adventure, sex, and humour to influence the target market. In the truck market, all of the major brands such as the Ford F-150, Chevrolet Silverado, and Ram appeal to the lifestyle of hardworking, outdoor-oriented, adventurous males. The message focuses on the strength and toughness of the vehicle. Advertisements for the Silverado use phrases such as "Silverado. True North Strong" to establish its desired brand image. The phrase "Built Tough" plays a key role in advertisements for the Ford F-150. Refer to the image in Figure 3.17.

FIGURE
3.17

Chevy Silverado Trucks Are Positioned to Appeal to the Lifestyle of Hardworking, Adventurous Males

Source: © Rolling Stock/Alamy Stock Photo

REPOSITIONING

As a brand evolves and faces changes in the marketplace, an organization may decide to reposition the brand. For example, conditions in the economy change, new competitors might enter the market, or consumers' preferences change. **Repositioning** is defined as changing the place a product occupies in the customer's mind, relative to competing products. When a positioning strategy is working, a company should avoid the temptation to change things. That old expression "If it ain't broke, don't fix it" applies here.

Marketers must continuously monitor changes in the marketplace and adjust their strategies accordingly. Out of necessity, a few years ago Buick (a brand marketed by General Motors Canada) launched a new vehicle called the Verano with a completely new image. Buick is traditionally the preferred ride of older men. While GM can't ignore its older target, the path to future success lies with the brand's ability to attract new, younger customers. The solution was Melina, the internal name GM gave to the new target market Buick would pursue. Melina is a tech-savvy urbanite making a good salary who likes to treat herself with spa treatments, nice clothes, and nights out with the girls. GM launched the Verano with Melina in mind. The advertising for the car featured young women enjoying fine coffee, relaxing at the beach, and enjoying driving the new car.[9]

PLANNING AND IMPLEMENTING MARKETING AND MARKETING COMMUNICATIONS PROGRAMS

To build brand loyalty and firmly position a brand requires effective marketing programs: activities that produce a strong and favourable association with a brand in a consumer's memory. It is an information transfer process that considers two essential factors. First, decisions must be made about how to employ various brand elements. These decisions involve brand names, trademarks, and characters. Second, appropriate marketing strategies must be developed to communicate the brand values and brand positioning strategy.

The most common brand elements are brand names, logos, symbols, characters, packaging, and slogans. The content of most advertising in any medium, from television to print to websites, usually includes these elements. Characters, whether they be paid actors employed in a commercial or something that an organization creates, help portray the personality of a brand. Think of the manager in A&W's television commercials or the actor who appeared in countless Trivago commercials to help you find just the right hotel room. Even cartoon characters such as Tony the Tiger (Frosted Flakes) and the Michelin Man (Michelin tires) play key roles in brand advertising.

Slogans are also important in brand advertising, as they tend to summarize what a brand stands for—the brand's positioning strategy. When creating a slogan, creative planners attempt to suggest a key benefit and to reflect the brand's personality, while keeping the slogan short enough so that it is easy for consumers to remember.

Here are some famous slogans from the past:

Molson Canadian	"I Am Canadian"
Red Rose Tea	"Only in Canada? Pity."
Tim Hortons	"Always got time for Tim Hortons"
Budweiser	"The king of beers"
Campbell Soup	"M'm, M'm good"
M&M Candy	"Melts in your mouth, not in your hands"
KFC	"Finger-lickin' good"

Based on the numerous examples already cited in this chapter, it should be abundantly clear that marketing communications are the "voice" of a brand's (or company's)

ING Bank Becomes Tangerine

Good communications plans call for effective collaboration between creative planners and media planners. The goal of both is always to place the right message in the right medium, and, when they do, good things happen. Here's a brief summary of a campaign that clicked for Tangerine.

What is Tangerine, one might ask? Well that was the precise situation Scotiabank faced when it embarked upon a rebranding effort for ING DIRECT Canada. Scotiabank acquired ING DIRECT and a legal requirement of the transition called for a new brand name and visual identity within 18 months of the acquisition.

ING DIRECT was successfully positioned as a challenger to the big banks—it was a bank that did things differently and more simply. After 12 months of consumer research Scotiabank decided on the Tangerine name. It stood for simple, unique, progressive banking. And it offered an element of fun, even though banking is considered a serious business.

The advertising objectives for the rebranding campaign were three-fold.

1. To achieve an unaided brand awareness of 7 percent within six months
2. To drive customer acquisition based on the bank's value proposition
3. To ensure existing clients were aware of the name change and acclimatized to the transition before it occurred

Analysis of the situation by John St. (the ad agency used by Scotiabank) determined that simplicity would play a key role in messaging. The big banks are associated with complexity and doing things the old-fashioned way. Tangerine would stand for accessibility, innovation, and flexibility—money would be simpler to manage.

Strategically, timing would play an important role in message delivery and transparency was crucial throughout the process. The bank maintained dialogue with employees and clients to ensure a smooth transition. Internal communications included live streaming of messages, events to help create buzz, and a micro-site outlining how the name change was just another step in the history of the bank. A direct mail piece was sent to all clients informing them of the change and how they would be affected.

The initial launch was in two phases. The first phase explained the transition of ING DIRECT to Tangerine. The message helped acclimatize Canadians to the name change and established Tangerine as a credible and trustworthy bank. The message was informative in nature; the focus was on the name and what wasn't changing: "We're changing our name, but we'll never change what we do."

The second phase was designed to make Canadians take notice. The message would encourage Canadians to stop and think about how they do their banking. Why were people staying with their existing bank when Tangerine was a simpler and superior alternative?

In the media, the first phase of the launch was TV-driven, supported by print ads and a micro-site. Ad placements were in media traditionally used for information: newspapers, digital banners, and news and information sites. In the second phase the objectives focused on awareness so a multimedia approach was recommended. In addition to 30-second and 60-second TV spots, large-scale transit dominations, transit shelters, digital display ads, and pre-roll video were added to the media mix.

The transition campaign was a success. There was a sizeable uptick in customer acquisition—a 90 percent increase in applications in the first two months of the campaign. Unaided brand awareness reached 15 percent within three months—well above the target. News and media coverage achieved 81 million earned media impressions (free brand exposure), and there were 188 unique news stories about the name change transition.

Source: © Torontonian/Alamy Stock Photo

Based on Cassies 2015, "Off to a Good Start (Silver)" http://cassies.ca/entry/viewcase/17998.

positioning strategy. Regardless of the medium selected, that voice must deliver a message with clarity and continuity. If the communications strategies are executed effectively and with sufficient financial support, the desired message and image should be planted in the customer's mind.

Advertising in any medium and in social media communications should have a blanketing effect on the audience it reaches. Advertising is the most visible communication—a form that creates awareness and interest in a brand and gets people talking about it.

The other forms of marketing communications play more specific roles and should be viewed as surround sound. Sales promotions, experiential marketing, and public relations generate buzz and create desire and action. They provide the stimulus that gets the wallet out of the pocket or purse. Therefore, with all points of contact delivering a unified message, a brand begins to build momentum—the brand-building process has begun.

To demonstrate the process of planning and implementing a marketing communications campaign, as well as the role of various communications elements, consider the situation that Scotiabank faced when it acquired the Canadian operations of ING DIRECT Canada. Part of the acquisition agreement called for a new brand name for ING within 18 months of the takeover. For more insight into this exercise in branding and marketing communications read the IMC Highlight: **ING DIRECT Becomes Tangerine**.

Packaging and Brand Building

The package is what consumers look for when they are contemplating a purchase. For new products especially, the look of the package must be instilled in the customer's mind. For that reason, it is very common for the package to play a key role in introductory marketing communications programs.

The colour of a package is an important element of the brand building equation. Given the way in which consumers scan merchandise on store shelves, colour plays a role in attracting people's attention. Many brands actually own a colour, at least in marketing terms, which is a concept known as brand blocking. For example, the colour red is a sign of power. In the soft drink market, Coca-Cola owns the colour red, and it is no coincidence that Coca-Cola is a market leader. Colours are an emotional trigger and consequently are powerful marketing tools. Dark colours project richness and are common in the coffee aisle on brands such as Maxwell House and Nabob. When Unilever launched Dove Men+Care, it used a medium grey colour—a colour unique to the product category. Refer to the image in Figure 3.18.

In today's competitive environment, packaging is playing a more significant role in differentiating one brand from another. Over the life cycle of a product, the packaging may change several times to spruce up the image of a brand. As well, a common package design across all product lines that make up a brand (that is, various sizes, shapes, and formats) helps maintain brand identity.

A revolution is occurring in packaged goods marketing, as marketers see packages having a growing influence on purchase decisions amid ongoing media fragmentation. The majority of purchasing decisions are made in the store: up to 70 percent (40 percent in supermarkets) by people navigating aisles, scanning shelves, and making spur-of-the-moment decisions.[10]

The package is a very important touch-point with consumers. Familiarity with a package helps build trust between the consumer and the brand, so ultimately the package is a factor that can influence consumer loyalty. A good package serves four functions: It protects the product, it markets the product, it offers convenience to consumers, and it is environmentally friendly.

FIGURE
3.18

**Dove Men+Care Uses Grey
Packaging and White Lettering
to Present a Consistent Image
to Consumers**

Source: © Mark Von Holden/Invision for
Dove Men/AP Images.

PROTECT THE PRODUCT

How much protection a product needs depends on how often it changes hands in the distribution process. For example, how long does it sit in a warehouse, how will it be transported, what kind of handling will it experience, and how much protection from exposure to heat, cold, light, and moisture will it need? Snack foods such as potato chips for example, require larger than needed packages (air-filled to remain somewhat rigid) so that the fragile contents are cushioned. Nobody wants a bag of crushed chips!

MARKET THE PRODUCT

In its marketing role, the package does the same thing an advertisement in any medium would do. The design and colour scheme should be coordinated so that the overall look of the package creates a good impression. The package should be attractive and eye-catching to grab the attention of consumers. It should contain useful information and tell consumers what the product's benefits are so they will have a reason to buy it. To demonstrate, refer to the image in Figure 3.19.

Packages can also be used to communicate information about promotional offers such as coupons, contests, and giveaways. Since promotions of this nature are temporary, a package "flash" is usually added to the front panel of the package to draw attention to the offer. Details of the offer would appear on the side, back, or inside of the package (see Figure 3.20).

PROVIDE CONVENIENCE

A package should be easy to carry, open, handle, and reseal (if appropriate). Liquid detergents, for example, should be easy to pour without spills (on some brands the plastic lid is the measuring device for dispensing the product). Squirt spouts on products such as mustard and ketchup also offer convenience. If a product is heavy or bulky, handles should be built into the package design. The Tide package appearing in

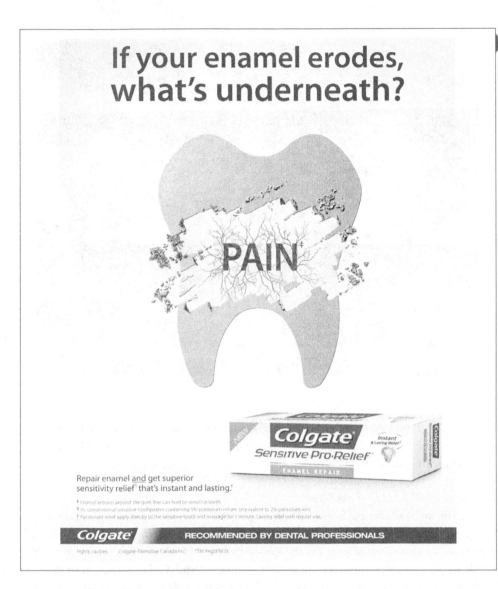

FIGURE
3.19

Colgate's Package Clearly Communicates the Key Benefit: It Helps Repair Enamel Damage

Source: © Colgate Palmolive Company

FIGURE
3.20

A Package Face Often Communicates Details of a Promotional Offer

Source: © Dick Hemingway.

FIGURE
3.21

**Bulky and Heavy Products
Should Be Designed So That
They Are Easy to Carry**

Source: © Keith Tuckwell

Figure 3.21 demonstrates this principle. Other examples of convenience include resealable plastic lids on margarine containers, twist-off caps on beer and wine, and straws on fruit juice containers.

BE ENVIRONMENTALLY FRIENDLY

Packaging, or wasteful packaging, is an important issue for marketing organizations today. As many studies have shown, consumers are more willing to do business with organizations that show respect for the environment, and respect extends to marketing goods in packages that are environmentally friendly. Pepsi-Cola recently introduced a bottle made entirely of plant material. The bottle is made from switch grass, pine bark, corn husks, and other materials. The new bottle looks and feels like plastic, and protects the drink just as plastic bottles do. PepsiCo also introduced a fully compostable bag for its Sun Chips line of snacks, although the loud noise the bag makes is disturbing to some consumers. The company is investigating ways to reduce the noise factor.

Branding by Design

Not all kinds of product are sold in a package. What attributes sell an appliance, an automobile, a computer, the services offered by a bank, and so on? For durable goods such as cars and computers, the key influencer in the buying decision could be the design—the look and style of the product and the image it projects about itself. For products like mutual funds, trusts, and other financial offerings—products that are truly intangible—consumers are primarily influenced by the brand image as perpetuated by effective marketing communications programs.

brand design A concept that attempts to include an experience in the design of a product (for example, the design may trigger an emotional response).

Brand design integrates the brand experience into the product or service. It's about creatively designing innovative approaches in order to create a unique brand

FIGURE
3.22

The Design of a Product Plays a Key Role in Building a Brand's Image in the Minds of Consumers

Source: Courtesy of KitchenAid ® Canada

experience.[11] In the durable goods market, designers traditionally followed one basic premise: Form follows function. They responded to consumers wanting goods that performed specific functions dependably and reliably. Things have changed. Consumers now want products that fit in with their lifestyle or the decor of their home furnishings. They are more style conscious, and are purchasing durable goods like automobiles, appliances, and electronics based more on emotion and style than function. Refer to the illustration in Figure 3.22.

Advancing technology has an impact on design. As mentioned earlier in the chapter, Apple's products have always been perceived as sleek and stylish. Apple's phones, tablets, and laptop computers are an ideal fit with the lifestyle of consumers who want them. Have you noticed that people who hang out in coffee houses display their Apple laptops—sort of a badge of honour? Samsung's Galaxy line of smartphones also boasts sleek design. The slim profile and larger screen have been a hit with consumers. Refer to the image in Figure 3.23.

FIGURE 3.23

Effective Brand Design and Brand Strategy Are the Keys to Samsung Galaxy's Success in the Smartphone Market

Source: © Samsung

SAMSUNG
Galaxy S6 | S6 edge

►► SUMMARY

Developing a sound brand strategy and positioning strategy is the first step in the brand-building process. Having the right strategy is important because consumers form their impressions about a brand based on what they hear and see about it. Therefore, marketing organizations use branding as a means of identifying products and building an image.

Over time, consumers come to trust what a brand stands for and express their satisfaction in varying degrees of brand loyalty. Loyalty is expressed in terms of brand recognition, brand preference, and brand insistence. Brand equity is the value a consumer derives from a brand beyond its physical attributes. Such equity is based on how aware

consumers are of a brand, their degree of loyalty, and perceptions held about quality. Brand equity may also be described in monetary terms, as brands are a valuable asset of a company.

Branding offers several benefits for consumers. It suggests a consistent degree of quality, provides psychological rewards (for example, a better self-image) for possessing certain brands, and distinguishes competing brands from one another. Good brands are personal, and they often become integral parts of people's lives. For manufacturers, the brand name communicates a point of difference, allows for the creation of an image, and helps build brand loyalty.

The brand-building process involves four essential steps: identifying brand values and positioning strategy, planning and implementing a brand marketing program, measuring and interpreting brand performance, and growing and sustaining brand equity. Brand values are the primary attributes (descriptive features) and benefits (the values consumers attach to a brand). Positioning refers to the image a marketer wants the brand to have in the customers' minds. A positioning strategy is based on an important element of the marketing mix. Some of the common positioning strategies include product differentiation, brand leadership, head-on (comparative) positioning, innovation, price and value, and lifestyle.

When implementing a brand strategy, all elements of the marketing mix and the marketing communications mix come into play. The marketing communications mix is the voice of a brand's positioning strategy. A good strategy that is executed efficiently should instill the desired image about a brand in the customer's mind. In this regard, all elements of the communications mix work together to deliver a consistent message.

Packaging and product design play key roles in differentiating brands and help determine consumer perceptions. Therefore, it is important that a brand, in all of its different sizes, formats, and variations, have a consistent and distinctive package design. The ability of a package to stand out in a cluttered point-of-purchase environment is a key factor influencing buying decisions.

A good package design will protect the product, market the product, provide consumers convenience in handling and using the product, and be environmentally friendly. Package designs should be unique and attractive to grab the attention of consumers as they pass by. Expensive durable goods rely on the design of the product to create images in the consumer's mind. The design must be functional yet attractive to the eye. Style and appearance are important influences on buying decisions for cars, appliances, computers, and other consumer electronic goods. Goods such as these are often an expression of one's self-image.

KEY TERMS

attribute   75
benefit   75
brand   66
brand design   88
brand equity   71
brand insistence   71
brand logo   68
brand loyalty   70

brand manager   75
brand name   67
brand preference   70
brand recognition   70
core values   75
head-on positioning   78
image positioning   81
innovation positioning   80

leadership positioning   78
lifestyle positioning   81
positioning   76
price positioning   81
product differentiation strategy   78
repositioning   83
trademark   68
unique selling point (USP)   74

REVIEW QUESTIONS

1. Identify and briefly explain the key components of a brand.
2. Identify two benefits of branding for consumers and two benefits of branding for organizations.
3. Identify and briefly explain the three stages of brand loyalty.
4. What is brand equity, and how does a brand build it?
5. "A brand is a set of core values." What does this statement mean?
6. Define what positioning is and state the importance of having a clearly worded positioning strategy statement.
7. What is the difference between head-on positioning and brand leadership positioning? Provide an example of each not mentioned in the chapter.

8. If a brand is using a product differentiation positioning strategy, what will the advertising message focus on? Provide an example of this strategy not mentioned in the chapter.
9. If a brand is using a lifestyle positioning strategy, what will the advertising message focus on? Provide two examples of this strategy not mentioned in the chapter.
10. What essential roles does a package perform in the marketing of a brand? Briefly explain.
11. Explain the role and influence that the design of a product can have on prospective buyers.

DISCUSSION AND APPLICATION QUESTIONS

1. "A brand is more than the physical product." Explain.
2. "Selecting the name for a new product is a critical decision." What are the essential issues in naming a brand? Conduct some online secondary research to get to the bottom of this issue.
3. Select a lifestyle advertising campaign that you think is particularly effective. Write a brief report or make a brief presentation on why you think it is effective.
4. Explain the relationship between brand positioning and the development of an effective marketing communications strategy.
5. Evaluate the marketing situation for one of the following companies or brands. What makes this company (brand) unique and what is its differential advantage(s) compared to the primary competitors? Based on what you know of this company (brand) and what you see or hear in terms of marketing communications, develop a positioning strategy statement for the company (brand).

   a) President's Choice
   b) Alexander Keith's beer
   c) H&M
   d) Doritos
   e) BioSteel sports drink

6. Using a company or brand of your choosing, examine the relationships among its name, logo, and advertising slogan. Are these brand and communications elements permanently entwined or can any of them change in order to build the brand's image? What are the benefits and risks associated with any kind of change?
7. Assess the role that package design plays in building a brand's image. To justify your position, provide an example of a package design that you perceive to be good and a design that you perceive to be less than good. What is the relationship between the package design and other forms of marketing communications?

ENDNOTES

1. Definition of a Brand, About.com. http://marketing.about.com/od/marketingglossary/g/branddef.htm
2. Katherine Lukovitz, "Brand Experience, Values Increasingly Driving Loyalty," *Marketing Daily*, February 6, 2012, www.mediapost.com.
3. David Dunne and Julia Moulden, "Personal Branding: Applying the Lessons of Successful Brands to Yourself," *The Globe and Mail*, October 21, 2002, p. B9.
4. "25 Best Brands in Canada, *Canadian Business,* http://www.canadianbusiness.com/lists-and-rankings/best-brands/canadas-best-brands-2016-the-top-25/image/26/
5. Russ Martin, "The 10 Most Reputable Brands in Canada," *Marketing*, www.marketingmag.ca/brands/the-10-most-reputable-brands-in-canada-174412.
6. Dale Beckman, David Kurtz, and Louis Boone, *Foundations of Marketing* (Toronto: Holt Rinehart and Winston, 1988) pp. 316–317.
7. "Apple Overtakes Google for Top Spot in the 10th Annual Brandz Top Most Valuable Global Brand Rankings," Millward Brown, http://www.brandz100.com/#/article/brandz-top-100-most-valuable-global-brands-2015-report/932?back_url=%2F
8. Kevin Forssmann, "Is My Brand Losing Focus?" *Brandchannel*, July 28, 2008, www.brandchannel.com/brand_speak.asp?bs_id=198
9. Susan Krashinsky, "There's Something about Melina," *The Globe and Mail*, November 23, 2012, p. B5.
10. "Retail Therapy," The Australian Centre for Retail Studies, Monash University, April 2009, p. 3; "2012 Shopper Engagement Study," Point of Purchase Advertising International (POPAI), www.popa.com/engage/docs/Media-Topline-Finalpdf.
11. Larry Light, "Brand Design Takes More Than Style," *Advertising Age*, November 6, 2006, p. 74.

Planning for Integrated Media

Part 2 examines the steps, considerations, and procedures for developing message and media strategies for television, radio, newspapers, magazines, various forms of out-of-home advertising, direct response media, and interactive media.

In Chapter 4, the basic elements of the communications process are introduced along with the various stages of creative (message) planning. Because creative plans are based on clearly defined objectives, strategies, and executions, the chapter draws clear distinctions among these three planning concepts. It finishes with a discussion of various creative appeal techniques and execution techniques that advertisers employ to present compelling messages to customers.

Chapter 5 describes the media planning side of advertising. Media planning involves identifying media objectives, creating media strategies, and executing those plans. The development of a sound media strategy is crucial, so considerable time is devoted to discussing primary issues that influence the strategy. Strategic decisions are largely influenced by the budget available.

Chapter 6 examines the growing field of direct response communications. Direct response plans rely on database management techniques, and the chapter devotes considerable time to how organizations use information sources. Various direct response media options are introduced, and the strengths and weaknesses of each option are examined.

In Chapter 7, the focus is on digital communications. The various strategies for delivering effective online messages are discussed, and perspectives are offered regarding how to effectively integrate online messages with offline messages and related communications strategies. Social media and mobile communications are also examined in this chapter.

Advertising Planning: Creative

After studying this chapter, you will be able to

1. Identify the basic elements of the communications process

2. Explain the various stages of creative planning

3. Explain the role of a creative brief and describe the content of such a document

4. Distinguish among creative objectives, creative strategies, and creative execution

5. Describe the role of creative objective statements

6. Appreciate the variety of appeal techniques for developing creative strategies

7. Identify various execution techniques for best presenting creative strategies

In Chapter 3 you learned about the strategic planning process and saw how various elements of the marketing and marketing communications mix converge in a master plan of some kind. The role and nature of the individual plans—the plans for advertising, direct response, interactive, sales promotion, public relations, experiential marketing, and personal selling—are the focus of the remainder of the book. Separate external organizations may be responsible for developing these plans. Therefore, in the planning and development stages there is much communication between a company and its external suppliers.

This chapter will focus specifically on one aspect of advertising: the development and implementation of the message. The initial section discusses some fundamental communication concepts that are common to all components in the marketing communications mix. It is followed by a discussion of the creative planning process. Creative planning relies upon essential input from the marketing plan and involves the development of a separate plan that outlines the creative objectives, creative strategies, and creative execution (tactics).

Communications Essentials

The marketplace is dynamic, and consumers are exposed to hundreds of messages each day from all kinds of sources. What do consumers recognize and recall at the end of the day? Can they say with certainty they saw a posting about Molson Canadian on their Facebook news feed? Can they recall who the NHL hockey player is in a Sport Chek TV commercial? Do they recall the name of the bank that says: "You're richer than you think"? The answer is not likely. In very simple terms, there is so much commercial clutter out there that consumers remember very little. The challenge, therefore, is to develop a message that will break through the clutter and leave a lasting impression on the audience. Easier said than done!

An understanding of the communications process and how consumers receive and interpret messages is essential. In Chapter 1, various consumer behaviour concepts were introduced—concepts such as needs and motives, attitudes and perceptions, and reference groups and family influences.

communication The transmission, receipt, and processing of information between a sender and a receiver.

Communication is defined as transmitting, receiving, and processing information. Communication occurs when the message that was sent reaches its destination in a form that is understood by the intended audience. Simply stated, an organization develops a message, selects the right media to deliver it, and, if all things are planned effectively, it will reach the consumers and have an impact on them. Developing the message is referred to as **encoding**; that is, the message is transformed into some attention-getting form, such as a print advertisement, a direct response mailing piece, an article about the product in a newspaper, and so on. The message is then **transmitted**, usually by the media (television, radio, newspapers, magazines, outdoor advertising, online, and so on). Refer to Figure 4.1 for an illustration.

In the delivery of the message, however, certain complications arise along the way. For example,

- The message was not in line with customer attitudes.
- The message did not reach the intended target with the desired frequency.
- The message delivered by the competition was more convincing.
- The competition spent more on advertising and had higher share of mind.
- New competitors entered the market and invested heavily in advertising.

Circumstances such as these are referred to as **noise**; they dilute the impact of an advertiser's message. Whether or not a message breaks through the clutter is usually determined by the relationships among three factors: the quality of planning when developing message strategy, the execution of the plan being on target with the right timing and frequency, and the impact of competitive messages. The advertiser has control over the first two factors but no control over the third.

Competing products are sending very similar messages to the same target market, creating noise. The objective, therefore, is to break through the noise. To do so, the message must be relevant to the consumer. For instance, the product's benefits must satisfy a need or suit the lifestyle of the target and be presented in such a manner that the brand becomes a preferred alternative.

If the message does not break through (if it is perceived as dull, uses the wrong types of appeals, or is simply confusing to the target), no action will occur. Lack of action indicates a need to revisit the creative strategy and execution and make changes where necessary. For example, many soap and skin care brands make similar claims and usually include good-looking females in their ads. Some years ago, Dove, in an effort to stand out, launched a "real beauty" campaign that encouraged women to celebrate themselves as they are. It was a bold and compelling message that regular women of all ages and sizes identified with—it broke through the clutter. The love-your-beauty attitude expressed by Dove led to the launch of many new Dove skin care products.[1]

encoding   The transformation of a message into a meaningful format, such as an advertisement, a mailing piece, or an article in a newspaper.

transmission   The sending of a message through a medium such as television, radio, newspapers, magazines, outdoor advertising, online, and so on.

noise   Any potential form of disruption in the transmission of a message that could distort the impact of the message; competitive advertising or the clutter of advertising messages in a medium are forms of noise.

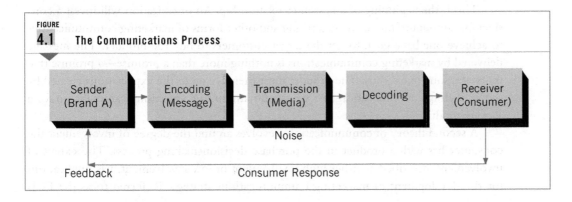

FIGURE 4.1   The Communications Process

A consumer passes through a series of stages on the way to taking action. Advertising can influence the consumer at each stage. One such model is referred to as ACCA— awareness, comprehension, conviction, and action. This model is part of a theory called DAGMAR, which stands for Defining Advertising Goals for Measured Advertising Response. An advertising goal is a specific communication task to be accomplished among a defined audience in a given period. The task should be measurable, with benchmarks in existence to assess achievements.

The effectiveness of an advertising campaign is usually linked back to this model. For example, an advertiser wants to know (in percentage terms) the level of awareness of its product among the target market, and whether or not it is perceived as being a preferred brand. Furthermore, the advertiser may want to know what percentage of the target market has tried the product (in the case of a new product campaign). Post-campaign marketing research studies measure the achievement of the objectives.

An advertisement (or campaign) that achieves good scores with respect to awareness, comprehension, and conviction is likely to succeed. The desired action in the form of someone buying the product will likely occur. To protect its investment in advertising, an organization may also conduct marketing research while the message strategy is in the development stage. The message is tested for likeability, persuasiveness, and likelihood of purchase. Research measures that exceed the norms of other products in the category would suggest the advertiser is onto something. The various marketing research techniques used to evaluate advertising effectiveness are discussed in Chapter 12. The following is a description of each behaviour stage:

- **Awareness:** In this stage, the customer learns something for the first time. In an advertising context, a message tries to plant the brand name and the primary benefit offered in the customer's mind. Awareness can be measured by aided and unaided recall tests.

- **Comprehension:** At this stage, the consumer is expressing interest. The message is perceived as relevant. The brand is evaluated on the basis of need satisfaction. It is in the consumer's cognitive realm and becomes a candidate for potential purchase. A like or dislike for a brand can be measured using attitude scales.

- **Conviction:** At this stage, the consumer expresses stronger feelings toward the brand based on the perceived benefits it offers. The brand has moved higher in the consumer's frame of reference and become a preferred brand in his or her mind. In other words, a new attitude or a change in attitude about something has occurred. There may be sufficient motivation to take action and buy the product.

- **Action:** At this stage, the desired action occurs. The consumer buys the brand for the first time, visits the dealer showroom, or calls that 1-800 number!

This is the beginning of a customer relationship. An organization will invest a considerable amount of money in advertising and other forms of marketing communications to achieve one basic goal: to get the target customers to buy the product. The message delivered by marketing communications is nothing more than a promise—a promise that motivates someone to buy. The product must then live up to the expectations created by the marketing communications. As we say, no amount of advertising can make up for a shoddy product.

A second theory of communications revolves around the degree of involvement the consumer has with a product in the purchase decision-making process. The extent of involvement, described as either high involvement or low involvement, has implications for the development of marketing communications strategy. Referred to as the FCB

FIGURE

4.2   An Illustration of the FCB Grid

High Involvement	
Quadrant 1 High Importance (expensive) Rational Decision **Example:** Automobile or computer	**Quadrant 2** High Importance (expensive) Emotional Decision **Example:** Designer clothing
Quadrant 3 Low Importance (less expensive) Rational Decision **Example:** Detergent	**Quadrant 4** Low Importance (less expensive) Emotional Decision **Example:** Soft drink, beer
Low Involvement	

Source: Based on www.public.iastate.edu/~geske/FCB.html.

Grid, the grid was developed by Richard Vaughn, a senior vice-president of Foote, Cone, and Belding Advertising (see Figure 4.2).[2]

Products that are included in Quadrant One are expensive and require a rational decision-making process during which alternatives are evaluated. Since the consumer will probably spend an extended period of time assessing alternatives, the message strategy should have an informative tone and style, and the media selected to deliver the message should be conducive to a long copy format (for example, newspapers, magazines, and websites). Products in Quadrant Two are also high involvement, but consumers evaluate alternatives more on emotion. For example, designer clothing is bought to make the consumer feel good, feel sexy, or show status. Marketing communications must generate emotional responses and create an image that people will buy. The message will appeal to higher-level needs, the looking-glass self (how you think others see you), and the ideal self (how you would like to be). Television ads, glossy and visually appealing magazine ads, and special inserts are effective media for such products.

Products that are included in Quadrant Three are low-involvement products that require rational decisions. Products such as household cleaning products, paper products, and other everyday items are in this category. Marketing communications should give the consumer a compelling reason to buy (for example, it lasts longer, as in a battery; it acts quickly, as in a headache remedy; or it is convenient to use, as in a household product). The focus of the message is on the key benefit, so the message must be short. A catchy slogan might act as a reminder. The illustration in Figure 4.3 offers a good example where an ad gives the viewer a compelling reason to buy. Here, Tylenol aptly demonstrates a need for its product. The image says it all. Television, magazine ads with strong visuals, and point-of-purchase material are effective media choices for these kinds of products.

Products that are included in Quadrant Four are low-involvement products purchased on emotional decisions. The products are not expensive, but they make the consumer feel good. Examples of such products include snack foods, beer and alcohol, and soft drinks.

FIGURE
4.3

Tylenol Appeals to a Person's Need to Avoid Pain Quickly When It Occurs

Source: © Johnson & Johnson Inc.

There are not many rational reasons for buying these types of products, so it is common for messages to adopt a "feel good" strategy. For example, there is an abundance of lifestyle-oriented messages among popular Canadian beer brands such as Coors Light and Bud Light. It is the image or lifestyle association that the consumer buys into. Television, outdoor advertising, interactive advertising, and point-of-purchase material play a role in delivering messages for these products.

MARKETING COMMUNICATIONS PLANNING PROCESS

The various elements of the strategic planning process were presented in Chapter 2. This chapter concentrates on the advertising planning process, but will recognize the relationships between advertising and the other forms of communication. Once the relationships are established, the chapter will then focus on creative planning. Media planning concepts for traditional media alternatives are presented in Chapter 5.

All aspects of a marketing communications plan are based on the same set of information. The current situation a brand or company faces is analyzed, a problem or opportunity is identified, and a plan of action is developed and implemented. As part of the planning process, the role and contribution of the various elements in the marketing communications mix are identified and those that are most appropriate are included in the plan. Separate plans, designed to achieve specific objectives, are developed for each element of the mix. Once completed, the key elements of these plans are integrated into the master plan—the marketing plan (see Figure 4.4).

With reference to Chapter 2 again, marketing communications plans are devised to meet a variety of challenges and are usually documented as communications objectives in the marketing communications plan. As you will see in this chapter and subsequent chapters, certain elements of the marketing communications mix are better suited to achieving certain objectives. Marketing communications objectives can be diverse and tend to involve challenges, such as

• Building awareness about and interest in a product.

• Encouraging trial purchase.

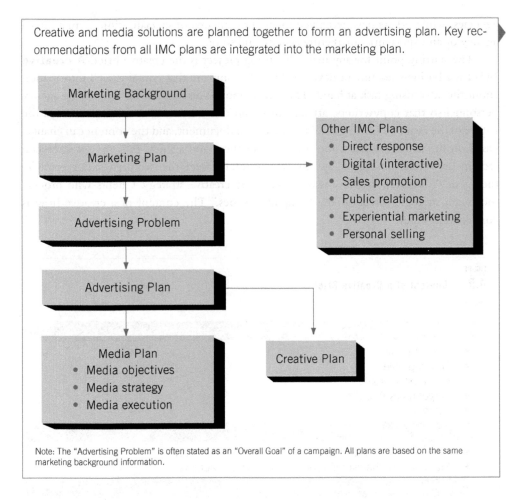

Creative and media solutions are planned together to form an advertising plan. Key recommendations from all IMC plans are integrated into the marketing plan.

FIGURE
4.4

Creative Planning

Note: The "Advertising Problem" is often stated as an "Overall Goal" of a campaign. All plans are based on the same marketing background information.

- Attracting new target markets.
- Encouraging brand preference.
- Altering perceptions held by consumers.
- Creating goodwill and fostering a positive public image.
- Motivating distributors to carry a product.

As indicated previously, certain components of the marketing communications mix are more appropriate than others for achieving specific communications objectives. In this chapter, you will see how advertising helps achieve some of these objectives.

ADVERTISING PLANNING: CREATIVE

Advertising is defined as a paid-for message communicated through the media by an identified sponsor. The goal of an advertisement is it to stimulate a response from the target audience the message is delivered to.

The advertising plan is usually developed by an advertising agency, an external partner that works closely with the client. The agency is responsible for developing and managing the client's advertising. Historically, agencies focused their energy on creative and media planning, but in today's environment they have expanded into other areas, such as direct response, marketing research, digital communications, and public relations. In this industry, many agencies have evolved into full-service marketing communications

advertising A paid-for media-delivered message by an identified sponsor designed to stimulate a positive response from a target audience.

agencies, while others have remained focused on an area of specialization, as in a digital agency or an experiential marketing agency, and so on.

The starting point for any new advertising project is the creative brief. A **creative brief** is a business document developed by the company that contains vital information about the advertising task at hand. The information is discussed with advertising agency personnel so that copywriters, art directors, and creative directors fully understand the nature of the assignment. The brief is a discussion document, and the content can change, based on the nature of discussion between the client and agency. In some cases, certain sections are actually left blank, awaiting discussion between the two parties. For example, the agency's key responsibility is to develop the creative strategy. Clients who provide too much strategic direction are "stepping on toes." The content of a creative brief is contained in Figure 4.5.

creative brief   A document developed by a client organization that contains vital information about the advertising task at hand; it is a useful tool for discussions between the client and its advertising agency.

FIGURE 4.5   Content of a Creative Brief

Market Information (information from the marketing plan)
- Market profile
- Brand profile
- Competitor profile
- Target market profile
- Budget

Problem and Overall Objective
- Identification of the problem that advertising will resolve
- Statement of the overall goal for advertising to achieve

Advertising Objectives (based on problem or goal)
- Awareness
- Interest
- Preference
- Action
- New image
- New targets

Positioning Strategy Statement
- A statement of brand benefits, brand personality, or desired image

Creative Objectives
- Key benefit statement
- Support claims statement

Creative Strategy
- Central theme ("big idea")
- Tone and style
- Appeal techniques

Creative Execution
- Tactical considerations
- Production decisions

Note: The nature and content of a creative brief varies from company to company. A working model is presented here to show the typical content of a creative brief. Some companies include a problem statement or an overall goal, while others include both. Advertising objectives usually concentrate on one or two issues so the campaign remains focused on the problem at hand.

Information provided by the client includes essential market background information, a statement identifying the problem to be resolved or the overall goal to be achieved, and a list of communications objectives. The client also provides a positioning strategy statement to guide the development of the creative plan. The positioning strategy statement directly influences the creative objectives. For our discussions here, creative objectives deal with the content of the message to be delivered (that is, what is the primary attribute and benefit to be communicated to the target market?). The remaining elements of the creative brief—the creative strategy and creative execution—are the responsibility of the agency. That's what they get paid to do.

Once the creative brief is finalized, the spotlight shines on the copywriter and art director, a team charged with developing the **creative concept** or "big idea," as it is often referred to, that will be the cornerstone of the campaign. At this point, the agency's creative team immerses itself in details about the brand, target market, and competition so that it can fully appreciate the current situation.

Let's examine the content of the creative brief in more detail. Since the market background information is drawn from the marketing plan, that section will not be discussed in this chapter. Simply refer back to Chapter 2 if you need more details. The market background section includes information about the market, brand, key competitors, a profile of the primary target market, and budget. Knowing a brand's market position and how consumers perceive it is important to developing message strategies. Knowing how competitors advertise their products is also important. The agency wants to ensure it recommends new and innovative ideas to its clients. An example of a creative brief is presented in Figure 4.6.

creative concept The basic sales message (a key idea) that an advertisement communicates through verbal and visual devices.

PROBLEM IDENTIFICATION Advertising plans are usually designed to resolve a particular problem or pursue an opportunity. For example, an established brand will review its marketing strategy each year and make changes in strategic direction when necessary. Factors such as the stage at which a brand finds itself in the product lifecycle, the intensity of competition, and changing preferences among target consumers are evaluated in the review process. Changes in these areas have an impact on marketing communications strategies.

Based on this creative brief model, the situation is encapsulated in a **problem statement**. Other models may require a statement that describes the **overall goal** of the campaign. Regardless of which option is used, advertising can accomplish only one thing at a time. A campaign must have a central focus. Simply stated, it's "Here's what we want to achieve!" To illustrate, consider the following examples:

problem statement A brief statement that summarizes a particular problem to resolve or an opportunity to pursue and serves as the focus of a marketing strategy.

overall goal The objective of an advertising campaign.

- To create or increase brand awareness.

- To alter perceptions currently held by consumers about a brand.

- To present a completely new image for a brand.

- To launch a new product into the marketplace.

- To attract a new target market to a brand.

- To encourage trial purchase.

These examples suggest focus. To demonstrate how an advertising campaign can focus on achieving an overall goal, consider a recent campaign by the Egg Farmers of Canada. To get Canadians to consume more eggs the focus will be on health and nutritional issues. People will be reminded that they can trust the goodness and purity of

FIGURE
4.6   An Example of a Creative Brief

Harley-Davidson

Market Information

- Market volume has been affected by the economic downturn and an aging rider population; unit sales for the industry dropped 20 percent versus one year ago.
- Market divided into two segments: the heavyweight segment, which Harley dominates, caters to older buyers wanting style, quality, and status; the lightweight segment appeals to younger buyers seeking speed, agility, and affordability in a motorcycle.
- Harley generates 70 percent of its sales in the United States and 30 percent internationally.
- Canada accounts for 15 percent of Harley's international sales.

Market Shares

Harley-Davidson dominates the heavyweight segment. Current market shares are estimated to be:

Brand	Share %
Harley-Davidson	50.0
Honda	15.1
Suzuki	12.9
Yamaha	8.6
Kawasaki	6.8

Brand Profile

Harley competes on design and quality (intentionally unique-sounding engines).

Harley's past growth and continued success is closely tied to its brand loyalty (Harley owners have been known to tattoo the brand's trademark on their bodies and are members of HOG—Harley Owners Group.)

Harley has distinguished itself from other brands based on its heritage, image, and reputation—a "rebellious" image the company doesn't have control over.

Harley does not promote functional benefits like power and performance; advertising messages portray the emotional connection between brand and rider.

Brand Insight from Loyal Customers

"I love everything about a Harley. From the bike and clothing to the people you meet when riding, and the instant friends everywhere you go."

"When you ride a Harley you feel a Harley. When you ride a [Honda] Gold Wing, you don't feel anything. The Harley engine has a soul. And a lot of Japanese bikes don't have soul."

Competitor Profile

Japanese competitors offer heavyweight models that appeal to price-conscious buyers more interested in the motorcycle's technology.

Features such as fuel injection and ABS brakes make Japanese bikes a sensible buy, but they lack the outlaw image of a Harley.

Target Market Profile (Current)

- Demographics: 45 to 59 years old; 88 percent male and 12 percent female; $75 000 plus annually; reside in urban markets
- Psychographics: adventurous, like to travel, break away from routine on weekends, enjoy the freedom of the open road
- Behaviour: current customers are extremely brand loyal and emotionally connected to brand. "Weekend Warrior" is a nickname describing the customer.

FIGURE

4.6   *(Continued)*

Problem

The current customer is aging, and younger potential customers see a Harley as a bike that looks like their father's or grandfather's bike—it is the motorcycle of choice for aging baby boomers. Future growth depends upon Harley's ability to attract new, younger customers. How does Harley-Davidson attract a younger customer?

Communications Objectives

- Attract a younger customer in the 30 to 45 age range.
- Alter perceptions held by younger customers about the brand.
- Present an image more in line with the lifestyles of the younger target.

Positioning Statement

Harley-Davidson represents a sense of freedom, independence, a chance to live on your own terms for a while, even rebelliousness. For individuals wanting to be a kindred spirit with others of like mind, Harley-Davidson is the brand for you.

Creative Objectives

- To communicate an image or set of images more in line with younger lifestyles.
- To portray the feeling of freedom and independence a younger rider will enjoy when riding a Harley.
- To communicate an emotional connection between Harley-Davidson and the rider (younger rider).

Creative Strategy

Strategy is left to the discretion of the agency but it must be in line with the brand's overall positioning strategy. Emotional and lifestyle appeals that focus on freedom and independence have been successful in the past, but Harley-Davidson is open to new ideas. The recommended strategy must be suitable for print, broadcast, and digital media.

Creative Execution

- 4-colour print ads (magazine and outdoor executions).
- 30-second television spots.
- Online video ads.

All images must portray the core positioning strategy of the brand while appealing to the younger target audience.

This brief was prepared by the author for illustration purposes. Based on Nathan Vanderklippe and Richard Blackwell, "Passionate Riders, Few Buyers," *The Globe and Mail,* July 28, 2009, pp. B1, B4; Martin Patriquin, "Booting the Outlaw Off the Chopper," *Maclean's,* August 24, 2009, p. 53; and Joseph Tirella, "Is Harley-Davidson Over the Hill," *MSN Money,* March 30, 2009.

Canadian eggs. A real Canadian farmer was featured in the initial television spot.[3] Refer to the image in Figure 4.7.

ADVERTISING OBJECTIVES   Once the overall goal is determined, specific **advertising objectives** are identified. Wherever possible, advertising objectives should be quantitative in nature so that they can be measured for success or failure at a later date. Advertising objectives might be behavioural in nature or they might focus on issues related to the overall problem. For example, an objective might focus on creating a new image or on attracting a new target market.

Advertising objectives should deal only with issues that advertising (the creative plan and media plan) can resolve. For example, a new product campaign will focus on

advertising objectives   Goal statements for advertisements that include quantitative measures related to behaviour or other relevant issues.

awareness objectives. The objective is to build awareness gradually by presenting a message that informs consumers about what the product is and what it will do for them. If the market is very competitive and several brands are strong, the advertising objectives will focus on building preference. The message will focus squarely on unique attributes that show how the advertised brand performs better than other brands.

To demonstrate how advertising objectives are written, consider the following examples:

- To achieve an awareness level of 60 percent for Brand X in the defined target market within 12 months of product launch.

- To achieve a trial purchase rate of 25 percent for Brand Y in the defined target market within 12 months of product launch.

- To reposition (or re-image) Brand Z in the customer's mind by presenting images that will attract a younger target market.

The first two examples are quantitative in nature and can be easily measured for achievement at the end of the plan period. If the objectives are achieved, it indicates that current advertising strategies are working. If they are not achieved, the client and agency can re-evaluate the situation and make appropriate changes. The third example is not quantitative in nature, but it can be measured. Assuming the current image of the brand is known, a marketing research study near the end of the campaign period can be conducted to determine if the brand has caught on with younger customers.

Let's examine a few of these challenges in more detail and determine how they influence the direction of creative planning and the message strategy that is ultimately employed.

CREATING OR INCREASING BRAND AWARENESS Creating awareness is always the first challenge for advertising. The higher the level of awareness, the stronger the likelihood consumers will buy the product. Achieving high levels of awareness depends on how memorable the message is and, perhaps, how frequently the message is delivered.

CHAPTER 4   Advertising Planning: Creative   **107**

4.8

A Clear Message and a Memorable Presenter Character Helped Create Brand Awareness for Trivago

Source: © Trivago

The medium used to deliver the message will also influence awareness levels. The right plan will use the right medium, but the size of the budget often dictates media selection.

When Trivago entered the North American market, its primary objective was to create brand awareness. An intensive television and digital campaign featured a character (now well-known as the TrivagoGuy) with a casual and laid back demeanour, who some saw as an unconventional character, and others saw as attractive. Regardless of the reaction, the guy inspired all kinds of buzz in social media. The message emphasized the brand name while the presenter showed how easy it was to use the Trivago hotel reservation website. The campaign was effective. Travellers' awareness of Trivago now ranks just below Priceline (the market leader) and ahead of Expedia and Trip Advisor. Refer to the image in Figure 4.8.

ENCOURAGING TRIAL PURCHASE Creating awareness and interest in a brand is one thing, but getting people to open their the wallets is another. Sometimes incentives have to be offered to give consumers an extra nudge. If the timing of the incentive is right, positive action will be taken. Therefore, many advertisements are designed specifically to include special offers—anything from cents-off coupons to manufacturers' rebates to low-cost financing. These incentives serve a specific purpose. They help reduce the risk associated with purchasing something for the first time. Refer to the incentive offered for a cookie purchase in Figure 4.9. For expensive goods such as cars and computers, where the risk is very high,

incentives help encourage consumers to buy in a time frame that is desirable for the manufacturer.

Considering how the consumer's mind works, people want to know they are making the right decision. If the product lives up to the promise presented in the advertising, subsequent purchases will be made without incentives. Consumers today are looking for better value in the products and services they buy, and, as a result, incentive-oriented advertising is now more prominent than in the past.

ATTRACTING NEW TARGET MARKETS   In order to attract a new target market, for example, a younger age group than the audience the brand currently appeals to, a new message strategy is necessary. The tone and style of advertising may have to change. To illustrate, consider a recent effort by luxury carmaker Jaguar. Jaguar wanted to go younger to attract new buyers in their late twenties and early thirties. To reach this tech-savvy group a digital campaign that included an interactive video was used to engage viewers. This was quite a departure from Jaguar's approach to its older target. Axe (personal care products) wanted to reach an older target (its concentration had been on teenagers), and to do so it toned down its message so that it was more in keeping with the aspirations of 20-something males. For insight into how the new Axe campaign was developed read the IMC Highlight **Axe Goes Older**.

ENCOURAGING PREFERENCE   The objective for an established brand in growth or mature markets is to stand out from competing brands. Therefore, the thrust of marketing activities is product differentiation. Advertising messages focus on the attributes the brand offers. Where continuous improvement programs are in place, it is possible for a brand to become better with age, so there may be new things to communicate.

Mr. Clean is a mature brand in a mature market, and faces competition from many other brands that can do the same thing—clean things around the house. Mr. Clean needed a campaign that would create preference in the consumer's mind. Insight from the brand's Facebook page revealed that women thought of Mr. Clean as a real guy (interesting!); there was a relationship there. That insight was parlayed into a mass media campaign that presented Mr. Clean as almost real. He would be presented with a story about how he came to be the king of clean. The campaign had impact. Sales increased 6 percent during the campaign, which is a testament to good advertising.[4]

Typically, it is the unique attributes of a brand that differentiate it from another and create preference for one brand over another. Sometimes, it's just a good idea about how to present the brand that succeeds. Such was the case for Mr. Clean. It was enough to position the brand in a better light with consumers.

ALTERING CONSUMERS' PERCEPTIONS   Building a brand sometimes requires consumers to adopt a different view of the brand. The quickest way to alter an image is to launch a completely new advertising campaign with an entirely different message. The style and personality of the message will be different to create a new image in the customer's mind.

Such was the case when Bosch assessed its position in the appliance market. Consumers knew Bosch made good dishwashers, but they associated the brand with just dishwashers. Consumers didn't know that Bosch made a complete range of kitchen appliances. Bosch's agency (Bob's Your Uncle) recommended a campaign that leveraged the brand's strength in one product category to build equity across the rest of the line.[5]

Axe Goes Older

You may remember those Axe commercials that showed male teenagers spraying themselves with Axe and then being chased by a mob of females. The guys who bought into the brand promise may have been naïve but ads like that helped make Axe a brand leader in the male grooming market.

Some research by Unilever, the maker of Axe, revealed that that type of message wasn't going to continue to resonate with this generation of teens, and it wouldn't necessarily keep current customers loyal—the brand had to grow up—a new advertising strategy was necessary.

The male grooming market is growing and there are other brands out there competing for the teen and 20-something target. The Old Spice campaign known as "The Man Your Man Could Smell Like" had a positive impact on market share at Axe's expense. To appeal to a slightly older target market, Axe launched a new product, toned down the scent, and offered a more mature message.

The new Axe White Label is positioned as a brand that gives 20-something males the confidence to go after more than just dates: they can go after whatever they want. Insight for the new advertising campaign was based on the fact these males grew up with good grooming habits; habits that were influenced by campaigns from brands like Axe and Old Spice. It was okay for young males to look after their appearance. The message for a slightly older male has to be more mature and serious, however.

One of the initial ads for Axe White Label featured actor Kiefer Sutherland recalling a story about the girl who got away. Another commercial, called "Peace," featured scenes of would-be despots declaring their love through grand gestures; the message: make love, not war. That's serious! The new positioning strategy comes alive in the 2015 commercial that shows a good-looking man walking through a hotel. People muse about what he does. Is he a spy? Is he a Russian fight champion? No. He is simply a hotel employee, but his confidence gives him the aura of a near-mythical man.

The key to the campaign is in understanding the attitudes of the target market. Unilever knows that guys are changing. They know there are many things that are timeless about attraction and how young men want to present themselves to the world. For now, the hope is that the aspirational tone of the message will have an impact on that target.

© Slaven Vlasic/Getty Images for AXE

Source: Based on Megan Haynes, "Axe Bromances the Older Gent," *Strategy*, February/March 2015, pp. 22–24.

Print advertisements showed the entire line of products in one kitchen setting. Refer to the advertisement in Figure 4.10 for details.

Positioning Strategy Statement

Positioning strategy has been discussed in the previous two chapters. Therefore, comments here will simply reinforce the necessity of having a clearly worded positioning strategy statement and discuss how to apply it in developing an ad campaign. The positioning strategy statement identifies the key benefit a brand offers, states what the brand stands for, and is a reflection of a brand's personality. These are the essential inputs assessed

FIGURE
4.10

This Campaign Showed Consumers That Bosch Offered More Products Than Dishwashers

Source: © Patti McConville/Alamy Stock Photo

by the creative team when it develops the message strategy. It can be the trigger that leads to discovery of the "big idea."

To illustrate how the positioning strategy influences creative planning, consider the success a brand like Secret deodorant has experienced. You are probably very familiar with Secret's advertising tagline: "Strong enough for a man, but made for a woman" or more recently "fearless." These taglines capture the positioning strategy of the brand—it is dependable, lasts long, and offers the user confidence. The message appeals to females on an emotional level. It tells a woman she can do anything she wants. In its advertising, slice-of-life images such as being active, being nervous, and lifting your arms bring the positioning strategy to life. The brand message is always about the issues of the day and inspiring woman to be fearless.[6]

Victoria's Secret dominates the retail lingerie market. Its positioning strategy is all about "captivating" as in captivating its female customers with its merchandise mix. The company has a highly refined marketing and advertising strategy. The brand's advertising team carefully selects models for its ads who they believe female customers can relate to. The company does however, use sexy models in its ads—after all it is lingerie. The company also recognizes that images of a woman as a wife and mother play well with all age groups, whereas that ultimate sexy model might be threatening to female customers. Victoria's Secret has achieved mass appeal by striking the right balance between sexy and approachable.[7] Refer to the image in Figure 4.11.

CREATIVE OBJECTIVES

Creative objectives are statements that clearly indicate the information to be communicated to the target audience. The creative brief usually includes what to say about a brand in general terms. While formats may vary, objective statements tend to involve a key benefit statement and a claims statement to support that benefit, because the content of an ad or an ad campaign needs focus.

creative objective A statement that clearly indicates the information to be communicated to the target audience; usually involves a key benefit statement and a supporting claims statement.

FIGURE
4.11

Victoria's Secret Strikes a Balance between Sexy and Approachable

Source: © Ty Wright/Bloomberg via Getty Images

When determining what to say about a brand and how to say it, creative planners refer to the advertising objective for context. As discussed earlier in the chapter, the advertising objective may be to achieve brand awareness, encourage trial purchase, attract a new target, encourage preference, or alter a perception. Somehow, the objective and the primary reason for buying the brand must be related so that a cohesive message is presented to the consumer.

key benefit statement A statement of the basic selling idea, service, or benefit promised to the consumer by the advertiser; appears in the creative plan section of an advertising plan.

- **Key Benefit Statement:** The key benefit statement expresses the basic selling idea, service, or benefit that the advertiser promises the consumer. This benefit should be the primary reason for buying a particular brand instead of competitive brands. The benefit can be something tangible, such as better performance, better quality, longer lasting, and so on, or it can be something intangible or psychological, such as the status and prestige that come with ownership. It is a promise to the consumer. For example, Dairy Farmers of Canada are repositioning milk by demonstrating its benefit as an excellent post-workout recovery beverage. The advertisement in Figure 4.12 encourages people to include milk in their training routines.

support claims statement A substantiation of the promise made in the key benefit statement; appears in the creative plan.

- **Support Claims Statement:** A support claims statement describes the characteristics that will substantiate the promise. It provides proof of the promise based on

FIGURE
4.12

Dairy Farmers of Canada Urge Athletes to "Recharge with Milk"

Source: © Dairy Farmers of Canada

criteria such as technical performance data, comparative product testing, and any other data generated from marketing research. Good support claims give customers a real reason why they should buy the product.

To demonstrate the concept of support claims refer to the ad in Figure 4.13. The Dove Advanced Hair Series of shampoo products promise women fuller, more youthful looking hair. Phrases such as "formulated with proteins and collagen, it nourishes and replenishes essential nutrients lost with age" contained in the body copy of the ad, offer proof of promise.

Support claims statements are less important for brands touting intangible benefits. Lifestyle imagery, for example, relies on the image presented and the connection between the image and the consumer who sees it to substantiate the promise.

CREATIVE STRATEGY

With the decisions about what to say in advertising determined, the creative team turns its attention to creative strategy. This is where the advertising agency starts to earn its keep. What the team searches for is the "big idea," or the central concept or theme that an entire campaign can be built around. All kinds of discussion and experimentation take place. It is an exercise in brainstorming. The guiding light is the positioning strategy. When the ad agency pitches its ideas to the client, the client evaluates the ideas based on how they fit with the positioning strategy. Simply put: Is the "big idea" on strategy or off strategy?

The **creative strategy** is a statement of how the message will be communicated to the target audience. It deals with issues such as the theme, the tone and style of message

creative strategy   A plan of action for how the message will be communicated to the target audience, covering the tone and style of message, the central theme, and the appeal techniques.

Unveil beautifully rejuvenated hair

New Dove Vitality Rejuvenated
Perfectly nourished + 2x fuller*
more youthful looking hair

Did you know? With age your hair can lose essential nutrients and become
more coarse, dull and can appear thinner. That is why Dove Advanced
Hair Series created the new Vitality Rejuvenated range. It is a specifically
designed ritual for aging hair. Formulated with proteins and collagen,
it nourishes and replenishes essential nutrients lost with age.
Unveil thicker looking hair, full of vitality.
www.dove.ca

* Vitality Rejuvenated Range vs flat, limp hair.

Source: Reproduced with kind permission of Unilever PLC and group companies.

that will be adopted, and the appeal techniques that will be employed. It is a statement about the personality a brand will project to consumers.

- **Central Theme:** The **central theme** is the glue that binds the various creative elements of the campaign together. As such, the theme must be transferable from one medium to another. For example, when people see an ad in print form (newspaper, magazine, or billboard), it should conjure up images and meaning from something they have seen on television (a 30-second commercial). What the theme will be is truly the key decision the creative team makes. For the theme to see the light of day, it must be presented to the client in a very convincing manner.

  A good theme can last through many campaigns—the message is simply executed differently in each campaign. For instance, Molson Canadian beer has used a "patriotic" theme for a long time. Images such as wheat fields, mountains, hockey rinks, and people travelling abroad are common backdrops in ads, and slogans such as "Made from Canada" and "I AM CANADIAN" strongly suggest Canadian pride. More recently a red beer fridge travelling around the world was the focus of Molson Canadian advertising. Refer to Figure 4.14.

- **Tone and Style:** In an attempt to break through the clutter of competitive advertising, copywriters and art directors agonize over decisions about tone and style. Such fundamental decisions have a direct impact on how a campaign evolves over time and how the brand's personality gets ingrained into the customer's mind. Single words often describe the tone and style that is recommended. For example, the message will be presented in a persuasive manner, an informative manner, a conservative manner, a friendly manner, a contemporary manner, a straightforward manner, an upbeat manner, and so on. What approach will have the most impact on the target audience? Knowledge about the target audience plays a key role in this decision.

The Molson Canadian campaign featuring a red beer fridge demonstrates how good decisions about theme, tone, and style have a positive impact on consumers. Facing stiff competition from craft beers and other types of alcohol beverages, Canadian's sales volume was declining. A turnaround campaign was needed, but the advertiser was insistent upon retaining the brand's core identity—based on Canadian patriotism. The ad agency recommended a strategy based on what triggers that identity. Some very specific moments would transform quiet, internal expressions of national pride into exuberant celebrations when Canadians find themselves away from home or when Canada competes on the world

central theme The glue that binds various creative elements of a campaign together; transferable from one medium to another.

FIGURE
4.14

Patriotism and Canadian Pride Have Long Been a Theme of Molson Canadian Advertising

Source: © Molson Coors Canada

stage. The Molson Canadian beer fridge would somehow harness these celebratory emotions. The video portion of the campaign went viral, with 6.5 million views. On Facebook there were over 1 million likes and 337 000 shares. The campaign achieved widespread engagement leading to a sales turnaround, which is proof that good advertising works.

For more insight into how creative strategies are developed and evolve over time, read the IMC Highlight: **At Scotiabank, "Richer" Means "New and Improved."**

APPEAL TECHNIQUES

Another key decision is how to make an advertisement appealing to the customer. What techniques will be employed to bring the product benefit claims and theme to life? What can we do creatively to break through the perceptual barriers in the consumer's mind? There isn't a single, definitive formula for success, but appeal techniques can be classified into several categories. For example, when you see an ad, does it make you snicker? Does it draw a tear? Does it make you think? How consumers respond to an ad is usually related to the effectiveness of the appeal. Here are some of the more common appeal techniques.

POSITIVE APPEALS Presenting the message in a positive manner is always a safe approach. However, it is also a very common approach. If combined effectively with the right theme, positive appeals will work. If the creative execution lacks impact, it will wind up being just another ad. The positive appeal stresses the positive benefits of the product and how a person can gain by purchasing the product. McDonald's is one of the country's biggest advertisers and it dominates its market. The company is proud of its accomplishments, so its ads reflect its position. The theme of McDonald's advertising does change from time to time, but the ads remain consistent in how they appeal to their target. McDonald's campaign using the theme and tagline "I'm lovin' it" appealed to people in a positive manner. Typically, McDonald's ads include music and positive interactions among family members.

Kraft Canada launched a campaign for Kraft peanut butter that shows a variety of symbols drawn into the peanut butter spread on toast. A heart, happy face, and peace symbol are among 10 symbols used in the campaign. Kraft is reminding people of all the good feelings they get when eating peanut butter and telling them they should "spread the feeling."

NEGATIVE APPEALS Unless you are Buckley's cough mixture, you don't say bad things about your product. "Tastes awful, but it works" is now a famous slogan coined by Buckley's. Following a philosophy of "do what your momma says and you will get better," Buckley's has experienced new popularity and a positive increase in market share, based solely on its negative advertising style.

For other products, though, negative appeals usually present a situation the consumer would prefer to avoid. Nobody wants to be in a car collision. But to dramatize the safety features of the Jetta, Volkswagen created a TV spot in which two young men suddenly collide with a truck backing out of a driveway. In a split second the front of the car implodes, and the men's heads snap forward, making contact with the exploding airbags. The dramatic demonstration makes its point: In another car they would be dead.

HUMOROUS APPEALS Taking a light-hearted approach to communicating benefits can work effectively. In fact, many critics believe that for advertising to be successful it must entertain the audience. If true, then an advertisement that causes the audience to break into a smile or giggle should break through the clutter.

IMC HIGHLIGHT

At Scotiabank, "Richer" Means "New and Improved"

You have probably seen television ads for Scotiabank telling people, "You're richer than you think." These ads have been on the air since 2006. That's the sign of a creative strategy that is enjoying its intended impact. The initial objective of the campaign was to spread a sense of optimism throughout the country during troubled economic times. The ads encouraged people to visit Scotiabank for a second opinion on their financial situation. When people visited the bank, they learned their situation wasn't as bad as they had thought.

The campaign was based on insights gained from consumer research that revealed people were concerned about their financial struggles—struggles that didn't necessarily depend on income level. That insight was the impetus for a marketing communications campaign to make people feel more comfortable and confident about their finances.

Courtesy of Scotiabank.

This campaign raised the bank's advertising awareness level significantly and attracted new customers to the bank. In 2012, Scotiabank redefined the campaign to give new meaning to the term "richer." Canadians define their own wealth. The new strategy was based on research that revealed "richness" meant different things to different people. It had a lot to do with a person's stage in life, for example, having a baby, retiring, striking out on your own, or paying off a mortgage—events that involve money! The campaign reflects such events. For example, in a commercial where a woman gives birth, the tagline is "Richness is a 7-pound 4-ounce fresh perspective."

The "Richer than you think" strategy is sound, but it continues to evolve. The latest installment integrates a new tagline: "financially new and improved." One television commercial shows a young couple discovering they have enough money to send their two kids to summer camp—the joy for them, two weeks of freedom. After giving the kids the good news there's a moment of celebration by the parents.

Commercials throughout the campaign focused on the personalized service offered by the bank. They show friendly bank representatives sitting down, discussing financial matters with people. Scotiabank's marketing strategy focuses on the human side of banking rather than specific bank products. It is the dialogue between the banker and the customer that makes things work.

If there's a moral to the story, it is this: If a strategy is working, resist the temptation to change it. Find new ways to keep it fresh.

Based on Jeff Fraser, "Scotiabank introduces 'New and Improved,'" *Marketing*, December 3, 2014, www.marketingmag.ca; and Kristin Laird, "Scotiabank Redefines 'Richer' Campaign," *Marketing*, January 23, 2012, www.marketingmag.ca.

Volkswagen uses a "dry" style of humour in many of its television commercials. One recent commercial showed a young man behind the wheel of a Volkswagen in a parking garage. He glances to his right and notices a beautiful young woman in a short skirt carting a few grocery bags. Eager to see her legs as she passes by, he fumbles to get the backup camera working. By the time he can see things the woman has passed by and a view of a hairy-legged male appears on the screen. The driver's expression is priceless.

A major weakness of using humour is that it can wear out prematurely. After a few exposures, the audience may not find the message funny. Advertisers must also be wary of sarcastic humour that could insult cultural groups. Humour can backfire and bring on unwanted negative publicity. Since the use of humour allows for creative latitude, the creative team must ensure that the humour does not get more attention than the product. To keep the message fresh, a pool of commercials is needed so that individual spots can be rotated in and out of a media schedule.

SEXUAL APPEALS   Sex in advertising! It will spark controversy: some good, some not so good. When sexual appeals are used in advertising, certain values and attitudes toward sex are being sold to consumers along with the products. To demonstrate, consider the images that Diesel shows in its jean advertisements. Diesel uses sexual imagery effectively to market jeans to 20-something males and females. Diesel's ads typically show lots of skin and couples enjoying each other's company; the ads are provocative and attention-grabbing. Refer to the image in Figure 4.15.

Sex is a strong physiological need, just behind self-preservation, so why not use it in advertising? The only real issue is the way in which it is used. Clearly, explicit sex increases the risks for the advertiser, since it may alienate consumers at large. However, if core customers do not find it offensive, the advertiser may truly be onto something.

EMOTIONAL APPEALS   Emotional appeals presented effectively will arouse the feelings of an audience. To demonstrate, consider the style of advertising used to promote social causes: anything from drinking and driving to spousal abuse to quitting smoking. In one TV ad that encourages people to stop smoking, a mature woman talks about the perils of second-hand smoke. Her husband, a smoker, is dead, and she suffers from emphysema due to second-hand smoke. Such a message leaves the viewer with a disturbing feeling.

On a more positive note, people have an emotional connection to animals, and their presence in advertising can have a persuasive influence. Budweiser beer, for example, has used their iconic Clydesdale horses in television commercials for years. The horses are synonymous with the brand. However, it's the relationship between the horses and their

FIGURE
4.15

Diesel Effectively Uses Sexual Imagery in Print Ads to Market Its Jeans

Source: Diesel "East Meets West" FW 2005.

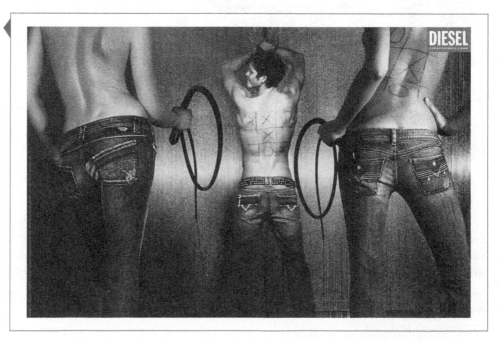

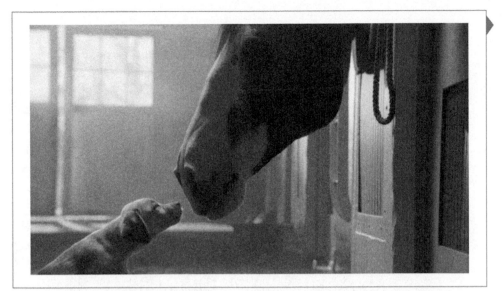

FIGURE
4.16

Budweiser Uses Emotional Appeal to Connect with Consumers

Source: © Used with permission of Anheuser-Busch, LLC. All rights reserved.

handlers that bring out the emotion. More recently, it's the relationship between one of the horses and a puppy that stirred the emotional juices. An initial commercial portrayed the loving relationship developing between a horse and a Labrador puppy—they played together in the field and rubbed noses in the barn. The second commercial called "Lost Dog" shows the puppy escaping from his master's truck when he hears a loud sound. The puppy faces several dangerous situations as he tries to find his way back home. When the master sees the puppy slowly trotting up the farm laneway in a ragged-looking condition followed by the four horses, the viewer's tears start flowing. Both of these ads were judged the best in two successive Super Bowls. They show the power of emotional appeals in connecting a brand with consumers. Refer to the image in Figure 4.16.

LIFESTYLE APPEALS Advertisers using lifestyle appeal techniques try to associate their brand with the lifestyle or desired lifestyle of the audience they are trying to reach. Some of the appeals already discussed, such as sexual appeals and emotional appeals, are frequently included as elements of a lifestyle campaign. Other elements may include action, adventure, and excitement to stimulate desire. Lifestyle appeals are popular among advertisers owing to the greater availability of psychographic information about Canadian consumers. Many beer brands use lifestyle appeals to establish an image firmly in the minds of drinkers 19 to 29 years of age. If you are what you drink, then there is a brand of beer for you.

The automobile industry uses lifestyle messages extensively. The need to experience adventure, for example, is effectively portrayed by simply placing a vehicle in an exciting situation. As shown in Figure 4.17, the Ram truck projects an image of strength, power, and toughness. It is a truck ideally suited for a hardworking male in any kind of physical occupation or pursuit. The slogan "Guts. Glory. Ram." aptly summarizes the positioning strategy of the brand.

COMPARATIVE APPEALS In comparative advertisements, the promise and proof are shown by comparing the attributes of a given product with those of competing products—attributes that are important to the target market. The comparison should focus on the primary reason for buying the product. Comparisons can be direct, such as when the other brand is mentioned and shown, or they can be indirect, with only a reference to another leading brand or brands.

The battle among leading truck brands is fierce so comparisons are often used to demonstrate some aspect of superiority. A commercial for a Chevy Silverado showed a handful of Silverado truck owners make it through a disaster (the scene looked like it was right out of 9/11 showing lots of dust and debris), but pause for a moment to mourn a friend who didn't make it because "he drove a Ford." Naturally, Ford didn't like the ad and didn't agree with some of the claims Silverado made about durability.[8] For the record, the Ford F-150 is the top-selling truck in the United States and Canada, well ahead of Silverado. The entire matter is now in the hands of lawyers.

Comparative campaigns are usually undertaken by a "challenger" brand, a brand that ranks behind the category leader in market share, as in the Ford F-150–Silverado situation. Showing comparisons where the challenger performs better than the market leader is a convincing presentation. It will make consumers think more about the brand they currently use. There are risks, however. The leader could fight back and force the challenger to spend more money on advertising than originally intended. As well, any claims made must not mislead the public. If they do, legal proceedings can occur. Critics of comparative appeals firmly believe a brand should stand on its own merits. Why cloud the issue by bringing in competing brands?

FACTUAL APPEALS   Certain product categories lend themselves to a straightforward style of advertising. The ads simply state what the product will do and back it up with information that is easy for the customer to understand. Over-the-counter pharmaceuticals use this technique frequently. Brands in this category rely on technical information or scientific data to validate claims. Advil says it's for "today's kind of pain." Advil offers fast relief for the things that slow you down. Phrases such as "safe, reliable, and doctor recommended" verify the claim. Category leader Tylenol says, "Doctors recommend Tylenol more than all other brands combined to reduce fever and temporarily relieve minor aches and pains." The third-party endorsement by doctors has a definite impact. These competitive examples aptly depict the intent of factual appeals.

CREATIVE EXECUTION

In the **creative execution** stage of creative planning, specific decisions are made regarding how to best present the message. If product comparisons are used, what kind of demonstration technique will be employed? Will sexual appeals be subtle or blatant? If lifestyle appeals are used, what kind of backdrops and settings will be needed? If music is called for, what kind of music will it be? If it is a print campaign, will the ads be copy dominated or image dominated? Will artwork or photography be the key visual element? How big will the ads be? There are a host of decisions to be made.

The agency creative team evaluates specific ideas that it thinks have the potential to convert its vision of an ad into reality. In doing so, the team must answer two basic questions:

1. What is the best or most convincing way to present the brand's benefits to motivate the consumer to take action?
2. Is there a specific technique that will effectively convince consumers that this is the right brand for them?

For example, if a decision is made to use a celebrity as a spokesperson, who will the celebrity be? Will it be a famous rock star, movie star, or sports personality? A lot of behind-the-scenes discussion goes on for decisions of this magnitude. The following are some of the more commonly used presentation tactics.

PRODUCT DEMONSTRATIONS   For products that want to make claims regarding performance (for example, dependability, reliability, speed), demonstrations work well. As mentioned above, the simplest appeal is to say or show the product and what it will do. On television, showing the product in use is often the simplest and most direct way to make a claim. In print advertising, "a picture says a thousand words." The image in Figure 4.17 could be a still from a television commercial. The truck demonstrates its strength and reliability when performing a certain task.

TESTIMONIALS   Advertisers that follow a traditional approach to advertising frequently use testimonials. In a **testimonial**, a typical user of the product presents the message. Real people in ads are often perceived to be more credible than models and celebrities who are paid handsomely to sell a certain brand. Walmart, for example, will use people of various ethnic backgrounds to make the point that Walmart offers the value that their respective families are looking for. Such a tactic broadens the reach of Walmart in cosmopolitan markets. Tim Hortons has established an emotional connection with Canadians partly based on a campaign

creative execution   The stage of creative planning at which specific decisions are made regarding how to best present the message.

testimonial   An ad in which a typical user of the product presents the message.

that featured real Canadians travelling across Canada, stopping at Tim Hortons shops along the way. The people tell their story about the role Tim Hortons plays in their lives.

endorsement A situation where a celebrity speaks highly of an advertised product.

ENDORSEMENTS Star power is the heart of an **endorsement** execution. Stars from stage, screen, music, and sports form the nucleus of celebrity endorsers.

When celebrity is used, the advertiser capitalizes on the popularity of the star. Brands such as Gatorade, Tim Hortons, SportChek, and adidas certainly see star potential in Sidney Crosby. His lofty position as an NHL superstar along with his pleasant personality makes him an ideal fit for these brands. Mark King, Group North America President for adidas, says, "There is no one like Sidney in the game. He's an iconic athlete who transcends his sport and will go down as one of the best ever to play. When an athlete like that wants to join your brand it means something." Refer to the image in Figure 4.18.[9]

Chanel No 5, a luxury brand of perfume, recently signed movie actor Brad Pitt as an endorser. He was the first male to ever endorse the brand. According to Chanel, the perfume brand is the most iconic fragrance of our time and Brad Pitt is the most iconic actor of our time.[10] Chanel sees it as a good marriage.

Do celebrities work? That's a tough question to answer, but one asked frequently by clients. There isn't a definitive answer, but let's look at a situation and try to pass judgment. Where would Nike be in the golf business without Tiger Woods? Nike has invested millions in Woods, and in return, he alone has put Nike on the golf map. The association of Chanel with Brad Pitt may seem like an odd one on the surface, but buying perfume is an emotional choice. Will the Chanel–Brad Pitt relationship work? Is using a man to sell women's perfume a wise choice? It's too early to tell.

TAGLINES AND SLOGANS Despite all the time, energy, and money that go into developing an ad campaign, consumers remember only bits and pieces of the message.

FIGURE 4.18 Celebrities Matched with the Right Product Can Be an Effective Advertising Combination

Source: Hand-out/adidas Canada Limited/Newscom

The most important thing for them to remember is the brand name and the primary benefit. To reinforce the primary benefit and the central theme of a campaign, and to reflect the positioning strategy of the brand, the creative team develops a **tagline** for individual ads or a **slogan** that will appear in all forms of advertising. The slogan provides continuity within an advertising campaign. The purpose of a slogan is to summarize the intention of the message. Various slogans appear in ads in this chapter, including "I'm lovin' it" for McDonald's; "I am what I am" for Reebok; and "Guts. Glory. Ram." for Ram trucks.

Of the things that consumers remember about a brand, the slogan is something they have a tendency to recall. The repetition of messages over an extended period helps ingrain the slogan in the customer's mind. From time to time the slogan will change, especially when a brand or company wants to change its image. However, it is more common for the slogan to remain in place even if the creative strategy and creative execution are completely new.

The best slogans are short, powerful summations that companies use alongside their logos to drive the brand message home to consumers. Some of the more popular and longstanding slogans appear in Figure 4.19.

NATIVE ADVERTISING

In an era where the potential audience receiving an advertising message is fragmented, based on the abundance of options people can choose from, advertisers are concerned about whether or not their message is breaking through the clutter, and, when it does break through, what impact does it have? At the same time, the audiences for traditional media (newspapers, magazines, and television networks) are declining. Readers and viewers are spending more time online and with their mobile devices. The competition for consumers has forced companies to look at communications options beyond traditional forms of advertising.

As a result of these trends, the media are introducing new options to deliver messages—options that may have more impact than traditional advertising. One of those options is called native advertising. Native advertising is a sub-component of a marketing strategy called content marketing. **Content marketing** is defined as the marketing process of creating and distributing relevant content to attract, acquire, and engage a target audience. Typically, it involves the creation of detailed information in an environment where time and space are not factors. Traditional advertising faces time and space constraints. A marketing

tagline   A short phrase that captures the essence of an advertised message.

slogan   A short phrase that captures the essence of an entire advertising campaign; it reflects the positioning strategy of the brand and is shown in all ads in all media.

content marketing   The marketing process of creating and distributing relevant content to attract, acquire, and engage a target audience.

FIGURE
4.19   Some Popular Brands and Slogans

- Subway "Eat fresh"
- KFC "It's finger lickin' good"
- McDonald's "I'm lovin' it"
- Nike "Just do it."
- M&Ms "Melts in your mouth, not in your hands."
- Maxwell House "Good to the last drop."

A slogan is a key element of brand identification. Many of these slogans have stood the test of time. They are strongly associated with the brand name and appear in all forms of advertising.

organization that uses blogs, webcasts, podcasts, social media, newsletters, video messaging, and mobile applications is following a content marketing strategy.

Red Bull demonstrated the power of content marketing. It produces its own content that often is not about the brand, but rather about an event or happening that can be aligned with the characteristics and values of the brand. The Red Bull Skydive from space was a media happening. With so much advance publicity it became a must-watch event. It generated 8 million live views on YouTube, was broadcast in 40 networks in 50 countries, and generated more than 3 million tweets.[11]

Native advertising is a form of paid advertising that matches the form and function of the user experience in the platform on which it appears. It does not look like advertising and is identified as sponsored content. In a newspaper or magazine it will look similar to the editorial content appearing on the same page or adjoining page. When readers look at it (and, hopefully, read some of it), they won't realize immediately that it is advertising content. Typically, native advertising in print media is long copy oriented— it is the execution of a factual appeal technique. Refer to the image in Figure 4.20.

In social media, it will be identified as a sponsored post. No doubt you have noticed that there are many more sponsored posts in your news feed these days. Clicking on a sponsored post on Facebook leads the viewer to another page where more detailed information is presented. On Twitter, native ads appear as promoted tweets.

In television, what looks like a program is actually content marketing produced by a marketing organization. It is identified as paid programming. The Ford Motor Company and Cottage Life Television have partnered in a content marketing venture. The 12-part web series housed at Ford.CottageLife.com features TV host Tara Gaucher visiting various off-the-beaten-path locales across Canada in a Ford Escape. According to Ryan Fuss, senior vice-president of Blue Ant Media (owner of the Cottage Life brand), "The partnership between Cottage Life and the Ford Escape seemed natural, as our readers and Escape owners enjoy exploration."[12] It's a great way to extol the merits of owning a Ford Escape.

native advertising A form of paid advertising that matches the form and function of the user experience in the platform on which it appears.

FIGURE 4.20

Native Advertising: Sponsored Content in Print Media

Note: The native advertising on the right side page looks similar to the editorial content on the left side page.

Source: © Keith Tuckwell

The increasing use of native advertising has met with criticism. Critics cite the blurring of the division between news and advertising. Is it fair to consumers if they can't readily distinguish between news and advertising? From a media perspective there is no other option. Revenue generated from native advertising is absolutely necessary in order for those outlets to survive in a very competitive environment. The media believe that if the advertising content is relevant, consumers won't object to it.

SUMMARY

The marketing communications process begins with a sender (the advertiser) developing a message to be sent by the media to the receiver (the consumer or business customer). The goal of marketing communications is to break through consumers' perceptual barriers while recognizing that competitors' messages are trying to do the same. When messages are developed, consideration is given to how consumers receive and interpret messages. The consumer's mind goes through a series of stages: awareness, comprehension, conviction, and action.

Creative planning is a sequential process that involves analyzing market and customer information, identifying problems and opportunities, setting goals and objectives, and developing creative strategies and tactics. The planning cycle starts with a creative brief, a document prepared by the client for discussion with the advertising agency. The brief includes relevant background information and identifies problems, goals, and advertising objectives. The document acts as a guideline for the creative team when it is brainstorming for new ideas.

Once the advertising objectives are identified, the creative team begins work on creative objectives, strategies, and execution. Advertising objectives provide focus to the creative challenge (for example, the objective is to create awareness, build preference, alter perceptions, encourage trial purchase, and so on). Creative objectives are statements that clearly identify the information to be communicated to the target market. They include a key benefit statement (a promise) and a support claims statement

(proof of promise). Usually the client and agency collaborate when finalizing these statements.

Creative strategy is concerned with the theme, tone, style, and appeal techniques that are used to influence consumers to take action. Among the more commonly used strategies are positive and negative approaches using humorous, sexual, emotional, and lifestyle appeals; offering factual information; and comparisons with other products.

At the creative execution stage, specific decisions are made on how to implement the strategy. Some of the specific techniques that are commonly used include product demonstrations, testimonials from everyday users of the product, and celebrity endorsements. A good campaign will include a slogan. The slogan serves two essential roles. First, it communicates the essential idea the advertiser wants associated with the product; and second, it maintains continuity within an advertising campaign. In combination with the brand name, a good slogan helps build brand equity.

Advertisers also take advantage of a new execution technique called native advertising. Native ads are presented in a format similar to the editorial content of the medium in which it appears. For example, a printed article identified as sponsored material appears in a newspaper or magazine. A sponsored post on Facebook and or a promoted tweet on Twitter are also examples of native advertising. Native ads provide advertisers a new means of breaking through the clutter of traditional advertising while publishers benefit from a new revenue stream.

KEY TERMS

advertising   101

advertising objectives   105

central theme   115

communication   96

content marketing   123

creative brief   102

creative concept   103

creative execution   121

creative objective   111

creative strategy   113

encoding   97

endorsement   122

key benefit statement   112

native advertising   124

noise   97

overall goal   105

problem statement   105

slogan   123

support claims statement   112

tagline   123

testimonial   121

transmission   97

REVIEW QUESTIONS

1. Briefly explain the behavioural stages a consumer passes through prior to making the decision to buy a particular product.
2. What is a creative brief, and what role does it play in the development of an advertising campaign?
3. In the context of creative planning, what is meant by the "big idea"?
4. Ad campaigns should have focus and aim toward an overall goal. Identify and briefly explain three specific goals a campaign may try to achieve.
5. How important is a positioning strategy statement, and what role does it play in creative planning?
6. What is the difference between a key benefit statement and a support claims statement?
7. Briefly describe the various appeal techniques commonly used in advertising.
8. Briefly explain the following creative execution terms:
   a) testimonial and endorsement
   b) tagline and slogan
9. What is native advertising? Briefly explain how it works.

DISCUSSION AND APPLICATION QUESTIONS

1. Are humorous advertising campaigns effective? Conduct some online secondary research on humour in advertising and present a case for or against the use of humour.
2. "Lifestyle advertising strategies are ineffective because they communicate little about the product." Is this statement true or false? Conduct some online secondary research about lifestyle advertising and present a position on this issue.
3. From a magazine in your household, clip out an ad that catches your attention. After assessing the ad, try to determine the advertising objective, the creative objective (key benefit statement), and the creative strategy (appeal technique). Can you figure out what the advertiser intended when the ad was in the development stages?
4. Assess a series of advertisements for one brand (pick a popular brand that uses several media). Based on what you know of the brand and its marketing communications, prepare a positioning strategy statement that reflects the intentions of the brand. What message or image does the company want to instill in the customer's mind?
5. Select two brands that compete directly against one another. Assess the creative strategies and creative executions used by each brand. Since both brands are trying to reach and influence the same target market using advertising, which brand has more impact on consumers? Which style of advertising is more effective? Justify your position.
6. Find separate products or services that use the following creative appeal techniques. What is your assessment of the impact these techniques have on the target market?
   a) negative appeals
   b) humorous appeals
   c) emotional appeals
   d) lifestyle appeals
7. Assess a brand advertising campaign that features a celebrity spokesperson. Will that spokesperson have an influence on the intended target? What are the benefits and drawbacks of using a celebrity spokesperson?

ENDNOTES

1. Theresa Howard, "Ad Campaign Tells Women to Celebrate Who They Are," *USA Today*, September 7, 2005, usatoday30.usatoday.com/money/advertising/2005-07-07-dove-usat_x.htm.
2. "Ad Education," Iowa State University, www.public.iastate.edu/"geske/FCB.html.
3. Alicia Androich, "New Egg Farmers Campaign Focuses on Natural Goodness," *Marketing*, April 21, 2014, www.marketingmag.ca.
4. "Putting the Mr. back into Mr. Clean," *Strategy*, February/March 2015, p. 39.
5. Michelle Dipardo, "Bosch Wants You to Know It's More Than Just Dishwashers," *Marketing*, July 7, 2014, www.marketingmag.ca.
6. Bob Garfield and Doug Levy, "How Secret Found Inspiration in Perspiration," *Advertising Age*, January 2, 2012, www.adage.com.
7. Ashley Lutz, "How Victoria's Secret Will Continue to Crush the Competition," *Business Insider*, September 8, 2014, www.businessinsider.com.
8. Stephen Williams, "Ford versus Chevy's Super Bowl Spot: Is Any Publicity Still Good Publicity?" *Advertising Age*, February 6, 2012, adage.com/article/special-report-super-bowl/ford-chevy-proof-publicity-good-publicity/232551.
9. "NHL All-Star Sidney Crosby Joins adidas," press release, October 6, 2015, HYPERLINK "http://www.newswire.ca/news-releases/nhl-all-star-sidney-crosby-joins-adidas-530854891.html" www.newswire.ca/news-releases/nhl-all-star-sidney-crosby-joins-adidas-530854891.html.
10. "A First for Man-kind," *Marketing*, October 31, 2013, p. 37.
11. Chris Pow, "Branded Content Offers High-Growth Opportunity for Canadian Producers: Study," *Marketing*, November 13, 2013, www.marketingmag.ca.
12. Chris Powell, "Ford Hits the Road with Cottage Life," *Marketing*, August 13, 2014, www.marketingmag.ca

Advertising Planning: Broadcast, Print, and Out-of-Home Media

Learning Objectives

After studying this chapter, you will be able to

1. Describe the steps involved in media planning

2. Distinguish among media objectives, media strategies, and media execution

3. Describe the various factors that influence media strategy decisions

4. Outline the characteristics, strengths, and weaknesses of various mass media advertising alternatives

As mentioned in Chapter 4, the creative plan and media plan are developed at the same time. This chapter will focus specifically on the development and implementation of the media plan. Developing a media plan is a complex process. The primary goal of the agency media planners is to reach a target market efficiently. In doing so, they consider all kinds of strategic issues, along with conditions in the marketplace and what competitors are doing.

Efficiency in media planning can be loosely defined as gaining maximum exposure at minimum cost. In following this mantra, the agency planners must develop and execute a plan that achieves the client's objectives within certain financial constraints. The media plan is part of a broader marketing communications plan and marketing plan. Therefore, the direction a media plan takes must fit in with and be coordinated (timed) with activities recommended in other marketing communications areas. Coordinating various communications activities creates synergy and maximizes the impact the plan will have on the target market.

Trends Influencing Media Planning

Much of today's media planning is influenced by technology and changes in consumer behaviour. How information is collected, analyzed, and utilized is another factor that must be considered—and there's an abundance of analytical information available to planners.

Devices such as tablets and smartphones generate data about people's behaviour that shed light on how best to reach them through advertising messages. Presently, 68 percent of Canadians have a smartphone and 76 percent of these people watch video on their device.[1] Further, digital media now hold the largest investment of advertising dollars in Canada compared to all other media. Dollars are being shifted away from other media.

Today many buying decisions are technology-based (due to quick access to information) and in real time. Comparison shopping on the fly is becoming commonplace. As a consequence, media planning and media buying have changed. A new system called programmatic buying has been introduced for digital media. In this system advertisers bid on available advertising spots in real time. The highest bid gets the spot. While currently in its early stages, the system is poised for significant growth in the future. The system could be applied to other media such as television given the increased penetration of smart TVs. Programmatic buying is discussed in more detail in Appendix 1.

Generally, people are spending less time with traditional media and more time with digital media. A recent research report indicates a divide between younger and older groups regarding television viewing. Young consumers, described as millennials, consume more TV online than on a regular television set. The reverse is true for older groups.[2] Since millennials are the next big group of consumers, their needs, preferences, and behaviours will have to be carefully considered by marketers and media planners.

New media strategies must also consider the ever-increasing mobility of consumers and their desire to stay connected. The combination of mobile devices, GPS collection points including Wi-Fi hotspots, mobile search queries, and social media sites allow advertisers to target customers where they are. The planner's mindset must be more in the now, as opposed to six months from now, which was the old way of doing things.

Media Planning

Media planning involves developing a plan of action for communicating messages to the right people (the target market), at the right time, and with the right frequency. Both the client and the agency play a role in media planning (see Figure 5.1). The client's role focuses on providing necessary background information and then evaluating the recommendations that the agency makes. The agency assesses the information provided by the client and then prepares a strategic plan that will meet the client's objectives. Because there is a considerable amount of money involved, the client scrutinizes media plans carefully.

media planning Developing a plan of action for communicating messages to the right people (the target market), at the right time, and with the right frequency.

Decisions made by the creative team about message strategy will influence media strategy (for example, the choice of media). There should be good communications between the creative team and the media team.

FIGURE
5.1

Media Planning Model

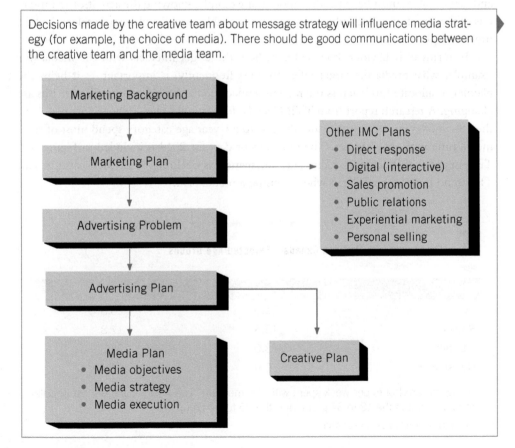

Information provided by the client is contained in a **media brief** (much like the creative brief discussed in Chapter 4). The media brief is a document that contains essential information for developing the media plan and is used as a starting point in the discussion between a client and the agency. It includes some or all of the following information.

MARKET PROFILE

Any relevant information about the current state of affairs in the market is useful to media planners. Such information includes historical sales data for leading brands, market share trends of leading brands, and rates of growth in the market. Is the market growing, flat, or declining?

COMPETITOR MEDIA STRATEGY

In general terms, what media do major competitors use, and how much money do they invest in media advertising? What the competitors are doing has some influence on the strategic directions that will be recommended. For example, if key competitors dominate a particular medium, it may be prudent to select another medium to reach the same target. Whatever competitive information is available should be in the hands of the media planners.

TARGET MARKET PROFILE

Perhaps the most important ingredient for a media plan is a thorough understanding of the target market. Targets are described on the basis of demographic, psychographic, geographic, and behaviour response variables. The target profile must be clearly defined, and key variables must be expanded upon. For example, knowing the activities and interests of the target (psychographic considerations) enables a media planner to select the best times and places to advertise.

In terms of behaviour, knowledge of how the target interacts with the media (for example, what media the target refers to most frequently) is important, as it helps the planner to allocate funds across the recommended media. Media consumption habits are changing. A research report from TVB Canada, for example, clearly shows that people in the 18- to 34-year age category and the 25- to 54-year age category spend most of their media time with the Internet. The most recent data for 2014 is included in Figure 5.2. Time spent with television, radio, and newspapers is declining with each passing year. This trend must be considered when devising a media plan.

FIGURE 5.2 Time Spent with Media in Canada—Selected Age Groups

Medium	18–34 Years	25–54 Years
TV	15.3	20.3
Radio	13.3	17.3
Internet	33.0	24.3
Newspaper	0.9	1.4

All figures are hours per week spent with the medium. The Internet is the most popular medium among the 18 to 34 group and the 25 to 54 group.

Source: Numeris RTS S Canada Fall 2014.

MEDIA OBJECTIVES

Based on marketing priorities, the client usually identifies key objectives. Objectives tend to focus on target market priorities by identifying primary targets and secondary targets, the nature of the message and its influence on media selection, the best time to advertise, and the geographic market priorities. Depending on the problem at hand or the overall goal of the campaign, the client may also identify priorities for reach, frequency, continuity, and engagement. For example, if it's a new product launch, reach and frequency over a short period may be the priority; if it's a promotional effort that invites consumer participation with a brand, engagement may be the priority.

MEDIA BUDGET

Since media advertising is but one media expenditure, the funds available come from the marketing plan budget. In most cases, the client has already identified the amount that will be allocated to media advertising. Knowing the size of the budget is essential because it provides the framework for the media planner's strategic thinking. Is there enough for television? Will this be strictly a print campaign? Is this a national campaign or will it be restricted to regional markets? The budget points the planners in a certain direction.

Once the media planners have been briefed on the assignment, they begin discussing potential alternatives. Their goal is to devise a media strategy and tactical plan (execution) that will achieve the stated objectives. Once the media plan has been presented to the client and approved, agency media buyers negotiate with the media to buy the time and space. The media buyer's task is to deliver the maximum impact (on a target audience) at a minimum cost (client's budget).

Media planning is quantitative by nature. Agency personnel are experts in media trends and have all kinds of statistical information available to figure out which media are best suited to the client's needs. Furthermore, media software enhances the ability of media planners to generate efficient media plans. Once a plan has been implemented, the agency evaluates the plan in a post-buy analysis. A **post-buy analysis** is an evaluation of actual audience deliveries calculated after a specific spot or schedule of advertising has been run. The actual audience may be different from the estimated audience that was identified in the plan. The question to be answered is whether the plan delivered the audience it was supposed to.

> **post-buy analysis**   An evaluation of actual audience deliveries calculated after a specific spot or schedule of advertising has run.

The Media Plan

The **media plan** is a document that outlines the relevant details of how a client's budget will be spent. Objectives are clearly identified, strategies are carefully rationalized, and execution details are precisely documented. The costs associated with every recommendation are put under the microscope when the agency presents the plan to the client. Because of the money involved, media plans often go through numerous revisions before being approved by the client. The structure and content of a media plan are the focus of this section of the chapter. Figure 5.3 summarizes the content of a media plan, although the content of a media plan varies from one agency to another. This model is strictly a guideline.

> **media plan**   A document that outlines the relevant details about how a client's budget will be spent; it involves decisions about what media to use and how much money to invest in the media chosen to reach the target audience effectively and efficiently.

MEDIA OBJECTIVES

Media objectives are clearly worded statements that outline what the plan is to accomplish. They provide guidance and direction for developing media strategies. If worded correctly, priorities will emerge. For example, there could be customer priorities, regional market priorities, and timing priorities. These priorities are based on historical

> **media objective**   A statement that outlines what a media plan is to accomplish (who, what, when, where, or how).

FIGURE
5.3 **The Structure and Content of a Media Plan**

Media Budget

- Total budget available (from client's marketing plan)

Media Objectives

- Who (is the target market)
- What (is the message)
- When (is the best time to advertise)
- Where (are the priority markets)
- How (important are reach, frequency, and continuity)

Note: Media objectives are usually clear, concise statements.

Media Strategy

- Target market matching strategy (shotgun, profile match, rifle)
- Market coverage
- Timing
- Reach considerations
- Frequency considerations
- Continuity considerations
- Engagement considerations
- Media selection rationale
- Media rejection rationale

Note: Media strategies expand upon the objectives and provide details about how the objectives will be achieved.

Media Execution

- Blocking chart (calendar showing timing, weight, and market coverage)
- Budget summary (allocations by media, time, and region)

information, the current situation a brand finds itself in, and the problem that the advertising plan must resolve. Such issues are part of the background information included in the media brief. For example, a plan may have a national or regional focus, or it may simply run in a few urban markets that are given priority.

Media objectives typically deal with the following issues:

- **Who:** Who is the target market? The target market profile is defined in terms of demographic, psychographic, and geographic characteristics. Media planners use this profile to match the target with a compatible media profile. For example, magazines know their readership profile, radio stations know their listener profile, and television networks know who watches specific shows. If there is a means to reach the target directly (as a group with special interests or as an individual), that too is considered.

- **What:** What is the nature of the message to be communicated? Media planners must be informed about the message strategy. For example, is the message strategy information intensive (lots of copy) or image intensive (lots of visuals)? Does the budget permit television, and if so, is the creative team giving television due consideration? Issues such as these strongly suggest that basic creative and media decisions be made at the same time.

- **Where:** Where are the market priorities geographically? The budget plays a key role in this decision. Typically, a brand has regions of strength and weakness. A media plan could be devised to correct a situation in a problem region. In such cases, a decision could be made to reduce media spending in a strong region and allocate more to a weaker region. In other situations, regions may be treated equally with media funds allocated based on population patterns, or a plan may simply consider advertising in key urban markets. The budget is a determining factor here.

- **When:** When is the best time to reach the target market? For example, is the product a seasonal product, such as barbecues or ski boots? If so, the media strategy will consider a heavier schedule of advertising in the pre-season, a time when consumers are starting to think about summer or winter activities. Knowledge of the target's daily schedule also plays a role in timing decisions. For instance, a busy executive who rises early and arrives home late may not have much time to spend with the media. How and when is the best time to reach this person?

- **How:** The question of how conjures up all kinds of media issues. How many people to reach, how often to reach them, and for what length of time? These are strategic issues that are best left to the media planners at the ad agency. However, some basic guidance from the client is provided. For example, if the plan is for a new product, the absolute number of people reached and how often they are reached may be given priority. If a product is firmly established and the goal of the plan is to simply remind the target, then length of time may be given priority.

MEDIA STRATEGY

Media strategy focuses on how media objectives will be achieved while outlining how to reach the target market as effectively and efficiently as possible. Given the scarcity of clients' financial resources and their demands for accountability, having the right media strategy is crucial. Clients want to see a reasonable return for their investment. A media strategy addresses how often to advertise, how long to advertise, where to advertise, and which media to use. It also rationalizes why only certain media are recommended and others rejected. Strategic decisions are linked directly to the media objectives. The various factors that influence media strategy are discussed next.

media strategy A plan for achieving the media objectives stated in the media plan; typically justifies the use of certain media.

TARGET MARKET PROFILE   For some products and companies, the target description may be broad in scope. For example, a newspaper's primary readers include adults of all ages and income groups. In contrast, the primary buyer for a performance-based Lexus is described in more specific terms. Lexus targets business executives 30 to 55 years of age, earning $100 000 annually, and living in an urban market of 1 million plus. Certain Lexus models are designed and marketed with these customers in mind. The extent of the target's description directly influences media strategy decisions.

The task of the media planner is to match the profile of the target market as closely as possible with the profile of the medium (for example, the readership profile of a magazine or the viewer profile of a television show). The more compatible the match, the more efficient the strategy will be. For example, executive-oriented business magazines such as *Financial Post Magazine*, *Canadian Business*, and *Report on Business* are good matches to reach that Lexus buyer just described. Figure 5.4 illustrates a readership profile. The same executive may watch television, but to place an ad in prime time hours on a television network would reach buyers beyond the target description. This would not be efficient. However, placing a print ad in a highly targeted magazine such as

FIGURE
5.4

Readership Profile of *Financial Post* Magazine

Characteristic	Audience	
Circulation	159 000	
Readers per copy*	5.8	
Total readership	924 000	
Male readers	674 500	
Female readers	249 500	
Demographics	**Readers**	**Index[†]**
Adults 25–54	399 000	98
Personal Income $75K	228 000	198
Household incomes $75–$100K	146 000	118
Household Income $100K+	355 000	146
Managers, owners, professionals, executives	340 000	194
Average household income	105 000	129
C-Suite (CEO, Chairman, President)	56 000	268
Sr. Manager/owners/professionals	302 000	171
Business Decision Makers		
Purchase influencers	300 000	145
Purchase authorizers	228 000	158
Education		
College/university degree	229 000	184
Post-grad degree	118 000	181
Spend over $100 on credit cards monthly	180 000	159

Notes

*Circulation multiplied by readers per copy equals total readership.
†The Index in the right column shows how *Financial Post Magazine* reads compared to the Canadian average. The index is calculated by dividing the percentage of *Financial Post* readers by the percentage of Canadian adults in the various categories being measured. *Financial Post* readers are equal to or above average in all categories.

Interpretation

Based on the above readership statistics, *Financial Post Magazine* is a good profile match for advertisers wanting to reach individuals with above average incomes, including senior managers, professionals, and business owners. These individuals are decision makers in their places of employment.

Source: Based on data from National Post Media Kit, 2015, Post Media.

Financial Post Magazine is efficient. Consideration will also be given to reaching this individual on the smartphone—another more efficient opportunity.

There are three basic target-market matching strategies: shotgun, profile matching, and rifle.

shotgun strategy   A tactic involving the use of mass media to reach a loosely defined target audience.

• If a **shotgun strategy** is used, the target market's profile has a broad scope. The message is placed in media that reach a broad cross-section of the population. For example, if the target market is described as adults 18 to 49 years old with no other demographic or psychographic characteristic being important, the media selected can be more general in nature. Members of a prime time (8 pm to 11 pm) television audience watching a drama or comedy show will range in age, embrace both genders, and have a variety of incomes and lifestyles. Therefore, television is a good medium for reaching the 18- to 49-year age group.

Television can be an effective medium for advertisers with significant budgets to reach a broad target market. That said, the cost of reaching that audience on a national scale is expensive. A popular show such as *Big Bang Theory* or *NCIS* will cost an advertiser as much as $60 000 for a 30-second spot. *Big Bang Theory* attracts as many as 4 million viewers weekly; *NCIS* as many as 2.8 million.[3] Less popular shows would cost less, as would specialty cable channels, which reach fewer people.

For advertisers on a tighter budget but with a diverse target market, options such as daily newspapers and out-of-home advertising are attractive. They reach a diverse population in key markets and generally cost less than television.

- If a **profile-matching strategy** is used, the target market profile is carefully defined by demographic, psychographic, and geographic variables. For example, assume a target profile described as follows: female head of household, working or stay-at-home mother, college or higher education, $65 000 household income, suburban lifestyle, with interests that include home decorating, entertaining, and travel. Several magazines are good possibilities for reaching such a woman: *Chatelaine, Canadian Living,* and *Style at Home.* The primary reader of each magazine is reasonably close to the description of the target. In contrast, *Canadian Business* magazine appeals to upper-income males and females commonly referred to as MOPEs (managers, owners, professionals, and entrepreneurs).

  Profile matching can extend to television as well, specifically on specialty networks where content attracts a particular type of audience. Among the most-watched specialty networks are YTV (youth programs), CBC News Network (news and information programs), and TSN and Rogers Sportsnet (sports programs).[4]

profile-matching strategy A media tactic that involves matching the demographic profile of a product's target market with a specific medium that has a similar target profile.

- In the **rifle strategy**, a common characteristic such as an activity or interest binds a target market together. A recreational interest such as gardening or golfing could be the common interest of a group. The demographic profile of such a group might be diverse, but the fact that members of the group garden or golf is important to garden supply manufacturers and golf equipment manufacturers and golf destinations. A specific medium can be used to reach each target group. *Canadian Gardening* (magazine) would be an appropriate publication to reach gardeners, and *Golf Canada* (magazine) would be appropriate to reach golfers. Advertisers should also consider the digital versions of these and similar magazines that offer content on tablet and mobile platforms.

rifle strategy A strategy that involves using a specific medium that effectively reaches a target market defined by a common characteristic.

NATURE OF THE MESSAGE Creative strategy and media strategy should be developed simultaneously to ensure that the right message is delivered by the right medium. For example, if a rational appeal technique is combined with factual information in the message, then print media options take precedence. If emotional appeals are used and if action and adventure are prominent in the message, television and interactive options (online video) are good options. If engagement with the audience is a concern, the Internet (for example, digital media advertising and sponsored posts on social media) presents opportunities for delivering the message.

GEOGRAPHIC MARKET PRIORITIES With regard to where to advertise, strategic decisions must be made on how to divide a budget among the areas where advertising will be scheduled.

A company or brand rarely advertises nationally on a continuous basis. It is common for some national advertising to occur during the course of a plan, but it is supplemented by additional advertising in markets where specific problems need to be resolved. In other instances, a brand might decide just to advertise in key urban markets. The top six Canadian urban markets (Toronto, Montreal, Vancouver, Calgary, Ottawa-Gatineau, and Edmonton) reach about 46 percent of the total population—and much of the success (or failure) in Canada is governed by how successful a brand is in those six markets. Usually, the budget determines the extent of market coverage. Some of the coverage options include the following.

National Coverage   Such a strategy assumes widespread availability of the product, with all geographic areas figuring equitably in the success of the product. For example, if product sales expressed as a percentage of total sales by region are close to population splits by region, a national strategy is an option. Funds can be allocated across media that reach the national market. Network television shows in prime time, such as *Survivor, Big Bang Theory*, and *NCIS*, (to name only a few), and national magazines such as *Maclean's* and *Reader's Digest* are good alternatives. Prime time television and general interest magazines reach a broad cross-section of the population. Digital media including social media are other good alternatives.

Regional Coverage   A regional strategy involves an evaluation of each region's contribution to a brand's (or company's) success. Funds are allocated so that no particular region has an advantage or disadvantage—at least, that's the theory. The reality is different. Some regions will over-contribute to sales, while others will under-contribute. An organization might assess the value of a region by analyzing its brand development index.

A **brand development index (BDI)** is a percentage of a brand's sales in an area in relation to the population in that area. For example, if Secret deodorant has 15 percent of its Canadian sales in BC and only 12 percent of the female population lives there, the BDI for BC would be 125 (15 divided by 12). This would indicate that BC is an important area for the brand; the brand is very popular there. See Figure 5.5 for some additional calculations of the brand development index, which help explain why certain regions get disproportionate funds. There is only so much money to be allocated. For example, in a market where a brand is underdeveloped but potential for growth is present, that brand may temporarily receive additional funds that will be taken away from a region where the brand is doing well. The BDI is commonly used when determining regional media budgets.

When determining which media to use, a planner will focus on regional opportunities to reach the target market. Television networks offer regional packages (for example, all stations within a region), and national magazines, such as *Chatelaine, Canadian Living*, and *Reader's Digest*, offer numerous regional editions.

Key Market Coverage   A third alternative is to give priority to those members of the target market residing in key urban markets. Usually there are predetermined criteria to establish which markets will receive media support. If population is the criterion, a planner will consider other strategic factors first and then go down the market list until the media budget is exhausted. Canada's top six cities account for 46 percent of the population. Given that the population is migrating steadily toward cities, a key market plan is a good option.

While this strategic approach seems equitable, smaller cities may never receive media support. Such would be the case in Atlantic Canada for the scenario described in the

brand development index (BDI)
The percentage of a brand's sales in an area in relation to the population in that area; determines if the brand is underdeveloped or overdeveloped in each area.

FIGURE
5.5   Considerations for Allocating Budgets by Region

One method of determining the importance of a region for a brand (company) is to compare actual sales volume (as a percentage of total sales) to the region's population (as a percentage of Canada's population). Such an analysis is called a brand development index (BDI), which is determined by dividing the sales volume percentage by the regional population percentage.

Region	Sales Volume %	Population %	BDI
Atlantic Region	7.6	7.6	100.0
Quebec	21.5	23.9	89.9
Ontario	42.5	38.5	110.4
Prairie Region	13.4	16.8	79.8
British Columbia	15.0	13.2	113.6
Total	**100.0**	**100.0**	—

Example: The BDI in Ontario is 110.4. The BDI was determined by dividing 42.5 by 38.5.

Analysis: Based on the BDI in each region, Ontario and BC over-contribute to sales while Quebec and the Prairies under-contribute. The media planner can concentrate advertising dollars in areas where the brand enjoys most usage. Another option is to transfer some funds from Ontario and BC to Quebec and the Prairies to help improve sales in those regions. Other factors can influence such a decision.

---

previous paragraph. If the Atlantic region doesn't receive media support, expectations for the brand should be lowered appropriately. Key market plans offer the most flexibility and choice for media selection. Local market television stations, daily newspapers, outdoor and transit advertising, and radio are attractive alternatives. Geographic targeting based on a person's location also makes mobile communications a good option. The combination of media to recommend depends on the media preferences of the target market and the budget available in the plan.

TIMING OF ADVERTISING   Information about the target market and cyclical patterns in sales influence decisions about when to schedule advertising. The best time could refer to the time of day, day of week, or time of year. For products with a cyclical sales pattern, the media schedule may follow the ebb and flow of sales. If the media plan is for a new product, the planners may decide to hit the market heavily and frequently over a short period. Lower levels of advertising are scheduled later in the plan cycle. Typically, a media schedule is planned in flights. A **flight** is a period of time in which advertising is scheduled. There are many options available for planning the timing of a media schedule, all based on unique situations a brand (company) faces. See Figure 5.6 for an illustration of various media schedules.

flight   A period of time in which advertising is scheduled.

- A **skip schedule** calls for scheduling advertising on an alternating basis. For example, ads are scheduled one week and not the next, or one month and not the next. This cyclical pattern is maintained for the duration of the campaign. A skip schedule strategically stretches a budget over an extended period while maintaining the effect of the advertising in the marketplace.

skip schedule   The scheduling of media advertising on an alternating basis, such as every other week or every other month.

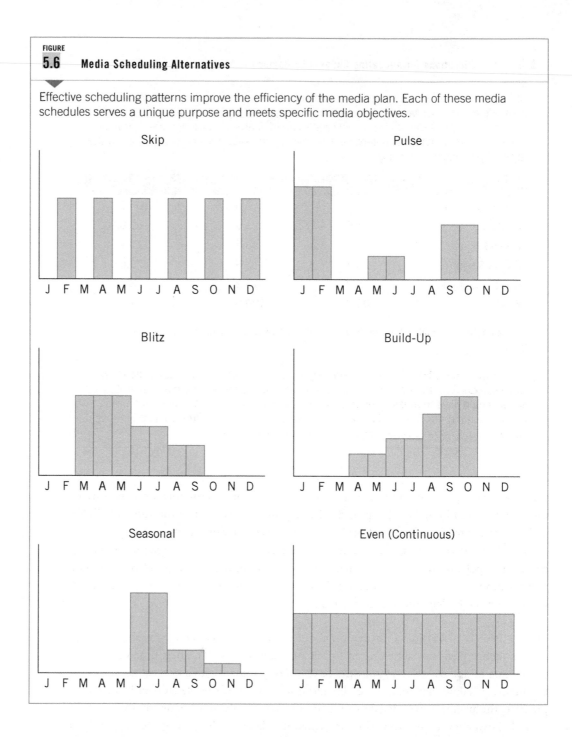

FIGURE 5.6 Media Scheduling Alternatives

Effective scheduling patterns improve the efficiency of the media plan. Each of these media schedules serves a unique purpose and meets specific media objectives.

pulse schedule A scheduling of media advertising in flights of different weight and duration.

seasonal schedule Scheduling media advertising according to seasonal sales trends; usually concentrated in the pre-season or the period just prior to when the bulk of the buying occurs.

- A **pulse schedule** involves scheduling advertising in flights but with different weights (the amount invested in media) and durations (the length of time). Such a schedule looks random, but the weight and frequency of the spending patterns are carefully rationalized. To demonstrate, assume a schedule has three flights. The first is four weeks long and heavy, the second is six weeks long at a low level, and the third is four weeks long and heavy. There is a period of four weeks with no advertising between each flight. The variation in flights creates a "pulsing" effect.

- Many products are seasonal in nature, so media advertising follows a **seasonal schedule**, with most of the advertising in the pre-season to create awareness and interest prior to the beginning of the seasonal purchase cycle. Banks and financial institutions have a heavy schedule of RRSP advertising in January and February, for example, as the tax-deduction deadline for contributions is the end of February.

- A **blitz schedule** is best suited for new products that want to hit the market with a bang—a multimedia strategy at a heavyweight level. Lots of money is spent in a very short period. Once the blitz is over, media spending tapers off considerably, and some media are dropped from the schedule.

- In a **build-up schedule**, often referred to as a teaser strategy, media advertising is scheduled at low levels initially and gradually builds (as more weight is added) over time. Often a teaser campaign is launched well before the product is available on the market (hence the name). The advertising creates a pent-up demand for the product when it becomes available. Hollywood movie releases and manufacturers of video game hardware and software frequently use this strategy.

- The **even schedule**, often referred to as a continuous schedule, involves the purchase of advertising time and space in a uniform manner over a designated period. This schedule is best suited for large advertisers that need to sustain a certain level of advertising spending due to competitive pressures. Such a spending pattern is not very common. Even in markets such as the quick-serve restaurant market, where various companies seem to be advertising all the time, the level of advertising actually scheduled does vary from month to month.

REACH/FREQUENCY/CONTINUITY   Media planners must decide on the reach, frequency, and continuity needed to achieve advertising objectives. Much like a riddle, these three factors interact and, if planned effectively, will have a synergistic effect on the target market. It is unrealistic to have maximum reach, frequency, and continuity at the same time. Priorities are based on the situation and the budget.

- **Reach** is the total unduplicated audience (individuals or households) exposed one or more times to an advertiser's schedule of messages during a specific period (usually a week). It is expressed as a percentage of the target population in a geographically defined area. For example, an ad on Ottawa's CJOH-TV may reach 40 percent of the households in the Ottawa region.

- **Frequency** is the average number of times a target audience has been exposed to an advertising message over a period of time, usually a week. It is calculated by dividing the total possible audience by the audience that has been exposed at least once to the message. In newspapers, frequency would be the number of times an ad appears in a publication (for example, two ads per week in a daily newspaper); on television, it is the number of times a commercial is aired in a week. The media planner must decide what combination of reach and frequency is appropriate for achieving the advertising objectives. For example, a new product that has a high awareness objective may place greater emphasis on reach (and frequency, if the budget will accommodate it). A campaign with the objective of changing consumer attitudes will usually call for more frequency.

- Media planners use gross rating points as a method of designing a media schedule. **Gross rating points (GRPs)** are calculated by multiplying the total reach (the unduplicated audience) of the proposed schedule by the frequency (the average amount of exposures) in the proposed schedule. It is an expression of the weight of advertising in a market. To illustrate, assume the weekly reach is 50 percent of targeted

blitz schedule   The scheduling of media advertising so that most spending is front-loaded in the schedule; usually involves a lot of money spent in a short period.

build-up schedule   The scheduling of media advertising so that the weight of advertising starts out light and gradually builds over a period of time; also called a teaser campaign.

even schedule   The uniform scheduling of media advertising over an extended period; also referred to as a continuous schedule.

reach   The total unduplicated audience exposed one or more times to a commercial message during a specific period (usually a week).

frequency   The average number of times an audience has been exposed to a message over a period of time, usually a week.

gross rating points (GRPs)   An expression of the weight of advertising in a media schedule; calculated by multiplying reach by frequency.

households in a particular city, and the average number of exposures is 3.5. The GRP level would be 175 (50 × 3.5). Depending on how important particular markets are, an advertiser usually varies the weight level (the GRP level) from one market to another. For more detailed illustrations of GRPs, refer to Appendix 1, "Media Buying Principles and Media Information Resources," at the end of the book.

continuity The length of time required in an advertising medium to generate the desired impact on the target audience.

- **Continuity** refers to the length of time required to ensure impact has been made on a target market through a particular medium. During that period, a consistent theme is communicated (for example, "I'm lovin' it," the theme for McDonald's or "eat fresh," the theme for Subway). Since advertising is scheduled in flights, continuity decisions deal with how long a flight will be. Will the schedule be four weeks, six weeks, or eight weeks?

Media planners must juggle reach, frequency, and continuity throughout a campaign. An increase in any one of these variables will increase the cost of advertising, so there would have to be a corresponding decrease in another variable to stay within budget. Very often continuity is the first of these variables to "give way" when budget becomes a factor. Figure 5.7 offers more information about the relationships among reach, frequency, and continuity.

engagement The degree of involvement a person has with the medium when using it.

ENGAGEMENT **Engagement** refers to the degree of involvement a person has with the medium when that person is using it. It is a response driven by emotion and whatever happens inside a person's mind. Both the message and the medium play a role in encouraging engagement.

In a fragmented media universe, planners struggle to find ways of engaging the audience. People are easily distracted, or they multi-task when using a medium. For example, a television viewer might avoid commercials by channel surfing during commercial

---

FIGURE
5.7   **The Relationship Among Reach, Frequency, and Continuity**

Reach is the number of people potentially exposed to a message in one week.
Frequency is the average number of times a person is exposed to a message in a week.
Continuity is the length of time required to generate impact on a target market.
 The relationship among these three variables is dynamic. Since the media budget is usually a fixed amount of money, if one variable is given more priority, another variable will be given less priority. Otherwise, you will spend beyond the budget. Examine the numbers in the chart. Each plan is different, but they all achieve the same number of gross impressions.
 Gross impressions are calculated by multiplying reach × frequency × continuity.

Variable	Reach	Frequency	Continuity	Impressions
Plan 1	500 000	4	6 weeks	12 000 000
Plan 2	250 000	8	6 weeks	12 000 000
Plan 3	125 000	8	12 weeks	12 000 000

Interpretation
Each plan is different. The first plan stresses reach, the second stresses frequency, and the third stresses continuity. The costs of each plan would be about the same. It's all in the numbers.

breaks, or he or she can do something on a tablet while watching television. In contrast, an Internet user, intent on what he or she is doing, or someone scrolling through the news feed on a social media outlet, could be more involved, and consequently take more notice of advertising messages. A magazine reader might spend 30 minutes of uninterrupted time with a favourite magazine—that's engagement! Earlier in the chapter (see Figure 5.2), it was noted how much time people spend with the media. Time spent does not necessarily translate into engagement.

From a strategic point of view, creative planners and media planners have determined that, if engagement is a strategic priority, online and mobile advertising messages must be entertaining. As well, planners encourage engagement with the brand by using an ad in one medium (TV, radio, or print) to encourage consumers to go online to a website or social network page for more information. Taking the time to go online suggests engagement. From a planning perspective, adopting an integrated approach to message strategy and execution will help achieve customer engagement with a brand.

Engagement is an important strategic factor to consider. By selecting the right media, the advertiser will start to develop a relationship with the consumer, a relationship that can thrive if planned properly. For this reason media planners now recommend more use of the Internet in the media mix—a reflection of the time consumers spend with the medium and how they interact with it.

MEDIA EXECUTION

The final stage of the media planning is media execution. **Media execution** is a process of fine tuning the media strategy and translating it into specific action plans. This involves comparing various options within a class of media for cost efficiencies, finalizing a schedule in the form of a calendar or blocking chart, and allocating the budget in detail by specific activity. Then the agency buys the media time and space.

media execution   The translation of media strategies into specific media action plans; involves recommending specific media to be used in the plan and negotiating the media buys.

MEDIA SELECTION   Selecting the right media to resolve the problem at hand is a three-step decision process: selecting the general type of media, selecting the class of media within the type, and selecting the particular medium. Of the media discussed in this chapter, the first decision involves what mix of media to use. Among television, radio, newspapers, magazines, and out-of-home, any combination is possible (direct response and interactive media are discussed in separate chapters and they too are part of the selection process). For the second decision, let's assume that magazines and television are the media chosen and that the campaign is national in scope. Will general interest magazines, men's or women's magazines, or special interest magazines be chosen? What television networks will be chosen? The characteristics of the target market will influence these decisions.

For the third decision, let's also assume the target market is men and women between 25 and 49, living in major cities across Canada. Magazines that reach both males and females would be selected: *Maclean's, Chatelaine*, and *Reader's Digest* are good candidates. Conventional television networks such as CTV, CBC, and Global are also good candidates.

When selecting specific media, the cost efficiencies of each alternative are analyzed. To demonstrate, magazines are compared on the basis of **cost per thousand (CPM)**. CPM is the cost incurred in delivering a message to 1000 readers. It is calculated by dividing the cost of the ad by the circulation of the publication in thousands. Therefore, if an ad costs $40 000 and the circulation is 500 000, the CPM would be

cost per thousand (CPM)   The cost of delivering an advertising message to 1000 people; calculated by dividing the cost of the ad by the circulation in thousands.

FIGURE 5.8   Comparing Media Alternatives for Efficiency

Women's Magazines	Cost (1P, 4-colour)	Circulation	CPM
Chatelaine	$53 480	524 000	$102.06
Canadian Living	$52 905	520 000	$101.74
Style at Home	$18 955	238 000	$79.64
Business Magazines			
Report on Business	$22 395	265 000	$84.50
Financial Post	$21 125	159 000	$132.86
Canadian Business	$21 698	64 000	$339.03

Observations

Among women's magazines, the lowest circulation magazine (*Style at Home*) is the most efficient at reaching women as it has the lowest CPM (the cost of reaching 1000 readers). However, advertisers with reach objectives would consider the highest circulation magazines (*Chatelaine* and *Canadian Living*), even though the CPM is higher.

Among business publications, *Report on Business* is more efficient, since its CPM is lowest. *Report on Business* is distributed for free to all *Globe and Mail* subscribers, a significant benefit to an advertiser with reach objectives. In contrast, *Canadian Business* has a much higher CPM but its audience is paid subscribers—people who truly value the magazine's content. That too, is worth something to an advertiser.

Source: Based on data from Online Media Kit for each publication, 2015 rate cards, retrieved April 30, 2015. Circulation data from Canadian Media Directors' Council *Media Digest,* 2014–15, p. 81.

$80 ($40 000 divided by 500). When comparing publications that reach the same target market, the ones with the lowest cost per thousand are the most efficient at reaching the target.

Media planners also assess media alternatives qualitatively. In other words, do numbers tell the complete story? Factors such as editorial content, quality of reproduction, and demographic selectivity can lead the media planner to prefer one magazine over another, even if the preferred magazine has a higher CPM. Perhaps there are more pass-along readers of one publication than another. If more people are exposed to the ad, then the real costs of reaching the target are lower than the CPM. Daily newspapers, television networks, and radio stations can be compared on a similar basis. For an illustration of a few cost comparisons within certain media, see Figure 5.8. Appendix 1, "Media Buying Principles and Media Information Resources," has additional information about media selection and how various alternatives are compared when making decisions about what media to use.

media calendar (blocking chart)
A document that shows allocation of a brand's media budget according to time of year and type of medium; shows coordination of various media recommendations.

MEDIA SCHEDULE AND BUDGET ALLOCATIONS   The final stage for media planners is developing the media calendar and assigning estimated costs to all activities. A **media calendar** or **blocking chart**, as it is also referred to, summarizes in a few pages all the details of the media execution (for example, media usage, market coverage, weight levels, reach and frequency, and the timing of the campaign). Accompanying the calendar is a detailed budget. Typically, the media budget classifies spending by medium, region or key market, and time of year. Because plans change during the course of the planning cycle, clients and agencies must know how much money is committed at any point in time, in case there is a need to cancel activities. Taking the axe to the budget while the plan is in midstream is both common and frustrating for managers.

MEDIA BUYING   Once the client approves the media plan, media buyers execute the plan. Buyers work with media representatives to negotiate final prices for the various activities. If the required elements of the plan are unavailable, buyers are responsible for making replacement buys that will achieve the same objectives. The demand for key time periods in television and preferred spaces in magazines and newspapers means that good timing and effective negotiation skills on the part of the buyer are critical elements of the media buy. In the role of negotiator, the media buyer seeks favourable positions and rates to maximize efficiency and achieve the objectives set out in the plan. Appendix 2 includes an example of a media plan that shows applications of the various media strategy and execution principles discussed in this chapter.

Assessing Media Alternatives

Typically, a planner will include several media in the plan, as people refer to more than one medium for information. In the hectic world of today's consumers, the simultaneous use of media is popular. Teens, for example, are online or texting on their cellphones while watching television. Adults frequently read the newspaper or a magazine while watching television. Knowing the right combinations for various age groups will influence media decisions.

Because consumers refer to so many different media, media planners usually recommend a **primary medium**, which will be allocated a higher percentage of the budget, and support it with **secondary media**, which complement the primary medium and receive less of the budget. As mentioned earlier, a medium such as television is ideal for creating awareness quickly, whereas print media are good for communicating detailed information over a longer period. The combination of the two media is usually effective. This section will analyze the major mass media alternatives and highlight the pros and cons of each. Chapters 6 and 7 will focus on direct response and interactive forms of communication.

primary medium   A medium that receives the largest allocation of an advertiser's budget; the dominant medium in a media plan.

secondary media   Media alternatives used to complement the primary medium in an advertising campaign; typically less money is allocated to these media.

TELEVISION

For what seems like forever, television has been the preferred medium for advertisers, assuming sufficient funds are available. Traditionally no medium has bettered television in creating brand awareness across a wide cross-section of the population. But television as a medium for advertising is in a state of transition as consumers' eyeballs move from the "big screen" to the "small screen" (laptops and mobile devices). Consequently, media planners should include an online media recommendation in combination with a television recommendation.

Many advertisers are even questioning the value of television advertising. Several trends conspire against the medium. The first is audience fragmentation because of the diversity of program choices available to viewers. The combination of conventional networks and stations with specialty channels, digital channels, pay-TV, and streaming services such as Netflix have resulted in smaller audiences for popular shows. Audience size is the key determinant of advertising rates and for selecting shows to advertise on.

The second trend is the growing presence of personal video recorders (PVRs) that allow viewers to record programs and edit out commercials in the process. PVR penetration in Canada has reached 50 percent. Research from the United States reveals that viewers skip 90 percent of the ads in recorded programs—a statistic that frightens broadcasters and advertisers. To compensate, advertisers are looking at options such as product placement, branded content, and sponsorship opportunities.

The third trend involves the alternate viewing behaviour of Canadians. Consumption habits are changing, particularly among younger age groups. Presently, one in six Canadians has abandoned their television set and now watches all their programs on a digital device. People are cutting the cord; cable and satellite providers such as Bell and Rogers are worried. The convenience and interactivity of online video content that can be consumed anytime, anywhere is attractive to time-pressed viewers. In the 18- to 24-year age group, one in four people are cord cutters, compared to one in five in the 24- to 35-year age group. Consumers aged 45 and older are likely to only watch TV.[5]

The fourth trend relates to the amount of time people actually spend watching television. The number of hours spent with television on a weekly basis has been gradually drifting downward. Such a drift is largely due to our obsession with the Internet and mobile devices. There is a correlation between these media however, as people are multitasking—using two or sometimes three different devices at the same time. Although the audience may be distracted, there is an opportunity to reach them one way or another.

Advertisers must be mindful of these trends if they want their campaigns to keep reaching their intended audience. If a target audience is migrating to different platforms, the advertiser must follow. From a planning perspective, an advertiser must consider a program's availability on conventional television and online in a variety of platforms, and allocate the budget accordingly. Things are a little more complicated these days.

All things considered advertisers are still magically drawn to television. It is a multi-sense medium that is ideal for product demonstrations and appeals to consumers on an emotional level. People perceive television to be an engaging medium, a perception not overlooked by media planners. Furthermore, a research study conducted by Numeris revealed that Canadians perceive television to be the "most influential, most effective and most persuasive advertising medium."[6] That's good news for the industry and advertisers.

With television, media planners have four options: network advertising, selective-spot advertising, local-spot advertising, and sponsorships. Newer options such as product placement and branded content can also be added to the mix.

network advertising Advertising from one central source broadcast across an entire network of stations.

- **Network advertising** on networks such as CTV, CBC, and Global is suitable for products and services that are widely distributed and have large media budgets. When a spot is placed on the network, the message is received in all network markets. The CTV network, for example, comprises 21 stations and reaches 99 percent of English-speaking Canadians. Popular prime time shows, such as *Big Bang Theory* (over 3 million viewers each week), *Criminal Minds* (2.3 million viewers), *Survivor* (2.3 million viewers), and *The Odd Couple* (2.2 million viewers), attract big-budget advertisers.[7]

selective spot Commercial time during a network show that is allocated back to regional and local stations to sell; advertisers buy spots on a station-by-station basis.

- At the regional or local level, stations fill the balance of their schedules with non-network programs and sell **selective spots** directly to interested advertisers. Local stations are also allocated a certain portion of a network program to sell directly to local advertisers. That's why you may see an ad for a local restaurant or retailer on *Hockey Night in Canada*.

  Strategically, selective spots benefit advertisers using a key market media strategy. For a large-budget advertiser, there is an opportunity to increase the level of advertising in local markets that are judged as priorities. Small-budget advertisers can simply choose the markets they wish to advertise in.

local spot Advertising bought from a local station by a local advertiser.

- With **local spots**, local advertisers such as independent retailers and restaurants buy time from local stations. Since local market advertisers don't usually work with an advertising agency, the stations usually provide assistance in the development and production of commercials for local clients.

- **Sponsorship** allows an advertiser to take "ownership" of a property that is targeted at its consumer audience. If the fit is right, the advertiser can leverage the sponsorship by extending the relationship to include consumer and trade promotions, alternate media exposure, and social media exposure.

sponsorship The act of financially supporting an event in return for certain advertising rights and privileges.

One of the most prominent sponsorship opportunities in Canada is *Hockey Night in Canada*, which was a Saturday-night institution on CBC television. *HNIC* is now the property of Rogers Communications based on its 12-year deal with the NHL. During the broadcasts, special segments of the show are sponsored by advertisers. For instance, Scotiabank sponsors the preview show that precedes the game and Subway sponsors a player biography segment.

Scotiabank is active in many television sponsorships, its latest being a six-year deal to sponsor *Wednesday Night Hockey* on Rogers Sportsnet and *Hockey Day in Canada*. The bank is also the presenting sponsor of *Sunday Night Hockey* on Rogers Sportsnet. Scotiabank says it's no longer about simply buying commercial time during the broadcast. The sponsorship presents an immense opportunity to integrate the second screen (mobile) for online content. The bank is tapping into Canada's national obsession to boost business; hockey is a natural connecting point for reaching customers.[8]

For more insight into sponsorship opportunities read about Budweiser's decision to associate with *Hockey Night in Canada* in the IMC Highlight: **Bud and Don: A Good Mix**.

Television provides advertisers with a means of reaching huge numbers of people in a short time with a compelling message. Companies that can afford to advertise in prime time on popular shows and on live sports programs have high reach potential instantaneously. However, if reaching a well-defined target is a priority, television is not a good option. The audience in prime time, for example, spans all ages. You will reach your target, but you're also paying for everyone else who is watching. Clutter is a problem on television. There are simply too many ads. Does an advertiser want to be the third or fourth ad in a **cluster** of six commercials? Refer to the discussion about CPM in the Media Execution section for more details, and consult Figure 5.9 for a summary of the advantages and disadvantages of television advertising.

cluster Ads grouped in a block of time during a break in a program or between programs, or in a section of a publication.

FIGURE 5.9   Advantages and Disadvantages of Television Advertising

Advantages
- **Impact**—sight, sound, motion; demonstration; emotion
- **Reach**—high reach in short space of time
- **Some targeting**—sports and specialty cable channels reach niche targets
- **Coverage flexibility**—local, regional, and national options

Disadvantages
- **High cost**—desired frequency (message repetition) increases absolute cost
- **Clutter**—too many spots in a cluster negates potential impact
- **Audience fragmentation**—abundance of channels lowers audience size (reach potential)
- **Technology**—electronic equipment records programs and edits out commercials

Bud and Don: A Good Mix

Beer wars between Labatt and Molson are nothing new. Each company tries to get an edge on the other by getting involved in unique advertising opportunities. Advertising plays a major role in building brands in the beer category. Therefore, both companies aggressively pursue advertising opportunities on CBC's *Hockey Night in Canada*.

Hockey Night in Canada is the longest-running and most influential program in Canadian television history. The broadcast offers an advertiser excellent reach among 25- to 54-year-old males and females across Canada, and while the cost of 30-second spots can be pricey, being associated with the broadcast brings a certain element of prestige. Prominent beer, automotive, hardware, and financial institutions are among the advertisers.

Since the 2013–14 season Labatt's Budweiser brand has been the exclusive sponsor of the well-known and very popular (if not controversial) Coach's Corner segment featuring Don Cherry and Ron McLean. The multiyear agreement with CBC also includes advertising spots during the game and digital ads on tablets and mobile devices.

Labatt feels strongly that the association with Coach's Corner will give Budweiser a clear advantage in terms of brand recognition and recall among viewers. Labatt views the Coach's Corner sponsorship as a tactical means of muscling into the sport without paying huge sponsorship fees to the league—a form of guerrilla marketing perhaps.

What are the true benefits of Budweiser's relationship with *Hockey Night in Canada* and Coach's Corner? According to Budweiser marketing director Kyle Norrington, "There's no better place to bring your brand to life than Saturday night hockey! We are, and have been, committed to hockey for a long time." Mr. Cherry's love of the frosty brew makes it a natural partnership. Don makes it very clear that beer is his drink of choice. Now that's influence!

Source: Based on Susan Krashinsky, "Labatt strikes back against Molson with Hockey Night deal," *The Globe and Mail*, January 17, 2013, www.globeandmail.com.

NEW STRATEGIES FOR REACHING A TELEVISION AUDIENCE Television and television advertising is not about to disappear, but new solutions for reaching viewers must be found to retain the economics of the system. Many advertisers have already found more compelling ways of delivering advertising messages on television—product placement, branded content, and shorter commercials.

product placement The visible placement of brand name products in television shows, movies, radio, video games, and other programming.

Product placement refers to the visible placement of branded merchandise in television shows, films, or video games. For example, Coca-Cola glasses or containers were prominently displayed in front of the judges on *American Idol* for 13 years. The sponsorship deal ended in 2015. Mazda now plays a prominent role in *Property Brothers*, a popular show on W Network. The shows' two stars drive a Mazda 6 and a Mazda CX-5 to transport homeowners to house listings and retail stores. Various features of the car such as energy efficiency, design, and technology are showcased. Mazda sees the show as a high-reach opportunity and a means of distinguishing itself in a crowded and highly competitive category.[9]

branded content (product integration) The integration of brand name goods and services into the script (storyline) of a television show or movie. The brand name is clearly mentioned and sometimes discussed.

Branded content or **product integration** takes product placement a step further by integrating the brand into the script of the television show. Many networks and independent production companies actively seek sponsors interested in integration opportunities. Mazda was used as an example in the product placement section. Yes, the two brothers will be driving the car and viewers will see the vehicle. While driving people around however, the two brothers can also verbally present various features of the vehicles—that's brand integration.

Over at TSN, Tim Hortons has been very active sponsoring various broadcasts. Tim Hortons is the title sponsor of *That's Hockey* and the show has been renamed *Tim Hortons That's Hockey*. For instance, a segment of the show that examines notable stats and facts is called Timbit Tidbits. Within the segment there are mentions of the Timbits hockey program that supports more than 300 000 young Canadians each year. The brand is also integrated into regional broadcasts of games featuring the Toronto Maple Leafs, Ottawa Senators, and Winnipeg Jets.[10]

Shorter commercials are another option for effectively delivering television ads. Shrinking attention spans (of multi-tasking viewers) and shrinking advertising budgets are the impetus for shorter commercials. Research is showing that shorter commercials (15 seconds long) hold onto more eyeballs than longer ones (30 seconds long), so why should an advertiser spend more on the longer format? That is an argument for a creative planner and a media planner to wrestle over!

The changes occurring in the television industry have direct implications for advertisers. Essentially, advertisers have two basic options: They can reduce investment in television advertising, making it less important in the mix than previously, or they can shift their investment entirely. While the latter option seems radical, many large advertisers are doing a lot of soul searching about their TV budgets. Other advertisers firmly believe that television will remain the dominant medium and that it's mandatory if the goal is to build brand image.

RADIO

There are just over 700 commercial radio stations in Canada. FM stations are much more popular than AM. FM stations reach 79 percent of persons over 12 years of age, while AM reaches 26 percent. All radio stations are self-regulating, with no restrictions on the number of commercial minutes or on the placement of those minutes.

Despite the high reach figures, Canadians are listening to the radio less with each passing year. Radio's reach among younger age groups, particularly teens, continues to decline, because young people have more entertainment options available to them than before and more places to get music (for example, downloading songs to iPods and smartphones).

The radio industry is in transition and is being influenced by newer technologies such as **Internet and digital radio**, and satellite radio. Most stations broadcast in both analogue (old) and digital (new) formats since the projected growth of digital radio has not materialized. Consequently, the industry has shifted its emphasis to websites where digital music can be streamed to laptops, tablets, and mobile devices, and additional information can be communicated to listeners. For instance, listeners visit websites to seek news and weather reports or podcasts from radio personalities.

Internet and digital radio   A digitized audio service transmitted via the Internet.

Podcasting describes audio programming that is downloadable to iPods, laptops, tablets, and smartphones. Listeners listen when it is convenient for them to do so.

Satellite radio offers commercial-free programming and is available by subscription through one supplier in Canada: SiriusXM. Conventional radio is local in scope, while satellite radio offers similar content but is broader in scope due to its national presence. Presently, there are 2.2 million satellite radio subscribers in Canada.[11]

podcasting   Audio programming that is downloadable to iPods and other portable digital media devices; allows listeners listen when it is convenient for them to do so.

satellite radio   A radio service that offers commercial-free programming for a monthly fee.

Where people listen to the radio is a factor a media planner must consider. Presently, about half of all radio listening hours occur in the home. A vehicle is the second most popular place to listen to radio, while listening at work ranks third.

One of the major advantages of radio is its ability to reach selective target markets. In fact, radio is a one-on-one medium more in tune with the lives of its listeners than television or newspapers, which appeal to a mass audience. Radio's ability to connect personally with listeners helps explain why it can be effective. For advertisers, this means that messages need to speak to listeners as individuals, not as a group.[12]

format The type and nature of the programming offered by a radio station.

The audience reached depends on the format of the station. **Format** refers to the type and nature of the programming offered by a station. The content is designed to appeal to a particular target group, usually defined by age and interests. In radio, everything is based on demographics.

The most popular radio formats among adults are adult contemporary, news and talk, country, and classic rock. Adult contemporary (AC) stations play popular and easy-listening music, both current and from the past, and they generally appeal to an audience in the 25- to 49-year-old range.[13]

The preference for FM is largely due to the better sound quality. The news/talk format has generated a renaissance for AM stations that moved in that direction. The news/talk format encourages interactivity with listeners and has attracted active rather than passive listeners. This format has been extended further to all-sports stations such as THE FAN 590 in Toronto, TSN 1040 in Vancouver, and Sportsnet 960 in Calgary. These are niche stations popular with sports-minded males who like to talk about sports news and rumours.

Because of its ability to reach precisely defined demographic targets in local markets, radio can be an ideal component of a "key market" media plan. As well, it is a relatively inexpensive medium. An advertiser can achieve high frequency on a weekly basis. In fact, radio is often referred to as the "frequency medium." If frequency is the strategic priority, then radio is a good fit.

Unlike TV, which is an evening medium, radio is a morning medium. In fact, breakfast time—between 8 and 9 am—is the highest daily period for tuning in by all demographics. There is a downward drift in listening as the day progresses, with a slight blip upward in the afternoon drive-home period (4 to 6 pm). Refer to Figure 5.10 for details. Listening trends such as these can influence the placement (timing) of an advertiser's message.

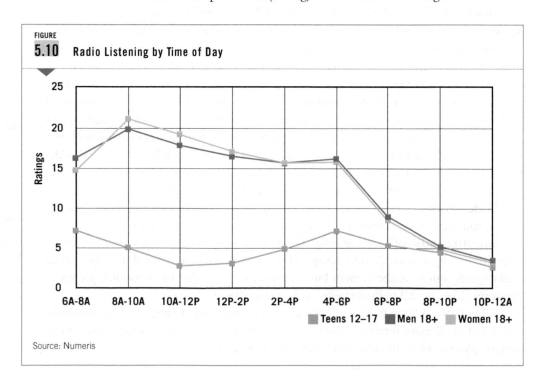

FIGURE 5.10   Radio Listening by Time of Day

Source: Numeris

FIGURE

5.11   **Advantages and Disadvantages of Radio Advertising**

Advantages

- **Target selectivity**—station format attracts a defined audience (profile matching possible)
- **Frequency**—reach plans rotate messages through entire audience weekly
- **Cost**—very favourable compared to other media
- **Flexibility**—stations and markets selected according to priority (key market strategy)

Disadvantages

- **Audience fragmentation**—multiple stations competing for the same demographic reduces station's audience potential
- **Message retention**—sound-only medium; clever creative required

---

For additional information about the advantages and disadvantages of radio advertising, refer to Figure 5.11.

NEWSPAPERS

Canada has 120 daily newspapers, with a total average daily circulation of 5.6 million copies.[14] **Circulation** is defined as the average number of copies per issue of a publication that are sold by subscription, distributed free to predetermined recipients, carried within other publications, or made available through retail distributors.

Industry research indicates that 50 percent of Canada's adult population reads a daily newspaper on any given weekday. Technology is having a significant impact on the newspaper industry, as more and more reading is done online and through mobile and tablet devices. The challenge for the industry is to encourage advertisers to see the value in placing ads in digital versions of newspapers. Newspapers are a popular medium among advertisers, particularly local market advertisers. Net advertising revenue generated annually by newspapers has been declining in recent years, which is a reflection of consumers' shift to digital alternatives for news and information. Newspaper ad revenues rank third in Canada behind television and the Internet.

Newspapers are produced in two formats: broadsheets and tabloids. A **broadsheet** is a large newspaper with a fold in the middle. Most Canadian dailies are published as broadsheets, including circulation leaders such as the *Toronto Star*, *The Globe and Mail*, and the *National Post*. A **tabloid** has a smaller surface area. It is sold flat and resembles an unbound magazine. The Sun newspaper chain (*Toronto Sun*, *Ottawa Sun*, *Calgary Sun*, and others) publishes all of its newspapers in tabloid format. Among the highest circulation newspapers in Canada are *The Toronto Star*, *The Globe and Mail*, *Le Journal de Montreal*, and *La Presse*.

There are also "free" daily newspapers covering major markets in Canada, marketed under the Metro banner (e.g., *Metro Ottawa* and *Metro Calgary*). These newspapers have had an impact on the circulation and readership of "paid for" dailies in many urban markets. Metro targets YAMs—youthful, active metropolitans—through hard copy, online, and mobile formats.[15]

Community newspapers are small-circulation newspapers usually published weekly. The community paper is the voice of the community. As such, it is well read. In fact, 61 percent of adults read a community newspaper each week. The readership of community newspapers parallels the demographics of the community. For that reason, they are an

circulation The average number of copies per issue of a publication sold by subscription, distributed free to predetermined recipients, carried with other publications, or made available through retail distributors.

broadsheet A large newspaper with a fold in its middle.

tabloid A smaller newspaper that is sold flat (not folded).

excellent advertising medium for local businesses and are a popular medium for inserts and advertising supplements.

Newspapers generate revenues from different types of advertising:

- **National Advertising:** National ads are sold to advertisers and ad agencies by a national sales department. Advertisers in this category include products and services marketed nationally or regionally. Brand name food and beverages, automobiles, airlines, banks and financial institutions, and telecommunications products and services fall into this category.

- **Retail Advertising:** Retail advertisers include department stores, supermarkets, drug stores, restaurants, and a host of other independent retailers. These retailers usually advertise sales or re-advertise the nationally branded merchandise they sell. Retail advertising generates a majority of revenue for a newspaper.

- **Classified Advertising:** Classified ads provide an opportunity for readers and local businesses to buy, sell, lease, or rent all kinds of goods and services. Publishers have shifted much of their classified advertising from their printed edition to their digital edition. The section is well-read whether in print or digital format.

- **Preprinted Inserts:** The preprinted **insert** (often referred to as a free-standing insert or flyer) is a dedicated piece of advertising inserted into the fold of a newspaper. Heavy users of inserts include department stores, supermarkets, drugstores, and large general merchandise stores. While not a glamorous medium they are important sources of information—some 84 percent of Canadian adults check grocery flyers before they shop and 56 percent read digital flyers.[16] People see inserts as a good means of comparing prices for goods. Refer to the image in Figure 5.12.

retail advertising   Advertising by a retail store; involves advertising the store name, image, location, and the re-advertising of branded merchandise carried by the store.

classified advertising   Print advertising in which similar goods and services are grouped together in categories under appropriate headings.

insert   A preprinted, free-standing advertisement (for example, a leaflet, brochure, or flyer) specifically placed in a newspaper or magazine.

FIGURE
5.12   **Newspaper Inserts Remain a Vital Component of Retail Advertising; Shoppers Use Them to Compare Prices**

© Keith Tuckwell

> **FIGURE**
> # 5.13   Advantages and Disadvantages of Newspaper Advertising
>
> ## Advantages
>
> * **Targeting capability**—reaches a diverse adult audience in key geographic markets
> * **Reach**—ideal for reaching consumers in local markets frequently
> * **Media environment**—readers engage with paper based on editorial content; they are receptive to messages
> * **Merchandising**—national advertisers have cooperative advertising opportunities with local market retailers
>
> ## Disadvantages
>
> * **Life span**—daily; exposure to message reduced if paper not read on day of publication
> * **Audience diversity**—not suitable if target market profile is precisely defined (an exception may be *The Globe and Mail*)
> * **Clutter**—lots of space devoted to advertising (many ads on one page)
> * **Reproduction quality**—primarily a black and white medium; adding colour does improve brand awareness and recognition scores

* **Sponsored Content:** The concept of native advertising was introduced earlier in the book. Newspapers have embraced this concept and now offer space to devoted sponsored content. Typically, this content looks very similar to editorial content. Even though the material is designated as sponsored, readers may not realize they are reading advertising material. This technique is proving effective in delivering detailed advertising messages.

For advertisers, newspapers offer geographic selectivity and high reach in local markets. Furthermore, newspapers and readers have a relationship with each other. Readers have a tendency to read the entire newspaper in their own unique and sequential manner—they are engaged when reading. Newspapers are an effective choice for reaching broadly defined adult target markets. Unfortunately, the papers' lifespan is very short (one day for dailies). As the old saying goes, "There's nothing as stale as yesterday's news." Newspapers also suffer from a clutter problem. **Clutter** refers to the amount of advertising in a medium. About 60 percent of newspaper space is devoted to advertising, so standing out in the crowd is a design challenge for the creative team. See Figure 5.13 for a summary of the advantages and disadvantages of newspaper advertising.

clutter   The amount of advertising in a particular medium.

The growing popularity of tablets and mobile devices indicate that digital distribution of news, information, and advertisements will be more important to newspapers and advertisers in the future. *The Globe and Mail* and the *National Post* have discovered that mobile activity peaks when people are commuting to the office and that desktop visitors and page views increase as the day goes on. It is important for advertisers to know how and when people consume newspaper content.[17]

MAGAZINES

Magazines have managed to stay relevant with consumers in the digital media era. New titles continue to launch in Canada, readership remains stable, and magazines continue to engage large numbers of consumers from all age groups. Recent research data reveal that three quarters of Canadians have read a magazine in the past three months, each magazine is read by an average of five people, and readers spend an average of 49 minutes with a magazine.[18]

FIGURE 5.14 Magazines Have Adapted; Digital Content Reaches Readers Anytime, Anywhere

The provision of fresh content across all digital platforms (websites, tablet editions, and mobile editions) has kept magazines relevant. As well, there are Facebook pages and Twitter feeds that readers follow. Such availability allows advertisers to reach and motivate readers whenever and wherever they are. Refer to the image in Figure 5.14.

paid circulation The circulation of a newspaper or magazine that is generated by subscription sales and newsstand sales.

Canadian consumer magazines are distributed on the basis of paid circulation or controlled circulation. **Paid circulation** refers to subscriptions and newsstand sales. Magazines such as *Maclean's, Chatelaine,* and *Canadian Business* are paid circulation magazines and rely on subscriptions, newsstand sales, and advertising space to generate revenues. Canada's most popular consumer magazines sold by subscription or at newsstands include *Chatelaine* (524 000), *Canadian Living* (520 000) and *Reader's Digest* (480 000 circulation).[19]

controlled circulation The circulation of a publication that is distributed free to individuals in a specific demographic segment or geographic area.

Some magazines are distributed free to a predetermined target audience based on demographic, geographic, job function, or other characteristics. These are **controlled circulation** magazines. *CAA Magazine* is an example of a controlled-circulation magazine. It is distributed free to all members of the Canadian Automobile Association (CAA). Entertainment magazines distributed free in movie theatres also fall into this category. *Cineplex,* for example, is distributed monthly to 727 000 Cineplex Odeon patrons.[20]

Business magazines are divided into various industry categories: food manufacturing and distribution, hardware trade, hotels and restaurants, engineering, and so on. These magazines are very specialized, their content appealing to people employed in a certain industry or a particular job function. Some magazine titles include *Canadian Grocer, Hotel & Restaurant, CA Magazine,* and *Marketing Magazine*.

For advertisers using a profile-matching strategy or rifle strategy, magazines serve a useful role. Magazines are often referred to as a "class" medium rather than a "mass" medium. In other words, readership is well defined on the basis of demographic and psychographic variables (profile matching), and there are all kinds of magazines devoted to a particular interest or activity (rifle strategy). As well, many large-circulation consumer magazines offer regional editions, so if geography is a factor influencing the media strategy, magazines can be part of the solution. Many studies have proven that readers are more engaged with magazines, and they consider advertising in magazines to be more acceptable and enjoyable than in other media. Among mass media alternatives, magazines rank first in moving readers to websites, motivating web searches, and favourably influencing attitudes toward a brand.[21]

Advantages

- **Targeting capability**—good reach based on readers' demographic (profile-matching strategy) and psychographic (rifle strategy) characteristics
- **Coverage flexibility**—city, regional, and national magazines available
- **Life span**—magazines tend not to be discarded right away; opportunity for multiple exposures to message
- **Quality**—excellent colour reproduction
- **Environment**—message benefits from the prestige of association with the magazine's quality and image
- **Pass-along readership**—actual readership goes beyond the subscriber (added reach)

Disadvantages

- **Clutter**—abundance of ads appearing in the initial section (advertising domination in some magazines)
- **Cost**—colour is an added cost in production of ad
- **Frequency**—distribution is usually monthly or bi-monthly

Clutter remains a problem in most consumer magazines. The clustering of ads at the beginning of a publication, for example, may mean that a reader skips over an entire section of ads on the way to reaching editorial content. Advertisers combat the problem by requesting specific locations in a magazine. Covers, for example, are preferred positions and command a higher price. If frequency is a key objective, magazines are not a viable option. Most are published monthly or bi-monthly, so they are good for achieving reach among a defined target audience and delivering continuity of message from month to month. More information about the advantages and disadvantages of magazine advertising appears in Figure 5.15.

OUT-OF-HOME ADVERTISING

Out-of-home advertising is a highly visible and effective alternative for advertisers. Think about it: If you drive a car, travel by transit, or stroll through shopping malls, you are constantly exposed to out-of-home advertising messages. Presently, 15.4 million Canadians commute to work each day and the average commute time using public vehicles (bus, subway, or light rail) is 45 minutes.[22] This time presents a great opportunity for advertisers.

Advertising investment in out-of-home advertising is increasing at a much greater rate than in other media. It seems that advertisers are intrigued by new creative possibilities presented by digital boards that are popping up everywhere. Digital messaging allows advertisers to modify a campaign on the fly or simply implement planned changes—something that couldn't be done using static outdoor boards. Presently outdoor advertising generates $514 million in revenue and accounts for 4.0 percent of all advertising revenue in Canada.[23] If the goal of an advertising campaign is to reach as many people as possible, then out-of-home should be the medium of choice.

The major classifications of out-of-home media include outdoor advertising and transit advertising.

poster (billboard)   A common form of outdoor advertising; usually a picture-dominant advertisement with a minimum of copy.

OUTDOOR ADVERTISING   **Posters** or **billboards**, as they are commonly referred to, are large sheets of poster paper mounted on a panel of some kind. To maximize reach potential, they are strategically located on major travel routes leading to or within a community's business and shopping districts. To maximize the frequency of message and to extend daily viewing by consumers, posters are often illuminated. A powerful light beams upward from the bottom of the poster.

backlit (backlight) poster   A luminous outdoor sign printed on polyvinyl material.

A step up in quality is the **backlit poster**. On a backlit, the advertising message is printed on translucent polyvinyl material. When the posters are erected, lights shine through the material from behind the sign. The primary advantage is the image enhancement offered by the lighting; there is strong visual impact both day and night. Backlits are strategically located at major intersections and on high-volume traffic routes. They cost the advertiser more.

superboard (spectacular)   Outdoor advertising that is larger than a normal poster and much more expensive to produce; can include extensions beyond borders, and electronic messaging.

A **superboard** or **spectacular** is an extremely large display unit positioned at the highest-volume traffic locations. It is created to the advertiser's specifications and can include space extensions, flashing lights, rotating faces, and electronic messaging. Since superboards are one-of-a-kind structures that are illuminated and frequently include moving objects, they require a long-term commitment from the advertiser due to the high expense of designing and constructing them. Spectaculars are beyond the budgets of most advertisers, but for those inclined to use them, they offer the "wow" factor—incredibly large creative executions that create a high degree of consumer interest and media interest—and can generate buzz for a brand! Refer to the image in Figure 5.16.

mural advertisement   A hand-painted outdoor ad seen on the side of a building.

Mural advertisements are hand-painted outdoor extravaganzas placed on the sides of buildings. They are very large—often the entire height of the building. If size really matters, these kinds of ads are real attention grabbers.

digital video boards   Outdoor advertising boards capable of displaying video content.

Technology is providing a means for outdoor advertising to be interactive. New **digital video boards** have rejuvenated interest in outdoor advertising. The new boards can display multiple messages at the same time (e.g., a manufacturer could rotate ads for many brands) or ads can be integrated with news and weather information. Rona recently launched a campaign for its Sico line of paints using digital superboards. The decision to use the large format video board was based on the belief they could leverage its flexibility (in what message to deliver) and that any changes in message could be made in real time. For example, different paint colours and situations could be featured in the ads.

FIGURE 5.16   Superboards Offer Larger Than Life Message Delivery

Print advertisement provided courtesy of Honda Canada Inc.

FIGURE
5.17

Transit Shelter Advertising Has a Strong Impact on Motorists, Pedestrians, and Transit Riders

Source: © Imago/ZUMApress.com/
Keystone Press.

Street-level posters are rear-illuminated units consisting of two- or four-sided advertising faces. Street-level advertising includes transit shelters and blocks or columns with advertising faces. They are primarily available in urban centres. Transit shelters offer high levels of exposure to motorists, pedestrians, and transit riders. Transit shelter advertising offers the advertiser strong visual impact, as the colour reproduction is of superior quality. For an illustration see Figure 5.17.

Mall posters differ from the posters described above because they rely only on pedestrian traffic and aren't exposed to vehicle traffic. Located in shopping malls, they are directed at consumers who are actually shopping; therefore, they are a useful medium for the mall's retailers.

The various forms of outdoor advertising are ideal for advertisers using a shotgun strategy. Posters reach a large cross-section of a market's population in a short period. Frequently, outdoor boards are included in a blitz or build-up schedule because they are good for launching new products where creating awareness for the brand name, brand logo, and package are important. Outdoor posters are also ideal for advertisers who want geographic flexibility; the advertiser selects only those urban areas that are given priority.

Messages are brief on outdoor boards but they can ignite action. Recent research evidence indicates that 57 percent of consumers over 18 have taken one or more actions (e.g., visiting a website or store for more information) after viewing an out-of-home advertisement.[24]

There are a few drawbacks as well. The message must be brief, considering the circumstances in which people view outdoor boards. Since they reach a wide cross-section of the population, they are not a targeted medium. The message reaches people well beyond the target, which will increase the cost of reaching an actual target customer.

For additional insight into tie usefulness and impact of out-of-home advertising read the IMC Highlight: **Bigger, Bolder, and Now Quicker.**

street-level poster   A rear-illuminated unit consisting of two- or four-sided advertising faces, such as transit shelters and blocks or columns with advertising faces.

mall poster   A form of advertising located inside shopping malls; relies on pedestrian traffic only.

Bigger, Bolder, and Now Quicker

Reaching a mass audience with a huge visual image has always been a benefit of outdoor advertising, but marketers often perceived outdoor options as add-ons to a media plan. In the digital era outdoor advertising has adapted quickly and it now offers advertisers a good option for reaching potential customers in real time. The medium now plays a more important role.

There are two critical considerations for outdoor advertising. Experts tell us that location is the first priority followed closely by the creative (the message). An advertiser must make sure the message is properly delivered. For instance, a good television commercial may not have the same effect on a digital board. If used correctly, certain forms of outdoor advertising will effectively link location with the message. Outdoor provides an opportunity to customize content according to criteria such as location demographics, traffic volume, and the weather.

Pattison Outdoor, a large supplier of outdoor boards in Canada, offers smartAD technology. Advertisers using their exterior digital posters and spectaculars can update ads according to the weather, date, and time of day, or in response to market conditions. Coca-Cola has used these digital boards for its Simply Lemonade beverage. Ads for the brand only appear when the temperature reaches 25°.

Rona painted the town many different colours in an outdoor campaign for its Sico Pure brand of paints. The outdoor boards featured a colour sample linked to a different, regularly changed activation. On St. Patrick's Day, the digital board read "Get Your Green On." Rona's ad agency recommended digital superboards in order to add flexibility to the campaign and to deploy a real-time communications strategy. The ability to be responsive gave the creative team a lot of latitude for developing new ideas.

New technologies have helped boost the role of outdoor in many media plans. While it remains a static medium for the most part, the growing presence of digital boards offers advertisers all the functionality of the Internet in a public environment. If the strategic priorities of a campaign include mass reach, frequency, and flexibility, outdoor digital ad space must be given consideration.

Source: Based on Jordan Pinto, "Rona Paints the Town," *Media in Canada*, April 15, 2015, www.mediaincanada.com and Chris Powell, "Pattison Outdoor Adds SmartAd Technology to Outdoor Inventory," *Marketing*, July 13, 2014, www.marketingmag.ca.

TRANSIT ADVERTISING   People who use public transit are a captive audience for advertising messages. To relieve the boredom of travelling, ads offer a form of visual stimulation. Passengers read the same ad over and over again while riding a subway car or bus. Transit advertising is classified as interior or exterior. Interior options include transit posters, door cards, and station posters.

Transit posters are print advertisements (in a horizontal format) contained in racks above the windows of transit vehicles (buses, streetcars, subway cars, and rapid transit cars). The average commuting time allows ample time for brand exposure.

Door cards are vertically oriented posters usually located beside the doors of subway cars or light rapid transit (LRT) commuter trains. Typically the traveller sees the ad when exiting the vehicle. Advertisers may include take-away items such as coupons with both transit posters and door cards.

transit poster   A transit ad in the rack above the window or near the door of a bus or subway car.

door card   A vertically oriented poster usually found beside the doors of subway cars and light rapid transit (LRT) commuter trains.

Station posters are advertisements located on platforms and at the entrances and exits of subway and LRT systems. They are available in a variety of sizes and are either paper posters or backlit posters. Passengers waiting on platforms are exposed to the advertising message.

Another concept, called **station domination**, gives a single advertiser control of all advertising space in a subway station, which includes wall murals, turnstiles, stairs, and floors. These are good options for advertisers looking for new ways of standing out amid the clutter of out-of-home advertising.

Exterior transit options include king posters, seventy posters, full wraps, bus murals, and bus backs.

Two different posters are available on the outside of buses. The **king poster** is a very large poster that stretches along the side of a bus. A **seventy poster** is smaller and located either on the side or tail end of the vehicle. The unique characteristic of bus posters is their mobility. They move through the city and are seen by lots of motorists and pedestrians.

The **full wrap**, **bus mural**, and **bus back** options are vinyl coverings that take up all of the transit vehicle or parts of the vehicle. Full wraps cover both sides and the back of the vehicle; bus murals cover one side; and bus backs occupy the tail end. Due to the cost, the advertiser must commit to a long-term contract (13 or 26 weeks) with the transit company.

From an advertising perspective, transit offers continuous exposure. That commute provides ample opportunity to deliver an advertising message while delivering both reach and frequency. Transit riders cut across all demographics, with the heaviest concentration being adults. Factors such as the increasing cost of operating a car and the increasing numbers of commuters travelling to, from, and within a city each day have a positive effect on the reach potential of the medium. Like outdoor advertising, transit advertising is suited for media strategies designed to reach a diverse audience in key markets. Refer to Figure 5.18 for additional details about the benefits and drawbacks of the various forms of out-of-home advertising.

OTHER FORMS OF OUT-OF-HOME ADVERTISING   It's everywhere! It's everywhere! There are all kinds of unique opportunities to reach consumers when they least expect it. Among the more popular options with advertisers are washroom advertising, elevator advertising, and cinema advertising.

Washroom advertising involves the placement of mini-posters in public washrooms, usually above urinals in men's washrooms and on the backs of stall doors. They are located in colleges and universities, sporting facilities, hospitals, restaurants, and bars. Beer brands such as Budweiser and Molson Canadian have employed washroom advertising as it offers a certain degree of targeting. It is a good fit, for example, to reach college and university students on campus.

Elevator advertising is available in two forms: posters contained in display frames on the walls of elevators and slim-line televisions usually mounted in the top corner and tilted downward toward the passengers. The Elevator Network delivers print ads and video ads in more than 1500 high-rise buildings in seven major cities across Canada. Ads of this nature reach business decision makers and consumers alike. Strategically, the message engages a rather "captive" audience.

Arena and stadium advertising opportunities extend across North America and offer targeted reach for advertisers. In arenas that are home to professional hockey teams, advertising starts right above the front door, with companies paying megabucks

---

station poster   An advertisement located on the platform or at the entrance or exit of subways and LRT systems.

station domination   One advertiser purchases all advertising inventory available in a subway station.

king poster   An oversized poster attached to the side of a bus.

seventy poster   A small poster usually affixed to the side or back of a bus.

full wrap   An advertisement in the form of a vinyl covering that covers both sides and the back of the vehicle.

bus mural   An advertisement in the form of a vinyl covering that appears on one side of the vehicle.

bus back   A vinyl wrap advertisement that appears on the back end of a vehicle.

washroom advertising   A mini-poster ad located in a public or institutional washroom; usually placed above the urinal or on the back of the stall door.

elevator advertising   Advertising in display frames on elevator walls or on televisions mounted in the corner or above the door.

arena and stadium advertising   Advertising within arenas and stadiums, from the door to the court, rink, or playing field.

FIGURE
5.18

**Advantages and Disadvantages
of Out-of-Home Advertising**

Outdoor Posters

Advantages

Reach and frequency—reach a large general audience daily
Coverage flexibility—markets selected geographically (key market plan)
Compatibility—a good complementary medium to reinforce a message
(name, logo, slogan)
Awareness—often included in teaser and blitz campaigns for new products due to
reach potential

Disadvantages

Creative limitations—message must be concise; good visuals mandatory
Targeting—not suitable for reaching precisely defined targets
Cost—absolute costs high compared to other media (minimum four-week cycles)
Image—often referred to as "urban clutter"

Transit

Advantages

Reach and frequency—riders receive same message daily, weekly, and monthly
Continuous exposure—trapped riders view same ad many times
Coverage flexibility—markets selected geographically, based on priority
(key market strategy)

Disadvantages

Targeting—a diverse cross-section of population, therefore some circulation wasted
Environment—cluttered and crowded environment in peak periods makes
message less visible

to have an arena adorned with their name. Rogers Arena in Vancouver, Air Canada Centre in Toronto, Canadian Tire Centre in Ottawa, and Bell Centre in Montreal are just some examples. See the illustration in Figure 5.19. In hockey arenas, there is also on-ice advertising and signs behind the players benches and penalty box. At ballparks, rotating signs behind home plate are popular, and there are courtside signs on basketball courts. These signs receive additional exposure when a game is broadcast on television.

Cinema advertising in Canada offers a variety of options from various on-screen commercial lengths for pre-show and post show-time placement, digital lobby signs, digital backlits, in lobby brand activations and sampling, interactive screen executions, and more. Cineplex Entertainment's media division, Cineplex Media, represents cinema advertising options for Cineplex Entertainment (Canada's largest movie exhibitor) as well as a number of additional exhibitors and independent theatres, reaching a combined average 8 million moviegoers monthly. There is a clear benefit to cinema advertising. Unlike most other media in which ads can be avoided cinema delivers an engaged audience for on-screen advertising that cannot be avoided and is actively viewed and experienced. A captive audience and engaging content on the big screen and in Dolby sound offer a high degree of impact. Refer to the image in Figure 5.20.

cinema advertising   Print advertising inside film theatres and broadcast advertising on screens; options include television-style ads on screen, slides, posters, and ads printed on tickets.

FIGURE
5.19

Advertising Starts Right above the Front Door

FIGURE
5.20

A Captive Audience Is the Key Benefit of Cinema Advertising

SUMMARY

Media planning is the process of developing a plan of action for communicating messages to the right people at the right time. The end result is a media plan prepared by an advertising agency that covers all relevant media strategies and tactics. It is a document that is presented to the client for approval and, once approved, is put into action.

The key elements of the plan are media objectives, media strategies, and media execution. Media objectives deal with five key issues: who to reach, what and how to present the message creatively, where to advertise, when to advertise, and how often to advertise. Media objectives establish priorities for the plan and provide guidance for developing media strategies.

Media strategy deals with the selection of appropriate media to accomplish the objectives. Strategies are influenced by variables such as the characteristics and behaviour of the target market; the nature of the message; the degree of market coverage desired; the best time to reach the target; competitive activity; reach, frequency, and continuity; engagement; an assessment of the benefits and drawbacks of the various media options; and the available budget.

The advertising agency makes specific recommendations regarding the media a client should use. Depending on the assessment of the situation, there are numerous alternatives: television, radio, newspapers, magazines, outdoor advertising in a variety of forms, and transit advertising. Digital formats for each medium must also be considered in the media mix. Some unique and newer options are also considered: washroom advertising, elevator advertising, advertising in arenas and stadiums, and advertising in cinemas. To meet the challenge, the advertising agency usually recommends a combination of media. Typically, there is one primary medium (a medium that receives a significant portion of the budget) supplemented with secondary media.

Media execution is the section of the media plan that outlines the specific tactics for achieving the media objectives. These include the specific media usage recommendations and summaries of how media funds will be allocated. Once the plan is approved, the agency's media buyers negotiate the best possible prices with media representatives. The plan is then put into action.

KEY TERMS

arena and stadium advertising   157
backlit (backlight) poster   154
billboard   154
blitz schedule   139
blocking chart   142
brand development index (BDI)   136
branded content   147
broadsheet   149
build-up schedule   139
bus back   157
bus mural   157
cinema advertising   158
circulation   148
classified advertising   158
cluster   145
clutter   151
continuity   140
controlled circulation   152
cost per thousand (CPM)   141
digital video board   154
door card   156
elevator advertising   157
engagement   140
even schedule   139

flight   137
format   148
frequency   139
full wrap   157
gross rating points (GRPs)   139
insert   150
Internet and digital radio   147
king poster   157
local spot   144
mall poster   155
media brief   130
media calendar   142
media execution   141
media objective   131
media plan   131
media planning   129
media strategy   133
mural advertisement   154
network advertising   144
paid circulation   152
podcasting   147
post-buy analysis   131
poster   154
primary medium   143

product integration   147
product placement   146
profile-matching strategy   135
pulse schedule   138
reach   139
retail advertising   150
rifle strategy   134
satellite radio   147
seasonal schedule   138
secondary media   143
selective spot   144
seventy poster   157
shotgun strategy   134
skip schedule   137
spectacular   154
sponsorship   145
station domination   157
station poster   157
street-level poster   155
superboard   154
tabloid   149
transit poster   156
washroom advertising   157

REVIEW QUESTIONS

1. What are the essential differences among media objectives, media strategies, and media execution?
2. Identify and briefly describe the key issues usually covered by media objective statements.
3. What is the difference among a profile-matching strategy, a shotgun strategy, and a rifle strategy? What media are best suited for each strategy?

4. What is the difference among the following market coverage strategies: national coverage, regional coverage, and key market coverage? What media are best suited for each strategy?

5. Briefly describe how the timing and amount of spending vary in the following media schedules: pulse, skip, blitz, and build-up.

6. Briefly describe the impact of reach, frequency, continuity, and engagement on strategic media planning.

7. What role does CPM play in media selection? How is it calculated?

8. Identify two key strengths and weaknesses for each of the following media: television, radio, magazines, newspapers, outdoor boards, and transit.

9. In television advertising, what is the difference between a network spot and a selective spot?

10. What is the difference between product placement and branded content?

11. Briefly describe the following media terms:
    a) format (of a radio station)
    b) broadsheet and tabloid
    c) paid circulation and controlled circulation
    d) posters and backlit posters (outdoor)

DISCUSSION AND APPLICATION QUESTIONS

1. Should the budget determine the media plan or should the media plan determine the budget? Briefly explain and establish an opinion on this issue.

2. Is it possible to implement a rifle media strategy by using television advertising? Justify your position by providing branded advertising campaigns that are scheduled effectively or ineffectively on television networks and channels.

3. Assuming you can't have both high reach and high frequency, under what circumstances should reach take precedence? Under what circumstances should frequency take precedence? Be specific and provide examples.

4. Given the nature of Canada's population and where the bulk of the population is located, when is it practical to implement a national media campaign? When do regional media campaigns or key market media campaigns make economic sense?

5. Using resources that are available in your library or online, compare the CPMs for three magazines that compete with each other. They must be magazines that reach a similar target audience and attract similar advertisers. Which magazine is the most efficient at reaching the target audience?

6. Assume you are about to devise a media plan to launch a new luxury automobile (such as a BMW, Audi, Lexus, or Infiniti). The new model is a very sleek-looking sporty car. The target market is males aged 35 to 49 living in urban markets. What media (be as specific as possible) would you use to reach this target and why would you recommend them? What target market media-matching strategy would you use? Justify your position.

ENDNOTES

1. "Nielsen Adds New Mobile Metric," *Media in Canada*, April 21, 2015, www.mediaincanada.com.

2. Wayne Friedman, "Millennials Watch More TV Online," *Media Daily News*, Media Post publications, August 19, 2011, www.mediapost.com/publications/article/156252/millennials-watch-mor-tv-online.html.

3. Val Maloney, "The Big Bang Theory Takes the Week: Numeris," *Media in Canada*, March 11, 2015, www.mediaincanada.com.

4. "Canada's Most-watched Cable Channels," *The Globe and Mail*, November 28, 2011, www.theglobeandmail.com.

5. "Number of Cord Cutters Is Growing, 16% of Canadians No Longer Watch TV," *Marketing*, July 11, 2013, www.marketingmag.ca.

6. TVB Canada, *TV Basics, 2014–15*, p. 27.

7. "Top Programs—Total Canada (English), March 2–March 8, 2015," Numeris, www.numeris.ca.

8. Morgan Campbell, "Scotiabank to Sponsor Hockey Broadcasts," *Toronto Star*, May 29, 2014, p. B2.

9. Chris Powell, "Mazda Hits the Road with Property Brothers," *Marketing*, October 8, 2014, www.marketingmag.ca.

10. Josh Kolm, "Tim Hortons Makes Major Hockey Play," *Media in Canada*, October 8, 2014, www.mediaincanada.com.

11. Canadian Media Directors' Council *Media Digest*, 2014–15, p. 57.

12. Patti Summerfield, "Radio Connects with Consumers," *Strategy*, September 2, 2004, www.mediaincanada.com.

13. "Radio Listening Time by Format and Age Group," Statistics Canada, 2008, www.statcan.gc.ca/tbles-tableaux/sum-sum/101/cst01/arts17-eng.htm.

14. Matthew Chung, "NADbank: Newspaper Readers Still Prefer Print," *Media in Canada*, October 27, 2014, www.mediaincanada.com.

15. "About," metronews.ca, www.metronews.ca/about.

16. Josh Kolm, "When It Comes to Flyers, Print Still Has Pull," *Media in Canada*, November 18, 2014, www.mediaincanada.com.

17. Matt Semansky, "Paper Tigers," *Marketing*, February 8, 2011, www.marketingmag.ca/uncategorized/paper-tigers-22290.

18. NADbank and PMB Release 2015 Readership Studies," press release, Newspapers Canada, April 22, 2015.

19. Canadian Media Directors' Council *Media Digest*, 2014-2015, p. 81.

20. Ibid.

21. "Magazines Engage Across Multiple Platforms and Devices," Canadian Media Directors' Council *Media Digest*, 2011–12.

22. Oliver, "The Canadian Commute, by Car, Alone," *The Globe and Mail*, June 27, 2013, pp. A8–A9.

23. Canadian Media Directors' Council *Media Digest*, 2014–15, p. 9.

24. Chris Powell, "Digital Puts the Awe into OOH," *Marketing*, May 2014 p. 16.

Planning for Direct Response Communications

Learning Objectives

After studying this chapter, you will be able to

1. Describe the direct response marketing communications planning process

2. Describe the various forms of direct response communications

3. Assess the role of database management techniques in the design and implementation of direct response strategies

4. Evaluate various external sources of list information and evaluate the role of lists in building an effective direct response campaign

5. Explain the role and nature, and advantages and disadvantages, of the various forms of direct response communications

Some of the discussion in previous chapters indicates that consumers' media habits are changing. There is a migration away from mass media, such as print and broadcast media, and toward direct and interactive media. As well, advancing technology has created a means for organizations to communicate with customers on an individual basis. In Chapter 1, the concepts of customer relationship management (CRM) and database marketing were introduced. Both concepts influence the development of programs that are designed to attract, cultivate, and maximize the return for each customer with whom the company does business. The end result is that companies are combining mass communications and marketing techniques with micro-marketing techniques. Database management and its influence on integrated marketing communications programs are discussed in more detail in this chapter. Information—that is, quality information—is the backbone of a direct response communications strategy.

Direct response communications include direct mail, direct response communications in the mass media (mainly television, magazines, and newspapers), telemarketing, and catalogue marketing. Direct mail is the most common means of delivering messages directly to consumers, but advances in technology and database management techniques offer great potential for catalogues and the Internet to become more important in the mix. Internet communications are discussed in detail in Chapter 7. Using database management techniques, a company can look at a customer over an entire lifetime and plan appropriate strategies to encourage customers to buy more often or in larger quantities. Communicating directly with customers makes the entire process much more personal.

Direct Response Communications and Direct Marketing

Just how important are direct response communications and other direct marketing practices in Canada? Recent statistics suggest direct response communications and direct marketing have a significant impact on advertising expenditures and sales revenues for goods and services. Direct mail advertising alone accounts for $1.24 billion in net advertising revenues in Canada. As an advertising medium, direct mail ranks fifth, just behind online, television, and newspapers.[1] When investments in direct response television, telemarketing, and catalogue marketing are included, the total investment in direct response communications is much higher.

Direct response communications are playing a more prominent role in the overall media mix of Canadian companies. Some of Canada's largest corporations have successfully integrated direct response communications with traditional forms of communications. These companies see the real value to be gained by managing customer relationships. Among these companies are Bell Canada, Rogers Communications, Shoppers Drug Mart, Mountain Equipment Co-op, and financial institutions such as RBC Financial Group and BMO Bank of Montreal.

Direct marketing and direct response communications will continue to grow for several reasons. First, companies want managers to be more accountable for the expenditures they oversee. Executives are looking for more immediate sales returns for the dollars they invest. The success of direct response advertising can be measured quickly. Second, the expanded use of customer relationship management techniques by organizations demonstrates the importance of forming good relationships with customers. Because direct response communications can be personalized, they constitute an ideal medium for nurturing relationships. Third, the availability of database management techniques provides the fuel that direct response communications run on. Assuming a database is available, an organization can now deliver unique and tailored messages to individual customers. Advantages such as these clearly indicate why prudent marketing organizations include direct response as part of their communications mix.

It is important to remember that direct response communications is a subset of direct marketing. In other words, the communications program is a component of a much larger direct marketing program. What is the distinction between the two practices? In **direct marketing**, products are developed, messages about the products are sent directly to customers (business-to-consumer or business-to-business) through a variety of media, orders are accepted, and then products are distributed directly to customers. In true direct marketing, all wholesale and retail intermediaries are eliminated.

In contrast, **direct response advertising** is advertising placed in any medium that generates an immediate and measurable response from the intended target. A direct response advertising plan involves the design and development of appropriate messages and the placement of messages in appropriate direct response media to encourage immediate action by the intended target. Alternatively, direct response advertising may be designed to build brand image, alter a perception, or attract a new target, much like other forms of advertising. Therefore, direct response advertising can be part of a fully integrated marketing communications campaign. Figure 6.1 illustrates the direct response planning process and its relationship with other components of marketing communications.

A direct response advertisement comprises three essential components: product information, a convincing sales message, and a response mechanism. The response mechanism or call to action is the most important component. The message should include a 1-800 number, a return mail address, or a website address where more information can be obtained or an order placed. In direct response advertising, the marketer must tell the customer what to do and how he or she will benefit. The inclusion of time-sensitive offers is an effective means of stimulating immediate action.

Unlike other mass media, direct response advertising is capable of making a sale. Assuming adequate order taking and fulfillment strategies are in place, the entire transaction process from creating awareness to delivering the product is possible in a short span of time. Further, the results of a direct response plan can be tracked and measured daily, providing a daily and weekly return on investment—significant information that is not available through other media. Return on investment in direct mail is significant. In the United States, advertisers spend $167 per person on direct mail, earning $2095 worth of goods sold, a 1300 percent return on investment.[2]

direct marketing   A marketing system for developing products, sending messages directly to customers, and accepting orders through a variety of media, and then distributing the purchase directly to customers.

direct response advertising   Advertising placed in a medium that generates an immediate and measurable response from the intended target.

FIGURE
6.1

The Direct Response Planning Process

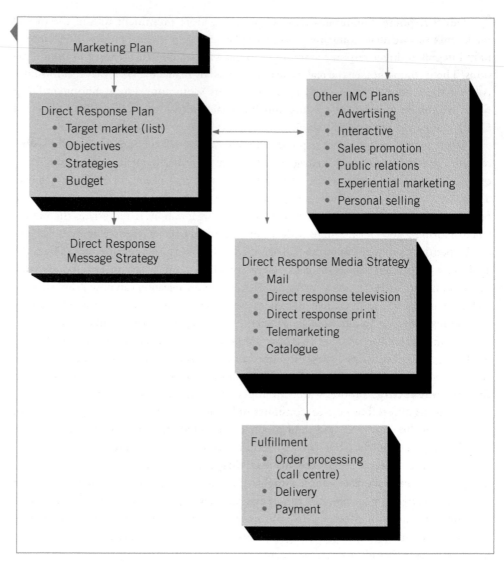

Direct response communications can be divided between online communications and more traditional forms. Online communications are presented in Chapter 7. The traditional forms of direct response communications are direct mail, direct response in the mass media (TV or print), telemarketing, and catalogue marketing:

- **Direct mail** is a printed form of communications distributed to prospective consumers by Canada Post or independent delivery agents (for example, leaflets and flyers that can be dropped on a doorstep).

- **Direct response television (DRTV)** is a form of advertising communicated to prospects by television commercials that may be 30 seconds long, 60 seconds long, or in a program that could be 30 minutes long. Call-to-action information is included in the advertisement.

- **Direct response print** refers to ads that appear in magazines or newspapers that include call-to-action information so consumers can respond immediately to the offer.

- **Telemarketing** refers to outbound sales calls (a company calls the customer) or inbound sales calls (the customer contacts the company) to secure an order. All calls are usually handled through a call centre.

direct mail   A printed form of direct response advertising distributed by Canada Post or independent delivery agents.

direct response television (DRTV)   Advertising that appears on television and encourages viewers to respond by telephoning a toll-free number, by mail, or online; often referred to as infomercials.

Direct response print   A response-oriented ad delivered to prospects by magazines or newspaper advertisements.

telemarketing   The use of telecommunications to promote the products and services of a business; involves outbound calls (company to customer) and inbound calls (customer to company).

- **Catalogues** are important communications vehicles for retail organizations. Typically, they are mailed or hand delivered by independent agents to existing customers or they are distributed in stores.

catalogue A reference publication, usually annual or seasonal, distributed by large retail chains and direct marketing companies.

There was a time when direct response communications were a last-minute strategy—a technique to be used when things weren't working well. How the times have changed. Today, marketing organizations stress accountability and measurability. They want to know what they are getting for their investment. Consequently, most large full-service agencies now offer direct response expertise or have access to it. Many traditional advertising agencies have acquired direct response agencies. Such progression reinforces the importance of direct response communications in today's competitive business environment.

The Roots of Direct Response Communications: Database Management

Whether it's mail or telephone communications, there needs to be a convenient and efficient means of contacting customers. As experts in direct response communications often state, it's the list that makes or breaks the campaign. By list, they mean the list that will be used to contact current or prospective customers directly. That list is the backbone of the entire campaign; the quality of the list has a direct impact on the success or failure of the campaign.

Companies recognize that it costs about six times as much to acquire a new customer as it does to keep an existing customer. Consequently, companies compile databases to keep track of existing customers and form relationships with them through mail and electronic means. Obviously, the best list is a well-maintained and well-managed internal list of customers. Such a list is referred to as a **house list**. Since the best customers are current customers, it is much easier to get them to buy more of something than it is to attract a new customer. If the goal is to generate new business from new customers, lists can be obtained from external sources.

house list An internal customer list.

INTERNAL DATA SOURCES

A good database management system collects and maintains relevant information about customers. The information is stored in such a manner that managers have easy access to it when developing marketing strategies. For example, managers should be able to manipulate the data so that customer profiles will emerge and future purchase patterns can be forecast from those profiles. In other words, a thorough understanding of a customer's past purchasing behaviour should provide ammunition for predicting his or her future buying patterns. This is all part of a customer relationship management system, a concept presented earlier in the text.

COLLECTING DATA

The names and addresses of customers are the most common forms of internal data, but simply knowing who the customers are offers little perspective when developing a strategic plan. Factor in technology, and all kinds of information about customers can be combined. Keeping track of purchasing behaviour and then linking it to a name and address is very meaningful. Therefore, the database should identify what a customer purchases, how often the customer purchases, how much the customer spends on average, what brands of goods the customer prefers, and so on.

FIGURE
6.2

The Shoppers Optimum Database Provides Information that Produces Offers of Interest to Send to Shoppers Drug Mart Customers

Source: Courtesy of Shoppers Drug Mart.

Sophisticated retail organizations update this information automatically as goods are scanned through checkouts. Shoppers Drug Mart, for example, has an exhaustive database of customer information collected via its Shoppers Optimum loyalty program. From this information, buying behaviour profiles of a customer can be developed and special offers that are unique to an individual customer can be delivered to those who have consented to receive such offers. Refer to the image in Figure 6.2.

Adding external information to the database rounds out the profile of the customer. Information about customers using credit cards for purchases is readily available. Credit card companies, such as Visa and MasterCard, are sitting on nest eggs of information that marketing organizations can purchase. Statistics Canada makes available census data, which are updated every five years. This information is available at a reasonable cost to the marketing organization.

Demographic and psychographic information can also be obtained from commercial research companies such as Millward Brown, or a company can hire an independent research company to conduct primary research to uncover such information. The combination of information dealing with age, gender, education, income, marital status, and household formation; along with information about attitudes, lifestyles, interests, and hobbies forms an arsenal of information ready for use in strategic planning.

ACCESSING DATA

The second step in database management is devising a storage system that allows managers to access information easily when it is needed. In the realm of marketing communications, sales representatives and sales managers need instant access to customer sales records as they prepare for sales calls. Customer service personnel need access to historical information to handle complaints or simply serve customers better. Marketing managers and marketing communications managers need to clearly identify target customers and their behaviour to communicate directly with them and design special offers. To accomplish these kinds of tasks, relevant information must be convenient and accessible to all those who work with the database. Molson Canada, for example, has more than 1 million customers in its Molson Insider database. Molson uses the database to attract insiders to Molson-sponsored events and to inform customers about new products and promotional offers.[3] Refer to Figure 6.3.

The electronic era has resulted in an information explosion that allows for the storage and transfer of a large amount of data in a short time. What has emerged is a new concept called data mining. **Data mining** is a process in which raw data is turned into useful information. Special software looks in large batches of data for patterns that allow an organization to learn more about its customers and ultimately develop more effective marketing strategies to increase sales.

data mining The analysis of information to determine relationships among the data and enable more effective marketing strategies to be identified and implemented.

FIGURE

6.3   **Molson's Insider Database Is Used to Keep Members Informed about Product, Events, and Promotions**

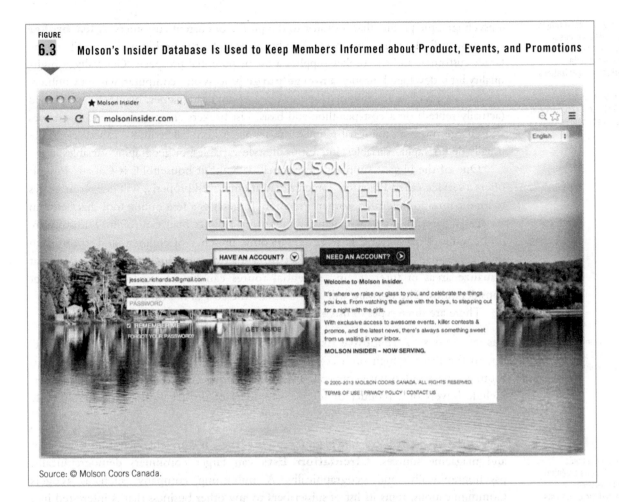

Source: © Molson Coors Canada.

The goals of data mining are to produce lower marketing costs and to increase efficiency by identifying prospects most likely to buy in large volume. A firm's competitive advantage in the marketplace will increasingly depend upon knowing the situation better than the competition and being able to take rapid action, based on that knowledge. Look no further than your local Walmart to see data mining at work. Walmart is the acknowledged leader in data mining, capable of tracking sales on a minute-by-minute basis. It can also quickly detect regional and local market trends. Such knowledge allows Walmart to customize each store's offerings while keeping suppliers abreast of how well their products are selling.[4]

Data mining offers an organization two essential benefits. First, it provides a means of profiling the "best" customers and the "worst" customers. Clearly, in these times, greater emphasis must be placed on customers who produce sales and high profit margins for an organization. As well, consideration can be given to dropping customers who cost more than they generate in profit. Why keep customers if they are not profitable? Second, data mining techniques give an organization a means to predict future sales. Continuous compiling and analysis of data about current customers' sales histories should result in more accurate forecasts about what the future holds. As well, when a company wants to expand its business by attracting new customers, it can use the internal customer profile information as a guideline and then rent from lists names who have similar profiles.

EXTERNAL SOURCES

People who have a history of responding to mail offers tend to be attractive prospects for new offers. Buying by mail or from offers seen on television is part of their behaviour. Therefore, the challenge is to find prospects who have a demographic profile, and perhaps

list broker A company specializing in finding or developing lists for direct response purposes; finds prospect lists based on target market criteria established by marketing organizations.

merge/purge A process in which numerous mailing lists are combined and then stripped of duplicate names.

a psychographic profile, that is similar to the profile of current customers. A **list broker** can assist in finding these prospects. The buyer provides the broker with a profile of the target customer, and the broker supplies a list of potential prospects. Generally, a high-quality list is developed through a **merge/purge** process on a computer, whereby numerous lists are purchased, combined, and stripped of duplicate names. Names are purchased (actually rented) on a cost-per-thousand basis. List brokers charge a base rate for names and charge more if additional requests are made. Additional requests, called *selects*, are usually demographic variables, interest or lifestyle variables, or geographic variables.

One of the biggest suppliers of external data about households is Canada Post. It offers a service called Precision Targeter that, if employed properly, will deliver messages to an organization's ideal customer. Precision Targeter is a free online tool that helps an advertiser determine the best delivery routes for a direct mail campaign. The software tool combines consumer data (e.g., age, income, presence of children, and so on) with interactive maps. Advertisers can select from 14 demographic categories, maps that visualize areas of interest, and potential routes can be adjusted based on budget considerations. The software will even estimate the cost of the campaign.

There are three types of lists available:

response list A list of direct mail buyers who have previously made purchases based on direct response offers.

Response Lists A **response list** is a list of proven direct response buyers. It's a "hot" list, so the price is high on a cost-per-thousand basis. Such lists include people who routinely place orders with cooperative direct marketing firms. Examples of response lists include buyers of a product or service, members of organizations, attendees at trade shows or events, and subscribers to trade journals.

circulation list A publication's subscription list that targets potential customers based on specified demographic characteristics, interests, or activities.

Circulation Lists The word "circulation" indicates these lists are obtained from newspaper and magazine sources. **Circulation lists** can target consumers demographically, psychographically, and geographically. A publishing company, such as Rogers Communications, rents its list of subscribers to any other business that is interested in a similar target. A list management company is usually responsible for managing and renting all of the lists made available by the publisher. The Cornerstone Group of Companies handles this service on behalf of Rogers Communications publications.

For instance, *Chatelaine* magazine reaches women aged 25 to 49 who have children and are busy with careers and family. The *Chatelaine* list has a base cost of $130/M (cost per thousand) that increases as certain characteristics are added. There are also additional costs for requesting specific formats for the list, such as FTP, secure file transfer, and CD-ROM.[5] An example of a circulation list appears in Figure 6.4.

compiled list A direct mail list prepared from government, census, telephone, warranty, and other publication information, or from surveys conducted by marketing organizations.

Compiled Lists **Compiled lists** are assembled from government, census, telephone, warranty, and other publication information or from surveys conducted by marketing organizations such as Epsilon TargetSource Canada. TargetSource's consumer survey captures a wide range of data on purchase behaviours and intentions, lifestyles, life stage, hobbies, interests, product ownership, and demographics. Marketers can target specific segments from a database of over 2 million households.[6] The base price for a TargetSource list is $125/M. There are additional charges of $15/M when the advertiser requests specific age ranges or other demographics.[7]

Names of prospects can be assembled from various print sources, such as *Fraser's Canadian Trade Index* and *Scott's Industrial Index*, for business-to-business marketing. Provincial and national associations such as the Canadian Medical Association provide lists of their physicians, as do other associations: accountants, engineers, purchasing managers, teachers, and so on.

Cornerstone
GROUP OF COMPANIES

List Management Datacards

CHATELAINE MAGAZINE - ENGLISH

CLASSIFICATION	MAGAZINES
TYPE	CONSUMER WOMEN
LIST SIZE	177,762
MINIMUM ORDER	5,000
BASE COST/THOUSAND	$130.00 CDN
BROKERAGE COMMISSION	20.00%
NAMES THROUGH	April 13, 2015
PROFILE UPDATED	April 28, 2015

Chatelaine - Canada's favourite women's magazine, delivers what women are looking for most - real value, real ideas, real inspiration, and real solutions.
Chatelaine subscribers index above the Canadian average for: bachelor or post grad degree (index 138); owning mutual funds (index 130); donors to Canadian charities (index 123).
Source: PMB 2010 Base: English adults 18+
Area data information has also been overlaid and a variety of averaged
statistical demographic information is available. Examples include:
Affluent Households over $75,000; High Contributing Donors $100-$300+.
This is an ideal list for offers related to Fundraising, Entertainment, Cooking, Crafts, Education, Catalogues, Finance and a variety of additional Consumer Products and Services.
Subscription sources: direct marketing including online and agency.
This list is updated bi-monthly.
Subscription Rate: $19.98/Year (12) Issues

TERMS:
Any order placed will incur a set up fee of $25.00.
$100.00 fee will apply to all cancelled orders. For shipped orders, applicable run charges plus format fees will also be incurred. Full charges will apply for orders cancelled after a Merge Purge and/or the Mail Date.

SELECTS	COSTS
Gender	$10.00 /M
Key Records	$5.00 /M
Nth	$0.00 /M
Province	$10.00 /M
FSA	$10.00 /M

OTHER SELECTS	COSTS
3 Month Hotline	$0.00 /M
6 Month Hotline	$0.00 /M
Actives (Base $130/M)	$0.00 /M
Address Type	$10.00 /M
Age	$10.00 /M
Change of Address	$10.00 /M
Donation Value	$10.00 /M
Income	$10.00 /M
New to File	$10.00 /M
Radius	$10.00 /M
Source	$10.00 /M

FORMATS	COSTS
FTP	$60.00 /F
Secure File Transfer	$60.00 /F
CD-ROM	$60.00 /F

SHIPPING	COSTS
Toronto Area	$0.00 /F
Other Areas	$0.00 /F
Abroad	$0.00 /F

PROVINCIAL BREAKDOWN

ON 51.82%	QC 3.24%	BC 12.55%
AB 12.81%	MB 5.10%	NB 2.59%
NL 0.81%	NS 3.03%	PE 1.01%
SK 6.75%	NT 0.16%	YK 0.13%
NU 0.01%		

List Owner asserts that this list is subject to and compliant with the Personal Information Protection and Electronic Documents Act (PIPEDA).

Status Recorded: October 03, 2000
Today's Date: May 26, 2015

ONLINE DATABASES

online database An information database accessible online to anyone with proper communications facilities.

Due to advancing technology, there has been a surge in developing online databases. Information from commercial sources can now be transferred to an organization almost instantly. An **online database** is an information database accessible to anyone with proper communications facilities. For example, census data from Statistics Canada are readily available online. Most of Statistics Canada data are based on census data collected every five years. The nature of the information and reporting of the information is very detailed, covering dozens of demographic and socio-economic topics such as family and household structures, income, occupation, education, ethnic background, and marital status. Knowledge about and understanding trend data are essential skills for a marketing organization to plan effective marketing strategies.

directory database A commercial database that provides information about a company (for example, size, sales, location, number of employees).

From commercial sources such Dun & Bradstreet (D&B), marketing organizations can access information through directory databases. A **directory database** provides a quick picture of a company and its products (for example, ownership, size in terms of sales revenue, company locations, number of employees, key management personnel, and profitability). Examples of business directories that are available online include the *Canadian Business Directory* and the *Canadian Trade Index*. The *Canadian Business Directory* provides some 830 000 listings of companies in Canada. The *Canadian Trade Index* identifies organizations and their purchase decision-makers by industry. These types of directories help an organization locate and qualify potential customers in Canada.

The Tools of Direct Response Communications

Essentially, five primary media compose the direct response tool kit: direct mail, direct response television, direct response print media, telemarketing, and catalogues. Among these options, direct mail still dominates, but other options are growing in importance. Let's examine each option in more detail.

DIRECT MAIL

The use of direct mail is widespread, thanks to the sender's ability to personalize the message by using names secured from internal databases or rented from external databases. Direct mail provides an opportunity to target customers demographically and geographically. For example, a national quick-serve restaurant chain might use a shotgun approach and deliver a leaflet containing coupon offers in the areas where restaurants are located. An upscale car maker such as BMW might decide to deliver a mail message to very selective upper income households in a concentrated area of a big city—those areas could be identified by the Precision Targeter software (discussed earlier) that is available through Canada Post.

Moreover, direct mail provides an opportunity to "tell a story." There's a saying in this business: "the more time you have to tell, the more time you have to sell." Since the average mailing includes several pieces, an expanded story can be told about the product or service. The advertiser is not restricted by time (30-second commercials on TV or radio) or space (one page or less in a newspaper or magazine). Benefits such as these make direct mail an attractive option. Although many perceive direct mail to be "junk" mail, research clearly indicates that consumers react positively to receiving direct mail offers. Refer to Figure 6.5 for details.

A typical direct mailing has several components, each designed to serve a specific purpose:

Envelope   The envelope is a critical component of the mailing. Since direct mail is usually unsolicited, the envelope has to suggest strongly why the recipient should read the contents. There should be a sense of urgency about opening the envelope.

FIGURE
6.5   Some Facts and Figures about Direct Mail in Canada

Canadians Opening Mail	
91%	are likely to open an item from a business they do business with
89%	will open direct mail if it looks official or important
84%	will open direct mail if it has their name and address on it

Canadians Reading Mail	
52%	will read direct mail if it informs them about product changes form a company they have a relationship with
43%	will read direct mail promotions just in case something catches their attention
41%	will read direct mail if they have seen the same concept/offer elsewhere (e.g., on television)

Communication Preferences	
79%	Mail is preferred over email, telephone or other means of communication for advertising correspondence and solicitations

Source: Based on data from "Canadian Attitudes toward Direct Marketing and Mail," Marketing Research Fact Sheet, Canada Post, www.canadapost.ca.

Letter   The letter introduces the prospective customer to the product or service and encourages the receiver to read more about the offer in the other pieces included in the mailing. The letter may be unaddressed (delivered to the householder) or personalized (with the person's name and address). Addressed mail produces a higher response. Typically, the language used in the letter is persuasive, because the goal is to generate interest and desire, and, ultimately, get the receiver to respond to the offer.

Leaflets and Folders   These types of direct mailing components can vary in size and structure. By definition, a **leaflet** is one page (though it may not be a full page), printed front and back, and contains vital information about the offer: Here's what the product is and here's why you should buy it. Again the language is persuasive in nature. Visuals frequently support the copy. A **folder** can be larger in size and contain multiple pages. For example, a double page folded once results in a four-page layout. That amount of space gives the marketer ample room to sell. When an offer is put together, an **incentive** is often included to stimulate a more immediate response. An incentive might nudge a recipient interested in buying closer to taking action. The objective is to get that person to take the appropriate action, call a 1–800 number, go online, or fill in the order form. A selection of leaflets and folders is included in Figure 6.6.

leaflet   A one-page flyer that offers relevant information about a direct mail offer.

folder   A direct response sales message printed on heavy stock that can be mailed with or without an envelope; may be several pages in length.

incentive   A free gift or offer included in a direct mail package.

Order Form   A well-designed order form is essential. It must be easy to read, and it must communicate all details regarding price, additional costs such as shipping and handling charges, and means of payment (usually credit card information). The recipient must be able to place the order effortlessly.

Postage-Paid Return Envelope   Eliminating the need for postage is another means of encouraging the recipient to take action. The combination of a clear and concise order form with a postage-paid return envelope makes it a no-hassle process from start to finish.

Statement Stuffers   A **statement stuffer** or **bounce back** is an additional offer that rides along with the delivery of another offer or with the delivery of a monthly statement. Capitalizing on the ease of purchasing by credit or on the knowledge that the customer uses

statement stuffer (bounce back)   An ad or offer distributed in monthly statements or with the delivery of goods purchased by some form of direct response advertising.

FIGURE
6.6

**A Selection of Leaflets
and Folders in Various Sizes
and Configurations**

Source: © Keith Tuckwell

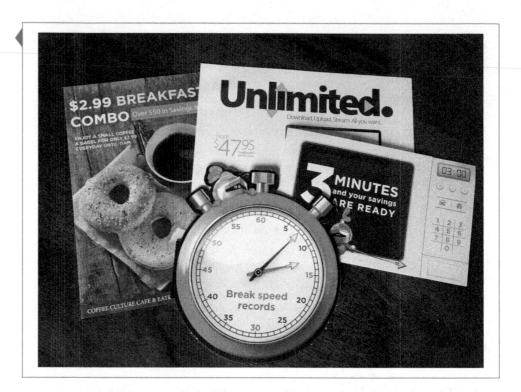

related products or services, such mailings make it convenient for the customer to take action. Bounce backs commonly arrive with Sears, The Bay, Visa, and MasterCard bills.

DIRECT MAIL STRATEGIES   There are two basic options for delivering direct mail. The first is to deliver the mailing as a standalone piece. In this option, the organization bears all of the costs associated with developing the offer and distributing it to the target market. The second option is to deliver the offer as part of a package that includes offers from other companies. In this option, the distribution costs are shared equally among all participants. That is the difference between solo direct mail and cooperative direct mail.

solo direct mail (selective direct mail) A unique advertising offer mailed directly to a target audience by a marketing organization.

Solo Direct Mail   With **solo direct mail**, also known as **selective direct mail**, the organization prepares a unique offer and mails it directly to the target market. It is a standalone offer. As discussed earlier, today's technology makes it very convenient for organizations to assess buying information, devise unique offers for existing customers, and deliver offers directly to those customers. Such a plan of action sounds much more efficient than delivering a message blindly to all consumers on prime-time television, or through daily newspapers or national magazines. Furthermore, solo direct mail can play a key role in an organization's CRM program. It is an effective means of keeping the channel of communication open.

Personalization is an important element of solo direct mail. Including a name and address (addressed direct mail) increases the likelihood of the mailing being read. According to Canada Post, 84 percent of Canadians open direct mail if their name is on it and 49 percent will read it just in case something catches their eye. Refer back to Figure 6.5 for more details. Addressed mail also achieves higher response rates than does unaddressed mail.

dimensional mail   Direct mail that can take any form other than the typical flat piece of mail.

Another type of direct mail that attracts more attention and gets higher response is dimension mail. **Dimensional mail** is a type of direct mail that can take any form other than the typical flat piece of mail. It could be something as simple as a pen or other object in an envelope or a unique box or package that contains the mail offer. Dimensional mail is meant to stand out—it is unique and often generates buzz for the product. Figure 6.7 demonstrates elements of solo direct mail and dimensional direct mail in one mailing piece.

FIGURE
6.7 **A Direct Mail Piece That Combines the Elements of Solo Direct Mail and Dimensional Mail**

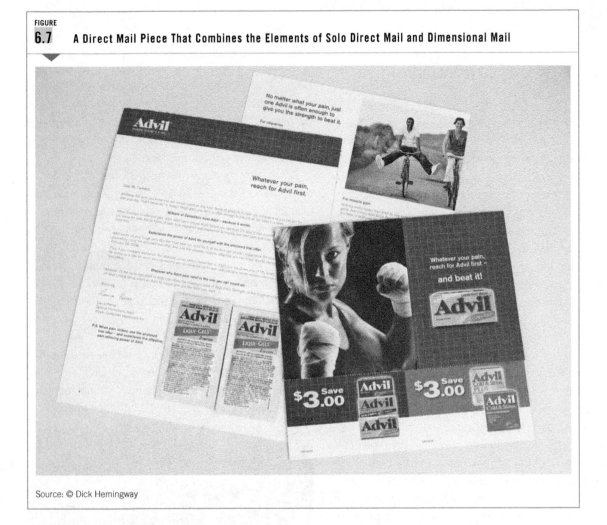

Source: © Dick Hemingway

For additional insight into the impact direct mail campaigns have on sales read the IMC Highlight: **The Power of Direct Mail.**

Cooperative Direct Mail   **Cooperative direct mail** refers to packages containing offers from non-competing products and services. Consumer goods companies commonly use this method; they are attracted to it because the costs are shared among all participants. A typical mailing might include coupons for packaged goods items, magazine subscription forms, order forms for direct mail offers, and so on. For packaged goods marketers in the food and drug industries, cooperative direct mail has proven to be an effective means of generating trial purchase. Response rates for coupon offers delivered by direct mail tend to be higher than coupon offers delivered by magazines or newspapers. The illustration in Figure 6.8 is representative of a typical cooperative direct mailing.

In deciding how and when to use direct mail, a manager evaluates the benefits and drawbacks of the medium. Refer to Figure 6.9 for details.

DIRECT RESPONSE TELEVISION

Direct response television (DRTV) is gaining in popularity with advertisers. There are two types of direct response television advertising (DRTV). **Short-form DRTV** is 30- or 60-second commercials that typically run on cable channels. **Long-form DRTV** is a program-like commercial, commonly referred to as an **infomercial** that can last

cooperative direct mail   A mailing containing specific offers from non-competing products.

Short-form DRTV   30- or 60-second commercials that run on cable channels.

long-form DRTV/infomercial   A long commercial (for example, 10 to 30 minutes) that presents in detail the benefits of a product or service; usually includes a call to action such as a 1-800 number.

The Power of Direct Mail

The best way to demonstrate the usefulness of direct mail advertising is to examine some real situations in which advertisers achieved success from it. The restaurant industry in Canada is very competitive, especially when you consider the number of quick-serve and fast casual dining options that are out there. On what basis do you decide which one to go to? Perhaps an incentive delivered by mail will tip the scales in favour of a particular restaurant.

Perhaps you have received some restaurant offers in the mail and taken advantage of them. They are quickly becoming a preferred tactic in the restaurant marketing. Unaddressed mail from McDonald's that offers a "Two for the price of one" entrée meal is hard to resist. Other chains will tempt you with similar offers!

Restaurants benefit from these and other kinds of offers. Direct mail can help achieve a variety of marketing objectives. It can generate brand and product awareness, build traffic, encourage purchases of particular menu items, and launch seasonal campaigns or other special promotions. The true benefit of a direct mail offer is immediacy—consumers will take advantage of a coupon offer for a meal soon after receiving it. Deadlines on the offer force consumers to take action . . . now!

Pizza Pizza is a strong believer in direct mail. It ran a mail campaign with the objective of increasing awareness of non-pizza items. Using Canada Post's Unaddressed Admail service Pizza Pizza distributed 4.1 million flyers promoting chicken wings to Canadian households. It was one of their most successful campaigns ever with 1.5 million Canadians taking advantage of the offer—an astonishing response rate of 37 percent. Pat Finelli, Chief Marketing Officer, says, "Direct mail continues to be our strongest performer in generating sales for our business."

Casey's, a casual dining restaurant, wanted to attract new customers. To do so, Casey's used a variety of media, but direct mail produced the best results. A mail campaign in neighbourhoods where their restaurants are located delivered a promotional offer and included its entire summer beverage menu. On average, each restaurant enjoyed an 8 percent lift in sales as a result of the offer. Jon McQuaid, brand marketing manager, says, "Direct mail is our most effective marketing tool to drive restaurant traffic."

Despite the fact we live in a digital media era, it seems people still love to receive old-fashioned mail. Statistics don't lie! People do read direct mail and they do take advantage of offers that catch their attention.

Source: Advertisements placed by Canada Post in *Canadian Business*, Direct Mail Delivered for Pizza Pizza and Direct Mail Put Casey's in the Hands of an Entire Neighbourhood.

30 or 60 minutes. It presents in detail, the benefits of a product or service, can include celebrities, and is well scripted.

The nature of direct response television advertising has changed over time. Once it was regarded as the "domain of schlock"; mainstream marketing organizations would not go near it. It was perceived as a last-resort tactic when all else failed. DRTV is now looked at in a more positive light due to the acceptance of infomercials and their improved quality.

Infomercials today are presented in a more entertaining manner. There is less "hard sell." The transfer of information is less intrusive. Consumers can simply evaluate the message and take action if they so desire. Unlike general TV advertising, direct response TV ads, including infomercials, ask the consumer to take action immediately—to

6.8   Contents of a Cooperative Direct Mailing Distributed by Open & Save

Source: © Dick Hemingway.

FIGURE
6.9

Direct Mail As an Advertising Medium

Advantages

- **Audience Selectivity**—Targets can be precisely identified and reached based on demographic, psychographic, and geographic characteristics. It is possible to secure external lists that closely match internal lists.

- **Creative Flexibility**—Unlike other media, the message can be copy oriented, visually oriented, or a combination of both. Because a mailing includes several components, there is ample time to expand on the benefits of the product.

- **Exclusivity**—Mail does not compete with other media or other ads upon receipt. In contrast, magazines and newspapers include clusters of ads and create a cluttered environment to advertise in.

- **Measurability**—Direct mail response is measured by the sales it generates. A sale can be directly linked to the mail offer (for example, receipt of a phone call or order form in the mail). The success of a campaign is determined in a relatively short period.

Disadvantages

- **Image**—Direct mail is not a prestigious medium. Often perceived as junk mail, it can be easily discarded by the recipient.

- **Cost per Exposure**—When all costs are included (for example, printing, securing list, mail delivery, and fulfillment), total cost can be higher than an ad placed in another print medium, although selective targeting reduces waste circulation.

- **Lack of Editorial Support**—As a standalone medium, compared to newspapers or magazines, it can't rely on editorial content to get people to read the message.

make the call, grab the credit card, and make the purchase. The effectiveness of the ad can be measured on the spot for its impact. Did it work or not? These ads are measured quantitatively based on response. Typical measures include cost per order, cost per lead, cost per call, or some other criterion.

Well-produced and highly informative infomercials are now produced by serious mainstream marketing organizations. By industry, pharmaceutical marketers, automotive marketers, packaged goods marketers, and financial institution marketers are all on board. Companies within these industries that use DRTV include Pfizer and GlaxoSmithKline, General Motors and Ford, Procter & Gamble and Unilever, and RBC Financial and TD Canada Trust.

These organizations evaluated the returns from their respective investments in mainstream advertising and decided that direct response communications would play a more vital role. Some companies' message could not be adequately conveyed in the usual 30-second television spot. Manulife Financial recently produced three 120-second commercials. According to Ian French, president and executive creative director at Northern Lights Direct Response, "We wanted to more clearly articulate the types of life circumstances that people would be in that lend themselves to insurance." For example, one commercial depicts a family facing child health care costs that are not covered by government insurance.[8]

Direct response commercials do not always have to sell something. In fact, a good infomercial can serve many marketing communications objectives: It can establish leads, drive retail traffic, launch new products, create awareness, and protect and enhance brand image. Procter & Gamble, for example, is not selling direct to consumers, but uses infomercials to promote products sold by retailers. Essentially, advertisers are pursuing a dual benefit—they are combining a brand message with a DRTV technique of encouraging action, either immediately or when the viewer visits a store.

Getting into direct response television, however, is not cheap. Experts say it costs as much as $250 000 to produce a 30-minute infomercial, and if celebrities are included, the costs can go much higher. By comparison the cost of a 30-second national television commercial can exceed $300 000—so the comparison is 30 minutes of airtime, perhaps at a late hour, versus 30 seconds of airtime in prime time. To keep media placement costs reasonable, shorter commercials (up to 60 seconds long) usually employ a station's run-of-schedule option where the ad is placed at the discretion of the station. Advertisers also use **remnant time**, which is unsold television inventory available on short notice at a lower cost.

For more insight into the effectiveness of direct response television, read the IMC Highlight: **Infomercials Move the Merchandise**.

remnant time Unsold television inventory available at lower cost to an advertiser.

DIRECT RESPONSE PRINT MEDIA

The print media—mainly newspapers and magazines—are good choices for communicating direct response offers or for fielding leads for future marketing programs. Given the local nature of daily newspapers, an organization can target prospects geographically. If the size of the budget restricts activity, markets can be assigned priorities until the budget is exhausted. Local market retailers that want to take advantage of direct response techniques have a good option in newspapers.

A majority of magazines are targeted at specific audiences based on demographic and psychographic characteristics, so the direct response message can be sent to specific audiences based on criteria established by the advertiser. For example, a company marketing floating docks or cottage designs might want to reach cottage owners. A direct response ad placed in *Cottage Life* magazine will reach that target market. The basic point is that it is possible to identify magazines that closely match the profile of a company's best customers. Resort destinations such as Whistler Blackcomb and Mont Tremblant adopt similar strategies, as do

IMC HIGHLIGHT

Infomercials Move the Merchandise

There are those who believe television is dead. They claim it's an old medium—it's out of touch with on-demand consumers who want to watch programs when they want to watch, not when the station wants them to watch. Not so fast, say many direct response industry experts! What about those direct response commercials? Tacky to some, impactful to others, these commercials can certainly move the merchandise.

Stop and think about these infomercials that have grabbed your attention late at night or on weekend mornings: the FlavorWave Oven, the Ab Rocket Twister, or Bowflex Max Trainer. The Bowflex Max Trainer boasts "The ultimate 14-minute workout!" Don't snicker. These ads work! A study conducted by the Electronic Retailing Association reveals that 63 percent of the population watches some form of DRTV advertising. The viewers are female and male, more affluent than the rest of the population, and are younger rather than older—a desirable target to pursue.

The television universe is becoming fragmented. There are too many stations—too much choice for viewers. Regular television spots can get lost amidst the clutter. With direct response it is possible to target consumers more accurately and at lower cost. Further, with conventional television or radio commercials, or a print ad, it is difficult to link the ad to sales since so many other variables come into play. After an infomercial, the phones start to ring right away, so the impact of the ad and the resulting sales are known almost immediately. For clients concerned about financial accountability, direct response television is an ideal fit.

So what makes a consumer pick up the phone to place an order? Experts in the industry say the message must be clear and concise, it must resolve a problem a consumer is experiencing, it must provide instant gratification, and it must be offered at a price point where the value is recognizable. Above all, the benefits of the product must be easy to demonstrate!

You may be too young to recall the George Foreman Grill but the DRTV campaign for the product met all of these criteria. George Foreman was a heavyweight boxing champion in the 1970s. Foreman estimates he made $200 million from the sale of grills bearing his name, which he neither invented nor initially wanted anything to do with. The success of the direct response campaign paved the way for retail distribution of the grill. The grill was produced and marketed by Salton Inc., an appliance maker that didn't expect the grill to be much of a hit. For Foreman and Salton it was like money falling from heaven, which was proof that good direct-response advertising serves a real business purpose. Those grills are still available for sale.

© Roy Letkey/Associated Press

Based on Simon Houpt, "Call Now to Take Advantage of This Special TV Advertising Offer," *The Globe and Mail*, December 16, 2011, p. B5; and Jon Nathanson, "The Lucrative Secret behind Infomercials," *The Week*, www.theweek.com.

provincial governments wanting to promote tourism. The print media are ideal for showing colourful pictures of local tourist attractions. See the ad in Figure 6.10 for an illustration.

Another option to consider is the insert, which was mentioned in Chapter 5 in the discussion of newspapers. An **insert** can be a single-page or multiple-page document that is inserted into the publication (see Figure 6.11). In some cases, the insert is actually glued onto a page (rubber-like glue that is easily removed when the insert is removed from the page). This type of insert is referred to as a **tip-in**.

Advertisers pay the publication insertion fees on a cost-per-thousand basis. A single-page insert in the *Toronto Star*, for example, costs $45.50/M, and a 16-page insert costs $61.50/M. Costs increase with the page count.[9] Preprinted inserts can be used for other communications purposes—they are good handouts at trade shows and other promotional

insert   A preprinted, free-standing advertisement (for example, a leaflet, brochure, or flyer) specifically placed in a newspaper or magazine.

tip-in   An insert that is glued to a page in the publication using a removable adhesive.

FIGURE
6.11   Inserts Are Flexible and Can Be Used in Print Media, Direct Mail, and at Point of Purchase

Source: © Jesse Johnston/CP Images.

events, and can be used to draw attention to products at the point of purchase. They can also be mailed directly to customers in the company's database.

TELEMARKETING

Telemarketers seem to call at the worst times, like suppertime, or just as you are sitting down to watch a favourite program. Can't telemarketers call at a more suitable time? Does that sound like a common complaint? To a telemarketer, it's simply a fact of life. The best time to call is when the prospect is at home, and that's suppertime or shortly thereafter. Despite the negative feelings consumers have about telemarketing's practices, it is growing in popularity with marketers as a means of communicating with customers. Telemarketing communications are often directly linked to direct response television and direct mail campaigns. Working together, they are a potent combination for achieving all kinds of marketing objectives.

Most telemarketing activities are conducted by call centres. A **call centre** is a central operation from which a company conducts its inbound and outbound telemarketing programs. In Canada, the latest data available from Statistics Canada reveals that the call centre industry generates $2.76 billion in revenues annually and that the industry is growing each year.[10] Telemarketing practices are having a positive impact on Canadian marketing strategies.

There are two forms of telemarketing: inbound and outbound. **Inbound telemarketing** refers to the calls received by an order desk, customer inquiries, and calls generated from toll-free telephone numbers promoted on direct response television commercials. **Outbound telemarketing** refers to calls made by a company to customers to develop new accounts, generate sales leads, and even close a sale.

call centre A central operation from which a company conducts its inbound and outbound telemarketing programs.

inbound telemarketing The calls received by a company from consumers, whether to place an order, inquire about products or services, or in response to a toll-free telephone number promoted on a direct response television commercial.

outbound telemarketing Calls made by a company to customers to develop new accounts, generate sales leads, and even close a sale.

The call centre is a vital link in the database management system because the telephone is a quick and convenient tool for capturing information about customers. Any information that is obtained can be added instantly to the database. Cost-effective software is available to manage this task.

In direct response communications, much emphasis is placed on message and media decisions. For example, how will the offer be communicated to entice the target market, and what media will it be placed in? Managing the inbound sales calls generated by commercials has traditionally been a weak link. Therefore, an organization must effectively plan its activities to meet call volume, capture data, present selling opportunities, and handle closing calls. The better a company can do these things, the better the economics of the direct response campaign. To illustrate, consider that a national TV spot on a cable network for a direct response lead generation campaign can easily generate 500 or more inbound inquiries, 85 percent of which will occur within the first three minutes of airing.[11] The call centre has to be ready. If it has to drop the call, or if the consumer hears a busy signal and hangs up, the marketer's return on investment is undermined. The ability to manage an inbound call requires precision planning to maximize returns.

The primary advantage of telemarketing is cost. Compared to traditional forms of mass advertising and the cost of having a salesperson make a business call, telemarketing offers considerable savings. In comparison to direct mail, the response rate for telemarketing is about 100 times higher. Even though direct mail may appear to be cheaper than telephone solicitation, it is actually more costly in the long run. To be effective, however, the telemarketing call must be carefully planned. Telemarketing representatives must be properly trained and prepared, just as field sales representatives are. Figure 6.12 summarizes the activities that can involve telemarketing.

FIGURE
6.12 **Telemarketing Performs Many Marketing Roles**

Fundraising
- Inbound (donations)
- Outbound (solicitations)

Sales Support
- Generating leads
- Qualifying prospects
- Securing appointments
- Marketing research

Personal Selling
- Opening new accounts
- Selling existing accounts
- Selling marginal accounts

Fulfillment
- Accepting orders
- Maintaining customer records
- Invoicing and payment processing

Customer Service
- Handling inquiries and complaints
- Help lines

Earlier in this section, the negative image of telemarketing was mentioned. Image is perhaps telemarketing's biggest drawback. People who react negatively to the calls simply hang up. In Canada, a National Do Not Call List (DNCL) was established in 2008 to protect consumers from unwanted telephone calls. By calling the registry number or by registering online, consumers can have their telephone number included on the DNCL. The registry requires that telemarketers check the registry at regular intervals. The Canadian Marketing Association (CMA) supports the registry, stating that "without reasonable laws regulating organizations that use the telephone to market goods and services, the industry risks losing this valuable marketing channel."[12] Organizations that call individuals or households on the list are subject to fines of "up to $15 000 per call"—ouch!

CATALOGUES AND MAGAZINES

Catalogues are reference publications, often annual, distributed by large retail chains and other direct marketing organizations. Catalogue marketing involves the merchandising of products through catalogue sales. When someone thinks of catalogues, the Sears catalogue comes to mind immediately, and for good reason. The Sears catalogue is the largest in Canada and is distributed to more than 3 million households. Sears publishes two semi-annual catalogues (Fall & Winter and Spring & Summer) as well as numerous seasonal catalogues, such as the *Christmas Wish Book,* and sale catalogues. Sears has outsourced call centre operations for catalogue ordering to IBM which handles English-language operations in the Philippines; French-languages services are handled in Europe.

Sears is a fully integrated marketing communications organization that generates $3.5 billion in revenues annually. Much of its business is generated from catalogue sales. Sears also operates one of the busiest commercial websites in Canada. Refer to Figure 6.13.

FIGURE 6.13   Sears Effectively Integrates Retail, Catalogue Marketing, and Web Marketing

Source: Used with permission of Sears Canada Inc; (far right) © Steve White/CP Images.

Other prominent catalogue retailers in Canada include Canadian Tire, Home Hardware, Mountain Equipment Co-op, and IKEA. These retailers have merged their retail operations with online buying. The catalogues they distribute drive traffic to their respective websites or to their retail stores. Selling via catalogues meets time-pressed consumer demand for more shopping convenience. As well, today's consumers are accustomed to multichannel shopping, and catalogues are one of the channels they pursue.

Rather than distribute catalogues, some companies have taken the concept a step further and publish their own magazines for distribution to current and prospective customers. The purpose is to stay in touch with customers after the sale and build a firmer relationship. Harry Rosen, a prominent, upscale menswear store, distributes *Harry* magazine in hard copy and online. The magazine keeps customers informed about fashion, health and lifestyle trends, and stories of interest to them. It is part of Harry Rosen's customer relationship program.

Mazda Canada also produces a magazine titled *Zoom Zoom*. It is distributed digitally to anyone interested in learning about Mazda products. Available in desktop, tablet, and mobile versions, the magazine keeps current and potential customers informed about new designs and technical innovations, offers stunning photographs and video content, and articles concerning adventure and lifestyles associated with automobiles and travel. Refer to the illustration in Figure 6.14.

FIGURE 6.14   Mazda Fosters a Relationship with Current and Prospective Customers through *Zoom Zoom* Magazine

Source: © Mazda

SUMMARY

Direct response advertising is the fifth-largest advertising medium in Canada. Companies seeking tangible returns for the money they invest in communications see value in direct response communications. Direct response is a natural extension of database management programs and is an ideal medium for enhancing customer relationships. The key components of direct response communications are direct mail, direct response television (DRTV), telemarketing, and catalogue marketing.

The foundation of direct response communications is the organization's database. An organization collects and analyzes data from internal and external sources. Customer or house lists record data about purchase transactions made by customers. This information is combined with demographic and psychographic information to form profiles of an organization's best customers. These customers are then targeted and reached through direct response communications. The analysis and manipulation of data constitute a process called data mining. The goal of data mining is to reveal useful information to create more effective marketing strategies.

The success of a direct response campaign depends on the quality of the list used by the advertiser. Lists are available from list brokers and other secondary sources such as directories and trade indexes. Lists provided by brokers are rented on a cost-per-thousand basis. Advertisers can choose between response lists, circulation lists, and compiled lists.

Direct mail is the most common form of direct response advertising. A direct mailing usually includes an envelope, letter, leaflet or folder, order form, and postage-paid return envelope. Each component performs a specific role in trying to get the recipient to take action. Advertisers choose between solo direct mail and cooperative direct mail. Solo distribution is more expensive but produces a higher response rate than cooperative distribution. An organization also has the option to use dimensional mail, which is mail of a different size and shape than traditional flat pieces. Dimensional mail draws attention to something inside the mailing piece and tends to break through the clutter of other mailings.

In recent years, direct response television has captured the attention of blue-chip marketing organizations. An advertiser can choose between short-form (30 and 60 seconds long) and long-form commercials (30 minutes long). Direct response commercials can establish leads, build image, launch new products, and complete transactions with customers.

Direct response ads in the print media are another option. Advertisers frequently use the print media to encourage prospective customers to call 1-800 numbers or to visit websites to get more information. Print is also is a good medium for distributing inserts. By selecting the right newspaper or magazine, the advertiser can target its primary customer.

There are two types of telemarketing. Inbound telemarketing refers to calls made by customers to an order desk. Outbound telemarketing refers to calls made by a company to prospective customers to generate leads and even close a sale. Companies are attracted to telemarketing because of its low costs. It is less expensive than face-to-face personal selling and mass advertising. Its major drawback is the negative perception people hold about this form of communication. Recent government legislation and the establishment of a National Do Not Call List now play a key role in determining whom a direct marketer may call.

Catalogues are a direct response medium often used by retail organizations. Catalogues include visual images, descriptions, and prices of the products offered for sale. Time-pressed consumers appreciate the convenience of catalogue shopping, and catalogues help direct consumers toward offline purchases (at retail) and online purchases (at a website).

KEY TERMS

REVIEW QUESTIONS

1. What is the difference between direct marketing and direct response advertising?
2. What are the major forms of direct response advertising?
3. Explain the concept of data mining. What impact does data mining have on marketing and marketing communications?
4. What is the role of the list broker in direct response advertising?
5. In the context of mailing lists, what does merge/purge refer to?
6. What are the differences among a response list, a circulation list, and a compiled list?
7. Briefly explain two advantages and two disadvantages of direct mail advertising.
8. Identify and briefly explain the components of a typical direct mail piece.
9. What is a statement stuffer?
10. What is the difference between a solo direct response campaign and a cooperative direct response campaign?
11. Identify and briefly explain how dimensional mail is different from other forms of direct mail.
12. Identify and briefly explain the various direct response television alternatives.
13. What is the difference between an insert and a tip-in?
14. What is the difference between inbound telemarketing and outbound telemarketing?

DISCUSSION AND APPLICATION QUESTIONS

1. Will direct response communications play a more significant role in the marketing communications mix in the future? Through secondary research, identify those factors that will encourage or discourage the use of direct response communications and formulate your position on the issue.
2. Direct mail advertising is a popular medium for not-for-profit organizations. Why? What are the benefits and drawbacks of using direct mail? Identify some organizations that successfully use direct mail advertising to help achieve their marketing goals.
3. Collect two or three direct mail pieces that have been delivered to your household address. Did the mailing reach the appropriate target market? What components did the mailing include, and how effective were they in communicating the message? Is the message convincing enough to act upon?
4. Assume you are about to develop a direct response advertising campaign that will encourage a select target audience to visit an Audi dealer to test drive a new Audi TT. The target is defined as male and female managers and executives who earn $100 000 or more and live in large metropolitan markets. The priority markets are Toronto, Montreal, and Vancouver. What direct response media would you use in the campaign? Assuming direct mail will be a component of the campaign, how would you find names for the mailing?
5. Conduct some research to find a company that has successfully used any form of direct response advertising as part of an integrated marketing communications campaign (such as a major bank, financial services company, or not-for-profit fundraising campaign). What role did direct response communications play? Describe the successes that resulted from the direct response effort.

ENDNOTES

1. Canadian Media Directors' Council *Media Digest*, 2014–15, p. 9.
2. Jim Wisner, "Direct Mail in Today's Digital World," Direct Marketing Association of Canada, October 20, 2014, www.directmac.org.
3. Mary Dickie, "Change Is Brewing," Strategy, July 1, 2007, strategyonline.ca/2007/07/01/biz-20070701/.
4. Susan Pigg, "Diapers, Drinking, and Data," *Toronto Star*, August 16, 2002, pp. E1, E10.
5. Costs Obtained from Cornerstone Group of Companies, *Chatelaine* Datacard, May 26, 2015
6. Epsilon TargetSource Canada, www.lists.epsilon.com.
7. Epsilon TargetSource Canada, Customer Data and Data Cards, retrieved May 26, 2015, http://lists-epsilon.com.
8. Matt Semansky, "Manulife Financial Flexes DRTV Muscle," *Marketing*, January 9, 2008, www.marketingmag.ca/news/marketer-news/manulife-financial-flexes-dret-muscle-12715.
9. *Toronto Star*, Media Kit, 2015, http://mediakit.thestar.ca.
10. Larry McKeown and Richard Vincent, "Trends in the Telephone Call Centre Industry," Statistics Canada, www.statcan.gc.ca/pub/63f0002x/63f0002x2008053-eng.pdf.
11. Maria Eden, "One Call, Multiple Sales Opportunities," *Direct Marketing News*, August 30, 2002, www.dmnews.com/one-call-multiple-sales-opportunities/article/78517.
12. "Do No Call Has Strong Support," *Marketing Daily*, November 1, 2007, www.marketingmag.ca.

Planning for Online
and Interactive
Communications

Learning Objectives

After studying this chapter, you will be able to

1. Assess strategies for delivering effective messages using online advertising

2. Describe the various roles played by online communications in a marketing and marketing communications environment

3. Evaluate the various advertising alternatives that are available online

4. Assess the potential of the Internet as an advertising medium

5. Assess the role of social media, mobile media, and video games as alternatives in integrated marketing communications campaigns

Online communications offer a high degree of personalization. Since personalization is one of the cornerstones of customer relationship management (CRM) programs, the Internet is an attractive communications alternative for marketers. The medium is unique, as it allows an organization to listen to customers, learn from them, and then deliver content and services tailored to their responses and actions. These benefits must be considered when devising an integrated marketing communications plan.

In the digital universe, control has shifted from the advertiser to the customer, a situation that marketing organizations must adapt to. It's no longer about delivering a message, but rather about allowing customers to participate in developing messages and interacting with brands—a concept referred to as engagement. As well, viewers now have unprecedented choice. They can access the Internet by computer, tablet, mobile phone, or smart TV.

More is spent on advertising on the Internet in Canada than any other medium. In the wake of changing consumer behaviour in how people consume media, there has been a clear shift in how advertisers allocate their communications budgets. Now that members of all age groups are online, agency media planners give greater consideration to the opportunities that various interactive media offer. In making recommendations however, one thing hasn't changed much: budgets have remained relatively stable, making the media choices more difficult. Any form of online communications can be expensive so the funds must come from other media an organization has traditionally used. The challenge remains the same: finding the best combination of media to reach and impact a target audience effectively.

This chapter examines in detail a host of new interactive marketing communications opportunities that should be considered when planning an integrated marketing communications campaign.

Internet Penetration

When compared to most other countries, Canada has one of the highest levels of Internet penetration and broadband access. The latest data available about consumer participation on the Internet reveals that 86 percent (29.7 million people) of Canadians are Internet users. Canadian participation ranks second in the world, just behind the United Kingdom. The amount of time Canadians spend online is a factor considered by media planners. More time online equals a greater opportunity to reach a target audience. The average time individual Canadians are online using a computer is close to 5 hours a day. Mobile device users are connected for an average of just under 2 hours a day.[1]

Medium	18–24 Years	35–54 Years	55+ Years
TV	1218	1572	2382
Internet	1384	1243	470
Radio	675	1135	1202
Newspaper	100	151	266
Magazine	26	34	39

Note: All figures are weekly minutes per capita

FIGURE
7.1

Time Spent by Canadians with Media

Source: Based on "2014: Internet in the Media Garden," The 2014 CMUST Report, IAB Canada.

Such high Internet penetration is having an impact on the time spent with other media, but it seems that Canadians have adopted digital technologies seamlessly while maintaining a strong appetite for traditional media. The amount of time spent online does vary by age category and younger age categories are leading the charge in digital media consumption. Television once ruled the roost, but among 14- to 24-year-olds the Internet leads the way. Among 35- to 54-year-olds the Internet ranks second to television. Not surprisingly, the Internet falls to third place in the 55+ age group. Among older Canadians television remains the dominant medium. For additional insight into how much time Canadians spend with various media, refer to Figure 7.1.

The data presented in this section strongly suggest the inclusion of online media in a marketing communications plan. The Internet is the ideal medium for reaching younger Canadians and a reasonably good one for reaching older Canadians. In the future, the smartphone will be the preferred method for accessing the Internet, hence the need for planners to reevaluate how budgets are allocated. Mobile devices enable advertisers to reach consumers anywhere and anytime, which is a significant advantage over any other medium.

Online and Interactive Marketing Communications

The Internet is revolutionizing how companies look at advertising and other forms of marketing communications. However, there is a gap between how much advertisers spend online and how much they should be spending. Canada's online advertising market has reached $4.3 billion and accounts for 34 percent of net advertising revenue in Canada. Presently, four industries account for about half of the Internet advertising revenue in Canada: consumer packaged goods, automotive, retail, and financial. Companies in these industries such as Procter & Gamble and Unilever, General Motors and Ford, Canadian Tire and Walmart, and RBC Financial and Scotiabank lead the way. There are a good many industries and companies that still don't recognize the true value of online communications.

For effective online communications, the communications planner must respect some essential differences between the Internet and traditional media. The Internet is a true source of information and entertainment for consumers and is a "participative" medium. For example, fans of a brand are known to produce their own commercials for the brand and post them on YouTube for others to view. In contrast, mass advertising through traditional media such as television, radio, magazines, and newspapers is "interruptive" and the communications are one way from the advertiser to the consumer. Therefore, an advertiser must adapt and produce advertising that is suitable for the online arena.

Planners are reluctant to place ads online. They want to be assured that ads are actually viewed and that real people are clicking on them. **Viewability** is a hot issue among

Viewability   A minimum of 50 percent of an ad in view for at least one second.

planners. Since companies are pouring more money into online advertising they want to be sure that their ads actually appear in front of humans. While this concern may appear odd, recent data show that less than 50 percent of ads appearing "in view" were actually seen. In view means that at least half of the ad was visible on a web page for one second or more. Such a brief view counts as an impression that advertisers pay for. Advertisers question the value of this kind of impression.

Click fraud When a bot imitating a legitimate user of a web browser clicks on an ad for the purpose of generating an advertising charge for the click.

Advertisers are also concerned about **click fraud**, a situation where bots that look like human web users click on advertisements. A click is a click, and advertisers must pay for ads that are seen by this non-human traffic. The fraud that the bots enable is a major problem. The various means of paying for online advertising are discussed in Appendix A. Concerns about viewability and click fraud must be addressed by the industry. Simply stated, an advertiser should not have to pay if a human does not see their ads.

The rapid growth in Internet consumption strongly suggests the inclusion of interactive media in a marketing communications strategy. To do so, marketing communications planners face a two-fold challenge. First, they must devise a plan that effectively integrates online advertising with other forms of advertising while recognizing a fundamental difference in behaviour that people exhibit when using digital media. Second, they must determine how much to invest (share of budget) in online communications while exercising concern for issues such as click fraud and the extent to which ads are actually viewed.

Unlike any of the traditional mass media, online advertising provides immediate feedback to advertisers regarding how effectively their message reached the target; it automatically gears ads to viewers' personal tastes, and it generally reaches receptive consumers—at least those consumers who click on the ads. The Internet also delivers on the corporate mandate for marketers to be more accountable; since online advertising is measurable, it is attractive to marketing organizations. Given the merits of online communications and its integral role in our daily lives marketers must acknowledge that anything interactive is a critical medium to engage consumers and create deeper brand experiences.

At the same time, online communications can go further than many other media because they can secure a purchase and make arrangements to have goods delivered.

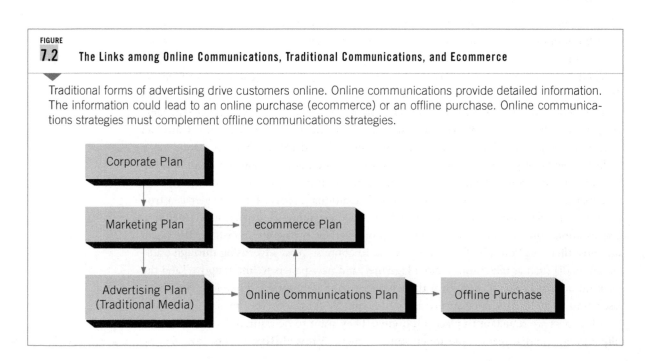

FIGURE 7.2　The Links among Online Communications, Traditional Communications, and Ecommerce

Traditional forms of advertising drive customers online. Online communications provide detailed information. The information could lead to an online purchase (ecommerce) or an offline purchase. Online communications strategies must complement offline communications strategies.

IMC HIGHLIGHT

Nissan Altima Goes with Digital Media

The launch of a newly redesigned Nissan Altima embraced the concept of integrated marketing communications and included a significant digital media component. The creative for the campaign revolved around the tagline "Innovation that Excites." Naturally, the latest in technological developments are mentioned in the advertising; improvements such as the redesigned suspension; a category-unique, tire-fill alert system; zero-gravity seats; and a 3D driver display. Nissan decided to use "innovation" as a means to differentiate the Altima from competitor brands.

The campaign was launched with a 60-second spot shown on 2D and 3D cinema screens. Computer graphics show how the car has evolved from its predecessor. On the digital front, animated banners say things such as "Wouldn't it be cool if your car was as smart as your smartphone?" and "Wouldn't it be cool if your car was as fast as it looked?" Print ads use phrases such as "Go further. Go faster. Go lighter." Out-of-home ads use short messages such as "Vroomier," and include a beauty shot of the vehicle.

Nissan sees the digital component of the plan as absolutely vital. According to director of marketing

Vinay Shahani, "We know the majority of our customers are leveraging the Internet to do research and perform shopping tasks, so it makes sense to be there. The percentage of digital is much higher than in the past."

To engage consumers with the brand, Nissan offered an opportunity for customers to submit personal essays on why they should be chosen to participate in an Altima driving experience. In a contest format, five lucky people were then chosen to visit the automaker's proving grounds in Arizona to drive the new Altima. Videos of their driving experiences were produced and placed on Facebook, Twitter, and YouTube.

Nissan has been very active in social media; in fact, Nissan has the highest consumer engagement percentage on its Facebook brand page of any automaker. If "likes" are an important measure of success in social media, then Altima is a clear winner, with more than one million of them. According to Nissan's director of interactive and social media marketing Erich Marx, "Everybody at Nissan understands that social space is different and quirky, and we are trying to take advantage of that with what we do there."

Vinay Shahani acknowledges that the Honda Accord and Toyota Camry are key competitors and that the objective of the campaign is to gain market share at their expense. He says the Altima buyer is typically younger and more interested in the performance and uniqueness of a vehicle. The all-new Altima meets these buying criteria, and the new marketing communications campaign was designed to connect with the target audience on an emotional level. "We'll have to wait and see how the market responds," says Shahani.

© AP Photo/Mark Lennihan/CP Images.

Based on Karl Greenberg, "Nissan Rolls out Biggest Campaign for Altima," *Marketing Daily*, June 18, 2012, www.mediapost.com; and Rich Thomaselli, "Nissan Looks to Facebook to Help Launch Five New Models," *Advertising Age*, June 25, 2012, www.adage.com.

They are capable of closing the loop, from initial awareness to a buying decision, in a very short period, assuming a website has ecommerce capabilities. Figure 7.2 illustrates how Internet communications link with traditional advertising and ecommerce.

For more insight into the benefits of adding online advertising to the marketing communications mix, see the IMC Highlight: **Nissan Altima Goes with Digital Media**.

Online and Interactive Communications Planning

interactive communications The placement of an advertising message on a website, or an ad delivered by email or through mobile communications devices.

Interactive communications refers to the placement of an advertising message on a website, usually in the form of a banner, rich media ad, video ad, sponsorship at a website, or an ad delivered by email or mobile communications device.

When devising an interactive communications plan, decisions about which medium to use are largely based on the target market the advertiser wishes to reach, the communications objectives, and the budget available. Refer to Figure 7.3 for a visual review of the interactive planning process. The first step in the process is to identify the target market. The second step is to establish the objectives. The third step is to evaluate the various media options strategically. Will it be an online campaign, a mobile media campaign, a video game campaign, a social media campaign, or some combination of alternatives? Once the strategy is determined, the final step is execution. Here, decisions are made on specific media, how much to spend, and how to schedule media activities during the year.

ONLINE TARGETING

The reality of the Internet is that consumers voluntarily visit specific websites. To get what they want, they also divulge valuable information about themselves. Smart companies use the Internet as a means of obtaining information for their databases. Once the information is analyzed, it can be translated into specific messages, and marketing offers can be tailored to specific customer needs.

demographics The characteristics of a population that include gender, age, education, income, occupation, and culture.

The Internet is much like any other medium. Audiences can be targeted based on demographic and geographic variables, by time of day, day of week, and behaviour. All websites accumulate data on who visits and how long they visit. Such information aids media planners when they are devising target audience reach and frequency scenarios. In terms of **demographics**, a popular website like TSN.ca attracts a male audience and is over-indexed for males in the 18- to 24-year age category. On a monthly basis TSN.ca attracts 1.7 million visitors who average 14.3 visits.[2] It's no wonder that Molson Canadian advertises heavily on this site—it reaches the company's primary demographic! Ram trucks also see TSN.ca as good advertising value. The brand sponsors a daily contest called 1V1 that pits a challenging highlight (for example, a spectacular goal by a hockey player) against a reigning champion highlight. Visitors to the site vote to determine the winner. A website such as HGTV.ca has a strong female reach, particularly in the 35- to 49-year age category—an attractive target for any marketing organization in the home furnishing and decorating business.

Once targets are identified demographically they can be qualified further by geography. Advertisers can zero in on users in specific regions, cities, or postal codes. For example, in the RAM truck and TSN.ca example just cited, if Ram only wanted to reach younger urban males, for example, in Toronto, Montreal, and Vancouver, ads will only be placed in those markets.

Daypart targeting The placement of online ads based on time of day

Daypart targeting is another planning option. Unlike television, where prime time is during the evening, prime time online is during the day—when people are at work. Not only is the at-work online audience vast, it is comprises a demographically attractive group of individuals who have higher-than-average incomes, education, and the tendency to shop and buy online. To demonstrate the impact of daypart targeting, Best Buy ran a three-week campaign on Yahoo! Its ads ran Monday to Friday between 5 am and 11 am in Ontario and Quebec. The campaign generated a

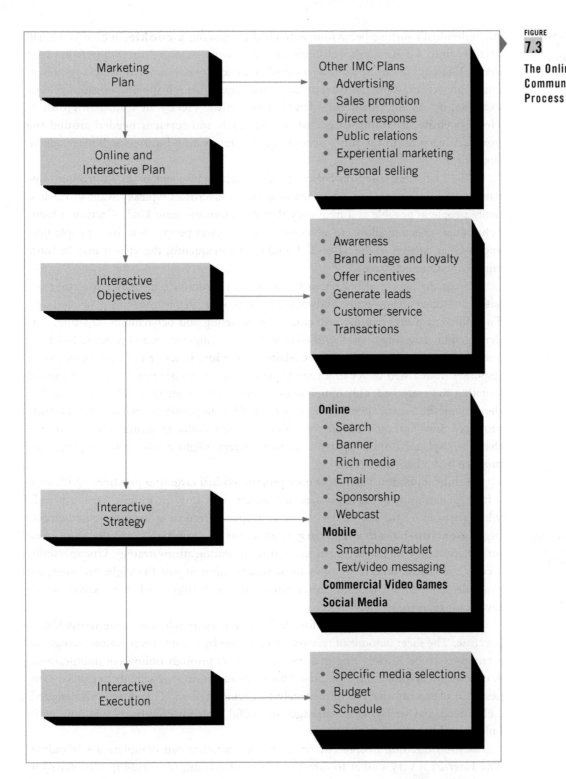

FIGURE
7.3

The Online and Interactive Communications Planning Process

200 percent conversion lift (consumers who took action based on the advertising) over previous campaigns.[3]

Unlike other media, the Internet is a medium that allows marketers to target customers on the basis of their behaviour. In its simplest form, **behavioural targeting** means delivering ads based on a consumer's previous surfing patterns.

behavioural targeting A means of delivering online ads based on a consumer's previous surfing patterns.

cookie An electronic identification tag sent from a web server to a user's browser to track the user's browsing patterns.

An individual's surfing behaviour is tracked by placing a **cookie**, which is a small text file onto a consumer's web browser and sometimes stored on that person's hard drive. The cookie can be used to remember a user's preferences. By tracking preferences, an organization can directly tailor messages to reach specific consumers. For example, if someone spent considerable time on the HGTV or Canadian House & Home website, it would trigger ads for products and services needed around the home. Advertisers in the food, decorating, and renovation business will place ads on these sites.

When targeting based on behaviour, the reach component of an advertising campaign is less important. In mass media campaigns, advertisers typically want to reach as many people as possible at a frequency that will motivate some kind of action. Online behavioural targeting allows an advertiser to reach fewer people, but those people have expressed an interest in the advertised product. Consequently, the viewer may be more engaged with the message.

impression (ad view) An ad request that was successfully sent to a visitor. This is the standard way of determining exposure for an ad on the web.

To test the impact of behavioural targeting, an automotive insurance advertiser targeted consumers who had recently visited automotive sites in order to generate leads. Two different plans were used: demographic targeting and behavioural targeting. The demographic targeting option resulted in 183 million impressions and generated 47 leads per 1 million impressions. An **impression** or **ad view** is defined as a measurement of responses from a web server to a page request from a user's browser. When behavioural targeting was employed, only 6 million impressions were made (at much lower cost), but those impressions generated 116 leads per 1 million impressions. Behavioural targeting produced three times the number of leads than demographic targeting. This test verifies that a well-planned online communications strategy might reach far fewer people yet produce better business results.

Mobile communications is also shaping individual targeting practices. With such a high penetration of smartphones in Canada, it is now possible to reach people while they are on the move, which is a concept referred to as location-based targeting. **Location-based targeting** is an effort to integrate consumers' location information into the marketing or marketing communications strategy. Unexpectedly, a consumer could receive an offer from an advertiser at just the right moment, for example, a restaurant discount offer when you are hungry and don't know which restaurant to visit!

Location-based targeting Integrating a person's location information into a marketing communications strategy.

Behavioural targeting is ideal for reaching consumers when they are researching a purchase. The sheer amount of research done online by consumers is reason enough for a company to be actively engaged with consumers through online communications. A user who sees something of interest (that is, an advertising message that creates awareness) can obtain information immediately by clicking the ad. Therefore, well-designed, well-placed, and well-targeted messages are useful tools for consumers who engage in online product research.

Beyond reaching people efficiently, an organization can complete a sale online. The Internet is very similar to direct response advertising (discussed in Chapter 6) in terms of securing action. Online storefronts such as those for Canadian Tire and Chapters/Indigo fall into this category. Finally, the Internet deals with the concept of mass customization. **Mass customization** refers to the capability of personalizing messages, and, ultimately, products, to a target audience of one—the ultimate form of targeting! How would you like a personalized pair of running shoes from Nike delivered right to your front door?

mass customization The development, manufacture, and marketing of unique products to unique customers.

Online and Interactive Communications Objectives

Online advertising performs the same or similar roles as traditional media advertising. It can help create brand awareness, build or enhance brand image, generate sales leads, provide a means to make a purchase, improve customer service and communications between customers and the company, and acquire meaningful data about potential customers (as in database management).

CREATING BRAND AWARENESS

Given the amount of time and the frequency with which consumers go online, there is ample opportunity for a company or brand to develop advertising that will generate brand awareness. The most obvious way to achieve awareness is to advertise on a web portal where the reach is extremely high. A **portal** is a website featuring several commonly used services, such as news or searching, and serves as a starting point or gateway to other services, such as shopping, discussion groups, and links to other sites. These sites are among the most visited sites and include Google (1.1 billion visitors), YouTube (1.0 billion), Facebook (900 million), Yahoo! (750 million), and Amazon (500 million).[4] In Canada the most visited websites are Google, Facebook, YouTube, Yahoo!, and Wikipedia. Presently, 19 million Canadians (54 percent of the population) have a Facebook profile. Statistics like these demonstrate the potential value of advertising online.

portal   A website that serves as a gateway to a variety of services such as searching, news, directories, email, online shopping, and links to other sites.

To create brand awareness and awareness of a brand's promise, a variety of advertising alternatives are available. Among the options are banner ads, rich media, and sponsorships (discussed later in the chapter). Recent research indicates that Internet advertising works best when utilized as part of a media mix. To illustrate, when Dove launched a new line of skin care products, a media mix of magazine, outdoor, television, and online advertising was employed. Key findings of the Dove study provided insight into how various media can work together synergistically. The key findings were:

- The addition of online and/or outdoor advertising to a combination of television and magazines improved awareness scores by 33 percent.

- The combination of television, print, and online was especially effective in increasing brand attribute scores among a very specific female target group versus television alone.

- Online advertising outperformed television in raising purchase intent; however, the combination of television, magazine, and online maximized purchase intent an astounding 47 percent higher than by using television alone.

If the objective is to create brand awareness and ultimately purchase intent, these data strongly promote the inclusion of online advertising in an integrated marketing communications plan.

BUILDING AND ENHANCING BRAND IMAGE

If the objective is to have the public perceive the brand positively, online communications must present a message and image consistent with and comparable to any traditional form of communication. Whether it be an online advertisement or brand/company website, it is important that the message and image projected be in keeping with the overall company image and its other forms of marketing communications.

It is common for consumers to be routed to sub-pages on a website (for example, a brand page) as they search for the information they are after. Therefore, the brand page must comply with the brand's image and persona. Most advertisers now encourage people to follow them on Facebook, Twitter, Instagram, and other social media sites. Therefore, it makes good sense that the look, appearance, and style of the message be integrated across all media. This helps produce a synergistic effect for the total communications effort.

Companies in the telecommunications, packaged goods, and financial services industries are masters at matching message strategies among traditional and non-traditional forms of media. Sports sites in particular do an excellent job of creating and building an image for male personal care products. A brand such as Gillette, which has a primary target of males 35 and under, can reach its target effectively using a combination of television and online communications. Placing ads on sites such as TSN or CBC Sports will reach the desired target. Refer to the images in Figure 7.4 for an illustration.

OFFERING INCENTIVES

The Internet is a good medium for implementing a variety of sales promotion activities. Price discounts are commonplace to encourage consumers to make their initial online purchase. Canadian Tire, for instance, offers unique and special deals online as a means of getting people comfortable with online buying. Once customers realize it is a safe and convenient way to buy, they go back for more. Companies that are active with customer

FIGURE 7.4   Gillette Reaches Its Primary Target Audience on the CBC Sports Website

© Procter & Gamble and CBC, © Gillette/CBC

relationship management programs are capable of delivering incentives to customers in their database by using email advertising.

Contests and sweepstakes are popular online promotions. Typically, they encourage consumers to buy for the first time, or they encourage brand loyalty (repeat purchases). Regardless, the true benefit to the company is the names and information that are collected through entry forms. It is surprising how much personal information an individual will divulge to a marketing organization for the chance of winning a prize. This information can be used either to start or expand a database.

GENERATING LEADS

The Internet is a useful medium for generating leads in a business-to-consumer or business-to-business marketing situation. As already indicated, consumers willingly disclose information when entering contests. Consumers and business people will also leave the same vital information when they are searching for information online. The stumbling block in retrieving the information they want is the transfer of personal or business information. However, online visitors are known to give out more details about themselves, or the business they are part of, so that they can retrieve the information they are searching for. Business sites often request information such as company size, number of employees, type of business, location, postal code, email address, and so on. It's a fact of life in doing business online. This type of information, once analyzed and mined (data mining), can be used to identify potential targets (one-to-one marketing) and to customize messages and products that are suited to that target.

PROVIDING CUSTOMER SERVICE

In any form of marketing, offering good customer service is crucial. Satisfied customers hold positive attitudes about a company and are likely to return to buy more goods. Again, the Internet plays a pivotal role. It can be an efficient and cost-effective way of providing service, assuming a company's website is well organized. Service demands by customers tend to be high. Therefore, any frustration a customer experiences when searching for service on a website will only compound the problem. Speed of service is a primary benefit offered by the Internet. It goes without saying that customers should have quick and open access to service information. Carefully indexed FAQs (frequently asked questions) or key word searches are common ways to access online information quickly.

For specific questions and concerns, email is another good option, although email response time can be an issue. Making customers wait a few days for a response is not the type of service they expect. Successful online businesses don't forget that online activities must be backed up by a human component. They must pay close attention to inbound sales, order tracking, out-of-stock issues, deliveries and returns, and all the service issues associated with these tasks. All of these activities are part of a good CRM program.

CONDUCTING TRANSACTIONS

Online shopping is becoming a big factor in the consumer and business purchase cycle. The presence of online retailers such as Amazon and eBay has had a negative impact on bricks and mortar retailers. Some have gone out of business (Mexx, Jacob, Smart Set, and Future Shop) while others have streamlined operations and closed underperforming stores (Sears and Best Buy). In today's marketplace it is necessary to have a website but surprisingly, in 2012, less than half of Canadian companies had one. Business-to-consumer ecommerce transactions are growing at a rate of about 10 percent annually

FIGURE
7.5   Canadian Tire Has Effectively Combined Online Buying with Traditional In-Store Buying

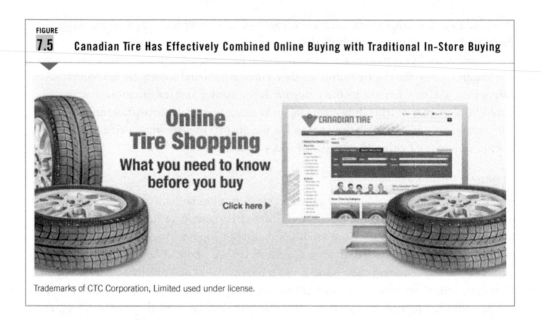

Trademarks of CTC Corporation, Limited used under license.

and reached $25.4 billion in 2014. Ecommerce sales account for 5.2 percent of all retail sales.[5] Customers in the 25- to 34-year-old category are the most prolific online shoppers; they have money, good credit ratings, and a high degree of comfort with buying online.[6]

Today it is important to have a website with ebusiness capabilities. The site plays a key role in the communications process and is a real means of generating sales. Companies such as Canadian Tire and Indigo use the Internet to communicate effectively with shoppers and these companies have combined emarketing with traditional methods of conducting business. Refer to Figure 7.5. To remain competitive, more businesses must do the same.

Online and Interactive Communications Strategies

As indicated by the increase in advertising revenues from year to year and the amount of time consumers spend online each week, advertisers have embraced online communications from a strategic perspective. Today's media planners are technologically savvy; they recognize the value of online communications and other forms of interactive communications, and make appropriate recommendations when devising an integrated marketing communications strategy.

From a media strategy perspective, the Internet and other forms of interactive communications offer high reach and frequency, although advertisers have to be careful about budgets when the various cost models are evaluated (see later section of the chapter for cost models). At portal sites such as Google and Yahoo, the number of unique daily visitors is incredibly high. In contrast, niche sites that focus on a particular interest, hobby, or activity reach fewer people, but are more targeted. Both scenarios should be considered when devising an online media plan.

There are a variety of creative opportunities available to online advertisers. The advertising options include search advertising, display advertising (banner ads), video ads, sponsorships, and email advertising. Video is becoming more popular with advertisers due to its similarity to television ads by including sight, sound, and motion.

FIGURE
7.6   **Online Advertising Revenues by Types of Advertising**

Type of Advertising	$M 2013	$M 2014	% Change
Search	1802	2051	+14
Display	1091	1274	+17
Classifieds/Directories	289	171	−41
Video	208	266	+28
Email	18	19	+8
Video Games	11	11	+/−0
Total	3419	3792	+11

Source: Based on data from IAB Canada, Canadian Online Advertising Revenue Survey, detailed report.

Presently, search and display advertising account for the largest portion of online advertising investment. For details refer to Figure 7.6.

Beyond the Internet, an advertiser might consider social media, mobile communications opportunities, and advertising in video games. As with other media, the planner must evaluate the alternatives and devise a media selection and rejection rationale for the online and interactive components of a media plan.

Prior to examining the various online advertising alternatives, some basic terminology should be understood. All terms relate to how Internet ads are measured for strategic variables such as reach, frequency, and engagement:

- **Impression (Ad Views):** An ad request that was successfully sent to a visitor. This is the standard way of determining exposure for an ad on the web.

- **Frequency (Online):** The number of times an ad is delivered to the same browser in a single session or time period. A site can use cookies to manage frequency.

- **Clicks (Clickthroughs):** This refers to the number of times that users click on a banner ad. Such a measurement allows an advertiser to judge the response to an ad. When viewers click the ad, they are transferred to the advertiser's website or to a special page where they are encouraged to respond in some way to the ad.

- **Click (Clickthrough) Rate:** The ratio of clicks to impressions. It is calculated by dividing the total number of clicks by the total number of impressions. For example, if during 1 million impressions, there are 20 000 clicks on the banner, the clickthrough rate is 2 percent. A high click rate indicates the banner ad was effective in its purpose.

- **Unique Visitor:** The number of unduplicated (counted only once) visitors to a website over a course of a specified time period. Visitors are determined by cookies, a small text file stored in a user's browser.

- **Visit:** A sequence of page requests made by one user at one website. A visit is also referred to as a session or browsing period.

A site's activity is described in terms of the number of unique visitors, the time they spend visiting, and how often they return to the site. A site that can report, for example, that it had 8 million page views, 100 000 visitors, and 800 000 visits last month would be

impression (ad view)   An ad request that was successfully sent to a visitor. This is the standard way of determining exposure for an ad on the web.

frequency (online)   The number of times an ad is delivered to the same browser in a single session or time period.

clicks (clickthroughs)   The number of times users click on a banner (clicking transfers the user to another website).

click (clickthrough) rate   The percentage of impressions (ad views) that resulted in a click; determines the success of an ad in attracting visitors to click on it.

unique visitor   The number of unduplicated visitors to a website during a specified period.

visit   A sequence of page requests made by a visitor to a website; also called a session or a browsing period.

doing very well. It means that the average visitor returns to the site 8 times each month and views 10 pages on each visit. That's incredible "stickiness" (most sites don't do that well)! **Stickiness** refers to the notion that the website has a compelling reason for users to stay for a longer visit or to come back frequently for more information. Offering relevant and interesting content is a key factor in getting visitors to return to a website.

stickiness A website's ability to keep people at the site for an extended period or to have them return to the site frequently.

SEARCH ADVERTISING

With **search advertising**, the advertiser's listing is placed within or alongside search results in exchange for paying a fee each time someone clicks on the listing. This is also known as **pay-per-click advertising**. Google, for example, offers a service called AdWords that allows companies, for a small fee, to have a link to their website when a user searches for a word that company has specified. For example, if a user types in mutual funds and Scotiabank has bought that term, an ad for Scotiabank appears on the screen. Google sets advertisers against one another in auction-style bidding for the highest positions on the search page. If Scotiabank bid the most for the word, it would appear first on the listing of ads. Other bidders can also appear on the same list; the highest bidder for the word or term is at the top of the list. When a consumer clicks on the sponsored link, he or she is immediately directed to the advertiser's webpage where detailed information is provided.

search advertising (pay-per-click advertising) An advertiser's listing is placed within or alongside search results in exchange for paying a fee each time someone clicks on the listing.

DISPLAY ADVERTISING (BANNERS AND RICH MEDIA)

Display advertising includes **banner ads** in a variety of sizes. Advertisers place banner ads on websites of interest to the target audience (users target content). A banner ad appears similar to an ad on an outdoor board or even a print ad with a limited amount of copy. Not much copy can be included in a banner. The combination of brand name, short message, and visual must convince the user to click on the ad, which links to another website.

banner Online, a graphic advertising image (usually horizontal or vertical in shape) that appears on a webpage.

The industry, through the Interactive Advertising Bureau (IAB), has established standard ad sizes based on width and height in pixels in order to make the planning and buying of online ads more efficient. Refer to Figure 7.7 for an illustration of the four ad sizes established in the initial standardization phase.

- **Rectangle Ad:** A box-style ad (180 × 150 pixels) that offers more depth than a standard-sized banner.
- **Big box:** A large rectangle (300 × 250 pixels) that offers greater width and depth to an ad.
- **Leaderboard (Super Banner):** An ad that stretches across the entire top of a webpage (728 × 90 pixels).
- **Skyscraper:** A tall, slim, oblong-shaped ad that appears at the side of a webpage (160 × 600 pixels).

rectangle ad A large ad, slightly wider than it is tall, on a webpage.

big box An online ad shaped like a large rectangle that offers greater width and depth to an ad.

leaderboard (super banner) An ad that stretches across the entire top of a webpage.

skyscraper A vertical, box-shaped ad that appears on a webpage.

Advertising research conducted by the IAB has concluded that larger formats, which are naturally more visible and provide more creative freedom, are more effective than smaller, standard-sized banners across all campaigns. Because of their size and better performance, they command a higher price. Cost must be factored into the equation when an advertiser decides to use online advertising. The average click rate for a banner ad is now 0.09 percent, meaning only one person in a thousand actually clicks on an ad, even though the ad, by its presence on the page, made an impression on the person. Low click rates are worrisome to advertisers, and, as a result, they are migrating toward video

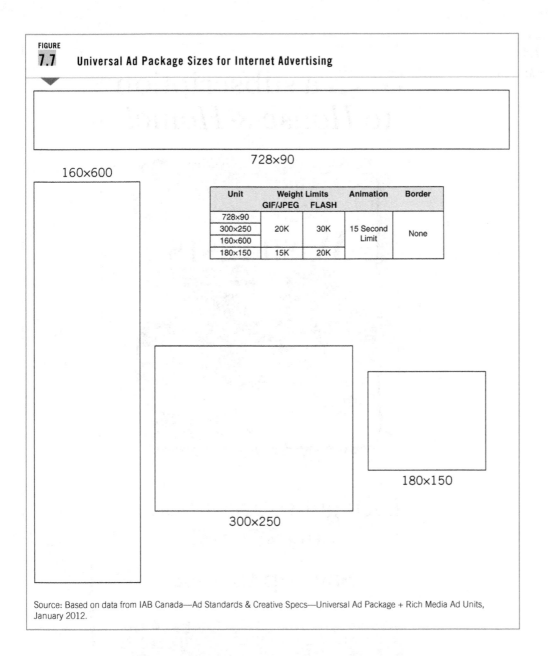

Source: Based on data from IAB Canada—Ad Standards & Creative Specs—Universal Ad Package + Rich Media Ad Units, January 2012.

advertising (a TV-style of advertising online) and online sponsorships as a means of reaching their target market more effectively. An example of a skyscraper banner ad appears in Figure 7.8.

Rich media are banner ads that include animation, sound, video, and interactivity. There are several inside-the-banner rich media options. An *expandable banner* employs multiple panels that are launched when the banner is clicked on. A *video strip* shows a strip of video in the banner space that, when clicked on, expands to reveal the video and audio in a full-sized panel. A *push down banner* slides advertising out of the way to reveal additional content rather than covering it up.

There are also some outside-the-banner options. A *floating ad* moves within a transparent layer over the page and plays within a specific area of the page. A *window ad* downloads itself immediately and plays instantly when a page is loading. A *wallpaper ad* is a large image that replaces the web background. Such a variety of styles can grab the viewer's attention in different ways. They can also irritate the viewer if they are too intrusive.

rich media   A form of online communication that includes animation, sound, video, and interactivity.

FIGURE
7.8

A Skyscraper Banner Ad

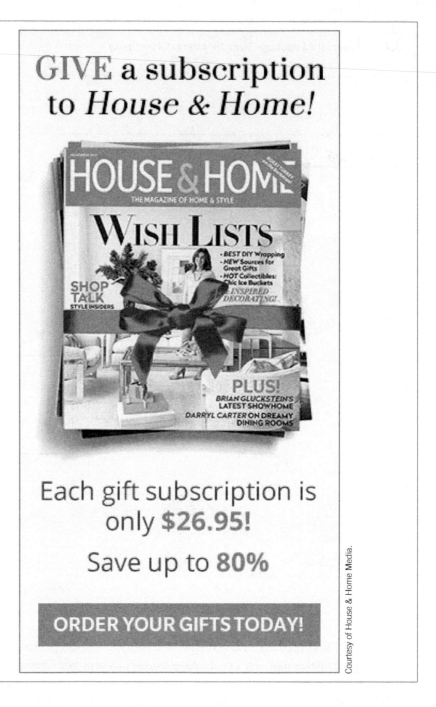

Consumer response to rich media banners is much better than static banners. Presently, the average click rate for a rich media banner is 0.27 percent meaning that almost three people click on the ad for every 1000 impressions.[7]

VIDEO ADVERTISING

Video advertising is the fastest growing option in online advertising. Advertisers are comfortable with online video ads because they are similar to television advertising. They offer the opportunity to connect with consumers on an emotional level. Now that more television shows and news and sports highlights are streamed online, there are some

Courtesy of House & Home Media.

good opportunities for advertisers. Streamed video content includes commercial breaks! The CTV Network offers popular shows from its main network on CTV.ca as well as many of its cable channels that include TSN, Comedy Network, MTV, Discovery, and Bravo, among others.

Production companies such as House & Home Media also stream their shows online or produce specific video content for online viewing. Having such content available reflects the on-demand nature of the present television market. Refer to Figure 7.9.

Video ads are delivered by a process called streaming. **Streaming** involves continuous delivery of small packets of compressed data that are interpreted by a software player and displayed as full-motion video. Having shows available online is a reflection of the on-demand nature of the present television market. People want to watch shows when and where they choose rather than abide by preplanned network schedules. Online shows include video ads. **Pre-roll ads** refer to ads at the start of a video, **mid-roll ads** refer to ads placed during the video, and **post-roll ads** appear after the video. When TV-style ads are embedded in programs or on news and sports highlight clips, it ensures an ad is viewed. In order to view the desired video content, viewers have no choice but to view the ads as well.

Advertisers have the option of creating unique video content for online consumption or showing the same commercials they show on television. At one time unique content was the preferred option, but consumers have gradually adapted their thinking and recognize the Internet as another mass medium. They expect advertising, so they are more receptive to ads that resemble television commercials. From the advertisers' perspective, being able to deliver the same message in all media offers greater impact and reflects a well-planned integrated communications effort. Showing the same message in different media also reduces production costs for advertisers.

streaming   Audio or video delivered online in small, compressed packets of data that are interpreted by a software player as they are received.

pre-roll ad   An ad placed at the start of a video.

mid-roll ad   An ad placed during a video.

post-roll ad   An ad that appears after the video.

SPONSORSHIPS

An **online sponsorship** is a commitment to advertise on a third-party website for an extended period. Advertisers are attracted to sponsorships on the basis of web content. If the content of a site is particularly interesting to an advertiser's target market, visitors are

online sponsorship   A commitment to advertise on a third-party website for an extended period.

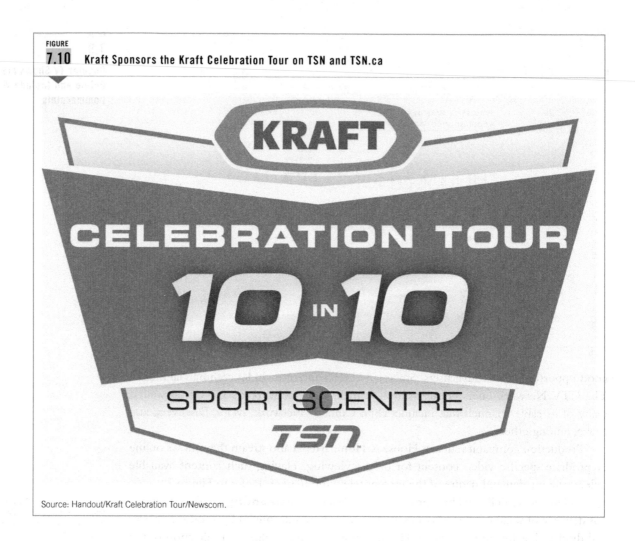

Source: Handout/Kraft Celebration Tour/Newscom.

FIGURE 7.10 Kraft Sponsors the Kraft Celebration Tour on TSN and TSN.ca

apt to visit the site frequently. For example, investors in the stock market frequently visit BNN.ca, which broadcasts business news online, and sports junkies frequently visit TSN.ca. Brands that are closely linked to the content of these networks pursue sponsorships. TSN, for example, runs various sports contests during the year. Kraft Canada sponsors the annual Kraft Celebration Tour on TSN and TSN.ca. Each year, Kraft and TSN go on the road to visit 10 towns in 10 days. A TSN live sportscast and numerous community events occur in each town. The winning communities, as voted by the public, each receive $25 000 to upgrade local sports facilities. Refer to Figure 7.10.

In sponsorship arrangements such as these, the sponsor benefits from the popularity of the website and the traffic it draws (high reach and frequency). TSN is one of the busiest websites in Canada and is a key site for reaching young males who visit regularly. Consumers trust the sites they visit frequently, so a brand associated with the site through a sponsorship could be perceived more positively. The Kraft sponsorship on TSN.ca described in the previous paragraph, demonstrates this principle.

EMAIL ADVERTISING

One of the most promising applications in online advertising is permission-based email. **Permission-based email** is sent to recipients who agree to receive information in that form. In other words, people actively subscribe to the email service. This form of

permission-based email   Email sent to recipients who have agreed to accept email advertising messages.

advertising is relatively inexpensive, response rates are high and easy to measure, and it is targeted at people who want information about certain goods and services. An offshoot of email advertising is sponsored email. With **sponsored email**, the email includes a short message from a sponsor along with a link to the sponsor's website.

Email is an attractive opportunity for businesses of all sizes. It is less expensive than direct mail, and allows for greater frequency of distribution and an incredible level of customization. Email also delivers good return on investment. Email typically costs a marketer a fraction of a cent to send, and, when compared to other online advertising formats, delivers a good return. It can be an efficient method of delivering new product information and information about promotional offers.

Email advertising is similar to direct mail advertising, but at the same time it is different. Email advertising programs operate from a list contained in a database and target customers specifically interested in something. This type of advertising generates higher responses, which is what attracts advertisers' attention. Unlike other forms of online advertising, sending messages by email seems quite acceptable to Internet users. Users can subscribe and unsubscribe to email lists as they wish. How often a marketer communicates with customers by email is an issue. "Many experts say there is a fine line between sending emails to customers on a consistent basis and crossing into annoyance marketing territory."[8]

Similar to direct mail, the success of an email campaign depends on the quality of the list. The lists are called **opt-in lists**, an appropriate name because consumers agree to have their names included. There are two kinds of opt-in lists. A *first-party list* comprises people who have specifically agreed to receive email from an organization. A *third-party list* is composed of names and addresses compiled by one company and sold to another.

Unsolicited email messages, referred to as **spam**, were a problem in the past. *Canadian Anti-Spam Legislation (CASL)* is now in effect to protect consumers from receiving unsolicited email. The legislation prohibits sending a commercial electronic message to an electronic address unless the person to whom the message is sent has consented to receive it, and the message complies with prescribed form and content requirements. This is the concept of permission-based email already described. With regard to prescribed form, the email must clearly identify the sender of the message, provide information regarding who a person can respond to, and offer an unsubscribe mechanism. The legislation includes a few exceptions. For example, the consent requirement does not apply to email that solely provides requested product or service quotes; completes an ongoing commercial transaction; involves product warranty or recall; or deals with ongoing subscriptions, memberships, or similar relationships. It should be noted that consent is implied if there is an existing business or non-business relationship.[9]

In the age of database marketing, the compilation of an in-house list is essential. Since all forms of advertising should invite people to visit a website, the site should include a section where people can sign up for email newsletters or email updates that could announce the introduction of new products. In other words, the list should comply with anti-spam legislation. Online promotions such as contests provide another opportunity to secure email addresses. Sending email to customers and prospects who specifically request the mail will almost always work better than using a rented list.

One of the key objectives of email advertising is to establish and maintain a relationship with customers, and ultimately generate sales. As shown in Figure 7.11, Staples sends email offers to customers in its database. Typically, these mailings include financial incentives to encourage customers to take action within a certain period.

sponsored email Email that includes a short message from a sponsor along with a link to the sponsor's website.

opt-in list A list of people who have agreed to receive messages via email.

spam Unsolicited email.

FIGURE
7.11

**An Incentive Communicated to
Consumers by Email to
Encourage a Purchase**

© Staples Canada, Inc.

CONTENT MARKETING: WEBSITES AND SOCIAL MEDIA

Traditional forms of advertising can tell a story but not necessarily the complete story. Therefore, traditional media combined with effective web content give an advertiser ample opportunity to tell the whole story. In any form of traditional advertising (broadcast or print) part of the message should encourage the viewer or reader to visit a website or follow a brand (company) on a social media network. The common phrase is "Follow us on Facebook, Twitter, Instagram, Google+, and LinkedIn."

Companies are creating unique video content about their products and services and posting it on their own websites or their YouTube channel and Facebook page. **Content marketing** is the marketing practice of creating and distributing relevant content to attract and engage a target audience. Unlike a television commercial where time restrictions apply, a video can be longer, offer more entertainment value, and be more creative in order to engage viewers. It is also tends to be less "sales-driven."

In order to reach a younger audience, Mercedes-Benz Canada devised an integrated campaign that included online webcasting and mobile applications. A spy-themed movie, entitled *Drive & Seek,* features a James Bond–like character and his female accomplice

content marketing   The marketing practice of creating and distributing relevant content to attract and engage a target audience

eluding police—by employing fancy driving maneuvers in a C–Class coupe—to deliver a mysterious suitcase. Viewers participate in the movie by using keyboard sequences to drive the action.[10] The mobile application included a contest that used GPS technology to guide users to one of 10 virtual briefcases in their vicinity. When they approached the briefcase, the driver would see a 3D rendering of the car espousing the latest technological advancements. The grand prize for one of the top 125 game players was a new C–Class coupe. Refer to the image in Figure 7.12.

FIGURE 7.12 A Spy-themed Web Movie Attracts a Younger, Tech-savvy Consumer to Mercedes-Benz C-Class Coupe

Source: Courtesy of Mercedes-Benz Canada Inc.

Although the number of potential viewers of video content is much lower than for a conventional television ad, the fact that viewers choose to watch it indicates the benefit of producing video content. People behave differently on the web and will watch advertising content as long as it is enjoyable and engaging. Further, it isn't necessary to camouflage the brand—people expect the brand to play a key role. The Mercedes videos demonstrate how consumers will engage with a brand, either online or through a mobile device.

Video content is ideally suited for inclusion on a company website. To illustrate, consider how much more meaningful content a manufacturer of cars can present about a new model in a 5-minute video, compared to a 30-second television commercial. On television or in print, the message focuses on image but does little in terms of telling buyers about design and technical specifications. If a potential buyer visits an automobile manufacturer's website, he or she wants detailed information and demonstrations that will influence a buying decision.

Having informative and engaging content on a website helps people do research before they make a buying decision. One study revealed that some 57 percent of consumers felt product videos made them more confident in a purchase. Further, 41 percent of consumers are more likely to share product videos than other product content.[11] In an era of marketing where consumer recommendations (word of mouth on Facebook and Twitter) are important, marketers must react accordingly and produce content that consumers are willing to share.

Organizations also establish microsites that serve unique purposes. A **microsite** is an individual webpage or series of pages that functions as a supplement to a primary website. For example, Unilever has a corporate website in which all brands have a page.

microsite An individual page or series of pages that is a supplement to a primary website.

FIGURE
7.13 Advantages and Disadvantages of Online Marketing Communications

Advantages

- **Targeting Capability**—Advertiser reaches individuals based on browsing behaviour and preferences.
- **Broad and Flexible Reach**—The online audience continues to grow in size; since ads can be bought by the impression, you can buy as much or as little of the audience as you desire.
- **Timing**—Messages can be delivered 24 hours a day, 7 days a week.
- **Interactivity**—Messages encourage consumers to interact with brands while online (performing a task, playing a game, and so on).
- **Tracking and Measurement**—Detailed information about who saw an ad, in what context, and how many times, is available immediately.
- **Transaction**—Assuming ebusiness capability at a website, an online purchase can occur.

Disadvantages

- **Low Click Rates**—Average click rates of only 1 percent are common, which significantly reduces the number of visitors to a website (the intended action).
- **Advertising Overload**—Too much advertising clutter on a webpage reduces the potential impact of any ad appearing on the page.
- **Consumer Frustration**—The barrage of unexpected banner ads frustrates consumers; advertisers must deal with their wrath.
- **Too Measurable**—A marketer can be overburdened with the amount of data available from an online advertising campaign.

However, some of their more high-profile brands have their own site. For example, Axe, a very popular grooming product line, has its own site that encourages young males to look their best. All it takes is a visit to the AXE.ca website. When Axe launched a new line of dry spray antiperspirant, a short video appeared on the website and the brand's YouTube channel. For a brand such as Axe that appeals to a youthful target, web communications are a critical component of the communications mix.

For a summary of the advantages and disadvantages of the various forms of online communications, refer to Figure 7.13.

Social Media Networks

A **social media network** connects people who share interests on a website. Social networking is a bit of a phenomenon—in a very short period it has become a fundamental aspect of the online experience. Social network sites, such as Facebook, Twitter, and YouTube, are among the most visited sites in the online world. Refer to Figure 7.14.

Canadians are married to the social web and that makes it a good advertising option for planners. In fact, Canada has the highest social media network penetration in the world. Presently, 82 percent of Canadians use a social network and 91 percent of Canadian Internet users have a social media account.[12] Facebook is the most popular followed by Twitter, Google+, and LinkedIn. However, social media usage is starting to peak. To illustrate, year-over-year usage data for Facebook in the United States show that user growth rate is slowing down. The number of unique visitors peaked at 168 million in April 2014. By April 2015 the number of unique visitors dropped to 149 million.[13] As with any product, Facebook has to find ways of remaining relevant. It must continuously offer new features to keep people coming back. This principle also applies to all other social networks.

In the context of marketing communications planning, who's online and how much time they spend there are key factors in the media strategy and media selection process. All Canadian age groups are active online, some more than others. As indicated earlier, younger Canadians spend more time online than they do watching television. The demographic profile of social media users in Canada is presented in Figure 7.15.

social media network   A social website (for example, Facebook and Twitter) that connects people who share interests.

FIGURE
7.14

Facebook Is by Far Canadians' Most Popular Social Network Destination

© REUTERS/Dado Ruvic

FIGURE
7.15   **Demographic Profile of Social Media Users in Canada**

	% respondents in each group			
	Facebook	Linkedin	Twitter	Instagram
Gender				
Female	60	25	22	18
Male	59	37	27	14
Age				
18–34	75	30	36	32
35–44	68	37	31	19
45–54	63	41	23	11
55–64	47	31	15	4
65+	32	12	9	2
Language				
French	65	23	19	16
English	58	33	26	16
Total	59	30	25	16

Note: Social Networks on which Canadians have a profile, January 2015

Source: Based on data from Forum Research, "The Forum Poll," January 6, 2015.

With businesses operating in an era of social media marketing, you would think that all companies and brands would be actively devising strategies to engage consumers on social networks. A good many marketing executives feel unprepared however. One recent study among marketing and advertising executives by The Creative Group found that 71 percent of executives feel it is "somewhat challenging" to stay abreast of social media trends.[14] Other executives expressed concerns such as what is the value of a "like," do people actively engage with brands on social networks, and what is the impact on sales?

These executives needn't look far for the answers. Another recent research study concluded that social media chatter drives consumer purchasing. Data from the study revealed that 50 percent of Canadians have made a purchase decision based on social media conversations. Millennials account for 42 percent of those influenced by network interactions. Apparently, they use social media throughout the purchase process as a source of reviews, recommendations, price and product comparisons; and to trigger ideas for things to do spontaneously.[15] So, an organization has to be either part of the conversation or not. Remaining on the social media sidelines could be damaging.

Social networks fall into two categories. Broad-based sites, such as Facebook, Twitter, and YouTube, offer an interactive, user-created network of friends, personal profiles, blogs, music, and videos. A lot of content sharing occurs on these sites. Niche sites also exist. LinkedIn is a site where business professionals can network. Pinterest lets people post pictures (on a pinboard) of things they love. Users can also browse pinboards created by other people, which can be a fun way to discover new things and to share interests.

ADAPTING TO THE SOCIAL MEDIA ENVIRONMENT

Organizations are operating in an era in which consumers have more control over marketing communications. Previously, marketers would push their communications onto consumers. In the social media era, the communications process is more participative— the goal is to get consumers talking about brands and promoting brands on behalf of the organization. This shift in control is often referred to as **brand democratization**.

Once the marketer adapts to this change and sees the benefit of allowing consumers to participate in the creation of brand content, the easier it will be to integrate social media into a marketing communications strategy. For example, if a marketer puts out a call for input based on some broad-stroke direction (for example, request that consumers submit a video and enter a contest), the public might submit some very worthy content that the marketer could use. It is often surprising what a brand enthusiast can do for a brand.

Much of the content on social media networks is created by amateurs. **Consumer-generated content** is content created by consumers for consumers. It is done without provocation, and, in many cases, presents the brand effectively. People who do this are often called "brand evangelists" or "brand advocates" and will do anything to promote their favourite brand. Visit YouTube for video examples! For many people, this type of content carries more weight than marketer-generated content.

When a company invites the public to participate in the marketing of its brands, it is employing a technique referred to as crowdsourcing. **Crowdsourcing** uses the "collective intelligence of the public at large to complete business-related tasks that a company would normally perform itself or outsource to a third-party provider (for example, an ad agency or production company)."[16] Crowdsourcing capitalizes on the vision, creativity, and enthusiasm people have for the brand.

Perhaps no brand demonstrates the principle of crowdsourcing and the power of social media better than Doritos. Each year Doritos invites the public to submit content for its "Crash the SuperBowl" contest. The winning video, as judged by public voting on the finalists, is shown during the Super Bowl. The contest has produced some of the most effective advertising during the game, despite the fact that the ads compete for attention against professionally produced ads from other brands. All of the ads from the group of finalists are posted on the Doritos website and on YouTube.

Marketers must take advantage of this shift in power. The expression "Any publicity is good publicity" applies here. If consumers can create and upload content that is viewed by millions of people, there must be some benefit for the brand. All marketing organizations must find ways to tap into this phenomenon and strategically add social media to their marketing communications arsenal. It sounds almost frightening to let consumers take charge, but consumer control is the ultimate form of engagement that consumers are searching for.

OPTIONS FOR SOCIAL NETWORK ADVERTISING AND MARKETING COMMUNICATIONS

Several advertising and marketing communications opportunities exist on social networks. Many of the online advertising options discussed earlier are available, along with some interesting brand-sponsored opportunities, such as blogs, that allow an organization to publish ongoing information about its brands.

DISPLAY ADVERTISING

Display advertising in the form of banner ads is available on social networks. Given the abundance of information that social networks collect about users, there is a significant targeting advantage available to advertisers. Sites such as Facebook and Twitter offer

brand democratization A concept that states consumers are now in charge of brand marketing (because of the amount of consumer-generated content produced and distributed online) rather than brand marketers being in control.

consumer-generated content Online content, often brand oriented, that is created by consumers for consumers.

crowdsourcing A technique that uses the collective intelligence of the public at large to complete business-related tasks a company would normally perform itself or outsource to a third-party provider.

a sophisticated demographic filtering process that can be combined with behavioural data collected about individual users. For example, if an advertiser wants to reach females 35 to 49 years old who are interested in home decorating and renovations, that target request could be entered into the Facebook database. The advertiser would know the approximate number of women fitting the profile and plan a campaign to reach them.

Click rates on a site such as Facebook are low. One recent study observed that an average click rate for display ads at 0.4 percent on Facebook, about half that for display ads across the Web.[17] Low click rates are causing advertisers to look at other marketing communications options on social networks.

SPONSORED (SUGGESTED) POSTS IN A NEWS FEED

sponsored post An advertisement delivered to a social media user's news feed based on the interests they express on social media; the ad may be presented as a suggestion.

Appearing much like news from friends, a **sponsored post** ad appears within an individual's news feed. The ads contain a minimum amount of copy and rely heavily on a visual image to attract a person's attention. People receive these ads as "suggestions" based on their online behaviour (for example, the interests they express and the activities they associate with) or because the person fits a demographic profile an advertiser wishes to reach. An illustration of a sponsored post appears in Figure 7.16. The average click rate for a sponsored post on Facebook is 2.09 percent, significantly better than display ads across the Web. In a social media environment, a person will share sponsored posts that they like with their friends. Sharing expands the reach of the advertiser's message.

Sponsored posts on Twitter are called promoted tweets. They are available in a variety of sizes and typically include body copy (to a prescribed limit) and a small visual image (square or rectangular). For advertisers, a popular option is the product card that allows users to share information, product photos, and video content directly through tweets. The images will help an ad to stand out in a sea of text on a Twitter stream and increase the likelihood that customers will click on and retweet an advertiser's post.

Mazda Canada recently used targeted promoted tweets to encourage potential car buyers to take a test drive. The brand launched two lead-generating campaigns (a trial campaign and a follow-up) that took advantage of the many conversations on Twitter revolving around automobiles. Promoted tweets targeted users talking about comparable vehicles. Mazda's message focused on the superior capabilities of its vehicles and offered a strong call to action to encourage a test drive. The targeting and tracking capabilities on Twitter allowed Mazda to trace leads from the corporate level right down to the showroom floor.[18]

Sponsored posts and promoted tweets on Facebook and Twitter do not seem to interfere with how people engage with a feed.

FIGURE 7.16

Sponsored Posts on Facebook Appear Within a Person's News Feed

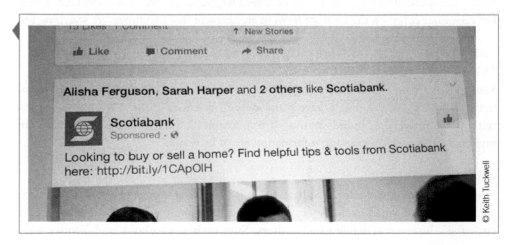

VIDEO ADS

Video ads are the fastest growing advertising alternative online in general and in social media in particular. Facebook recently introduced a new ad unit called "premium video," a 15-second ad that starts playing automatically as a user scrolls past it in their news feed. The ads play without sound until a person pauses on the ad. If the person taps on the ad it will fill the full screen and the sound starts. Since 15-second television commercials are now popular with advertisers, they now have another medium on which to play them.

BRAND PAGE (FAN PAGE)

Marketers can create their own page on Facebook that users choose to join. Users who click on a brand's like button become members of the brand's fan page. Contests or other forms of incentives motivate fans to visit the page, resulting in an expanded base that can be used for future marketing programs.

The value of a "like" is often questioned by advertisers. Presently, many marketers equate social media success to the number of likes they have, and they implement programs to build their number of likes. However the value of a like remains elusive. Apparently, only 5 percent of people who "like" a brand go back to that brand page.[19] A prudent marketer must shift his or her way of thinking and devise strategies that give "engagement" a priority over "likes."

Engaging people with a brand in social media is a challenge. Certain motivation (for example, offering incentives and deals) delivered by sponsored posts and other media are required, as well as the constant updating of the content on the fan page. Updating the fan page requires a commitment in time and financial resources, which is a necessary regular budget allocation. Simply put, if the marketer's goal is to engage consumers with the brand, the marketer must also be more engaged by continuously providing fresh content—it's a two-way, participative form of communication.

COMPANY BLOGS

A **blog** is a website where journal entries are posted on a regular basis and displayed in reverse chronological order. Blogs provide commentary on news or particular subject areas of interest—politics, food, fashion, even marketing-related material! A blog can include text, images, video, and links to other blogs.

blog   A frequent, chronological publication of personal thoughts at a website.

A company blog is proving to be an effective means of presenting relevant information in a positive manner. It gives an organization an opportunity to be part of the discussion on matters that are important to customers. People read blogs because they are interested in the content. A blog allows an organization to communicate with customers in a more relaxed way. With a blog, a brand has an opportunity to develop an online personality that goes beyond what can be accomplished in traditional media communications. Most company blogs are not written to sell products or services, but to provide useful information that can indirectly influence a purchase decision.

YOUTUBE CHANNELS

Everyone views video content on YouTube, don't they? With that in mind, doesn't it make sense for an organization to have its own YouTube channel, where it can show some dazzling videos about its brands? On YouTube, a channel is the word used for a user's profile. Other users can access a channel/profile to find out what videos have been uploaded. You can also subscribe to a user's profile and be notified when that user uploads new videos to the site.[20]

The principle just described can certainly apply to a company and its brands. Axe, a very popular brand of male grooming products, is all over social media and recently launched a dedicated channel on YouTube: www.youtube.com/AXECanada. Similar to Axe communications in other media, the YouTube channel offers a highly sexualized perspective on topics of male interest. According to Shelley Brown, president and CEO of CP+B (Axe's ad agency), "Axe is a brand that, as it moves through social space, needs to stay very relevant, very fresh. It needs to be in a state of continual renewal."[21]

VIRAL MARKETING AND SOCIAL MEDIA COMMUNICATIONS

Successful campaigns in social media can be measured by how people engage with a brand and share information with friends. Sharing information introduces the concept of viral marketing. **Viral marketing** is a strategy that encourages individuals to pass along information to others, creating the potential for exponential growth in the message's exposure and influence.

An organization can't plan a viral campaign; the receivers of the message determine if a campaign goes viral. One of the most talked about campaigns that did go viral was Old Spice's "The Man Your Man Could Smell Like" campaign. The videos featured the rather handsome actor Isaiah Mustafa. The original videos were viewed 36 million times and the final video in the series was viewed 23 million times in 36 hours—that's viral! Why the Old Spice campaign took off remains a mystery but the entertainment value apparently broke through the clutter of competitive advertising. Offline, the campaign garnered much publicity, all of which benefited the brand. This campaign illustrates that "brands don't make viral videos, users make videos go viral"[22]

KEY BENEFITS OF SOCIAL MEDIA MARKETING COMMUNICATIONS

There are several key benefits available for a marketing organization that engages in social media communications. From a targeting perspective, all age groups are engaged with social networks. Some 91 percent of Internet users have a social media account and those users embrace all age groups. Therefore, social media is an ideal complementary medium in the marketing communications mix. More specifically, given the media consumption behaviour of people under the age of 35, social media is an essential medium to include.

One of the most potent forms of influence on brand decisions is *word-of-mouth*, a situation that marketers have no control over. As demonstrated earlier, a significant amount of word-of-mouth happens among friends on social networks. Perhaps the primary benefit is an intangible one—the fact that consumers willingly engage with brands. While such engagement may not produce an immediate sale, it is part of the relationship-building process that could produce a sale later on.

A survey of U.S. marketing executives revealed that customer *engagement* with a brand is the single most important benefit of advertising on social media. Engagement is an essential element of the relationship-building process that has an indirect impact on sales. As well, the ability to communicate with customers provides quick insights about how people feel about the brand that can be used to modify marketing strategies.

Despite these benefits, many companies are reluctant to invest in social media communications. The *absence of sound metrics* (beyond click rates) to determine return on investment is a stumbling block. Despite the abundance of available analytical information (for example, reach, clicks, time spent, and so on) marketers are looking for

Social Media Gives Stratford Festival a Boost

One of the keys to success for any annual event such as the Stratford Festival is attracting former patrons back to the theatre. You need the combination of current patrons and new patrons to fill the seats. Many people attend a play or two, enjoy the experience tremendously, but don't return. The Festival needed a new marketing communications strategy to reach out to lapsed and new patrons.

The Festival had never used the targeting capabilities of Facebook before so a plan was hatched to enter social media. Facebook's audience insight tools allow advertisers to target sponsored posts to users based on interests, liked pages, and attended events. Being able to target people who like theatre productions was a real attraction.

The impact of the campaign was easy to measure since Stratford's advertising budget did not change from the previous year—the only change was the addition of social media. The results were significant: a three-fold increase in the number of tickets sold, revenue generated, and sales, specifically to new and lapsed patrons. Anita Gaffney, the executive director of the Festival commented that it was a bigger return on its dollar than ever before and attributed the success to the targeted advertising.

Direct mail had always been the backbone of the festival's marketing effort. The inclusion of targeted social media was a natural extension of the direct mail effort. Stratford had a lot of insight into the interests and habits of its audience and provided very accurate profiles to the audience insight tool at Facebook. Stratford also has a Facebook page to generate discussion about the festival's productions and answer questions from patrons.

The plan for the future is to include more targeted social media communications in a bigger way. Both direct mail and social media allow Stratford to measure results and evaluate its return on investment—a key benefit of both media.

© Stratford Festival

Based on Josh Kolm, "The Verdict: Much Ado About Facebook Targeting," *Media in Canada*, August 21, 2014, www.mediaincanada.com/2014/08/21/the-verdict-much-ado-about-facebook-targeting

something more tangible such as a link to sales performance. Embarking on a social media program requires ***time and financial commitment***. Information must be constantly refreshed if an organization expects a consumer to engage with a brand for an extended period. Out-of-date information could ultimately have a negative impact on how consumers perceive a brand.

Staying abreast of social media trends poses a challenge for marketing executives. Erich Marx, director of interactive and social media at Nissan, puts social media communications into perspective for modern-day advertisers effectively. He says, "From an ROI standpoint, are we selling hundreds of cars through social? No. But, you have to be there. It's not about ROI, it's about COI—cost of ignoring. It's too big to ignore."[23]

Social media advertising played a key role in improving ticket sales for the Stratford Festival. For insight into its campaign, read the IMC Highlight: **Social Media Gives Stratford Festival a Boost.**

Mobile Communications

The screen is small, the audience's attention span is short, and the environment—a park bench or a busy subway station—is variable. Yet the possibilities of mobile marketing are capturing the attention of advertisers. Data from 2013 indicate there are 28.4 million wireless phone subscribers in Canada and that smartphone penetration has reached 73 percent. Further, six in 10 Canadians access the Internet via a mobile device.[24]

Generally speaking, Canadians are emotionally attached to their phones (check your own behaviour)—79 percent of people don't leave home without it![25] Such behaviour suggests the need to include mobile in the marketing communications mix. It is an ideal medium for reaching people on the go with advertising messages.

Mobile advertising revenue has surged in Canada in the past few years. As of 2014, mobile advertising revenue (including on tablets) reached $903 million and accounted for 24 percent of Internet advertising revenue.[26] Only four years earlier, mobile generated only $82 million in revenue. Factors such as the penetration of smartphones, the ability to offer location-based messages, and consumers' willingness to make online transactions have attracted mobile-minded advertisers. Leading the way are packaged goods companies, retailers, telecommunications, and automotive companies.

Earlier in the chapter, the issue of time spent with the media was discussed. It is a critical factor to consider when developing a media plan. Data from 2014 reveal that Canadians spend 2.5 hours a day with their mobile device (phone or tablet) and 80 percent of their mobile time is on an app.[27] These data confirm the need for an advertiser to consider advertising in social media applications such as Facebook, Twitter, YouTube, and so on. Facebook reported that mobile ads now account for 61 percent of its revenue.[28]

MOBILE MARKETING COMMUNICATIONS OPPORTUNITIES

Advertising on mobile devices is similar to Internet advertising only the ads are smaller. Many of the same advertising options are available, including text messaging, banner ads, and video. Each of these formats is deliverable directly to a smartphone or tablet. The ads will appear when a person visits a website or when using an application such as Facebook, Twitter, or Instagram. Similar to the Internet on a laptop or desktop computer, mobile advertising messages can be delivered to consumers in a highly targeted manner.

Targeting is a key element of mobile communications. Through mobile media, an advertiser can reach targets wherever they are at any time—a concept referred to as location-based targeting. Essentially, a person's location information (available through GPS chips in smartphones) is factored into a marketing communications effort. Let's assume that a fast-food restaurant such as Dairy Queen or A&W knows where you are; they can instantly send you an incentive (coupon) to encourage you to visit a nearby location.

Let's examine the primary means of communicating with consumers through mobile media.

TEXT MESSAGING

text messaging The transmission of short text-only messages via cell phone.

Text messaging refers to the transmission of text-only messages. The popularity of so-called smartphones has allowed text messaging to emerge as a popular communications tool. Believe it or not, Canadians send 270 million text messages a day.[29] Texting is popular because of its speed, portability, and low cost.

Marketers interested in reaching younger targets are experimenting with text messaging, running promotions that include "call to action" short codes. Codes are usually mentioned in other media used to create awareness for the promotion. Scotiabank entered the cell phone arena successfully. Its initial effort was a contest in support of the bank's sponsorship of the Canadian Football League. Contest entrants earned the chance to win a VIP Grey Cup Experience and a selection of secondary prizes. The objectives of the promotion were to encourage participation, broaden reach beyond that of traditional media channels, and drive the brand's association with the sponsorship among consumers. The campaign was a multimedia effort with web, email, online media, TV, stadium advertising, and mobile components. A full 20 percent of all entries were through the text short code "Scotia" (726842). The mobile component helped make the contest a success.[30]

Marketers must consider some potential drawbacks of a text message strategy. If the messages are too intrusive, they could be perceived much like a telemarketing call and have a negative impact on brand image. Further, wireless companies must be careful about renting their databases to commercial interests without their customers having opted in. Opt-in means customers agree to allow calls or messages to be sent to them.

DISPLAY ADVERTISING (BANNER ADS)

Banner ads very similar to those displayed on a computer screen can also be sent to mobile communication devices. A standard banner ad (320 × 50 pixels) usually appears at the top of bottom of a mobile screen. Due to the size of the ad and absence of meaningful content, click rates for them are quite low. For strong brands such as RBC Financial or BMO that simply want to leave a brand impression the standard banner works well. No additional information is needed.

A graphical banner can appear in a variety of settings and be of different shapes and sizes. For example, it can appear in the middle of a news article a person is reading—a box-like format is most common. A person can scroll by the ad, which counts as an impression, or click on the ad for more information. A graphical banner can also take up an entire screen. With more space available, additional content can be added, there can be a clearer call to action, and the creative can be more sophisticated, perhaps aided by the addition of animation. Refer to the image in Figure 7.17.

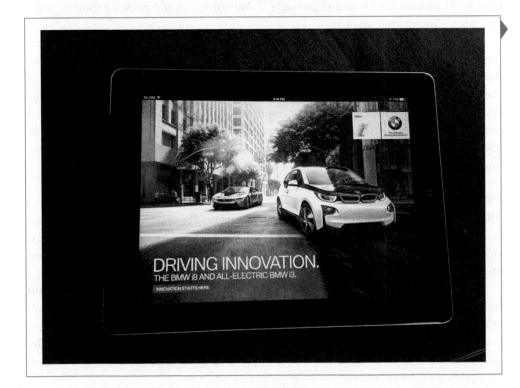

FIGURE

7.17

This Ad Occupies The Full Screen as the Reader Scrolls Down

Source: Keith Tuckwell

VIDEO ADS

Video is the fastest growing form of mobile advertising and for good reason. People are watching long-form video content on their mobile phones—in fact, some 41 percent of all video viewing occurs on a smartphone.[31] Viewing embraces streamed television shows, news and sports highlights, sports events, and YouTube videos. (It's ironic that these same consumers want the largest flat screen television in their family room.)

The sweet spot for mobile users is the 15- to 29-year-old age category, but the industry is growing across all demographics. Teens and young adults have grown up with technology. Mobile phones are ubiquitous among teens and are becoming popular with younger kids. These consumers will carry their mobile behaviour forward, and it will have a dramatic impact on how they learn about and buy products. Some research reveals that consumers are receptive to video advertising; they are willing to sit through ads in order to access the content they want if it means saving a few dollars. The Interactive Advertising Bureau (IAB) found that 78 percent of respondents in a survey would rather watch free mobile videos with ads, while only 15 percent would rather pay a monthly mobile video subscription fee with no ads.[32]

Mobile devices are helping reshape Canadians' shopping behavior. People use their phones much like a shopping assistant to research products, check product availability and prices, and send product information to friends. A 2013 study found that about three-quarters (75 percent) of respondents had searched for a product on their phones, and that 27 percent had made an online purchase using their devices.[33] With the burgeoning addition of mobile payment options, it certainly makes sense to ad mobile advertising to the marketing communications mix.

It can be costly to produce a 15- or 30-second video advertisement. To save money, brands that advertise on television will often show the same commercial on a mobile device. This tactic is questionable since mobile users prefer shorter messages. A 2014 study observed that Canadians are more attentive to shorter ads and exhibit a 98 percent completion rate for messages that are 7- to 10-seconds long. The completion rate plummets to 37 percent for 15-second messages.[34] Advertisers should consider shorter, snappier ads to deliver their message.

Are mobile ads effective? Recent research indicates that mobile ads are outperforming standard banners on the Internet. Different sources publish different click rates but the average for mobile ads is in the range of 0.38 to 0.41 percent. Ads on tablets have an average click rate of 0.59 percent.[35] These click rates are higher than those on a laptop or desktop computer. The emotional connection people have with their phones combined with higher click rates (user participation with mobile ads) clearly indicates that mobile advertising is, and will continue to be, a worthwhile component of a marketing communications campaign. For additional insight see Figure 7.18.

MOBILE APPLICATIONS

All smartphone suppliers, such as Apple and Google, offer applications that encourage in-application advertising. Within an application an advertiser can have a full-screen video ad or select from less intrusive forms of advertising. The number of apps available on the market is mind boggling—Google has 1 500 000 and Apple 1 400 000.

Although placing ads on popular social media apps such as Facebook, Twitter, and Instagram may be easy decisions, given so much choice, how does a planner select which other apps to place ads on? One possible planning option is to simply follow a target market's media consumption behaviour. For example, people are reading less print media and seeking their news, sports, and weather information through an app. A good many

FIGURE

7.18   Mobile Communications Have an Impact on Consumers

Mobile devices are becoming the device of choice among consumers. They are used to gather product information, make purchases, and conduct transactions. Here are some interesting facts on mobile device usage and impact:

- 17.8 million Canadians (50.2% of the population) used a smartphone in 2014
- Among 18- to 34-year-olds, 80% have a smartphone
- 81% of consumers say they research products via smartphone before visiting a store
- 73% of consumers say they engage with mobile ads before visiting a store
- 72% of consumers say they research goods via mobile; 23% buy their goods via mobile
- 70% of consumers say they have tried a new packaged good after seeing a mobile ad

These survey results suggest marketers would be well advised to ensure their brands deliver a high quality mobile media experience to consumers. Mobile will continue to grow in importance in the marketing communications mix.

Source: Based on Jeff Fraser, "Half of Canadians used smartphones last year," *Marketing*, January 5, 2015, www.marketingmag.ca and "Mobile's Impact on the Path to Purchase," April 23, 2015, http://www.pymnts.com/in-depth/2015/mobiles-impact-on-path-to-purchase.

former *Globe and Mail* readers (of the print edition) now get their information through the *Globe and Mail* app. Luxury automobile advertisers who follow a target market matching strategy have always advertised in the *Globe and Mail*. Given readership trends, brands such as BMW and Mercedes-Benz have transferred dollars to the *Globe and Mail* digital edition. Refer to the illustration in Figure 7.17.

Some companies are developing their own applications that perform some essential tasks for consumers who use them. Tim Hortons has an app called Timmy Run. The application allows users to take orders for up to 20 people. It makes the run easier and more convenient for those who volunteer on behalf of friends and colleagues. Logistically, when a member of a group initiates a run, everyone in the group is notified and given a specified period of time to opt-in. When the time is up, the runner is notified of the order, which is compiled on one list. The runner can pay for the order through his or her mobile device.[36]

Media companies such as Rogers and Bell have applications for their more popular media outlets on television and radio. These apps allow users to view live and on-demand video content on their mobile devices. Regular, scheduled programs are available to mobile users. Bell Media offers a TV app and a Fibe TV app that accommodates program downloads through an in-home wifi system. Program streaming from networks such as CTV, CBC, TSN, HBO, AMC, and Crave TV is available. The applications give advertisers the ability to reach consumers on a greater variety of platforms—online, tablet, and mobile. Pre-roll and mid-roll video ads are sold to advertisers. Refer to the image in Figure 7.19.

QR CODES

A **quick response (QR) code** is a two-dimensional barcode that can be scanned and read by smartphones. Made up of small squares in black and white patterns, the code allows for sharing of text and data. To read the code, a person needs to download a QR code reader, available at various app stores (for example, Tag Reader for an iPhone).

To secure information, a user takes a picture of a code and is then linked to a website, a phone number, or perhaps a YouTube video that offers more information

quick response (QR) code   A two-dimensional barcode that can be scanned and read by smartphones to allow sharing of text and data.

FIGURE
7.19

Television Apps Allow Program
Viewing On-Demand

about a product or service. The process sounds simple, but thus far consumers seem reluctant to use the codes. One U.S. study revealed that only 21 percent of smartphone owners ever scanned a code. Many experts believe low usage is attributed to poor communications with consumers on how to use them. Marketers have a different view. A recent study among marketing executives revealed that 66 percent of the respondents felt they were effective.[37]

So far, Canadian advertisers have enjoyed mixed results using the codes; their effectiveness in stimulating interest and ultimately a desired action is yet to be proven. The gap between consumers' acceptance of the technology and marketers' belief that they are a useful tactic has to be narrowed before any significant results can be achieved. Assuming the gap can be narrowed, QR codes offer an important benefit: they can communicate additional information to consumers in a cost-efficient manner and when customers snap the picture, they are instantly engaged with the brand. Refer to the illustration in Figure 7.20.

Video Game Advertising

The video game industry is huge. In 2014, industry sales in the United States reached $15 billion. The emergence of online games has produced a significant revenue generator for the games industry. Advertising in video games refers to the placement of ads in commercially sold games or in games played online or on mobile devices.

The notion that video games are male (especially young male)-dominated initially restricted the level of interest in the medium by marketing organizations. However, new data suggest that video games are growing in popularity across genders and all age categories. The average gamer today is 34 years old, and 40 percent of gamers are women.[38] Games are now an accepted form of family and adult entertainment. This information is an important targeting consideration for a media planner.

From a planning perspective, integrating a brand into games helps achieve several objectives: It can generate positive brand awareness and higher brand preference ratings, as well as help stimulate purchases. The tactic is seen as more effective than product placements on TV shows, mainly due to the intensity of the behaviour while gamers are playing—they see and recall the brand messages!

FIGURE
7.20   **A QR Code Can Communicate More Detailed Information about a Product**

Banking solutions as unique as your business.

BMO® Business Bundles – simple, flexible solutions designed for businesses like yours.

We'll help you take care of your finances, so you can focus on running your business smoothly. Customize a bundle that's right for you and enjoy 6 months of FREE business banking¹. Talk to your BMO representative and learn how you can also receive 6 months of FREE personal banking² by adding a BMO Personal Bundle.

Let's talk about your business. Make an appointment today.
Call 1-877-818-0339, or visit bmobundles.ca

Scan for more details.

BMO ⬥ Bank of Montreal

Making money make sense®

¹"Free business banking" is defined as the Everyday Banking for Business Plan fee being waived for 6 months. The customer is responsible for all fees of any transactions, services and products not included in the business bank plan. Promotion runs from September 1 to December 31, 2012. ²"Free personal banking" is defined as the monthly Everyday Banking for Personal Plan fee being waived for 6 months. The customer is responsible for all fees of any transactions, services and products not included in the personal banking plan. Promotion runs from September 1 to December 31, 2012. ®Registered trade-marks of Bank of Montreal.

Source: Courtesy of BMO Bank of Montreal. Used with permission.

ADVERTISING OPPORTUNITIES IN VIDEO GAMES

There are several kinds of advertising opportunities in video games. Generally, placement opportunities are classified as around-game, in-game, and advergames. Let's briefly describe each option:

- **Around Game Ads** These ads are displayed in conjunction with or alongside a game. Typically they appear as a banner, digital video, or downloadable content on a console system. The ads are delivered before and after the game.

- **In-Game Ads** These ads are either described as *environment ads* or *immersive ads*. Environment ads are branded displays within the game that a player sees but can't interact with (for example, a branded billboard ad or storefront); immersive ads invite the player to take some action (for example, a branded automobile is driven by a game character).

- **Advergames** Advergames are structured entirely around a specific brand and act as de-facto ads in themselves. A branded message is blended with a fun, interactive gaming experience.

An advertiser has the option of placing ads in commercially sold games and games available online or by creating its own branded game. In commercially sold games and online games, there is a diverse range of possibilities, including fully integrated opportunities (having a game designed around a brand or brands), interactive product placements, outdoor-style billboards, and 30-second video spots. Refer to Figure 7.21. Many brands have developed their own games for visitors to play at their website. Such games promote interactivity and offer good entertainment value—things people are looking for when they visit a website.

IMPACT OF VIDEO GAME ADVERTISING

Gamers do not seem to mind the presence of ads. In fact, they expect to see ads, and are receptive to their presence. A study conducted by IGA Worldwide (a game vendor) discovered 70 percent of respondents felt that the ads made them feel better about the brands. Further, brands running ads in games experienced an average 44 percent increase in brand recall among consumers, when compared to awareness prior to seeing the brand in the game.[39]

Another study released by Nielsen Entertainment on behalf of Microsoft-owned in-game advertising specialist Massive Inc., showed that average brand familiarity increased by 64 percent due to in-game advertising; average purchase consideration increased by 41 percent, and average recall scores increased by 41 percent.[40] Statistics such as these are attractive to potential advertisers. However, the video game market is very fragmented and difficult for advertisers to navigate. Determining the best opportunities to pursue remains a puzzle for many marketing organizations.

FIGURE
7.21

Ads in Video Games Offer Players a Sense of Reality

© Chris Ratcliffe/Bloomberg via Getty Images

SUMMARY

The Internet is the largest advertising medium in Canada. With all age groups online, advertisers have shifted a significant portion of their advertising budgets to digital media and away from traditional media such as print and broadcast. With the younger generation of consumers being avid users of technology, there is little doubt that digital media will play a more dominant role in the future.

Internet penetration continues to rise. Canada ranks second in the world in Internet usage. Canadians are spending more time online than any other country; overall the Internet ranks second only to television in time spent with the media. Canadians under the age of 35 spend more time with the Internet than with television. The interactive nature of the medium allows a brand to engage consumers and create deeper brand experiences. The challenge for advertisers is to create useful and entertaining messages that will capture the imagination of Internet users who want to be entertained.

Marketers raise two key concerns about online advertising: viewability and click fraud. Fewer than half of the ads appearing in view are actually seen and non-humans (bots) are clicking on ads to produce unnecessary advertising charges that advertisers must pay. With these issues in mind, marketers question the effectiveness and efficiency of the medium.

The Internet is a medium that allows marketers to target customers on the basis of demographics, geographics, and behaviour. Of particular interest to advertisers is the concept of behaviour targeting. By tracking preferences, unique messages are delivered to consumers on an individual basis. As well, there is the capability to design unique products for customers, a concept referred to as mass customization.

Interactive marketing communications refers to the placement of an advertising message on a website in a variety of formats. The messages are communicated by computer, smartphone, tablet, smart TV, and video games. Advertising online plays a key role in achieving specific marketing objectives. It helps create brand awareness for the launch of new products, is an excellent medium for building and enhancing brand image, and is a good medium for distributing buying incentives. In a business-to-business context, online advertising is a means of generating leads and completing transactions.

There are a variety of advertising alternatives to choose from. Among the options are search advertising, banner ads in static and rich media formats, video ads, sponsorships at other websites, email ads, and unique video content for the Web. Video ads are growing in popularity mainly due to their similarity to television ads. Permission-based email is also growing in popularity. Using lists generated from in-house databases or from other sources (rented lists), email advertising represents a cost-efficient way to reach prospects and current customers. Beyond these advertising options, companies also use company and brand websites to communicate detailed information.

As an advertising medium, the Internet provides targeting capability at a very reasonable cost and also offers tracking capabilities that measure effectiveness in a variety of ways (for example, impressions, clicks, clickthrough rates, leads, and purchases). It is also a 24/7 medium, offering ample opportunity for brand and company exposure and engagement with consumers. Some drawbacks of the Internet include low click rates for ads and advertising overload (the sheer number of ads that may appear on a webpage).

Canadians are married to the social web. All age groups are involved with social media. Many advertisers have enjoyed much success with social media communications campaigns while others have struggled to find the right formula. Marketing executives say it is challenging just to stay abreast of the changes that are occurring in the social media environment, and claim that their lack of knowledge is what's holding them back. Nonetheless, people are spending considerable time with social media, so advertisers must be there.

In the social media era, the communications process is more participatory, a situation that advertisers must adapt to. The goal is to get consumers talking about the brands and promoting the brands on behalf of the organization. Advertisers must also understand that control of the message is in the hands of consumers in social media.

Advertising options in social media include display advertising, sponsored posts, video ads, blogs, and YouTube channels. Ads can be specifically targeted, which is an important benefit to advertisers. Social media encourage word-of-mouth about brands among friends, and the engagement possibilities between the brand and consumers is a key step in the relationship-building process. The ability to measure return on investment is a common concern that advertisers raise about social media.

Mobile communications now represent one-quarter of all online advertising spending in Canada and will continue to grow in importance. The mobile phone has made shopping easier and more convenient. Factors such as smartphone penetration and consumers' increased comfort level with online shopping have attracted advertisers to the medium.

Marketers see several benefits with advertising on mobile devices. Messages can be delivered to people while they are on the go, a concept referred to as location-based targeting. They also like the immediacy and intimacy that mobile offers. Mobile media advertisers must be careful regarding the frequency of communications with consumers. If the advertiser is too intrusive, there could be a negative impact on brand image. Mobile advertising opportunities include text messaging, display ads (banners), video ads, ads in applications, and QR codes.

Video games are proving to be an effective means of reaching all age groups. Some age groups spend more time playing games (often in prime time) than watching television. Gamers don't mind the presence of ads. In fact, they say ads make the game more real. Recall scores for brands that appear in games are quite high. The advertising opportunities include around-game ads, in-game ads, and advergames. Advergames are specifically produced for a brand. A branded message is blended with a fun, interactive gaming experience.

KEY TERMS

ad view   194
banner   200
behavioural targeting   193
big box   200
blog   213
brand democratization   211
click (clickthrough) rate   199
click fraud   190
clicks (clickthroughs)   199
consumer-generated content   211
content marketing   206
cookie   194
crowdsourcing   211
daypart targeting   192
demographics   192
expandable banner   201
floating ad   201
frequency (online)   199

impression   194
interactive communications   192
leaderboard   200
location-based targeting   194
mass customization   194
microsite   208
mid-roll ad   203
online sponsorship   204
opt-in list   205
pay-per-click advertising   200
permission-based email   204
portal   195
post-roll ad   203
pre-roll ad   203
push down banner   201
quick response (QR) code   219
rectangle ad   200
rich media   201

search advertising   200
skyscraper   200
social media network   209
spam   205
sponsored email   205
sponsored post   212
stickiness   200
streaming   203
super banner   200
text messaging   216
unique visitor   199
video strip   201
viewability   189
viral marketing   214
visit   199
wallpaper ad   201
window ad   201

REVIEW QUESTIONS

1. What does click fraud refer to?
2. What is behavioural targeting, and how is it applied in online marketing communications programs?
3. What is location-based targeting?
4. What is mass customization, and how do online communications facilitate its practice?
5. What are the primary marketing objectives that online communications can help an organization achieve? Identify and explain each objective briefly.
6. Explain the following terms as they relate to online advertising:
   a) impressions
   b) clicks
   c) click rate
   d) unique visitor

7. What is banner advertising, and how does it work?
8. Identify and briefly describe the various types of banner ads.
9. What does rich media refer to, and how does it work? What does streaming media refer to?
10. Briefly explain how an online advertising sponsorship works. What benefits does it provide? Illustrate the benefits with some examples.
11. Briefly explain the following email advertising terms:
    a) permission-based email
    b) sponsored email
    c) opt-in list
    d) spam

12. What does consumer-generated content refer to and how might an advertiser use it?

13. In a social media context, what is a sponsored post?

14. Briefly explain two benefits and two drawbacks of advertising on social media.

15. In a mobile communications context, how does location-based targeting work? Briefly explain.

16. What is the difference between in-game ads and advergames?

DISCUSSION AND APPLICATION QUESTIONS

1. What future lies ahead for email advertising? Will it continue to grow, or will consumers and businesses turn away from it? Conduct some online research on the issue and present a brief report on your findings.

2. How pervasive is click fraud on the Internet? Conduct some secondary research on this issue and determine how concerned advertisers should be about it.

3. Visit some commercial websites of your choosing. Evaluate these websites in terms of their ability to achieve certain marketing and marketing communications objectives such as building brand image, offering incentives, generating leads, and providing customer service. Are communications on the websites coordinated with any other form of marketing communications?

4. Assess how consumer goods marketing organizations are using social media communications to their advantage. Is it an effective medium for building relationships with customers?

5. Canadians are married to their smartphones. Will consumers accept or reject the notion of delivering frequent advertising messages on mobile devices? Examine the issues surrounding this emerging practice and formulate a position on the matter.

6. Is it possible to launch a new product using online communications as the primary medium for creating awareness and interest? What strategies would be necessary to make such a plan work?

ENDNOTES

1. Melody McKinnon, "Canadian Digital, Social and Mobile Statistics on a Global Scale 2014," January 23, 2014, http://canadiansInternet.com/canadians-digital-social-mobile-statistics

2. Tim Nichols, Video Advertising Builds Brand Awareness," ExactDrive, June 4, 2014, www.exactdrive.com/news/video-advertising-builds-brand-awareness

3. "Interactive Marketing + Online Advertising," IAB Canada Conference, May 20, 2009, p. 145.

4. "Top 15 Most Popular Websites, July 2015," eBiz/MBA Guide, www.ebizmba.com/articles/most-popular-websites

5. "Retail Ecommerce Sales in Canada to near C$30 billion, eMarketer, January 15, 2015, www.emarketer.com/Article/Retail-Ecommerce-Sales-Canada-Near-C30-Billion/1011853

6. "Online Shopping Becomes Mainstream in Canada," Marketing, November 8, 2008, www.marketingmag.ca.

7. David Chaffey, "Display Advertising Clickthrough Rates," n.d., Smart Insights, www.smartinsights.com/internetInternet-advertisinginternetInternet-advertising-analytics/display-advertising-clickthrough-rates/

8. Maureen Morrison, "Consumers Balance on Verge of Offer Anarchy," Advertising Age, February 13, 2012, p. 24.

9. "Overview of Canada's Anti-Spam Legislation," Information + Privacy Law Blog, Alexander Holburn Beaudin + Lang LLP, http://informationandprivacylawblog.ahbl.ca/2014/03/20/overview-of-Canadas-anti-spam-legislation

10. Chris Powell, "Mercedes Take an 'Appy' Path to Younger Consumers," Marketing, October 14, 2011, www.markeingmag.ca/news/marketer-news/mwecedes-take-an-app-path-to-younger-consumers-37945.

11. Daisy Whitney, "57% of Consumers Rely on Product Videos," Video Insider, Media Post Publications, March 28, 2013, www.mediapost.com/publications/video-insider/

12. Melody McKinnon, "Canadian Digital, Social and Mobile Statistics on a Global Scale 2014," Dotster.com, http://canadians.com/canadian-digital-social-mobile-statistics

13. "Number of Unique U.S. Visitors to Facebook between April 2011 and April 2015 (in millions)," Statistica, www.statista.com/statistics/265831/number-of-unique-us-visitors-to-facebookcom?

14. Chris Powell, "Marketers Struggling with the Speed of Social Media: Study," Marketing, August 16, 2010, www.marketingmag.ca/news/marketer-news/marketers-struggling-with-speed-of-social-media-study-4590

15. Sonya Fatah, "Social Media Chatter Drives Purchasing: Report," Media in Canada, August 6, 2015, http://mediaincanada.com/2015/08/06/social-media-chatter-drives-purchasing-report

16. Jenifer Alsever, "What Is Crowdsourcing?" MoneyWatch, CBS News, March 7, 2007, www.cbsnews.com/8301-505125_162-51052961/what-is-crowdsourcing

17. "Facebook Ad CTR Study—Newsfeed versus Display: From the Wolfgang Lab, Wolfgang Digital, www.wolfgangdigital.com/blog/digital-marketing/facebook-ad-ctr-study-newsfeed-display-wolfgang-lab/

18. "Mazda Canada: How Can an Automotive Company Drive Qualified Leads with a Simple Tweet" https://biztwitter.com/success-stories/maxda-canada

19. Mark Walsh, "Engagement: Brands Should Drive Traffic to Facebook Page," *Online Media Daily*, June 14, 2012, www.mediapost.com/publcations/article/176841/engagement-brands-should-drive-traffic-to-facebook.html

20. Michael Miller, "Joining the YouTube community—and Creating Your Own Channel," May 4, 2007, www.quepublishing.com.

21. Chris Powell, "Axe Launches Its Own Web Channel," *Marketing*, August 25, 2011, www.marketingmag.ca/news/marketer-news/axe-launches-its-own-web-channel-34902

22. "The Old Spice Social Media Campaign by the Numbers," *Mashable*, July 15, 2010, http://mashable.com/2010/01/15/pld-spice-stats

23. Rich Thomaselli, "Nissan Looks to Facebook to Help Launch Five New Models," *Advertising Age*, June 25, 2012, www.adage.com/article/digital/nissan-facebook-launch-models/235616/

24. Canadian Wireless Telecommunications Association, www.cwta.ca/facts-figures/

25. "The State of Canadian Connectedness: Internet Usage, Mobile, Search, and Social Media," 6S Marketing, http://6smarketing.com/blog/infographic-canadian-internetInternet-usage

26. Canadian Internet Advertising Revenue Survey 2014, IAB Canada, June 29, 2015, www.iabcanada.com

27. Michael Oliveira, "Video and Mobile Use Doubles Canadians' Time Spent Online, Research Says," *The Globe and Mail*, November 12, 2014, www.theglobeandmail.com.

28. Susan Kraschinsky, "Mobile Ads Fuel Facebook Revenue Surge," *The Globe and Mail*, July 24, 2014, www.theglobeandmail.com.

29. "CWTA: Canadians Love for Text Messaging Is Declining," *MobileSyrup.com*, December 2, 2013, http://mobilesyrup.com

30. "Take Possession," Mobile Marketing Supplement to *Strategy*, August 2008, p. S32.

31. "Mobile Phones Strengthen Lead for Mobile Video Viewing," *eMarketer*, July 2, 2015, www.emarketer.com/Article/Mobile-Phones-Strengthen-Lead-MObile-Video-Viewing/1012683

32. Ibid.

33. "Smartphones: Canadians increasingly attached to their mobile devices," *The Toronto Star*, July 29, 2013, www.thestar.com/business/tech_news/2013/07/29/canadians_addicted_to_smartphones_ownership_zooms_study_says.html

34. Jordan Pinto, "Canada Likes Its Mobile Ads Short and to the Point," *Media in Canada*, April 24, 2014, http://mediaincanada.com/2015/04/24/Canada-likes-its-mobile-ads

35. Robert Hof, "Study: Mobile Ads Actually Do Work–Especially in Apps," *Forbes.com*, August 27, 2014, www.forbes.com/sites/roberthof/2014/08/27/study-mobile-ads-actually-do-work-especially-in-apps/

36. Kristin Laird, "Updated: Tim Hortons Makes Group Buying a Little Easier," *Marketing*, April 17, 2012, www.marketingmag.ca/news/marketer-news/tim-hortons-makes-group-buying-a-little-easier-50546

37. Lindsay Kolowich, "Are QR codes Dead?" Hubspot.com, August 14, 2014, http://blog.hubspot.com/marketing/qr-codes-dead

38. "Platform Status Report Game Advertising," IAB, 2010, www.iab.net/media/file/IAB-games-PSR-update_0913-pdf

39. Mike Shields, "IGA: Most Gamers Cool with In-game Ads," *AdWeek*, June 17, 2008, www.adweek.com.

40. "Platform Status Report Game Advertising," p.3, Interactive Advertising Bureau, www.iab.net/media/file/iab-games-PSR-update_0913.pdf.

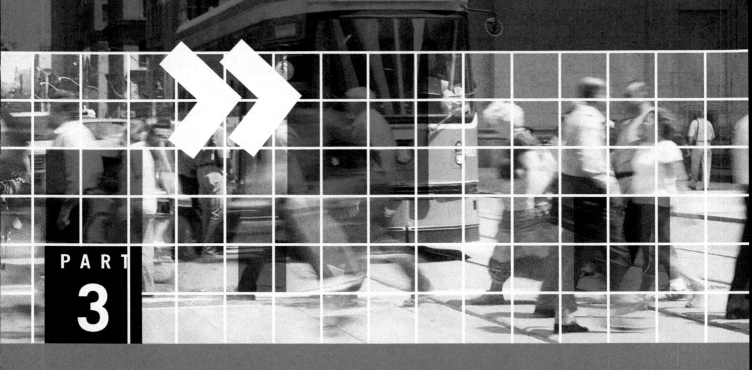

Planning for Integrated Marketing

Part 3 looks at marketing communications choices beyond the media that enhance the communications plan.

Chapter 8 introduces various sales promotion alternatives that are frequently used in integrated marketing communications plans. Discussion is divided between consumer promotions and trade promotions, with each area examined for its ability to achieve marketing and marketing communications objectives.

Chapter 9 describes the role of public relations communications in the marketing communications mix. Various public relations techniques are introduced. The process of planning public relations activities is examined in detail, along with various measurement techniques used to determine the effectiveness of public relations messages.

Chapter 10 discusses the role of experiential marketing techniques that embrace street marketing strategies along with event marketing and sponsorships. The criteria for participating in event marketing, and the steps and procedures for planning an event are introduced, along with evaluation techniques for this activity.

In Chapter 11, the role of personal selling in a variety of business settings is examined. Personal selling adds a human component to the integrated marketing communications mix and, for this reason, plays a very important role in an era where customer relationship management practices dominate.

Sales Promotion

Learning Objectives

After studying this chapter, you will be able to

1. Distinguish between consumer promotions and trade promotions

2. Describe the steps in the sales promotion planning process

3. Assess the role of consumer promotions in achieving specific marketing communications and marketing objectives

4. Assess the role of trade promotions in achieving specific marketing communications and marketing objectives

5. Outline the nature of various consumer promotion and trade promotion activities

6. Assess various criteria for integrating sales promotion strategies with other integrated marketing communications strategies

This chapter examines the role of sales promotions in the marketing communications mix. Promotions are activities that focus on making a sale, usually in a short period of time. When planning and implementing promotions, the marketing organization provides an offer to customers in return for something they must do. Because the offer is valid only for a certain period, the impact of the offer—and its success or failure—can be measured quickly.

A wide variety of promotion offers are presented here, all of which are suited to achieving specific marketing and marketing communications objectives. The right promotion must be offered at the right time if the offer is to bring true benefit to the brand or company. In order to create awareness and interest in the promotion, there must also be media advertising to support it, and possibly some publicity generated by public relations and social media campaigns. A coordinated effort is usually required to make a sales promotion a success. This chapter focuses on two distinct yet related areas of sales promotion: consumer promotion and trade promotion. An organization must consider strategies for both if it is to grow and prosper.

Sales Promotion

Sales promotion is defined as an activity that provides special incentives to bring about immediate response from an organization's sales force, distributors, and customers. It is a strategy that encourages action by the recipient. According to the definition, three distinct groups are considered when planning sales promotion strategies. First, the consumer or final user must be motivated to take advantage of the offer. Second, the distributor (reseller of goods) must be motivated to support the offer by providing merchandising support. Third, the company's sales force must be motivated to sell the promotion to its trade customers. Because the intent of a promotion is to provide some added excitement to the product, an organization's sales representatives must present it enthusiastically to the trade distributors.

Consumer promotions are designed to stimulate purchases or to encourage loyalty. Among the options readily available are coupons, free samples, contests, rebates, price incentives, and rewards programs. These types of promotions are planned to help **pull** the product through the channel of distribution. An organization creates demand for the product by directing its promotional efforts directly at the consumer. The combination of advertising and promotions, for example, creates demand and causes consumers to look for the product

sales promotion An activity that provides incentives to bring about immediate response from customers, distributors, and an organization's sales force.

consumer promotion An incentive offered to consumers to stimulate purchases or encourage loyalty.

pull Demand created by directing promotional activities at consumers or final users, who in turn pressure retailers to supply the product or service.

FIGURE
8.1

Pull and Push Promotion Strategies

Pull—The promotion strategy is directed at consumers, who in turn request the product or service from distributors and pull it through the channel.

Push—The promotion strategy is directed at distributors, who resell the product. Incentives help push the product from one distributor to another.

in stores or request a service; by asking for it specifically, they put pressure on the retailer to provide it. Many companies now include experiential marketing activities in their promotion strategies.Experiential marketing is presented in detail in Chapter 9.

Consumer promotions can play a key role in an integrated marketing communications plan. A poll conducted by Delvinia Data Collection asked a sampling of Canadian consumers, "What would best convince you to try a new brand of beer?" Product sampling and tasting events garnered a 42.6 percent response, giveaways (clothing and hats) 20.6 percent, and contests 14.3 percent. In comparison, television advertising garnered only a 7.8 percent response.[1] Despite these responses, media advertising typically receives the lion's share of a beer brand's marketing budget. Consumer promotions are often added to a beer brand's marketing mix during the peak summer selling season.

trade promotion An incentive offered to channel members to encourage them to provide marketing and merchandising support for a particular product.

push Demand created by directing promotional activities at intermediaries, who in turn promote the product or service among consumers.

Trade promotions are less visible activities, given that they are offered to members of the channel of distribution. These promotions include options such as discounts and allowances, cooperative advertising funds, dealer premiums and incentives, and point-of-purchase materials. Offering financial incentives to distributors encourages them to support a manufacturer's promotion plans. Such promotions **push** the product through the channel of distribution. Refer to Figure 8.1 for an illustration of pull and push promotion strategies.

To be successful, an organization must determine what type of promotion will contribute the most to achieving its objectives. In most cases, it is a combination of consumer and trade promotions. The real decision is to determine the extent to which each type of promotion is offered. Such a decision is based on the market analysis that precedes the development of any sales promotion plan. Sales promotion planning is discussed in the following section.

Sales Promotion Planning

Like any other component of the marketing communications mix, a sales promotion plan is but one component of a much larger plan. It must directly fit into the marketing communications plan and play a role in achieving the specific objectives that are identified in that plan. Whereas advertising plans have a long-term perspective and longer-term objectives, the sales promotion plan adopts a short-term view and achieves objectives of a more immediate nature. While advertising is building a brand's image, sales promotions are implemented to encourage a spike in sales.

To demonstrate the difference between the roles of advertising and sales promotions, consider a recent campaign by Deeley Harley-Davidson in Canada. Harley's "Live the

Dream" campaign combined the renowned Harley mystique with a more friendly tone to attract newcomers to the brand. The theme of the television advertising captured a young boy's love of his bicycle and drew parallels to the feelings of riding a Harley motorcycle. Harley also used advertising to connect with the individuality and rebel in everyone. The promotion side of the campaign included a dedicated website that offered a chance to win a made-to-measure Harley. The contest encouraged consumer engagement with the brand, because sharing information with friends via Facebook, Twitter, or email increased a person's chances of winning the motorcycle.[2]

Sales promotions are activities that complement advertising. When you consider the primary goals of advertising—awareness, comprehension, conviction, and action—the primary goal of sales promotion is to focus on one specific area—action. A well-planned promotional offer that coincides with an image-building advertising campaign—as in the case of the Harley-Davidson example or Tim Hortons' annual spring "Roll up the Rim" contest—could be just the incentive needed to get the customer's money out of that wallet or purse. Such a relationship suggests that integration of advertising strategies and promotional strategies is essential, and, on a larger scale, that their integration with online communications, events and sponsorships, and public relations is what promotes a brand or company with a sense of continuity.

Sales promotion planning involves developing a plan of action for communicating incentives to the appropriate target markets (consumers and trade customers) at the right time. Very often, an external company that specializes in sales promotion will assume responsibility for developing and implementing the consumer promotion plan. As with developing an advertising plan, the specialist must be briefed. The client's role is to provide the necessary background information and then evaluate the promotion concepts put forth by the agency. The promotion agency must assess the information provided by the client and then prepare a strategic plan that will meet the client's objectives. Figure 8.2 outlines the promotion planning process.

A sales promotion brief typically includes some or all of the following information.

MARKET PROFILE

An overview of sales and market share trends provides market perspective to the promotion planners. Knowing if the brand is a leader, challenger, or follower has an impact on the nature of the promotion they will ultimately recommend. It is important to know if the market is growing and what brands are growing in the market.

COMPETITOR ACTIVITY PROFILE

In general terms, what marketing communications strategies do key competitors rely upon? The role of the various elements of the mix will vary from one brand to another. What brands dominate the market, and what are their mixes? An evaluation of this kind of information may suggest that various combinations of activities have more or less impact on customers. A review of competitors' recent sales promotion activities is essential.

TARGET MARKET PROFILE

Perhaps the most important aspect of planning a promotion is a good understanding of the target customer. As discussed earlier in the text, customers are described according to demographic, psychographic, geographic, and behavioural characteristics. Additional information about shopping behaviour usually plays a role in developing a sales promotion plan. For example, many of today's consumers are time challenged and value

FIGURE
8.2

The Sales Promotion Planning
Process

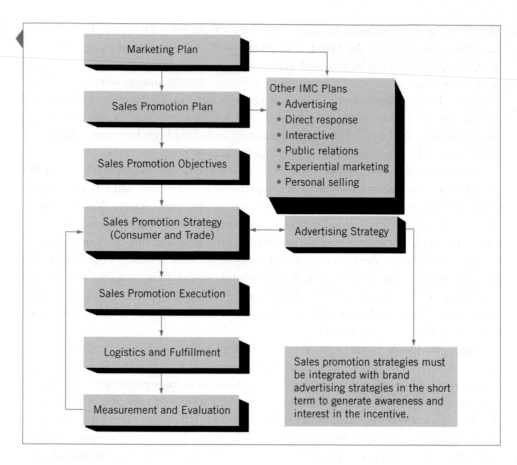

conscious, and are looking for good deals they can take advantage of quickly. When planning the promotion, the value must be immediately evident to the consumer.

SALES PROMOTION OBJECTIVES

A variety of background factors will determine the objectives of the promotion campaign. Essentially, sales promotion plans focus on three distinct objectives: generating trial purchases, encouraging repeat or multiple purchases, and building long-term brand loyalty. Objectives for trade promotion plans concentrate on building sales and achieving merchandising support. These objectives are discussed in more detail in the "Consumer Promotion Execution" and "Trade Promotion Execution" sections of this chapter.

BUDGET

Funds for the sales promotion plan come from the overall marketing budget. In most cases, the client has already determined how much money is available for promotions. Knowing the size of the budget is crucial when the promotion agency is thinking about potential concepts. Will this be a large-scale national promotion, or will it be restricted to specific regions? Will it involve an expensive grand prize, or will there be a series of smaller prizes? How much media advertising support will be needed to create awareness for the promotion?

The Sales Promotion Plan

sales promotion plan An action plan for communicating incentives to appropriate target markets at the right time.

The **sales promotion plan** is a document that outlines the relevant details about how the client's budget will be spent. Objectives are clearly defined, strategies are justified, and tactical details are precisely documented. Similar to direct response communications plans, back-end

---

FIGURE
8.3   The Content of a Sales Promotion Plan

Situation Analysis

- Market profile
- Competitor activity profile
- Target market profile

Budget

- Funds available

Sales Promotion Objectives

A. Consumer Promotion
- Trial purchase
- Repeat purchases
- Multiple purchases
- Brand loyalty

B. Trade Promotion
- New listings
- Sales volume
- Merchandising support

Sales Promotion Strategy

- Incentive or offer (save, win, or reward)
- Merchandise, cash, or combination
- Balance between consumer and trade

Advertising Strategy

- Broadcast
- Print
- In-store
- Digital
- Social

Sales Promotion Execution

- Details of consumer offer (coupon, sample, contest, premium, rebate, loyalty promotion)
- Details of trade offer (trade allowance, performance allowance, cooperative advertising funds, dealer premiums, collateral materials, display materials, trade shows)

Logistics and Fulfillment

- Back-end plan to administer and implement the promotion

Budget and Timing

- Activity costs
- Calendar of events

---

considerations are very important. For example, if a fulfillment program is part of the package, details about how the offer will be handled from the time the consumer responds to the time the goods are delivered must be precisely planned. Promotions that include coupons, free samples, contests, rebates, and premiums might involve other companies that handle various aspects of the promotion. The structure and content of a sales promotion plan are the focus of this section. Figure 8.3 summarizes the content of a sales promotion plan, but because the content of a plan varies from one company to another, it is only a guideline.

SALES PROMOTION OBJECTIVES

Sales promotion objectives are statements that clearly indicate what the promotion plan is to accomplish. Similar to other communications plans, objective statements should be realistically achievable, quantitative in nature to facilitate measurement, and directed at a carefully defined target market.

The nature of the promotion plan (that is, consumer promotion versus trade promotion) determines the objectives. Although objectives for both are quite different, they complement each other when implemented. Let's start with consumer promotion objectives.

The most common objective of consumer promotion is to encourage consumers to make a *trial purchase*. When a product is new, for example, an organization wants to establish acceptance as quickly as possible. Therefore, trial-oriented promotions are common (see Figure 8.4). Even when a product is in the growth stage of development, there is a need to distinguish one brand from another. At that stage, incentives that encourage

FIGURE
8.4

Coupon Offers Are an Effective Means of Achieving Trial Purchase

Source: © Karen Bleier/AFP/Getty Images.

purchase of a specific brand remain essential. Media-delivered coupons are an excellent promotion tool for encouraging trial purchase, as are product samples.

The second objective is to stimulate **repeat purchases** by existing customers. An extension of this objective is to encourage consumers to make multiple purchases at one time. Quaker offered consumers a "Buy Two Get One Free" offer on its Harvest Crunch and Life Cereal brands, which is a significant savings. Such an offer reduces the likelihood of a consumer purchasing competitor brands, at least temporarily. A contest such as Tim Hortons' "Roll Up the Rim" promotion encourages consumers to visit Tim's more often—more visits mean more sales! Refer to the image in Figure 8.5.

The third objective deals with customer relationship management (CRM). Here, the objective is to encourage **brand loyalty** for an extended period. Traditionally, promotions encourage instant activity, but there are promotion alternatives that can meet both short-term and long-term brand objectives. Something as simple as the loyalty card offered by a local coffee shop helps keep a customer. Rewards bring customers back.

The overall goal of trade promotions is to give sales a jolt in the short run. Such an accomplishment is usually the result of promotion strategies combined with other marketing strategies to influence trade customers and consumers. Therefore, trade promotion objectives must be confined to what they can realistically achieve. Generally speaking, trade promotion plans are designed to encourage distributors to carry a product and then sell it to retailers, and to increase the volume sold for products they already carry.

FIGURE
8.5

**A Consumer Promotion
Designed to Encourage Repeat
or Multiple Purchases**

Source: © Keith Tuckwell

In the case of a new product, the first objective is to *secure a listing* with distributors. A listing is an agreement made by a wholesaler to distribute a manufacturer's product to the retailer it supplies. For example, when the head office of Canada Safeway or Sobeys agrees to list a product, it is then available to all of their retail outlets. Typically, trade promotions in the form of financial incentives are used to secure listings.

A second objective is to *build sales volume* on either a seasonal or a predetermined cyclical basis throughout the year. For example, baking products are promoted in the pre-Christmas season, and there are usually displays of such products in retail stores. In other cases, it is common for a company to offer temporary discounts for its key brands on a quarterly basis because it recognizes that consistent activity keeps a popular brand in a preferred position with the trade and consumers. The nature of competition often dictates such a strategy.

A third trade objective is to *secure merchandising support* from distributors. Their support is crucial, because once the product leaves the manufacturer's warehouse, the manufacturer is no longer in control of how it is sold. Consequently, funds are allocated to activities that get the product out of a distributor's warehouse and into displays on the retail sales floor. As well, the manufacturer will look for a sale price and perhaps a brand mention of the sale price in a retailer's advertising flyer. These activities constitute merchandising support.

Sales Promotion Strategy

Decisions about sales promotion strategy focus on the selection of the best promotion activity to meet the objectives. Decisions point the organization in a certain direction, and, if agreed to, the tactical details are then developed. For example, on the consumer side of things, an organization can choose among coupons, free samples, contests, rebates, premiums, and loyalty programs. Other decisions might involve the selection of prizes.

Should they be cash, merchandise, or a combination of both? The organization can use any one of these options or combine several to maximize the potential of the promotion.

Each of these options provides a different kind of incentive. For example, coupons and rebates save people money; contests give people a chance to win something; and samples, premiums, and loyalty programs offer something free with a purchase. As a result, the first decision relates directly to the incentive. Should the promotion program offer savings, a chance to win something, or a reward?

Key decisions about trade promotion strategy involve the allocation of funds among the various alternatives. Depending on the promotion objectives, preference may be given to listing allowances, trade and performance allowances, and cooperative advertising allowances. Alternatively, some combination of several of these allowances might be employed. The manager must also decide about the balance between consumer promotions (pull) and trade promotions (push). Successful promotions use both and are carefully integrated with other forms of marketing communications to maximize impact on the intended target audience.

The second component of the sales promotion strategy involves integration with the advertising strategy. You need to promote a promotion! In many cases, a brand will already be planning a brand-image campaign, and several media might be involved. Is special creative needed for the sales promotion? What media will be used to advertise the sales promotion?

With creative, the ideal situation is to have promotional creative blend effectively with existing brand creative. For example, in March each year, Tim Hortons implements its "Roll Up the Rim to Win" promotion. Separate creative and a variety of media (television, outdoor boards, online communications, and in-store signage) are employed to announce details of the promotion. A promotion is an added incentive, so it temporarily becomes the brand's unique selling point. The combination of a strong ongoing sales message with the added bonus of a special offer will help achieve short-term and long-term objectives. Refer to Figure 8.6.

FIGURE 8.6

A Consumer Promotion Offer Can Be the Temporary Focal Point of a Marketing Communications Strategy

Source: All Tim Hortons trademarks referenced herein are owned by Tim Hortons. Used with permission.

A good sales promotion incentive is designed so that it offers consumers meaningful value. For example, any savings on the price of a product should be meaningful in relation to the regular price. Any prizes that are offered in a contest should be of interest to the core customers who typically buy the product or visit the retail store. The Tim Hortons contest fits these criteria and has been successful in building sales for over 25 years.

A sales promotion will work only if it receives the necessary media support, so another decision must be made about allocating funds specifically for promotion-related programs. Once that decision is made, the media strategy will focus on two objectives: creating awareness for the promotion and providing details about how the consumer can take advantage of the promotion (for example, how to submit order forms for premium offers or entry forms for contests).

Typically, a variety of broadcast, print, and online media are selected. Television is an ideal medium for creating instant awareness of the promotion. High-impact television advertising in a short period (a blitz strategy) is common. In the case of a contest or sweepstakes promotion, television is ideal for creating excitement and for conveying a sense of urgency to consumers. It encourages them to take advantage of the offer right away. Social media can also play a role in generating buzz for the promotion. Sharing among a friend network expands the reach of the message.

In-store advertising can also assist in achieving awareness objectives while playing a key role in communicating details of the offer. Consumers are conditioned to look for details at point of purchase. In conjunction with trade promotion strategies, the ideal situation is to have brand displays in stores supported by posters and shelf cards at the product's regular shelf location to draw attention to the promotion. See the illustration in Figure 8.7.

Obviously, the nature and size of the promotion will dictate the degree of media support. It is common for brands such as Pepsi-Cola, Gillette, and Kellogg's cereals to

FIGURE
8.7

In-store Displays and Signage Draw Attention to a Contest Promotion and Encourage Immediate Purchases

Source: © Keith Tuckwell

invest in media advertising to promote contests that offer huge grand prizes. In contrast, a premium offer may simply be announced to the target market on the package itself and by shelf cards at point of purchase. The investment in media advertising in this case would be low.

The manufacturer's sales representatives have the task of making trade customers aware of consumer promotion offers. The manufacturer commonly prepares specific sales literature such as brochures, pamphlets, and display material for representatives to use to introduce the promotion. The sales representatives will integrate the consumer promotion offer with their trade promotion plans (a combination of pull and push) to maximize the impact of the dollars being invested in the promotion. The sales representatives must sell the promotion to the distributors and show how it will affect their business positively. Their objective may be to secure a listing for a new product or to ensure the distributor orders sufficient inventory of an existing product to cover the anticipated demand and to encourage adequate merchandising support in its stores. If the trade customers are on board, the promotion will be successful. Their support is crucial.

LOGISTICS AND FULFILLMENT

The final phase of planning a promotion campaign involves working out all of the details of the offer. Depending on the nature of the promotion, there will be a variety of dates and deadlines, other companies will be involved in planning and implementing the offer, and a system needs to be in place to deliver the goods to consumers, if the promotion so dictates. These are only a sampling of the potential decisions to be made.

To demonstrate the fulfillment process, let's assume that a major contest is the sales promotion offer. The grand prize is a trip to Disneyland with a series of smaller prizes to be awarded to runners-up. Answers to the following questions start to create a plan of action for implementing the awareness and fulfillment sides of the promotion:

- When will the promotion be announced to the trade and to consumers?

- Who are the contest prize suppliers, and what are the costs?

- How will consumers enter the contest? Who will design the entry form? Will it be an online entry form?

- What is the deadline for receiving entries?

- Who will draw the prizes?

- How will the prizes be delivered to the winners?

- What costs are associated with contest administration by a third-party organization?

- Who will the third-party organization be?

- Who will prepare in-store promotional materials?

- Who will print the promotional literature, and what will it cost?

- How will media advertising be coordinated with the sales promotion offer?

- Who will ensure the contest is legal in all jurisdictions?

Such a list of questions reveals the logistical implications for running a sales promotion offer. Needless to say, the entire promotion must operate seamlessly from the front end (announcing the promotion) to the back end (delivering prizes to winners). Smart marketing organizations outsource the administration of the promotion to a specialist in this industry.

MEASUREMENT AND EVALUATION

Similar to any other marketing communications program, sales promotion activities must be evaluated for success or failure. As indicated earlier, a boost in sales is the immediate goal of most forms of promotion, but other factors beyond promotion also influence sales. Therefore, a promotion must be evaluated based on the objectives that were established for it. If the objective was to generate trial purchases, how many new users were attracted to the product? If the objective was loyalty, are current customers buying the product more frequently? To answer these questions, some pre- and post-promotion marketing research is necessary.

Specific promotions are also measured by response rates of consumers. For example, a coupon promotion could be assessed by the number of coupons returned. If the average return rate for coupons distributed by magazines is 1 percent and an offer draws a 2 percent response, the promotion could be judged a success. A contest is evaluated on the basis of the number of entries received. If the objective was 10 000 entries and only 7500 were received, the promotion could be judged a failure.

If there is a method of projecting revenues generated by a promotion, then it is possible to estimate some kind of financial payout from the promotion. The difference between revenues and costs would be the return on investment, because the costs of the promotion are known. Figure 8.8 illustrates how to evaluate the financial payout of a coupon offer.

FIGURE
8.8   Evaluating the Financial Impact of a Sales Promotion Offer

This example shows the return on investment for a coupon offer distributed to households by co-operative direct mail. Costs and revenues are estimated to determine the return on investment.

Coupon Plan	
Face value of coupon	$1.00
Printing cost (digest-sized ad with perforated coupon at bottom)	$12.00/M
Handling charge for retailer	$0.15
Handling charge for clearing house	$0.05
Distribution cost	$18.00/M
Distribution	2 million households
Redemption rate (estimated)	5.0%
Retail price of product	$3.89
(Manufacturer receives about 65 percent of retail price when distributors' mark-ups are deducted.)	

Costs	Cost Calculation	Total	Grand Total
Printing	2 000 000 × $12/M	$24 000	
Distribution	2 000 000 × $18/M	$36 000	
Coupon redemption	2 000 000 × 0.05 × $1.20	$120 000	
Total cost		**$180 000**	**$180 000**
Cost per coupon redeemed	180 000/100 000	$1.80	

Revenues			
Per unit of revenue	$3.89 × .065	$2.53	
Total revenue*	2 000 000 × 0.05 x 0.80 × $2.53	202 400	$202 400
Return on investment			$22 400

*In any coupon offer, there is a risk of coupons being returned without a purchase being made. This is referred to as *misredemption*. In this example, the misredemption rate is 20%, hence the 0.80 factor in the revenue calculation equation.

IMC HIGHLIGHT

Quick Serve Coffee Wars

Coffee is the beverage of choice among Canadians and 35 percent of all coffee is consumed in restaurants. It's a huge market and one that McDonald's wanted a piece of. But the competition is fierce. How does McDonald's (with a 2 percent market share in the restaurant coffee) lure customers away from Tim Hortons, Starbucks, Second Cup, Coffee Time, and a host of independent coffee shops?

As in any market, the right combination starts with a good quality product supported by media advertising for awareness and impactful sales promotions to encourage initial purchases. McDonald's introduced its premium blend Arabica medium roast coffee in 2009 with a promotion that gave it away to customers for two weeks for free; it was the beginning of an annual tradition.

Not only was the coffee good, but the cup was superior to any competitor—a nifty double-walled cup with a lid that could be easily opened in a car without spills! The key objective for McDonald's was to get people to try the coffee. According to CEO John Betts, "We needed to do something bold to disrupt the market and get people talking—and nothing works like free." Over a

five-year period starting in April 2009, 113 million cups of coffee were given away, and during that time market share moved from 2 percent to 13 percent, which was a very good return on investment. The market share increase suggests customers altered their routines and now visit McDonald's for the coffee. The free sample promotion has exceeded company expectations.

Phase 2 of McDonald's foray into coffee saw the launch of McCafés in 2011. The remodelled restaurants offer customers a more relaxed environment that includes flat screen televisions, gas fireplaces, long communal tables, and armchairs that encourage patrons to linger over their coffee and chat with friends. The introduction of a solid loyalty program with a tangible benefit keeps customers coming back for more coffee. After purchasing seven cups of coffee the customer gets one free—a meaningful benefit.

Phase 3 of the coffee strategy involves a partnership with Kraft Canada that introduced McCafé coffee to Canada's grocery aisles. McDonald's coffee is now available in bags and pods for single-serving machines. Kraft's expertise in retail distribution plays a key role in this part of McDonald's plans.

While Tim Hortons still dominates the restaurant coffee market in Canada, McDonald's is a global juggernaut and it is on the attack. The goal is to continue to build market share. Thus far, the combination of improved coffee beverages, free week-long promotions, and ambience seems to be working. We'll have to wait and see what's next!

© Alex Segre/Alamy Stock Photo

Source: Based on Hollie Shaw, "McDonald's Making Gains in Canadian coffee Wars, as U.S. Sales Decline Deepens," *Financial Post*, December 10, 2014, http://business.financialpost.com and James Cowan, "McDonald's in Trouble. Meet The Canadians Engineering Its Comeback," *Canadian Business*, April 28, 2014, http://www.canadianbusiness.com.

A side benefit of consumer promotions is the collection of names. The names on entry forms from contests and order forms for premium offers and rebate offers can be added to the organization's database. Smart marketers seek additional information about consumers on promotion entry forms to develop more thorough customer profiles and determine who their primary target market is. Having more and better information about customers will assist in the development of customer relationship management programs.

For more insight into the role sales promotion strategies play in building market share, read the IMC Highlight: **Quick Serve Coffee Wars**.

CONSUMER PROMOTION EXECUTION

As indicated earlier, an organization will combine various consumer promotion activities with trade promotion activities so that there is balance between the pull and push strategies. It is that combination of pull and push that creates a synergistic effect in the marketplace. This section will discuss the various forms of consumer promotions that are often included in sales promotion plans.

The major types of consumer promotions include coupons, free samples, contests, cash rebates and related incentives, premiums, and loyalty programs. The popularity of the various alternatives varies from one industry to another. In the packaged goods industry, all alternatives are used, but coupons and free samples tend to be very popular. In the appliance and automobile industries, rebates are the preferred tactic. Automobile manufacturers frequently offer cash-back rebates and extremely low financing terms. Does anyone actually buy a car that doesn't have some kind of incentive offer attached to it? Let's analyze the various consumer promotions and determine the conditions for which each type of promotion is best suited.

COUPONS   **Coupons** are price-saving incentives offered to consumers to stimulate quick purchase of a designated product. The motivation for distributing the coupons is the same across all industries, although the value of the coupons varies considerably. Grocery coupons, for example, might be valued at $0.75 or $1.00, while a trial coupon for a restaurant may be valued at 50 percent of the cost of the meal. See Figure 8.9 for an illustration.

coupon   A price-saving incentive offered to consumers to stimulate quick purchase of a specified product.

Data available from the Canadian Deals Association, which keeps records on coupon distribution and redemption rates in Canada, reveal that more than 6.8 billion coupons are distributed annually. A total of 86 million are returned, for an average redemption rate of 1.26 percent. Coupons save Canadians over $100 million in redeemed value annually. The most popular categories for distributing coupons are food, personal care, and household products.[3]

FIGURE
8.9

The Coupons in This Illustration Are Distributed As Part of the Display

Source: © Keith Tuckwell

Coupons are an excellent medium for achieving several marketing objectives at various stages of the product life cycle. First, coupons can encourage *trial purchase* among new users (and encourage competitive brand users to switch brands), and they can encourage *repeat purchases* by current users. In the latter situation, the coupon is a means of building brand loyalty.

How coupons are distributed to consumers is based on the objectives of the coupon offer. When a product is new or relatively new, trial purchase is the marketer's primary objective, so **media-delivered coupons** are popular. Options for delivery include **free-standing inserts (FSI)** in newspapers, magazines, direct mail, and in-store distribution. Websites such as Save.ca distribute coupons on behalf of manufacturers. Many companies distribute coupons to consumers who request them while visiting their website. Procter & Gamble firmly believes in the power of coupons and distributes them online at www.pgbrandsaver.com and www.pgeveryday.com.

The distribution of digital coupons online or by mobile devices is becoming very popular. Digital distribution provides consumers an array of money-saving opportunities. According to Nielsen's Digital Consumer Report 87 percent of U.S. smartphone and tablet users use their devices to shop, and nearly half have used mobile coupons.[4] Refer to Figure 8.10. Digital coupons save consumers time. There is no need to clip anything

media-delivered coupon Coupon packaged with another medium, such as newspapers, magazines, direct mail, in-store distribution, and on the Internet.

free-standing insert (FSI) A booklet featuring coupons, refunds, contests, or other promotional advertising distributed by direct mail or with newspapers, magazines, or other delivery vehicles.

FIGURE
8.10

Coupons Distributed by Mobile Devices Can Deliver Offers to People Based on Their Location and Behaviour

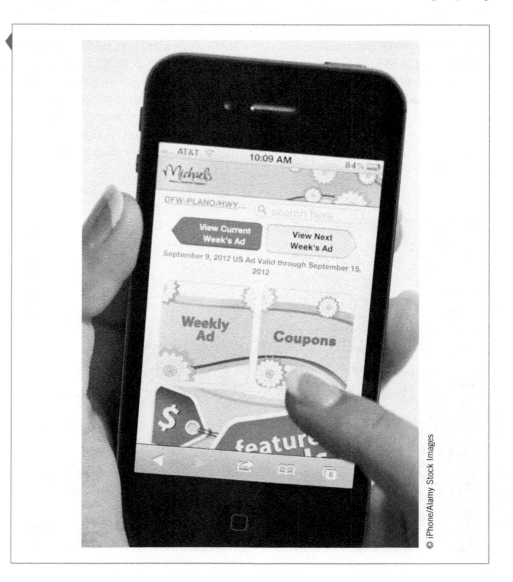

© iPhone/Alamy Stock Images

and they can be redeemed quickly at the checkout counter. Retailers who distribute digital coupons see them as a means of improving the customer's shopping experience. Smartphones also let people access deals while they are on the go—deals that are relevant based on their location, behaviour, and timeliness.

Once a product moves into the late growth and early mature stages of its life cycle, a marketer's attention shifts from trial purchase to *repeat purchase*. By now there are many competing brands, all of which have a certain degree of consumer loyalty. As a defensive measure, it is important to reward current customers in one form or another. The package itself becomes an important medium for distributing coupons. The insertion of a coupon in or on a package, for example, is an incentive for a customer to keep buying the product.

Coupons contained inside a package are called **in-pack self-coupons**, because they are redeemable on the next purchase. Usually the face panel of the package makes mention of the coupon contained inside. A coupon that appears on the side panel or back panel is called an **on-pack self-coupon**. Another option is the **instantly redeemable coupon**, which is attached to the package in some fashion and can be removed immediately and used on the purchase of the product. Sometimes two products collaborate on a coupon offer. To illustrate, Tetley Tea includes an in-pack coupon for Christie cookies, and Christies places a Tetley Tea coupon in its package. The relationship between the two brands is obvious. Each brand capitalizes on the other's consumer franchise in its effort to attract new users. This type of coupon is called a **cross-ruff** or **cross-coupon**.

The success or failure of a coupon offer is often determined by the redemption rate that is achieved. The **redemption rate** refers to the number of coupons returned to the manufacturer expressed as a percentage of the total coupons in distribution. If, for example, 1 million coupons were distributed and 45 000 were returned, the redemption rate would be 4.5 percent (45 000 divided by 1 000 000).

For budgeting purposes, it is important to know the average redemption rates for the various methods of delivering coupons. For example, the 2014 Nielsen Coupon Facts Report reveals that print coupons have an average redemption rate of 1 percent. That may seem low but the redemption rate varies based upon the method of distribution. Coupons in magazines have a range of 1 to 7 percent, addressed direct mail coupons have an average redemption rate of 6.5 percent. and Nielsen reports that digital coupons have a much higher average redemption rate—14 percent![5] Clearly, people are enticed to take action when they receive a digital coupon. The perceived value of the offer in relation to the regular price will also influence the redemption rate. If it is not a worthwhile incentive, it won't be acted upon.

PRODUCT SAMPLES

Product sampling is a powerful, yet expensive, way to promote a product. It is an effective strategy for encouraging trial purchase, but due to the costs involved, many manufacturers do not select this option. Traditionally, **free sample** programs involved the distribution of trial-size packages (small replicas of the real package) or actual-size packages. The latter option is obviously an expensive proposition.

In order to implement a sampling program, the marketer must appreciate the true benefit of such an offer. In a nutshell, it is unlike any other form of promotion in that it is the only option that will convert a trial user to a regular user solely on the basis of product satisfaction. Essentially, the marketing organization has eliminated any risk the consumer might perceive in buying the product. That's a compelling reason for using samples.

in-pack self-coupon   A coupon for the next purchase of a product that is packed inside the package or under a label.

on-pack self-coupon   A coupon that is printed on the outside of a package redeemable on the next purchase of the product.

instantly redeemable coupon   A removable coupon often located on the package or a store shelf that is redeemable on the current purchase of the product.

cross-ruff (cross-coupon)   A coupon packed in or with one product that is redeemable for another product. The product the coupon is packed with is the means of distributing the coupon.

redemption rate   The number of coupons returned expressed as a percentage of the number of coupons that were distributed.

free sample   Free distribution of a product to potential users.

FIGURE
8.11

**In-store Sampling Motivates
Consumers to Purchase a
Product**

Source: © Casey Rodgers/AP Images for
Kellogg Company.

A tried-and-true approach, particularly for food products, is in-store sampling. Costco uses this approach extensively by setting up sample stations at the ends of food aisles. A smart shopper can practically have a free lunch while shopping at Costco on a Saturday. When packaged goods grocery manufacturers do sample tasting in local supermarkets, they usually outsource the promotion to an independent company that specializes in this activity. Booths are strategically set up in stores to intercept customers as they shop. Refer to the image in Figure 8.11.

Other alternatives for delivering free samples include solo or cooperative direct mail (provided the sample is small and light enough to be accommodated by a mailing envelope), home delivery by private organizations, and providing samples at events.

When deciding whether to use a free sample program, a review of the benefits and drawbacks is essential. Samples are an expensive proposition due to product, package, and handling costs. In spite of these costs, samples rank second to coupons among marketers, so clearly the long-term benefit outweighs the short-term costs. Further, sampling combined with a coupon is the best way to gain a trial purchase and convert a trial to immediate purchase. Refer to the image in Figure 8.12. The fact that samples eliminate the risk usually associated with new product purchases is a key benefit.

On the downside, a sample is the fastest and surest way to kill an inferior product. In terms of timing, sample programs are best suited to the early stage of the product life cycle, when the primary objective is to achieve trial purchase. For certain, the delivery of samples adds excitement to any new product launch.

contest   A promotion that involves awarding cash or merchandise prizes to consumers when they purchase a specified product.

sweepstake   A chance promotion involving the giveaway of products or services of value to randomly selected participants.

CONTESTS   **Contests** are designed and implemented to create temporary excitement about a brand. For example, offering a grand prize such as an automobile, vacation, or dream home can capture the consumer's imagination, even though the odds of winning are very low. Contests can be classified into two categories: sweepstakes and games. A **sweepstake** is a chance promotion involving the giveaway of products and services such as cars, vacations, and sometimes cash. It's like a lottery—winners are

FIGURE
8.12

Some Examples of Free Samples and Coupons Delivered by Direct Mail Campaigns

Source: © Keith Tuckwell

randomly selected from the entries received. Typically, consumers enter a contest by filling in an entry form that is available at point of purchase, through print advertising, or on a website.

When companies are searching for the right sweepstake idea, their objective is clear: It must light a fire under sales. In the world of promotional contests, experts generally agree that offering cash, cars, and travel are effective. PepsiCo is an avid user of contests to support its key brands. For its popular Lay's Potato Chips it offers Canadian consumers a chance to create a potato chip flavour in a contest called "Lay's Do Us a Flavour." The 2015 version of the contest sought flavour recipes that were inspired by the various regions of Canada; the contest was promoted as "Tastes of Canada" and the winner received a cash prize of $50 000 plus 1 percent of future sales of the flavour. A judging panel narrowed the flavour entries down to four finalists and Canadians got an opportunity to vote for the winning flavour. Winning flavours in the first two contests were Jalapeno Mac N' Cheese for Lay's Wavy chips and Maple Moose for Lay's Original chips. The contest is an ideal means of engaging consumers with the brand.[6] Refer to Figure 8.13.

Games are also based on chance, but can be more involving because they often require repeat visits for game pieces. This makes them a good device for encouraging continuity of purchase by consumers. McDonald's is somewhat of an expert in this area. Its "Monopoly" game is a regular feature in annual marketing plans. As the saying goes, "You have to play to win," and the only way to play is to go to a McDonald's restaurant.

An offshoot of the game contest is the **instant-win promotion**, which involves predetermined, pre-seeded winning tickets in the overall fixed universe of tickets.

Tim Hortons' annual "Roll Up the Rim to Win" is an example of an instant-win promotion. Although most of the prizes involve food products, it is the roster of bigger prizes that draws the consumer in. "Roll Up the Rim to Win" is an example of a

game (instant-win promotion)
A promotional contest that includes a number of pre-seeded winning tickets; instant-win tickets can be redeemed immediately.

FIGURE
8.13

Pepsico's Contest That Encouraged Canadian Consumers to Name the Next Great Chip Flavour Was a Hit

Source: Handout/PEPSICO CANADA/ Newscom.

longstanding successful promotion. It delivers a consistent theme and has a catchy and memorable slogan. According to Tim Hortons, the promotion is now less of a promotion and more like a brand unto itself: "Roll Up the Rim to Win" is recognized as an entity, much like a product is. The promotion is an integral part of Tim Hortons' annual marketing plan. Sales increase by 10 to 15 percent during the promotion period.

Planning any kind of contest is a challenge. Most manufacturers rely on external suppliers to develop and implement a contest. In this regard, there is much upfront discussion with suppliers to ensure proper briefing on objectives and expectations. The success of a contest depends on the consumer's perception of the value and number of prizes being awarded and on the odds of winning. As well, the prizes must match the image of the product and the lifestyle of the target market. Contests that are combined with other purchase incentives provide added stimulus for consumers to take action. Refer to the illustration in Figure 8.14.

A cost–benefit analysis should be done prior to getting involved with a contest. In terms of benefit, a contest is a good device for achieving repeat purchase objectives. A well-designed contest encourages customers to come back or buy more frequently. By returning to buy more goods, consumers exhibit a certain degree of loyalty. As such, contests are ideal promotions for products in the mature stage of the product life cycle. They can boost brand sales in a time of need.

On the cost side of things, a contest requires a significant investment in media advertising to create awareness and interest. Contests such as "Roll Up the Rim to Win" are supported by multimedia advertising campaigns. A combination of media advertising, social media, and in-store promotional materials tends to be effective. To encourage support by retail distributors, a trade promotion program involving price allowances and display materials is necessary. When the cost of prizes, trade promotion allowances, and having an external organization implement the contest are factored in, the amount required for a contest promotion can be a sizeable portion of a marketing budget.

Legal issues are another concern for marketers when they get involved in contests. The manager must be familiar with some of the basic laws that govern contests in Canada.

FIGURE
8.14

An Example of a Promotion that Combines a Coupon and Contest Communicated by In-Store Shelf Pads

Source: © Keith Tuckwell.

Section 189 of the *Criminal Code* and sections 52 and 59 of the *Competition Act* regulate most contests in Canada, and there are certain fairly standardized rules and regulations for what information must be communicated to participants. The following information must be clearly conveyed:

- The number of prizes and the value of each
- The odds of winning, if known
- Whether a skill-testing question will be administered
- Whether facsimiles are acceptable in the case of a sweepstakes
- How to enter and what proof of purchase is required
- The contest's closing date

For some tips on planning an effective contest, see Figure 8.15.

REBATES   A **rebate** is a predetermined amount of money returned directly to the customer by the manufacturer after the purchase has been made. It is an incentive to get consumers to buy in greater volume during the promotion period. Initially, rebates were the promotion of choice among packaged goods marketers, but they are now an integral element of marketing programs for durable goods such as automobiles, major appliances, and consumer electronics.

The most common type of rebate is the *single-purchase refund*, in which consumers receive a portion of their money back for the purchase of a specified product. Such an offer is one method of achieving trial purchases. Other variations of rebates include making an offer according to an escalating schedule. For example, an offer could be

rebate   A predetermined amount of money returned directly to customers by the manufacturer after the purchase has been made.

FIGURE
8.15

Tips for Planning an Effective Contest

Effective contests do not happen by chance. They are carefully planned to spark interest and action, and to achieve specific marketing objectives. Here are some pointers from those in the business:

- Choose prizes that spark wish-fulfillment fantasies.
- Give consumers a decent chance of winning (low odds of winning create ill will).
- Plan an engaging media component to drive consumer awareness and generate publicity.
- Keep the company name in the contest moniker (again for positive press).
- Use strategic partnerships; co-brand the contest to leverage each other's equity.
- Make sure contest rules are clear and unambiguous.
- Ensure that fulfillment (awarding of prizes) occurs quickly.
- If it ain't broke, don't fix it! Stay with a successful contest if it's producing desired results.

Source: Based on "Tips for Creating Killer Contests," Special Report on Premiums and Incentives, *Strategy*, August 26, 2002, p. 24.

structured as follows: Buy one and get $1.00 back, buy two and get $2.00 back, and buy three and get $5.00 back. The nature of the offer encourages consumers to buy three items at one time, thus helping achieve multiple purchase objectives.

Though many people buy a product because of the possibility of a rebate, many rebates go uncollected due to the hassle of filling out the form and mailing it in with the proof of purchase documentation a manufacturer requires. This phenomenon is referred to as **slippage** when the consumer collects labels but fails to follow through and request the refund, even for a refund with a $100 value. Time-pressed consumers often forget about the rebate offer. Technology at point of purchase is now eliminating problems associated with slippage. Once a transaction is complete in a retail store, for example, it can transfer appropriate information about the customer to the source of the rebate offer.

In recent years, incentives and rebates have become commonplace among automobile manufacturers. Automobile companies trying to recover from the 2008 recession offered "cash back" rebates as high as $5000 on cars and $8000 on trucks. The rebates move the cars but place a financial strain on the company. Consumers are adapting to rebates so well, it seems they won't buy a new car without some kind of financial incentive. In the long term, this promotion tactic is not in the best interests of the industry.

Rebate offers are best suited to products in the mature stage of the product life cycle. As indicated, they are a good incentive for encouraging multiple purchases of inexpensive packaged goods products. Encouraging multiple purchases or building frequency of purchases is a common objective for mature products. At this stage in the life cycle, maintaining customer loyalty is critical. Apart from the rebates offered by automobile companies, which tend to be very high, a rebate promotion is not that expensive to implement. Since it is current users who tend to take advantage of rebate offers, advertising support can be confined to the package and various in-store opportunities, such as shelf cards and product displays.

PREMIUM OFFERS   A **premium** is an additional item given free, or greatly discounted, to induce purchase of the primary brand. The goal of a premium is to provide added value to tempt consumers to buy.

Premiums are offered to consumers several ways: as a mail-in, by sending in proofs of purchase so the item can be delivered by mail; as an in-pack or on-pack promotion, where the item is placed inside or attached to a package; by an order form that is usually available at point of purchase; or by electronic registration at a website. Packaged goods

slippage   A situation in which a consumer collects labels in a promotion offer but fails to follow through and request the refund.

premium   An additional item given free, or greatly discounted, to induce purchase of the primary brand.

FIGURE
8.16

In-pack Premiums Encourage Impulse Purchases at Point of Purchase

Source: © Keith Tuckwell.

companies frequently use their packages to distribute free premiums. Refer to the illustration in Figure 8.16.

Many marketers firmly believe that there is something to be said for offering a tangible, quality gift, which can surprise the consumer and build long-term equity through association. Others see the benefits of premiums as largely misleading, citing large increases in sales followed by an equally large tumble once the giveaway ends. Both Molson and Labatt experienced this feast-or-famine phenomenon when they packed everything from golf balls to T-shirts to ball caps in their beer cases. Both companies found the promotions expensive, and rather than create loyalty, they simply encouraged drinkers to switch brands constantly.[7]

An offshoot of a premium offer is the **bonus pack**. The traditional bonus pack offers the consumer more for less. For example, a brand offers a package size that gives the consumer 20 percent more product for the regular price. Another option is to bundle a product in pairs and offer a deal like "Buy One, Get One Free." Offers like these, if implemented properly, will attract new users and reward current users. If done wrong, they can cheapen the image or value perception of the brand.

Marketing managers tend to rank premiums lower in terms of popularity, but they do offer some tangible benefits. They achieve several marketing objectives: They can increase the quantity of brand purchases made by consumers during the promotion period; they help to retain current customers, therefore building brand loyalty; and they provide a merchandising tool to encourage display activity in stores. A good premium offer will help differentiate one brand from another at a crucial time—when consumers are deciding which brand to buy.

bonus pack   The temporary offering of a larger package size (for example, 20 percent more) for the same price as the regular size.

LOYALTY PROGRAMS

Loyalty programs take the short-term premium offer a step further—they encourage long-term brand loyalty. How many loyalty cards do you have in your wallet? It seems that consumers are collecting points to obtain something for free years from now. In the meantime, we keep going back to the loyalty sponsor to earn more points. By definition, a **loyalty program (frequent buyer program)** offers consumers a small bonus, such as points or play money, each time they make a purchase. The bonus accumulates and can be redeemed for merchandise or some other benefit at a later date.

Shoppers Drug Mart has a frequent buyer program that is updated electronically. Their Shoppers Optimum cards are scanned each time members make a purchase. Shoppers can cross-reference transaction data electronically, and tailor offers and services to specific customers. One such offer included free samples of a variety of brand-name grooming and personal care products. These samples were distributed by mail to a select group of Shoppers Drug Mart customers. As discussed elsewhere in this text, the true benefit of a loyalty program is the information it collects for database marketing. See the illustration in Figure 8.17.

The Intercontinental Group of Hotels, which operates in all price and quality segments of the lodging industry, has a program called "Priority Club Rewards." In this program the customer can redeem accumulated points on merchandise such as coffee makers, food processors, and small consumer electronic items, or the points can be used for hotel rooms and special travel packages sponsored by the hotel chain and its airline partners.

Perhaps the longest-running and most successful loyalty program in Canada is Canadian Tire money. Canadian Tire rewards regular shoppers who pay by cash or Canadian Tire credit card with Canadian Tire money, worth up to 4 percent of the value of the purchase. Now at an advanced stage, the program allows customers to collect virtual money at Canadian Tire's website. Canadian Tire money represents the true essence of a loyalty program: Customers actually can receive something for free. In contrast, a program like AIR MILES takes considerable time before the consumer can get even the smallest of rewards. For insight into Canadian Tire's program, read the IMC Highlight: **Canadian Tire Money Keeps Customers Happy**.

FIGURE
8.17

An Illustration of a Rewards Loyalty Program at Shoppers Drug Mart/Pharmaprix

Source: Courtesy of Shoppers Drug Mart.

Canadian Tire Money Keeps Customers Happy

Canadian Tire money is a simple concept. Yet it is the cornerstone of Canadian Tire's marketing mix. Canadian Tire money is a most successful and popular customer reward program, with a 90 percent redemption and participation level. It is the very heart of what Canadian Tire stands for in today's competitive marketplace.

The program has evolved since it was introduced in 1958, but stays true to its original premise: reward good customers for their loyalty! To keep customers truly happy, the program lets customers determine what their reward will be. Unlike many other loyalty programs that are much more complex and allow customers to select only rewards from predetermined merchandise,

Source: Courtesy of Canadian Tire Corporation, Limited.

Canadian Tire's program allows customers to claim their reward anytime and on anything the store sells. That formula still works today. It encourages people to come back to the store.

Canadian Tire money is part of the customers' shopping experience. From a marketing perspective, it allows the company to differentiate itself and provides immense competitive advantage. For the record, Canadian Tire is the most-shopped store in Canada: 90 percent of Canadians shop there. And the Canadian Tire brand is one of the top five most recognized brands in Canada.

The "money" is extremely popular among older customers, who feel deep connections to the currency. The rewards program has gone digital so that it can do what loyalty programs are designed to do: Track customer purchase patterns to help customize marketing and select products for shelves.

As a loyalty program, and regardless of whether it's paper money or electronic money, the Canadian Tire rewards program is successful because of its simplicity. It offers instant rewards to its customers, and it keeps them coming back!

Based on Marina Strauss, "Canadian Tire's 'Funny Money' Dilemma," *The Globe and Mail*, February 16, 2012, p. B3; and Sharon Adams, "Canadian Tire Got the Ball Rolling," *Loyalty & Its Rewards*, supplement in the *National Post*, April 26, 2007, p. IS6.

Loyalty programs are popular with Canadian customers. In fact, a recent study revealed that 90 percent of Canadians have a loyalty card, and, on average, Canadians have four cards in their wallet. The presence of loyalty cards indicates Canadian consumers are looking for added value when they shop; they also show a preference for cards with no annual fees.[8]

Free rewards are a real incentive, but consumers don't realize they may be paying for the privilege. The true benefit for the organization is the information it is collecting about customer shopping behaviour. The ability to mine such data is very useful as organizations move further toward individualized marketing programs.

A plastic card can function as both a loyalty card and a gift card. Gift cards are a booming market. Presently, the gift card market is estimated to be worth $6 billion. Card buyers benefit from having a convenient option for gift giving. Retailers benefit through what is known as float and slippage. **Float** refers to the fact that the issuer of the card receives the money without offering goods or services right away. **Slippage** (often called **breakage** as well) refers to those cards that go unredeemed; it is estimated that

float Money received by the issuer of a gift card without yet having offered any goods or services.

slippage (breakage) Gift cards that go unredeemed.

10 to 15 percent of cards are not redeemed, which becomes easy money in the pocket of the card seller![9] Retailers like gift cards because, in the hands of a brand-new customer, the card could be the starting point of a new and long-term relationship.

TRADE PROMOTION EXECUTION

Trade customers are the link between manufacturers and consumers, and in Canada they have incredible control in many markets. In the grocery industry, for example, the combination of two large wholesale/retail operations, Loblaw and Sobeys, controls more than half of all food store sales. In the hardware market, the combination of Canadian Tire, The Home Depot, and Home Hardware control a significant portion of volume. Distributors make money by selling your products, but they are also in business to sell anyone's products. Consequently, their loyalty to any supplier can waver if they do not receive trade promotion offers they feel they deserve.

Simply stated, the trade looks for the best offers from suppliers and makes buying decisions accordingly. As with consumer promotions, trade promotions must be designed to deliver the highest possible value to the trade while costing as little as possible for the manufacturer. Manufacturers have a variety of trade promotion offers to choose from when developing a promotion plan. Typically, the offers work together to generate a high degree of impact during the promotion period. This section explores the various trade promotion options.

trade allowance A temporary price reduction that encourages larger purchases by distributors.

TRADE ALLOWANCES   A **trade allowance** is a temporary price reduction that encourages larger purchases by distributors. It can be offered several ways: a percentage reduction from the list price, a predetermined dollar amount off the list price, or free goods. A free goods offer may be something like "Buy 10 cases and get 1 free."

In addition to encouraging larger volume purchases, the manufacturer would like to see a portion of the allowance devoted to lowering the price of the product at retail for a short period. In the grocery industry, products are commonly offered on sale for one week. The manufacturer absorbs the discount offered to consumers. Trade allowances can be deducted from the invoice immediately, and in such cases are called *off-invoice allowances*. Or they can be offered on the basis of a *bill-back*, in which case the manufacturer keeps a record of all purchases shipped to the distributor and, when the deal period expires, reimburses the distributor for the allowances it earned.

performance allowance A discount offered by a manufacturer that encourages a distributor to perform a merchandising function on behalf of the manufacturer.

PERFORMANCE ALLOWANCES   A **performance allowance** is a discount that encourages the distributor to perform a merchandising function on behalf of the manufacturer. As indicated, a trade allowance helps lower prices, but additional incentives are required to make the promotion a real success. It is common for the manufacturer to request automatic distribution of goods to retail stores, displays in stores, and a mention of the sale price in the retailer's weekly advertising flyer. The additional funds provided in the performance allowance help cover the distributor's costs of implementing these activities. The distributor may or may not comply with all of the manufacturer's requests, but some kind of deal is negotiated and agreed to. Before paying the allowance, the manufacturer requires proof of performance by the distributor.

Given this information, you can now appreciate that many of the advertising flyers and in-store promotional activities that are undertaken by large retail chain stores are actually subsidized by the manufacturers' brands involved in the promotions. The costs of trade promotions are significant and take a considerable portion of a brand's marketing budget each year.

COOPERATIVE ADVERTISING ALLOWANCES   A **cooperative advertising allowance**, or **co-op allowance** as it is commonly referred to, is a fund allocated to pay for a portion of a distributor's advertising. Marketing organizations often pay a percentage (often 50 percent or more) of the distributor's ad cost, provided the marketer's brand is featured prominently.

To maximize the effectiveness of allowances offered to the trade, these allowances are frequently combined to develop an integrated promotion plan. If a bigger plan is in place, the trade promotion plan will be integrated with consumer promotions and brand advertising. Combining the allowances is attractive to the retailers. The financial rewards will be much greater, and the funds available are sufficient to support their own advertising and merchandising activities. Financial incentives are a great motivator among distributors.

> **cooperative advertising allowance (co-op allowance)**   The sharing of advertising costs by suppliers and retailers or by several retailers.

DEALER PREMIUMS   A **dealer premium** is an incentive offered to a distributor by a manufacturer to encourage the special purchase of a product or to secure additional merchandising support from a retailer. Premiums are usually offered in the form of merchandise and distributed by sales representatives of the company offering the premium. Some common premiums include golfing equipment, cameras, audio equipment, and leisure clothing.

The offering of premiums is a controversial issue. Some distributors absolutely forbid their buyers to accept them. They argue that the buyer is the only beneficiary and that the buying organization might be purchasing more goods than it really needs. Many believe the practice of offering buyers premiums, often referred to as "payola," is unethical. However, dealings between sellers and buyers sometimes occur under the table.

An offshoot of a premium offer is a **spiff**. Next time you're in a sporting goods store, ask yourself why that retail sales representative recommended an expensive pair of Reebok (or any other popular brand) running shoes over the others. It could be that the manufacturer encouraged the sales representative to promote its brand by providing some kind of incentive. The retail sales representative stands to gain if more Reebok products are sold. Such a practice is common in product categories where consumers have a tendency to ask for recommendations. Since there are so many good running shoe brands to choose from, you value the salesperson's advice, but you may also play right into their hands by doing so!

Clearly, the use of premiums and spiffs achieves certain marketing objectives. Many companies employ them when they are facing unusual circumstances, such as when trying to meet year-end sales objectives and it's a touch-and-go situation. Compared to other forms of sales promotion, though, they are not the kinds of activities that will be used regularly.

> **dealer premium**   An incentive offered to a distributor to encourage the special purchase of a product or to secure additional merchandising support from the distributor.

> **spiff**   An incentive offered to retail salespeople to encourage them to promote a specified brand of goods to customers.

COLLATERAL MATERIAL   The role of the sales representative cannot be underestimated, particularly in business-to-business selling situations. Companies invest significant sums in programs that tell consumers about their goods and services but, as indicated, it is also important to invest in programs that help push the product through the channel. Sales representatives need selling resources, and that's where collateral material comes into play. **Collateral materials** are visual aids that are specific to special promotions or simply ongoing aids for the variety of products being sold. Collateral materials include price lists, catalogues, sales brochures, pamphlets, specification sheets, and digital sales aids.

> **collateral materials**   Visual aids used by sales representatives in sales presentations, such as price lists, sales brochures, and digital materials.

DEALER DISPLAY MATERIAL   As indicated, one of the objectives of trade promotion is to encourage merchandising support from retail distributors. The manufacturer can assist in this area by providing **dealer display material** or **point-of-purchase material** as

> **dealer display (point-of-purchase) material**   Temporary display material placed in retail stores that advertises a product and encourages impulse purchasing.

it is often called. Dealer display material includes posters, shelf talkers (mini-posters that hang or dangle from store shelves), channel strips (narrow bands that fit into the side of a store shelf), and advertising pads (tear-off sheets that hang from pads attached to shelves). Refer to the image in Figure 8.18.

Material of a more permanent nature includes display shippers (shipping cases that convert to display stands when opened and erected properly) and permanent display racks. One of the problems with display material is that it frequently goes to waste. In many retail outlets, permission to erect displays must be granted by the store manager and sometimes by the head office of the retailer. Some retailers do not allow manufacturer-supplied display material at all. To be effective, displays must be erected in a visible location. The retailer makes the location decision, which may not be to the liking of the manufacturer. A poor location will diminish the intended impact of the display.

trade show An event that allows a company to showcase its products to a captive audience and generate leads.

TRADE SHOWS   Trade shows are an effective way for a company to introduce new products to the marketplace. There is no better opportunity to showcase something special than at a trade show. Where else will a manufacturer find as many customers, all in one place, actively and willingly seeking product information? All industries seem to have trade shows, and in many cases they move around the country to make it more convenient for prospective customers to visit. Depending on the nature of the show, it may attract consumers, trade distributors, or both.

The automobile industry and the recreation and leisure products industry are among the largest users of trade shows. Here, all manufacturers gather to show their latest models. Auto shows are magnets for the media, so they generate all kinds of positive press for the participating companies. From a manufacturer's perspective, a trade show provides an opportunity to develop a prospect list that the sales force can follow up on. When visiting a trade show, customers leave a trail of valuable information about themselves that can be quickly added to a database for analysis and use later. The very nature of a trade show, however, requires considerable planning by participants, along with a considerable financial investment. There is a simple rule of thumb about participating in trade shows: "If you are going to do it, do it right." It's a great opportunity to outshine the competition.

Additional Considerations for Sales Promotion Planning

Sales promotions are not usually the focal point of a brand's marketing communications strategies but, as mentioned above, play a complementary role in achieving certain objectives. Therefore, sales promotions must be carefully planned so they effectively integrate with advertising, public relations, social media, and any other marketing communications plans. Decisions must be made regarding how frequently promotions are offered, what types of promotions will have a positive effect on brand image, and how they will build brand value in the long term. Let's look at each situation briefly.

FREQUENCY OF PROMOTIONS
How frequently should a brand offer sales promotions? All kinds of factors influence this decision: the type of product, the activities of the competition, the stage of the product life cycle the brand is in, and the receptiveness of customers toward promotions. A theme running throughout this chapter is that promotions are complementary in nature, so they should never disrupt the flow of regular and more dominant communications activities. There is a risk that too many promotions could cheapen the image of a brand—short-term gain for long-term pain! In general, coupon activity can be implemented more frequently than cash refunds, premium offers, and contests. It is less disruptive to the regular message expressed through media advertising.

BRAND IMAGE AND PROMOTIONS
Much of the discussion about promotion strategies in this chapter mentioned lowering prices so that consumers get a better deal. In the short run, such a strategy brings positive results. However, if this practice becomes frequent, consumers will perceive the sale price to be more of a regular price. In the long term, such a practice will hurt the brand's image and lower profit margins. Domestic automobile manufacturers are facing this dilemma right now. Advertising is so focused on rebates and low financing packages that much less time is devoted to building an image, the former priority of these companies. That said, these manufacturers have to deal with current economic realities.

BUILDING BRAND EQUITY
The cumulative force of all marketing communications is a key factor in building brand equity. Marketers must be aware that sales promotions are a rather chaotic sequence of deals and events that create noise in the marketplace. They are not a sustaining message. It is preferable to adopt a view about promotions that will pay attention to long-term brand values and a consistent approach that will build good relationships with the trade and consumers. A few of the promotions mentioned in this chapter do just that. Among them are Lay's "Do Us a Flavour" contest, Tim Hortons' "Roll up the Rim to Win" contest, Shoppers Drug Mart's Optimum loyalty program, and Canadian Tire's reward money. Promotions like these become a positive part of the brand's heritage and reinforce relationships with customers.

>> SUMMARY

Sales promotions are incentives offered to consumers and the trade to encourage more immediate and larger purchases. Strategically, consumer promotions are designed to help pull a product through the channel of distribution, while trade promotions help push a product through the channel of distribution. A good sales promotion plan usually balances between pull and push.

Sales promotion planning involves a series of steps or decisions. After an assessment of the situation is made, specific objectives and strategies are established and the appropriate offers or incentives are determined. The plan must also consider fulfillment obligations at the back end, and a means of assessing the effectiveness of the plan must be in place.

A key to a successful sales promotion plan lies in how it is integrated with other marketing communications strategies. For certain, sales promotion strategies must be integrated with advertising strategies. Because sales promotions are short term in nature, they often become the focus of the advertising message while the promotion is in place. When the overall plan is implemented, media advertising and social media strategies create awareness of the promotion, while in-store displays and websites provide additional details.

Some specific objectives of consumer promotions are to achieve trial purchase by new users and repeat and multiple purchases by current users. The types of activities commonly used to achieve these objectives include coupons, free samples, contests, rebates, premium offers, and loyalty programs.

Specific marketing objectives of trade promotions are to secure new listings and distribution, build volume on a pre-planned cyclical basis, and encourage merchandising support at point of purchase. Trade promotion activities that help achieve these objectives include trade allowances, performance allowances, cooperative advertising funds, dealer premiums, point-of-purchase display materials, collateral materials, and trade shows.

The impact of sales promotions is short term in nature, and therefore promotions complement other integrated marketing communications strategies. As such, sales promotions should not disrupt regular brand advertising. They must be integrated into advertising strategies to enhance the overall impact on consumers and trade customers. When planning promotions, a manager should guard against running them too frequently so as to not harm the image of the brand. A good sales promotion concept will fit with the brand's image and help build brand equity.

KEY TERMS

bonus pack   249
breakage   251
collateral materials   253
consumer promotion   229
contest   244
co-op allowance   253
cooperative advertising allowance   253
coupon   241
cross-coupon   243
cross-ruff   243
dealer display material   253
dealer premium   253
float   251

free sample   243
free-standing insert (FSI)   242
frequent buyer program   250
game   245
in-pack self-coupon   243
instantly redeemable coupon   243
instant-win promotion   245
loyalty program   250
media-delivered coupon   242
on-pack self-coupon   243
performance allowance   252
point-of-purchase material   253
premium   248

pull   229
push   230
rebate   247
redemption rate   243
sales promotion   229
sales promotion plan   232
slippage   248
spiff   253
sweepstakes   244
trade allowance   252
trade promotion   230
trade show   254

REVIEW QUESTIONS

1. What is the difference between a pull strategy and a push strategy, and how do sales promotions complement both strategies?
2. What are the primary objectives of a consumer promotion plan?
3. What are the primary objectives of a trade promotion plan?
4. Briefly explain how sales promotion strategies are integrated with advertising strategies. Why is such integration essential?
5. In sales promotion planning, what is meant by logistics and fulfillment?
6. Briefly describe the following consumer promotion terms:
   a) redemption rate
   b) in-pack self-coupon
   c) cross-ruff
   d) instant-win promotions
   e) slippage
   f) bonus pack
7. What types of coupon distribution are appropriate for the early stages of the product life cycle? What distribution is appropriate for the later stages? Why?
8. What are the benefits and drawbacks of a free sample offer?
9. What elements contribute to the success of a contest offer?
10. What is the objective of a consumer premium offer, and when is the best time to implement such an offer?
11. What are the benefits and drawbacks of loyalty promotions?
12. How do trade allowances, performance allowances, and cooperative advertising funds complement each other when implementing a trade promotion plan?
13. Briefly describe the following trade promotion terms:
    a) spiff
    b) dealer premium
    c) collateral materials
    d) point-of-purchase material

DISCUSSION AND APPLICATION QUESTIONS

1. Assume you are a brand manager launching a new snack food or confectionary product. What balance would you recommend among consumer promotion, trade promotion, and media advertising? What specific sales promotion activities would you recommend? Justify your choices.
2. Conduct some secondary research on consumer and trade promotion budgets and spending patterns in various industries. Is there undue pressure placed on marketing organizations to spend more on trade promotions and less on other activities? Does the situation vary from one industry to another?
3. A common criticism of consumer premium offers is that they encourage only temporary brand switching. Once the offer is over, consumers switch back to their regular brand. Therefore, in the long run, the promotion will not contribute to sales objectives. Conduct some secondary research on this issue and determine if such a criticism is valid.
4. Consumers could be suffering from "loyalty promotion fatigue." Conduct some secondary research on loyalty promotions to find out how organizations view loyalty promotions. Do loyalty promotions provide real benefits to consumers and the sponsor? What are the elements that make a loyalty promotion a success?
5. What forms of sales promotion are best suited for the following brands? (Hint: you may want to consider the life cycle stage the brand is in.) Justify your position.
   a) Secret deodorant
   b) Quaker Chewy Granola Bars
   c) Blue Mountain Resort (or any similar ski or golf resort)
   d) Valvoline motor oil
   e) Gatorade
   f) New Balance running shoes
6. Evaluate the sales promotion strategies used by Tim Hortons. What marketing and marketing communications objectives do they meet? How does Tim Hortons integrate sales promotions with other components of the marketing communications mix?
7. Automobile manufacturers have used rebate programs for years to provide consumers with an incentive to buy (and buy now!). Is this an effective sales promotion strategy? Conduct some secondary research on rebate incentives and develop some kind of cost–benefit analysis for using this form of promotion.

ENDNOTES

1. "Asking Canadians," *Strategy*, March 2008, p. 12.

2. Evra Taylor, "Harley-Davidson Rides Out with 'Live the Dream' Promotion," *Marketing*, April 13, 2012, www.marketingmag.ca.

3. "Coupon Redemption Canada: Some Interesting Data," Canadian Deals Association, www.canadiandealsassociation.com.

4. Julie Landry Laviolette, "Digital Coupons Rise in Popularity," *Miami Herald*, November 14, 2014, www.miamihearld.com.

5. Lynn Cook, "CPG Slow To Realign Coupon Programs for Growing Popularity Of Digital," Greenwood Group, October 9, 2014, www.greenwoodg.com/news/item/130-cpg-slow-to-realign-coupon-programs.

6. "The Lay's Do Us a Flavour Contest returns: The Tastes of Canada Edition Asks Fans to Draw Flavour Inspiration from Canadian Regions," press release, PepsiCo Canada, February 23, 2015, www.pepsico.ca.

7. John Heinzl, "Beer Firms Rethink Giveaways," *The Globe and Mail*, March 3, 2003, p. B5.

8. Rebecca Harris, "Loyalty Programs: What's in It for Marketers?" *Marketing*, March 31, 2015, www.marketingmag.ca.

9. Rob Carrick, "Not All Gift Cards are Created Equal," *The Globe and Mail*, December 1, 2009, www.theglobeandmail.com.

Public Relations

Learning Objectives

After studying this chapter, you will be able to

1. Identify and assess the various roles of public relations communications in achieving marketing and business objectives

2. Describe the various steps in public relations planning

3. Identify and evaluate various public relations execution techniques for potential application in public relations plans

4. Identify and assess the various techniques that evaluate and measure the impact of public relations strategies

Public relations (PR) are an often-misunderstood form of marketing communications. The term can conjure up negative images of a company trying to cover something up or trying to put its own spin on a situation. Certainly, with all the news coverage that companies receive when they are in trouble, there is some truth to such perceptions. However, public relations can have a very positive impact on a brand or company's performance, and are responsible for communicating all kinds of positive information.

The theme of this text deals with how messages from various disciplines in communications are integrated, and that, whatever the discipline, all must work together to give the consumer a unified message. In fact, with the media landscape and technology transforming the way in which consumers receive information, many PR experts believe public relations should be at the forefront of the communications mix. With social media, public relations communications can move from *earned media* (the traditional press coverage they still desire) to *shared media* (where consumers interact and exchange information they find interesting with others).

Technology and social media are changing the nature of public relations practice. It is taking off as a profession. Organizations now use new job titles such as "strategists" and "connectors" to reflect how things are changing. Public relations now play a key role in building brand image and brand equity.

In the age of heightened competition and advancing electronic technology, marketers are looking for multiple solutions to brand building. This position further suggests the need for the integration of various forms of marketing communications. To rely on any one medium or channel of marketing communications could be harmful, since consumers' media habits are constantly changing. An organization must embrace all communications channels in order to build better relationships with consumers and to achieve its business objectives.

Defining Public Relations

public relations A form of communication designed to gain public understanding and acceptance.

Public relations is a form of communication that is primarily directed toward gaining public understanding and acceptance. Unlike advertising, which is a form of communication paid for by the company, public relations use publicity that does not necessarily involve payment. Public relations communications appear in the news media and social media, and, as such, offer a legitimacy that advertising does not have. Recently, companies have been using public relations to extol the merits of a product

260

by assisting in new product launches or reporting eventful occurrences of the product. This form of communications is often referred to as marketing public relations or marketing PR.

The practice of public relations is used to build rapport with the various publics a company, individual, or organization might have. These publics are either internal or external. **Internal publics** involve those with whom the organization communicates regularly and include employers, distributors, suppliers, shareholders, and customers. **External publics** are more distant and are communicated with less frequently. They include the media, governments, prospective shareholders, the financial community, and community organizations.

The goal of public relations is to conduct communications in a way that an organization builds an open, honest, and constructive relationship with its various publics. In comparison to advertising, public relations communications are not controlled by the organization. Instead, the media determine what is said about the company, regardless of what information the company provides. In other words, the media act as a "filter" for the information an organization releases.

In the age of social media, an organization can actually bypass traditional media channels and post information directly online through Facebook, YouTube, Twitter, and other social networks. That said, it takes a significant investment in time, people, and money for an organization to keep information in the social media fresh. As well, organizations must adapt to the reality that consumers will comment on brand communications. Those comments can be positive or negative. A shift in who controls the message is taking place.

internal publics   The publics with which an organization communicates regularly; can include employees, distributors, suppliers, shareholders, and customers.

external publics   Those publics that are distant from an organization and are communicated with less frequently.

The Role of Public Relations

Toyota has learned the true value of public relations. A few years ago the company had to recall 4 million vehicles in North America because of gas pedals getting caught in the floor mats. The recall certainly damaged Toyota's reputation as the leader in automotive quality, and, needless to say, Toyota initially experienced much negative publicity. After carefully analyzing the situation, Toyota implemented a well-thought-out public relations plan over a long period. The plan helped re-establish its quality position in the minds of consumers. Toyota's case demonstrates how public relations communications fit into an organization's overall marketing communications plans.

As a management function, public relations will help an organization anticipate and interpret public opinion that will have an impact on its actions. PR will also provide the means to plan and implement communications strategies that are in the best interest of the organization—for example, to devise communications intended to change public attitudes if necessary. Good PR will help launch new products, and create awareness and excitement for them, just as advertising can, and at a much lower cost. In an era where marketing budgets are being squeezed, that's music to an executive's ears.

The role of public relations is varied, but generally falls into seven primary categories: corporate communications; reputation management; product publicity; product placement, branded content, and product seeding; community relations; fundraising; and internal communications. The diversity of this list indicates how public relations can be company oriented or product oriented. Let's examine each category in more detail.

CORPORATE COMMUNICATIONS

corporate advertising Advertising (paid for) designed to convey a favourable image of a company among its various publics.

A good public relations plan strives to maximize communications in an unpaid manner, but there are times when paid communications are necessary. Such communications may be in the form of **corporate advertising**, a paid form of advertising designed to convey a favourable image of a company to its various publics.

Corporate advertising shows how the resources of the organization resolve customers' problems by promoting goodwill or by demonstrating a sense of social responsibility. The Good Purpose survey conducted by global PR firm Edelman revealed that Canadians support brands that have a societal purpose associated with them. Some 70 percent of Canadians are more likely to recommend a brand that supports a good cause than one that doesn't.[1] Domtar Canada shows how it integrates economic progress with environmental issues, often a delicate challenge for a company in the pulp and paper business (see Figure 9.1). Domtar is committed to the responsible use of paper and to communicating paper's place and value to the businesses and people who use their products every day. The advertisement in Figure 9.1 is an example of social responsibility marketing; it reflects Domtar's position on the importance of sustainability in business practice.

REPUTATION MANAGEMENT

Chances are that a company in the headlines is there for all the wrong reasons. Something went wrong and key executives are being called upon to defend the company's position. Public relations play a vital role when a company finds itself in a crisis situation, because the final outcome often depends on how effectively an organization manages its communications during the crisis.

An organization might also be guilty by association and have to defend its position to the public. Such was the case for leading companies such as Scotiabank, VISA, and Coca-Cola in the wake of the FIFA corruption allegations that surfaced in 2015. FIFA is the governing body for World Cup soccer. Allegedly, prominent FIFA officials accepted bribes, laundered money, and then voted in favour of awarding the World Cup of Soccer to undeserving countries. Scotiabank, a North American sponsor, immediately announced it would review its involvement with World Cup soccer; the bank doesn't want to be associated with inappropriate business ethics and disturbing and ongoing media coverage of the scandal.

On the same issue VISA provided an acute criticism, saying it expects the organization to take swift and immediate steps to address its issues, and warned it was prepared to jump ship. "This starts with rebuilding a culture with strong ethical practices in order to restore the reputation of the games to fans everywhere. Should FIFA fail to do so, we have informed them that we will reassess our relationship." Coca-Cola also took a hard stance, saying "the lengthy controversy has tarnished the mission and ideals of the FIFA World Cup." Coca-Cola questioned its continued involvement under such circumstances.[2]

The irony of this situation is that World Cup soccer is one of the crown jewels of marketing, and these corporations have long-term connections to it. To disassociate themselves would open the door to competitors. It's economics versus ethics. Who wins?

FIGURE
9.1

An Illustration of Corporate Advertising with a Social Responsibility Message

Source: © Domtar.

When facing a crisis situation, acting quickly and decisively is the approach recommended by experts. The objective is to reassure the public that everything possible is being done to correct the situation. Maple Leaf Foods faced a serious crisis a few years ago, a crisis that put considerable strain on the company's resources. Maple Leaf responded in a quick and professional manner. For details, read the IMC Highlight: **Maple Leaf Effectively Manages Crisis**.

Maple Leaf Effectively Manages Crisis

When it comes to handling a crisis situation, the best strategy for an organization is to be open, honest, and forthcoming. Clearly, Maple Leaf Foods adopted the right strategy in 2008 in dealing with a listeriosis outbreak. Tainted meat from a Toronto processing plant was responsible for the deaths of 20 people.

Michael McCain, CEO of Maple Leaf, took quick and decisive action. McCain's first step was to apologize publicly. At a press conference, McCain stated, "Tragically our products have been linked to illnesses and loss of life. To Canadians who are ill and who have lost loved ones, I offer my deepest sympathies. Words cannot begin to express our sadness for your pain. We have an unwavering commitment to keeping your food safe with standards well beyond regulatory requirements, but this week our best efforts failed and we are deeply sorry." His apology was heartfelt.

McCain went on to explain the actions the company would be taking to ensure the safety of the public. His plan included an immediate recall of all meat products produced at the plant. The announcement received national coverage and helped position the company positively in the eyes of the public. To reassure the public and to inform the public of the actions the company was taking, Maple Leaf ran full-page newspaper ads in all major daily newspapers in Canada.

Much is at stake if a company is less than forthcoming. Michael Dunne, a marketing professor at the University of Toronto, commended Maple Leaf for its proactive approach. He said, "They were very proactive about it, unusually so, because most companies that go through crises of this nature tend to hide. Maple Leaf is protecting the brand, and it's the brand that matters in the long term for Maple Leaf. Without the brand they don't have anything."

Maple Leaf suffered a serious blow in this situation. Sales of Maple Leaf products declined by 35 percent following the recall, and the profits of the meat division were wiped out. The recall alone cost the company about $30 million. The company's stock price dropped to $6.15 from a high of $15.00. McCain also decided to quickly settle the class-action lawsuits brought by those affected by the illness and deaths by agreeing to pay $27 million. McCain said settling the lawsuit was part of understanding that "you can't accept accountability without accepting a consequence."

To summarize, hiding from the public doesn't work. The best approach for handling a crisis is to clearly and quickly communicate to the public an action plan that will reassure them that all that can be done is being done. Having the CEO, who is the face of the organization, deliver the message is an effective strategy to employ.

© Norm Betts/Bloomberg via Getty Images

Based on Kristine Owram, "A Real Example of How to Do It Right," *The Kingston Whig-Standard*, January 3, 2009, p. 24; Hollie Shaw, "On Road to Recovery," *National Post*, September 5, 2008, p. FP15; and "Maple Leaf Brand Should Rebound in Months: Experts," *Marketing Daily*, August 27, 2008, www.marketingmag.ca.

Situations like these clearly show how important it is for organizations to be prepared. Having a plan in place to meet disaster head on makes more sense than simply reacting to an unforeseen circumstance. Senior executives must be ready to act instantly and demonstrate they are in control of the situation. Company executives must be ready to meet the demand of a more sophisticated and more demanding consumer audience, or suffer the consequences of its wrath. Some tips for handling a crisis situation appear in Figure 9.2.

An organization never knows when it will be caught off guard. Circumstances can arise quickly and get out of control if an organization is not prepared. Here are some tips for handling a crisis situation properly.

1. Take responsibility. If your name is on the problem, you have to take responsibility for it. This is different from accepting blame. The public respects an organization that accepts responsibility.
2. Respond quickly and communicate directly and sincerely. Show the public you are going to resolve the problem.
3. Embrace the three fundamentals of good crisis communication:
   • Communicate very clearly what has gone wrong.
   • Communicate what you are doing about it.
   • Describe the steps you are taking to ensure it doesn't happen again.
4. Have access to a former journalist who knows how to deal with the media (knowing what to expect when the media calls is essential).
5. Offer an apology if an apology is warranted. If the public is satisfied with your efforts in rectifying the problem, they will forgive and move on.

FIGURE 9.2

Tips for Handling a Crisis Situation

Based on David Menzies, "Silence Ain't Golden: Media Crisis Dos and Don'ts," *Marketing*, August 1/8, 2005, p. 18.

PRODUCT PUBLICITY

Publicity is news about an organization, product, service, or person that appears in the media. There is a tendency for people to confuse publicity and public relations, thinking they are one and the same. Publicity is but one aspect of many public relations activities. Essentially, publicity is something that a company and the media deem to be newsworthy. Newsworthy information can include things like a discovery, securing a significant contract that will generate new jobs, and celebrating product or company success.

publicity News about an organization, product, service, or person that appears in the media.

To demonstrate how publicity works: Kraft wanted to celebrate the hundredth anniversary of its popular Oreo cookie. Everybody loves Oreos, don't they? An anniversary itself isn't that special to the media, but the events that surround it are. Once there's consumer involvement with the anniversary, the press takes note. Celebrating the anniversary on a global scale is not easy, but, to the credit of Kraft, it kept things fairly simple. There was a special website with lots of interactivity, tons of social media tie-ins on Facebook and Twitter, special events and music concerts featuring popular country music bands, live special events that included flash mobs, and an oversized Oreo birthday cake.[3] Refer to the image in Figure 9.3.

The Oreo celebration points to two trends reshaping marketing. First, there's a growing interest in authenticity, and consumers are searching for brands that have stood the test of time. Second, heritage brands are changing their marketing strategies to demonstrate how they have stayed in touch with change. Kraft set out to do something authentic yet fresh and current.[4] The Oreo campaign used the theme "Celebrate the kid inside," which appeared in video and print ads, online at oreo.com/birthday, and in social media such as Facebook, where the brand has more than 25 million "likes" on its fan page. The Oreo celebration campaign included television advertising, online video ads, experiential marketing, and sales promotions—a truly integrated marketing communications campaign!

PRODUCT PLACEMENT, BRANDED CONTENT, AND PRODUCT SEEDING

Product placement refers to the visible placement of branded merchandise in television shows, video games, films, or other programming. Product placement was discussed in Chapter 5 as it can be part of a well-planned media strategy—a strategy that stems from public relations roots. It seems that no brand does product placement better than Apple. During one year, Apple products appeared in just over 1000 television shows and

product placement The visible placement of brand-name products in television shows, movies, radio, video games, and other programming.

FIGURE
9.3

Oreo's 100th Anniversary Is Celebrated by Legions of Fans across the Country

Source: © JJ Thompson/Kraft Canada Inc./Newscom.

40 percent of Hollywood's top grossing movies. Apple's venture into product placement started with the first *Mission Impossible* movie in the 1990s, an arrangement that has continued with each new movie. Apple does not pay for the product placement but they are more than willing to hand out their products (computers, tablets, and iPhones) for free.[5] Apple products also appear in the popular show *House of Cards* on Netflix. In one episode, Apple products actually had 31 minutes of exposure. Apple is Kevin Spacey's main computer in the show.[6] In an extraordinary way, the movies and television shows have capitalized on the aura of Apple—it's a two-way street.

Product placement offers an organization two key benefits. First, the product is present at a time when the audience is paying attention—they can't avoid the brand impression.

Second, there may be an opportunity to associate the brand with the character beyond the television show. It presents an opportunity to extend the brand/actor relationship and build buzz for the brand elsewhere, not to mention the brand chatter that could follow on Facebook.

Branded content, or **product integration**, takes product placement a step further by weaving the name of the brand right into the storyline of a show, movie, or video game. In one episode of *Modern Family*, Apple played a dominant role as the show focused on Phil Dunphy's (a main character) excitement about getting Apple's first iPad.

Tim Hortons received a boost of celebrity publicity when a fictitious doughnut (a chocolate Timbit stuffed into a strawberry-vanilla doughnut) was integrated into the popular sitcom *How I Met Your Mother*. The episode featured well-known Canadians Jason Priestly, Alex Trebek, and Paul Shaffer. All of them mentioned Tim Hortons by name. Once it aired, people started tweeting about it, and customers started asking for a Priestly at Tim Hortons. To capitalize on the publicity, Tim Hortons created the doughnut and posted photos of it on Facebook and Twitter. They also started a contest in which consumers could submit ideas for new doughnut varieties. The winning entry would be sold in the restaurants.[7]

The extent to which a brand can and should be integrated into a show is an issue. Too much of it and the viewer could be turned off—they see enough commercials already. So far viewers have not had too much. Their reaction has been more on the positive side of things. Apparently, actors doing things with real products and talking about them makes the show more real.

Product seeding is an activity that involves giving a product free to a group of trendsetters who, in turn, influence others to become aware of and, the company hopes, purchase the product. The trendsetters or influencers are people who marketers use to pass on product information. These people use technology and their own social networks to spread their opinions about products. Marketers, therefore, can take advantage of their knowledge and their access to consumers—a concept referred to as **word-of-mouth marketing**.

One form of product seeding is celebrity product placement. When a product is used or worn by the celebrity it appears to be a choice the celebrity made according to his or her individual preferences. Marketers have long known the power of celebrity to influence consumer purchasing decisions. For instance, if George Clooney walks the red carpet and clearly exposes an Omega watch in the process, Omega benefits. Clooney appears in advertisements for the watch brand so it would be a natural for him to wear the watch—but consumers may not know that.

Product seeding offers several advantages. First, putting a product in the hands of trendsetters helps create buzz for the brand. Second, it is a low-cost strategy that is nowhere near the cost of an advertising campaign. There is a potential disadvantage as well. If the product does not meet expectations, influencers could tell others about that experience—word of mouth can backfire.

COMMUNITY RELATIONS

Companies today are operating in an environment where social responsibility is very important. Consequently, they place much higher value on programs that foster a good public image in the communities where they operate. Sponsoring community events, local groups, and sports teams is part of being a good corporate citizen. The effect of such an investment on sales is indirect and long term. Very often, being part of the fabric of a community takes precedence over sales. Leaders of companies that place a high value on public relations will

branded content (product integration) The integration of brand-name goods and services into the script (storyline) of a television show or movie. The brand name is clearly mentioned and sometimes discussed.

product seeding Giving a product free to a group of trendsetters who promote the product to others by word of mouth.

word-of-mouth marketing The transfer of a product message by people (often using technology) to other people.

tell you that the public has to "like you before they will buy you." Tim Hortons is a good example of a community-minded company. It supplies sports jerseys to local hockey and soccer teams through its Timbits Sports program, offers free ice skating in local communities during the Christmas break, and sends thousands of needy children to camps each summer through the Tim Horton Children's Foundation. Refer to the image in Figure 9.4.

FUNDRAISING

In the not-for-profit sector, public relations play a key role in fundraising. National organizations such as the Canadian Cancer Society, the Canadian Heart and Stroke Foundation, and the United Way face huge financial challenges each year. Public relations help these and similar organizations educate the public about how funds are used. The message is designed to predispose people to give, to solicit commitment, and to make people feel good about giving. The overall goal of such campaigns is to create a positive image and secure support by sending a message that clearly states what the organization is all about. Such campaigns require an integrated communications plan and employ a variety of techniques to deliver the message. In addition to public relations communications, media strategies include direct mail, telemarketing, print advertising (outdoor, newspapers, and magazines), and websites (see Figure 9.5).

INTERNAL COMMUNICATIONS

Internal communications refers to a system whereby employers, employees, and colleagues share information and talk to each other. It is also a system that will help ensure mutual understanding between management and staff, particularly on issues such as the vision and mission of the company, the objectives a company sets, and the performance expectations of employees. Therefore, how communications are worded, the nature of the content, and the timing of delivery make the planning of internal communications similar to external communications. For example, important news information that could positively or negatively affect employees should follow a carefully planned strategy. It is important for employees to understand why change is occurring and what impact it will have on them personally.

Internal communications are important because they have an influence on employee morale. Employees don't want to be communicated at; they want to be communicated with. Being allowed to offer feedback or to engage in discussion as new policies and procedures are being formulated helps create a more collaborative working environment and a motivated workforce. Poor or ineffective internal communications can have the opposite impact.

FIGURE
9.5   A Public Relations Advertisement Encouraging the Public to Support an Important Social Cause

I believe
in possibility.

Please give to United Way's Community Fund

www.unitedwayhalifax.ca

United Way

Source: © United Way Halifax.

Many companies fall into the trap of withholding information. Access to information is typically based on organizational hierarchy—top management has complete access, mid-management less access, and frontline staff even less. Ironically, it is frontline staff who interact the most with the public. Companies that realize this benefit the most. They will implement an internal communications system that provides sufficient access to relevant information so frontline employees can effectively respond to public inquiry. How they respond has a direct impact on the the public's attitude toward the company.

Several tools are called upon to create good internal communications. Most organizations of size will distribute a company *newsletter* on a predetermined cycle. A good newsletter includes information produced by people from all areas of the company and all levels of management. A newsletter can't be seen as simply a top management propaganda tool. Planning *small group meetings* is a viable option. In the age of abundant non-personal digital communications (internal emails), face-to-face communications are refreshing and appreciated by employees. Finally, *suggestion boxes* that allow employees to offer comments anonymously, and *posters* placed in high traffic, high visibility areas of offices and manufacturing facilities are useful internal communications tools.

Public Relations Planning

As a component of the integrated marketing communications mix, public relations plans are designed to complement the needs of the organization's marketing objectives. They can be active (help support a brand or company positively) or reactive (help out in a crisis situation). Regardless of the situation, as already stated, a plan must be in place.

A good public relations plan can help build an image and assist in developing relationships with customers. Furthermore, a well-timed public relations plan can play a crucial role in the launch of a new product, especially in times when budget resources are scarce. Advertising is a very expensive endeavour; public relations are much more economical. To companies searching for greater effectiveness at lower cost, public relations look like a better option than advertising, or, at the very least, the two disciplines must work effectively together to achieve objectives efficiently.

To demonstrate how public relations and advertising should work together, Richard Edelman, president and CEO of Edelman Public Relations Worldwide, says it often makes sense for public relations to take the lead in marketing communications campaigns. He says his job "is no longer doing a press conference to break the ads, it's to engage with enthusiasts to create a runway of credibility for a new brand or campaign."[8] That occurs long before a product is available on the market.

The planning of public relations communications is best left to specialists. It is not an area of expertise in most organizations, although many have a senior-ranking officer assigned the responsibility. Typically, the in-house public relations specialist liaises with outside agencies that prepare and implement public relations plans. There is a tendency to hire an organization that specializes in the preparation and implementation of corporate and product public relations plans. Hill and Knowlton, Edelman Canada, and NATIONAL Public Relations are examples of leading public relations agencies in Canada. The organization briefs the specialist on its needs and expectations. Then, the specialist assesses the information and prepares a strategic plan that will meet the client's objectives. Such a plan must consider the timing of other components of the marketing communications mix—all plans must fit together. Figure 9.6 illustrates the public relations planning process.

Let's discuss each stage of the planning process in more detail.

PUBLIC RELATIONS OBJECTIVES

Public relations objectives typically involve creating awareness, shaping attitudes, and altering behaviour. As marketing campaigns become more integrated and seamless, the ability both to quantify and to measure objectives becomes more difficult. On the surface, public relations objectives are very similar to advertising objectives. Therefore, to try to distinguish between the two is difficult. Increased awareness and predisposition to buy are influenced by numerous factors well beyond the scope of public relations, so trying to evaluate public relations in terms of sales and increased market share is next to impossible.

What can be measured is the level of publicity generated (or earned media) by a public relations plan. Typically, the goal of public relations is to achieve media exposure,

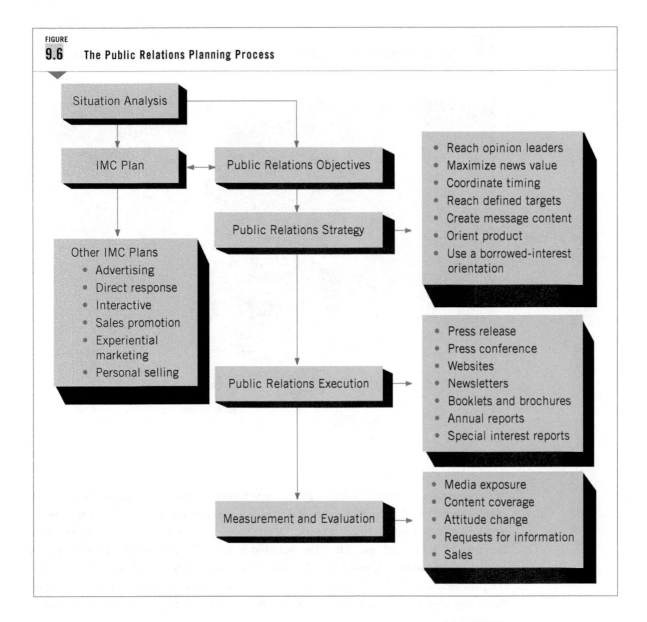

FIGURE 9.6   The Public Relations Planning Process

so quantifiable objectives can be established in this area. Publicity objectives should consider the media through which the message will be communicated and the target audience reached by the media. Surprisingly, even very targeted public relations plans can catch the attention of the national media, because good stories, no matter where they come from, are good stories on national news broadcasts, in national newspapers, and in general interest magazines.

Media exposure can be measured in terms of *gross impressions*, the number of times an item was potentially seen. If a news story appears in a large-circulation newspaper, what is the circulation or readership (circulation multiplied by the readers per copy) of that newspaper? An objective can be stated in terms of impressions. For example, the objective may be to achieve 10 million gross impressions nationally in Canadian daily newspapers.

Another objective could focus on *engaging consumers* with a brand. Degree deodorant did just that when it devised a campaign centred on content that "guys" were interested in. Unilever decided to split its Degree brand of deodorant into specific men's and women's lines. The PR challenge was to engage the male target—men in their twenties—in a

> **FIGURE**
> **9.7**   Degree Adrenaline Appeals to Males in Their Twenties in a Manner Relevant to That Target

manner relevant to them. Unilever's PR agency Weber Shandwick recommended a dedicated website called "The Adrenalist." The site featured news, videos, and information on gear and gadgets for the target audience. Degree enticed males to the website by reaching them where they hang out. The plan included links to the company's Facebook pages, earned media (publicity), and paid ads online. The word "Adrenaline" was also added to the package. Refer to the illustration in Figure 9.7. Within four months of the launch, The Adrenalist tallied more than 750 000 unique visitors, representing nearly 18 500 hours of engagement.[9]

PUBLIC RELATIONS STRATEGY

Every form of marketing communications has its strengths and weaknesses. With public relations, the company cannot control the media or dictate the manner in which the message is communicated. Getting past the media gatekeepers is the first challenge. **Media relations** involve working with the media and developing a good relationship with the strategic people for the purpose of distributing an organization's messages to the public. In this regard, an organization or its public relations agency must be familiar with what topics and news certain people are responsible for (for example, newspaper feature writers, blog specialists in social media, TV assignment editors, reporters, and so on). Typically, these people are listed on a media list (local and national) that can be consulted when needed.

The second challenge is ensuring the message is communicated with reasonable accuracy. On the positive side, public relations messages provide enhanced credibility. When the consumer reads a story in a newspaper, hears and sees something positive

Media relations   Working with the media and developing relationships with key people in the media, for the purpose of distributing an organization's messages to the public.

on a news broadcast about a product or company, or receives branded information from friends in their social network, it is much more authentic than an advertisement.

The role of public relations is determined in advance and is outlined in the marketing communications plan. As mentioned, that role is to reach influential media representatives and bloggers, as well as industry analysts and early adopters of products.

The strategic role of public relations should be examined based on how best to

• Reach the opinion leaders, including professionals, industry analysts, trade audiences, and media, well in advance of the public.

• Maximize the news value of new product introductions, new advertising campaigns, and event sponsorships. Messages must be written creatively and visuals must grab attention.

• Time public relations events to reinforce advertising and promotion campaigns, and to maintain visibility between campaigns.

• Reach markets that are defined by demographics, psychographics, or geographic locations that might not be targeted by advertising.[10]

A public relations strategy allows an organization to tell a longer story about itself and its products. Strategy deals more with informing and educating rather than motivating someone to buy something. Therefore, when claims are made about a product, proper substantiation should be provided. Unlike advertising, where time and space are often restricted, public relations communications can spend additional time expanding on something of importance. Granted, a news editor can shorten the story.

A company might employ a **borrowed-interest strategy** to generate publicity. A borrowed-interest strategy will typically promote a newsworthy marketing activity that is related to the product. For example, participation in and sponsorship of a community event or national event is news. Canadian Tire's "We All Play for Canada" program involves an eight-year sponsorship agreement with the Canadian Olympic Committee and much of the marketing communications for the program encourages young children to be more active—to play and participate in sport and recreation activities. One of the objectives of the communications is to build an emotional connection between Canadian Tire and its customers.[11] This campaign drew considerable media attention.

> **borrowed-interest strategy**   A plan to promote a marketing activity that is related to a product.

Many brands garner publicity by announcing sales promotion incentives. Old Dutch, for example, often uses contests for its brands to generate excitement. One such contest gave a lucky Canadian consumer the chance to win $1 000 000 for shooting as many pucks as possible into an empty net within a limited time.

In these types of situations, marketing communications will shift away from brand-oriented image advertising to focus on the event, sponsorship, or promotion; the goal of which is to stimulate immediate excitement for the product or company. The Canadian Tire "Jumpstart" and "We all can play" campaigns encouraged Canadian children to be more active. Refer to the image in Figure 9.8.

The news reporters and bloggers on social media can't be controlled. They determine what information a company provides to publish. Therefore, a key element of any public relations strategy revolves around building a professional relationship with people in these roles.

On the surface, following basic procedure often gets the job done. The PR professional prepares the press release, it is sent to a predetermined list of reporters, and, low and behold, some news coverage occurs. The challenge is to maximize the news coverage in order to achieve stated public relations objectives. This is where good media relations has an influence— the better the relationship with the press, the greater the likelihood of news coverage. Reporters are inundated daily by emails and press releases. Why should they cover your story?

Strategically, it is important to be in contact with the right people on a frequent basis, while providing them with useful information that makes their job easier.

The relationship with the media is a two-way street. On occasion, the media will contact a company or its PR agency seeking information on industry issues or the company itself. Therefore, having the ability to offer comments when necessary is an influencing factor in the relationship-building process. Helping out a reporter with a news story is an intangible that can influence the extent of news coverage that reporter will give your company. Devising an effective media relations strategy involves a few essential steps. For insight into these steps refer to Figure 9.9.

FIGURE 9.8

A Borrowed-Interest Strategy Works Effectively in a Public Relations Campaign

Trademarks of CTC Corporation, Limited used under licence.

FIGURE 9.9

Key Steps in Developing a Media Relations Strategy

In order to secure media coverage, efforts must be devoted to building a positive, professional relationship with key people in the media who cover particular industries.

1. Develop a News Media Source Book

Identify the reporters that cover your industry on a local or national basis (e.g., food reporter, business reporter, sports reporter, entertainment reporter). The goal is to reach the right target audience with your message.

2. Research the Reporters

Conduct a review of their news coverage to get a feel for who they are and how they think and communicate. Such knowledge will offer hints on how to prepare information for them.

3. Provide Information on a Regular Basis

Ongoing communications of a predetermined frequency keeps a company on the media's radar screen. There is a delicate balance between media stalking and persistence; don't burden the media with emails and unnecessary communications, but be persistent—it pays off!

4. Be Familiar with Your Industry

As an industry participant it is important to know what's going. Being able to comment on issues that are happening in an industry is important. Expressing such knowledge can help a reporter who is writing an article on the industry. Establishing a Google Alerts system for key terms in an industry or an advanced Twitter search to follow relevant companies will keep a PR person informed.

5. Follow-up

Securing news coverage is a game of percentages. You can't win them all. If a reporter tells you to get back to them because they are busy, do so. Open and ongoing communications helps build the relationship.

PUBLIC RELATIONS EXECUTION

The tools available to execute public relations programs are diverse. Some are used routinely to communicate newsworthy information, and some are brought out periodically or only on special occasions. This section examines some of the more routinely used media tools.

PRESS RELEASE   A **press release** is a document containing all the essential elements of the story (who, what, when, where, and why). Editors make very quick decisions on what to use and what to discard, so the release must grab their attention quickly. Copies of the release are delivered to a list of preferred editors, for example, those with whom an organization has a good relationship. Alternatively, the release could be distributed to a national wire service as well as being posted on the company's website. A press release is a quick way to spread the news about a company and its products.

press release   A document prepared by an organization containing public relations information that is sent to the media for publication or broadcast.

A good press release should be clearly written with essential details carefully explained in the opening few paragraphs (editors receive all kinds of releases). The goal is to grab attention early. Many practitioners follow a very simple formula: Focus on who, what, when, and where, and then end the release with whom to contact should more information be needed. Refer to the illustration in Figure 9.10.

PRESS CONFERENCE   A **press conference** is a meeting of news reporters invited to witness the release of important information about a company or product. Because a conference is time consuming for the media representatives, it is usually reserved for only the most important announcements. A crisis, for example, is usually handled by an initial press conference (see the IMC Highlight about Maple Leaf Foods that appeared earlier in the chapter). When a professional sports team is about to announce a new star player entering the fold, a press conference is very common. For instance, when the Toronto Maple Leafs signed Mike Babcock to an eight-year $50-million contract to be their new head coach that was big news! A huge press conference broadcast live by TSN was held at the Air Canada Centre in Toronto. A conference allows the media to interact by asking questions, which results in the transfer of additional and perhaps more meaningful information for the story they will publish or broadcast.

press conference   A meeting called by an organization to present information to representatives of the media.

A media kit is usually distributed at a press conference. A **media kit** can include a schedule of conference events, a list of company participants including biographical information, a press release, a backgrounder that tells something about the character of the organization and the nature of what it does, a page of stand-alone facts about the company, sample products, photographs, digital material, contact information, and any other relevant information. The recipe to developing a good media kit is to evaluate who will use it and what that person is likely to need. For example, a media kit for a special event or new sales promotion activity would be very different in tone, style, and content from one needed for a crisis situation.

media kit   A package of relevant information associated with a product or organization that is distributed at a press conference.

WEBSITE   Since the primary purpose of a website is to communicate information about a company or brand, it can be a very useful public relations tool. Visitors to a website quickly form an impression about the company based on the experience they have at the site. Therefore, the site must download quickly and be easy to navigate. Providing some kind of entertainment or interactive activity also enhances the visit. Unlike other media, the website can be updated easily and quickly, so the very latest news about a company and its products can be made available for public consumption. In large companies, it is now common to have dedicated pages for specific brands or for current sales promotions. All press releases about the company and its brands are also posted at the company website, usually in chronological order starting with the newest releases.

FIGURE
9.10

The Essential Elements of a
Good Press Release: Who,
What, When, and Where

Source: © Nova Scotia Community College.

NEWSLETTERS   The **newsletter** is a very common public relations tool. By nature, it is a concise reporting of the news related to the organization and is very clear and to the point. A successful newsletter conveys information in a unique way so that the people who receive it pay attention to it. Newsletters are distributed regularly to their intended audience, so they are an efficient method of conveying information.

There are various types of newsletters, but most are published by companies that want to communicate regularly with employees and customers, by recreation and sports clubs that wish to keep in touch with their members, and by professional associations that regularly convey information to members who are geographically dispersed. It is now common to distribute newsletters digitally. Newsletters are usually distributed based on a predetermined frequency (for example, monthly, quarterly, and so on).

BOOKLETS AND BROCHURES   A **booklet** or **brochure** is a brand-sponsored, multiple-page document that is distributed to consumers and other interested stakeholders. The information in a booklet is usually related to a product or service. For example, it may promote usage of a product in a variety of ways, or it may appeal to the lifestyle of its target audience. Campbell's Soup is well known for distributing recipe booklets in food stores, through direct mail, and through its website. These booklets encourage consumers to use Campbell's products more frequently in cooking as well as in other non-traditional ways. Greater usage equals greater sales.

In the automobile market, Mazda Canada publishes a semi-annual magazine that is distributed digitally to all car owners in its database. The magazine can also be read by visitors to the Mazda Canada website. The publication, appropriately titled *Zoom Zoom*, has a lifestyle orientation and includes general interest articles along with articles and advertisements about the company's newest models. See the illustration in Figure 9.11.

ANNUAL REPORTS AND SPECIAL INTEREST REPORTS   The primary purpose of an **annual report** is to provide current and prospective investors and stakeholders with financial data and a description of an organization's operations. It can do much more to promote the company. It is a good public relations opportunity for the organization to tell the public where it stands on social and environmental issues, for example. In fact, the annual report is often seen by audiences beyond the primary target, such as the media, community leaders, and employees. Word can spread fast about what a company stands for.

Special interest reports can be integrated into an annual report or can be stand-alone documents. For companies that want to portray to the public that there is more to business than a healthy bottom line, a special interest report is an ideal vehicle to get a different message out. To illustrate, Royal Bank of Canada issues a Corporate Responsibility Report each year. The report focuses on issues such as integrity in business; commitment to clients, employees, and the community; commitment to diversity; and commitment to the environment. The information is also published online at the RBC Financial website (rbc.com). Refer to the illustration in Figure 9.12 for an illustration of RBC Financial's public relations initiatives.

SOCIAL MEDIA   **Social media** are the online tools that people use to share content, profiles, opinions, insights, experiences, perspectives, and media itself, thus facilitating conversations and interaction online among groups of people. The emergence of social media has shifted control of the message from the organization to the consumer—the consumer can read the message, formulate an opinion on it, and communicate that opinion to others. Social media have changed communication from monologue (one to many) to dialogue (many to many).

newsletter   A document sent to a predetermined audience that contains news about an organization (for example, a newsletter sent to alumni of a school or to all employees of an organization).

booklet (brochure)   A multiple-page document distributed to consumers and other interested stakeholders.

annual report   A document published annually by an organization primarily to provide current and prospective investors and stakeholders with financial data and a description of the company's operations.

social media   Online tools that people use to share content, insights, experiences, and various media, thus facilitating conversations and interaction online between groups of people.

FIGURE
9.11 **Mazda Distributes a Magazine to Current Customers to Keep Them Informed about New Car Models**

Source: Used with the permission of Mazda Canada Inc.

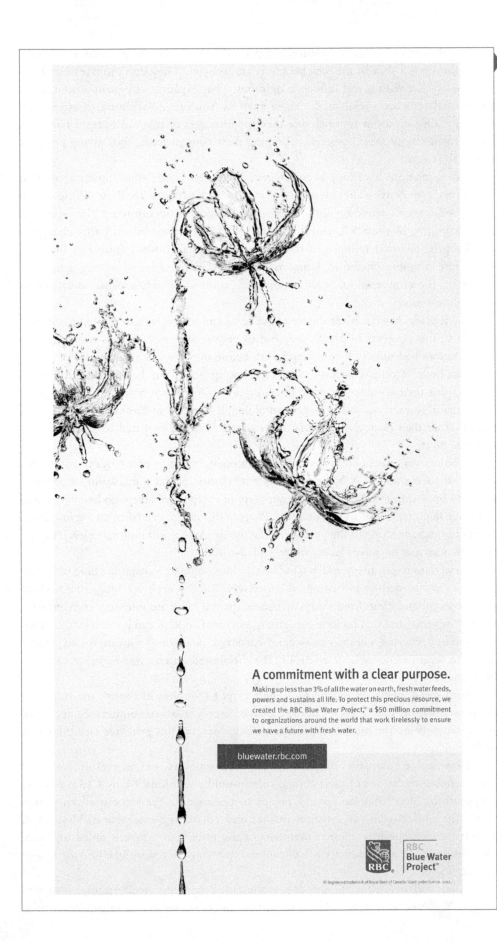

Social media have had a significant impact on public relations practice. Furthering the evolution is a shift in the way people relate to news. They don't just read it. They want to interact with it and influence opinions. That explains why many of the most-visited websites are social media sites, such as YouTube, Facebook, Twitter, and Google+. Organizations routinely use these popular sites to their advantage. The challenge organizations face, however, is keeping their content fresh, thus giving people a reason to return.

Public relations have long been associated with the word "spin." Spin implies that marketers can deliver the message in a tone and manner to their liking. Such an approach won't work on social media. Many experts recommend "less spin and more humility in their PR communications."[12] Their rationale for this change is based on the fact that millions of Internet users simultaneously scrutinize a brand in the public domain. Therefore, being as transparent as possible, while engaging consumers in the conversation, is an important consideration when using social media communications.

Social media has also made the timing of communications an issue. Practitioners used to refer to the "Golden 24 hours" they had to prepare and respond to a crisis situation. Organizations had time to take a deep breath before they responded. Now it's called the "Golden hour." Companies must monitor breaking stories on Twitter that may affect them so that their comments can be offered quickly. To demonstrate the significance of social media, it is estimated that 50 percent of people learn about breaking news via social media rather than through an official news source.[13] Being prepared has a whole new meaning now!

blog A frequent, chronological publication of personal thoughts on a website.

Social media present an opportunity for an organization to post blogs to communicate with their publics. A **blog** is a frequent, chronological publication of personal thoughts on a website. They can be the property of everyday people who like to rant and challenge the integrity of an organization. Blogs of this nature can harm an organization's reputation, which is one of the perils of social media. An organization must learn to deal with the idea that negative things will be said about it.

Viewed more positively and in a public relations context, a corporate blog can be an effective way to deliver the company's message. Today, corporate blogs that include video content and blogs from everyday people (people who are intensely engaged with specific subjects) and that include consumer-generated content can be an effective combination in delivering a brand's message. A corporate blog is also a means for an organization to regain some message control in the social media arena. See Figure 9.13 for an illustration.

With social media, an organization must adapt to the shift in control and recognize the power that the public has regarding message. Simply stated, consumers are in control and consumers are the media. Organizations that disregard this principle face the wrath of the public.

Blogs enable companies to speak directly to consumers, and, as a result, are pushing the news media out of their central role in public relations. Many CEOs of large corporations blog; they do so as a means to personalize the structured corporate world they operate in. To have an impact and encourage interaction, blogs must deliver the message in a manner members of the public are unaccustomed to. Since the CEOs are speaking directly to consumers, they must act more like journalists and less like executives.

Online video sharing sites are one of the fastest-growing media sectors, with sites such as YouTube attracting millions of visitors daily. Therefore, an organization must

9.13   Companies Employ Blogs to Communicate Current, New, And Relevant Information to Consumers

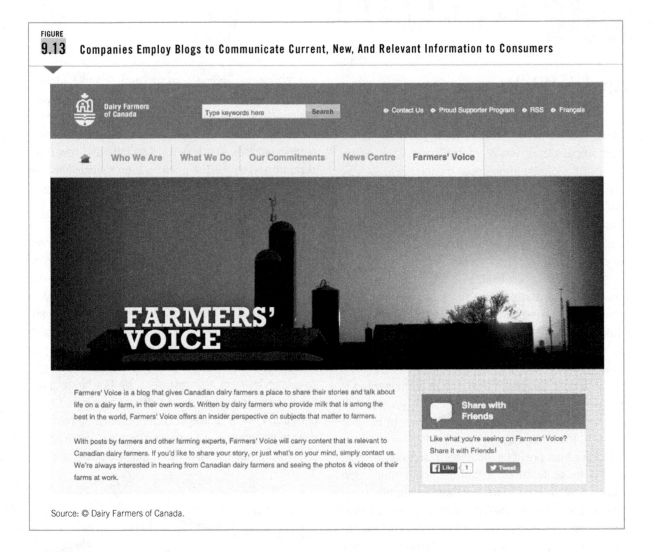

Source: © Dairy Farmers of Canada.

evaluate the benefits of including web videos in the communications mix. Many companies now have their own YouTube channels, where they can deliver video content nonstop. A web video is an enticing proposition, since production and distribution costs are much lower than the costs of creating traditional broadcast material. Unfortunately, a majority of web video content is simply an edited version of conventional broadcast material, an organizational cost-savings strategy that many communications experts question. For smaller businesses that compete with larger businesses, online video helps level the playing field.

Press releases for traditional media were discussed earlier. Social media provide an opportunity to communicate more detailed information. A social media news release can include a variety of elements such as photos and video, links to blogs, digital tags, and RSS feeds. These opportunities were discussed in Chapter 7.

In summary, social media offer new and innovative ways to help a business achieve its marketing communications objectives. The techniques described in this section are much less expensive than traditional advertising. When using social media, an organization must consider that some control of the message may be lost. That loss can be weighed against additional exposure and engagement opportunities with potential customers.

Apple's PR Buzz

Take a moment to think about how you first learned about Apple's latest version of its iPhone. Chances are you heard about them on social media, but knew very little about what made these products new. As time passed, more information became available—perhaps a sneak preview of what the product might look like. Regardless, there were lots of bloggers and ordinary people talking about the product.

So the question is: did this situation just happen or was it part of a master PR plan by Apple to drum up demand for its latest gadget? Apple is the master of PR strategy. Simply by following a few simple techniques but doing it in such a tantalizing manner, Apples product launches are always successful.

So what's the plan? First you determine what is newsworthy and then you leak just enough information on social media to create some buzz. For instance, the iPhone 6 and iPhone 6 Plus were lighter and larger than previous models—a story can be built around those features. Let the rumour mill begin online! A while later journalists and influential bloggers were sent more detailed information and images. The social media exploded with a frenzy of excitement as people shared new information. They couldn't wait to get their hands on the new phone! Closer to launch date, a big event was held and the CEO officially introduced the new phone. The cameras start flashing and photos and stories are placed everywhere. On opening weekend, 10 million iPhone6 phones were sold!

Why is this approach so successful? Apple adheres to a few basic rules but does so in a sneaky kind of way. It all starts with virtually no information. It's a model of thriftiness. Let the media speculate on what the new product will look like, how it will be different, how it will perform, and so on. The publicity is on steroids because Apple is behind everything! When Apple announces something big is coming down the pipe, it rattles the bones of social media. As additional information is released and timelines fall into place more stories will appear in print media, in online blogs, and television news broadcasts. Industry analysts will debate the potential merits. It's a gradual build leading up to the big day. The strategy is so successful competitor's don't dare copy it. They just couldn't pull it off the way Apple does!

Once the initial launch is over, Apple embarks upon a traditional-style multimedia advertising campaign. Television delivers a simple message but on an emotional level, and print ads in both consumer and business publications deliver important product information in a rational manner—a great combination! While all this is going on, Apple is working on the next great gadget.

© Hadrian/Shutterstock.com

TIMELINE AND BUDGET

A timeline is essential so that all activities can be carefully coordinated with other marketing communications activities. In the case of a new product launch, for example, public relations programs can be put in place well before the product is actually available. One strategy is to start the public relations communications in a small way, slowly building credibility, and proceed with a slow rollout. This strategy creates demand in such a manner that the public is eager to buy the product once it is launched. Apple uses this approach all the time. For more insight into Apple's strategy, read the IMC Highlight: **Apple's PR Buzz**.

Public relations programs cost much less than advertising programs, but, nonetheless, there are costs that must be accounted for. If a company employs corporate advertising, the costs are similar to brand advertising programs. There are costs associated with producing print and broadcast materials; and with buying time in the broadcast media, space in the print media, and in developing and maintaining websites and blogs.

MEASUREMENT AND EVALUATION

To justify a financial investment in any form of marketing communications, certain expectations and results must be delivered. There must be an increase in awareness, a change in behaviour, or some kind of financial return. Ketchum Public Relations, a leading international PR agency identifies three levels of measuring effectiveness: outputs, outcomes, and business results.[14]

- *Outputs* measure reach, frequency, visits, tone of message, prominence, and the inclusion of a recommendation or endorsement.

- *Outcomes* measure attitude and behaviour change, and considers factors such as awareness, comprehension recognition, credibility, image change, and purchase intentions. Surveys may be required to collect data.

- *Business results* are estimated by analytic techniques or from data collected in surveys. Typical measures include sales revenue, new clients secured, market share, purchase intentions, brand value, and reputation value.

Outputs are a measure of exposure and companies like to know how much exposure was actually received as a result of its public relations activities. This is referred to as *content analysis*. There are organizations that keep track of content. They record what is being reported, where, to how many people, over what period of time, in which media, and how the coverage changes over time. For example, if an article appears in the front section of the *Toronto Star*, a newspaper with a weekday circulation of more than 360 000, how many impressions will be made? If there are 2.5 readers for every newspaper, the potential number of impressions is 900 000 (360 000 × 2.5). If a similar story appears in other newspapers, the total impressions accumulate.

There is an abundance of analytical information available on social media to measure results of a campaign. Such measures include visits, likes, followers, and the number of active advocates a brand or company may have. Going a step further, an organization can get a feel for the sentiments held by people based on their comments and the general degree of audience engagement.

Another measurement commonly used is called **equivalent advertising value (AVE)**. AVE is a mathematical calculation that considers the scale of coverage and positioning of a PR article and then estimates what a comparable amount of advertising space would cost. A tracking firm examines the size of the article, the location in the publication, the number of brand mentions, and so on. The system includes multipliers (in the range of 3 to 10) to account for the integrity factor of news copy over advertising. The industry is moving away from this calculation and for good reason. First, the calculation does not consider message quality (for example, it doesn't consider the actual content and the tone of the coverage) or whether the target market actually saw it. Second, the use of multipliers is in the eye of the beholder. Inflated multipliers might make clients happy by overstating the true value of the PR effort. In simpler terms the value of public relations shouldn't be equated to the cost of advertising.[15]

equivalent advertising value (AVE) A mathematical calculation that considers the scale of coverage and positioning of a PR article and then estimates what a comparable amount of advertising space would cost

Measuring for outcomes involves determining whether the target audience received and understood the message. Collecting this information involves a combination of qualitative and quantitative research methodologies, so it is much more costly. As with research conducted for any other marketing activity, this form of evaluation involves pre-campaign and post-campaign research. The initial research firmly establishes a benchmark, and the post-research measures any change.

More detailed information about specific procedures for measuring and evaluating public relations activities is included in Chapter 12.

Public Relations as a Communications Medium

Senior executives today have a much better understanding of the role played by public relations in achieving their organization's marketing objectives. As a communications discipline, the status of public relations has been considerably elevated. The examples in this chapter show how public relations can play a key role in specific situations. That role will certainly continue to grow in its contribution to marketing communications strategies and the achievement of an organization's objectives. Those responsible for corporate and brand communications should be aware of the basic benefits and drawbacks of public relations communications.

ADVANTAGES OF PUBLIC RELATIONS

If public relations are done properly, they can be a *credible source* of information. Unlike advertising, public relations messages are delivered by third parties who have no particular interest in the company or product. They are communicating information that they deem useful to their readers, listeners, viewers, and so on. Consumers reading or viewing such messages perceive those messages to be more objective than advertisements.

Third-party endorsements by trusted media personalities can have a *positive impact on business results*. To illustrate, consider the ALS campaign and the "Ice Bucket Challenge" of 2014. The fundraising campaign went viral on social media. In a very short time people everywhere were taking the challenge, all the while raising funds for the ALS Association. In the period between July 29 and August 20, the ALS Association raised $31.5 million in donations compared to $1.9 million in the same period one year earlier. The ALS Association is a non-profit organization raising awareness about and funds for research on Lou Gehrig's disease (amyotrophic lateral sclerosis). This is an exceptional example, but it does demonstrate the potential impact a well-planned PR campaign can have.

Indirectly, public relations also play a role in developing sound *customer relationships*. Public relations campaigns offer a means to build rapport through ongoing dialogue with consumers and other stakeholders. Such a benefit is important, considering the rising costs of media advertising, the fragmentation of the media, and the clutter of commercial messages. Employing social media in PR campaigns enhances the relationship-building process.

DISADVANTAGES OF PUBLIC RELATIONS

One of the biggest drawbacks of public relations is the *absence of control* experienced by the sponsoring organization. Through press releases and press conferences, the company does its best to ensure that factual information is available and presented accurately to the public. In the process of communicating the information, however, the media might add their own opinions, which detract from the intent of the original message. Companies facing crisis situations often see stories in the media that misrepresent the company or mislead the public. In the case of blogs and other social media options, consumers act as publishers and control what is said about the product or company, be it good, bad, or indifferent.

A second disadvantage deals with the sheer *waste* of time, energy, and materials that go into a public relations campaign. This is not to say that the effort isn't worthwhile, but the challenge of catching the attention of editors (the media gatekeepers) and influential bloggers is an onerous one. Enormous amounts of material flow into media newsrooms daily, so standing out in the crowd is part of the public relations challenge. The same can be said about the clutter of information that is present in the diverse social media universe. Senior management must recognize the waste factor and be prepared to absorb the costs that go along with it. Finally, what is important to management may not be perceived as important by the media. End of story!

≫ SUMMARY

Public relations are a form of communications directed at gaining public understanding and acceptance. They are used by organizations to change or influence attitudes and behaviour. Unlike advertising, which is very costly, public relations go largely unpaid for. The organization presents information to the media in the hopes they will publish or broadcast it in a news story.

The primary roles of public relations are diverse. They constitute a useful channel for communicating corporate-oriented messages designed to build or repair an organization's image. At the product level, public relations help generate positive publicity by distributing news releases and holding press conferences when there is newsworthy information to announce. Other good alternatives that help generate buzz for a product or company include product placement, branded content, and product seeding. Employing social media in the PR effort today is almost mandatory. Although there is less control of the message, social media allow for consumer engagement and interaction with a brand (company) and its message. Information about a brand can be shared throughout a friend network. An organization must also develop an open and effective internal communications strategy that encourages employee input. The effectiveness of internal communications has an impact on employee productivity and morale.

Public relations planning begins with a situation analysis. Usually, the client organization provides a brief containing all relevant background information to a public relations agency. The public relations firm establishes the goals and objectives, develops the communications strategy, selects the best execution techniques, and, after receiving the client's approval, implements the plan.

The primary objectives of public relations programs tend to dwell on creating awareness, altering attitudes, and motivating a change in behaviour. The public relations strategy focuses on reaching opinion leaders, maximizing the news value of the story, and reinforcing other communications campaigns such as advertising, sales promotions, and experiential marketing activities. Securing good media coverage often depends on the relationship a company or its PR agency has with the media.

There are several techniques for getting a story into distribution. The most commonly used options include the press release, press conferences, websites, newsletters, booklets and brochures, and social media. Social media options include the use of blogs, postings on a variety of networks, including Facebook, Twitter, Instagram, and Google+. Posting video content on YouTube is another good option.

The impact of public relations is measured several ways. Output measurements are the most common technique. They measure message transmission—that is, the amount of exposure in the media, the number of placements and audience impressions. Outcome measurements involving changes in attitude and behaviour can be obtained by conducting pre-campaign and post-campaign research (budget permitting). Measuring business results must be done in conjunction with other forms of communications that are part of an integrated plan.

Public relations communications offer several benefits: They help build credibility for a product or company with its various publics, they help build brand awareness and interest, and they have an indirect impact on brand sales. There are some drawbacks as well. The organization has little control over the message that is delivered by the media, and there is often a lot of waste in the preparation of materials that are not distributed by the media.

KEY TERMS

REVIEW QUESTIONS

1. What are the essential differences between media advertising and public relations communications?

2. Identify and briefly explain the role of public relations in the following areas:

   a) corporate communications
   b) reputation management
   c) product publicity
   d) branded content
   e) product seeding
   f) community relations

3. What are the differences among product placement, branded content, and product seeding?

4. What are the key elements of a public relations strategy?

5. What is a borrowed-interest public relations strategy? Provide an example of this strategy that isn't in the text.

6. What is a media kit, and what role does it serve?

7. What are the roles of special interest newsletters and special interest reports that are distributed by companies, organizations, and associations?

8. Public relations effectiveness is measured based on outputs and outcomes. Briefly explain each form of measurement.

9. What are the advantages and disadvantages of using public relations as a marketing communications medium? Briefly explain.

DISCUSSION AND APPLICATION QUESTIONS

1. Considering the nature of the business environment today, do you think that public relations will play a more significant or less significant role in future marketing communications strategies? State your position and justify it, based on your vision of the future business environment.

2. What is your opinion of the newer PR techniques such as product placement, product seeding, and social media communications? Will these techniques continue to grow in importance as PR tools?

3. What role will social media play in future public relations practice? Will it change the very nature of the way an organization communicates with its publics? Conduct some secondary research on this issue and formulate an opinion on it.

4. Identify two companies that compete with each other (Coca-Cola and Pepsi-Cola, Nike and Adidas, and so on) in the same industry or markets. Analyze the information they provide on their Facebook pages in terms of public relations value. Are these companies maximizing the potential of Facebook in communicating vital information to customers?

5. Visit a company website of your choosing. Usually, there is a link to the press release section of the site. Review that company's five latest press releases. What subject matter did they deal with? Try to determine how the company uses public relations to its advantage.

ENDNOTES

1. Rebecca Harris, "Canadians Support Brands that Do Good," *Marketing*, May 16, 2012, www.marketingmag.ca/news/marketer-news/canadians-support-brands-that-do-good-52792.

2. "FIFA Sponsors Respond to Corruption Scandal," *Marketing*, May 28, 2015, www.marketingmag.ca/brands/fifa-sponsors-respond-to-corruption-scandal.

3. Tim O'Brien, "Oreo's 100th: An Anniversary Campaign with Taste, April 2, 2012, simplifyingpr.bolgspot.ca/2012/04/oreos-100th-anniversary-campaign-with.html.

4. Stuart Elliott, "The Oreo Turns 100, with Nod to the Past," *The New York Times*, February 27, 2012, www.nytimes.com/2012/02/28/business/media/the-oreo-turns-1oo-with-a-nod-to-the-past-advertising.html.

5. "Apple Placement in TV Shows on the Rise, September 2012, http://applemagazine.com/apple-placement-in-tv-shows-and-movies-on-the-rise.

6. Ben Lovejoy, "Apple Product Placement Reaches New Heights in Netflix Show 'House of Cards'," February 5, 2013, www.macrumours.com.

7. Susan Krashinsky, "How I Met Your Marketer," *The Globe and Mail*, August 2, 2013, p. B5.

8. Julie Liesse, "The Big Idea," Special advertising section of *Advertising Age*, November, 28, 2011, p. C4.

9. Julie Liesse, "The Big Idea: Unilever/Degree," Special Advertising section of *Advertising Age*, November 28, 2011, p. 25.

10. Thomas L. Harris, "Value-Added Public Relations" (Chicago: NTP Publications, 1998), p. 243.

11. Chris Powell, "New Canadian Tire Campaign Bids Us to Go Play," *Marketing*, August 16, 2013, www.marketingmag.ca.

12. Kenneth Evans, "Stop the Spin," *Marketing*, Public Relations Report, June 1, 2009, p. 11.

13. Orlaith Finnegan, "Social Media Revolutionizes Public Relations," February 20, 2013, http://socialmediatoday.com/orlaith-finnegan/1249821/social-media-revolutionizes-public-relations-today.

14. "The Principles of PR Measurement," Ketchum Global Research & Analytics, www.ketchum.com.

15. "5 Reasons to Look Beyond Advertising Value Equivalency," Edelman Public Relations, www.edelman.com.

287

Experiential Marketing, Events, and Sponsorships

Ned Yeung/Dreamstime.com/GetStock.com.

After studying this chapter, you will be able to

1. Explain the role of experiential marketing as a vehicle for building relationships with customers

2. Explain the importance of event marketing and sponsorships in contemporary marketing

3. Differentiate among the various forms of event sponsorships

4. Evaluate the roles of event marketing and sponsorships in the marketing communications mix

5. Assess the criteria that a marketing executive considers before participating in event marketing and sponsorships

6. Identify and assess the various evaluation techniques that determine the effectiveness of event marketing and sponsorship activities

7. Describe the steps in event marketing planning

8. Evaluate various marketing strategies for making an event successful

9. Identify and explain the key elements of event marketing execution

Traditional forms of marketing communications tend to bombard consumers with messages. They emphasize reach and frequency, and the brand that barks the loudest gets the consumer's attention. In that scenario, there isn't a true connection between the brand and the consumer. In contrast, experiential marketing focuses on giving a target audience a brand-relevant customer experience that adds value to their lives. It involves effective two-way communication between the brand and the consumer. Consequently, marketers are rethinking how marketing budgets are allocated, and there is a shift in the direction of engagement-oriented activities.

Experiential marketing embraces several tried and true concepts, such as event marketing, sponsorships, and product sampling, but it is the event itself rather than the product that becomes the key component of an integrated marketing campaign. The ultimate goal of experiential marketing is to get consumers to engage actively with the brand, and, based on the experience, talk about the brand to others. A well-planned and implemented experiential marketing campaign can be the fuel for effective word-of-mouth marketing. This chapter explores the emerging world of experiential marketing, events, and sponsorships, and shows how a variety of companies reap the benefits of these forms of marketing communications.

An Introduction to Experiential Marketing

Experiential marketing is a form of marketing that allows consumers to be active participants in a brand's marketing effort, the purpose of which is to form an emotional connection between the brand and the consumer. Such programs are usually associated with planned consumer events such as product sampling and hands-on demonstrations that allow consumers to touch or use the product rather than just hearing or reading about it. A well-planned experiential marketing program will engage consumers and spark interest in a brand in an exciting and personal manner. The experience could be something as simple as a free sample distributed at an event or something as complex as a planned event where the brand is the centrepiece of the event.

The term *experiential marketing* is relatively new, but the fundamental concepts behind it are not. Brands have always employed product sampling, special product promotions,

experiential marketing A form of marketing that gets consumers participating in a brand's marketing effort in order to form a stronger emotional connection with the brand.

public relations stunts, product seeding, and special events in their marketing arsenal, but it is just recently that the concept of consumer engagement with a brand has taken hold. To engage consumers requires a carefully designed and emotive experience that often integrates various forms of marketing communications. Social media can play an important role in getting consumers to experience a product. Brands encourage digital participation by posting product demonstrations, games, and other interactive content on YouTube and other social media.

The product should be the focus in an experiential marketing campaign. Mio sponsored North by Northeast, a music festival in Toronto. In addition to the sponsorship, Mio ran an experiential campaign during the festival involving a concert series on a streetcar. Mio enhanced the experience of riding a streetcar by running a special double-long TTC streetcar along a downtown route. During the ride, a rotating roster of festival artists played a full set on the "Mio Squirt Car." Passengers and concertgoers got on and off at the various music venues along the way. The objective was to create an intimate concert experience never experienced before. Refer to the image in Figure 10.1.

When Speed Stick GEAR for men (a new deodorant) was launched, experiential marketing played a key role. The brand targeted the millennial market with an adventurous experiential event in downtown Toronto. A 20-metre freestanding, ice-climbing wall was erected, and a group of professional climbers hosted a climbing event. The professional climbers and a street team encouraged young men to take the climbing challenge. The event, which included samples being given away, generated significant publicity for

FIGURE 10.1   An Experiential Marketing Campaign Complemented Mio's Sponsorship of a Music Festival in Toronto

Source: © Sam Santos/WireImage/Getty Images

the brand, including national media coverage and social media conversations. Product samples were given away at the event.[1]

Another component of experiential marketing is shopper marketing. **Shopper marketing** involves understanding how consumers behave as shoppers in all channels (retail, catalogue, and online), and then targeting these channels with appropriate marketing communications to enhance the sales of a brand. Shopper marketing is essential since three out of four purchase decisions are made in-store. These purchase decisions are broken down into categories: 55 percent of the decisions are unplanned; 15 percent are generally or specifically planned; and 6 percent are substitutes.[2] These data, when combined with other known information about shopping behaviour (that is, shoppers feel time stressed and in a hurry to make purchase decisions), reinforces the importance of an effective shopper marketing communication strategy. The goal is to make the purchase decision easier.

Unilever Canada, a marketer of a variety of food products under brands such as Hellmann's, Knorr, and Becel, sees good value in shopper marketing programs, the goal of which is to motivate consumers to select their products for consumption or for use in favourite recipes. For several years in conjunction with IGA stores in Quebec, the company has implemented a shopper-marketing program. The multi-brand program for 2015 included well-known Quebec chef Mélanie Marchand. Marchand was chosen because she was a good fit for the target—moms 35 to 55. "She's a mom, she is a Quebecker, she is a chef, and she has her own way of expressing herself." The theme of the program is a cooking class with our friend Mélanie Marchand. The campaign included in-store displays, recipe booklets and cooking tips prepared by Marchand, and coupons for participating products.[3]

shopper marketing Understanding how consumers behave as shoppers in all channels (retail, catalogue, and online), and then targeting these channels with appropriate marketing communications to enhance the sales of a brand.

One of the greatest challenges facing a company is where to invest its marketing dollars at a time when there are more choices than ever.

Experiential marketing is growing in popularity, and companies are investing in it because consumers respond to it. Nine out of ten consumers say they would purchase a good or service if they experienced it and were satisfied.

Here are a few unique examples of experiential marketing:

Nutella

Nutella kicked off a Canadian road trip with a branded food truck that visited major cities. At each stop on the truck tour, there were complimentary all-day breakfast options (a Belgian waffle or a fresh fruit skewer with the spread) with interactive activities such as personalized Nutella jar labels, a claw machine game for prizes, and an opportunity to have a photo taken with a giant jar.

Wine Country Ontario

Wine Country Ontario launched a mobile wine sampling tour called "Dare to Compare" showcasing Ontario wines. The 16-week tour stopped in various cities across Ontario. A patio environment set up beside the food truck tempted people to sample various wines they hadn't tried before. The objective was to draw comparisons and get people thinking about the quality of Ontario wines. Social media spread the word about the program.

Lexus

To reach their target market of business travellers between the ages of 35 and 54, Lexus dealers in Montreal offered returning passengers at Montreal's Pierre Elliot Trudeau Airport an opportunity to drive home in a Lexus. On-site signage using the theme "We pick you up" greeted travellers as they arrived at the airport, along with messages at departure gates and a video that aired throughout the airport. A Lexus branded booth was set up where brand ambassadors offered information and encouraged people to sign up for the test drive.[4]

FIGURE
10.2

Some Unique Experiential Marketing Campaigns

Source: Based on Harmeet Singh, "Nutella hits the road," *Strategy*, June 15, 2015, www.strategyonline.ca; Rebecca Harris, "Wine Country is on the Move with Sampling Program, *Marketing*, June 24, 2014, www.marketingmag.ca; and "Mio Brings Music to Transit Riders During NXNE," *Media In Canada*, June 10, 2014, www.mediaincanada.ca.

A successful shopper marketing campaign calls for collaboration between a supplier and a retailer. Both parties must establish mutually agreeable objectives and commit the necessary resources to make the program a success. The Unilever–IGA example demonstrates this point. They wouldn't run the program for six consecutive years if they weren't achieving good business results.

Organizations are investing more money in experiential marketing, and that investment is justified based on changing market conditions. In the past, an organization was concerned about making impressions on people (a staple means for measuring the effectiveness of advertising and public relations communications). Presently, emphasis has shifted so that the objective is to make quality impressions (fewer but better impressions) while engaging the consumer with the brand. When consumers interact with the brand, it creates a stronger reason to buy the product and to build a relationship over an extended period. For some additional examples of experiential marketing refer to Figure 10.2.

Event Marketing and Sponsorships

Event marketing and sponsorships are important components of many experiential marketing programs. Over the past five years, investment in these areas has continued to grow—a sure sign that marketers see the value in such activity. In 2014, total investment in event marketing and sponsorships in Canada amounted to $2.85 billion, which is comprised of $1.75 billion in rights fees and $1.1 billion in activation.[5] Activation refers to any form of advertising or other activity that makes people aware of the brand's connection with the event.

event marketing The process, planned by a sponsoring organization, of integrating a variety of communications elements with a single event theme.

Event marketing is the design and development of a "live" themed activity, occasion, display, or exhibit (such as a sporting event, music festival, fair, or concert) that promotes a product, cause, or organization.[6] Both of Canada's leading breweries, Molson Coors and Labatt, include events as a key component of their marketing mix. The companies see events as a means of creating excitement for their brands. Honda has a similar view, and actively participates in motorsports activities and professional golf as a means of reaching its target audiences. Honda is the title sponsor of the annual Indy-style race held in Toronto each year—marketed as the Honda Indy Toronto (refer to Figure 10.3). The company is also the title sponsor of the Honda Classic, a major golf event on the men's PGA Tour.

event sponsorship The financial support of an event in exchange for advertising privileges associated with that event.

Event sponsorship is the financial support of an event, for example, a sports event, theatre production, or cause marketing effort, in return for advertising privileges associated with the event. On the grandest scale, the Olympics and FIFA World Cup soccer are the most expensive sponsorship investments a company can make. Global brands such as Coca-Cola, Visa, and McDonald's commit significant funds to sponsor both events and plan advertising campaigns and promotions around them. These organizations see great value in being associated with global events.

For brands such as Nike and Adidas, sponsorship of FIFA World Cup soccer, national soccer teams, and star soccer players play an essential role in building sales and market share for their soccer equipment and apparel. The battle for supremacy between these brands rages on. As of 2014, global soccer-related revenue for Adidas in U.S. dollars was $2.7 billion; for Nike $2.3 billion.[7]

Usually, an event marketer offers sponsorships on a tiered basis. For instance, a lead or title sponsor or sponsors would pay a maximum amount and receive maximum privileges. Sponsors who pay lesser amounts receive fewer privileges. For instance, the title sponsor of the Canadian stop on the men's PGA golf tour is RBC Financial and the event is called the RBC Canadian Open. On the tiered system, Shaw is a premier partner; BMW is a platinum partner; and TaylorMade, Molson Canadian 67, and PepsiCo are classified as partners.

© ZUMA Press, Inc. / Alamy Stock Photo

FIGURE
10.3

Honda Is an Active Participant in Racing Events, an Ideal Fit for an Automobile Company

Event marketing is big business. According to IEG, LLC, a Chicago-based sponsorship measurement firm, the North American sponsorship market is estimated to be valued at $20.6 billion (2014).[8] As mentioned, the Canadian sponsorship market is estimated to be worth $2.85 billion. Growth in event marketing is fuelled by deals with traditional broadcast properties that include a sponsorship element. As well, marketers today are reluctant to rely on traditional forms of marketing communications. With television viewership waning and newspaper and magazine readership declining each year, marketers are shifting their dollars to other alternatives such as event marketing and social media.

A recent survey among North American marketing executives indicates that events deliver the greatest return on investment over other customary tools, including advertising. There are a few other reasons why sponsorships offer value to an organization. First, the company or brand can form an emotional connection with the fans simply by being there and participating (fans expect sponsors to be at events). Second, an event has the potential to reach a target market (a certain demographic) more effectively than advertising. For example, BMO is a strong supporter of professional and community soccer in Canada. Its logo is emblazoned across the jerseys of three Canadian professional teams in the MLS league, the soccer stadium in Toronto is called BMO Field, and the bank provides team jerseys to community soccer leagues. The sport of soccer is growing in popularity in Canada and it attracts a diverse ethnic audience. Such sponsorship is an ideal fit for the bank's marketing strategy.

Investment in event marketing and sponsorships is mainly divided among five areas: sports, entertainment, festivals and fairs, culture and the arts, and causes. Ongoing sponsorships on television shows can also be included in the sponsorship mix. A list of the leading event marketing and sponsorship companies in North America appears in Figure 10.4. In Canada, RBC Financial is a leading sponsor of sports and community events. Each year RBC invests some $100 million in a variety of national and local programs. RBC's sponsorships include the Olympics and Paralympics, the RBC Play Hockey program, RBC Canadian Open (golf), the Canadian Freestyle Ski Association, and the Canada Snowboard Federation. RBC has a philanthropic side, making annual contributions to educational, civic, arts, social, and environmental causes.

FIGURE
10.4

Leading Sponsorship Investors in North America

Source: Based on *IEGSR Sponsorship Report,* Chicago, 2013.

Rank	Company	Amount ($ million)
1	PepsiCo.	$350M–$355M
2	The Coca-Cola Co.	$290M–$295M
3	Nike, Inc.	$260M–$265M
4	Anheuser-Busch InBev	$255M–$260M
5	AT&T Inc.	$175M–$180M
6	General Motors Co.	$175M–$180M
7	Toyota Motor Sales	$155M–$160M
8	Ford Moto Co.	$145M–$150M
9	Adidas North America	$ 120M–$125M
10	Miller Coors LLC	$ 115M–$120M

SPORTS MARKETING SPONSORSHIP

Sports sponsorship occurs at amateur and professional levels, and can be subdivided into classifications from local events to global events (see Figure 10.5). Among the various categories of sponsorships, sports sponsorship is by far the largest in terms of dollars invested by marketing organizations. In Canada, sports presently accounts for about 58 percent of all sponsorship investments; festivals and fairs accounts for 16 percent; cause marketing, 5 percent; entertainment, 4 percent; and the arts, 1 percent.[9]

The investment in sports sponsorship increases at each level moving upward on the chart. Organizations choose between spending locally to support community events at relatively low cost to investing in national and international sponsorships at significantly higher cost. Such decisions are based on how sponsorships fit with other marketing communications strategies and the overall marketing strategy of the organization.

Sports sponsorships tend to be dominated by certain industries and manufacturers. In Canada, for example, the automobile industry is well represented by General Motors and Ford, the brewing industry by Molson and Labatt, and the financial industry by RBC Financial Group, BMO Financial Group, Scotiabank, VISA, and MasterCard.

Sponsorships are a key component of Tim Hortons marketing mix. At the national level the company is active with curling and professional hockey—two of our favourite pastimes. For instance, it is the title sponsor of the Tim Hortons Brier, the national men's curling championship and lead sponsor of hockey broadcasts on TSN. It is also the title sponsor of *Tim Hortons That's Hockey,* a popular show on TSN. At the local level Tim Hortons provides uniforms for community soccer and hockey associations. Both types of sponsorships fit nicely with the target market Tim Hortons is trying to reach. Refer to the image in Figure 10.6.

An organization's involvement in sports sponsorship does not have to be extravagant; involvement and commitment depend upon the organization's marketing objectives and its overall strategy. To illustrate, Visa associates with national and international events, a reflection of the card's status around the world, while Tim Hortons divides its sponsorship dollars between national and local opportunities.

A recent phenomenon associated with event sponsorship is the practice of ambush marketing. **Ambush marketing** is a strategy used by non-sponsors to capitalize on the prestige and popularity of an event by giving the false impression they are sponsors. Nike is an expert at ambush marketing dating as far back as the 1996 Olympic Games in Los Angeles. At the 2012 Olympic Games in London, Adidas paid $155 million to be an

ambush marketing A strategy used by non-sponsors of an event to capitalize on the prestige and popularity of the event by giving the false impression they are sponsors.

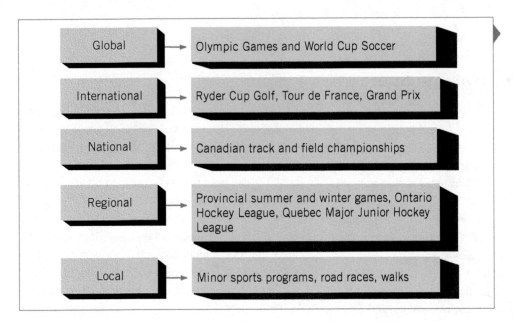

10.5

The Various Levels of Sports Event Marketing

Global	Olympic Games and World Cup Soccer
International	Ryder Cup Golf, Tour de France, Grand Prix
National	Canadian track and field championships
Regional	Provincial summer and winter games, Ontario Hockey League, Quebec Major Junior Hockey League
Local	Minor sports programs, road races, walks

FIGURE
10.6   **Tim Hortons Is an Active Supporter of Events at the National and Local Level**

All Tim Hortons trademarks referenced herein are owned by Tim Hortons. Used with permission; © Curling Canada

official sponsor. However, Nike upstaged Adidas by having athletes, including the world's fastest human, Usain Bolt, wear chartreuse Nike Volt Flyknit shoes.

Such tactics have led to more assertive anti-ambushing strategies by subsequent Olympic organizing committees and by organizers of other world events such as the FIFA World Cup of Soccer. The ethics of ambushing has to be questioned as such action will ultimately affect an event's capability to attract sponsors. Without protection rights, fees would have to be lowered, a situation that impacts the viability of large-scale events.

For more insight into ambush marketing and its merits, read the IMC Highlight: **All is Fair in Love and Sport**.

IMC HIGHLIGHT

All is Fair in Love and Sport

To ambush almost seems like an unethical tactic; you catch someone off guard and perhaps do harm to another party. In contemporary marketing it seems all is fair in love and war. At Nike they actually have a creative director for the Olympics (Nike does not sponsor the Olympics) whose primary role is to plan and implement strategies that ambush legitimate Olympic sponsors. It's big business with lots of money at stake.

The creative director's focus is on the Nike products that some 3000 Olympic athletes wear on and off the field, from design to deployment. At the 2012 summer Olympics in London, athletes from many countries wore the same shoes. At the Games, Nike's trademark execution was the chartreuse Nike Volt Flyknit shoe—a colour that really stood out in the crowd. Apparently, this combination of green and yellow is the colour most visible to the human eye, so it wasn't selected by accident. Nike acknowledges that the whole point was to create impact, and it did. The shoe garnered all kinds of broadcast, print, and online media exposure during the Games. The result was one of the most iconic images of the 2012 Olympic Games.

Archrival Adidas was an Olympic Games sponsor who paid dearly for the privilege—$155 million. Although Adidas complained about the presence of the shoes and the broadcast coverage Nike was receiving, the company couldn't do much about it. Rather than complain, perhaps Adidas should be spending more time devising programs that make their shoes and apparel stand out. Adidas did not renew its deal for the 2016 Olympics in Rio.

Leslie Smolan, co-founder of Carbone Smolan Agency, said "Nike's use of the garish shoes was absolutely brilliant. Nike managed to integrate themselves into the games by showing the product, not just talking about it." Nike has been an Olympic ambusher for a long time. As far back as 1984 at the summer Olympics in Los Angeles, it ran ads of athletes backed by the Randy Newman song, "I Love LA." After those Games, research found that consumers thought Nike was the official sponsor, not Converse, which was the official sponsor.

Fair or foul? Is this good marketing strategy or not? You be the judge.

© Rodrigo Reyes Marin/AFLO/Newscom

Source: Based on Shareen Pathak, "How Nike Ambushed the Olympics with this Neon Shoe," *Advertising Age*, August 20, 2012, p. 1, 19; and Thom Forbes, "Nike Scores with Ambush Products, Ads, PR," *Marketing Daily*, August 13, 2012, www.mediapost.com.

---

venue marketing (venue sponsorship) Linking a brand name or company name to a physical site, such as a stadium, arena, or theatre.

Venue marketing or **venue sponsorship** is another form of event sponsorship. Here, a company or brand is linked to a physical site such as a stadium, arena, or theatre. See the illustration in Figure 10.7. In Canada, there is the Air Canada Centre (home of the Toronto Maple Leafs and Raptors), the Bell Centre (Montreal Canadiens), and Canadian Tire Place (Ottawa Senators). Rogers Communications firmly believes in placing its name on buildings. There's the Rogers Centre in Toronto (Blue Jays home), Rogers Arena (Vancouver Canucks), and Rogers Place (the new home of the Edmonton Oilers).

Sony, the Japanese electronics giant, paid $10 million to put its name on a performing arts centre in downtown Toronto (formerly the O'Keefe Centre, then Hummingbird Centre). As part of the deal, the centre has been fitted with the most technically advanced audio and video equipment made by Sony.[10] Naming rights to buildings is expensive. For additional insight into how much it costs see Figure 10.8.

FIGURE
10.7   The Branding of Sports Venues Helps Improve Brand Awareness

Source: © Tom Szczerbowski/Zuffa LLC/Zuffa LLC via Getty Images.

AIR CANADA CENTRE ($20 MILLION, 20-YEAR DEAL)

Sponsor: Air Canada
Toronto Maple Leafs (hockey), Toronto Raptors (basketball), Toronto Rock (lacrosse)

BELL CENTRE ($60 MILLION, 20-YEAR DEAL)

Sponsor: Bell Canada
Montreal Canadiens (hockey)

JOHN LABATT CENTRE ($2.9 MILLION, 10-YEAR DEAL)

Sponsor: Labatt Breweries of Canada
London Knights (Ontario Hockey League)

TD GARDEN ($80 MILLION, 20-YEAR DEAL)

Sponsor: TD Bank
Boston Bruins (hockey) and Boston Celtics (basketball)

AT&T STADIUM ($400 MILLION, 20-YEAR DEAL)

Dallas Cowboys (football)

Note: The AT&T deal is the richest in history. It is a 100 000 seat stadium with a retractable roof.

Source: Data from Revenues From Sports Venues, 2009 and "The biggest stadium naming rights deals," *The Richest*, November 20, 2013, www.therichest.com.

FIGURE
10.8

Venue Marketing Is Popular Among Corporations

There are also sponsorship opportunities within an arena or stadium for naming rights owners and other sponsors. The Rogers deal in Vancouver includes extensive branding and advertising placements, including in-ice, in-building, and rink board signage; Canucks.com, in-game features; and interactive hockey-themed concourse displays and mobile applications. The Vancouver and British Columbia marketplace is a priority for Rogers because it is not presently an area of strength. The partnership with the Canucks is a step in the business building process.[11] In the same arena PepsiCo secured exclusive beverage and snack rights (through its Lay's brand) for a five-year period. The partnership gives Pepsi branding and advertising placements at all concessions, restaurants, bars, and other outlets in the arena. "The partnership is a major win because of the sheer volume of visitors to Rogers Arena," says Robb Hadley, director of marketing for PepsiCo Beverages Canada.[12]

What's thriving in sports marketing is the concept of *value-added sponsorships*, where hefty doses of public relations and media exposure accompany a marketer's sponsorship agreement. The key in this strategy is a lucrative player endorsement. Reebok International was quick to strike an endorsement deal with hockey sensation Sidney Crosby—a five-year deal worth $2.5 million, more money than any hockey company has ever paid established stars. When interviewed by the media, Crosby is always seen wearing a Reebok hat. To maximize the benefits of the partnership with Crosby, the company launched the Reebok SC87 training collection of footwear and apparel. Refer to the image in Figure 10.9. Crosby is also a partner with Tim Hortons, PepsiCo (Gatorade), and SportChek (retail sporting goods and apparel).

10.9

The Partnership Between Reebok and Sidney Crosby Led to the Launch of the SC87 Line of Training Footwear and Apparel

© CP PHOTO/Halifax Daily News/Jeff Harper

Adidas, a brand that is struggling to find its place in the basketball shoe market, recently signed an annual $2-million partnership agreement with rising star Anthony Wiggins (a Canadian who plays in the NBA for the Minnesota Timberwolves). Should Wiggins become the superstar he is projected to be, the contract will be renewed at a much higher rate and very likely a shoe model will be marketed under the Wiggins brand.

How effective is an organization's investment in sports marketing? The true benefits of event marketing are discussed later in the chapter. For now, simply consider that key indicators of success are brand awareness and brand association with the event or, in some cases, celebrity. For example, which quick-serve restaurant sponsors the Olympics? Which company sponsors the men's national curling championships? Whose name appears on the building where the Maple Leafs play? If you can or can't answer these questions, it helps a company justify the benefits and drawbacks of investing in sports sponsorships.

ENTERTAINMENT SPONSORSHIPS

Canadian corporations invest huge amounts of money to sponsor concerts and secure endorsements from high-profile entertainment personalities in the hopes that the celebrity–company relationship will pay off in the long run. Companies like Molson and PepsiCo, which are interested in targeting youth and young adult segments, use entertainment sponsorship as a vehicle for developing pop-music and youth-lifestyle marketing strategies.

Coca-Cola recently decided to end its sponsorship of the Academy Awards citing a shift in marketing strategy that focused on a younger target. For other companies the show has considerable marketing power. The Academy Awards show has an audience of 40 million in the United States alone—an audience that is 62 percent female, the majority of whom are well educated and affluent.[13] This audience is an ideal fit for sponsor brands such as Apple, Samsung, and JC Penny. Samsung, for example, has invested $43 million in advertising on the show over a 5-year period; JC Penny, $50 million.[14] Advertising insiders refer to the show as the "Super Bowl for women."

FESTIVAL AND FAIR SPONSORSHIPS

Festivals that embrace film, theatre, and comedy are enticing because they reach a cross-section of adult target audiences. At a top film festival, a corporate sponsor hitches a ride on the most glamorous coattails of all—movie stars! There are waiting lists for platinum sponsorships for two prominent film festivals: the Toronto International Film Festival and the Festival des Films du Monde in Montreal. These events showcase branded products not only to filmgoers, but also to the thousands of deep-pocketed domestic and international wheeler-dealers who do business at festivals. Key clients get to hobnob with the movie stars.

Sponsorship revenue for the Toronto International Film Festival (TIFF) averages $4 million annually, with the top sponsor spot occupied by Bell Canada. The venue in which many of the films are shown is called the Bell Lightbox (Figure 10.10). Other major sponsors of TIFF include RBC Financial Group, L'Oréal Paris, and Visa. Visa provides its cardholders with exclusive benefits. Visa cardholders can purchase tickets and special ticket packages in advance of the general public, and enjoy priority access to the Visa Screening Room—Visa-branded theatres during the film festivals. Visa Premium cardholders (Visa Gold, Visa Platinum, and Visa Infinite cardholders) also have exclusive access to the Visa Premier Lounge in Toronto, where they can enjoy refreshments and complimentary snacks one hour before evening screenings at the Visa Screening Room.

Film and other types of theatre festivals are now popular with marketing decision makers, as organizers are offering customized packages better suited to a sponsor's unique needs.

FIGURE
10.10 Bell Capitalizes on Entertainment Sponsorships to Reach a More Exclusive Audience

Source: © Christopher Drost/ZUMAPRESS.com/Keystone Press.

From a marketing strategy perspective, a festival like the Toronto International Film Festival reaches a "class" audience rather than a "mass" audience. The TIFF audience is described as young, urban, and affluent: 47 percent are 18 to 34 years old; 92 percent have a university education; 73 percent have a household income of $50 000+, 33 percent, in excess of $100 000; and all are culture and experience seekers who spend money on entertainment.[15]

CULTURE AND THE ARTS SPONSORSHIPS

Arts and cultural event opportunities embrace such areas as dance, film, literature, music, painting, sculpture, and theatre. What separates cultural events from sports and entertainment events is the audience size. Depending on the sponsor, this is an advantage or a disadvantage. A company such as Molson might prefer the mass audience reach of a sports event, whereas Mercedes-Benz and BMW might prefer to reach a more selective and upscale audience through an arts event. Perhaps only 2500 people attend the arts event, but those people can be powerful. Typically, their education level is above average, as is their income. Such an audience profile is a good match for promoting a new luxury car. A financial services company such as RBC Financial Group or MasterCard sponsor both large-audience and small-audience events given the diversity of age and income of its customers.

The primary benefit these companies gain by sponsoring the arts is goodwill from the public. Most firms view this type of investment as part of their corporate citizenship objectives; that is, they are perceived as good, contributing members of society. For example, BMO is the lead sponsor of the Toronto Symphony Orchestra and is a longstanding sponsor of numerous cultural events and organizations that include the Governor General's Literary Awards, the Stratford Festival, the national Business Book Award, and the National Ballet School.

CAUSE MARKETING SPONSORSHIPS

Progressive organizations are now at a stage where consideration for the environment and other social causes has come to the forefront of strategic planning and decision making. Organizations are operating in a socially responsible manner. A **socially responsible marketing** organization is one that conducts all of its operations in an ethical manner and in the best interests of consumers and society.

Cause-related marketing falls under the umbrella of social responsibility marketing. It is defined as an organization's support of causes that benefit society, such as cancer research, helping underprivileged children, literacy programs, and so on. Bell Canada is a good example of an organization supporting a worthwhile cause. Since 2010 Bell has been associated with mental health issues in Canada. Knowing that one in five Canadians will experience some kind of mental illness in their lifetime, Bell's objective was to reduce the stigma attached to mental illness by encouraging dialogue. To initiate dialogue, Bell actively markets Let's Talk Day, an annual event, through a multimedia advertising campaign. On Let's Talk Day Bell donates five cents for every text or long distance call made by Bell customers. Since 2010, Bell and its customers have raised $73.6 million for mental health research and awareness. Clara Hughes, one of Canada's most distinguished athletes, suffered from mental illness, and she plays a cornerstone role in Bell's campaign. Refer the image in Figure 10.11.

> **Socially Responsible Marketing** A form of marketing in which an organization conducts its operations in a manner beneficial to consumers and society

Being associated with a worthwhile cause can have a positive impact on the consumer's perception of the brand. Such is the feeling for Bell for its association with mental health. CIBC derives a similar benefit from its ongoing title sponsorship of the Canadian Breast Cancer Foundation CIBC "Run for the Cure," where the overall goal is to raise funds to help find a cure for breast cancer.

In today's competitive business world, brands drive marketing. But as brand loyalty diminishes, marketing executives are searching for new ways to connect with consumers emotionally. By associating with causes that have a high degree of interest among the public, even the biggest of corporations can connect with consumers on an emotional level. This is what Bell and CIBC have been doing for years.

TELEVISION SPONSORSHIPS

Due to the waning impact of the 30-second TV commercial, the television industry and programs are offering branded sponsorship opportunities. One of the hottest sponsorship properties in Canada is on Rogers Sportsnet channels and TSN regional hockey broadcasts. Hockey is a natural fit for companies such as Molson, Canadian Tire, Scotiabank, and Tim Hortons.

The hockey broadcasting landscape changed in Canada in 2015 with the new partnership between the NHL and Rogers Communications—a 12-year, $5.2 billion broadcast and multimedia rights deal. Rogers is now the primary broadcaster for NHL games in Canada. Scotiabank was a sponsor of hockey broadcasts on the CBC and TSN so it was a natural for them to continue the relationship with Rogers. The bank is the title sponsor of *Wednesday Night Hockey* on Sportsnet as well as Hockey Day in Canada. Hockey Day in Canada is an annual event that involves three games broadcast during one day, culminating a week of community activities and events celebrating the grassroots of the game. What could be more Canadian than that? Refer to Figure 10.12.

FIGURE
10.11

**Bell Actively Supports Efforts
to Destigmatize Mental Illness
in Canada**

FIGURE
10.12

Marketers Value Sponsorship Opportunities Associated with Hockey Broadcasts in Canada

Source: Courtesy of CBC/Scotiabank.

Scotiabank is also the presenting sponsor of *Sunday Night Hockey* on CityTV and a featured sponsor throughout *Hockey Night in Canada* broadcasts. A Scotiabank sponsored minor hockey team introduces *Hockey Night in Canada* every Saturday night. Over the course of the deal that runs until 2020 Rogers and Scotiabank will develop a range of fan initiatives and community programs.[16] The bank's commitment to hockey broadcasts sponsorships is significant; it sees real benefit in being associated with Canada's favourite pastime.

Strategic Considerations for Participating in Event Marketing

When companies enter into events and sponsorships, they typically are trying to achieve two basic objectives. First, they are trying to create a favourable impression (build awareness and/or enhance their image) with their target audience. Second, they are trying to engage the target audience directly with the brand. Unlike other forms of communication, an event provides an environment where people are more receptive to the message—they expect to hear from the sponsors when they attend. To achieve these objectives, the fit between the event and the sponsor must be a good one. The most effective sponsors generally adhere to the following principles when considering participation in event marketing:

• **Select Events Offering Exclusivity:** If a company needs to be differentiated from its competition within the events it sponsors, it calls for exclusivity so direct competitors are blocked from sponsorship. For example, McDonald's ongoing sponsorship of the Olympic Games shuts out all other quick-serve restaurants from the event. Also, sponsors are often concerned about the clutter of lower-level sponsors in non-competing categories that reduce the overall impact of the primary sponsor. There is a lot of clutter, for example, in sports events such as NASCAR (brand logos seem to be everywhere, as can be seen in Figure 10.13).

• **Use Sponsorships to Complement Other Promotional Activities:** The roles that advertising and promotion will play in the sponsorship must be determined first.

Sponsoring the appropriate event will complement the company's other promotional activities. For example, Pepsi-Cola and Frito Lay (both PepsiCo brands) sponsor the Super Bowl and place several ads during the broadcast. To leverage the association with the Super Bowl, both brands advertise a Super Bowl contest (game tickets and other major prizes) in the months preceding the game. Huge in-store displays accompanied by coupon or cash refund offers promote the Super Bowl connection, and encourage consumers to buy products. Pepsi's integrated strategy embraces advertising, sales promotion (consumer and trade promotion), and event marketing and sponsorships across key company brands.

- **Choose the Target Carefully:** Events reach specific targets. For example, rock concerts attract youth; symphonies tend to reach audiences who are older, urban, and upscale. As suggested, it is the fit—or matching—of targets that is crucial, not the size of the audience.

- **Select an Event with an Image That Sells:** The sponsor must capitalize on the image of the event and perhaps the prestige or status associated with it. For example, several brands of automobiles place a high value on associating with professional golf and sponsor various tour events: BMW Championship Tournament, Buick Open, and Honda Classic are examples. The prestigious image and status of such events have an impact on the sale of products that project a comparable image: the image and status that come with ownership of a BMW automobile, for example.

- **Formalize Selection Criteria:** In addition to using the criteria cited here, companies should make sure they formalize the decision process. For example, the short-term costs must be evaluated against the long-term return on investment that sponsorship offers. Before committing financial resources to an event, a company should also consider whether it is likely to receive communications exposure through unpaid media sources and whether the event organizers will be able to administer the event efficiently. The company must establish objectives in terms of awareness and association scores, image improvement, sales, and return on investment, so it can properly evaluate its participation in the activity.

For insight into how various organizations make sponsorship decisions, refer to Figure 10.14. The key to a successful event or sponsorship is the fit between the brand or company, the event (or celebrity in the context of value-added marketing opportunities), and the target market. Several leading brands see P.K. Subban, star defenceman for the

---

FIGURE
10.14 **Companies Have Different Reasons for Participating in Event Marketing and Sponsorships**

General Motors Canada	
Sponsorship	**Rationale**
Chevrolet Canada sponsored the Toronto 2015 Pan/Parapan American Games. Leading up to and during the event, the company provided 1000 vehicles for event organizers and volunteers. The vehicles featured various green technologies.	"This partnership allows Chevrolet to be part of an event that will inspire and engage a generation of Canadians," said Kevin Williams, president of GM Canada. "This major commitment is an extension of Chevrolet's long history of supporting Canadian athletes, from novice players to elite players at an international level."

Molson Coors Brewing Company	
Sponsorship	**Rationale**
Molson Coors is the lead sponsor of the Honda Indy car race in Toronto after signing a 3-year deal as the official beer and cider partner.	The deal gives Molson pouring rights for its entire brand portfolio, including Coors Light, Molson Canadian, Creemore, Granville Island, Molson Canadian Cider and Heineken. "The company was sensitive to the fact that the audience is changing so this was an opportunity to gets some of their craft products available on site. The sociability of a beer garden will give Molson Coors a great fan engagement experience."

Coca-Cola	
Sponsorship	**Rationale**
Coca-Cola signed tennis star Eugenie Bouchard to a three-year sponsorship deal. Eugenie works with two brands, Coke and Diet Coke, as she competes in global tournaments. She also appears in brand advertising and promotions.	"Bouchard's demeanor both on and off the court embodies happiness and active, healthy living; and because of this, she is truly an inspiration to Canadians and a perfect fit for our company," said Michael Samoszewki, vice-president of Coca-Cola's sparkling business unit.

Based on Chris Powell, "Molson Coors returns as sponsor of Honda Indy Toronto," *Marketing*, May 27, 2015, www.marketingmag.ca; Meagan Kashty, "Tennis star Eugenie Bouchard aces sponsorship deal with Coke," *Marketing*, July 3, 2014, www.marketingmag.ca; and Evra Taylor, "Chevrolet teams up with Pan/Parapan American Games," *Marketing*, November 11, 2011, www.marketingmag.ca

Hockey Star Subban in Demand

Since entering the National Hockey League, P.K. Subban has made quite a splash. He's a controversial figure at times but you can't deny his enthusiasm for the game of hockey. He's become a leader of the Montreal Canadiens and an all-star player. For many good reasons, several key brands including Samsung and Gatorade have chosen Subban to be their marketing partner.

Mark Childs, the Chief Marketing Officer for Samsung Canada, said Subban was offered the partnership because he's a fan favourite and represents Samsung's brand. "Young-minded Canadians are our primary audience. They're technologically engaged, they're passionate. What we found in P.K. was the complete embodiment of the passion and energy that is a young-minded Canadian." The partnership with Subban extends Samsung's connection to hockey. It offers the NHL mobile application on its devices, which gives fans access to statistics, scores, and personalized content.

Gatorade also likes the qualities that Subban offers. Claudia Calderon, director of marketing for Gatorade Canada, says, "He embodies so much of what our brand stands for. He is someone who puts in hard work, has the inherent desire to win and is a leader in the game. His performance on the ice and commitment to the community make him a natural fit for the Gatorade brand."

Their is no doubting Subban's hockey success. He is a top player in the NHL, he has won the award as the league's best defenceman, and has won gold for Canada at amateur and professional levels. What's interesting however, and perhaps what's truly attractive to sponsors, is his unorthodox approach to the game and his on-ice persona. He is one of those players that players on other teams don't like. He's a pest, a hard-working pest who likes to stir things up. Fans take notice of that and that's what the sponsors like.

Based on "Gatorade Canada Announces Addition of P.K. Subban to Growing Athlete Roster," Press release, June 24, 2015, www.newswire.ca/en/story/1561412/gatorade-announces and Sarah Cunningham-Scharf, "Hockey Star P.K. Subban signed by Samsung and Gatorade," *Marketing*, June 24, 2015, www.marketingmag.ca.

Hand-out/PEPSICO BEVERAGES CANADA/Newscom

Montreal Canadiens as an ideal sponsor partner. For insight into why he was chosen read the IMC Highlight: **Hockey Star Subban in Demand**.

Measuring the Benefits of Event Marketing and Sponsorship

One reason many companies are reluctant to enter into sponsorship programs is that results are difficult to measure. Large sums of money are spent at one time for a benefit that may be short-lived. Will the investment produce a reasonable return on investment

(ROI)? The basic appeal of event marketing is that it provides an opportunity to communicate with consumers in an environment in which they are already emotionally involved. Beyond this, companies conduct marketing research to determine the impact of the sponsorship association. The following indicators, many of which are obtained from research, are used to measure the benefits of sponsorship.

- **Awareness:** How much awareness of the event is there within each target group? How well do people recall the brand or product name that sponsored the event? Such an association takes time and financial commitment. For instance, fans of professional tennis have a high level of awareness of the Rogers Cup, a tournament held each year in Canada.

- **Image:** What change in image and what increase in consumer perception of leadership or credibility result from the sponsorship? Market research may be necessary to determine this.

- **New Clients:** How many new clients were generated as a result of the company's sponsoring an event? Entertaining prospective clients in a luxury box at an event goes a considerable way in building a relationship.

- **Sales:** Do increases in sales or market share occur in the period following the event? Be aware that the real sales benefit may take years. It takes time for a sponsor to become closely associated with an event.

- **Specific Target Reach:** Do the events deliver constituency? Carefully selected events reach specific targets that are difficult to reach by conventional communications. For example, pre-teens and teens are difficult to reach through conventional media but can be reached effectively through sponsorship of concerts and music tours. As discussed earlier, events need not be big in terms of attendance to attract constituency.

- **Media Coverage:** What value was derived from editorial coverage? Did the sponsorship result in free publicity for the sponsor? Did participation create any buzz on social media? The industry benchmark for sports sponsorship is currently four to one, meaning $4 in exposure (for example, free air time) for every $1 spent on sponsorship and its marketing support.

For sponsorships to be successful they must be seamlessly integrated into corporate marketing and marketing communications plans. All forms of communications must be complementary. The organization must leverage the use of its website, Facebook page, and Twitter feed; incorporate the sponsorship into public relations campaigns; and run thematic promotions to get all customer groups (trade and consumers) involved. Above all, it has to make a financial commitment above and beyond the rights fees. A general ratio for spending should be three to one: $3 should be spent to promote the relationship to the event for every dollar spent on securing the rights.[17]

For smaller events, success or failure is determined by the financial outcome of the event. Key indicators of success would be the profit the event generated. The event planner and perhaps a financial executive would scrutinize all the revenues and costs associated with planning and operating the event to determine if a profit or loss was ultimately generated.

An organization must choose between event marketing (planning and implementing its own event) and event sponsorships (providing financial support in return for advertising privileges). Either option presents challenges and opportunities.

Planning the Event

Should an organization decide to develop its own event, it must be comfortable with an exhaustive planning process. Putting the plan into place is one thing—executing it is quite another! As in the case of many other forms of marketing communications, a more prudent approach may be to outsource the activity, allowing experts in this field to do the job.

An organization's marketing team carefully considers the role of an event or sponsorship to ensure it is an appropriate opportunity for achieving the company's business objectives. The organization's primary role is to identify the overall goal and marketing objectives, identify the target audience and timing, consider the financial implications (revenues, costs, and profit), and evaluate the results. Working with the client organization, the event planner develops the event theme, identifies the best venue, and establishes the marketing strategy and implementation plan. The event planner's role is tactical in nature at the implementation stage, as all kinds of concerns need to be addressed. Among these are staging the event, having adequate and trained staff, operations and logistics planning, and safety and security. Successful events run smoothly, moving like clockwork from one activity to another. A successful event requires careful planning down to the minutest of details (see Figure 10.15).

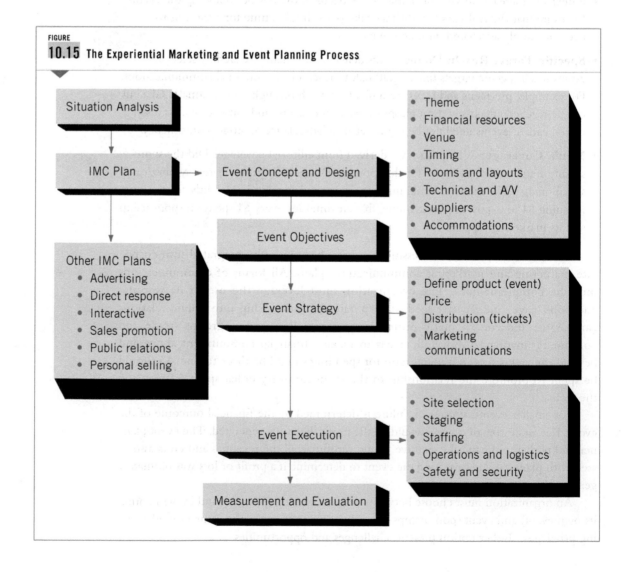

FIGURE 10.15 The Experiential Marketing and Event Planning Process

EVENT CONCEPT DEVELOPMENT

The initial stage of planning is developing the concept. In determining the nature of the event, the planner considers the event's purpose, the audience it will reach, available resources, potential venues, and timing. In terms of *purpose*, an event that is designed to transfer information to prospective clients would be quite different from one intended to entertain an audience. The former might have a business tone and style, while the latter would be much more upbeat and participative. To illustrate, an event with a trade-show orientation (for example, some kind of business fair where new products are introduced to the market) is different from the annual Calgary Stampede. The Calgary Stampede is a community event that is presented with all the enthusiasm and passion that the people of Calgary and all of Alberta can muster. The Stampede represents the historical and cultural fabric of the West.

The *theme* of the event should be linked to the purpose and consider the needs of the audience. Events tend to adopt a colour scheme and a tagline that tie various components of the event together. For example, tickets, programs, promotional literature, and signs are usually designed to look like they are all part of a package. What influences the theme development are imagination and money. The latter always brings a sense of reality to the planner's imagination! Potential themes could involve history (the organization's history), geography and culture (the location of the organization or the event), sports (being part of a sports event that fits with the product), music and entertainment (offers significant appeal for younger audiences), and so on.

Once the theme is determined, the next decision is *venue*. Will the venue be a traditional setting such as a hotel, convention centre, arena, or stadium (see Figure 10.16)? Or will it be something unusual, such as a parking lot or a site at a company facility? Or will it move from location to location, as in the case of branded product promotional tours? Regardless of the venue, the planner must carefully consider factors such as sound,

FIGURE 10.16 Hotel and Conference Centres Actively Market Their Facilities to Conference Planners

Source: Courtesy of The Old Mill Inn & Spa, Toronto, Canada.

lighting, other technical issues, and availability of parking and public transportation. And of course, there's always the unpredictability of the weather. Should the event be inside or outside?

The *financial resources* must be considered immediately. The event's budget quickly determines the degree of extravagance. What an event planner would like to do and what the planner can actually do are usually quite different—a good idea is only a good idea if it is financially viable. Therefore, the event planner must carefully balance creative instincts with the financial resources of the organization.

The *timing* of an event is often linked to the season or weather. For example, the National Home Show, an annual show held at the Enercare Centre in Toronto, is held mid-March each year. The show is timed to coincide with the public's interest in home improvements and renovations, which tends to peak in the early spring. Essentially, there are four time-related factors to consider: season, day of the week, time of day, and duration of the event. Business trade shows, for example, are usually scheduled on weekdays. In contrast, home and leisure shows cover weekends as well as weekdays, with traffic at the show peaking on the weekends.

DESIGNING THE EVENT

Once the concept decisions have been made, the next stage is design. For the purpose of illustration, let's assume we are planning a two-day business conference at which several prominent speakers will make presentations about various aspects of marketing communications. Attendees will include advertising agency personnel; marketing executives; and managers employed in digital communications, sales promotion, and public relations. The theme of the conference is "How to Communicate Effectively with Youth," a hot topic among marketing communications practitioners.

In designing this conference, key decision areas include venue, room layout, technical requirements, food and beverage requirements, material suppliers, and hotel room availability. Regarding *venue*, a downtown hotel location in a major city would likely be a logical choice because the target audience works in that environment. The hotel's banquet room facilities will be considered, because a room for 250 to 300 attendees is required, and an additional banquet room will be needed for some of the meals. For example, it is common for keynote speakers to make their presentations after a meal in the main banquet room. Meals without keynote speakers are often in an adjacent room where the atmosphere is less formal.

The *layout* of the banquet room has a bearing on how well the audience and speakers interact with each other. A common layout at this type of conference includes carefully spaced round tables with eight people seated at each. Attendees usually like this arrangement because a table can be reserved for a large group from one company. Such an arrangement encourages collegiality at the table, even if the people did not know each other initially. The speakers usually address the audience from an elevated podium at the front of the room.

In today's technologically driven world, the use of proper and effective *technology* is crucial. Most speakers today use digital presentations as their primary visual aid to illustrate their main points. Therefore, an event planner must consider all possible audiovisual needs in advance. Typically, the audiovisual aspect of the conference is outsourced to an company expert in this field. This company brings in the equipment (sets it up and tears it down) and is responsible for coordinating the visual aspect of the presentation with the speaker. For extremely large conferences where attendees are distant from the speaker, it is common to have additional screens that display the speaker making the presentation.

Food and beverage requirements are another decision area. Since attendees are investing their time and money in the conference, they expect good-quality food and efficient service by hotel staff. A poor experience in this area can negate any other positive experiences the attendee has at the conference. Buffet-style meals, for example, seem efficient, but only if there are enough serving stations so the lineups aren't too long. If the meal is served directly to tables, adequate staff must be on duty so that the meal is served within the time allocated. Conferences must stick to their schedule. Light snacks and beverages must be readily available in convenient locations during the break periods.

Dealing with **suppliers** behind the scenes is another important decision area. In our example of the marketing communications conference, print materials are prepared and copied by a printing company to be distributed at registration. It is quite common to have a booklet containing an event schedule, profiles of the various speakers, information about the host sponsor, and copies of the various presentations. Often conference highlights or summaries of speeches are available on flash drives that are also part of the conference package. AV people will record speakers for later broadcast on the organization's website or YouTube channel. As indicated earlier, audiovisual supply requirements must also be confirmed in advance. Food and beverage supplies are the responsibility of the hotel, but all meal requirements must be confirmed ahead of time between the event planner and catering manager.

The final decision area involves having adequate **hotel rooms** available for the anticipated number of attendees. Hotels usually block off rooms until a specified date before the conference. If there aren't enough rooms at the host hotel, additional rooms should be reserved nearby. All promotional materials should include hotel information and indicate the key dates and reservation procedures.

SETTING OBJECTIVES

As indicated earlier in the chapter, an organization must establish concrete objectives to justify any financial investment in event marketing. Therefore, quantitative objectives are identified—objectives that are realistic, achievable, and measurable. They must be within the realm of what event marketing is capable of achieving. A direct link to sales is not possible, but it may be possible to measure changes in awareness or intentions to purchase a company's product as a result of event participation.

Other objectives might relate to the size of audience reached, the ability to reach a specific target audience (for example, the quality of reach), sponsor recognition levels, sales of sponsor products, the economic impact of the event, and profit. In the example of the marketing communications conference, the event's objective may have been to attract 300 participants (perhaps any number above 200 participants would produce a profit for the event). Since the event will attract a quality target audience of marketing communications practitioners, it could attract additional sponsors who will help defray the costs of planning and executing the conference.

PLANNING TOOLS

The initial stage of planning is the preparation of an event proposal. The **proposal** should include the objectives of the event as well as details about organization, layout, venue, technical requirements, and any other key considerations (see Figure 10.17). Certain planning tools are essential in the planning stages. Most important is a **timeline chart** that indicates when various planning activities start and finish. As well, a schedule of daily events, often called a **run sheet**, is essential to list the various dates, times, and

timeline chart   A chart indicating when various planning activities start and finish.

run sheet   A schedule of daily events that shows the various dates, times, and locations of activities at an event.

FIGURE
10.17

Key Elements of an Event
Proposal

An event proposal is drafted in the preliminary stages of planning to highlight key elements. As planning progresses, the proposal becomes more detailed and execution oriented.

Event Description

- Type of event and event name
- Location
- Timing
- Event concept (including goals and objectives)

Event Management

- Management responsibilities
- External supplier requirements
- Facility requirements (venue, rooms, layout)
- Identification of target audience

Marketing

- Assessment of audience needs
- Competitor analysis (similar events, timing)
- Product (event definition)
- Price strategy (price ranges, ticket availability)
- Marketing communications strategy (media advertising, web, public relations, social media)
- Distribution strategy (registration procedures, methods)

Financial

- Budget (consideration of all associated costs)
- Profit-and-loss statement

Staging

- Theme
- Decor
- Layout

- Sound and lighting
- Catering
- Services (parking, transportation, vehicle requirements, electricity)

Staffing

- Recruitment of staff
- Staff training (roles and responsibilities)
- Recruitment of volunteers
- Volunteer training

Safety and Security

- Risk identification and management
- Safety strategy (audience, presenters, entertainers)
- Security strategy (premises, equipment, cash)
- Reporting procedures and communications
- First aid

Operations and Logistics

- Bump-in (setup)
- Room layout
- Technical execution (sound, lighting, computers, projectors)
- Attendee traffic flow (venue layout, room locations, meeting rooms)
- Contingencies (weather, technology failure, accidents)
- Bump-out (teardown)

Evaluation

- Actual versus plan (based on objectives)
- Profitability

locations of activities (see Figure 10.18). The importance of the timeline chart will become clear in the discussion of execution issues later in this chapter. With so many logistical things to consider, it is important to identify a critical path for those elements of the plan that are essential for a successful outcome.

Marketing the Event

Marketing an event is no different from marketing a product; an integrated plan is needed. The key decisions involve carefully defining the product (event) and then positioning it in the minds of the target audience in a favourable way. Motivating people to attend the event depends on the quality and quantity of marketing communications activities. This section examines some of the essential strategic planning elements.

A run sheet is an indispensable planning tool that is updated as needed during planning. It is particularly useful for hotels and conference centres at the execution stage of an event. The schedule below was used at the Ambassador Resort Hotel and Conference Centre, Kingston, Ontario, when it hosted the Ontario Colleges' Marketing Competition.

FIGURE
10.18
A Sample Run Sheet

Thursday, November 14	
2:00–4:00 pm	Registration and Team Photographs *(Atrium)*
5:30–7:00 pm	Complimentary Buffet Dinner *(Ballroom)*
7:00–7:15 pm	Opening Ceremonies *(Ballroom)*
7:15–9:30 pm	Marketing Quiz Bowl *(Ballroom)*
10:00–11:30 pm	Faculty Social *(Prime Minister's Suite)*
Friday, November 15	
7:00–8:00 am	Judges' Breakfast *(East Ballroom)*
7:00–8:00 am	Continental Breakfast, Students and Faculty *(West Central Ballroom)*
8:00 am	First Participants Enter Prep Rooms *(refer to event schedules)*
8:00 am–12:00 pm	Judging Begins for Cases, Job Interview, and Sales Presentation
12:00–1:00 pm	Judges' Lunch and Faculty Lunch *(East Ballroom)*
1:00–4:00 pm	Competition Continues
6:30–7:30 pm	Reception *(Ballroom)*
7:30–10:00 pm	Awards Banquet *(Ballroom)*

All activities take place at the Ambassador Resort Hotel and Conference Centre.

PRODUCT STRATEGY: DEFINING THE EVENT

In defining the event, the planner must identify the essential features and benefits of the event that can ultimately be used in messages directed at the target audience. For example, is the purpose to entertain, to provide a learning experience, or to simply have fun with friends? The marketing communications conference cited earlier offers a learning experience for participants, who gain from the success and expertise of others. In contrast, attending the Rogers Cup Tennis Championships brings tennis enthusiasts together to cheer and celebrate tennis at the highest level of performance. Clearly, the nature of communications to motivate attendance for these two events would be very different. Promotional information for the Rogers Cup stresses words such as intense competition, excitement, and emotion.

In defining the product (event) and understanding the motivation of the target audience, the event planner discovers what buttons to press to motivate participation.

PRICING STRATEGY

Price also plays a role in motivating attendance. Literature promoting professional seminars and conferences is easily discarded if the price–value relationship is incongruent. Charge too much for a conference, and the value is questioned. Charge too little, and people may think they won't learn anything important by attending. All things considered, the pricing decision is a delicate one. To put things in perspective, the registration fee for our example of the one-day marketing communications conference could be in the range of $600 to $700. Such an event might attract 200 people and could prove to be profitable for the sponsoring organization. However, if the price were lowered to less than $600 (say $595), would it attract a larger audience? Pricing an event is much like pricing a product—a lot of psychology is involved.

In contrast, the Rogers Cup (a professional tennis tour event) prices tickets on an individual basis or offers group rates, varies prices for individuals or groups based on factors such as proximity to the court (for example, platinum seats are the most expensive, and upper deck red seats are the least expensive), day of the week, weekend, or what stage the tournament is in (for example, tickets for matches in the preliminary rounds will be less than tickets for matches in the quarter-final, semi-final, and championship rounds). In addition to regular seating there are package plans that include the best seats, reserved parking, and access to VIP lounges. For fans with bigger wallets there are also private suites that include catering and other special services. Pricing for an event sometimes has to be flexible and meet a variety of customer needs.

A second pricing consideration involves a plan for purchasing tickets. The sale and distribution of tickets for an event or the registration process for a business conference must be convenient for the participant. As well, the planning organization must decide if it will sell the tickets directly or outsource this task to a specialist, such as Ticketmaster or StubHub. Consumers find online ticket buying and event registration very convenient. Therefore, registration could be handled by an organization's website or by the website of a ticket intermediary. All details about pricing and how to buy tickets should be clearly stated on the organization's website.

MARKETING COMMUNICATIONS STRATEGY

The success of any event is often dictated by the effectiveness of the marketing communications strategy. What message will be delivered to the target audience to motivate participation, and what media will be used to efficiently reach that audience? A separate budget must be drawn up for marketing communications, because it may take a considerable portion of the event's overall budget.

The initial marketing communications decisions are basically **branding** decisions. Typically, an event will adopt a distinctive name, logo, colour scheme, and image. Several examples appear in various figure images in this chapter. Every component of the communications mix, including tickets, will bear the same logo and colour scheme. Such consistency of presentation gives the event a branded look. The Rogers Cup logo plays a key role in all forms of communications and related materials for that tennis event. Refer to the image in Figure 10.19.

The **advertising strategies** for the event are based on the target market profile and how best to reach the target given the financial resources available. The content of the message and the style of delivery must combine effectively to meet the motivational needs of the audience. Media alternatives include television and radio advertising, magazine and newspaper advertising, direct mail (letters, brochures, and pamphlets), and the Internet. Most events now have a presence on Facebook as well.

The size of the media budget obviously dictates media decisions. An event such as the Rogers Cup Tennis Championships for both men and women, which attracts a broad cross-section of ages, will adopt a multimedia strategy to create awareness and will rely heavily on the Internet to communicate specific information and sell tickets.

Public relations are also essential in generating positive publicity for an event. Organizers of large events frequently hold press conferences, timed appropriately, to build some pre-event publicity. Organizers may also issue press releases, as in the case for annual national events such as the Tim Hortons Brier or the Rogers Cup. Smaller and more local events send a press release to all local media and then hope for the best—and take care to invite the press to the actual event.

Courtesy of Tennis Canada

Event Marketing Execution

Execution involves dealing with specific details about an event. A planner usually works from a checklist to ensure that all details are taken care of in the planning stage and the execution stage of an event. For the purpose of illustrating event execution, this section assumes that a planner is planning a marketing conference. Discussion will focus on several key areas, including site selection and staging, staffing, operations and logistics, and safety and security. Event execution is complex, and a full discussion of such a topic is beyond the scope of this text.

SITE SELECTION AND STAGING

In the theatre, the *stage* is the scene of action. The same is essentially true in event marketing. The scene of action for an event involves a site selected according to considerations such as theme development, sound and lighting, and availability of essential services. The venue chosen should be consistent with the event's purpose and theme, and it should provide all of the essential services that are required. Some of the key factors influencing site selection include

• The size of the event (for example, the number of participants).

• The suitability of the site for planned activities (for example, formal and informal activities).

• The primary field of play (for example, the theatre or conference room where the main event will be held).

- The availability of or proximity to accommodation, food, and attractions.
- The availability of on-site technical support and venue management experience.

Theme development was discussed earlier. At the event, the theme should be supported in every aspect, including sound and lighting, decor, and special effects. For example, the theme at a marketing conference could be very subtle and communicated only by signage and colour schemes. At much larger events of a longer duration, music and entertainment (for example, specific acts revolving around the theme) could be included, along with special props appropriately placed around the venue. If the latter is the choice, an event planner is wise to seek advice from staging and rental companies that offer specialized services in this area.

For the purpose of illustration, let's assume for our one-day marketing conference we need a hall that can accommodate 200 to 300 people. The conference theme will be billed as "Marketing in the Future: What Lies Ahead?" The purpose of the conference is to educate and inform concerned marketing managers about what trends and external environments will influence marketing strategies over the next decade. Influential guest speakers from the ranks of industry, government, and the service sectors will present their views on what the future holds and provide insights into how they are already responding.

At this type of conference, most of the speakers' presentations involve computer-generated shows, so a planner must be concerned about room layout—the stage where the speakers are positioned, sound, lighting, and vision. Let's start with *room layout*. Since a standard, rectangular-shaped banquet room is the theatre, the speakers will be placed at one long side of the room, reducing the distance between the front and back of the room. The seating will be laid out in a way conducive to taking notes. For this type of a presentation, there are four basic seating layouts: cabaret, banquet, classroom, and theatre (see Figure 10.20). Of the options available, the cabaret layout seems most appropriate because it allows for good eye contact for all participants and encourages communication among participants at each table.

FIGURE 10.20

An Event Planner Can Choose from a Variety of Room Layouts

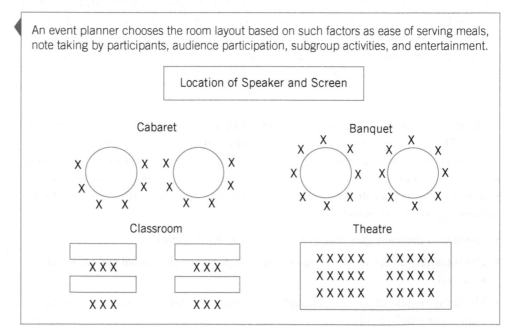

An event planner chooses the room layout based on such factors as ease of serving meals, note taking by participants, audience participation, subgroup activities, and entertainment.

The guest speakers will be on an elevated platform at one side of the room. The height of the platform considers the sight lines of the audience. The audience must be able to see the speaker and the screen clearly. Appropriate backdrops should be on stage to isolate the presentation area and create a more intimate feeling. At such a conference, the speaker rarely controls the slide presentation—technical coordination is usually the responsibility of an audiovisual expert who is located at the side of the room.

Proper *sound and lighting* are essential to create mood and ambience. Professional advice from a sound and lighting expert is recommended. Such advice is usually readily available at conference centres. If audience communication is going to be important, microphones should be strategically situated throughout the conference room.

With all details addressed, the final aspect of staging is *rehearsal*. The rehearsal is an opportunity for everyone to integrate their efforts and to ensure that all technical glitches are remedied. Contingency plans should be established in case the unexpected occurs, which it often does! For example, there should be a plan in place in case a speaker falls ill at the last minute or the projector breaks down.

Additional staging considerations include making arrangements for *catering and accommodations*. Since the marketing conference is being held at a conference centre, food and beverages are readily available. Decisions involve the style of service (for example, buffet or set menu with table service), the timing and availability of snacks and beverages (for example, during planned breaks), and choosing the menu for each meal. Hotels and conference centres usually offer food and beverage packages that are available in a range of prices. Of course, the planner must negotiate room rates with the host hotel or conference centre. Typically a group rate is negotiated based on number of rooms that will be booked.

STAFFING

Planning and executing an event are complex undertakings and, depending on the size and scope of the event, the human resources required can vary considerably. Can you imagine the number of people who are required (paid and volunteers) when a city hosts the Olympic Games or a national sports championship? For example, over 15 000 people volunteered for the 2015 PanAm/ParapanAm games. For large-scale events, the roles and responsibilities of all individuals must be spelled out in detail. Therefore, organization charts are needed for various stages of event planning: pre-event, event, and post-event. In the pre-event stage, the focus is on planning, so anyone connected with marketing, financial, and human resources planning is involved. During the event itself, human resources capacity expands to its fullest, so it is essential that reporting relationships for all operations be delineated. After the event, only those people involved with evaluation and financial planning play a key role.

OPERATIONS AND LOGISTICS

To illustrate the importance of operations and logistics, consider the planning required to get a major golf championship, such as the RBC Canadian Open, up and running. For the participants alone, a plan is needed to ensure that

- All golfers, their entourage, and their equipment arrive on time.
- Golfers are settled in the correct accommodation, and all equipment is safe and secure.
- The golf course is in immaculate condition (a process that starts months before the competition), and spectator stands, scoreboards, and crowd barriers are in place.
- Golfers arrive in time for their tee-off each day.

bump-in (setup) The setting up of structures and other equipment at an event.

This set-up process is referred to as the bump-in. **Bump-in**, or **setup**, involves setting up structures and facilities required for an event. For an event such as our marketing conference example, tasks such as installing sound and lighting equipment, computers, projectors, and screens involve the services of a specialist. Regardless of how the bump-in occurs, it is essential that all facilities and equipment are in place and in good working condition prior to the official start of the event. Simply stated, logistics is about getting equipment and people into the right place at the right time so that things run smoothly, and then, once the event is complete, taking everything down. The process of dismantling is referred to as **bump-out**, or **teardown**.

bump-out (teardown) The process of dismantling everything after an event.

SAFETY AND SECURITY

Imagine the potential safety and security concerns there would be for a Grand Prix racing car event where the race is conducted on city streets. For that matter, any sports event where large numbers of fans congregate requires a detailed plan outlining safety and security measures. The plan must consider potential crowd behaviour and methods for controlling crowds, should the need arise.

At an event, everyone must feel safe, including the audience, the staff, and the subcontractors (for example, technical crews). At large events, accidents can occur, people might fall ill, or something completely unexpected may happen. Potential risks include fires, bomb threats, gas leaks, overzealous fans (even riots), and so on. A few years back, some NBA basketball players and fans were involved in an ugly brawl, a situation that threatened the safety of both fans and players. Crowd management—the orderly flow of spectators into and out of the venue—is very important. Signage indicating direction and staff barking out commands where necessary play a key role in moving audience pedestrian traffic smoothly.

Proper security measures for property, equipment, and cash must also be planned for. As well, the planner must ensure that only certain people have access to specific areas and must act responsibly in case of emergency. Typically, people in positions of authority or special responsibility wear badges identifying their role at the event. Vehicles may be necessary to transport security personnel to areas where emergencies occur. Event planners have a choice of hiring private security firms or members of the local police force. Since safety and security is such a critical issue, it is recommended that organizers of large events employ external organizations that are experts in this field to take care of all of the planning and implementation.

►► SUMMARY

Experiential marketing is a growing component of marketing communications campaigns. Organizations see greater value in activities that actively engage a target audience with a brand, and that is what experiential marketing does. Activities such as free product samples, product promotional tours, shopper marketing programs, and event marketing and sponsorships are potential components of an experiential marketing campaign. Typically, experiential marketing strategies reach fewer consumers than traditional advertising strategies,

but the quality of the association a brand develops with consumers is stronger.

Event marketing and sponsorships are now an important element of a firm's marketing communications mix. Sponsorships tend to be concentrated in five areas: sports, entertainment, festivals and fairs, culture and the arts, and causes. Ongoing sponsorships on television shows can also be included in the sponsorship mix. Events and sponsorships can be local in nature, or they can be expanded to become regional, national, or international in scope. Sports sponsorships and events draw the majority of the sponsorship pie, but interest is now growing faster in the other areas.

Prior to getting involved with sponsorships, an organization should establish specific criteria for participation. Factors to consider include product category exclusivity, relationships with other marketing communications programs, the event's ability to reach the desired target market effectively, and the image-building potential offered by the event.

Once the event is over, attention turns to evaluation. In relation to objectives that were established for the event, measures are determined for criteria such as awareness, image enhancement, new business clients, product sales, target market reach, and media coverage. There will be an assessment of all revenues and costs to determine profitability and to make recommendations for improvements should the event be planned for another occasion.

Should an organization decide to plan its own event, it must be comfortable with a rather exhaustive planning process. The first decision is to evaluate the role of the event or sponsorship to ensure it offers a good opportunity for achieving business objectives. The organization is responsible for establishing goals and objectives, identifying the target audience, determining the best time for the event, providing adequate financial resources, and evaluating the event for effectiveness. The event planner develops strategies for staging the event, making available properly trained staff to execute the event, planning operations and logistics to make

sure everything runs smoothly, and preparing for safety and security issues that could arise during an event.

The first stage in developing an event is to determine the event's concept and design. This involves decisions about the type of event, the name, and the theme of the event. Once these decisions are made, attention focuses on issues such as venue alternatives, financial resources required, timing, room layouts, and technical requirements. Technical support is commonly outsourced.

As with other forms of marketing communications planning, objectives are established. Typically, event marketing objectives focus on target audience reach, potential new business and product sales, the economic impact of the event, and profit. Event marketing strategies involve carefully defining the product (the event) and then positioning it in the minds of the target audience. A good event title and theme become the foundation for building an effective communications strategy for motivating attendance at the event. An effective price strategy is also crucial because prospective participants evaluate the potential benefits against the cost of attending. To promote the event, a combination of media advertising and public relations is an effective mix. All communications must have a branded look and present a similar message to the target audience.

At the execution stage, concerns focus on specific details in the following areas: site selection and staging, staffing, operations and logistics, and safety and security. All details must be checked and rechecked to ensure a smooth flow of activities and people.

KEY TERMS

ambush marketing   294
bump-in   318
bump-out   318
event marketing   292
event sponsorship   292
experiential marketing   289
run sheet   311

setup   318
socially responsible marketing   301
shopper marketing   291
teardown   318
timeline chart   311
venue marketing   296
venue sponsorship   296

REVIEW QUESTIONS

1. Briefly explain how experiential marketing is different from other forms of marketing communications activities. What benefits does it offer?
2. What is shopper marketing? Briefly explain and offer a new example of this concept.
3. What is the difference between event marketing and event sponsorship?
4. What is ambush marketing, and what benefits does it offer?

5. Identify and briefly explain the main classifications of event marketing.
6. Briefly explain the strategic criteria an executive considers before pursuing an event marketing opportunity.
7. What are the measures commonly used to evaluate the effectiveness of event marketing participation?
8. Identify the basic steps in the event marketing planning process.

9. Developing the event concept is the initial stage of planning an event. What are the key decision areas in this stage? Briefly explain each.

10. Designing the event is the second stage of event planning. What are the key decision areas in this stage? Briefly explain each.

11. Briefly explain the purpose of the following planning tools:
   a) timeline chart
   b) run sheet

12. A key element of event marketing strategy is defining the event. What decisions are associated with defining the event?

13. Briefly explain the following stages of event marketing execution:
   a) site selection and staging
   b) staffing
   c) operations and logistics
   d) safety and security

DISCUSSION AND APPLICATION QUESTIONS

1. Why are companies becoming more actively involved in cause-related event sponsorships? Conduct some secondary research on this issue and formulate a position on the matter.

2. Do value-added sponsorships, such as the one between Reebok and Sidney Crosby, offer significant benefits to the sponsoring organization? If so, what are the benefits? Discuss.

3. What classification of event sponsorship is appropriate for the following companies or brands? (More than one can apply.) Justify your decision.
   a) Becel margarine
   b) Rolex Watches
   c) BMW automobiles
   d) McDonald's

4. Assume you are responsible for planning an event such as a marathon/half-marathon race to raise funds for the Alzheimer's Association of Canada or some similar not-for-profit organization. What are your objectives? Consider both qualitative and quantitative objectives. Provide examples of a few objective statements. What marketing strategies will you employ to create awareness and interest in the event? Provide details of the activities you recommend.

5. Provide some examples of companies and brands that are involved with "experiential marketing." Based on your observations of their activities, identify the strengths and weaknesses of this form of marketing communications.

ENDNOTES

1. Rebecca Harris, Colgate-Palmolive Takes Deodorant Marketing to New Heights," *Marketing*, March 18, 2014, www.marketingmag.ca.

2. "2012 Shopper Engagement Study," *Point of Purchase International* (POPAI), www.popai.com/engage/docs/Media-Topline-Final.pdf.

3. Rebecca Harris, "Unilever Whips up Shopper Marketing Campaign," *Marketing*, June 9, 2015, www.marketingmag.ca.

4. Matthew Chung, "Lexus Greets Airport Arrivals," *Strategy*, May 22, 2014, http://strategyonline.ca/2014/05/22/lexus-greets-airport-arrivals

5. Susan Krashinksy, "A Blind Faith in Sponsorships," *The Globe and Mail*, July 12, 2014, p. B2.

6. "Event Marketing," *Business Dictionary*, www.businessdictionary.com/definition/event-marketing.html.

7. Brian Milner, "The Other Battle in Brazil," *The Globe and Mail*, July 15, 2014, pp. B1, B6.

8. "Sponsorship Spending Growth Slows in North America As Marketers Eye Newer Media and Marketing Options, *IEGSR*, January 7, 2014, www.sponsorship.com/iegsr/2014/01/07/Sponsorship-Spending-Growth-Slows-In-North-America.aspx

9. 9th Annual Canadian Sponsorship Landscape Study, 2015, www.sponsorshiplandscape.ca.

10. "Sony Takes over the Hummingbird," *Marketing Daily*, September 10, 2007, www.marketingmag.ca.

11. "Rogers Arena: New Name for Home of Vancouver Canucks," *Canucks.NHL.com*, n.d., http://canucks.nhl.com/club/newsprint.htm?id=533891

12. "Pepsi Ousts Coke in Rogers Arena Deal," *Marketing*, October 5, 2011, www.marketingmag.ca/uncategorized/pepsi-ousts-coke-in-rogers-arena-deal-37322

13. Anthony Crupi, "Two of the Oscar's Biggest Sponsors Have Decided not to Return This Year," *Ad Week*, February 2, 2014, www.adweek.com/news/television/two-oscars-biggest

14. Brand Adgate, "100+ Oscar 2015 Funfacts to Drop in Conversation this Weekend," *Forbes*, February 19, 2015, www.forbes.com/sites/bradadgate/2015/02/19/fun-facts-about-the-oscars/

15. Toronto International film Festival, "Lights, Camera, Festival!" www.tiff.net/contents/pdfs/SponsorshipFestival2013.pdf

16. Michael Kolberg, "Rogers and Scotiabank Ink Six-Year NHL Sponsorship Deal," *Media in Canada*, May 28, 2014, www.mediaincanada.com/2014/05/28/rogers-and-scotiabank-ink

17. Wendy Cuthbert, "Sponsors Pump ROI with Experiential Approach," *Strategy*, March 12, 2001, p. B7.

Personal Selling

Learning Objectives

After studying this chapter, you will be able to

1. Understand the role of personal selling in retail, business-to-business, and direct selling environments, and its relationship to integrated marketing communications

2. Describe the evolution of personal selling strategies and evaluate the role that relationship selling plays in integrated marketing communications programs

3. Identify the human variables that contribute to the successful application of personal selling strategies

4. Learn how to apply this knowledge to a variety of personal selling situations

5. Identify the fundamental roles and responsibilities of a sales representative

6. Identify the essential steps in the selling process and the key elements required for preparing a successful sales presentation

7. Assess how selling strategies need to adapt to a changing business environment

Among the various components of the integrated marketing communications mix, personal selling differentiates itself due to its personal nature. Other forms of marketing communication are non-personal. Advertising and promotions rely on the media to deliver a message; public relations uses various tools to seek the media's support in spreading the word; and direct response communications rely on the mail, the Internet, and mobile communications. In spite of all of the changes that have occurred in the marketplace and in spite of the fact that industry has come to rely on technology as a means of communication, personal selling still remains a vital component. Organizations continue to sell—they just sell differently than they used to.

To demonstrate, customer relationship management (CRM) practices affect all forms of communication, but none more than personal selling. The human contact and the ability to negotiate form the foundation of CRM practices. Furthermore, all the technical wizardry in the world can go only so far. Once the show is over, someone has to ask for the order. And that's the responsibility of the sales representative. This chapter examines the role of personal selling in the context of integrated marketing communications.

Personal Selling and Integrated Marketing Communications

personal selling   Face-to-face communication involving the presentation of features and benefits of a product or service to a buyer; the objective is to make a sale.

Personal selling is a personalized form of communications that involves sellers presenting the features and benefits of a product or service to a buyer for the purpose of making a sale. It is an integral component of marketing communications because it is the activity that in many cases clinches the deal. Advertising and promotions create awareness and interest for a product; personal selling creates desire and action. In creating desire and action, the interaction between the seller and buyer is crucial.

Personal selling can be divided into three main areas: retail selling, business-to-business (B2B) selling, and direct selling, either to consumers or other businesses (see Figure 11.1). In all these areas, personal selling is connected to other aspects of integrated marketing communications planning. For example, a sales representative for Procter & Gamble who calls on the head office of a grocery chain such as Safeway or Sobeys does

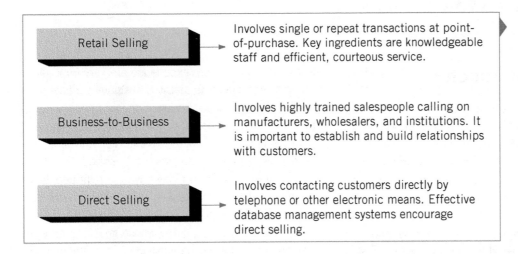

FIGURE
11.1

Classifications of Personal Selling

more than just communicate the benefits of various product lines. If the salesperson's presentation involves a new product launch, the objective is to get the product listed by the chain's head office so that retail stores in the chain can order it. Buyers want to know what kind of marketing support Procter & Gamble will provide. In the sales presentation, the salesperson will include information about advertising plans and sales promotion plans (both consumer and trade promotions) that will help create demand for the new product. Details about when advertising is scheduled, what markets it will run in, and what incentives will be offered to the consumer and the trade are all critical factors that influence the buying decision.

RETAIL SELLING

Transactions occur on the sales floor of a department store, in a bank, at an insurance agent's office, and at the service desk of an automobile maintenance shop, to name just a few examples of retail selling. In these situations, the nature of the sale is defined as a single transaction or a repeat transaction. The quality of service offered at the point of purchase and the degree of satisfaction the customer receives usually influence repeat transactions. In fact, the retail salesperson is the face of the organization. How that person deals with customers affects the buyer's experience.

Successful retailers continuously stress the importance of customer contact at point of purchase. How a retail salesperson interacts with the customer has a significant impact on how the customer perceives the retailer and helps determine if that individual will make a purchase. It is the seller's responsibility to clarify what the customer actually needs, usually by politely asking a few questions. The seller must then offer some product suggestions and demonstrate knowledge by presenting the essential benefits of the products to the customer.

The nature of information offered and the level of service provided will also influence whether or not a person will return to the retail store. People like to feel comfortable when making important buying decisions. For example, customers will return to the same automobile repair shop after getting to know the people who are working on their cars. The relationship between the buyer and seller is usually based on factors such as trust, respect, and satisfaction with the goods or services provided.

When the purchase decision is made, the seller should look for opportunities for add-on sales or suggest service warranties to protect the customer's long-term interests. In doing so, the seller should not be too aggressive, as that may lead to customer frustration.

The Personal Touch

Harry Rosen is a very successful men's fashion retailer, operating 15 stores in key urban markets across Canada and two outlet stores in the greater Toronto area. Larry Rosen has been in charge of the company business since 2002. The business was founded by his father, Harry Rosen.

One of the foundations of the company, and a key factor that has contributed to ongoing success, is staying in touch with customers. When Harry was in charge it was very common for him to patrol the retail floor, interact with customers, and help them select just the right piece of clothing.

Now that son Larry is in charge, nothing has changed. "My dad taught me. I hold the same values," says Larry. Larry admits to being old school but he firmly believes that customers want knowledgeable staff who are prepared to work hard to ensure customers buy the right piece of clothing and receive the proper level of service. In this regard, Larry's frequent presence on the retail floor sets the bar high for his staff.

The emphasis on personal interaction with customers and customer service is a wise strategy to follow as it fits well with the needs and expectations of Canadian shoppers. Some recent research on consumer buying considerations indicates that 70 percent of Canadians enjoy their retail shopping experience. They say that loyalty and the in-store experience are very important. The research suggests that it is absolutely critical that retailers focus on the experience and on understanding their customers' needs. A host of Canadian fashion retailers have gone out of business in the last few years—perhaps they didn't get the message.

Successful retailers today have the right people in place to assist customers with their buying decisions. Nobody does it better than Harry Rosen. Harry Rosen is a customer-centred company whose goal is to provide fashion goods that fit the lifestyle of its customers. Of course, the level of service provided goes well beyond the retail stores. Harry Rosen has an active website that counsels current and prospective customers about fashion trends and how to build just the right wardrobe.

Source: Based on Jon Stoller, "Why the personal touch never goes out of fashion," *The Globe and Mail*, December 13, 2012, p. B10.

© THE CANADIAN PRESS IMAGES/Mario Beauregard

Generally speaking, a low-key approach involving positive customer contact in a pleasant and courteous manner is the main ingredient for retail selling success. In retail, the salespeople are the most essential point of contact in the purchasing process—integral to a well-planned integrated marketing communications program.

Harry Rosen is a successful Canadian men's fashion shop. For insight into its approach to personal selling read the IMC Highlight: **The Personal Touch**.

BUSINESS-TO-BUSINESS SELLING

Business-to-business salespeople either sell products for use in the production and sale of other products, or sell finished products to channel members who in turn resell them. For example, a Xerox sales representative sells photocopiers to another business for use in its daily operations; a representative from Sun Life sells another company a health insurance plan to that will benefit all the buying company's employees.

Thoroughly trained and adequately prepared sales representatives are crucial in these examples. Investment in other forms of marketing communications could be all for naught if the personal selling execution is weak. B2B organizations usually have different types of sales personnel. A **field sales force** is composed of sales representatives who call on customers regularly. They make presentations to existing and new customers, and provide ongoing customer contact to establish a good business relationship. A company may also operate with an **inside sales force**, who seek out new customers and provide them with useful information. Working from the organization's premises, the inside sellers accept orders generated by telephone and online sources.

field sales force   An organization's external sales representatives who regularly call on customers to pursue orders.

inside sales force   An internal group of sellers, who accept orders from customers by telephone and online sources.

DIRECT SELLING

Direct selling to customers either by telephone or the Internet can be accommodated in the retail selling and B2B selling situations just described. **Telemarketing** involves using the telephone as an interactive medium for a marketing response. It uses highly trained people and database marketing techniques to seek and serve new customers. Figure 11.2 summarizes the role that telemarketing can play in the selling process. Telemarketing improves productivity by reducing direct-selling costs, specifically the costs associated with keeping sales representatives on the road (automobiles, accommodations, and related travel expenses). It is also useful in screening and **qualifying** incoming leads, generating leads from various database directories and mailing lists, calling on current customers to secure additional orders, and determining the level of customer satisfaction.

telemarketing   The use of telecommunications to promote the products and services of a business; involves outbound calls (company to customer) and inbound calls (customer to company).

qualifying (a customer)   Assessing if a prospect needs a product, has the authority to buy it, and has the ability to pay for it.

Online selling refers to the use of websites to conduct sales transactions. Consumers who are looking for convenience now include the Web as part of their shopping experience. Ecommerce in Canada in the business-to-business sector (B2B) and the business-to-consumer sector (B2C) is growing each year. In 2013, B2B sales rose to $138 billion, a 13 percent increase over the previous year. Almost one-quarter of the total sales of companies selling online came from online transactions.[1]

online selling   Using the Internet to conduct sales transactions.

The latest data for B2C online sales show sales of $25.4 billion. By 2017, online sales are expected t reach $38.7 billion. Online retail sales are outpacing bricks-and-mortar retail sales by a wide margin. It is estimated that seven in 10 Internet users will make at least one online purchase in 2015.[2] The trend toward online buying and selling will continue because it has been influenced by the rapid increase in use of smartphones. Canadians use their phones to research products, compare prices, and buy products. To stay relevant, marketing organizations must adapt their selling strategies accordingly.

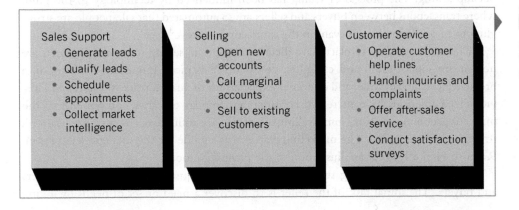

Sales Support
- Generate leads
- Qualify leads
- Schedule appointments
- Collect market intelligence

Selling
- Open new accounts
- Call marginal accounts
- Sell to existing customers

Customer Service
- Operate customer help lines
- Handle inquiries and complaints
- Offer after-sales service
- Conduct satisfaction surveys

FIGURE

11.2

Some of the Roles Played by Telemarketing in Personal Selling

FIGURE
11.3

**Online Selling Offers
Convenience to Consumers**

Source: Courtesy of Grocery Gateway.

Figure 11.3 shows how Grocery Gateway, an online supermarket, provides its consumers with convenience. Websites of companies such as Grocery Gateway are capable of accepting and processing orders, receiving payment, and arranging for the delivery of goods and services directly to consumers and businesses. Indigo Books & Music, operator of Chapters and Indigo stores, sells goods in a similar fashion. Since all transactions are electronically recorded, companies accumulate huge databases of information that can be used for marketing purposes in the longer term.

The Evolution of Selling

Over the years, the nature of selling has changed dramatically. It has moved through a series of stages from consultative selling to strategic selling to relationship selling to partnership selling. The process of selling has been influenced by technology to the point where transactions between buyers and sellers are so automated that salespeople are struggling to make themselves relevant in the transaction process.[3]

Changes in the marketplace have dictated changes in selling strategies. Products are now more sophisticated and complex; competition is more intense and occurs on a broader (even global) scale; and customer expectations of quality, price, service, and individualized solutions have increased considerably. Similar to other components of the marketing communications mix, selling strategies are influenced by an organization's strategic marketing plan. The marketing plan acts as a guide for the strategic selling plan. Refer to Figure 11.4 for an illustration of the planning model.

Consultative selling stresses open, two-way communication between sellers and buyers. The initial task of the seller is to discover a need or set of needs by asking

consultative selling   A form of selling
that stresses open, two-way communication
between a buyer and seller.

> **FIGURE**
> **11.4   Personal Selling Planning Model**

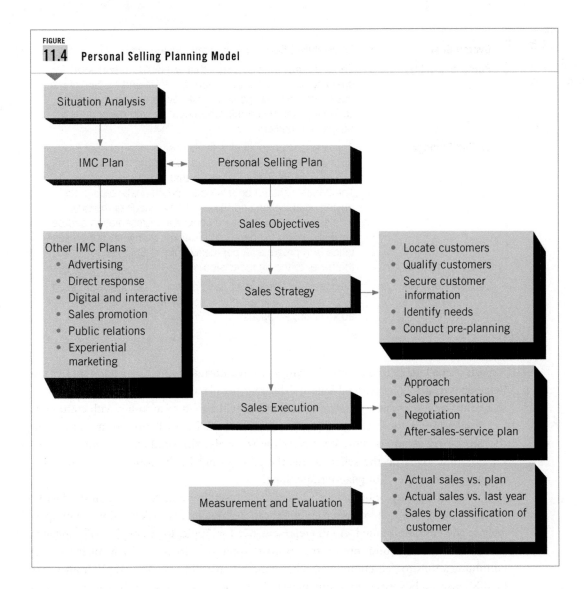

questions and listening carefully. The seller then uses that information to formulate appropriate product recommendations, acting as a consultant. Once the sale is complete, the seller gets involved with after-sales service and customer care programs. A satisfied customer remains a customer. The Harry Rosen story that appeared earlier in the chapter demonstrates this concept.

Strategic selling takes consultative selling to the next level. It considers the changing conditions in the marketplace, adds technology to enhance the methods of presenting products to buyers, and focuses on serving customers one customer at a time. The goal is to be flexible while providing solutions that are unique to each customer. There are three core factors to be considered in strategic selling: the seller must form a good relationship with the customer, the seller must effectively match products and position them to meet customer needs, and the seller must develop a compelling presentation that will clearly portray the usefulness of a product in resolving a customer's problem.

In **relationship selling**, the goal is to develop a plan of action to establish, build, and maintain customers. It involves taking a long-term perspective on selling and considers the fact that good relationships don't necessarily form very quickly. Instead, a seller must take the necessary steps to form a relationship, such as establishing rapport and building trust and

strategic selling   A form of consultative selling that involves dealing with each customer as an individual, stressing that in the transfer of product information.

relationship selling   A form of selling with the goal of developing a plan of action that establishes, builds, and maintains a long-term relationship with customers.

FIGURE
11.5

**The Key Elements of
Relationship Selling**

Overall Goal	To establish, build, and maintain customers.
Personal Strategy	The seller must initiate steps that will build rapport with customers. The seller must earn the trust and respect of the customer. The salesperson must have a strong and positive self-image and be flexible when dealing with many different people and personalities.
Selling Strategy	The salesperson must effectively position the product (a solution) in the customer's mind by relating the right benefits to a unique problem or situation that the customer presents. The benefits should be related to the rational needs of the buying organization and the emotional needs of the buyer. A salesperson must make a convincing presentation and be flexible enough to adapt to the unexpected while the presentation is in progress. A persuasive presentation should lead the buyer to the right decision.
Building Relationships	Customers not only want good products, but also want good relationships. Selling today is not about selling products—it's about selling solutions!

respect, over a long period of time. Having a positive attitude, projecting a good image, and being able to get along with all kinds of different people and personalities are key factors that contribute to a sales representative's ability to build a solid relationship with customers.

Establishing a good relationship depends on how well the seller positions products in the minds of customers, how effectively (persuasively) the product's benefits are presented, and how well the seller guards the relationship in the long run. Figure 11.5 reviews the key aspects of relationship selling.

With relationship selling, it is the seller's responsibility to match the right product to the customer and then develop the communications strategy that will position it appropriately in the customer's mind. A sales representative for Apple, for example, will capitalize on the user-friendly positioning strategy that Apple uses in other forms of marketing communications to sell computers. The representative differentiates Apple from other brands based on benefits such as uniqueness, degree of innovation, performance capabilities (for example, speed of performing functions), and reliability. A wise representative will also build in the lifestyle imagery associated with the brand (for example, it is perceived as a sleek and sexy brand, a lifestyle brand compared to other brands).

The formation of the right positioning strategy depends largely on the seller's knowledge of the customer. The more knowledge the seller has going into the presentation, the easier it is to structure the presentation. A good salesperson continuously updates customer files with new information. In the age of technology, such a practice is easy and vital to success.

presentation strategy A plan of what to say to a customer in a sales presentation to identify customer needs, summarize benefits, and prepare for potential objections.

A good salesperson formulates a **presentation strategy** that focuses on what to say to customers when presenting the product. A good plan is based on the seller's knowledge of the customer and the customer's immediate needs; it summarizes potential benefits that will be stressed (often prioritized from most important to least important) and considers potential objections that the buyer might raise. As with most marketing communications strategies, a sales strategy must remain flexible. The seller, for example, must be able to adapt the presentation based on new information that surfaces during a presentation, or to rephrase relevant benefits if the buyer introduces the benefits of a competitor's product. The importance of knowledge in a variety of areas and the key elements of a presentation are discussed in more detail later in this chapter.

PARTNERSHIP SELLING

Partnership selling is an extension of relationship selling. It involves a strategically developed, long-term relationship to sell products; provides comprehensive after-sales service; and encourages effective two-way communications to ensure complete customer satisfaction. The goal is to form partnerships with customers in a manner that fosters prosperity between partners.

Changing marketplace conditions have fostered the concept of partnership selling. There was a time when companies could rely on the strength of their company, product, and service components to secure stability and growth. Now, however, the intensity of competition, the availability of copycat products, the need to constantly reduce costs, and the speed with which innovative products are introduced necessitates strong buyer–seller partnerships. As well, buyers are simply more informed today. With so much information available online, they can access information about competing brands and formulate opinions prior to even meeting with a sales representative.

In the current business environment, it is essential that an organization transform its selling methods to build formal relationships with other organizations in the channel of distribution. It is part of the CRM philosophy introduced earlier in this text. CRM involves managing an organization's interactions with customers, clients, and sales prospects by using technology to organize, automate, and synchronize marketing and selling procedures. Successful organizations today are those that invest time and money into systems that help create good solutions for customers.

To operate successfully in this environment, a salesperson must show a deep understanding of a prospect's business needs. According to Mark Stuyt, a successful sales force trainer, "A sales representative needs to understand how the business operates. Industry content is absolutely critical. Sales people know their product but not much about the industry they are selling into. Today, business acumen trumps traditional sales tactics."[4]

To illustrate the importance of understanding how customers' businesses operate, consider a change implemented by UPS in the courier service market. Rather than having a short-term perspective where building the business was based on offering good prices and fast service to customers, UPS realized it could offer its customers much more in terms of distribution services. UPS moved from being a courier service to becoming a supply chain management company with the goal of assisting customers with their long-range growth needs. The company has evolved with changes in the marketplace and with the changing needs of its customers. Shipping goods is a complex business that many organizations prefer to outsource. UPS is equipped to serve those organizations.

> **partnership selling** A strategically developed long-term relationship that involves selling products and providing comprehensive after-sales service and effective two-way communications to ensure complete customer satisfaction.

Personal Selling: The Human Communications Element

If establishing and building effective relationships are the keys to modern-day success, what strategies must the salesperson use to form a good working relationship with customers? To be successful, a salesperson must focus on three primary areas: personal characteristics, verbal communications, and non-verbal communications. A well-prepared and energetic salesperson knows how to communicate effectively both verbally and non-verbally, and, as a result, will be successful. Let's examine each area briefly.

PERSONAL CHARACTERISTICS

To survive in selling, certain personal characteristics are required. Typically, successful salespeople are self-confident, motivated, flexible, optimistic, and project a good image when confronted with social and business situations. These characteristics can be learned and practised. Given time and proper training, poorly performing salespeople can be transformed into prosperous salespeople. All that is required are dedication and a desire to confront the challenges of selling.

self-image Your own idea about yourself and your relationship with others.

Self-image is a psychological term referring to your attitude and feelings about yourself and your roles in relation to others. It certainly plays a key role in selling. Perhaps the most important aspect of self-image is confidence. For example, an individual who approaches a challenge with enthusiasm, or possesses that "I'm going to win" attitude, is likely to succeed. In contrast, an individual who tends to forecast failure, or has a "doom and gloom" attitude, will almost certainly get disappointing results. To succeed, therefore, you have to think you can succeed.

Among all the theories about building self-confidence, three essential strategies stand out. First, a positive self-image will exist if a person does not dwell on past mistakes. Instead, people must learn from their mistakes and move forward. Second, a salesperson should develop some expertise in a certain area, because there is special status in being an expert. Others will call upon you for advice. Third, a salesperson should develop a positive outlook. For example, taking courses that reinforce the principles of success and simply associating with other positive and successful people are both good practices to follow.

VERBAL AND NON-VERBAL COMMUNICATIONS

verbal skills Comfort and ability with speaking and listening.

Typically, good salespeople have good **verbal skills**. They are generally comfortable when addressing a buyer, buying committee, or even a larger audience. When one thinks of a salesperson, the stereotype of the fast talker often comes to mind, but the reality is that listening skills are just as important. A salesperson who listens carefully to what the buyer says can respond better. Communications in a selling situation is a two-way street.

non-verbal communication (body language) The expression of thoughts, opinions, or information using non-verbal cues such as body movement, facial expressions, and eye contact.

Non-verbal communication or **body language** is another essential aspect of self-confidence. Non-verbal communication refers to the imparting of thoughts, opinions, or information without using spoken words. An observer (in this case the buyer) will notice non-verbal cues such as body movement, facial expressions, and eye contact.[5] A buyer's perceptions of a salesperson are often determined by body language. For example, does the seller squirm in the chair while conversing, or does the seller fidget with a small object while speaking? Such body language could be perceived as a lack of confidence. Alternatively, does the seller make direct eye contact? Was that handshake firm and friendly? Such body language suggests self-confidence. For a summary of some essential characteristics and traits for successful selling, refer to Figure 11.6.

Other non-verbal characteristics that influence buyers' perceptions include facial expressions, personal appearance, and manners. The old expression that "the lips say one thing, but the eyes say another" applies to selling situations. Facial gestures can communicate confidence, as does a smile; boredom, as does a grin; or evaluation or judgment, as in a frown or perplexed expression. Given that the goal in selling is to express confidence, successful salespeople always wear a sincere and winning smile when they approach customers and when they present information to them.

Dress codes have changed drastically in recent years. The business world moved away from formal attire (business suits) and toward informal attire (business casual) for a period of time. Recently, however, there has been a return to more formal dress. Wardrobe experts believe clothing makes a significant difference in building a person's credibility and likeability with customers. Experts offer different opinions on how to dress, but generally there is one common theme: The situation (or appropriateness) dictates the style of dress.

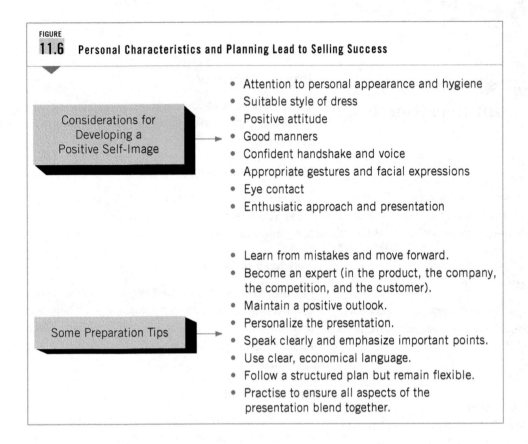

FIGURE
11.6 **Personal Characteristics and Planning Lead to Selling Success**

Considerations for Developing a Positive Self-Image

- Attention to personal appearance and hygiene
- Suitable style of dress
- Positive attitude
- Good manners
- Confident handshake and voice
- Appropriate gestures and facial expressions
- Eye contact
- Enthusiatic approach and presentation

Some Preparation Tips

- Learn from mistakes and move forward.
- Become an expert (in the product, the company, the competition, and the customer).
- Maintain a positive outlook.
- Personalize the presentation.
- Speak clearly and emphasize important points.
- Use clear, economical language.
- Follow a structured plan but remain flexible.
- Practise to ensure all aspects of the presentation blend together.

For example, if you are meeting your customer in a business office or boardroom setting, formal dress is appropriate. If the meeting is in a factory or at a construction site, less formal attire is suitable. Other traditional guidelines for wardrobe focus on simplicity, quality, and the selective use of accessories. Accessories such as large, dangling earrings and facial jewellery could be a distraction for the buyer, and anything causing a distraction should be avoided.

There is a relationship between verbal communication and non-verbal communication in a selling situation. Successful salespeople effectively blend together verbal and non-verbal communications. They communicate the message in a positive and enthusiastic manner, and reinforce it with body language that is consistent with what they say. Such a combination builds confidence in the buyer and gives the buyer the impression the salesperson can be trusted. Such perceptions certainly go a long way in building and maintaining a business relationship.

Beyond these personal characteristics, good salespeople possess other intangible characteristics that have an impact on their performance. For some insight into these characteristics, see the IMC Highlight: **What Separates Successful Salespeople from Everyone Else?**

PREPARATION AND THE IMPORTANCE OF KNOWLEDGE

In a nutshell, the primary task of a salesperson is to provide a customer with a solution to a problem by providing the right product or service at a price that is agreeable to the customer. It sounds so simple! It requires much advance preparation. That preparation is divided into three primary areas: product knowledge, company knowledge, and competitor knowledge. With regard to product knowledge, the salesperson must become an

What Separates Successful Salespeople from Everyone Else?

Successful salespeople possess intangible skills that go beyond product, company, and competitor knowledge. These salespeople know it is the "little things" that separate successful salespeople from the rest of the pack. So, what are some of these intangibles? Here are a few of them.

They Are Persistent

Successful salespeople don't let obstacles stand in their way. They are tenacious and are constantly looking for new solutions.

They Set Goals

Successful salespeople establish specific goals, then visualize their target, determine how they will achieve their goals, and take action daily.

They Listen

Effective salespeople know the customer will tell them what they need to know; therefore, they listen and learn.

They Are Passionate

When you love what you do, you put more passion into it. Effective salespeople are passionate about their company and products.

They Are Enthusiastic

Effective salespeople remain positive, even in tough times. When faced with negative and challenging situations, they always focus on the positives.

They Keep in Touch

Effective salespeople go well beyond routine follow-up. They keep track of key dates, such as birthdays and anniversaries, and deliver communications on a more personal level in order to enhance the relationship.

They Work Hard

Successful salespeople start early, make more calls, and stay late when necessary. They know that making more presentations will produce more sales.

Based on Kelley Robertson, "Characteristics of Successful Salespeople," *SOHO*, Summer 2006, pp. 14, 15.

---

expert and know exactly what benefits to stress with any particular customer. For example, two different customers might require the same product, but one customer is motivated by quality, the other by service. The salesperson would have to adapt the presentation to offer different perspectives based on each buyer's unique needs and priorities. In complex situations, such as when various products must be combined to form a solution, the salesperson must be capable of bringing the right products and services together. This process is called **product configuration**.

product configuration The bringing together of various products and services to form a solution for the customer.

PRODUCT KNOWLEDGE

Essentially, product knowledge can be classified into four crucial areas: product development and quality improvement processes, performance data and specifications, maintenance and service, and price and delivery. The various combinations of this information make up the essential elements of a planned sales presentation. To grow, companies develop new products to solve new needs. It is important for a salesperson to know how a product was developed, how much it cost to develop, and why it was developed. This sort of information strongly suggests to a customer that the company takes research and development seriously and strives to build better products for its customers.

In terms of performance and quality, a salesperson should be familiar with quality control standards so that information regarding product claims can be substantiated and compared with claims made by competitors. Knowing that a product meets or exceeds certain standards often provides a competitive advantage in a sales presentation.

A buyer usually poses questions or raises objections about performance data and specifications in the middle of a sales presentation. To illustrate, assume you are planning a business conference and considering various conference centres. What kinds of questions would you ask the sales manager of a potential conference centre? Here are a few examples:

- What kind of technical support does the conference centre offer if we need it?

- Is wifi available to delegates and at what cost?

- Is there sufficient accommodation for 200 delegates?

- How efficient is the catering department in serving a buffet dinner to 200 people?

Certainly the list could be longer and much more diverse—and that is the point. A good salesperson must be ready to respond to the expected and the unexpected.

If the competing products are similar, perhaps information about maintenance and service provide product differentiation. If service is provided as part of a package deal, all specifications regarding additional services must be part of the sales presentation. Specifications must be agreed upon: who is responsible for what service, when it will happen, how often it will happen, and so on. It is very common for selling companies to draw up official service contracts based on specific requirements provided by the buying organization. Such contracts play a vital role in the relationship-building process.

Other knowledge that helps differentiate one product from another is knowledge about price and delivery. The easiest and most common objection that buyers raise is price: "Your price is too high!" Knowing how to respond appropriately is crucial to closing the sale. If your price is higher than the competition, that fact must be acknowledged, and additional and tangible product benefits must be presented to justify the higher price. In such situations, the buyer simply wants more information; the salesperson must show good product knowledge.

COMPANY KNOWLEDGE

Since the salesperson is the customer's primary source of contact, the salesperson *is* the company. The perceptions formed by a customer, or prospective customer, about a company depend largely on the attitude, style, behaviour, and communications abilities of the salesperson. If perceptions are positive, there is a stronger likelihood of making the sale and developing a long-term business relationship. A salesperson, therefore, should integrate essential information about the company into a sales presentation.

Business organizations exist to serve their customers, and all employees must recognize that they contribute to this effort. This attitude, often referred to as **corporate culture**, is defined as the values, norms, and practices shared by all employees of an organization. A good corporate culture always puts the customer first.

corporate culture   The values, beliefs, norms, and practices shared by all employees of an organization.

CIBC identifies customer needs and develops innovative products to satisfy those needs. Such information should be passed on to prospective customers by sales representatives because it sends out a clear signal about the type of company CIBC is: a company willing to develop new products and to respond to new challenges in an ever-changing marketplace. Introducing mobile payments for retail purchase transactions is but one example of how CIBC responded to the changing marketplace. Refer to the image in Figure 11.7.

FIGURE

11.7

CIBC Responds to the Challenge of Developing New and Innovative Products for a Changing Marketplace

Source: Handout/Giesecke & Devrient/ Newscom.

What services a company provides after the sale is also crucial information to provide to customers. Many experts say, "The relationship begins once the sale is made." Therefore, after-sales service, which is a function that is usually implemented by other departments of a company, must be integrated into a sales presentation. It is important for a company to track the level of satisfaction that customers are experiencing, so it is quite common for organizations to contact customers directly by telephone or mail. The results of surveys, for example, can be passed on to sales representatives for follow-up.

COMPETITOR KNOWLEDGE

Good salespeople know the competitor's products almost as well as their own. In a sales presentation, comparisons inevitably crop up, making it essential to know the benefits and weaknesses of competing products and adapt the selling strategy accordingly. If a seller cannot respond to the challenges posed by a buyer, the chances of making a sale are lost.

Talking about competing products is usually awkward. Obviously, a salesperson does not want to acknowledge a competitor's strengths, but at the same time a seller cannot be too critical of competitors' products. The customer may already be doing business with the competition. Here are a few basic guidelines for dealing with competing products:[6]

- Do not deliberately include reference to competitors in your presentation as it shifts the focus off your own product. Do, however, respond to questions about the competition.

- Do not make statements about the competitor if you are uncertain of the facts. Your credibility will suffer if you make inaccurate statements.

- Do not criticize the competition. State the facts as you know them and avoid emotional comments if you have to make a comparison.

Remember, prospective customers are forming perceptions of you and your company when you are making the sales presentation. How you handle competing products goes a long way toward creating a favourable or unfavourable impression.

Roles and Responsibilities of Salespeople

The primary tasks of a salesperson, particularly in a business-to-business environment, are to gather market intelligence, solve customers' problems, locate and maintain customers, and provide follow-up service. This section examines each responsibility.

GATHERING MARKET INTELLIGENCE

In a competitive marketplace, salespeople must be attuned to the trends in their industry. They must be alert to what the competitor is doing, to its new product projects, and to its advertising and promotion plans; and they must listen to feedback from customers regarding their own products' performance. As indicated earlier, competitive knowledge is important when the salesperson faces questions involving product comparisons. Data collected by a salesperson can be reported electronically to the company's head office. Managers can retrieve the information and use it appropriately at a later date.

PROBLEM SOLVING

The only way a salesperson can make a sale is to listen to what a customer wants and ask questions to determine the customer's real needs. Asking, listening, and providing information and advice that are in the best interests of the customer are what relationship selling is all about. The seller must demonstrate a sincere concern for the customer's needs.

LOCATING AND MAINTAINING CUSTOMERS

Salespeople who locate new customers play an important role in a company's growth. A company cannot be satisfied with its current list of customers, because aggressive competitors are always attempting to lure them away. To prevent shrinkage and to increase sales, salespeople actively pursue new accounts. Their time is divided between finding new accounts and selling to and servicing current accounts.

FOLLOW-UP SERVICE

The salesperson is the first point of contact should anything go wrong or should more information be required. Maintenance of customers is crucial, and, very often, it is the quality of the follow-up service that determines if a customer will remain a customer. Since the salespeople are the company's direct link to the customer, it cannot be stressed enough how important it is that they handle customer service well. The sale is never over! Once the deal has closed, numerous tasks arise: arranging for delivery, providing technical assistance, offering customer training, and being readily available to handle any problems that might emerge during and after delivery. The personalized role of the sales representative is instrumental in building relationships.

Personal Selling Strategies

Before discussing the various steps involved in successful personal selling, let's first explore the difference between features and benefits. A product **feature** is anything that can be felt, seen, or measured. Features include such things as durability, design, and economy of operation. They provide a customer with information, but do not motivate a

feature Tangible aspect of a product, such as durability, design, and economy of operation.

benefit The value a customer attaches to a brand attribute.

customer to buy. A **benefit** provides the customer with advantage or gain, and shows how a product will help resolve a specific problem. Benefits provide motivation. To demonstrate, consider all the technical features usually associated with a laptop computer. The list seems endless and includes much technical jargon. Assuming the customer wants quick access to information when using the computer (information the seller would seek out by asking a few questions), the seller can quickly zoom in on the appropriate features and translate them into benefits that are appropriate for and meaningful to the customer.

Regardless of the sales situation—whether retail selling, business-to-business selling, or direct selling—the steps in the selling process are similar. They are simply adapted to each situation. This section covers the seven essential steps in the selling process (see Figure 11.8).

PROSPECTING

prospecting A procedure for systematically developing sales leads.

The first step is **prospecting**, which is a procedure for systematically developing sales leads. If salespeople do not allocate enough time to finding new customers, they risk causing a decline in sales for their company. If their income is geared to the value of the business they produce, they risk the loss of personal compensation as well. Prospecting is

FIGURE 11.8

The Seven Essential Steps in the Personal Selling Process

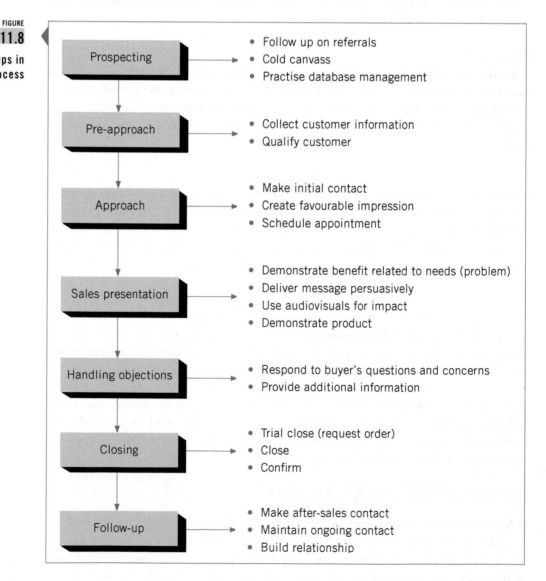

also important because of attrition. Attrition refers to the loss of customers over a period of time. Even with extensive CRM programs in place to retain customers, buyers switch suppliers when better products and services become available.

Potential customers, or prospects, are identified by means of published lists and directories, such as *Scott's Industrial Directory*, *Hovers Business Directory*, and the *Canadian Key Business Directory*. Another strategy for seeking new customers is the referral. A **referral** is a prospect who is recommended by a current customer. The salesperson also seeks new customers by **cold canvass**, the process of calling on people or organizations without appointments or advance knowledge of them. Other sources of leads include names obtained from trade shows, advertising, direct response communications, telemarketing and online communications, sales promotion entry forms, and channel members.

referral A recommendation by a current customer of a potential new customer to a sales representative.

cold canvass The process of calling on people or organizations without appointments or advance knowledge of them.

PRE-APPROACH

The **pre-approach** involves gathering information about potential customers before actually making sales contact. During the pre-approach stage, customers are qualified, which is the procedure for determining if a prospect needs the product, has the authority to buy it, and has the ability to pay for it. There is little sense in pursuing customers who lack the financial resources or have no need to make the business relationship successful. In the process of qualifying customers, the seller also gains insights that can be used in the sales presentation: information such as the buyer's likes and dislikes, personal interests and hobbies, buying procedures, and special needs and problems.

pre-approach The gathering of information about customers before actually making sales contact.

APPROACH

The **approach** is the initial contact with the prospect, often in a face-to-face selling situation. Since buyers are usually busy, little time should be wasted in the approach. The salesperson must capture the attention and interest of the buyer and create a favourable first impression in the first few minutes of a sales interview, so that there is an effective environment for the presentation of the product's benefits.

approach The initial contact with a customer.

SALES PRESENTATION

It is common for a salesperson to make presentations to individuals (one-on-one selling) or to buying teams (one-on-group selling). Buying teams are classified as buying centres (an informal grouping of people in the buying group) or buying committees (a formal group with a structured buying procedure in place). In dealing with buying committees, the salesperson must listen attentively and observe body language to determine which members of the group are the real influencers and decision makers.

The actual **sales presentation** consists of a persuasive delivery and demonstration of a product's benefits. An effective sales presentation shows the buyer how the benefits of the product satisfy specific needs or help resolve a particular problem. In doing so, the seller focuses on the benefits that are most important to the buyer. Critical elements usually focus on lower price, the durability of the product, the dependability of supply, the performance of the product, and the availability of follow-up service.

sales presentation A persuasive delivery and demonstration of a product's benefits; shows buyers how the product's benefits will satisfy their needs.

At this stage, asking proper questions and listening attentively are particularly important to uncover real needs. A salesperson listens to and analyzes what buyers are saying, then uses what has been discovered when presenting the appropriate benefits. Being flexible and adapting a presentation in mid-stream could be the difference between making a sale and not making a sale.

Demonstrations play a key role in a sales presentation. A **demonstration** is an opportunity to show the product in action and substantiate the claims being made about

demonstration A sales technique that involves showing the product in action to portray its benefits to a buyer.

FIGURE
11.9

**Useful Reminders for Planning
a Sales Presentation**

- Ask the buyer questions and listen attentively to the responses.
- Include useful information about the company.
- Watch for cues by observing body language.
- Include a product demonstration (rehearse to make sure it works).
- Involve the buyer in the presentation.
- Remain flexible throughout the presentation and adapt it based on feedback.
- Add technology where appropriate to enhance the presentation.
- Respond to objections pleasantly (be prepared for the expected and unexpected).
- Ask for the order (always be closing).

the product. A good demonstration (something the buyer can see) adds to the convincing nature of the presentation. It helps hold the buyer's attention and creates interest and desire. It is wise to rehearse the demonstration so that what the salesperson says and what the salesperson demonstrates are in harmony with each other. Portable technologies allow for multimedia presentations and effective demonstrations. The salesperson must be certain that all equipment is in good working condition; any failure with technology is embarrassing. Figure 11.9 lists useful reminders for planning a sales presentation.

HANDLING OBJECTIONS

objection   An obstacle that a salesperson must confront during a sales presentation.

An **objection** is an obstacle that the salesperson must confront during a presentation and resolve if the sales transaction is to be completed. An objection is a cue for more information. The buyer is suggesting that the presentation of a product has not revealed how the product will satisfy a particular need. The objection, therefore, is feedback to be analyzed and used. It might enable the salesperson to discover another benefit in the product, a benefit that can then be presented to the buyer.

Typical objections involve issues related to the following: product quality and the level of service and technical assistance; the price or the level of discounts suggested, for example, the price may be too high, discount too low, or credit terms unacceptable; and sourcing issues such as how the buyer feels about the company in comparison to other potential suppliers. Objections are a normal response from buyers, so salespeople should not take them personally. Instead, the salesperson should ask questions to clarify the buyer's concern, answer the objection, and then move on to the next benefit or attempt to close the sale.

A good salesperson develops effective strategies for handling objections; being prepared for the expected and unexpected is essential. When responding to objections, the salesperson can call upon the product itself, testimonials and case histories of success, test results shown in a variety of formats (for example, graphs and charts), and other forms of audiovisual support.

CLOSING

closing   Asking for the order at the appropriate time in a sales presentation.

trial close   A failed attempt at closing a sale; the buyer said "no."

Does the buyer voluntarily say, "Yes, I'll buy it"? The answer is, "rarely"! Getting the buyer to say "yes" is the entire purpose of the sales interview, but this task is accomplished if only the salesperson asks for the order. **Closing** consists of asking for the order; it is the most difficult step in the process of selling. Salespeople are reluctant to ask the big question, even though it is the logical sequel to a good presentation and demonstration. In fact, a good salesperson attempts a close whenever a point of agreement is made with the buyer. If the buyer says "no," the close is referred to as a **trial close**, or an attempt to close that failed. The salesperson simply moves on to the next point in the presentation.

The close can occur at any point in a sales presentation. Knowing when to close is essential. Therefore, as the sales presentation progresses, the salesperson must be alert to closing cues. A **closing cue** is an indication that the buyer is ready to buy. The cue may be verbal or non-verbal. If a cue is detected, a close should be attempted. Verbal cues include statements such as "What type of warranty do you provide?" Such a statement shows that the buyer is thinking ahead. Another cue is "The delivery and installation schedule fits well with our factory conversion schedule." Such a statement suggests confirmation of a key benefit. Or another could be "We need the product in one week." In other words, if you can supply it, we'll buy it! Statements such as these are closing cues that must be acted upon.

Positive non-verbal communications include changing facial expressions, a change in the buyer's mood (for example, the buyer becomes more jovial, or the buyer nods in agreement. Good salespeople do not miss such opportunities, even if they have not finished their presentation. The buyer is telling you it is time to close—do it!

Timing a close is a matter of judgment. Good salespeople know when to close—it is often referred to as the "sixth sense" of selling. The salesperson assesses the buyer's verbal and non-verbal responses in an effort to judge when that person has become receptive, and at the right moment, asks the big question with a high degree of self-confidence. A list of commonly used closing techniques appears in Figure 11.10.

Once the sale has been closed, it is time to reassure the customer that a good decision has been taken and to confirm that you will provide all the essential services that were promised in the presentation. Parting on a positive note is crucial, because buyers very often experience cognitive dissonance. **Cognitive dissonance** in this case, refers to a feeling of doubt or regret once the buying decision has been made. The buyer wants to be reassured that the best choice has been made. This is the start of the relationship-building process.

cognitive dissonance   A feeling of doubt or regret in a consumer's mind once a buying decision has been made.

FOLLOW-UP

There is an old saying: "The sale never ends." There is truth to this statement, because a new sale is nothing more than the start of a new relationship. Keeping current customers satisfied

---

The objective of the sales presentation is to get the order. To do so, the seller must close the sale by asking for the order. Asking for the order can be accomplished in a variety of ways.

Assumptive Close

The seller assumes the buyer has already decided to buy. The seller says, "I'll have it delivered by Friday," or "What is the best day for delivery?" An agreement or answer confirms the seller's assumption.

Alternative-Choice Close

The seller assumes the sale is made but asks for clarification on another point. For example, the seller may say, "Would you prefer metallic blue or cherry red?"

Summary-of-Benefits Close

At the end of the presentation, the seller calmly reviews the key points the buyer has already agreed to (price, service, quality, reliability, and so on). Once the summary is complete, the seller says, "When would you like it delivered?"

Direct Close

No beating around the bush here. The seller confidently says, "Can I deliver it on Friday?" Then the seller stops talking and awaits the response.

Take-Away Close

It is human nature to want what you can't have. The seller says, "This product isn't for everyone. It's a certain kind of person who can appreciate the finer qualities of this product."

FIGURE
11.10

Successful Closing Techniques

follow-up Maintaining contact with customers to ensure that service has been satisfactory.

is the key to success. Effective salespeople make a point of providing **follow-up**; that is, they keep in touch with customers to ensure that the delivery and installation of the goods were satisfactory, that promises were kept, and that the expectations of the buyer were met. When problems do occur, the salesperson is ready to take action to resolve the situation.

In the current competitive business environment, good follow-up strategies help reduce customer attrition. Companies realize that a satisfied customer is a long-term customer. As discussed elsewhere in this text, customer relationship management programs now act as a foundation for long-term business success. Keeping track of customer transactions and customer preferences provides an opportunity for incremental sales. Larry Rosen, president of upscale clothier Harry Rosen, firmly understands this concept. Harry Rosen has implemented programs that ensure the utmost in customer service and care. "We don't look at a person in terms of an immediate sale. We look at him in terms of potential lifetime value."[7]

Success in selling requires dedication, determination, and discipline. What separates the successful salesperson from the unsuccessful one usually boils down to how well an individual follows an established set of principles. While the wording of these principles might vary from one source to another, the intent behind them is consistent. See Figure 11.11 for some pointers on what separates the professionals from the average salespeople.

FIGURE
11.11

Tips for Successful Selling

1. Selling skills are learned skills

Successful salespeople take the time to develop their skills. They ask meaningful questions, listen attentively, and observe buyer behaviour. Through learning, they can relate appropriate product benefits to the customer's needs. Knowledge of the product, company, the customer and their industry, and the competition is essential.

2. The salesperson is the most important product

Successful salespeople sell themselves. They project a positive image about themselves and their company. A customer who isn't sold on you won't buy your product.

3. Emotions, feelings, and relationships are important

Successful salespeople present more than just facts. They create positive emotions about themselves, their products and services, and their company. Through effective communications, they bring the buyers into the relationship, showing how their problems will be resolved.

4. Preparation is crucial

Be prepared! A sales presentation is like a stage performance. You may not get a second chance. Command the buyer's attention immediately and encourage participation throughout the presentation. Through participation, the buyer will discover the product's benefits. Ensure that all components of the presentation are coordinated and all electronic aids are in working condition.

5. Negotiation skills are important

A successful salesperson can deal with any and all concerns raised by the buyer. Be prepared to meet challenges by offering additional information, and package together all points of agreement in order to close the sale.

6. Always be closing

Closing begins at the start of a presentation. The challenge is to build agreement and help the prospect decide how to buy, not whether to buy. When the prospect agrees, ask for the order. If the buyer refuses, continue with the presentation and ask for the order again when the prospect agrees. Persistence pays off!

Selling in a Changing Business Environment

The nature of selling is changing rapidly. To be successful in the future, the salesperson and the company must consider the importance of teamwork in communicating with customers (another aspect of integration), the importance of building long-term relationships, and the importance of adapting to technologies that directly influence the selling process.

SELLING IS A TEAM EFFORT

Traditionally, selling has been thought of as an individual effort (for example, the salesperson calling on the customer and presenting a product to an individual or to a committee of buyers). Today, selling is often a team effort involving people from several departments of an organization. To sell sophisticated technical equipment in a B2B environment requires a team of experts, including research and design specialists, engineers, and other marketing personnel in addition to the salesperson. They all bring different expertise to the presentation and make the customer feel more at ease with the decision-making process.

Buyers also form teams comprised of members from across an organization who share responsibility for making a decision. The team can better evaluate the product offerings of sellers, as the product can be evaluated from various perspectives. The team approach also reduces the risks that are associated with large and complex buying decisions.

COMPANIES SELL RELATIONSHIPS, NOT PRODUCTS

Organizations abiding by contemporary corporate culture—that is, those that believe in relationship marketing—actively pursue relationships in the selling process. Making a sale or getting the order is simply one step in the sales continuum. It symbolizes the start of a new relationship or the solidification of an existing one.

The strategic decision for the seller is to determine how the company's resources can give the customer an edge. It is a consultative process in which the seller proves to the buyer that there is an advantage in doing business together. The search for a good fit between sellers (suppliers) and buyers stems from customers' relentless search for value in everything they purchase.

TECHNOLOGY IS CHANGING SELLING

The nature of selling is changing in many industries due to the advances in communications technology. Members of a channel of distribution that includes raw material suppliers, manufacturers, wholesalers, retailers, and end users are working cooperatively on supply chain management programs. By electronically transferring information among the participants in the supply chain—a cornerstone of true CRM programs—basic buying decisions are automated. Therefore, the challenge facing creative sellers is how to get their products into such a system.

Technology-based CRM programs and a company's ability to sell goods online also have consequences for salespeople and the way they communicate with customers. Technology makes it possible to use fewer people in personal selling, and these sellers find themselves spending less time in personal contact with customers and more time in electronic contact with them. Companies using technology to help market goods and services are finding that geographical boundaries are being eliminated as buyers search for the best value in what they require. Because customers contact companies in a variety of ways (such as by telephone, in person, by email, or through websites), it is important to send out a consistent and integrated marketing communications message.

In summary, even though business operates in an era of automated purchasing, downsized sales teams, and state-of-the art customer relationship management technology, many experts still insist the human element remains important. People like to buy from people they like.

SUMMARY

Personal selling refers to personal communications between sellers and buyers. Typically, personal selling is divided into three main areas: retail selling, business-to-business selling, and direct selling. In all forms, the immediate goal is to complete a sales transaction and then adopt appropriate strategies to encourage repeat transactions, thus building a relationship with the customer that will last for an extended period.

The nature of selling has evolved with the changing marketplace. Selling has moved from consultative selling to strategic selling to relationship selling. Relationship selling involves strategies to establish, build, and maintain customers. It approaches selling from the perspective of the lifetime value of a customer and the concept that retaining satisfied customers is much more profitable than constantly finding new ones. Relationship selling has extended into partnerships between sellers and buyers. Partnership selling is but one aspect of customer relationship management programs and is strategically developed to encourage a profitable long-term relationship.

There are several essential attributes for successful selling today. A good salesperson possesses the right combination of personal characteristics (characteristics that can be learned and practised) and communication skills (both speaking and listening). A good self-image and positive approach to selling are essential—a successful outlook breeds success! The ability to read a customer is also necessary. Observing and interpreting verbal and non-verbal cues from the customer allow the salesperson to adapt a presentation while in progress and to close the sale at the appropriate time.

Adequate advance preparation is another key to successful selling. Good salespeople possess sound knowledge of the product and company they represent, the customer and the industry they operate in, and the competition. The task of the salesperson is to match the right product or combination of products and services with the customer's needs. In doing so, the salesperson plans a presentation strategy that shows how the products meet customer needs better than the competition's products. Other essential roles of the salesperson include gathering market intelligence, solving problems, locating and maintaining customers, and providing follow-up service.

The selling process involves seven distinct steps: prospecting, pre-approach, approach, sales presentation, handling objections, closing, and following-up. A good presentation shows how the benefits of a product meet the buyer's needs. During the presentation, a seller's negotiation skills are called upon to respond to the buyer's objections and concerns. Once those are answered, the seller closes the sale by asking for the order. Assuming a satisfactory response, the sale is confirmed and follow-up strategies are implemented. This is the start of the CRM process that, if nurtured carefully, will profit both parties.

Advances in technology are changing the nature of personal selling. Less time is now spent in personal contact, and more time is devoted to electronic contact and activities designed to service and retain customers. As in other forms of marketing communications, the challenge is to develop effective strategies to solidify relationships.

KEY TERMS

approach 337
benefit 336
body language 330
closing 338
closing cue 339
cognitive dissonance 339
cold canvass 337
consultative selling 326
corporate culture 333
demonstration 337
feature 335
field sales force 325
follow-up 340
inside sales force 325
non-verbal communication 330
objection 338
online selling 325
partnership selling 329

REVIEW QUESTIONS

1. What are the fundamental differences among consultative selling, strategic selling, and relationship selling?
2. In relationship selling, what is meant by the phrase "positioning the product in the customer's mind"?
3. Briefly define partnership selling and explain its importance.
4. What personal and non-personal characteristics are essential for successful selling?
5. Advance preparation is crucial to successful selling. Briefly describe the importance of knowledge in the following areas: product, company, and competition.
6. Briefly explain the roles and responsibilities of a salesperson.
7. List and briefly describe the seven steps in the selling strategy process.

DISCUSSION AND APPLICATION QUESTIONS

1. "Advances in communications technology will dramatically change the role and nature of selling in the future." Discuss this statement and provide examples of changes that are already influencing selling strategies or will have an influence on them in the future.
2. Conduct some secondary research on the concept of partnership selling. How prevalent is partnership selling in business today? Provide some examples of organizations that have adopted this strategy.
3. Assess the role of follow-up in the context of customer relationship management practices. How important is it, and how much emphasis do sales representatives place on this aspect of selling?
4. Conduct a brief interview with a business-to-business sales representative for a company in your area. Inquire about the representative's role in the context of integrated marketing communications. Are there links to other aspects of marketing communications that offer assistance in selling goods and services? Explain the various links as best you can.
5. Pre-planning is an essential step in making a sales presentation. Assume you are working for Apple (or any other marketer of computers) and plan to make a sales presentation to your school. The school is going to purchase or lease desktop computers for a new 50-station lab and is in the process of securing information from various suppliers. What questions would you ask to determine your prospect's specific needs? What benefits would you stress when planning the sales presentation and why? What objections do you foresee being raised by the buyer? You may wish to discuss this question with the individual responsible for information technology at your school.

ENDNOTES

1. "E-Commerce in Canada Worth $136 billion in 2013, up from $122 billion in 2012, *TechVibes*, June 11, 2014, www.techvibes.com/blog/e-commerce-in-canada-worth-136-billion-in-2013-2014-06-11
2. "Retail Ecommerce Sales in Canada to Near $30 billion," *eMarketer*, January 15, 2015, www.emarketer.com/Article/Retail-Ecommerce-Sales-Canada-Near-C30-Billion/1011853
3. John Lorinc, "Death of the Salesman," *Canadian Business*, November 2, 2011, pp. 49–50.
4. John Lorinc, "Death of the Salesman," *Canadian Business*, November 21, 2013, pp. 50–51.
5. Jane Imber and Betsy-Ann Toffler, *Dictionary of Marketing Terms* 2nd Edition (Hauppauge, NY: Barron's Educational Series Inc., 1994), p. 367.
6. Gerald Manning, Barry Reece, and H.F. Mackenzie, *Selling Today*, 3rd Edition (Toronto: Prentice Hall, 2004), p. 137.
7. "Relationship Marketing," *Venture* (Canadian Broadcasting Corporation), broadcast on April 7, 1998.

Measuring Performance

Part 4 takes a look at the role of marketing research in evaluating the effectiveness of marketing communications programs. Because so much of the evaluation process relies on the collection of qualitative and quantitative data, it is essential to develop an appreciation of the various research techniques and procedures available.

Chapter 12 introduces some fundamental methodologies for collecting primary research data and distinguishes between qualitative and quantitative data. It discusses the relationship between data analysis and interpretation, and their impact on the development and evaluation of marketing communications strategies and executions.

Evaluating Marketing Communications Programs

Learning Objectives

After studying this chapter, you will be able to

1. Define the role and scope of marketing research in contemporary marketing organizations

2. Describe the methodologies for collecting primary research data

3. Distinguish between qualitative data and quantitative data

4. Determine the influence of primary data and information on the development of marketing communications plans

5. Assess a variety of marketing research procedures and methodologies that measure and evaluate behavioural responses to communications messages

6. Identify the unique methods that measure the effectiveness of individual components of marketing communications

Because a considerable amount of money is invested in marketing communications activities, a marketing organization is very concerned about protecting its investment. In addition, its desire to remain competitive and be knowledgeable about consumers' changing needs makes it necessary to collect appropriate information before and after critical decisions are made. Certainly, a firm understanding of relevant and contemporary consumer behaviour will play a major role in the development of a marketing communications campaign (refer to Chapter 1 for details). Carefully planned and well-timed marketing research is the tool that provides organizations with the insight necessary to take advantage of new opportunities. This chapter will discuss some fundamental concepts about the marketing research process and present various specific research techniques that are used to measure and evaluate the effectiveness of marketing communications programs.

The Role and Scope of Marketing Research

Research provides an organization with data. The data do not guarantee that proper decisions and actions by the firm will be taken, because data are always open to interpretation. The old saying that "some information is better than no information" puts the role of marketing research into perspective. A vital marketing tool, marketing research is used to help reduce or eliminate the uncertainty and risk associated with making business decisions. Of course, this principle applies to marketing communications decisions as well.

In many ways, marketing research is a form of insurance. It ensures that the action a company might take is the right action. A manager would want to have good information (a foundation, so to speak) available before making a multi-million-dollar marketing decision to make sure the right one is made. To demonstrate, assume you are developing a new product and the product requires an attractive package that will catch the consumers' attention. Will you simply ask for a few package designs and select one that you like or will you consult with a research company that will have consumers make the decision for you? Explorer Shopping Solutions offers a lab facility that simulates a real store environment. Staged like a grocery store, it is equipped with eye-tracking technology on the shelves and on packaging that can determine what a shopper is and isn't looking at.[1] You can easily discover how your new package attracts a consumer's eye. Surely this kind of information will be useful in deciding on the final package design.

marketing research A marketing function that links the consumer/customer/public to the marketer through information; the information is used to define marketing opportunities and problems, generate marketing strategies, evaluate marketing actions, and monitor performance.

Marketing research links the consumer/customer/public to the marketer through information—information used to define marketing opportunities and problems; to generate, refine, and evaluate marketing actions; to monitor marketing performance; and to improve the understanding of marketing as a process. It designs the method for collecting information, manages and implements the information collection process, analyzes the results, and communicates the findings and their implications.[2]

The scope of marketing research seems endless. In a marketing communications setting, research is useful for identifying consumer insights that can be considered when developing message strategies, for measuring the impact and effectiveness of message and media strategies, for tracking brand awareness during the life of a campaign, for pretesting and post-testing advertising strategies, and for measuring changes in behaviour based on the effects of all forms of marketing communications. Any information obtained will assist managers in their decision making.

The very nature of marketing research, however, requires a significant investment by a marketing organization. Due to the diversity of marketing communications and the complementary ways in which the various components blend together, it is difficult to isolate one communications component and state definitively that it determined success or failure.

How do managers go about collecting information? Prudent marketing decision makers combine their intuition and judgment with all other information sources available. They use the scientific method, which implies that the data generated are reliable and valid. **Reliability** refers to the degree of similar results being achieved if another study were undertaken under similar conditions. **Validity** refers to the research procedure's ability to measure what it was intended to measure.

reliability (of data) Degree of similarity of results achieved if another research study were undertaken under similar circumstances.

validity (of data) A research procedure's ability to measure what it is intended to measure.

Research Techniques for Marketing Communications

When an organization attempts to measure the potential impact on consumers of its advertising messages, it implements a variety of primary research techniques. Students should be aware of the basic steps involved in planning various research procedures to appreciate the value of the data. Essentially, the evaluation of advertising messages or any other form of marketing communications involves the collection of primary data.

PRIMARY RESEARCH

primary research The collection and recording of primary data.

primary data Data collected to resolve a problem and recorded for the first time.

Once the organization decides it requires input from customers and potential customers before making a decision, the research process moves to the stage of collecting primary data. **Primary research** refers to the process of collecting and recording new data, called **primary data**, to resolve a specific problem, usually at a high cost to the sponsoring organization. Primary research is custom designed and focuses on resolving a particular question or obtaining specified information. A procedure is developed and a research instrument designed to perform the specific task. Figure 12.1 summarizes the steps involved in collecting primary data.

research objective A statement that outlines what the marketing research is to accomplish.

hypothesis A statement of outcomes predicted in a marketing research investigation.

In directing the primary research, the marketing organization identifies the precise nature of the problem, the objectives of the study, and the hypotheses associated with it. **Research objectives** are statements that outline what the research is to accomplish, while **hypotheses**, which are statements of predicted outcomes, are confirmed or

FIGURE
12.1

The Steps Involved in Primary Research

refuted by the data collected. The outcome of the research often leads to certain actions being taken by the marketing organization. Consider the following example:

- **Research Objective:** To determine the impact of a humorous style of advertising on adults 25 to 49 years of age.

- **Research Hypothesis:** A humorous style of advertising will generate significantly higher recognition and recall scores than other types of message appeal techniques.

- **Action Standard:** Assuming the research findings indicate a significant preference for a humorous style of advertising and that preference can be sustained for an extended period, a new creative campaign based on a humorous style will be requested for the next planning cycle.

SAMPLE DESIGN

Prior to implementing a research study, the researchers identify the characteristics of the people they would like to participate in the study. This process is referred to as sample design. A **sample** is defined as a portion of an entire population used to obtain information about that population. The sample must form an accurate representation of the population if the information gathered is to be considered reliable. Some basic steps must be taken to develop a representative sample:

- **Define the Population (Universe):** A **population (universe)** is a group of people with specific age, gender, or other demographic characteristics. It is usually the description of the target market or audience under study. For the purposes of primary research, a description of a population might be "single or married females between the ages of 21 and 34 years living in cities with more than 500 000 residents."

- **Identify the Sampling Frame:** The **sampling frame** refers to a list that can be used for reaching a population. If Canadian Tire wanted to conduct research among its current customers about the style of advertising it uses, it could use its credit card

sample   A representative portion of an entire population that is used to obtain information about that population.

population (universe)   In marketing research, a group of people with certain age, gender, or other demographic characteristics.

sampling frame   A list used to access a representative sample of a population; it is a means of accessing people for a research study.

account holder list as a means of access. Canadian Tire could also survey visitors to its website. Online feedback is quick, convenient, and less costly than traditional forms of research, although the population is self-selected, which can skew the results somewhat.

probability sample A sample of respondents who are known to have an equal chance of selection and are randomly selected from the sampling frame.

- **Determine the Type of Sample:** The researcher has the option of using a probability sample or a non-probability sample. If a **probability sample** is used, the respondents have a known or equal chance of selection and are randomly selected from across the population. For example, the researcher may use a predetermined, systematic procedure for picking respondents through a telephone directory. The known chance of selection enables statistical procedures to be used in the results to estimate sampling errors.

  In a **non-probability sample**, the respondents have an unknown chance of selection, and their selection is based on factors such as convenience for the researcher or the researcher's judgment. The researcher relies on experience to determine who would be most appropriate. For example, Canadian Tire could randomly stop shoppers inside its stores to seek their input on a variety of marketing concerns. Factors such as cost and timing are other reasons for using non-probability samples.

non-probability sample A sample of respondents who have an unknown chance of selection and are chosen because of factors such as convenience or the judgment of the researcher.

- **Determine the Sample Size:** Generally, the larger the sample, the greater the accuracy of the data collected and the higher the cost. The nature of the research study is a determining factor in the number of participants required. Some researchers use a 1 percent rule (1 percent of the defined population or universe), while others state absolute minimums of 200 respondents. The accuracy of the sample is usually calculated statistically and stated in the research report. Therefore, a researcher considers the margin of error that is acceptable and the degree of certainty required.

DATA COLLECTION METHODS

There are three primary methods a researcher can use to collect data: surveys, observation, and experiments (see Figure 12.2). The data collected can be qualitative or quantitative in nature.

survey research The systematic collection of data by communicating with a representative sample by means of a questionnaire.

For **survey research**, data are collected systematically through some form of communication with a representative sample by means of a questionnaire that records

FIGURE **12.2**
Data Collection Methods

Surveys

- Data are collected systematically by communicating with a representative sample, usually using a questionnaire.
- Questionnaires can be disguised (purpose hidden) or undisguised (purpose known), and structured (fixed responses provided) or unstructured (open-ended question format).

Observation

- The behaviour of the respondent is observed by personal, mechanical, or electronic means.

Experiments

- Variables are manipulated under controlled conditions to observe respondents' reactions.
- Experiments are used to test marketing influences such as product changes, package changes, and advertising copy tests.

responses. Most surveys include predetermined questions and a selection of responses that are easily filled in by the respondent or the interviewer. This technique is referred to as **fixed-response (closed-ended) questioning**. Surveys may also include space at the end of a question where verbatim comments by the respondent are recorded, referred to as **open-response (open-ended) questioning**. Survey research can be conducted by personal interview, telephone, mail, or online. Computer software allows researchers to conduct surveys on electronic devices. The use of electronic devices ensures error-free transfer of data.

In **observation research**, the behaviour of the respondent is observed and recorded. In this form of research, participants do not have to be recruited; they can participate in a study without knowing it. In other situations, respondents are usually aware of being observed, perhaps through a two-way mirror, by a hidden camera while being interviewed, or by electronic measurement of impulses. All of these techniques can be used when consumers are asked to evaluate advertising messages.

Many companies now use ethnographic research to their advantage. Ethnographic research is a form of observation research that involves the study of human behaviour in a natural setting: for example, following people around the house or when they are out and about in their daily routine. The purpose is to observe how people interact with others, with the media, and so on. Scott Paper placed an anthropologist in selected homes to observe women 25 to 54 years old. The goal was to find out what goes on in the bathroom (really!). Scott observed that women see the bathroom as a place for a moment of solitude and privacy. That knowledge led to the repositioning of its Cashmere toilet paper as a luxury brand. It was aligned with the idea that solitude can be a luxury in a hectic life.[3]

In **experimental research**, one or more factors are manipulated under controlled conditions, while other elements remain constant so that respondents' reactions can be evaluated. Test marketing is a form of experimental research. In a marketing communications context, **test marketing** involves placing a commercial or set of commercials in a campaign (could include print ads as well) in one or more limited markets, representative of the whole, to observe the potential impact of the ads on consumers. Do the ads generate the desired level of awareness and preference? Do they provide sufficient motivation so that consumers take the desired action? Good test marketing provides valuable experience prior to an expensive regional or national launch of the campaign.

QUALITATIVE DATA VERSUS QUANTITATIVE DATA

According to the nature of the information sought, research data are classified as either qualitative or quantitative. There are significant differences between these two classifications.

Qualitative data are usually collected from small samples in a controlled environment. They result from questions concerned with "why" and from in-depth probing of the participants. Typically, such data are gathered from focus group interviews. A **focus group** is a small group of people (usually eight to ten) with common characteristics (for example, a target market profile), brought together to discuss issues related to the marketing of a product or service.

The word "focus" implies that the discussion concentrates on one topic or concept. A trained moderator usually conducts the interview over a period of a few hours. The role of the moderator is to get the participants to interact fairly freely to uncover the reasons and motivations underlying their remarks. Probing uncovers the hidden interplay of psychological factors that drive a consumer to buy one brand rather than another. With regard to advertising evaluations, it provides views on how effective a message

fixed-response (closed-ended) questioning   Predetermined questions with set answers for the respondents to choose from.

open-response (open-ended) questioning   Space available at the end of a question where the respondents can add their comments.

observation research   A form of research in which the behaviour of the respondent is observed and recorded; may be by personal or electronic means.

experimental research   Research in which one or more factors are manipulated under controlled conditions while other elements remain constant so that the respondent's actions can be evaluated.

test marketing   Placing a commercial, set of commercials, or print ad campaign in one or more limited markets that are representative of the whole to observe the impact of the ads on consumers.

qualitative data   Data collected from small samples in a controlled environment; the data describe feelings about and opinions of issues.

focus group   A small group of people with common characteristics brought together to discuss issues related to the marketing of a product or service.

might be. Consumers' reactions to the message, the characters that present the message, and the campaign theme and slogan can be discussed at length.

The major drawback of using focus groups concerns the reliability of the data. The sample size is too small to be representative of the entire population, and most people in a focus group do not like to show disagreement with a prevailing opinion. For that reason, interviews are usually held in several locations.

Marketing decisions involving considerable sums of money are very risky if based on such limited research. One of the most spectacular focus group failures, the launch of new Coke in the 1980s, came about because the soft-drink maker was not asking the right questions. Worried that archrival PepsiCo had a better-tasting product, Coca-Cola asked consumers if they liked its new formulation without ever asking if they wanted its tried-and-true beverage changed.[4] The new version of Coca-Cola failed miserably when it was launched, and the public backlash was so significant that Coca-Cola had to reintroduce the original Coke as Coca-Cola Classic.

Many organizations now conduct online focus groups. Advancing technology allows organizations to use chat and web conferencing software to conduct focus groups. Web conferencing programs include tools for chat and messaging, webcams to stream video, and screen sharing that allows participants to view content on the moderator's screen. This option is quicker and less costly than face-to-face focus groups.[5]

quantitative data Measurable data collected from large samples using a structured research procedure.

Quantitative data provide answers to questions concerned with "what," "when," "who," "how many," and "how often." This research attempts to put feelings, attitudes, and opinions into numbers and percentages. The data are gathered from structured questionnaires and a large sample to ensure accuracy and reliability. The interpretation of the results is based on the numbers compiled, not on the judgment of the researcher. Quantitative research will statistically confirm the attitudes and feelings that arose in qualitative research. Therefore, a manager will have more confidence in research-based decisions. Figure 12.3 briefly compares qualitative and quantitative research.

The wise organization should use both forms of data collection. Molson Coors, for example, does focus groups and qualitative research, but it also does quantitative research on all television ads before production of the ad takes place. Each ad must hit a specific persuasion level or it will not be used in a campaign.[6]

FIGURE 12.3

A Comparison of Qualitative and Quantitative Data

Qualitative Data

- Collected from a small sample, usually in a focus-group environment.
- Unstructured questions.
- Questions seek attitudes, feelings, and opinions.
- Data not always reliable because of small sample size.

Quantitative Data

- Collected from a large, representative sample of target market.
- Structured questions with predetermined responses.
- Deals with who, what, when, how many, and how often.
- Statistically reliable, with calculated degree of error.

SURVEY METHODOLOGY

There are four primary means of contacting consumers when conducting surveys to collect quantitative data: telephone, personal interview, mail, and the Internet. **Personal interviews** involve face-to-face communication with groups (for example, focus groups) or individuals and are usually done through quantitative questionnaires. Popular locations for interviews are shopping malls and the homes of respondents.

Telephone interviews involve communication with individuals over the phone. Usually, the interviews are conducted from central locations (that is, one location that can reach all Canadian markets), and, consequently, there is supervised control over the interview process. Telephone technology is now so advanced that research data can be transferred from the telephone directly to a computer. There is a very high refusal rate for telephone surveys.

Mail interviews are a silent process of collecting information. Using the mail to distribute a survey means that a highly dispersed sample is reached in a cost-efficient manner. The main drawbacks are the lack of control and the amount of time required to implement and retrieve the surveys.

Online surveys allow an organization to be much less invasive in collecting information. Some companies have found that consumers seem more willing to divulge information over the Internet compared with the more traditional means of surveying.

Online research is proving effective in testing new product concepts and getting feedback on new advertising ideas. For marketers, if time is an imperative and money is in short supply, online research answers the bell—you can quickly access and analyze information. On the downside, recruiting respondents can be a lot like fishing—participation is left to the fish. Consequently, the validity of information collected is questionable.

Figure 12.4 summarizes the advantages and disadvantages of each survey method.

personal interview   The collection of information in a face-to-face interview.

telephone interview   In marketing research, the collection of information from a respondent by telephone.

mail interview   In marketing research, the collection of information from a respondent by mail.

online survey   In marketing research, using an online questionnaire to collect data from people.

DATA TRANSFER AND PROCESSING

Once the data have been collected, editing, data transfer, and tabulation take place. In the **editing stage**, completed questionnaires are reviewed for consistency and completeness. In the **data transfer** stage, answers from questions are transferred to a computer. Answers are pre-coded to facilitate the transfer.

Once the survey results have been entered into a computer, the results are tabulated. **Tabulation** is the process of counting the various responses for each question and arriving at a frequency distribution. A **frequency distribution** shows the number of times each answer to a question was chosen. Numerous cross-tabulations are also made. **Cross-tabulation** is the comparison and contrast of the answers from various subgroups or from particular subgroups with the total response group. For example, a question dealing with brand awareness could be analyzed by the age, gender, or income of respondents.

editing stage   In marketing research, the review of questionnaires for consistency and completeness.

data transfer   In marketing research, the transfer of answers from the questionnaire to the computer.

tabulation   The process of counting various responses to each question in a survey.

frequency distribution   The number of times each answer in a survey was chosen for a question.

cross-tabulation   The comparison of answers to questions by various subgroups with the total number of responses.

DATA ANALYSIS AND INTERPRETATION

Data analysis refers to the evaluation of responses question by question, a process that gives meaning to the data. At this point, the statistical data for each question are reviewed, and the researcher makes observations. Typically, a researcher makes comparisons between responses of subgroups on a percentage basis.

Data interpretation, on the other hand, involves relating the accumulated data to the problem under review and to the objectives and hypotheses of the research study. The process of interpretation uncovers solutions to the problem. The researcher draws conclusions that state the implications of the data for managers.

data analysis   The evaluation of responses question by question; gives meaning to the data.

data interpretation   The relating of accumulated data to the problem under review and to the objectives and hypotheses of the research study.

FIGURE
12.4

The Advantages and
Disadvantages of Various
Survey Methods

Advantages	Disadvantages
Personal Interview	
• High rate of participation	• Higher cost due to time needed
• Visual observations possible	• Respondents reluctant to respond to certain
• Flexible (can include visuals)	questions
	• Interviewer bias possible
Telephone Interview	
• Convenient and allows control	• Observation not possible
• Costs less	• Short questions and questionnaires
• Timely responses	• Privacy concerns (bad time of day)
Mail Surveys	
• Cost efficient	• Lack of control
• Large sample obtainable	• Potential for misinterpretation by respondent
• Relaxed environment	• Time lag between distribution and return
• Impersonal nature produces	• Low response rates
accurate responses	
Online Surveys	
• Efficient and inexpensive	• Respondent voluntarily participates, so
• Less intrusive (respondent driven)	respondent authenticity is questioned
• Convenient for respondent	• Limited sample frame (Internet users only)
• Fast response time (days)	• Research by bulk email associated with spam
	• Reliability of information suspect

RECOMMENDATIONS AND IMPLEMENTATION

The recommendations outline suggested courses of action that the sponsoring organization should take in view of the data collected. Once a research project is complete, the research company will present its findings in a written report and highlight the key findings in a visual presentation.

For insight into how primary research can influence marketing communications strategy, see the IMC Highlight: **Research Insight Sparks Scotiabank Campaign.**

Measuring and Evaluating Advertising Messages

One of the first steps in measuring advertising messages is an evaluation of agency creative ideas by the client. It seems that a creative idea is just that—an idea—until it is sold to the client for approval. Very often, these kinds of evaluations are subjective in nature because they rely on the opinions of brand managers, marketing directors, and presidents of companies. The chain of command for approving advertising creative and media expenditures can go very high up in an organization.

CLIENT EVALUATION

Creative can be tested at several stages of the development process. The first step is usually a qualitative assessment by the client to determine if the message conforms to the strategic direction that was provided to the agency. This evaluation is conducted by means of a *managerial approach* whereby certain criteria are established and the

Research Insight Sparks Scotiabank Campaign

You've probably seen television ads for Scotiabank telling people, "You're richer than you think." The primary objective of the campaign was to spread a sense of optimism across the country during troubled economic times. The ads encouraged people to visit Scotiabank for a second opinion. When visiting the bank people would learn their position wasn't as bad as they thought.

The campaign was based on insights garnered from primary research the bank conducted. The research revealed people were concerned about their financial struggles that don't necessarily depend on income level. That insight was the impetus for a new advertising campaign to make people more comfortable and confident about their finances.

The campaign was successful. It raised the bank's awareness significantly and attracted new customers. A few years into the campaign, the bank altered the message of the advertising somewhat, again based on insights obtained from research. New research indicated that "richness" meant different things to different people. It had to do with the stage of life, such as getting married, having a baby, and sending children to college. The new advertising campaign showed people and scenes reflecting these events.

The moral to the story is a simple one. Good insights gained from marketing research will lead to profitable marketing decisions.

Richness is:
The moment everything changes.

Scotiabank's 5 Year Plan.
You define richness. With a 5 Year Plan that lets you adapt to anything, we can help with the money part.

scotiabank.com/5yearplan

You're richer than you think.

Ⓢ Scotiabank®

Courtesy of Scotiabank.

Based on Kristin Laird, " Scotiabank Redefines 'Richer' Campaign," *Marketing*, January 23, 2012, www.marketingmag.ca.

advertising ideas are measured against them. Typically, a client reserves the right to conduct research prior to making a decision to proceed.

Clients using the managerial approach for evaluating creative may apply some or all of the following criteria:

1. **Does the content of the advertisement communicate the creative objectives and reflect the positioning strategy of the brand (company)?** The client reviews the creative for its ability to communicate the key benefit and support claims that substantiate the benefit. The client determines if the message strategy and execution conform to the overall positioning strategy of the brand. If it is off strategy, the ad will be rejected.

2. **In terms of how the ad is presented (strategy and execution), does it mislead or misrepresent the intent of the message? Is it presented in good taste?** The client must be concerned about the actual message and any implied message since it is responsible for the truthfulness of the message. Legal counsel often has the final say regarding message content.

   Taste is always in the eyes of the beholder, and very often consumers complain if an ad is too offensive. Advertisers must be conscious of potential negative feedback and avoid it if they can.

3. **Is the ad memorable?** Breaking through the clutter of competitive advertising is always a challenge, and a lot of advertising that is approved doesn't quite cut it. Is there something that stands out that people will remember? For instance, characters in ads often build momentum for a brand and become strongly associated with the brand itself. For example, the voice (actor Sam Elliott) in a Ram truck commercial, the character (restaurant manager) in an A&W commercial, or the guy in the Trivago commercials.

4. **Is the brand recognition effective?** There must be sufficient brand registration in the ad. Some companies go as far as to stipulate how many times the package should be shown in a television commercial or how many times the brand name should be mentioned. The creativity of the commercial or print ad should not outweigh the product—it should complement the product. For example, people often recall funny ads, but when asked what brand was in the ad they can't remember. So much for the laughs!

5. **Should the advertisement be researched?** When it comes to assessing the impact and effectiveness of the advertisement, subjective judgments by the client have the disadvantage of not being quantifiable. Prior to spending money on production, the client may decide to conduct consumer research to seek quantifiable data that will help the decision-making process. Better to be safe than sorry!

The evaluation process can occur at any stage of the creative development process. Consumers might evaluate a television commercial, for example, at the storyboard, rough-cut, or finished commercial stage. Although it is not practical to test commercials at all stages, if the quality or effectiveness of the commercial is ever in question, the client should conduct research to avoid costly and embarrassing errors in judgment.

EXTERNAL RESEARCH TECHNIQUES AND PROCEDURES

Creative evaluation involves a variety of research techniques. The objective of most creative research is to measure the impact of a message on a target audience. Creative research is conducted based on the stage of creative development. It is either a pre-test or a post-test situation. **Pre-testing** is the evaluation of an advertisement, commercial, or campaign before it goes into final production or media placement to determine the strengths and weaknesses of a strategy and execution. **Post-testing** is the process of evaluating and measuring the effectiveness of an advertisement, commercial, or campaign during its run or after it has run. Post-testing provides information that can be used in future advertising planning.

Common techniques used to measure the effectiveness of creative are recognition and recall testing, opinion-measure testing, and physiological-response testing.

RECOGNITION AND RECALL TESTING

In **recognition tests**, respondents are tested for awareness. They are asked if they can recall an advertisement for a specific brand or any of the points made in the advertisement. For example, consumers who have read a publication in which an ad has appeared are asked if they remember what brand was advertised and what the basic message being communicated was.

Several factors affect the level of recognition of an ad. For example, a large print ad occupying a full page usually has a higher level of recognition than an ad occupying only a portion of a page. The inclusion of a celebrity might draw more attention to an ad simply because consumers like the celebrity.

pre-testing The evaluation of commercial messages prior to final production to determine the strengths and weaknesses of the communications.

post-testing The evaluation and measurement of a message's effectiveness during its run or after the message has run.

recognition test A test that measures a target audience's awareness of a brand, copy, or the advertisement itself after the audience has been exposed to the message.

In **recall tests**, respondents are tested for comprehension to measure the impact of advertising. The test can be an *aided* situation (some information is provided to the respondent to stimulate thinking) or an *unaided* situation (no information is provided). In either situation, respondents are asked to name or recall ads and asked to recall specific elements of an advertisement or commercial, such as its primary selling points, the characters in it as presenters, and its slogan. Test scores are usually higher when some form of aid is provided.

Recognition and recall both help develop a brand's image with consumers over a period of time. Therefore, once an advertiser finds an ad or advertising campaign that is performing well, it must resist the temptation to make changes. In the long run, effective advertising plays a role in building sales and market share.

Two of the most common methods for collecting recognition and recall information are Starch readership tests and day-after recall tests. A **Starch readership test** is a post-test recognition procedure applied to both newspaper and magazine advertisements. The objectives of the test are to measure how many readers saw an ad and how many actually read the ad.

In a Starch readership test, a consumer is given a magazine to read, after which an interviewer goes through it ad by ad with the respondent. For each advertisement in the magazine (the entire magazine is "starched"), responses are divided into three categories:

- **Noted:** the percentage of readers who remembered seeing the ad in this issue.
- **Associated:** the percentage of readers who saw any part of the ad that clearly indicated the brand or advertiser.
- **Read Most:** the percentage of readers who read half or more of the written material.

The Starch readership test offers several benefits. The client can measure the extent to which an ad is seen and read; by reviewing the results of other ads that were tested, the extent of clutter breakthrough can be determined; and by reviewing scores obtained by other products in previous tests, various layouts and design options can be evaluated for effectiveness.

In the broadcast media, particularly television, the use of **day-after recall (DAR) testing** is common. As the name implies, research is conducted the day after an audience has been exposed to a commercial message for the first time. By means of a telephone survey technique, a sampling of the client's target market is recruited and asked a series of questions to determine exposure to and recall of particular commercials. Respondents who saw the commercial are asked what the ad actually communicated.

For additional details about these research methodologies, visit the websites for G&R Research and Consulting (www.gandrllc.com) and Starch Research (www.starchresearch.com).

OPINION-MEASURE TESTING
Measuring attitudinal components is another means of evaluating advertising effectiveness. Attitudes and opinions can be gathered from surveys or focus groups. The intent of attitude surveys is to delve a bit deeper with consumers to determine their true feelings about an ad and the product.

With television commercials, **opinion-measure testing** exposes an audience to test-commercial messages in the context of special television programs. In a research setting, respondents view commercials on a large screen (theatre) or on television monitors. Once all of the ads are viewed, participants respond to a series of questions.

recall test A test that measures an ad's impact by asking respondents to recall specific elements (for example, the selling message) of the advertisement; can be aided (some information provided) or unaided.

Starch readership test A post-test recognition procedure that measures readers' recall of an advertisement (noted), their ability to identify the sponsor (associated), and whether they read more than half of the written material (read most).

day-after recall (DAR) test Research conducted the day following the respondent's exposure to a message to determine the degree of recognition and recall of the advertisement, the brand, and the selling message.

opinion-measure testing A form of research yielding information about the effect of a commercial message on respondents' brand name recall, interest in the brand, and purchase intentions.

The test commercial is usually presented twice during the program, in cluster situations. Also included in the cluster is a set of control commercials against which the test commercial or commercials (sometimes more than one commercial is being tested) can be compared. The position of the test commercial is different in each cluster. The test measures three key attributes: the audience's awareness of the commercial based on brand name recall, the extent to which the main idea of the ad is communicated, and the effect the commercial might have on purchase motivation—that is, the likelihood of the respondent buying the brand. This final measure is based on a comparison of pre-exposure brand purchase information and post-exposure brand preference data.

PHYSIOLOGICAL-RESPONSE TESTING

Advertisers also have access to a variety of physiological testing methods that measure involuntary responses to a specific element of an advertisement. In an **eye movement-camera test**, consumers read an advertisement while a hidden camera tracks their eye movements. Such a test gauges the point of immediate contact, how a reader scans the various components of an ad, and the amount of time spent reading it. The **pupilometer test** measures the dilation of a person's pupil to see how it changes based on emotional arousal. For example, a person's pupils widen when frightened or excited and are smaller when the response is negative.

These types of tests are popular with researchers because emotions trigger physiological responses that can be measured. Physiological responses to something a person sees or hears are difficult to mask. In the two tests just mentioned, reactions are monitored with no words being spoken. Sometimes respondents try to hide their true feelings by saying something that contradicts their physiological reaction. For example, a person might respond in the desired way physiologically to a print ad with sexual imagery, but might state that the ad should not be shown in a magazine. In such a case, physiological reactions speak louder than words.

Testing procedures and the need for them are controversial issues in the industry. Many creative directors argue that too much testing defeats the creative process (because it stifles creativity) and that what people say in research and do in the real world can be completely different. These same creative directors also realize it is the client's money at stake, so if the client is inclined toward research, the ad agency must deal with the situation as best it can.

Measuring and Evaluating Direct Response Communications

One method of measuring direct mail and direct response television messages is to include a toll-free telephone number or website address. The number of inquiries received or the actual sales that result from a particular offer can be compared to those of offers in the past. From this, an observation can be made about the effectiveness of a new offer. As well, a great deal of information can be collected about consumers responding to phone calls. Sales data can be recorded and demographic information gathered. Sales data can be tied to demographic information to determine who is actually buying the product. Knowing who is responding to each offer helps a firm better understand its customers and provides insight into how to develop better marketing communications strategies to reach particular targets.

Response cards are another means of assessing impact and collecting information about customers. Typically, these cards are filled in at the time of purchase. Any information

eye movement–camera test   A test that uses a hidden camera to track eye movement to gauge the point of immediate contact in an advertisement, how the reader scans the ad, and the amount of time spent reading.

pupilometer test   A device that measures pupil dilation (enlargement) of a person's eye when reading; it measures emotional responses to an advertisement.

response card   A card filled in, usually at the time of purchase that collects information about customers that can be added to the organization's database.

that is collected can be added to the organization's database and be combined with other information that may be available on a particular customer.

Measuring and Evaluating Internet Communications

In an online environment, a **cookie** (an electronic identification tag sent from a web server to a user's browser to track the user's browsing patterns) enables an organization to track online responses. The built-in technology of the Internet makes it a unique communications medium. In fact, Internet communications are much easier to measure in hard numbers than any other form of media advertising.

Online advertising campaigns are typically measured based on impressions, clicks (or clickthroughs), and click rates. An **impression** (also called an **ad view**) refers to the number of times a banner ad image is downloaded onto a user's computer. **Clicks** or **clickthroughs** refer to the number of times that users click on a banner ad. Such a measurement allows an advertiser to judge the response to an ad. When viewers click the ad, they are transferred to the advertiser's website or a special page where more information is available.

The **click (clickthrough) rate** is the percentage of impressions that result in a click (or clickthrough). The click rate is calculated by dividing the number of clicks by the number of impressions. For example, if during 1 million impressions there are 10 000 clicks on the banner, the click rate is 1 percent (10 000/1 000 000). Google reports that click rates for banners are not that high and average about 0.09 percent. Advertisers are concerned about low click rates so other means to measure the effectiveness of online advertising is considered.

Most online advertising campaigns are designed to transfer a person from an ad to a website—that is the desired action or objective. Therefore, a campaign can also be evaluated on the following criteria:

- **Increase in Web Traffic** By monitoring daily traffic flow to a website, a simple increase in traffic as determined by tracking software might indicate a campaign is a success.

- **Length of Visit** If time spent at a site is a key metric, the effectiveness can be evalutated based on the number of people who spend a minimum number of minutes at the site.

- **Page Views** If, for example, a campaign involves providing video content, an advertiser can evaluate how many people download or stream the content. How many people play the entire video is another measure of success.

An organization must invest in appropriate web tracking software technology to gain access to these metrics.

Measuring the Impact of Social Media Communications

People do not visit social network sites to view advertising; they visit to socialize. Very low click rates verify this notion. In a social media campaign, advertisers must look at a softer set of measurement tools to judge whether a communications effort was successful.

cookie   An electronic identification tag sent from a web server to a user's browser to track the user's browsing patterns.

impression (ad view)   The number of times a banner ad image is downloaded onto a user's computer.

clicks (clickthroughs)   The number of times users click on a banner (clicking transfers the user to another website).

click (clickthrough) rate   The percentage of impressions (ad views) that resulted in a click; determines the success of an ad in attracting visitors to click on it.

It's more about engagement and conversation than it is about selling a product. Essentially, there are two ways to measure social media communications: *on-going analytics* and *campaign-focused metrics*. Ongoing analytics tracks activity over time. For example, how much buzz did a campaign generate and what was the nature of the conversation?

In contrast, campaign-focused metrics generate hard and fast numbers that help justify the investment. Numeric indicators involving reach, engagement, share of voice, and conversions are evaluated. *Reach* figures are a reflection of the impact of the social content. Remember, the quality of the creative plays a role in attracting attention and conversation. Reach indicators include the number of likes on Facebook, followers on Twitter, video views, subscribers on a YouTube channel, and LinkedIn connections.

Engagement is measured by determining how many people actually interacted with a message. Therefore, if a campaign includes several messages (different creative) an advertiser can determine what type of message followers like the most. A follower engages with a brand message and cares enough to do something about it. The extent of engagement is determined by the number of clicks, shares, and comments on Facebook; retweets and mentions on Twitter; and ratings for videos on YouTube.

Share of voice, or how large a share of the conversation it has when compared to competitors, can be an important measure. Dividing the brand conversation by industry conversation will give a brand its share of voice. If a competitor has a much higher share of voice, it would be wise to analyze the social media practices of the competitor.

Conversion is a measure of how many people actually took the desired action after exposure to a message. Conversion metrics include actions such as email subscriptions, content subscriptions, registration for content downloads, and online sales. Obtaining figures like these typically requires the services of Google Analytics. Their service can track which visitors arrive at an organization's website from the links an advertiser provides on social media.

The *viral* nature of social media can be another means of measuring success. For example, Dove (a Unilever brand) created a video titled "Dove Beauty Sketches." The video featured an FBI-trained forensic artist sketching women to show them how their self-image differed from how others see them. In one month the video reached more than 100-million views across various social media channels.[7] The video also earned Dove much free publicity.

Marketers who realize the difference between offline and online communities reap the benefits of online communications. The Dove message was highly acceptable to members of the online community. It caught their attention, was innovative, and was discussed by millions of viewers. That's success!

For additional insight into social media measurement and evaluation read the IMC Highlight: **TD** Canada Trust **Takes Pride in Its Achievement**.

Measuring and Evaluating Sales Promotions

The overall goal of sales promotions is to produce an increase in sales in the short term and to build brand loyalty in the long term. As discussed in Chapter 8, promotions are classified as either consumer promotions or trade promotions. Consumer promotions (for example, coupons, contests, free samples, cash rebates, premium offers, and loyalty card programs) are designed to encourage trial purchase by new customers, repeat purchases by existing customers, and, generally, brand loyalty. Therefore, consumer promotions are measured against these objectives.

TD **Canada Trust** Takes Pride in Its Achievement

Many companies still struggle with social media campaigns, particularly the challenges presented by newer networks such as Pinterest and Instagram. Financial institutions, however, have invested heavily in Internet and social media communications, and are ahead of the curve when it comes to developing effective social media campaigns.

TD Canada Trust implemented a four-day social media campaign on Instagram in conjunction with Pride Week. The primary objective of the campaign was to build awareness about the bank's commitment to the LGBT community. Measurement for the campaign was to be focused on increasing brand metrics for awareness and association.

The campaign was promoted using the hashtag #ForeverProud and utilized five different pieces of creative. The visual effort was designed to reinforce the bank's long-term support of Pride Week. TD Canada Trust has been a sponsor for 11 years. The Instagram campaign came with an additional benefit. A custom audience was developed on Instagram through campaign response and then remarketed to people efficiently on Facebook. This expands the reach and frequency of the message.

The campaign reached 1.1 million people and delivered 3.8 million impressions. Engagement with the brand saw a 36-point lift in advertising recall and an 18-point lift in people's awareness of TD's support for the LGBT community. The campaign succeeded in achieving its objectives!

© NISARGMEDIA / Alamy Stock Photo

Source: Based on Sonya Fatah, "Measuring TD's pride campaign on Instagram," *Media in Canada*, August 25, 2015, http://mediaincanada.com/2015/08/25/measuring-tds-pride-campagn-on-instagram

---

Trade promotions include activities such as trade allowances, performance allowances, cooperative advertising allowances, dealer premiums, and dealer display materials. These activities are designed to secure listings of new products with distributors, build sales volume in the promotion period, and secure merchandising support from distributors. Trade promotions are measured against these objectives.

Specific sales promotion measures include **response rates** to coupon offers, the number of **entries received** for a contest, and the number of **cash rebate forms returned** to the company. A marketing manager typically compares response rates for current promotions to response rates received for past and similar promotions. For example, some brands may run a major contest each year in the peak season. Brands such as Pepsi-Cola and Coca-Cola and Coors Light and Bud Light usually run contests during the summer. If a particular contest generates significantly more entries than usual, the manager will attempt to isolate the elements of the promotion that led to the higher degree of interest.

Coupon offers are usually evaluated based on the **redemption rate**, which is defined as the number of coupons returned, expressed as a percentage of the number

redemption rate The number of coupons returned expressed as a percentage of the number of coupons that were distributed.

of coupons distributed. The higher the redemption rate, the more successful the coupon promotion was. For example, if a magazine coupon draws a 2 percent return rate and the norm for magazine coupons is only 1 percent, the offer is an overwhelming success. Historical redemption rates for coupon offers are used to develop budgets for new coupon offers. For an illustration of such a calculation, refer to Figure 12.5.

The absolute number of entry forms received from a contest or rebate offer is a means of measuring the effectiveness of these types of offers. Post Cereal recently offered consumers a high value premium on their packages—a free Reebok PlayDry T-shirt for just two proofs of purchase. Managers estimated that 60 000 T-shirts would be given away over the duration of the promotion. All of the shirts were gone in a matter of weeks! This case demonstrates that the perceived value of an offer has a significant impact on a promotion's success.

FIGURE 12.5

Measuring the Effectiveness of a Coupon Promotion

Assumption

A manufacturer offers a $1.00 coupon on a branded box of cereal that has a regular retail price of $4.59. The coupon is distributed through a cooperative direct mail package. For the purposes of budgeting, an average coupon redemption rate for cooperative direct mail will be used. A misredemption rate of 20 percent is considered, because on average only 80 percent of coupons redeemed are on valid purchases. The manufacturer receives about 65 percent of the retail price when wholesale and retail profit margins are considered.

Coupon Information

Face value	$1.00
Handling charge (retailer)	$0.10
Handling charge (clearing house)	$0.03
Distribution cost	$15.00/M
Printing cost	$10.00/M
Total coupons in distribution	2.5 million
Redemption rate	5.0%

Costs

Distribution	2 500 000 × $15.00/M	$37 500
Printing	2 500 000 × $10.00/M	$25 000
Redemption	2 500 000 × 0.05 × $1.13	$141 250
Total cost		**$203 750**

Revenues

Revenue from each purchase	$4.59 × 0.65	$2.98
Total revenue	2 500 000 × 0.05 × 0.80 × $2.66	**$266 000**

Payout

Total revenue minus total cost	$266 000 – $203 750	**$62 250**

From the total revenue line, it can be determined that the coupon offer generated 100 000 purchases (2 500 000 × 0.05 × 0.80).

The names collected from a contest, premium, or rebate offer provide an additional marketing benefit, as they can be added to the company's database and used for marketing purposes at a later time.

The use of dealer display materials affects the success of sales promotions. Point-of-purchase advertising helps create awareness of promotion offers and reminds consumers about a product at precisely the right time—the purchase decision time. Figure 12.6 shows that a significantly higher purchase response is achieved if various combinations of in-store merchandising activities are implemented. An often quoted figure about purchase decisions is that 70 percent of brand purchase decisions are made in-store. A recent study about purchase decisions in mass merchant retail stores conducted by the Point-of-Purchase Advertising Institute (POPAI) found that 82 percent of purchase decisions were made right in those types of stores. Regardless of the figure, such insight suggests the importance and persuasive tendencies displays can have on shoppers' purchase decisions.[8]

Form of Communication	Incremental Response Rate
Brand signage	+2 percent
Sign plus base wrap	+12 percent
Display stand and sign	+27 percent
Display stand, sign, and mobile	+40 percent
Display stand plus sign about sports tie-in	+65 percent

On average, point-of-purchase communication generates incremental sales ranging from +2 to +65 percent, independent of any price reductions. The above figures were based on research in 250 stores in 22 cities, and 94 brands in eight product categories (beer, salty snacks, cold and allergy products, dog food, soft drinks, laundry detergent, shampoo, and conditioner).

FIGURE
12.6

Measuring the Effectiveness of Point-of-purchase Communications

Based on "Initial Results from Supermarket Phase of POPAI/ARF Study Reveal Insights into POP Advertising," *Point-of-Purchase Advertising International*, March 27, 2000.

Measuring and Evaluating Public Relations Communications

There are several ways to evaluate public relations communications: counting clippings, calculating the number of impressions based on the numbers of clippings, and employing a mathematical model that equates public relations to an advertising value. The latter is referred to as an advertising equivalency.

Many organizations that are active in public relations subscribe to a **clipping service**, which scans the print and broadcast media in search of a company's name. Each time the name is found, it is recorded and compared to the number of press releases that were issued. For example, if 500 press releases were issued and there were 50 clippings, the return rate would be 10 percent. The success of the campaign would be based on historical comparisons of return rates.

The *number of impressions* generated is based on the circulation of the medium in which the organization's name is mentioned. For example, if an article appears in the *Toronto Star* on a Tuesday and the circulation that day is 350 000, the total number of impressions is 350 000. A company may also "gross up" the number of impressions by considering the actual readership of the paper. If the average number of readers is 2.8 per copy, the gross impressions would be 980 000 (350 000 × 2.8).

clipping service   An organization that scans the print and broadcast media in search of a company's or brand's name.

Counting clippings and impressions is a form of measurement, but the procedure ignores the nature of the article written or broadcast about the organization. Was it positive or negative? There is a presumption that an article critical of a company is of equal value to one that praises a company. It could be argued that positive articles and negative articles should be separated. For certain, companies receive a lot of negative publicity when they face a crisis situation, and such publicity negates much of the positive publicity that is generated by planned public relations communications. On the other hand, there are also those who believe that any publicity is good publicity.

Another PR measure is *website traffic*. An analysis of pre-campaign and post-campaign traffic a website receives will indicate some degree of success. Many sales leads are the result of calls-to-action listed on an organization's website. As well, *social media mentions* are a measure of success. In addition to mentions, social media measurement can focus on conversations about the brand. Any lift in social conversation during or post-PR campaign will indicate the PR campaign had some impact. Social media networks such as Facebook, Twitter, Pinterest, Vine, and others are overflowing with users who interact with and follow brands. For each brand there are countless influencers and brand advocates who share status updates, tweets, videos and pictures related to a brand. Granted, the potential impact of this type of activity is hard to measure but it does extend the reach of any planned advertising activity.

Trying to equate public relations to a corresponding advertising value is an attempt to eliminate the problems associated with clippings and impressions. A technique called **advertising equivalency** involves an evaluation of the space occupied by a public relations message and relating it to a similar amount of advertising space. To demonstrate, assume that a one-page article about a company appeared in *Canadian Business* magazine. If a one-page ad costs $25 000, then that is the value of the public relations to the organization. Similar calculations can be made for the broadcast media. Based on this type of calculation, the sum total of a public relations campaign can be considerable. Specialist companies exist to provide this service.

advertising equivalency
A mathematical model that equates public relations to an advertising value by evaluating the space occupied by a public relations message in relation to advertising space.

Measuring Experiential Marketing, Events, and Sponsorships

Among all of the integrated marketing communications components, event marketing and sponsorships are the most difficult to evaluate, particularly on a quantitative basis. At their best, sponsorships are a high-profile way to increase sales and improve brand recognition. At their worst, they're a haphazard form of promotion.[9]

Event marketing is attracting a bigger piece of the marketing communications pie each year, but it doesn't get the respect it deserves because there aren't any widely accepted, standardized methods of measuring its results. Despite the lack of measurement, event marketing and sponsorship programs continue to be a valued element in many marketing plans.

The most common measures of an event's success are *how well the event reaches the target audience* and *how well the brand or company is associated with the event*. If some form of return on investment can be added to the evaluation mix, so much the better. But, unless you are establishing leads or selling something at the event, the true impact of the sponsorship won't be felt immediately.

Nowhere are sponsorships more visible than in the world of sports. In professional football, basketball, and hockey leagues, there is no shortage of sponsors willing to jump in. Some research conducted right after the NHL playoffs in 2015 revealed that 60 percent of Canadians followed at least some of the playoffs. Scotiabank led all sponsors with an unaided recall score of 23 percent. Considering the clutter of advertising around NHL broadcasts Scotiabank would be pleased with this kind of a recall score.[10]

Big sports events are attractive to sponsors. An estimated 60 percent of Canadians watched at least some of the events of the PanAm Games held in Toronto in 2015. In unaided recall, CIBC, Coca-Cola, and Nike were the top three sponsors. CIBC fared very well with an unaided recall of 32 percent among people following the games.[11]

Most managers rely on less concrete evidence to justify investing in event marketing and sponsorships. Having Roger Federer playing tennis wearing a Nike shirt, for example, has a positive impact for Nike products that extends well beyond tennis products. Seeing Sidney Crosby wearing Reebok attire and equipment when he's being interviewed enhances the credibility of Reebok as a manufacturer of hockey equipment.

How beneficial are naming rights on a building? Canadian Tire has the name rights to the building where the Ottawa Senators play, which is called Canadian Tire Centre. Does it enhance Canadian Tire's brand image? Industry experts believe Canadian Tire gets lots of media exposure for its $20 million investment. *Media exposure* is a true benefit of event marketing, since hockey games are broadcast and covered by newspapers, radio, TV stations, and their digital media alternatives.

As discussed in Chapter 10, certain indicators are commonly used to measure the benefits of sponsorship. As described in the PanAm/CIBC example, an organization might look at *awareness* and *association* measures as well as changes in *image perceptions* among its customers. To do so, a company will have to conduct some of the pre- and post-test research described earlier in the chapter.

Another common measure is the impact on *brand sales*. Is it immediate, during the event period, or will it happen after the event? Such a measure is often difficult due to the impact of other marketing activities. Any increase in sales that cannot be attributed to another activity is likely the result of an association with an event sponsorship.

Measuring the Integrated Marketing Communications Effort

Because integrated marketing communications is a coordinated and collaborative effort among many individuals and organizations and many communications disciplines, perhaps the best form of measurement and evaluation is to look at the big picture. In other words, how healthy is a particular brand or the company as a whole, based on all the marketing and marketing communications strategies that have been implemented over the past year (a typical planning cycle)?

Some typical indicators of success or failure include market share, productivity, sales and profitability, customer satisfaction levels, and social responsibility. As in most evaluation systems already discussed in this chapter, the organization should look back at the corporate objectives it established in these areas to see how well it performed.

An increase in **market share** would indicate greater acceptance by more customers, a higher degree of brand loyalty among current customers, and a strong competitive position. A well-planned integrated marketing communications program would have contributed to such an outcome. *Productivity* measures are more difficult to come by, but where tangible results can be attributed to a specific communications activity, it should be noted. Did the integrated marketing communications program generate new customers? Was brand awareness higher than it was previously? Was the company's or

market share   The sales volume of one product or company expressed as a percentage of total sales volume in the market the company or brand is competing in.

brand's image altered in a positive way? These kinds of measures indicate whether or not a plan is working.

Marketing managers are responsible for producing sales while keeping marketing and marketing communications investments at reasonable levels. Sales must generate an adequate level of *profit* for the company to thrive and survive in the long term. Most brands in an organization have their own profit and loss statement that is reviewed continually to ensure that sales, costs, and profit targets are always within sight. Alterations and adjustments to a marketing plan or marketing communications plan will occur during the year when necessary.

As discussed elsewhere in the text, every employee of an organization plays a role in providing *customer satisfaction*; all employees must adopt a marketing attitude. Therefore, it is very important for all employees to be aware of the marketing and marketing communications strategies. Informed employees play a key role in implementing the strategies; they thus directly influence how customers perceive the organization.

Planned public relations programs play an important role with regard to *social responsibility* objectives. An organization must promote its positive contributions while eliminating, as best it can, the negative outcomes. Brand equity and company image are directly influenced by the quality of social programs and ethical behaviour that a company and its employees demonstrate to the public.

SUMMARY

Marketing research must be viewed as a tool that assists the manager in the decision-making process. It is a systematic procedure that, if used properly, will produce reliable and valid data.

The research process begins with a firm becoming aware of a problem situation. Problems associated with evaluating marketing communications typically involve primary research. Primary research is the gathering of new data from a representative sample. Primary data are collected from surveys, observation, and experiments. Survey data are either qualitative or quantitative in nature. Qualitative data are collected by focus group or one-on-one interviews and answer the question "why." Quantitative data are obtained by questionnaires through personal interviews or telephone, mail, or online surveys and involve translating thoughts and feelings into measurable numbers. Once the data are secured, they are processed for analysis and interpreted by the researcher.

Experimental research involves testing a marketing mix activity within a controlled situation to measure the effectiveness of the activity. Test marketing is an example of experimental research. In a test market involving marketing communications, an advertisement, commercial, or set of ads in a campaign is placed in designated geographic markets to evaluate the potential impact on consumers. Knowledge gained from such tests allows an organization to make changes to a campaign before it is launched in additional markets.

In order to measure the effectiveness of marketing communications programs, various research procedures are implemented. In advertising, several pre-test and post-test techniques are available. If recognition and recall are a concern, a Starch readership test, a day-after recall test, and opinion-measure tests can be applied. These tests generate data on brand identification and message comprehension.

Direct response communications can be measured quantitatively since they include a toll-free telephone number, a website address, or response cards. Inquiries can be tracked, and any sales that occur can be attributed to specific customers.

On the Internet, cookies allow an organization to track responses. Other Internet measures include impressions (ad views), clicks, and the actual click rate an ad generates. Most campaigns are designed to get a person to visit a website for more information. Therefore, other measures of success include any increases in website traffic, the length of time a person visits the site, and how a person interacts with the content (for example, downloading video content).

Social media measures are based on on-going, long-term analytics and campaign-focused metrics. Some key metrics for specific campaigns include reach, engagement, share of voice, and conversions. The viral nature of social media is another measure of success. An organization must adjust to the differences between social and mainstream media in order to reap the benefits of social media communications.

Sales promotion measures include response rates to coupon offers and the number of entries received for contest, premium, and cash rebate offers. Response rates for current promotions are compared to response rates for previous promotions. The manager will evaluate the various elements of the promotion to determine which elements contributed to success or failure.

The most common ways of measuring public relations communications include counting actual clippings that appear in the print and broadcast media, calculating the number of impressions that the press clippings generate, and converting the press coverage (the size of space or amount of time it occupies) to some kind of advertising equivalency. The latter places a monetary value on public relations and is a popular means of justifying investment in public relations. Some additional measures include PR's impact on generating website traffic and how it influences the conversation about a brand on social media.

Event marketing and sponsorships remain difficult to measure, but they are perceived as a high-profile way to increase sales and improve brand recognition. The most common measure of an event's success is determined by how well the event reaches the target audience. Other commonly used measures include changes in brand awareness levels and image, both of which are based on how well a brand associates with an event.

When measuring the success of an integrated marketing communications campaign, an organization looks at the bigger picture. Typical indicators of success or failure include shifts in market share, productivity, sales and profitability, employee performance and attitude, and the public's perceptions of an organization's social responsibility. A carefully planned marketing communications program contributes to achieving objectives in all of these areas.

KEY TERMS

ad view   359
advertising equivalency   364
click (clickthrough) rate   359
clicks   359
clickthroughs   359
clipping service   363
closed-ended questioning   351
cookie   359
cross-tabulation   353
data analysis   353
data interpretation   353
data transfer   353
day-after recall (DAR) test   357
editing stage   353
experimental research   351
eye movement–camera test   358
fixed-response questioning   351
focus group   351
frequency distribution   353

hypothesis   348
impression   359
mail interview   353
market share   365
marketing research   348
probability sample   350
observation research   351
online survey   353
open-ended questioning   351
open-response questioning   351
opinion-measure testing   357
personal interview   353
population   349
post-testing   356
pre-testing   356
primary data   348
primary research   348
probability sample   350
pupilometer test   358

qualitative data   351
quantitative data   352
recall test   357
recognition test   356
redemption rate   361
reliability (of data)   348
research objective   348
response card   358
sample   349
sampling frame   349
Starch readership test   357
survey research   350
tabulation   353
telephone interview   353
test marketing   351
universe   349
validity (of data)   348

REVIEW QUESTIONS

1. In the context of marketing research, what is the relationship between each of the following sets of terms?
   a) research objectives and hypotheses
   b) observation and experimental research
   c) population and sampling frame

   d) qualitative data and quantitative data
   e) probability sample and non-probability sample
   f) frequency distribution and cross-tabulation
   g) tabulation and cross-tabulation
   h) data analysis and data interpretation

2. Briefly explain the four steps in the sample design process.
3. What is a focus group? What are the benefits of focus group research?
4. Under what circumstances would you use the telephone for collecting survey data? When would you use the personal interview?
5. In measuring the effectiveness of advertising, what is the difference between pre-testing and post-testing? What benefits does each form of research provide?
6. What is the difference between a recognition test and a recall test?
7. What are the three categories of measurement in a Starch readership test? Briefly explain each category.
8. What are three primary ways of measuring the impact of social media communications? Briefly explain.
9. What are the three primary ways of measuring the effectiveness of public relations campaigns? Briefly discuss each form of measurement.
10. What are the primary ways of measuring the effectiveness of event marketing and sponsorship participation? Briefly discuss each form of measurement.

DISCUSSION AND APPLICATION QUESTIONS

1. Compare and contrast the nature of qualitative data and quantitative data. Is it essential to have both types of information prior to investing in a new advertising campaign? Prepare a position and provide appropriate justification for it.
2. "Too much information obtained from marketing research ultimately stifles creative thinking and the production of innovative creative." Many creative directors have expressed this opinion. Conduct some secondary research and present an opinion on the issue. Justify your position with appropriate examples.
3. Companies are now using online surveys to learn more about their customers and how they feel about the company's products. What are the benefits and drawbacks of using online research? Is it as useful and effective as traditional survey methodologies? Briefly discuss the key issues.
4. If event marketing and sponsorships are so difficult to measure for tangible business results, why do so many large and prosperous companies pursue such associations? What are the advantages and disadvantages of being involved in this form of marketing communications? Is it a worthwhile investment? Present an opinion supported with appropriate justification.

ENDNOTES

1. Kwlly Gadzala, "Explorer Group Launches High-Tech Shopper Insight Facility," *Strategy,* September 20, 2011, www.strategyonline.ca.
2. American Marketing Association, *Dictionary of Marketing Terms,* www.marketingpower.com.
3. Lisa D'Innocenzo, "Cozying up to Shoppers," *Marketing,* November 22, 2004, p. 31.
4. "Managers Should Rethink the Power and Limitations of Focus Groups," *Financial Post,* December 14, 1999, p. C4.
5. Jody Temkin, "How Focus Groups Work," http://money.howstuffworks.com/business-communicatons/how-focus-groups-work
6. Wendy Cuthbert, "Hold the Numbers," *Strategy,* June 4, 2001, pp. B6, B7.
7. Susan Krashinsky, "Marketing at the Speed of Social Media," *The Globe and Mail,* May 20, 2013, p. B9.
8. "POPAI Releases 2014 Mass Merchant Study Results," RetailCustomerExperience.com, www.retailcustomerexperience.com/news/popai-releases-2014-mass-merchant-study-results/
9. Patrick Maloney, "Do Sponsorships Measure Up?" *Marketing,* July 8, 2002, p. 13.
10. Chris Powell, "CIBC Most Noticed Pan AM sponsor: Solutions Research Group," Marketing, August 5, 2015, www.marketingmag.ca/brands/cibc-most-noticed-pan-am-sponsor
11. Ibid.

Media Buying Principles and Media Information Resources

This appendix presents the essential aspects of media buying and acquaints the student with a variety of media rate cards and how to read them. The rate cards used in this section have been gathered from online sources and *Canadian Advertising Rates and Data (CARD)*. Rate cards are usually posted on a media company's website under a title like "Advertise with Us" or "Media Kit." Students can refer to *CARD* (if your college or university has a subscription) by visiting cardonline.ca. *CARD* contains summary rate cards for all print and selected out-of-home media in Canada.

In addition, this section exposes the student to a variety of media information sources often referred to by marketing organizations and communications agencies. In most cases, specialized software available by subscription is required to access specific data. However, students are encouraged to visit the various websites listed under "Media Information Resources" to gain exposure to basic information that is available for free.

A set of review questions dealing with various media calculations is included at the end of the appendix.

Media Buying Principles

NEWSPAPER ADVERTISING

Newspaper space is sold on the basis of agate lines or a descriptive ad size (for example, ½ page, ¼ page, and so on). An **agate line** is a non-standardized unit of space measurement, equal to one column wide and 1/14″ deep. Width is generally measured in columns, which vary by newspaper. The combination of agate lines, depth, and width is used to calculate the actual size of a newspaper ad.

An alternative to the agate line format is modular advertising. **Modular advertising** involves selling ads by standardized sizes. To illustrate, an advertisement could be described as a 1/2 page vertical or 1/3 page horizontal.

Note that in this context "lines" and "columns" are not physical lines and columns. They are invisible lines and columns that the newspaper industry uses to measure the size of an ad.

The basic procedure for buying newspaper space is to determine the size of the ad, either in agate lines or by buying a standardized size offered by the newspaper. In the agate line situation, the size is calculated by multiplying the width of the ad (number of columns) by the depth of the ad (inches of depth). One column inch of depth equals 14 agate lines. Note that the newspaper world still operates in the imperial measurement system of inches.

Some newspapers offer standard-size ads that are easier to understand. In the case of *The Globe and Mail* (see Figure A1.1), some of the standard-size options are full page (2800 agate lines), 1/2 page horizontal (1400 agate lines), 1/3 page (930 agate lines), and 1/4 page horizontal (700 agate lines).

agate line A non-standardized unit of space measurement, equal to one column wide and 1/14″ deep, used in newspaper advertising.

modular advertising Selling advertisements based on standardized sizes.

FIGURE

A1.1 Some Standard-Size Page Options in Newspapers

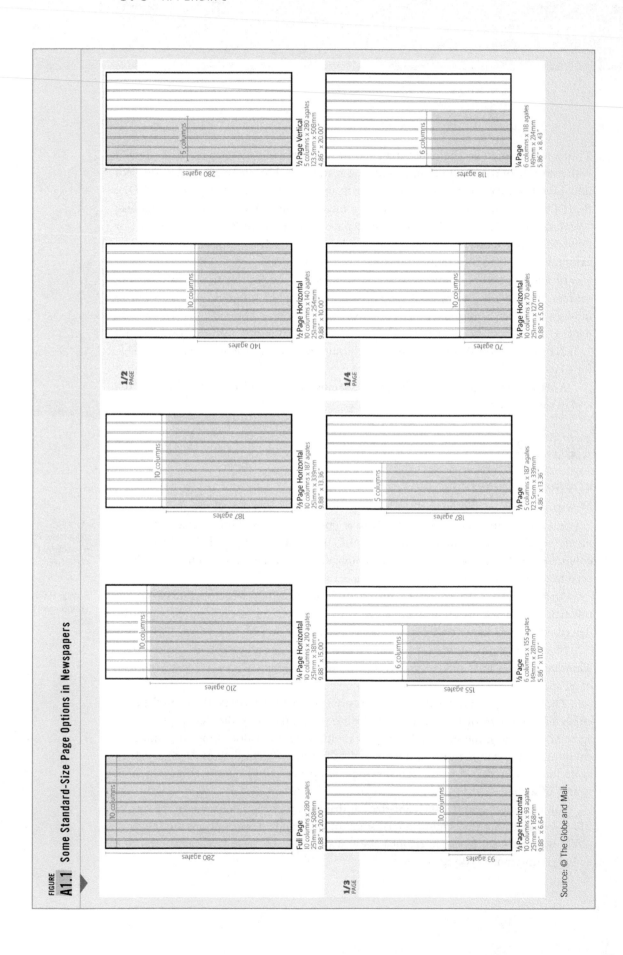

Full Page
10 columns x 280 agates
251mm x 508mm
9.88" x 20.00"

¾ Page Horizontal
10 columns x 210 agates
251mm x 381mm
9.88" x 15.00"

⅔ Page Horizontal
10 columns x 187 agates
251mm x 339mm
9.88" x 13.36"

½ Page Horizontal
10 columns x 140 agates
251mm x 254mm
9.88" x 10.00"

½ Page Vertical
5 columns x 280 agates
123.5mm x 508mm
4.86" x 20.00"

1/3 PAGE

⅓ Page Horizontal
10 columns x 93 agates
251mm x 168mm
9.88" x 6.64"

¼ Page
6 columns x 155 agates
149mm x 281mm
5.86" x 11.07"

⅓ Page
5 columns x 187 agates
123.5mm x 339mm
4.86" x 13.36"

1/2 PAGE

1/4 PAGE

¼ Page Horizontal
10 columns x 70 agates
251mm x 127mm
9.88" x 5.00"

¼ Page
6 columns x 118 agates
149mm x 204mm
5.86" x 8.43"

DETERMINING SPACE SIZE   To illustrate the concept of agate lines, let's assume the size of the ad is 4 columns wide by 10 column inches deep. Considering that each column inch of depth equals 14 agate lines, the size of the ad would be calculated by the following formula:

$$\text{Number of columns wide} \times \text{Inches of depth} \times 14$$
$$4 \times 10 \times 14 = 560 \text{ agate lines}$$

If the size of the advertisement is 5 columns wide by 8 inches deep, the size of the ad in agate lines will be:

$$5 \times 8 \times 14 = 560 \text{ lines}$$

These two examples illustrate that different configurations of ads (combinations of width and depth) can produce the same size ad in terms of space occupied and rates charged.

RATE SCHEDULES   **Line rate** is defined as the rate charged by newspapers for one agate line. With regard to rate schedules, several factors must be noted. First, rates charged by line go down as the volume of the lineage increases over a specified period. Second, costs for the addition of colour or preferred positions are quoted separately. Third, the line rates can vary from one section of the paper to another and from one edition to another (that is, a national edition versus a regional edition). Fourth, line rates may vary by day of the week. The *Toronto Star*, for example, charges more per line for its Saturday edition, since the circulation is significantly higher that day. It is important to scrutinize a rate card carefully when estimating costs of newspaper advertising.

line rate   The rate charged by newspapers for one agate line.

In the chart in Figure A1.2, the rates quoted start with a **transient rate**, which is defined as a one-time rate, or base rate, that applies to casual advertisers. *Discounts* are offered to advertisers as the number of lines purchased increases. Lines accumulate over a period of time, usually a year. The volume discount scale is clearly indicated in Figure A1.2.

transient rate   A one-time rate, or base rate, that applies to casual advertisers.

To illustrate how costs are calculated in newspapers, let's develop a hypothetical plan using the rate card for *The Globe and Mail*. For the illustration, assume *The Globe and Mail* uses the agate line format.

Newspaper: *The Globe and Mail* —News Section, National Edition, (Mon. – Fri.)

Size of ad: 4 columns wide × 10 column inches deep

Rate: Transient rate

Frequency: Once

The first calculation determines the total number of agate lines:

$$4 \text{ columns wide} \times (10 \text{ column inches deep} \times 14) = 560 \text{ lines}$$

The next step is to multiply the number of lines by the line rate by the frequency to determine the cost of the insertion. In this case, the transient rate applies because there is not enough lineage to earn a discount.

$$560 \times \$31.88 \times 1 = \$17\,852.80$$

If the advertiser were to run the ad four times over a period of a few weeks, the calculation for costs would be

$$4 \text{ columns wide} \times (10 \text{ columns inches deep} \times 14) = 2240 \text{ lines}$$
$$2240 \times \$31.88 = \$71\,411.20$$

FIGURE
A1.2 *The Globe and Mail* Rate Card

National Rates

2015 GLOBE MEDIA KIT NEWSPAPER | NATIONAL

JUNE 8, 2015

FULL PAGE = 2,800 LINES (10 COLUMNS X 280 LINES)

ALL RATES ARE GROSS

NEWS, REPORT ON BUSINESS, GLOBE T.O.

	MONDAY TO FRIDAY			SATURDAY		
	NATIONAL	CENTRAL (ON/PQ)	METRO	NATIONAL	CENTRAL (ON/PQ)	METRO
Transient	$31.88	$27.42	$25.18	$35.06	$30.16	$27.71
$15,000	27.91	24.00	22.04	30.69	26.38	24.24
$25,000	27.09	23.32	21.40	29.81	25.63	23.54
$50,000	26.30	22.62	20.78	28.94	24.88	22.85
$100,000	25.51	21.93	20.16	28.06	24.13	22.15
$150,000	24.70	21.26	19.52	27.18	23.38	21.48
$250,000	23.91	20.56	18.89	26.30	22.62	20.78
$350,000	22.96	19.75	18.14	25.26	21.72	19.94
$500,000	21.99	18.92	17.37	24.18	20.81	19.13
$750,000	21.03	18.09	16.61	23.14	19.91	18.29
$1,000,000	20.08	17.27	15.87	22.09	19.00	17.45
$1,500,000	19.14	16.46	15.12	21.03	18.09	16.61
$2,000,000	18.17	15.63	14.37	19.97	17.19	15.80
$2,500,000	17.22	14.80	13.61	18.94	16.29	14.95

NEWS
Daily All editions

ROB
Daily National

GLOBE T.O.
Saturday Metro

COLOUR

MONDAY TO SATURDAY	NATIONAL	CENTRAL	METRO
HALF PAGE PLUS	$10,697	$9,727	$8,950
LESS THAN HALF PAGE	$8,557	$7,782	$6,846

REAL ESTATE, TRAVEL, DRIVE

	MONDAY TO FRIDAY			SATURDAY		
	NATIONAL	CENTRAL (ON/PQ)	METRO	NATIONAL	CENTRAL (ON/PQ)	METRO
Transient	$19.77	$17.00	$15.62	$21.73	$18.70	$17.18
$15,000	17.29	14.86	13.75	19.02	16.36	15.03
$25,000	16.80	14.44	13.27	18.48	15.89	14.60
$50,000	16.31	14.04	12.88	17.94	15.42	14.17
$100,000	15.81	13.61	12.50	17.39	14.95	13.74
$150,000	15.32	13.18	12.11	16.85	14.48	13.31
$250,000	14.82	12.74	11.70	16.31	14.04	12.88
$350,000	14.23	12.74	11.24	15.65	13.45	12.36
$500,000	13.64	11.74	10.78	15.00	12.90	11.85
$750,000	13.05	11.22	10.30	14.36	12.34	11.33
$1,000,000	12.46	10.71	9.83	13.69	11.79	10.82
$1,500,000	11.86	10.20	9.36	13.05	11.22	10.30
$2,000,000	11.26	9.69	8.90	12.38	10.66	9.80
$2,500,000	10.69	9.17	8.44	11.75	10.10	9.27

REAL ESTATE
Friday Metro

TRAVEL
Tuesday in Life & Arts, National and Metro
Saturday National, Central and Metro

DRIVE
Thursday Metro

COLOUR

MONDAY TO SATURDAY	NATIONAL	CENTRAL (ON/PQ)	METRO
HALF PAGE PLUS	$8,557	$7,782	$6,846
LESS THAN HALF PAGE	$6,846	$6,846	$5,477

FIGURE
A1.2   (*Continued*)

Advertising Information

2015 GLOBE MEDIA KIT NEWSPAPER | NATIONAL
JUNE 8, 2015

COLOUR MANDITORY POSITIONS

Certain positions are colour mandatory. Please contact your Globe and Mail representative for more details.

PREMIUM STOCK SURCHARGE

$5,000 net per page except for Globe Style.

- The Front News section is wrapped in semi-gloss premium stock Monday through Saturday.
- These pages feature our front banner, page 2, inside back cover (IBC) and outside back cover (OBC) advertising positions.
- The Globe Style (Saturday) section is printed on our semi-gloss premium stock.

ADDITIONAL INFORMATION

- Double Trucks: Gutter is charged as full column.
- Regional material changes: $579 per split. Not available in Report on Business, Style, Books or Careers.
- Position charge: +25 per cent.
- Front News Banner: +50 per cent.
- Page 3, News: +40 per cent.
- Front Report on Business banner: +25 per cent.
- Pages 2 & 3, Report on Business: +40 per cent.
- Floating Banners: +50 per cent.

- Charge for Globe and Mail box number: $100.
- Charge for affidavits: $100.
- Cancellation charge: 50 per cent for ads cancelled after deadline. No cancellations accepted the day prior to publication.
- The Publisher shall not be liable for errors in advertisements beyond the actual space paid. No liability for non-insertions of any advertisement.
- There is a $100 production charge for ads under 50 MAL that are not camera-ready.

ADVERTISING SPECIFICATIONS

10 Columns, 9.88" wide x 20" deep

Column depth: 280 modular agate lines for full page ads (2,800 lines per 10 column page)

For complete layout, mechanical and digital specifications, please visit **globelink.ca/adformats**

PLEASE NOTE: Before booking any advertising, please review our terms and conditions available from **globelink.ca/mediakits**

CONTACT INFORMATION

TORONTO ONTARIO & MANITOBA
advertising@globeandmail.com
TOLL FREE 1.800.387.9012

WESTERN CANADA
advertisingwesternca@globeandmail.com
ALBERTA & SASKATCHEWAN
1.403.245.4987 or 1.403.774.8024
BRITISH COLUMBIA 1.800.663.1311
NORTHWEST TERRITORIES & NUNAVUT
1.604.685.0308

EASTERN CANADA
OTTAWA REGION, QUÉBEC & ATLANTIC CANADA
advertisingeasternca@globeandmail.com
TOLL FREE 1.800.363.7526

UNITED STATES, INTERNATIONAL
globeandmail@publicitas.com
TOLL FREE 1.212.946.0219

GLOBELINK.CA/NEWSPAPER
CONTACT DIRECTORY globelink.ca/contactdirectory

In this situation, the advertiser remains in the transient rate range even though the total number of lines purchased increased.

Advertisers earn discounted line rates based on annual dollar volume line commitment. To demonstrate, assume an advertiser commits to $100 000. At that level, the line rate drops to $25.51 if the ads are placed in the News section or Report on Business section. Therefore, if the dollar commitment is divided by the line rate ($100 000/$25.51), the advertiser can place ads in various sizes totaling approximately 3920 lines. From the previous example, the total line space was 560 lines for one ad, which means that this ad could run seven times (560 lines × 7) for a total of 3920 lines. When an advertiser commits (typically by a contract) to a certain dollar volume, a greater number of ads can be placed with the newspaper.

POSITION CHARGES Since one disadvantage of newspaper advertising is clutter, advertisers and agencies can request positions in the newspaper that are deemed to be favourable. The request may be for a particular type of ad that commands a higher rate, or it could be for the first few pages of the newspaper. With reference to Figure A1.2, *The Globe and Mail* charges more for preferred locations. A general request for a specific section will increase the rate by 25 percent, while a request for an ad to appear on page 3 (news section) will increase the rate by 40 percent. A banner on the front page of the news section will increase the rate by 50 percent.

position charge   The cost of requesting a preferred position in a newspaper.

The privilege of having a preferred position in a newspaper at a higher cost incurs a **position charge**. An advertiser usually justifies the additional expense of a position request by referring to the improved recognition and recall that will result from the better position.

COLOUR CHARGES Although newspapers are often referred to as the black-and-white medium, colour is available to advertisers willing to pay for it. With reference to *The Globe and Mail*'s rate schedule in Figure A1.2, a separate cost of $8557 is added if the ad runs in colour and is less than a half-page. The colour charge applies each time the ad is run. Other newspapers quote cost increases for each additional colour that is added. The addition of a particular colour is often referred to as **spot colour**. A newspaper will also indicate if there is a minimum size requirement for ads running in colour. Make sure you read the fine print on the rate cards!

spot colour   The addition of one colour to an otherwise black-and-white newspaper or magazine ad.

Generally speaking, there is higher recognition and recall of ads that appear in colour, but given the constraints of most budgets, the use of colour in newspaper advertising is reserved for very large advertisers.

RATES BASED ON MODULAR AD SIZES When advertising rates are based on descriptive sizes such as ¼ page or ½ page, costs are easier to calculate. The rate cards establish a cost for each size. With reference to Figure A1.3, the cost of a black and white ½ page horizontal ad (H), running any day Monday to Friday is $11 750. Therefore, if an advertiser ran four ads (one ad per week for four weeks) the cost calculation would be as follows:

$$\$11\ 750 \times 4 = \$47\ 000$$

The rate card (bottom section of card) shows volume discounts based on the dollar value of the space purchased. In this example, the advertiser would qualify for a 25 percent discount. Therefore, the net cost calculation would be:

$$
\begin{aligned}
\text{Gross Cost} &= \$47\ 000 \\
\text{Less Discount: } \$47\ 000 \times .25 &= \$11\ 750 \\
\text{Net Cost} &= \$35\ 250
\end{aligned}
$$

FIGURE
A1.3

Newspaper Rate Card Based on Standard Ad Sizes

This rate card has been created to demonstrate to the reader the key factors that influence a newspaper media buy in newspapers that sell space based on standard sized ad spaces.

Newspaper Rate Card
Standard Advertising Units

Black & White Transient Rates

Ad Size	Mon. - Fri.	Colour Net Rates
Double Page Spread	$50 000	$7 500
Full Page	$23 500	$3 750
½ Double Page	$25 000	$6 000
¾ Page	$18 100	$3 750
½ Page H or V	$11 750	$2 625
¼ page H or V	$5 875	$2 250
1/8 Page	$2 950	$1 875

Volume Discount Schedule

Net Contract Level	Discount
$25 000	25%
$50 000	27%
$100 000	30%
$300 000	32%
$500 000	35%

Additional Information
- Rates are based on standard ad sizes. Other sizes may be available.
- Discounts only apply to black & white rates.
- Weekend rates are quoted separately and will vary based on circulation increases or decreases.

PREPRINTED INSERTS Preprinted inserts, such as advertising supplements for super-markets, drug stores, and mass merchandisers, are inserted into most newspapers and distributed by them. Rates are usually quoted on cost per thousand. As the size of an insert increases (number of pages) or the delivery circulation increases, the rates on a cost-per-thousand basis also increase. For example, a 24-page catalogue insert would cost more than a 4-page folded insert. Insert rates are quoted separately and in many cases advertisers must contact the newspaper directly to obtain rate details.

COMPARING NEWSPAPERS FOR EFFICIENCY In large metropolitan markets where several newspapers compete for advertising revenue, advertisers must decide which papers to place advertising with. For instance, the *Toronto Star* and *Toronto Sun* compete for ad dollars in Toronto as do the *Calgary Herald* and *Calgary Sun* in Calgary. If using a shotgun strategy, the advertiser may use all newspapers. Conversely, if the budget is limited and the target market is more precisely defined, the advertiser might be more selective.

Since the circulation and the cost of advertising (line rates) vary among newspapers, the advertiser must have a way of comparing the alternatives. To make this comparison, the advertiser may use the standard **cost per thousand (CPM)**. CPM is the

cost per thousand (CPM) The cost of delivering an advertising message to 1000 people; calculated by dividing the cost of the ad by the circulation in thousands.

The CPM, or cost per thousand, is used to compare newspaper alternatives. It is calculated by dividing the cost of the advertisement by the circulation (in thousands) of the newspaper.

Specifications	Ottawa Citizen	Ottawa Sun
Ad size	1000 lines	1000 lines
Cost per line	$9.09	2.65
Ad cost (rate × lines)	$8181	$2385
Circulation	110 173	41 297
CPM	$74.23	$57.75

Interpretation: The CPM for the *Ottawa Sun* is lower than the *Ottawa Citizen* so it is a cost-efficient choice. However, the absolute reach of the *Ottawa Citizen* is much higher. To expand reach among adults in the Ottawa market both newspapers would likely be used.

Source: Line rates obtained from the 2015 display rate cards for each newspaper. Circulation data from Canadian Media Directors' Council *Media Digest*, 2014–2015, p. 69.

actual cost of reaching 1000 readers in a market. The formula for calculating CPM is as follows:

$$\frac{\text{Cost}}{\text{Circulation (in thousands)}} = \text{CPM}$$

To illustrate the concept of CPM, assume an advertiser wants to reach adults in the Ottawa market and is considering both the *Ottawa Citizen* and the *Ottawa Sun*. Refer to Figure A1.4 for specific details on how the newspapers are compared.

As shown by Figure A1.4, the newspaper CPM is strictly a quantitative figure and the results vary considerably. If the advertiser bases the decision of which newspaper to use solely on this principle, the decision is an easy one—the *Ottawa Sun* has a much lower CPM than the *Ottawa Citizen*. However, to reach the adult population of Ottawa effectively, the advertiser will realize that the circulation of both newspapers will be needed. Even though the *Ottawa Citizen* costs more, it will help an advertiser expand its reach in that market.

MAGAZINE ADVERTISING

The procedure for buying magazine space begins with deciding on the size of the ad, which involves choosing from among the variety of page options sold by the magazines under consideration. The rates quoted are based on the size of page requested. Other factors that influence the cost of advertising in magazines include the frequency of insertions and appropriate discounts, the use of colour, position charges, and the use of regional editions.

SIZE OF AN ADVERTISEMENT AND RATE SCHEDULES
Magazines offer a variety of page options or page combinations. For example, *Canadian Geographic* sells space in the following formats: full page, double-page spread, 2/3 page, 1/2 page, and 1/3 page. See Figure A1.5 for illustrations of various magazine ad sizes. The size selected for the advertisement determines the rate to be charged. Magazine rates are typically quoted for all page combinations.

To illustrate how costs are calculated, let's consider a simple example. Assume an advertiser would like to purchase a one-page, four-colour ad in *Canadian Geographic* for January/February and July/August editions (see Figure A1.6 for rate card details). *Canadian Geographic* is issued six times a year. The column headings on the rate card

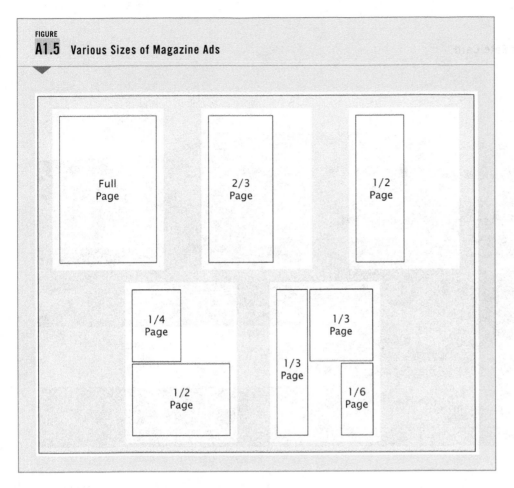

FIGURE A1.5 Various Sizes of Magazine Ads

(1X, 3X, 6X, and so on) refer to frequency (one time, three times, six times, and so on). In this example, the frequency is only twice. Therefore, the rates in the 1X column are used to calculate the campaign. A discount does not apply until the advertiser commits to three advertisements. The cost calculation is:

$$\text{One-page rate} \times \text{Number of insertions} = \text{Total cost}$$
$$\$17\ 290 \times 2 = \$34\ 580$$

DISCOUNTS Advertisers purchasing space in specific magazines with greater frequency will qualify for a variety of discounts. The nature of these discounts varies from one publication to another. Some of the more common discounts include frequency, continuity, and corporate discounts. In magazines, a **frequency discount (print)** refers to a discounted page rate, with the discount based on the number of times an advertisement is run. The more often the ad is run, the lower the unit cost for each ad. In the *Canadian Geographic* rate card, the unit rate is reduced when the ad is run three times, six times, nine times, and twelve times.

A **continuity discount (print)** is an additional discount offered to advertisers that agree to purchase space in consecutive issues of a magazine (such as buying space in 12 issues of a monthly magazine). When continuity discounts are combined with frequency discounts, lower unit costs per page of advertising result.

Large advertisers using the same magazine to advertise a variety of products (note that such an advertiser would likely be a multi-product firm with products that share similar target markets) may qualify for corporate discounts. A **corporate discount**

> **frequency discount (print)**
> A discounted page rate based on the number of times an advertisement runs.

> **continuity discount (print)** A discount offered to advertisers purchasing space in consecutive issues of a publication.

> **corporate discount** A discount based on the total number of pages purchased by a single company (all product lines combined).

FIGURE

A1.6 *Canadian Geographic* Rate Card

dates and rates

Material deadlines and rates

CANADIAN GEOGRAPHIC PUBLISHING SCHEDULE 2015

6 ISSUES ANNUALLY	EDITORIAL FEATURE	CLOSES	IN MARKET
January/February 2015	Wildlife issue	December 3, 2014	December 22, 2014
April 2015	Expeditions	February 25, 2015	March 18, 2015
June 2015	Raising *Erebus*	April 22, 2015	May 13, 2015
July/August 2015	Earthquakes	June 10, 2015	July 2, 2015
October 2015	Ultimate Canadian Geography Quiz	August 19, 2015	September 9, 2015
December 2015	Wildlife issue	October 28, 2015	November 18, 2015

NATIONAL ADVERTISING RATES 2015

NATIONAL	1X	3X	6X	9X	12X
Full page	$17,290	$16,770	$16,250	$15,730	$15,210
Double-page spread	$32,845	$31,855	$30,875	$29,885	$28,910
2/3 page	$13,830	$13,415	$12,995	$12,585	$12,170
1/2 page	$12,965	$12,575	$12,190	$11,790	$11,405
1/3 page	$8,640	$8,385	$8,120	$7,865	$7,595
IFC spread	$38,035	$36,895	$35,750	$34,610	$33,465
OBC	$22,470	$21,795	$21,125	$20,450	$19,780
IBC	$20,745	$20,015	$19,415	$18,840	$18,265
EAST/WEST SPLIT RUNS	**1X**	**3X**	**6X**	**9X**	**12X**
Double-page spread	$24,685	$23,950	$23,215	$22,530	$21,880
Full page	$12,995	$12,610	$12,220	$11,865	$11,515

*GROSS CANADIAN DOLLARS

Source: © Canadian Geographic.

involves consideration of the total number of pages purchased by the company (all product lines combined), and gives a lower page rate for each product. Companies such as Procter & Gamble or Unilever that advertise extensively in women's magazines such as *Chatelaine* and *Canadian Living* would earn preferred rates for the advertising pages they buy in those magazines.

COLOUR AND POSITION CHARGES   Most magazines publish in colour. Therefore, rates for black and white ads or ads that only include spot colour are usually quoted separately. Additional costs for requesting a guaranteed position are also quoted separately on the rate card. For a guaranteed position, such as the outside back cover (OBC) or the inside front cover (IFC) and inside back cover (IBC), the additional costs are usually in the +20 percent range. With reference to the *Canadian Geographic* rate card, the rate for the inside back cover is $20 745, compared to a full-page ad inside the magazine at $17 290. The outside back cover costs even more.

To illustrate the cost calculations of buying magazine space, let's develop a couple of examples based on the *Canadian Geographic* rate card (see Figure A1.6) and the following information:

Example 1:

Magazine:	*Canadian Geographic*
Size of ad:	full-page, 4-colour ad
Number of insertions:	full-page ad to run in 6 consecutive issues

The calculation for this buying plan will be as follows:

Costs for full page, four colour:

Base rate	6X rate applies
$16 250 × 6	= $97 500

Example 2:

Magazine:	*Canadian Geographic*
Size of ad:	double-page spread, 4-colour ad
Number of insertions:	6 issues

The calculation for this buying plan will be as follows:

Costs for double-page spread (DPS), four colour:

Base rate	6X rate applies
$30 875 × 6	= $185 250

COMPARING MAGAZINES FOR EFFICIENCY   Let's assume the advertiser has decided to use magazines because they usually have a well-defined target audience based on demographic variables. The advertiser still must choose particular magazines in which to advertise. Because costs and circulation figures vary, the advertiser needs a way to compare alternatives. As with newspapers, CPM is an effective quantitative means of comparing competing magazines.

In most magazine classifications, there is usually a group of publications competing for the same market. For example, *Chatelaine* and *Canadian Living*, among others, compete against each other in the women's classification. Although the editorial content varies from one magazine to another, each reaches a similar target, so advertisers must look at the efficiencies of each.

FIGURE
A1.7

Comparing Magazines for Efficiency

Similar to newspapers, CPM (cost per thousand) comparisons are made between magazines that reach similar target markets. In this case, *Chatelaine* and *Canadian Living* compete head-to-head for advertisers.

Specifications	*Chatelaine*	*Canadian Living*
1 time, 4-colour rate	$53 480	$52 905
Circulation	524 000	520 000
CPM	$102.06	$101.74

The magazines charge different rates and have different circulations. In this comparison, it appears that *Canadian Living* is marginally more efficient at reaching female adults. If the objective were to maximize reach, an advertiser would have to include both magazines in the media mix. Similar CPM comparisons can be made on the basis of total readership for each magazine (circulation X the number of readers per copy = total readership).

Source: Based on Canadian Media Directors' Council *Media Digest*, 2014–2015, p. 81.

Figure A1.7 contains the comparative calculations for two of the magazines in the women's classification. In terms of a purely quantitative measure, the two magazines are almost equal, which is why they attract the same types of advertisers. Advertisers wanting to reach the demographic profile of readers of these magazines have little choice but to allocate dollars to both. They reach different readers, but readers with the same profile. Therefore, to advertise in both increases the reach of the magazine campaign.

TELEVISION ADVERTISING

As indicated earlier, stations and networks tend not to publish a rate card. Therefore, it is difficult to demonstrate media buying procedures here. Simply stated, television rates are negotiated between buyers (advertising agencies) and sellers (television networks and local market stations). A variety of factors influence the costs of television advertising: the supply of advertising time available and the demand for that time, the type of program, the time of day the ad will appear, and the length of the commercial.

SUPPLY AND DEMAND For major networks such as CTV, CBC, and Global, fundamental economic principles rule the cost of advertising. The network's objective is to maximize revenue from top-rated shows. Top-rated shows such as *Big Bang Theory* (CTV), *NCIS* (Global), *Survivor* (Global), and *The Odd Couple* (CTV) attract advertisers willing to pay a premium price for being on a popular (highly watched) show. The low supply and high demand for the space drives the rates upward. Canada's top-rated shows are determined weekly by research organizations such as the Numeris and Nielsen Media Research. A sample of their research appears in Figure A1.8.

The rates ultimately paid for popular shows depend largely on the advertising agency's ability to negotiate with the networks. To illustrate, the quoted 30-second spot on a popular show like *Big Bang Theory* might be $60 000 or more, an indication of the show's popularity. But big budget advertisers often get lower rates. The **negotiated rate**, typically given to larger year-round advertisers after negotiations, packaging strategies, and agency agreements, will be much lower, possibly in the $40 000 to $45 000 range. Again, negotiation skills play a crucial role in the rates an advertiser actually pays.

negotiated rate The rate ultimately paid by an advertiser as a result of negotiations between an ad agency and a particular medium.

FIGURE
A1.8 Canada's Top TV Shows

 NUMERIS

Top Programs – Total Canada (English)
February 23 - March 1, 2015
Based on confirmed program schedules and final audience data including 7-day playback, Demographic: All Persons 2+

Rank	Program	Broadcast Outlet	Weekday	Start	End	# Aired	Total 2+ AMA(000)
1	BIG BANG THEORY	CTV Total	...T...	20:00	20:31	1	4098
2	NCIS	Global Total	.T.....	20:00	21:00	1	2841
3	SURVIVOR:WRLDS APART	Global Total	..W....	20:00	21:30	1	2553
4	NCIS: NEW ORLEANS	Global Total	.T.....	21:00	22:00	1	2376
5	THE ODD COUPLE	CTV Total	...T...	20:31	21:00	1	2273
6	CASTLE	CTV Total	M......	22:01	23:00	1	2156
7	GOTHAM	CTV Total	M......	20:00	21:00	1	2134
8	ARROW	CTV Total	..W....	20:00	21:00	1	2104
9	PERSON OF INTEREST	CTV Total	.T.....	22:00	23:00	1	1978
10	AMAZING RACE 26	CTV Total	..W.F..	21:30	23:00	2	1969
11	ONCE UPON A TIME	CTV Total	......S	20:00	21:00	1	1968
12	HNIC PRIME EAST	CBC Total	.....S.	19:08	22:03	1	1919
13	MARVELS AGENT CARTER	CTV Total	.T.....	21:00	22:00	1	1908
14	NCIS: LOS ANGELES	Global Total	M......	21:59	23:00	1	1891
15	HAWAII FIVE-O	Global Total	....F..	21:00	22:00	1	1848
16	CTV EVENING NEWS	CTV Total	MTWTF..	18:00	19:00	5	1791
17	GREY'S ANATOMY	CTV Total	...T...	19:00	20:00	1	1778
18	MASTERCHEF JUNIOR	CTV Total	.T.....	20:00	21:00	1	1733
19	HOW TO GET AWAY/MURD	CTV Total	...T...	21:00	23:00	1	1715
20	THE BLACKLIST	Global Total	...T...	21:00	22:00	1	1601
21	FOREVER	CTV Total	M......	21:00	22:01	1	1584
22	MASTERCHEF CANADA	CTV Total	......S	19:00	20:00	1	1448
23	MURDOCH MYSTERIES	CBC Total	M......	20:00	21:00	1	1441
24	MADAM SECRETARY	Global Total	......S	20:00	21:00	1	1432
25	BIG BANG THEORY	CTV Total	MTW.F..	19:30	20:00	4	1370
26	SCORPION	City Total	M......	21:00	22:00	1	1363
27	BATTLE CREEK	Global Total	......S	22:00	23:00	1	1343
28	BLUE BLOODS	CTV Total	....F..	22:00	23:00	1	1277
29	CTV EVENING NEWS WKD	CTV Total	.....SS	18:00	19:00	2	1270
30	CHICAGO PD	Global Total	..W....	22:00	23:00	1	1264

Understanding this report ...
This chart shows the Top 30 TV programs for all national networks and Canadian English specialty networks for the week indicated. Programs are ranked based on their AMA(000). AMA(000) is the average minute audience in thousands. The chart also indicates the broadcast outlet on which the program aired and the program's start and end time (shown in Eastern Time).

TYPES OF PROGRAMS Special programs such as drama specials, sports events, and miniseries are usually distinguished from regular programming. They are designated as special buys and are sold separately from regular programs. In the case of sports programs, for example, hockey and baseball broadcasts tend to appeal to a particular demographic: males between 18 and 49. They are attractive shows for certain types of advertisers. Networks need sponsors for these shows that are willing to make a long-term commitment, and there are separate rates and discount schedules for those that make such a commitment. For instance, Scotiabank, Canadian Tire, Tim Hortons, and Kraft are regular sponsors of *Hockey Night in Canada.*

Rates for one-time annual sports programming are usually separate from rates for regular programming because these special events attract a particular audience. For example, advertising rates for a special event such as the Super Bowl command extremely high prices. In the United States, networks such as CBS and Fox charge between $4.0 million and $4.5 million for a 30-second spot. Advertisers are attracted to the large audience— usually around 115 million people.[1] In comparison, the cost of a Super Bowl spot broadcast in Canada on the CTV network is in a range between $170 000 and $200 000.[2] That's still expensive for a Canadian advertiser.

TIME OF DAY Television is divided into three time categories: *prime time, fringe time,* and *day time.* Prime time is usually between 7 pm and 11 pm, fringe time between 4 pm and 7 pm, and day time from sign-on to 4 pm. Because television viewing is highest in prime time, the advertising rates are higher for that time period. Rates vary from show to show and are based solely on the size of viewing audience each show reaches. As indicated above, shows such as *NCIS, Big Bang Theory,* and *Survivor* reach a very large audience, so their rates are among the highest. Less popular shows (based on the audience size) command lower advertising rates.

Television viewing in fringe time and day time is much lower, so the advertising rates are adjusted downward. Program content is of a different nature: talk shows, children's shows, reruns of popular programs, and so on.

LENGTH OF COMMERCIAL Most advertisers run 30-second commercials, so rates are normally quoted based on that length. Due to the rising costs of television advertising, however, advertisers now use 15-second commercials more frequently. There is a slight premium for using 15-second commercials; rates are normally about 65 percent of the cost of a 30-second commercial on the same network or station. If an advertiser can accomplish creatively what is desired by using 15-second commercials, the cost to advertise will be less in absolute dollars. This is an important budget consideration.

GROSS RATING POINTS The weight of advertising in a market is determined by a rating system referred to as gross rating points. **Gross rating points (GRPs)** are an aggregate of total ratings in a schedule, usually in a weekly period, against a predetermined target audience. GRPs are based on the following formula:

gross rating points (GRPs) An expression of the weight of advertising in a media schedule, calculated by multiplying reach by frequency.

$$\text{GRPs} = \text{Reach} \times \text{Frequency}$$

To illustrate how GRPs work, assume a message reaches 40 percent of target households three times in one week. The GRP level would be 120 (40 × 3). If the message reaches 30 percent of households with an average frequency of 3.5 per week, the GRP level would be 105 (30 × 3.5). The reach of a television show is referred to as a rating. For example, if *Big Bang Theory* reaches 15 percent of households during its weekly time slot, the show has a 15 rating. Therefore, another way to calculate GRPs is to multiply a show's rating by the frequency of messages on that show. See Figure A1.9 for an illustration of this calculation.

The weight of advertising in a market or on a particular show is determined by a rating system. Media weight is expressed in terms of gross rating points (GRPs). GRPs consider two key variables: the size of the audience reached and frequency with which the ad is run against that audience. The chart shows some sample calculations to arrive at total GRPs.

Audience Demographic	Rating	Number of Spots	GRPs
18–49	15	2	30
18–49	20	2	40
18–49	10	2	20
18–49	18	2	36
Total		**8**	**116**

If the eight spots were scheduled in a one-week period, the weight level for the advertising would be expressed as 116 GRPs for the week.

To demonstrate a television media buy at a local market CBC station, refer to the information in Figure A1.10. This is a fictitious plan that was created to reach an adult target 25 to 54 years old in Nova Scotia. Thirty-second spots were placed on a variety of prime time shows all with different ratings. The media buy was scheduled over a three-week period. The unit price per spot shown in the schedule is the price for a local market spot (in this case on the Halifax station) during a network broadcast. Depending on the show, the number of spots purchased will vary from week to week, as do the ratings for each show.

A variety of discounts are usually available to television advertisers. A **frequency discount (television/radio)** is usually earned by purchasing a minimum number of spots over a specified period. A **volume discount** is linked to the dollar volume purchased over an extended period. The greater the volume purchased, the greater the discount. A **continuity discount (television/radio)** is earned when advertisers purchase a minimum number of spots over an extended period. With reference to the CBC discount schedule that appears in Figure A1.11, dollar volume discounts and continuity discounts are calculated based on 13-, 26-, and 52-week intervals.

frequency discount (television/ radio) A discount based on the purchase of a minimum number of spots in a specified period.

volume discount A discount based on the total number of spots bought in a specified period.

continuity discount (television/ radio) A discount for buying spots over an extended period.

RADIO ADVERTISING

The rates paid by radio advertisers are affected by several factors: the season or time of year in which commercials are placed, the time of day at which the commercials are scheduled, the use of reach plans, and the availability of discounts offered by individual stations.

SEASONAL RATE STRUCTURES Radio stations use grid-rate schedules that reflect seasonal listening patterns and reach potential. Refer to Figure A1.12 for an illustration of specific grid-level rates. Generally, radio rates fluctuate with the seasons as follows:

Time Period	Rate
May–August (summer) and December	Higher
September–October	Mid-range
March–April	Mid-range
January–February	Lower

FIGURE
A1.10 Sample Media Buy on CBHT–Halifax

CBC

CHANNEL: CBHT - Halifax

Purchaser: Time and Space Media
Attn: ANGIE REID

Plan ID:	9568472
From:	Mar-18-2013 To:
Target Grp:	A 25-54 / Primary demo
Source:	BBM
Advertiser:	Quest Vitamins
Phone:	
Fax:	
PO/Product:	

Rev. #: 0
Apr-07-2013

Submitted on:
Booked on:
Revised on:

GENERAL AVAILS CHART

Line #	Selling Component	Commercial Type	F/M	Unit	MTWTFSS	Time	* Brk	Pos	# Week	Unit Price	By spot GRPs	By spot AUD	CPP $	CPM $	Mar 18	Mar 25	Apr 01
4	Ron James Series	Regular	L	30	.W.....	20:30-21:00		N	3	49.33	1.1	14.0	46.98	3.52	X	X	X
5	Cracked	Regular	L	30	.T.....	21:00-22:00		N	2	78.33	1.6	12.0	50.21	6.53		X	X
6	Murdoch Mysteries	Regular	L	30	M......	21:00-22:00		N	2	103.33	1.8	13.6	58.38	7.60	X	X	X
8	Coronation St - Prime	Regular	L	30	MTWTF..	19:30-20:00		N	1	223.67	3.2	25.0	71.01	8.95			X
9	Dragons' Den	Regular	L	30	.....S.	20:00-21:00		N	2	168.00	2.7	31.3	61.31	5.36		X	X
11	HNIC Prime West	Regular	L	30	.....S.	23:00-26:00		N	1	80.67	1.2	10.5	67.23	7.68	X	X	X
12	CBC News: @ Six	Regular	L	30	MTWTF..	18:00-18:30		N	1	240.00	3.8	16.5	63.16	14.55	X	X	X
14	Disney	Regular	L	30	.....S.	17:00-19:00		N	1	28.33	0.8	8.5	37.77	3.33	X	X	
15	Republic Of Doyle	Regular	L	30	.....S	21:00-22:00		N	1	120.67	1.5	18.0	80.45	6.70			X
16	CBC Evening News	Regular	L	30	MTWTF..	17:00-18:00		N	3	79.67	2.4	14.5	33.90	5.49	X	X	X
17	Cdn Reflections - Sun	Regular	L	30	.....S	24:00-24:30		N	3	1.00	0.1	1.0	10.00	1.00	X	X	X
18	Fifth Estate - Sun	Regular	L	30	.....S	23:30-24:30		N	3	1.00	0.1	1.5	10.00	0.67	X	X	X
19	Dragons' Den Rotation	Regular	L	30	MTWTF..	16:00-17:00		N	2	8.00	0.2	1.5	40.00	5.33	X	X	X
23	HNIC Afternoon	Regular	L	30	.....SS	15:00-19:00		N	1	44.33	1.4	9.8	31.22	4.54			X

Sales Rep.: Wilson, Alexandra   (902) 420-4315 /
Sales Admin.: Veysey, Catherine   (506) 451-4132 /

Email:
Email: VEYSEYC@Fredericton.cbc.ca

GST/HST: 13975 0909 RT0001
QST: 1006020706 TQ0005

Accepted on behalf of Purchaser
X -   Date:

Rates protected for 5 working days from the date submitted

© CBC Halifax

FIGURE
A1.10 *(Continued)*

CBC

PROPOSAL   **CHANNEL:**   **CBHT - Halifax**

Purchaser: Time and Space Media
Attn: ANGIE REID

Plan ID:	9568472
From:	Mar-18-2013	To:
Target Grp:	A 25-54 / Primary demo
Source:	BBM
Advertiser:	Quest Vitamins
Phone:	
Fax:	
PO/Product:	

Rev. #:   0
Apr-07-2013

Submitted on:	February 14, 2013
Booked on:	-
Revised on:	February 14, 2013

RATING SUMMARY

Line#	Selling Component		By spot AUD
	ProRata	%	
	Total Cost (000's)	$	
	Avg Weekly Cost (000's) $	$	
	Total AUD/GRP		
	CPM/CPR	$	
	Avg Weekly AUD/GRP		

WEEKLY MARKET RATINGS

	Week Of	Occasions	By Week AUD
		Total Delivery	

DVD Rate Card

DVD THRESHOLDS ARE BASED ON INDIVIDUAL MARKET

Effective May 10, 2012

CBC CLIENT DEAL FLEXIBILITY 2012-13 BROADCAST YEAR	13 Week	26 Week Entire Regular Season	Full Season = Regular Season + Entire Playoffs
Continuity - HNIC only	5%	10%	15%
	13 Week	26 Week	52 Week
Continuity	5%	10%	15%
DVD	5%	10%	15%
Market/Tier Spend Thresholds	Gross $'s	Gross $'s	Gross $'s
National Tiers			
Network (incl. Mainchannel, Specialty & Digital*)	$750,000	$1,500,000	$2,500,000
CBC News Net	$75,000	$150,000	$300,000
Selective Markets (Mainchannel & Regional Digital)			
Pacific Region	$75,000	$125,000	$250,000
CBRT Calgary	$50,000	$100,000	$200,000
CBXT Edmonton	$40,000	$75,000	$175,000
CBKT Regina/Saskatoon	$10,000	$30,000	$80,000
CBWT Winnipeg	$15,000	$25,000	$50,000
Ontario Region	$80,000	$200,000	$600,000
CBLT Toronto	$75,000	$150,000	$400,000
CBET Windsor	$5,000	$15,000	$40,000
CBOT Ottawa	$20,000	$50,000	$100,000
CBMT Montreal	$20,000	$50,000	$100,000
Maritime Region	$10,000	$25,000	$50,000
CBHT Halifax	$10,000	$25,000	$50,000
CBCT Charlottetown	$7,500	$20,000	$40,000
CBAT Saint John/Moncton	$5,000	$12,500	$25,000
CBNT St John's/Cornerbrook	$15,000	$25,000	$50,000

*Digital Investment can count to overall Volume of spend on either your National buy or your Regional buy.
However DVD is NOT applied to the Digital elements, ONLY the broadcast schedule.
First calculate DVD discount and then apply Continuity discount on the new total.

Contact your account manager today

cbcrevenuegroup.ca

CBC

FIGURE
A1.12

CJAZ-FM Rate Card

CJAZ-FM Rate Card
CJAZ-FM Radio 101.7 JAZ-FM
Jazz that Rocks!

30-sec spot rates

Daypart/Grid	1	2	3	4	5
Breakfast 6:00 to 10:00 am	300	275	250	225	200
Daytime 10:00 am to 3:00 pm	245	225	205	185	165
Drive 3:00 to 7:00 pm	250	230	210	190	170
Evening and Sunday	220	200	180	160	140

Reach Plan - 30 sec spots

	1	2	3	4	5
Breakfast 25% Daytime 25% Drive 25% Evening and Sunday 25%	250	225	200	175	150

Discount Schedule

Contract Buy (Continuity)		*Volume (Spots)*	
14 to 26 weeks	Grid 3	250	Grid 3
27 to 39 weeks	Grid 4	450	Grid 4
40 to 52 weeks	Grid 5	700	Grid 5

DAYPARTS   Since the size and nature of the audience vary according to the **daypart** (a broadcast time period or segment), different rates are charged for each. Generally, the dayparts are classified as follows:

daypart   A broadcast time period or segment on radio or television.

Classification	**Time**
Breakfast	6 to 10 am
Midday	10 am to 4 pm
Drive	4 to 7 pm
Evening	7 pm to midnight
Nighttime	Midnight to 6 am

Dayparts vary from one station to another, with some stations having more or fewer classifications than those listed above. In addition, weekend classifications are often different from weekday ones, as the listening patterns of the audience change on weekends.

REACH PLANS   Radio advertisers can purchase specific time slots and schedule a particular rotation plan during the length of the media buy, or they can purchase a reach plan. For the first option, a **rotation plan**, the advertiser specifies the time slots and pays the rate associated with them. Two types of rotation plans are available:

rotation plan   The placement of commercials in time slots purchased on radio; can be vertical according to the time of day or horizontal according to the day of the week.

vertical rotation The placement of radio commercials based on the time of day (within various dayparts).

horizontal rotation The placement of radio commercials based on the day of the week (same daypart on different days).

reach plan Rotation of commercials in various dayparts on radio according to a predetermined frequency.

- **Vertical Rotation:** the placement of commercials based on the time of day (within various dayparts).

- **Horizontal Rotation:** the placement of commercials based on the day of the week (same daypart on different days).

Radio stations sell reach plans so that advertisers can maximize reach. In a **reach plan**, commercials are rotated through the various dayparts according to a predetermined frequency to reach different people with the same message. As shown in Figure A1.12, the reach plan divides spots equally between breakfast, daytime, drive, and evening/Sunday dayparts. For the advertiser, the benefit of the reach plan is twofold. First, the reach potential is extended; and second, the rates charged for the reach plan collectively are lower (because of the discounts) than those that would result from the individual purchase of similar time slots. Reach plans do require a minimum spot purchase on a weekly basis (16 spots per week is common).

DISCOUNTS OFFERED BY RADIO   Advertisers who purchase frequently from specific stations qualify for a variety of discounts.

A **frequency discount** is a discounted rate earned through the purchase of a minimum number of spots over a specified period of time, usually a week. Having earned such a discount, advertisers are referred to a lower-rate grid schedule, or could be quoted a percentage discount, such as 5 percent for 15 to 20 spots per week, 8 percent for 21 to 30 spots per week, 10 percent for over 31 spots, and so forth. With a **volume discount**, the advertiser is charged a lower rate for buying a large number of spots; the discount might be 5 percent for 260 spots, for example, or 10 percent for 520 spots. A **continuity discount** applies when an advertiser agrees to place ads over an extended period such as intervals of 26, 39, and 52 weeks.

Advertisers can increase reach by buying a reach plan. The **reach plan** offers a minimum number of weekly spots across all dayparts in return for a packaged discount rate. Refer to Figure A1.12 for examples of discounts.

BUYING RADIO TIME   A strategic plan guides the purchase of radio commercial time. To get the best possible rate from a station or network of stations, all details of the plan must be known by the radio station. Factors such as volume and frequency (the total number of spots in the buy), the timing of the schedule (time of day or season in which the plan is scheduled), and continuity (the length of the plan) collectively affect the spot rate that is charged the advertiser. It places an advertiser on a particular grid with the station. Refer to Figure A1.11 for a listing of grid rates and how an advertiser arrives at a certain grid. For advertisers who purchase large amounts of time, the discounts just described usually apply.

To illustrate some basic cost calculations used in buying radio time, let's develop some examples based on the CJAZ–FM rate card in Figure A1.12.

Example 1:

30-second spots

10 breakfast spots per week

15 drive spots per week

12-week schedule

Cost Calculations:

The advertiser does not qualify for a continuity discount. Therefore, the first calculation is to determine the total number of spots in the buy to see if a volume discount applies.

Total number of spots	= Spots per week × Number of weeks
Breakfast	= 10 per week × 12 weeks = 120
Drive	= 15 per week × 12 weeks = 180
Total spots	= 300

Based on the total number of spots (300), the rate charged will be from Grid 3. In this case, the 30-second rate is $250 for breakfast and $210 for drive time. The cost calculations are as follows:

Total cost	= Number of spots × Earned rate
Breakfast	= 120 spots × $250 = $30 000
Drive	= 180 spots × $210 = $37 800
Total cost	= $67 800

Example 2:

The advertiser would like to evaluate a reach plan (involving 16 commercials per week) against a specific buying plan. Details of each plan are as follows:

Plan A: Reach Plan (30-second spots)

16 spots per week (reach plan)

Rotated between breakfast, drive, day, and evening/Sunday

Schedule over 16 weeks, June through September

Plan B: Specific Plan (30-second spots)

8 breakfast spots per week

8 drive spots per week

16-week schedule

Cost Calculations for Plan A:

The advertiser qualifies for a continuity discount because of the 16-week schedule. The rate would be in Grid 3 in the reach plan. The earned rate is $200 per spot.

Total Cost	= Total number of spots × Earned rate
	= (16 spots per week × 16 weeks) × $200
	= $51 200

Cost Calculations for Plan B:

The total number of spots is as follows:

Breakfast	= 8 spots per week × 16 weeks = 128 spots
Drive	= 8 spots per week × 16 weeks = 128 spots
Total spots	= 256

Based on this calculation, the advertiser qualifies for either a volume or a continuity discount. The advertiser is charged the rate from Grid 3.

Breakfast	= 128 spots × $250 = $32 000
Drive	= 128 spots × $210 = $26 880
Total cost	= $58 880

In conducting a comparative evaluation of Plan A and Plan B, the advertiser must weigh the more selective reach potential of Plan B against the savings of Plan A. Perhaps the advertiser wants to reach business commuters in drive time to and from work. With Plan A, the advertiser can reach a somewhat different audience by means of a daypart rotation of spots. The net result is a cost difference of $7680 in favour of Plan A. Should the advertiser decide to go with the cost savings of Plan A, or with the more selective reach of Plan B at greater cost?

OUT-OF-HOME ADVERTISING

Out-of-home advertising offers a variety of outdoor poster options, street-level advertising, wall murals, transit shelters, vehicles, and station advertising. Regardless of the alternative, the media buying procedure is similar. Out-of-home rates can be based on GRPs or on a per-panel basis.

Referring to Figure A1.13, a rate card for Outfront Media (formerly CBS Outdoor) transit shelters, let's assume an advertiser wants to buy 50 GRPs in Halifax. That means the advertiser will reach the equivalent of 50 percent of Halifax's population. The word "equivalent" is important because vehicle and pedestrian traffic in a city is partly habitual; that is, people tend to travel the same routes each day. Therefore, in the Halifax example, the advertiser might reach 25 percent of the population twice a day for a total of 50 daily GRPs.

All out-of-home advertising rates are quoted on a four-week basis and are sold on a market-by-market basis. Posters and transit shelters are typically sold on the basis of a four-week minimum purchase. More elaborate outdoor executions such as a superboard will have an extended minimum time requirement. To illustrate outdoor cost calculations, let's consider a couple of media buying examples. Rates and data from Figure A1.13 (transit shelter rates) and Figure A1.14 (outdoor poster rates) are used to calculate costs.

Example 1: Outdoor Buying Plan

Medium:	Transit shelters
Markets:	Halifax (CMA), Hamilton (CMA), and Calgary (CMA)
Weight:	25 GRPs weekly in Halifax and Hamilton; 50 GRPs weekly in Calgary
Contract length:	16 weeks in all markets

Cost Calculations:

The costs for a four-week period for each market would be as follows:

Halifax	$4 686
Hamilton	$10 120
Calgary	$56 430
Total	$71 236

Because the contract is for 16 weeks, the costs are multiplied by four (16 weeks divided by four-week rates). The gross cost would be as follows:

$$\$71\ 236 \times 4 = \$284\ 944$$

FIGURE
A1.13   Outdoor Rate Card for Transit Shelters

2013 CBS Outdoor RATEBOOK: Street Furniture - Transit Shelters, APTs, Mapstands, Kiosks, Mediacolumns (68 1/4" x 47 1/4")

Province	Code	Market	Operator	2013 Est. Population	Avg. Daily Circ. In-Market Oct '12 CDR Column2	Single Panel Rate $ Net $ Rate	Average # of Panels to deliver GRPs 25	50	75	100	4 week net rate 25 GRPs (+5%) @25	50 GRPs flat @50	75 GRPs (-5%) @75	100 GRPs (-10%) @100
Newfoundland	005	St. John's CMA (Nfld.)	St. John's Trans.C	190,500		$ 530	6	11	17	23	$ 3,180	$ 5,214	$ 8,058	$ 10,534
Nova Scotia	019	Halifax CMA	CBS	393,600	9,451	$ 750	11	21	32	42	$ 4,686	$ 8,925	$ 12,718	$ 16,065
Nova Scotia	025	Cape Breton CA (Sydney)	CBS	95,600	12,274	$ 709	2	4	6	8	$ 851	$ 1,620	$ 2,309	$ 2,916
Nova Scotia	23	Annapolis Valley & Region	Atcom	61,900	8,200	$ 613								
New Brunswick	48	Saint John CMA (NB)	CBS	125,300	9,047	$ 667	4	8	11	15	$ 1,600	$ 3,048	$ 4,343	$ 5,486
Quebec	065	Saguenay (Chicoutimi-Jonquiere) CMA	CBS	153,700	10,247	$ 613	4	8	12	16	$ 1,470	$ 2,800	$ 3,990	$ 5,040
Quebec	77	Trois-Rivieres CMA	CBS	150,000	7,386	$ 548	6	11	16	21	$ 1,808	$ 3,443	$ 4,906	$ 6,197
Quebec	088	Sherbrooke CMA	CBS	198,500	14,869	$ 740	4	7	10	14	$ 1,555	$ 2,961	$ 4,219	$ 5,330
Quebec	057	Blainville (Montreal CMA)	Imagi	53,510		$ 510								
Quebec	123	Boucherville (Montreal CMA)	Imagi	40,753		$ 510								
Quebec	118	Brossard (Montreal CMA)	Imagi	79,273		$ 510								
Quebec	141	Chambly/Richelieu/Carignan (Montreal CMA)	Imagi	39,004		$ 365								
Quebec	130	Chateauguay (Montreal CMA)	Imagi	45,904		$ 365	non standard format size 55 1/4" H x 48"W							
Quebec	070	La Prairie (Montreal CMA)	Imagi	23,357		$ 365								
Quebec	119	Longueuil (Montreal CMA)	Imagi	231,409		$ 450								
Quebec	135	Repentigny (Montreal CMA)	Imagi	82,000		$ 450								
Quebec	081	St. Constant/Ste. Catherine/Delson (Montreal CMA)	Imagi	49,204		$ 365	non standard format size 55 1/4" H x 48"W							
Quebec	085	St-Jérôme (Montreal CMA)	Imagi	68,456		$ 365	non standard format size 55 1/4" H x 48"W							
Quebec	136	Saint-Philippe (Montreal CMA)	Imagi	5,495		$ 365								
Quebec	111	Terrebonne & Mascouche (Montreal CMA)	Imagi	148,813		$ 510								
Quebec	105	Varennes (Montreal CMA)	Imagi	20,994		$ 365	non standard format size 55 1/4" H x 48"W							
Quebec	144	Ottawa-Gatineau CMA-Quebec (incl. Gatineau, Hull & Aylmer)	Imagi	265,349		$ 365	9-11	19-21	27-31	37-41	$ 4,477	$ 8,550	$ 12,000	$ 15,765
Quebec	108	Drummondville CA	Imagi	71,852		$ 450								
Quebec	098	Joliette CA	Imagi	19,621		$ 365	non standard format size 55 1/4" H x 48"W							
Quebec	137	Mercier/Ste-Martine/Ormstown	Imagi	20,145		$ 365	non standard format size 55 1/4" H x 48"W							
Quebec	143	St-Hyacinthe CA/Ste-Madeleine	Imagi	58,777		$ 365								
Quebec	139	Saint-Jean-Sur-Richelieu Terminal	Imagi	92,394		$ 510								
Quebec	100	Shawinigan CA	Imagi	50,060		$ 365	3	5	7	9	$ 1,535	$ 2,500	$ 3,405	$ 4,235
Quebec	140	Sorel (Sorel-Tracey CA)	Imagi	34,600		$ 365								
Ontario	182	Toronto CMA	CBS	5,572,700	20,962	$ 1,790	67	133	199	265	$ 71,431	$ 136,059	$ 193,884	$ 244,906
Ontario	199	Hamilton CMA (+ 10% discount with Toronto)	CBS	705,700	9,320	$ 912	19	37	56	74	$ 10,120	$ 19,277	$ 27,470	$ 34,699
Ontario	224	London CMA	CBS	462,800	12,538	$ 781	10	19	28	38	$ 4,449	$ 8,474	$ 12,075	$ 15,253
Ontario	243	Windsor CMA	CBS	304,100	10,617	$ 901	8	15	22	29	$ 4,056	$ 7,725	$ 11,008	$ 13,905
Ontario	284	Sault Ste. Marie CMA	Superior 7	77,100	7,300	$ 503								
Ontario	309	Timmins CA	BK Corp. Mktg.	41,500		$ 700	2	4	6	8	$ 1,300	$ 2,500	$ 3,600	$ 4,600
Ontario	311	Greater Sudbury CMA	BK Corp. Mktg.	155,900	13,700	$ 850	3	6	9	12	$ 2,250	$ 4,350	$ 6,300	$ 8,100
Manitoba	318	Winnipeg CMA	CBS	722,800	18,829	$ 726	10	20	29	39	$ 4,358	$ 8,300	$ 11,828	$ 14,940
Alberta	362	Calgary CMA	CBS	1,218,200	9,199	$ 1,500	33	66	99	131	$ 29,626	$ 56,430	$ 80,413	$ 101,574
Alberta	387	Red Deer CA	Reid Signs	96,600		$ 400								
Alberta	395	Edmonton CMA (Mediacolumns/kiosks)	CBS	1,165,500	13,462	$ 1,120	23	46	69	92	$ 15,456	$ 29,440	$ 41,952	$ 52,992
British Columbia	430	Vancouver CMA	CBS	2,338,000	20,084	$ 2,126	29	58	87	116	$ 36,997	$ 70,470	$ 100,420	$ 126,846
British Columbia	431	Vancouver Core	CBS	600,000		$ 2,755								

Source: Courtesy of Outfront Media.

FIGURE
A1.14 Rate Card for Outdoor Horizontal Posters

2013 CBS Outdoor RATEBOOK: Horizontal Posters (10' X 20')

Province	Code	Market	Operator	2013 Est. Population	Avg. Daily Circ. In-Market Oct '12 CDR Circ In-Market	Single Panel Rate $ Net $ Rate	25	50	75	100	(+5%) @25	flat @50	(-5%) @75	(-10%) @100
							Average # of Panels to deliver GRPs				4 week net rate			
Newfoundland	004	St. John's CMA	E.C. Boone	190,500	13,800	$ 1,325	3-4	7	9-11		$ 5,010	$ 8,510	$ 10,025	
Nova Scotia	019	Halifax CMA	CBS	393,600	14,377	$ 1,400	7	14	21	28	$ 8,232	$ 15,680	$ 22,344	$ 28,224
Nova Scotia	020	Acadian Peninsula	Media 2000	15,700	4,100	$ 850								
Nova Scotia	023	Bridgewater/Lunenburg County	Atcom	47,300		$ 700								
Nova Scotia	025	Cape Breton CA (Sydney)	CBS	95,600	9,807	$ 1,456	3	5	8		$ 3,058	$ 5,825	$ 8,301	
New Brunswick	024	Bathurst CA	Media 2000	32,800	5,400	$ 950								
New Brunswick	026	Miramichi CA	Media 2000	27,300	10,200	$ 950								
New Brunswick	039	Fredericton CA	CBS	93,400	7,348	$ 1,350								
New Brunswick	043	Moncton CMA	CBS	137,600	9,738	$ 900	4	7	11	14	$ 2,646	$ 5,040	$ 7,182	$ 9,072
New Brunswick	048	Saint John CMA	CBS	125,300	11,060	$ 900	3	6	9	12	$ 2,268	$ 4,320	$ 6,156	$ 7,776
Quebec	049	St. Lawrence Basin/Matapedia (see below)	CBS	60,000		$ 700								
Quebec	051	Rimouski CA	CBS	50,100	6,118	$ 1,000								
Quebec	063	Riviere du Loup CA	CBS	27,300	7,603	$ 1,500								
Quebec	050	Matane CA	CBS	17,800	2,280	$ 1,000								
Quebec	074	Charlevoix	CBS	26,000		$ 1,000								
Quebec	056	Baie-Comeau CA	CBS	27,800	6,536	$ 1,000								
Quebec	059	Sept Iles CA	CBS	27,500	1,996	$ 1,000								
Quebec	054	Beauce District (see below)	CBS	28,400		$ 700								
Quebec	073	Saint-Georges CA	CBS	33,900	3,480	$ 1,500								
Quebec	071	Thetford Mines CA	CBS	27,300	4,826	$ 1,000								
Quebec	072	Victoriaville CA	CBS	45,900	4,974	$ 1,500								
Quebec	113	Plessisville	CBS	6,500		$ 930								
Quebec	114	Princeville	CBS	5,300		$ 930								
Quebec	117	Saint-Eulalie	CBS	900		$ 950								
Quebec	060	Quebec City CMA	CBS	756,200	21,165	$ 3,150	9	18	27	35	$ 19,845	$ 37,800	$ 53,865	$ 68,040
Quebec	065	Saguenay CMA (Chicoutimi-Jonquiere)	CBS	153,700	9,330	$ 1,403	5	9	13	17	$ 5,301	$ 10,098	$ 14,390	$ 18,176
Quebec	069	Alma CA	CBS	32,400	5,104	$ 1,000								
Quebec	082	Saint Bruno	CBS	2,400		$ 720								
Quebec	077	Trois-Rivieres CMA	CBS	150,000	12,105	$ 2,265	4	7	10	13	$ 6,659	$ 12,684	$ 18,075	$ 22,831
Quebec	078	Shawinigan CA	CBS	53,400	7,589	$ 1,545								
Quebec	084	Drummondville CA	CBS	87,200	7,000	$ 1,590								
Quebec	089	Granby CA	CBS	76,700	9,949	$ 1,590								
Quebec	088	Sherbrooke CMA	CBS	198,500	15,001	$ 2,265	4	7	11	14	$ 6,659	$ 12,684	$ 18,075	$ 22,831
Quebec	090	Montreal CMA	CBS	3,744,300	36,635	$ 4,418	26	52	78	103	$ 80,399	$ 153,140	$ 218,225	$ 275,652
Quebec	094	Joliette CA	CBS	46,900	13,538	$ 1,390								
Quebec	106	Saint-Hyacinthe CA	CBS	55,800	13,746	$ 1,390								
Quebec	109	Sorel-Tracy CA	CBS	47,200	8,960	$ 1,340								
Quebec	110	Salaberry de Valleyfield CA	CBS	39,200	7,994	$ 1,390								
Quebec	080	Cadillac/Malartic	CBS	3,500		$ 950								
Quebec	096	Rouyn-Noranda CA	CBS	40,700	3,463	$ 1,270								
Quebec	097	Val d'Or CA	CBS	32,200	4,397	$ 1,030								
Quebec	146	Ottawa-Gatineau CMA (Quebec) Hull	CBS	311,300	15,800	$ 1,794	6	11			$ 8,287	$ 15,785		
Ontario	125	Kingston CMA	CBS	157,000	14,362	$ 1,500	3	6	9	11	$ 3,780	$ 7,200	$ 10,260	$ 12,960

Source: Courtesy of Outfront Media.

FIGURE
A1.14 (*Continued*)

2013 CBS Outdoor RATEBOOK: Horizontal Posters (10' X 20')

Province	Code	Market	Operator	2013 Est. Population	Avg. Daily Circ. In-Market Oct '12 CDR Circ In-Market	Single Panel Rate $ Net $ Rate	25	50	75	100	(+5%) @25	flat @50	(-5%) @75	(-10%) @100
							Average # of Panels to deliver GRPs				\multicolumn 4 week net rate			
Ontario	124	Belleville CA/Trenton	CBS	89,300	10,786	$ 1,000								
Ontario	126	Brockville CA	CBS	37,600	5,248	$ 1,000								
Ontario	150	Picton/Prince Edward County	CBS	26,700		$ 950								
Ontario	149	Napanee	CBS	16,040		$ 950								
Ontario	148	Gananoque	CBS	5,600		$ 950								
Ontario	147	Ottawa-Gatineau CMA (Ontario)	CBS	919,600	14,000	$ 3,680	17	33	49	65	$ 42,498	$ 80,949	$ 115,352	$ 145,708
Ontario	134	Smith Falls	CBS	8,500		$ 1,000								
Ontario	132	Beckwith /Carleton Place	CBS	6,900		$ 1,000								
Ontario	131	Arnprior	CBS	7,200		$ 1,000								
Ontario	133	Perth	CBS	6,000		$ 1,000								
Ontario	165	Kawartha Lakes CA/Lindsay & Emily	CBS	70,400	6,474	$ 1,100								
Ontario	166	Peterborough CMA	CBS	115,900	5,904	$ 1,386	5	10			$ 5,822	$ 11,090		
Ontario	280	Beaverton/Brock	CBS	12,000		$ 650								
Ontario	182	Toronto CMA	CBS	5,572,700	24,964	$ 4,191	56	111	166	222	$ 139,569	$ 265,845	$ 378,829	$ 478,521
Ontario	195	Oshawa CMA	CBS	353,200	11,150	$ 1,769	8	16	24	31	$ 8,492	$ 16,176	$ 23,051	$ 29,117
Ontario	199	Hamilton CMA (additional 10% if sold with Toronto)	CBS	705,700	11,887	$ 1,871	15	29	43	57	$ 16,276	$ 31,001	$ 44,176	$ 55,802
Ontario	203	Kitchener CMA/Cambridge -distribution issues - check with chart|	CBS	467,700	12,403	$ 1,695	10				$ 11,865			
Ontario	219	Brantford CMA	CBS	131,900	4,852	$ 1,255								
Ontario	211	St. Catharines/Niagara CMA	CBS	379,600	9,582	$ 1,511	10	20	30	40	$ 10,574	$ 20,140	$ 28,700	$ 36,252
Ontario	224	London CMA	CBS	462,800	16,398	$ 1,641	8	15	22	29	$ 8,615	$ 16,410	$ 23,384	$ 29,538
Ontario	243	Windsor CMA	CBS	304,100	12,900	$ 1,416	6	12	18	24	$ 7,138	$ 13,596	$ 19,374	$ 24,473
Ontario	242	Chatham-Kent CA	CBS	97,900	3,719	$ 850								
Ontario	252	Leamington CA/Kingsville	CBS	47,600	3,900	$ 850								
Ontario	258	Essex	CBS	20,400		$ 850								
Ontario	250	Sarnia CA	CBS	86,600	7,844	$ 700								
Ontario	265	Collingwood CA	CBS	19,500	2,016	$ 1,400								
Ontario	264	Owen Sound CA	CBS	31,000	4,699	$ 1,400								
Ontario	266	Blue Mountain District (see below)	CBS	133,500		$ 1,000								
Ontario	278	Barrie CMA	CBS	183,800	9,236	$ 1,500	6	11	16	21	$ 6,930	$ 13,200	$ 18,810	$ 23,760
Ontario	281	Orillia CA	CBS	39,400	11,236	$ 1,400								
Ontario	277	Midland CA	CBS	34,400	5,374	$ 1,400								
Ontario	274	Muskoka District (see below)	CBS	62,000		$ 1,000								
Ontario	284	Sault Ste. Marie CA	Superior 7	77,100	10,200	$ 1,326	2	4	6	8	$ 2,652	$ 5,304	$ 7,956	$ 10,608
Ontario	295	Greater Sudbury CMA/North Bay CA/North Shore & Dist.	Outdoor Exposure	238,100	7,700	$ 1,100	8	16	23	31	$ 8,200	$ 17,600	$ 22,885	$ 29,400
Ontario	303	Thunder Bay CMA	CBS	116,800	9,687	$ 1,000								
Ontario	305	Timmins CA & District	Woodgreen	80,800	5,400	$ 1,005	4	8	11	15	$ 5,027	$ 8,684	$ 11,946	$ 16,830
Ontario	308	Timmins CA	Woodgreen	41,500	6,500	$ 1,100	2	3	5-8	8-10	$ 2,200	$ 4,200	$ 7,630	$ 8,864
Manitoba	318	Winnipeg CMA	CBS	722,800	21,614	$ 1,733	9	17	26	34	$ 8,836	$ 16,830	$ 23,983	$ 30,294

FIGURE
A1.14 (*Continued*)

2013 CBS Outdoor RATEBOOK: Horizontal Posters (10' X 20')

Province	Code	Market	Operator	2013 Est. Population	Avg. Daily Circ. In-Market Oct '12 CDR Circ In-Market	Single Panel Rate $ Net $ Rate	Average # of Panels to deliver GRPs				4 week net rate			
							25	50	75	100	(+5%) @25	flat @50	(-5%) @75	(-10%) @100
Saskatchewan	346	Prince Albert CA	20-twenty.ca	39,600		$ 950								
Saskatchewan	347	Yorkton CA	CBS	17,900	3,548	$ 715								
Saskatchewan	349	Regina CMA	CBS	207,000	15,156	$ 1,400	4	7	11	14	$ 4,116	$ 7,840	$ 11,172	$ 14,112
Saskatchewan	350	North Battleford CA	CBS	18,800	3,448	$ 715								
Saskatchewan	351	Rural Saskatchewan (Minimum 8 week buy)	CBS	437,000		$ 870								
Ontario	355	Moose Jaw CA	CBS	33,700	7,321	$ 1,060								
Saskatchewan	358	Saskatoon CMA	CBS	257,300	18,039	$ 1,400	4	8	11	15	$ 4,704	$ 8,960	$ 12,768	$ 16,128
Alberta	362	Calgary CMA	CBS	1,218,200	17,829	$ 1,938	18	35	52	69	$ 28,481	$ 54,250	$ 77,306	$ 97,650
Alberta	395	Edmonton CMA	CBS	1,165,500	16,923	$ 1,938	18	35	52	69	$ 28,481	$ 54,250	$ 77,306	$ 97,650
British Columbia	425	Vancouver CMA	CBS	2,338,000	30,720	$ 3,000	19	37	55		$ 46,601	$ 88,763	$ 126,487	

St. Lawrence Basin (049) includes: Cacouna, Grand Metis, Ile-Verte, Mont-Joli, Montmagny, Notre-Dame-Des-Neiges, Sayabec, St-Fabien, St-Simon, Ste-Luce, Trois-Pistoles, Val-Brillant

Beauce District (054) includes: Beauceville, Notre-Dame-Des-Pins, St-Come-Liniere, St. Joseph De Beauce, Ste-Marie Beauce, Vallee Jonction

Blue Mountain District (266) includes: Durham, Hanover, Hepworth, Kincardine, Markdale, Meaford, Nottawa, Port Elgin, Singhampton, Southampton, Stayner, Sunnidale Corners, Thornbury, Walkerton

Muskoka District (274) includes: Oro Township, Parry Sound, Ramara Township, Tiny Township, Wasaga

Although not shown in this particular illustration and rate card, outdoor media usually offer advertisers volume discounts (for example, a reduced rate based on dollar volume purchased) and continuity discounts (for example, a reduced rate for extended buys such as 12 weeks, 16 weeks, and so forth).

Example 2: Outdoor Buying Plan

Medium:	Horizontal posters
Markets:	Toronto (CMA), Montreal (CMA), and Edmonton (CMA)
Weight:	Toronto 25 GRPs; Montreal, and Edmonton 50 GRPs
Contract length:	12 weeks in Toronto; 8 weeks in Montreal and Edmonton

Cost Calculations:

Using the data from Figure A1.14, the appropriate costs for each market over a four-week period would be as follows:

Toronto	$139 569 × 3 = $418 707
Montreal	$153 140 × 2 = $306 280
Edmonton	$54 250 × 2 = $108 500
Gross costs	= $833 487

Because the length of the contract in Toronto is 12 weeks, the costs are multiplied by three (12 weeks divided by the four-week rate). In Montreal and Edmonton, the contract is 8 weeks. Therefore, the costs are multiplied by a factor of two (8 weeks divided by the four-week rate).

DIRECT MAIL ADVERTISING

Three basic steps are involved in buying direct mail: obtaining a proper prospect list, conceiving and producing the mailing piece, and distributing the final version.

OBTAINING DIRECT MAIL LISTS The direct mail list is the backbone of the entire campaign. Both the accuracy and definition of the list can have a significant bearing on the success or failure of a campaign. Since it is much less expensive to keep a current customer than to find a new one, companies should compile accurate lists of customers in their database, and form relationships with customers through mail and electronic means. Internal lists compiled from a database management system are referred to as **house lists**.

house list An internal customer list.

Prospective names are also gathered from external sources. People with a history of responding to mail offers tend to be attractive prospects for new offers. Buying by mail is part of their behaviour. Therefore, the challenge is to find prospects who have a demographic profile and, perhaps, a psychographic profile that mirror the profile of current customers. A **list broker** can assist in finding these prospects. The buyer provides the broker with the profile of the target customer, and the broker supplies a list of possible prospects on a cost-per-name basis. Generally, a high-quality list is developed through an automated **merge/purge** process, whereby numerous lists are purchased, combined, and stripped of duplicate names.

list broker A company specializing in finding or developing lists for direct response purposes; finds prospect lists based on target market criteria established by marketing organizations.

merge/purge A process in which numerous mailing lists are combined and then stripped of duplicate names.

Cornerstone Group of Companies, a database management company, compiles lists for various consumer, business, and professional targets. A consumer list can be compiled based on predetermined criteria such as income, home ownership, marital status, and type of dwelling. Business lists can be developed based on the type or size of business (for example, small, home-based businesses). Professional lists are available for medical, legal, and engineering practitioners, among many others.

Canada Post also supplies information vital to the accurate targeting of messages. For example, a postal code can isolate a small geographic area—say, a city block—and can then be combined with census data to provide relevant statistics regarding the ages and incomes of homeowners in the area and whether children are present in the households. Canada Post offers a free software tool called Precision Targeter that will assist marketing organizations in planning the best delivery routes for a direct mail campaign.

A few types of lists are available: response lists, circulation lists, and compiled lists. A **response list** is a list of proven mail-order buyers. Such lists include book-of-the-month-club buyers and people who order from cooperative direct mailing firms. Because these lists include proven mail-order buyers, they tend to cost more. A minimum rental of 5000 names is required in most cases.

Circulation lists are magazine subscription lists that target potential customers according to an interest or activity. A publishing company, for example, might rent its list of subscribers to another business interested in a similar target. Rogers Media offers a consumer database composed of unduplicated active subscribers to a host of its publications, including *Maclean's*, *Chatelaine*, and *Flare*. Typically, names are available on a cost per thousand basis (CPM). Cornerstone offers a list of subscribers to *Canadian Geographic* magazine at a base cost of $130/M. Requesting additional demographic variables such as age, gender, or income involves an additional charge.

Compiled lists are prepared from government, census, telephone, warranty, and other publication information, or from surveys conducted by marketing organizations such as Epsilon TargetSource Canada. Target Source's consumer survey captures a wide range of data on purchase behaviour and intentions, lifestyles, life stage, hobbies and interests, product ownership, and demographics. From a total universe of over 2 million households marketers can target specific segments. For example, there are 16 000 expectant mothers in the current TargetSource database available at a cost of $225/M.[3] That list would be of interest to marketers of baby foods and other baby needs.

response list A list of direct mail buyers who have previously made purchases based on direct response offers.

circulation list A publication's subscription list that targets potential customers based on specified demographic characteristics, interests, or activities.

compiled list A direct mail list prepared from government, census, telephone, warranty, or other publication information.

PRODUCTION Direct mail packages are usually designed by a specialist agency. Once the mailing package is designed, it is ready for printing. Various factors that influence cost include size, shape, number of pieces, use of colour, and so on. Costs are usually quoted CPM or on a cost-per-unit basis, with larger runs incurring lower unit costs. Once printed, the mailing pieces are turned over to a letter shop that specializes in stuffing and sealing envelopes, affixing labels, sorting, binding, and stacking the mailers. Once this task is complete, the mailing units are sent to the post office for distribution.

DISTRIBUTION Distribution costs of direct mail replace placement costs in traditional forms of media advertising. The most common means of delivery is Canada Post. Several options are available through the postal system: addressed mail, unaddressed mail, and business reply mail. Regardless of the option used, rates are determined by weight of the mailing. For example, an unaddressed mailing (for example, a restaurant flyer) weighing under 50 g costs 15.8 cents; a similar mailing weighing up to 100 g costs 18.1 cents.[4]

DIRECT MAIL BUYING ILLUSTRATION The procedures for estimating the cost of solo direct mail and cooperative direct mail are similar. However, with a solo direct mail campaign, the advertiser absorbs all the costs rather than sharing them with other advertisers.

Taken into consideration are factors such as costs of renting a mailing list, distribution costs, printing costs, mailing costs, and costs associated with fulfillment. For this example, we will assume a cooperative direct mail program will be undertaken in the Valassis Canada cooperative mailing package (see Figure A1.15). The Valassis Canada mailer is distributed to a predetermined list of households across Canada and contains offers from non-competing brands in various product categories.

FIGURE
A1.15

Valassis Canada Direct Response Rate Card

Direct Response Rate Card—Valassis Canada Inc.

Valassis is a full range media and marketing services company. We deliver value to consumers how, when, and where they want, achieved through exceptional targeting insights, results analysis and our diverse media portfolio.

Advertising Rates are effective **January 1, 2013.**

Rates are based on 1 side of page and exclusivity for one product category only. Additional categories extra. Multiple page, volume or frequency discounts available on request. Regional buys subject to a 10% surcharge with a minimum of $500 in each market purchased. Our Red Plum free standing insert delivers advertising messages and coupons through home delivered newspapers.

Rate Card

Size	Rate Per M
1P	$8.00
1/2P	$5.20
Front Cover	$12.50
Back Cover	$11.50
Front Tab	$9.50
Back Tab	$9.00

Note: Per M = $ cost per thousand

Source: Data from CARDonline, www.cardonline.com.

Buying Information:

Valassis Canada Cooperative Mailings

The offer:	One-page premium size (5.5" × 8.25") that includes a $1.50 coupon
Redemption rate:	2.5 percent
Distribution:	2 000 000 households
Frequency:	Once
CPM:	$8.00 (from rate card)

Cost Calculations:

Distribution costs

2 000 000 units to be delivered, therefore,

2 000 × $8.00 = $16 000

Printing costs (estimated at $7.50/M)

2000 × $7.50 = $15 000

Redemption costs (based on a 2.5 percent redemption rate)

2 000 000 × 0.025 × $1.50 = $75 000

Total cost $106 000

Depending on how the coupon offer is returned, there could be additional costs for the advertiser. For example, there is a handling fee provided to the retailer for conducting the coupon transaction. As well, coupons are usually sent from the retailer to a clearing house for processing. The clearing house pays the retailer and provides periodic reports to the advertiser about how many coupons are being redeemed. The advertiser pays a fee for this service.

INTERNET ADVERTISING

The most common model for quoting advertising rates on the Internet is CPM. An advertiser might pay each time an ad is downloaded to a browser, creating an impression or ad view. Or the advertiser may pay only when an ad is clicked on, a *pay for performance model*, or in some cases pay a *flat fee*.

CPM (online)   The price charged for displaying an ad 1000 times. The calculation for CPM is cost divided by impressions (number of impressions divided by 1000).

CPM MODEL   **CPM** is the price charged for displaying an ad 1000 times. The calculation for CPM is cost divided by impressions (number of impressions divided by 1000). For online advertising, an organization pays a rate for every 1000 impressions made. Therefore, if the total number of impressions desired is 500 000 and the CPM is $30, the total cost of the advertising campaign will be $15 000 (500 000 impressions/1000) × $30. In this pricing model the ad appears on a user's screen, so it makes an impression. The person may or may not click on the ad.

CPM rates vary according to the level of targeting desired by the advertiser. Typical options include *run of site*, *run of category*, *geographic targeting*, and *keyword targeting*. With reference to the rate card for globeandmail.com shown in Figure A1.16, if run of site is selected, the rates charged are those quoted for the various sizes and creative formats that appear in various sections of the newspaper. For example, a standard-sized banner ad anywhere in the news section costs $28/M. A bigger ½ page unit in the same section costs $38/M. Rates are also quoted for tablet and mobile editions of the newspaper.

targeting request   An ad placed to reach a specific target audience of a website, for which a premium is usually paid.

If **targeting requests** are applied, an additional charge will be added. Although not shown on the *Globe and Mail* rate card it is very likely that dollar volume discounts will also apply. Typically, discounts are offered on a graduated scale—the more dollars in the media campaign, the bigger the discount.

CPM rate cards vary from one site to another, but the high-traffic sites of course charge a higher CPM. Popular portal sites, such as Google, and various sports and media sites, such as TSN and Rogers Sportsnet, attract significant traffic and price their CPMs accordingly.

Here are a few illustrations to show how online advertising costs are calculated. Rate information is obtained from Figure A1.16.

Example 1:

Type of ad and Location:	Half-page unit, *Globe and Mail*, Lifestyle Section
Impressions desired:	3 000 000
CPM:	$36

FIGURE

A1.16 *The Globe and Mail* Digital Advertising Rate Card

Globe Digital and Alliance Rates

2015 GLOBE MEDIA KIT **DIGITAL**
APRIL 8, 2015

HOMEPAGE SPONSORSHIP PRODUCTS			ALL RATES ARE NET
Premium Globe and Mail Homepage Sponsorship	Billboard	$35,000	Single ad
Standard Globe and Mail Homepage Package	IAB Std	$30,000	3 Std IAB ad units/page
Standard Globe Alliance Homepage Package	IAB Std	$45,000	Std IAB ad units/page

GLOBE AND MAIL DIGITAL PRODUCTS	CORE CHANNELS			NICHE CHANNELS		
	NEWS	BUSINESS	LIFESTYLE	ADVISOR	AUTO	SMALL BUSINESS
DESKTOP DISPLAY						
GLOBE AND MAIL AND ALLIANCE PARTNER* NETWORK (STANDARD IAB FORMAT)						
Section Sponsorship	$32	$34	$30	$45	$36	$40
Run of Section/Run of Channel	$28	$30	$26	$40	$32	$35
Run of Site/Run of Network	$22	$22	$22	$22	$22	$22
Alliance partners: The Globe and Mail, Forbes, ABC News, Reuters, The Guardian, Washington Post, US Weekly, Rolling Stone, Elite Daily						
WALL STREET JOURNAL DIGITAL NETWORK						
WSJ Homepage	Flat fee: 300 x 250 = $5000/day, half pager = $7500/day (100,000 daily impressions)					
Run of Section	$35	$37	$33	——	——	——
Run of WSJDN	$32	$32	$32	——	——	——
CULTURAL DIVERSITY NETWORK						
South East Asia channel	$20	$20	$20	$20	$20	$20
SPECIAL AD FORMATS						
Half page unit (300 x 600) Available on all sites	$38	$40	$36	$50	$42	$45
IAB rising star units (portrait/filmstrip) Available on Globe and Mail only	$43	$45	$41	$55	$47	$50
Canvas unit (1000 x 700) Available on Globe and Mail only	$58	$60	$56	$70	$62	$65
SMALL AD FORMATS						
Tile (120 x 240)	Sponsorship $13.00; Std CPM $10.00					
VIDEO PRE-ROLL	$50	$50	$50	$50	$50	$50
TABLET AND SMARTPHONE (INCLUDES ALLIANCE PARTNERS)						
Tablet interstitial/Smartphone Interstitial	$45	$45	$45	$45	$45	$45
Tablet (Custom)	$35	$35	$35	$35	$35	$35
Tablet (Standard IAB)	$26	$28	$24	$35	$35	$35
Mobile Web/Smartphone (Standard 300 x 250, 300 x 450)	$28	$30	$26	——	$32	$35
Smartphone (Standard 300 x 50)	$18	$20	$16	——	$18	$18
Mobile Website (300 x 50)	$14	$15	$13	——	$18	$18
TARGETING PRODUCTS (INCLUDES ALLIANCE PARTNERS)						
Audience re-targeting based on behaviour – 1st party data	$25					
Custom audience segments – 3rd Party data	Prices available upon request					
EMAIL NEWSLETTER						
Editorial e-newsletters	$27	$27	$25	$35	$30	$30
Advertising exclusive e-blast (per 1000 sent)	$125	$125	$125	$125	$125	$125
PERFORMANCE PRODUCTS (ACROSS TGAM AND ALLIANCE SITES)						
Private exchange (RTB/Programmatic)	Prices subject to market for RTB and/or negotiation for direct programmatic deals					
Direct response campaigns	Varies based on program					

Rates effective Jan 1, 2015

Cost Calculation:	(3 000 000/1000) × $36 = $108 000

Once the ad achieves the desired number of impressions, it will be removed from the website.

Example 2:

Type of ad:	Canvas Unit, *Globe and Mail*, Business Section
Impressions desired:	2 500 000
CPM:	$60

Cost Calculation:	(2 500 000/1000) × $60 = $150 000

Although these are the quoted rates, the reality of the situation is similar to offline advertising. CPM rates are negotiable and depend on factors such as length of the campaign, season, and relationship between client and vendor. Effective negotiation skills in the media buying process could result in lower CPM rates. Rates are also influenced by a relatively new concept called programmatic buying and real time bidding. Both are discussed later in this section.

PAY FOR PERFORMANCE MODEL Advertisers must remember that the purpose of the banner is to create interest so that the viewer clicks the ad for more information. Once clicked, the viewer sees the ad in its entirety or is linked to the advertiser's website. Since clicking is the desired action, many pricing models are based on a **cost-per-click (CPC)** basis instead of CPM. The benefit of such a system is clear: The degree of clicking achieved by an ad indicates the effectiveness of the ad.

cost-per-click (CPC) An Internet advertising pricing strategy where advertisers pay based on the number of ad clicks received.

The question is often asked: What is a good click rate? The answer depends on a host of factors such as the size of the banner, whether or not animation or video content was included, and where the ad was located on a page. A recent report by MediaMind observes that standard banner click rates have stabilized at 0.09 percent, meaning there is just one click for every 1000 impressions made.[5] The same study showed click rates for mobile banner ads to average 0.64 percent. While the click rates may seem low, an advertiser has to assess the targeting capabilities of online and mobile ads. The ability to target individuals based on location and behaviour is a positive factor to consider when deciding to use mobile advertising.

FLAT-FEE MODEL Some websites charge a flat fee for advertising—typically, it is a set amount for the length of time the ad appears on the site. Sponsorships, for example, are usually sold on a flat-rate basis rather than on the number of impressions. For example, a site such as TSN.ca might offer a flat-fee sponsorship opportunity to an advertiser in combination with a CPM or CPC advertising package. At TSN, advertisers who opt for a sponsorship package will receive preferred positions for their banner ads. With reference to Figure A1.16, note that the *Globe and Mail* digital edition charges a flat fee for their home page sponsorship packages (refer to the top section of the rate card for details).

Programmatic media buying The practice of using algorithms to buy media space in online advertising campaigns.

AUTOMATION AND ONLINE MEDIA BUYING Online media buying is quickly moving toward automated media buying. **Programmatic media buying** is an automated system that considers an advertiser's budget, objectives, and audience data. The system rapidly adjusts dozens of variables in real time (in milliseconds), based on performance, to determine the right campaign settings to achieve a desired return on investment.

It sounds complicated but is simply algorithms that filter impressions based on behavioural data. The system is designed to produce impressions of greater value to the advertiser.

Within this automated system is another process called **real time bidding**. Real time bidding is an auction system in which advertisers bid against each other over individual ad impressions, as those impressions are shown to online users. Ad buyers seek out and bid on auctions that match their campaign criteria (for example, budget, objectives, and target audience). When the bidding is complete, the winning bidder's ad is delivered to the user.

real time bidding An auction system in which advertisers bid against each other over ad impressions, in real time.

From an advertiser's perspective automated media buying offers greater targeting capabilities and produces better impressions in a cost-efficient manner. From an agency's perspective it offers better control over campaign performance and improves spending efficiencies.[6]

SOCIAL MEDIA NETWORK ADVERTISING

The models for buying advertising space on social media involve CPM and CPC. To demonstrate their application we will use Facebook and Google. Which model to use is based on the primary objective of the campaign. For example, if awareness is the objective, the CPM model is chosen since the advertiser will want to maximize the number of impressions. If some kind of action is the objective, the CPC option is chosen.

Facebook gives an advertiser the option of reaching a broad audience, if so desired, or a targeted audience according to various criteria, therefore ensuring an optimum return on investment. There is a set procedure at its website that any advertiser can use to purchase space. It is a step-by-step process. Let's assume a sponsored post is being purchased. The initial step involves the composition of the advertisement. The ad is composed with a title (25 characters or less), body copy (maximum of 135 characters), and an illustration. The advertiser then selects the target audience. An advertiser can target an audience based on demographic variables such as location, gender, age, education, language, and relationship status. Interest-based targeting is also possible by choosing keywords. For example, if an advertiser chooses "soccer" an advertiser will have access to all people that have liked or shown interest in topics around that sport.[7] The advertiser then establishes a daily budget (the maximum an advertiser is willing to spend) and decides which pricing model is preferred (CPM or CPC). The price of the CPC model will be higher than the CPM model but the advertiser will only pay for the actual traffic the click generates.

Google offers a service called AdWords, an auction-style system that determines the ads that appear on the search results page. The advertising cost is based on what the advertiser is seeking (for example, awareness, website traffic, or conversion). If awareness is the objective, costs are based on a CPM basis. If web traffic is the objective, costs are based on CPC basis. Each time a person clicks on the ad, the advertiser pays a fee. For more seasoned advertisers, a CPA (cost-per-acquisition) system is available. In this system an advertiser pays a fee once the person takes specific action at the advertiser's website. The CPC system is the most widely used option on Google.[8]

Media Information Resources

Media planners rely on secondary research data provided by specialist media organizations. **Secondary research** refers to data compiled and published by others for purposes other than resolving a specific problem. In advertising, secondary sources are frequently used to gain access to media information that benefits media analysis and

secondary research Data compiled and published by others for purposes other than resolving a specific problem. In advertising, secondary sources are frequently used to gain access to media information that benefits media analysis and planning.

planning. This information is available through various media associations, specialized media research companies, and individual media outlets (for example, a daily newspaper, national magazine, or a local television station).

Most organizations that provide media data also provide appropriate software that can be used to sift through the data (for example, data can be cross-tabulated with product and service consumption data to determine the best way of reaching a specific target audience). Much of the information is made available through the media research companies and organizations mentioned in the text that follows, or through specialist companies that develop software for use with database information provided by these organizations. Agencies pay for the data provided by the various media research organizations.

BROADCAST MEDIA RESOURCES

The primary organizations that compile television and radio media data on a continuous (year-to-year) basis include Numeris, Nielsen Media Research, and the Television Bureau of Canada.

NUMERIS Numeris is the leading supplier of television and radio audience data to the Canadian broadcast advertising industry. Audience data is collected through a combination of electronic observation (portable people meter or PPM) and diaries that are returned by mail.

diary system A system to collect audience data in which participants complete a seven-day log by recording the television viewing for all television sets in the household for each quarter hour of the day.

When the **diary system** is used for television, participants complete a seven-day log over a three- to four-week period by recording the television viewing for all television sets in the household for each quarter hour of the day from 6 am to 2 am. Information from the returned diaries is scanned and databases of audience behaviour are compiled.

portable people meter (PPM) A form of electronic observation in which household members carry electronic metering devices that register what is being watched on television or listened to on radio every minute of every day.

In the case of the **portable people meter (PPM)**, a form of electronic observation is employed. The Numeris Meter Panel is a group of randomly selected households whose individual members carry special electronic devices—portable people meters (PPM). The meter electronically tracks their radio listening and television viewing habits. The data gathered is automatically downloaded at the end of each day. The compiled data are combined with that of other members in the panel to produce ratings about groups of people (for example, how many households watched particular television shows and for how long). Information can be provided to clients on a local, regional, or national basis.

Numeris data focus on national and local markets. Numeris conducts its diary surveys twice a year—spring and fall—in 40 television markets. Its reports contain current audience ratings and share data, as well as full coverage data for local market stations. The data are presented in four sections: time block, program, time period, and trend. People meter data is available nationally on a weekly basis. Each week the Top 30 programs are listed by audience size for the national market. Separate data are published for Quebec (French-language programs).

rating Television and radio audience estimates expressed as a percentage of a population in a defined geographic area.

The data collected from the diaries is used to establish program ratings. **Ratings** are audience estimates expressed as a percentage of a population in a defined geographic area. For example, if a show has a rating of 20, it reaches 20 percent of that market's population. For some examples of basic trend data available from Numeris, visit www.numeris.ca.

Numeris also compiles radio consumption data on a continuous basis by diary and electronically by portable people meters. Data from the portable people meters is published quarterly. The stations are ranked by market share and the number of people exposed to the station for a minimum amount of time. A sample of the electronically retrieved data published by Numeris appears in Figure A1.17.

FIGURE
A1.17 Radio Tuning Data for the Vancouver Market

PPM Top-line Radio Statistics

NUMERIS

Vancouver CTRL

Survey period: Radio Meter 2014/15 – March 2, 2015 - May 31, 2015
Demographic: A2+
Daypart: Monday to Sunday 2am-2am
Geography: Vancouver CTRL
Data type: Respondent

	March 2, 2015 - May 31, 2015 Average Daily Universe: 2,514,000			
Station	**Market**	**Share (%)**	**Cume (000)**	**Daily Cume (000)**
CBU+	Vancouver CTRL	12.2	772.4	195.0
CBU FM	Vancouver CTRL	3.0	865.0	99.0
CFBTFM	Vancouver CTRL	6.8	2,091.8	346.0
CFMIFM	Vancouver CTRL	7.4	1,614.5	216.0
CFOXFM	Vancouver CTRL	5.7	1,207.1	162.0
CFTE	Vancouver CTRL	0.2	312.6	18.0
CHLGFM	Vancouver CTRL	2.4	1,657.4	141.0
CHMJ	Vancouver CTRL	0.6	764.5	62.0
CHQMFM	Vancouver CTRL	11.4	2,367.5	414.0
CISL	Vancouver CTRL	3.4	542.6	78.0
CJAXFM	Vancouver CTRL	5.7	1,923.3	229.0
CJJRFM	Vancouver CTRL	5.7	1,325.8	157.0
CKKSFM*	Vancouver CTRL/Chilliwack	3.7	1,733.1	235.0
CKNW	Vancouver CTRL	8.1	559.8	158.0
CKPKFM	Vancouver CTRL	2.9	1,297.9	138.0
CKST	Vancouver CTRL	2.8	886.7	119.0
CKWX	Vancouver CTRL	5.7	867.1	201.0
CKZZFM	Vancouver CTRL	7.5	2,112.5	341.0
KWPZFM*	Vancouver CTRL/Abbotsford	1.4	451.7	42.0

*= spill station

TERMS

Share: Within a central market area, the estimated total hours tuned to that station expressed as a percentage of total hours tuned to Total Encoded Radio.

Cume (000): Expressed in thousands, this is the total number of people who were exposed to the stations for at least one minute during the analyzed period.

Average Daily Universe: The average daily universe for the analyzed period. The universe is expressed as daily averages because it changes slightly daily as the intab changes.

© Numeris

A more detailed report based on data collected from diaries is published twice a year. The report contains reach, hours, share data, and demographic profiles for each member station in major markets across Canada. The demographic data allow advertisers to better plan their buys, since they will know the exact profile of each station's audience. Audience data are available based on hours tuned per week, listening by daypart, and listening by location (for example, home, automobile, and other locations). For some samples of basic trend data published by Numeris, visit www.numeris.ca.

NIELSEN MEDIA RESEARCH   Nielsen Media Research provides advertising information services including advertising expenditures, GRP analysis, and creative monitoring services for advertising messages. Its advertising expenditure estimates are available for television (network and spot), radio, magazines, daily newspapers, and out-of-home media. These data allow an advertiser to compare its expenditures against those of its competitors.

Nielsen Media Research also offers a variety of competitive tracking services that provide the quantitative information necessary for strategic determination and tactical execution of communications plans. Advertisers and agencies use Nielsen Media's audience analyses and applications to estimate the future performance of television shows, to execute television buys, and to measure the performance of campaigns. Nielsen's software can be used to perform reach/frequency, duplication, and quintile delivery analyses.[9] For additional information about Nielsen Media Research, visit www.nielsenmedia.com/ca.

TELEVISION BUREAU OF CANADA   The Television Bureau of Canada (TVB) is a sales and marketing resource centre for the commercial television industry. Its mandate is to promote television as an effective advertising medium. Each year, this organization publishes a booklet, *TV Basics*, that contains the latest data on television trends. It covers viewing trends by demographic and geographic variables, programming preferences by demographic variables, and television-station circulation by gender and age for all station markets. The TVB provides such data as viewing by time of day, day of week, and time of year. For additional information about the data provided by the TVB, visit www.tvb.ca.

PRINT MEDIA RESOURCES

The companies and organizations involved in magazine and newspaper research and data collection include Vividata, the Alliance for Audited Media, and the Canadian Circulation Audit Board (CCAB). Vividata is a new data collection that was created by the merger between the Print Measurement Bureau and the Newspaper Audience Databank (NADBank) in 2014. Vivadata conducts one of the most comprehensive consumer surveys in the country, completed by 38 000 Canadians in over 50 markets. The survey generates a full year's database of consumer demographics, media usage, and lifestyle information, as well as attitudinal data and product usage in over three hundred categories. Vividata also offers complete readership metrics, revealing when and what consumers are reading in print and digital formats. This information helps advertisers and advertising agencies develop more efficient media plans to reach specific target markets. For additional information about Vividata, visit www.vividata.ca.

ALLIANCE FOR AUDITED MEDIA   The Alliance for Audited Media (AAM) issues standardized statements verifying circulation statistics for paid-circulation magazines (consumer and business publications) and most daily newspapers in Canada. All publications that are members of the AAM receive an audited **publisher's statement**. This statement is the authority upon which advertising rates are based (verified circulation is used to establish the advertising rate base as shown in the publication's rate card). The statement is issued twice each year. A publisher's statement includes the following information: average paid circulation for the past six months, paid circulation for each issue in the last six months, an analysis of new and renewal subscriptions, paid circulation by county size, and geographic analysis of total paid circulation. For a selection of sample data published by the AAM, refer to www.auditedmedia.com.

Statements include type of circulation (for example, paid or controlled circulation), recipient qualification (for example, distribution to a predetermined target based on demographic data), circulation for the past six months, average paid circulation per issue, and a geographical breakdown of the circulation. Additional information about the CCAB is available at www.bpaww.com.

The CCAB also audits web traffic for 12 daily newspapers. The metrics available include page impressions, user sessions, unique browsers and their frequency, page duration, and user session duration. The availability of web traffic data lets media buyers and advertisers evaluate greater brand reach instead of just circulation.

OUT-OF-HOME MEDIA

CANADIAN OUT-OF-HOME MEASUREMENT BUREAU The Canadian Out-of-Home Measurement Bureau (COMB) audits the circulations for a variety of out-of-home faces including outdoor posters and backlight posters, outdoor digital, mural advertising, street level advertising, and superboards. COMB also audits indoor media that include backlight boards, mini-boards, digital screens, and mall posters.

Audience data are location specific, full coverage, and in-market in nature. Circulation data concerning all outdoor media are based on municipal and provincial traffic counts and converted to circulations according to an established traffic-variation factor. Mall counts are based on observation (head counts) in each location by an independent research firm.

COMB publishes the *COMB Data Report* on a semi-annual basis. The report contains daily and weekly audience averages for each product in each market. Verification reports are also provided. These reports verify that suppliers are delivering what they are contracted to deliver and compare the percentage of audience delivered to what was contracted. Media planners can access COMB Navigator, a planning and reach-frequency analysis tool that adds insight to the outdoor advertising planning process. For more information about COMB, visit www.comb.org.

DIGITAL DATA SOURCES (INTERNET, SOCIAL, AND MOBILE)

Both the Interactive Marketing Bureau (IAB) and comScore Media provide useful information about online media and advertising consumption.

INTERACTIVE ADVERTISING BUREAU The Interactive Advertising Bureau (IAB) is a national organization of Internet publishers, advertisers, and agencies acting as the collective voice to represent companies engaged in selling advertising on Internet-based media. IAB promotes the value of Internet advertising to advertisers and agencies, and serves as an educational resource through which advertisers can increase their knowledge and gain a competitive edge in the marketplace.

publisher's statement A statement published by the Alliance for Audited Media (AAM) twice a year that is the authority upon which advertising rates are based.

Canadian Circulations Audit Board (CCAB) The CCAB, the Canadian division of BPA Worldwide, audits all paid, controlled, or any combination of paid and controlled circulation for business and farm publications, consumer magazines, and community and daily newspapers throughout Canada.

The IAB actively promotes advertising standards and guidelines that make it easier to plan, buy, execute, track, and evaluate online advertising plans. As well, it provides cross-media usage data via an annual research study and other interactive research.[10] For more information about the IAB, visit www.iabcanada.com.

COMSCORE CANADA   comScore Canada is an Internet audience measurement service that reports details of website usage, visitor demographics, and detailed information for online search behaviour.

A variety of quantitative data is available to advertisers, including measures for a website's unique visitors; reach; average usage days per user; average unique pages per user per month; average minutes spent per person per page per month; and age, gender, and other demographic characteristics of visitors.

Media Metrix Multi-Platform is one of comScore's analytic tools that offers the industry's first comprehensive view of digital consumer behaviour across desktop computers, smartphones, and tablets. Data is collected from more than 9000 digital media entities in Canada including unduplicated audience size, demographic composition, engagement, and performance within key user segments. All of these metrics can be compared across digital media platforms and can be used to understand incremental activity coming from each platform by expanding your potential audience.[11]

comScore also provides an array of media insights aimed at understanding and leveraging social media conversations and provides a full suite of media measurement metrics that can be directly compared to other types of media. comScore data include demographic and behavioural composition of a brand's social media audience, the reach and frequency of social media brand impressions, and the ability to tie social media exposure to desired consumer behaviours, including brand engagement and spending propensity. Similar information is available for mobile web audiences.[12] For more information, go to www.comscore.com.

Research Data by Individual Media

The specific media vehicles often conduct their own marketing research or use research data provided by independent sources such as those just described. These data provide advertisers and agencies with objective, reliable information showing the relative strengths of the given medium as an advertising vehicle. In local market situations, a daily newspaper or a local radio station provides advertisers and agencies with data to assist them in the decision-making process. Here, local media compete with each other for advertising revenue, so comparisons on criteria such as reach, readership, number of people listening and watching, and so on are inevitable. When assessing this type of data, the advertiser should ensure that the data have been audited and that they have been verified by an independent organization. Much of this data is available at the website of the particular magazine, newspaper, radio station, and so on.

The same situation exists for magazines and newspapers. All magazines and newspapers have their circulation and readership data readily available for review by advertisers and agencies. The viewer of such information should ensure it is audited data, possibly audited by the various research organizations cited in this appendix.

REVIEW QUESTIONS

1. Calculate the cost of the following newspaper campaign. Refer to Figure A1.2 for rate card information.

   Newspaper: *The Globe and Mail,*
   Metro Edition,
   Report on Business Section
   Ad Size: 4 columns wide by 6 column inches deep
   Colour: All ads are black and white
   Frequency: 2 ads per week (Wednesday and Friday)
   Continuity: 8 weeks
   Rate: Transient

2. Calculate the total cost of the following magazine campaign. Refer to Figure A1.6 for rate card information.

   Magazine: *Canadian Geographic*
   Ad Size: Double-page spread
   Frequency: 4 insertions

3. Calculate the total cost of the following magazine campaign. Refer to Figure A1.6 for rate card information.

   Magazine: *Canadian Geographic*
   Ad Size: 1/2 page
   Frequency: 8 insertions

4. Calculate the total cost of the following radio campaign. Refer to Figure A1.12 for rate card information.

   Station: CJAZ-FM
   Nature of Plan: Specific times requested during breakfast and drive periods

   Breakfast: 8 spots per week
   Drive: 8 spots per week
   Continuity: 6 weeks

5. Calculate the total cost of a 16-spot weekly reach plan for the same period of time as in Question 4 on CJAZ-FM radio. Refer to Figure A1.12 for rate card information. When the total costs of the reach plan are compared to the total costs of the specific request plan in Question 4, how much does the advertiser save by using the reach plan?

6. Calculate the total cost of the following outdoor campaign. Refer to Figure A1.13 for rate card information.

   Medium: CBS Outdoor Transit Shelters
   Markets and GRPs:
   Halifax (CMA), 50 GRP
   Calgary (CMA), 50 GRP
   London (CMA), 75 GRP
   Continuity: 16 weeks in all markets

7. Calculate the total cost of the following outdoor campaign. Refer to Figure A1.14 for rate card information.

   Medium: Outfront Media Posters
   Markets and GRPs:
   Montreal, 50 GRP
   Toronto, 25 GRP

Vancouver, 25 GRP

Continuity: Montreal and Vancouver, 16 weeks;
Toronto, 12 weeks.

8. Calculate the total cost of delivering a $2.00 coupon to 4 million Canadian households using Valassis Canada cooperative mailings. The estimated redemption rate for the offer is 2.5 percent. Refer to Figure A1.15 for rate card information.

9. Calculate the total cost of the following online banner campaign. Refer to Figure A1.16 for rate card information.

Medium: globeandmail.com
Ad Type: Canvas Unit
Location: Lifestyle Section
Impressions: 5 million

10. Calculate the total cost of the following online banner campaign. Refer to Figure A1.16 for rate card information.

Medium: globeandmail.com
Ad type: Standard IAB format, section sponsorship
Location: Business Section
Impressions: 6 million

ENDNOTES

1. Jay Busbee, "2015 Super Bowl Ads will cost $4.5 million apiece," *Yahoo Sports*, June 3, 2014, http://sports.yahoo.com/blogs/nfl-shutdown-corner/2015-super-bowl-ads-will-cost--4-5-million-apiece-135554114.html.

2. Susan Krashinsky, "A Super Bowl-sized Challenge for Canadian Advertisers," *The Globe and Mail*, January 22, 2015, www.theglobeandmail.com/report-on-business/industry-news/marketing/commercials-for-the-big-game-a-super-bowl-sized-challenge-for-advertisers/article22591070/.

3. Epsilon TargetSource Canada – Expecting a Baby Mailing List, http://lists.nextmark.com/market?page=order/online/datacard&id=224021.

4. Rates obtained from Canada Post, www.canadapost.com.

5. Esther Shein, "Banner Ads: Past, Present, and Future?" *CMO.com*, April 24, 2012, www.cmo.com/artices/2012/4/24/banner-ads-past-present-and-future.html.

6. "Real Time Bidding Explained," *Acuity*, October 30, 2015, www.acuityads.com/real-time-bidding.

7. Alicia Andrioch, "Facebook Rolling out New Targeting Options for Marketers," *Marketing*, February 21, 2014, www.marketingmag.ca.

8. "AdWords: Advertise Your Business on Google," Google, https://support.google.com/adwords/answer/1704424?hl=en.

9. "Television Data sources," Canadian Media Directors' Council *Media Digest*, 2011–12, p. 32.

10. www.iabcanada.com.

11. www.comscore.com.

12. www.comscore.com.

Market Background

MARKET ANALYSIS

The quick-serve restaurant (QSR) market is a mature market. The degree of competition among the various banners is intensive and extensive.

- The restaurant industry is growing only marginally (+1.0 percent a year).

- Quick-serve segment sales amounted to $25.1 billion in Canada (2014).

- The quick-serve segment is saturated and offers limited growth potential over the next five years.

- The casual dining segment, composed of mid-range establishments such as Montana's and Kelsey's, is experiencing higher growth (+3 percent a year).

- The sandwich segment of the market is presently worth $3.8 billion and accounts for about 15 percent of the quick-serve restaurant market.

- The sandwich segment is growing at the rate of +3.0 percent a year.

EXTERNAL INFLUENCES ON THE MARKET

ECONOMIC TRENDS

- The cyclical nature of the economy influences the volume of business in the QSR market segment. Canada's economic slowdown has had an impact on restaurant traffic and sales.

DEMOGRAPHIC TRENDS

- As the population ages, restaurants must reposition themselves to maintain customers.

- Youthful generations who are influenced less by traditional marketing methods are the next generation of customers.

- Ethnic Canadians are creating a demand for ethnic dishes in QSR establishments.

SOCIAL TRENDS

- A healthier lifestyle is an ambition for many people.

- People are maintaining an active lifestyle, but are subject to indulgences.

- Youthful generations favour non-traditional methods for learning about products; peer influences are very important.

- Time-pressed consumers are constantly searching for products and services offering convenience.

TECHNOLOGY

- Non-traditional methods of communication are popular with younger generations of consumers.

- Multi-tasking consumers refer to several media at the same time, so reaching consumers is now more challenging for marketing organizations.

409

CONSUMER DATA Consumers indicate that the following criteria are important when selecting a quick-serve restaurant:

- Value (in terms of food quality at competitive prices).

- Reduced wait times.

- Convenience (location in time of need is important along with drive-thru service).

- Food served "their" way.

COMPETITIVE ANALYSIS

Mr. Sub competes directly with Subway and Quizno's in the fresh sandwich segment. Quizno's is somewhat different, as it specializes in hot-served or toasted sandwiches.

Subway dominates the sandwich segment. Much of its strength can be attributed to the number of restaurant locations it operates across Canada.

McDonald's and Tim Hortons compete in the sandwich segment, but sandwiches account for only a portion of their business. Both restaurants offer only a limited selection of fresh and toasted sandwiches, but are very popular destinations for quick meals.

Market shares for the national chains (in the sandwich segment only) are as follows:

Chain	Share	Locations
Subway	25.0	3000
Tim Hortons	10.0	3500
Mr. Sub	6.5	375
McDonald's	3.5	1400
Quizno's	3.0	325

SUBWAY As the commercials say, "Subway . . . Eat Fresh." Subway is positioned as the premier destination for fresh sandwiches. Subway's success in the QSR market is due to the following factors:

- The brand name is synonymous with fresh food.

- High-quality and healthy food products are available.

- It has an association with social responsibility causes such as fighting childhood obesity.

- Subway reacts quickly to consumer taste preferences.

- Financial resources are available for marketing and marketing communications.

- It has extensive distribution with 3000 restaurants coast to coast.

- Its successful rewards program encourages loyalty.

QUIZNO'S The market share for Quizno's has tripled in the past two years. The company's success is based on the following factors:

- It claims to own the "toasted" and "grilled" segment (even though other brands offer similar items).

- An advertising campaign that included celebrities such as Don Cherry and Tie Domi helped establish the brand.

- A focus on quality justifies higher prices; consumers seem willing to pay more for a sandwich.

BRAND ANALYSIS (MR. SUB)

Mr. Sub was the original submarine sandwich retailer in Canada, but over the years it has not maintained marketing and marketing communications support at a sufficient level to build the brand. Mr. Sub has lost considerable market share to Subway.

Mr. Sub's present position in the marketplace is a result of the following factors:

- It is a popular destination for former generations of young people.

- Quality products are offered at competitive prices.

- Its product range includes popular items such as sandwiches, wraps, salads, and hot and cold beverages.

- Its present positioning fits with customer expectations and is based on "quality, freshness, and quantity."

- It has a loyal following among older age groups (45+ years).

- The brand is not well known among younger age groups.

- Only 375 locations (1:8 ratio of stores compared to Subway) exist coast to coast, with more than 60 percent of locations in Southern Ontario.

- Investment in advertising and marketing communications is much lower than that of its competitors.

SWOT ANALYSIS

BRAND STRENGTHS

- Products offered are as good as the leading brand.

- The brand is well known with older consumers (a sense of loyalty exists).

- Its good reputation will enhance new marketing initiatives.

BRAND WEAKNESSES

- Young consumers are unfamiliar with the brand and its offerings.

- It has low visibility among primary targets due to lack of marketing communications activity.

- Lack of availability (convenience); its key competitor has a significant distribution advantage.

MARKETING OPPORTUNITIES

- Fit the brand into healthier and contemporary lifestyles.

- Take a fresh marketing approach to attract a younger target audience.

- Appeal to consumer demand for value (a combination of convenience and quality).

THREATS

- The marketing and financial resources of direct competitors are extensive.

- Taste preferences among consumers (less demand for fresh) shift.

- Further encroachment from other fast-food restaurants and casual dining establishments is possible.

Marketing Communications Plan

TARGET MARKET

To rebuild/rejuvenate Mr. Sub requires that greater attention be given to younger generations of consumers because they are the primary consumers of QSR establishments.

PRIMARY TARGET

Demographic

- Males and females 15 to 29 years old.
- Secondary and post-secondary education level.
- Students and newly employed graduates.
- Income not important.

Psychographic

- Time-pressed and fast-paced daily routines.
- Socially active (peer groups are influencers).
- Technologically savvy (online and mobile communications generation).
- Active with a healthy outlook.

Geographic

- All across Canada, with emphasis on major urban markets.

SECONDARY TARGET

- Males and females 35+ years old.
- Young families.
- Active lifestyles.
- Located in major urban markets.
- More inclined to refer to traditional media for information.

MARKETING OBJECTIVES

1. To increase market share from 6.5 percent to 7.0 percent.
2. To position Mr. Sub as a restaurant offering healthy and hearty sandwiches at reasonable prices.

MARKETING COMMUNICATIONS GOAL (CHALLENGE)

- To create more top-of-mind awareness for Mr. Sub among younger generations of consumers and secure a place on their "consideration list."
- To associate Mr. Sub with a contemporary urban lifestyle that will appeal to the primary and secondary targets.

MARKETING COMMUNICATIONS OBJECTIVES

1. To achieve a 70 percent brand awareness level among the primary target market.
2. To achieve a trial purchase rate of 20 percent among the primary target market.

3. To communicate the quality, variety, and freshness of the various menu items offered by Mr. Sub.
4. To create an image for Mr. Sub that is in keeping with contemporary lifestyles.
5. To build buzz for Mr. Sub among a new generation of consumers currently unfamiliar with the brand.

MARKETING COMMUNICATIONS STRATEGY

BUDGET   For the first year of the campaign, a budget of $3.0 million is available to cover all marketing communications expenditures. The budget will cover a multimedia campaign and will include various integrated marketing communications activities.

POSITIONING STRATEGY STATEMENT   The current positioning strategy will be retained and is described as follows:

> "Mr. Sub is a restaurant that offers the best in terms of fresh, healthy food served quickly. Mr. Sub prides itself on giving the customer a little bit more for their money."

MARKETING COMMUNICATIONS MIX   A mix of marketing communications elements will combine to create a synergistic impact on the primary and secondary target markets. The various elements of the mix will each contribute to achieving the marketing communications objectives. The marketing communications mix will include traditional media advertising, sales promotions, event marketing, and online and interactive communications. The rationale for this combination of media is as follows:

- **Advertising:** Traditional forms of media advertising are needed to make a "visual impression" in key urban markets and to achieve the awareness objective.

- **Sales Promotion:** A variety of "incentives" are needed to achieve the trial purchase objectives. Some street-level activities will help achieve the "brand buzz" objective.

- **Event Marketing:** A significant event will be staged in Toronto that will start an association between Mr. Sub and basketball (a popular and growing sport). Basketball appeals directly to the primary male target, and the street-level marketing event will create buzz for Mr. Sub.

- **Online Communications:** The primary target audience is the biggest user of online and mobile technologies; therefore, these media are both effective and efficient for delivering Mr. Sub's message.

ADVERTISING PLAN: CREATIVE
CREATIVE OBJECTIVES

1. To communicate that Mr. Sub offers quality sandwiches, wraps, and salads.
2. To portray Mr. Sub as an appealing restaurant destination suited to a contemporary urban lifestyle.

CREATIVE STRATEGY   Mr. Sub does not have the physical presence of its primary competitor; therefore, the message will focus on the quality of the food (scrumptious shots of sandwiches and wraps) and people (teens and 20-somethings) enjoying the food. It's worth searching a little harder for!

Selected messages in various media will also include members of the secondary target enjoying the Mr. Sub experience.

Central Theme   All messages, regardless of media, will show the sandwich being created or the finished product; a mouth-watering selection of sandwiches that will satisfy any type of hunger will be visually presented in advertisements.

Appeal Technique   The message will combine a positive appeal (with an emphasis on the product and what it looks like) with a lifestyle appeal (the target will be shown enjoying the food).

Tone and Style   A straightforward approach will be used. All messages will be clear, product focused, and easy to understand. Print media will stress visual imagery by showing the "scrumptious" aspect of the sandwiches.

Tagline   Some options to summarize the message strategy include:

> "Mr. Sub. More than enough."

> "Mr. Sub. Enough and then some."

> "Mr. Sub. It's all about the sandwich."

CREATIVE EXECUTION   The campaign will include 30-second television spots, 4-colour newspaper inserts, outdoor posters, online banner ads, and a social media component. Selected messages will encourage consumers to visit the Mr. Sub website to participate in a variety of new video games.

Newspaper and outdoor media will be product focused, while broadcast media will feature consumer enjoyment and the fun associated with the Mr. Sub experience.

Integrated aspects of the campaign will include trial incentives delivered by newspaper inserts, a contest, a street-level marketing program in Toronto, and a television and online sponsorship element. Creating awareness for the brand and tagline will be a priority throughout the campaign.

ADVERTISING PLAN: MEDIA

BUDGET   A budget of approximately $2.0 million has been allocated for media advertising to cover a one-year period from January 2016 to December 2016.

MEDIA OBJECTIVES

Who   As described earlier, the primary target is teens and 20-somethings residing in urban locations. The secondary target is adults 35+ years residing in urban markets.

What   The message to be communicated will focus on the scrumptious quality of the food and people enjoying the Mr. Sub experience.

When   The launch phase of the plan will be given heavier support to set the new campaign in motion. Spending will be slightly higher than normal in the summer when promotions are in progress. A steady spending pattern will be implemented at other times of the year.

Where   The campaign will be national in scope with additional emphasis placed on key urban markets.

How   Creating awareness and developing a new image for a brand takes time; therefore, reach and frequency will be a priority in the initial phase of the campaign (the first three months). Continuity will be more important as the campaign progresses.

MEDIA STRATEGY

Target Market Strategy   In the initial phase of the campaign, a shotgun strategy is recommended to reach the primary and secondary target markets. A multimedia approach will be employed to achieve reach objectives. As the campaign progresses, there will be a shift to a profile-matching strategy to effectively reach the primary target.

Market Coverage   Since this is a national campaign, media that reach the national market will be used. Supplementary media will be added in urban markets to increase reach and frequency against the primary and secondary targets. The budget available will determine the extent of key market coverage.

Timing   Spending will be heavier in the initial phase (first three months), reflecting a blitz strategy. Spending will then taper off for a few months but rebound upward during the summer months when various integrated marketing activities are scheduled. For the remaining months of the campaign, spending will follow a moderate but steady pattern.

Reach/Frequency/Continuity   The initial phase of the campaign is devoted to attracting a new target market to Mr. Sub. Therefore, reach and frequency are the priorities. Various media will be employed to reach the target market in different ways. As the campaign progresses, continuity of message will be more of a priority. Media advertising will be scheduled in flights to ensure maximum impact, regardless of the media employed.

MEDIA SELECTION RATIONALE   A multimedia campaign that embraces network television, specialty television stations, key market daily newspapers (for inserts), out-of-home advertising, and online media is recommended.

Television   Television reaches the national target audience with a strong visual message (the message emphasis on food and friends is best delivered by television). Prime-time ad placements will ensure a high level of brand recognition. A television sponsorship opportunity will associate Mr. Sub with basketball, a popular and growing sport in Canada.

Print   A combination of targeted lifestyle magazines, newspapers, and inserts in selected daily newspapers will assist in creating brand awareness and distributing trial incentives. Inserts will be used exclusively to announce discounted meal combinations and special coupon offers to encourage trial visits.

Out-of-Home   In major markets, outdoor posters will deliver the message while people are "on the move." The decision about where to dine is often made when people are in transit, presenting an ideal opportunity to remind them about Mr. Sub.

Online   Since the primary target market spends a lot of time online there is an opportunity for consumers to interact directly with the brand. In conjunction with messages delivered by other media, the target will be encouraged to visit a new Mr. Sub website to play a variety of new sports games. Banner ads will also appear on two third-party sites with sponsored posts in social media to move viewers to the Mr. Sub website.

MEDIA EXECUTION   The CTV Network and TVA Quebec are recommended to reach a broad cross-section of the population. TSN and The Score are recommended to reach the primary target market.

Outdoor posters will complement television ads and reach a broad cross-section of the population in 12 major markets across Canada. Newspaper ads in local markets will deliver incentives to all members of the target audience.

Online and social media placements will effectively reach the primary target and encourage engagement with the brand.

For a summary of all media activity (timing and expenditures), refer to Figures A2.1 and A2.2.

FIGURE A2.1

Television Advertising

Network	# of Spots	Cost/Spot	Total Cost
CTV	40	$16 500	$660 000
TVA	30	$3000	$90 000
TSN	40	$2500	$100 000
Sportsnet	40	$2000	$80 000
Total	**185**		**$930 000**
Sportsnet sponsorship			$40 000
Total TV Costs			**$970 000**

Note: All ads are 30-second spots.

FIGURE A2.2

Outdoor Advertising

Market	GRPs	Weeks	Total Cost
Toronto/Hamilton	25	12	$295 800
Vancouver	25	12	$223 500
Ottawa	25	12	$108 600
Calgary	25	12	$64 800
Edmonton	25	12	$57 600
Quebec City	25	8	$40 800
Winnipeg	25	8	$20 800
London	25	8	$19 600
Kitchener	25	8	$22 200
Halifax	25	8	$13 400
Regina	25	8	$7200
St. John's	25	8	$8600
Total Cost			**$882 900**

Note: All ads are horizontal outdoor posters.

SALES PROMOTION PLAN

PROMOTION OBJECTIVES

1. To encourage trial purchase among primary and secondary targets.
2. To secure interactivity between the consumer and the brand by encouraging consumers to visit the Mr. Sub website.

PROMOTION STRATEGY   Trial coupons offering a discounted price for any sandwich or wrap will be distributed by daily newspapers in major urban markets. In many cases, the daily newspapers offer reach well beyond their designated market area.

Consumers visiting a Mr. Sub restaurant during the first two months of the campaign will receive a coded entry form for a contest. Consumers must visit the Mr. Sub website to enter their contest code.

SALES PROMOTION EXECUTION

Trial Coupon   A $1.50 coupon for the purchase of any sandwich or wrap (with a two-month expiry date) will be circulated. The initial coupon drop is timed for February/March.

Contest   A grand prize and two secondary prizes will be awarded:

- Grand Prize: $25 000 cash.
- Second Prize: One of three all-expenses-paid ski trips for two to Whistler/Blackcomb (value: $5000 each).
- Third Prize: One of five Sony HDTV flat-screen televisions (value: $2000 each).

The contest is open to all residents of Canada (excluding residents of Quebec), with winners randomly drawn from all entries received. Winners will be announced at the Mr. Sub website the day following the closing date of the contest. Complete contest details are available at the Mr. Sub website and all restaurant locations.

Trial Coupon   A second wave of $1.50 coupons (with a two-month expiry date) will be distributed by national daily newspapers in the August/September period.

The coupon inserts will be distributed via daily newspapers in the following markets: Toronto, Hamilton, Vancouver, Ottawa, Calgary, Edmonton, Quebec City, Winnipeg, London, Kitchener, Halifax, Regina, Saskatoon, St. John's, and Windsor.

Coupon inserts will be distributed by community newspapers in the following markets: Oshawa/Whitby/Clarington, St. Catharines, Niagara Falls, Cambridge, Barrie, Kingston, Peterborough, and Sudbury.

For cost details on these sales promotion activities, see Figures A2.3 and A2.4.

Component	Circulation	Cost/M	Frequency	Total Cost
Distribution	2 785 000	$40	2	$222 800
Printing	2 785 000	$10	2	$55 700
Coupon Redemption*				$83 500
Total Cost				**$362 000**

Note: * Circulation × Redemption Rate × Value of Coupon × Frequency = Coupon Cost
2 785 000 × .01 × $1.50 × 2 = $83 500

FIGURE A2.3

Sales Promotion Costs for Coupon Inserts

Prize	# Winners	Prize Cost	Total Cost
Cash Grand Prize	1	$25 000	$25 000
Ski Trips	3	$5000	$15 000
Sony HDTV Flat Screens	5	$2000	$10 000
Total Cost			**$50 000**

FIGURE A2.4

Sales Promotion Costs

ONLINE AND INTERACTIVE PLAN

OBJECTIVES

1. To increase brand awareness among teens and 20-something males.
2. To associate the Mr. Sub brand with a sporting activity popular with young urban males.

STRATEGY A combination that involves online banner advertising, social media, television and online sponsorship, and a brand new website will help build awareness among the primary target and help associate the brand with an urban lifestyle.

EXECUTION

Banner Ads Banners will be scheduled on the TSN and Sportsnet websites, which are popular with a younger male audience.

Sponsorship In conjunction with Sportsnet television channel, Mr. Sub will sponsor a highlight segment shown once a week during the last four months of the basketball season. The segment called "Plays of the Week" features all the exciting dunks and scoring plays from the previous week's NBA action. The same video clip sponsored by Mr. Sub will be available on the Sportsnet website.

Social Media Sponsored posts on Facebook and promoted tweets on Twitter will directly reach the primary and secondary targets. Sharing among friends will expand message reach.

Mr. Sub Website An entirely new website will be constructed that will offer essential product information and provide opportunities for consumers to engage in some entertaining activities. A variety of sports and action video games will be available for play at the site.

Refer to Figure A2.5 for online and interactive cost details.

FIGURE A2.5

Online and Interactive Costs

Site	Impressions/Month	CPM	#Months	Total Cost
TSN.ca	800 000	$30	6	$144 000
Sportsnet	400 000	$20	6	$48 000
Facebook	1 000 000	$15	9	$135 000
Twitter	500 000	$10	9	$45 000
Website				$200 000
Total Cost				**$572 000**

Note: Mr. Sub website costs include development and maintenance costs of the site.

EVENT MARKETING PLAN

To further develop the association between Mr. Sub and basketball, a street-level marketing event is planned in conjunction with the Toronto Raptors basketball team. This event fits with the Raptors' objective of being "more visible in the community" and provides an opportunity to generate positive publicity for the Raptors in the off-season.

OBJECTIVES

1. To encourage members of the primary target market to participate in a "3-on-3" basketball tournament.
2. To create buzz for Mr. Sub in a key urban market.

STRATEGY To associate Mr. Sub with the growing sport of basketball (playground, high school, college, and university level) in a key urban market.

To associate Mr. Sub with the Toronto Raptors (an exciting team that is creating its own "buzz" in Toronto, based on recent player acquisitions and performance).

EXECUTION

- The Mr. Sub Toronto Raptors 3-on-3 Tournament (straight elimination) will be held on half-size courts at Exhibition Place, Toronto, over one weekend in July.

- A predetermined number of teams (128 teams) will compete against each other in four age categories: 8 to 12 years, 13 to 16 years, 17 to 21 years, and 21 to 30 years. The youngest age category will attract the children of Mr. Sub's secondary target, while the older categories will attract the primary target. A total of 32 teams will be entered in each age category.

- Toronto Raptors players will participate in a skills competition to determine "the most skilled Raptor."

- Prizes will be awarded to each member of the winning team (five members on each team) in each category.

- Mr. Sub kiosks will be set up at the event to serve meals.

- The general public will be invited to the event, though all viewing of the games and Raptor skills competition will be on a "stand and watch" basis.

- A one-month outdoor ad campaign just prior to the event will create awareness and recruit teams for the event. A press release will also be issued to the media outlining all event-related details.

Cost details for this event marketing activity are included in Figure A2.6.

For summary details of all marketing communications expenditures and the timing of all activities, refer to Figures A2.7 through A2.9.

The marketing communications budget will be reviewed quarterly. Adjustments to the budget will be made when necessary.

FIGURE A2.6

Event Marketing Costs

Item or Activity	Estimated Cost
Equipment Rental	$50 000
Site Rental	$25 000
Bump-in (Setup)	$10 000
Staffing	$10 000
Security	$8000
Bump-out (Teardown)	$10 000
Administration Costs	$15 000
Prizes	$40 000
Miscellaneous Costs	$10 000
Total Cost	**$178 000**

Activity	Expenditure	% of Total
Television	$970 000	32.2
Outdoor	$882 900	29.3
Sales Promotions (Coupons and Contest)	$412 050	13.7
Online and Interactive	$572 000	18.9
Event Marketing	$178 000	5.9
Total	**$3 014 950**	**100.0**

Estimated Budget (Based on Activities)	$3 014 950
Plan Budget	$3 000 000
Expenditure Over Budget	$(14 950)

FIGURE
A2.9   **Marketing Communications Calendar**

Activity	Jan.	Feb.	Mar.	Apr.	May	June	July	Aug.	Sept.	Oct.	Nov.	Dec.
Television												
CTV	8	8	8	4	4				4	4		
TVA	5	5	5								5	5
TSN	8	8					8				8	8
Sportsnet	8	6	8	6					6	6		
Sportsnet Sponsorship	←			→								
Outdoor												
Top 5 Markets		←	→			↔						
Remaining Markets	↔					↔						
Sales Promotions												
Coupon Insert		←	→					←	→			
Contest		←	→									
Online												
TSN.ca						←		→			←	→
Sportsnet.ca	←			→							←	→
Facebook + Twitter				←								→
Mr. Sub Website	←											→
Event Marketing												
3-on-3 Basketball						↔						

Notes:

Television: Figures represent the number of spots on each network each month. All spots are 30-seconds long and run in prime time.

Outdoor: Top five markets include Toronto/Hamilton, Vancouver, Ottawa, Calgary, and Edmonton. Remaining markets include Quebec City, Winnipeg, London, Kitchener, Halifax, Regina, and St. John's. All ads are outdoor posters.

Magazines: Figures indicate one insertion in each month scheduled (*Maclean's* is a weekly magazine; others are monthly). All ads are 1P, 4-colour.

Online and Social: 800 000 impressions monthly on TSN.ca; 400 000 impressions monthly on the sportsnet.ca; 1 000 000 monthly on Facebook; and 500 000 impressions monthly on Twitter.

Coupon Insert: Coupons will be distributed in key market daily newspapers or community newspapers. Dailies include: *Toronto Star, Toronto Sun, Vancouver Sun, Vancouver Province, Ottawa Citizen, Ottawa Sun, Calgary Herald, Calgary Sun, Edmonton Journal, Edmonton Sun, Regina Leader Post, Saskatoon Star Phoenix, Winnipeg Free Press, Hamilton Spectator, Kitchener Record, London Free Press, Windsor Star, Halifax Chronicle Herald,* and *St. John's Telegram.* Community newspapers include: *Oshawa/Whitby/Clarington This Week, St. Catharines News, Niagara This Week, Cambridge Times, Barrie Examiner Complimentary, Kingston This Week, Peterborough This Week,* and *Sudbury Northern Life.*

Glossary

Acquisition strategy – A plan of action for acquiring companies that represent attractive financial opportunities.

Ad view – See Impression.

Advertising – A paid media-delivered message by an identified sponsor designed to stimulate a positive response from a target audience.

Advertising equivalency – A mathematical model that equates public relations to an advertising value by evaluating the space occupied by a public relations message in relation to advertising space.

Advertising objectives – Goal statements for advertisements that include quantitative measures related to behaviour or other relevant issues.

Advertising plan – A plan that includes creative and media components.

Agate line – A non-standardized unit of space measurement, equal to one column wide and 1/14 deep, used in newspaper advertising.

Ambush marketing – A strategy used by non-sponsors of an event to capitalize on the prestige and popularity of the event by giving the false impression they are sponsors.

Annual report – A document published annually by an organization primarily to provide current and prospective investors and stakeholders with financial data and a description of the company's operations.

Approach – The initial contact with a customer.

Arena and stadium advertising – Advertising within arenas and stadiums, from the door to the court, rink, or playing field.

Attitude – An individual's feelings, favourable or unfavourable, toward an idea or object.

Attribute – A descriptive feature of a product.

Backlit (backlight) poster – A luminous outdoor sign printed on polyvinyl material.

Banner – Online, a graphic advertising image (usually horizontal or vertical in shape) that appears on a webpage.

Behavioural targeting – A means of delivering online ads based on a consumer's previous surfing patterns.

Benefit – The value a customer attaches to a brand attribute.

Big box – An online ad shaped like a large rectangle that offers greater width and depth to an ad.

Billboard – See Poster.

Blitz schedule – The scheduling of media advertising so that most spending is front-loaded in the schedule; usually involves a lot of money spent in a short period.

Blocking chart – See Media calendar.

Blog – A frequent, chronological publication of personal thoughts at a website.

Body language – See Non-verbal communication.

Bonus pack – The temporary offering of a larger package size (for example, 20 percent more) for the same price as the regular size.

Booklet (brochure) – A multiple-page document distributed to consumers and other interested stakeholders.

Borrowed-interest strategy – A plan to promote a marketing activity that is related to a product.

Bounce back – See Statement stuffer.

Brand – An identifying mark, symbol, word or words, or combination of mark and words that separates one product from another product; can also be defined as the sum of all tangible and intangible characteristics that make a unique offer to customers.

Brand democratization – A concept that states that consumers are now in charge of brand marketing (because of the amount of consumer-generated content produced and distributed online) instead of brand marketers being in control.

Brand design – A concept that attempts to include an experience in the design of a product (for example, the design may trigger an emotional response).

Brand development index (BDI) – The percentage of a brand's sales in an area in relation to the population in that area; determines if the brand is underdeveloped or overdeveloped in each area.

Brand equity – The value (monetary or otherwise) of a brand to its owners; influenced by brand name awareness, degree of customer loyalty, perceived quality, and the brand's association with a certain attribute.

Brand insistence – A situation where the consumer searches the market for the specific brand.

Brand logo – A symbol that plays a key role in branding and creating an image.

Brand loyalty – The degree of attachment to a particular brand expressed by a consumer. There are three stages of brand loyalty: brand recognition, brand preference, and brand insistence.

Brand manager – An individual assigned responsibility for the development and implementation of marketing programs for a specific product or group of products.

Brand name – That part of a brand that can be spoken.

Brand preference – The situation where a brand is perceived as an acceptable alternative by a customer and will be purchased if it is available.

Brand recognition – Customer awareness of the brand name and package.

Branded content (product integration) – The integration of brand name goods and services into the script (storyline) of a television show or movie. The brand name is clearly mentioned and sometimes discussed.

Breakage – See Slippage (breakage).

Broadsheet – A large newspaper with a fold in its middle.

Brochure – See Booklet.

Build-up schedule – The scheduling of media advertising so that the weight of advertising starts out light and gradually builds over a period of time; also called a teaser campaign.

Bump-in (setup) – The setting up of structures and other equipment at an event.

Bump-out (teardown) – The process of dismantling everything after an event.

Bus back – A vinyl wrap advertisement that appears on the back end of a vehicle.

Bus mural – An advertisement in the form of a vinyl covering that appears on one side of the vehicle.

Business-to-business (B2B) market – A market of goods and services needed to produce a product or service, promote an idea, or operate a business.

Buying centre – An informal purchasing process in which individuals in an organization perform particular roles but may not have direct responsibility for the actual decision.

Buying committee – A formal buying structure in an organization that brings together expertise from the various functional areas to share in the buying decision process.

Call centre – A central operation from which a company conducts its inbound and outbound telemarketing programs.

Catalogue – A reference publication, usually annual or seasonal, distributed by large retail chains and direct marketing companies.

Central theme – The glue that binds various creative elements of a campaign together; transferable from one medium to another.

Cinema advertising – Print advertising inside film theatres and broadcast advertising on screens; options include television-style ads on screen, slides, posters, and ads printed on tickets.

Circulation – The average number of copies per issue of a publication sold by subscription, distributed free to predetermined recipients, carried with other publications, or made available through retail distributors.

Circulation list – A publication's subscription list that targets potential customers based on specified demographic characteristics, interests, or activities.

Classified advertising – Print advertising in which similar goods and services are grouped together in categories under appropriate headings.

Click fraud – A situation where bots that look like human web users click on advertisements.

Click (clickthrough) rate – The percentage of impressions (ad views) that resulted in a click; determines the success of an ad in attracting visitors to click on it.

Clicks (clickthroughs) – The number of times users click on a banner (clicking transfers the user to another website).

Clickthroughs – See Clicks.

Clipping service – An organization that scans the print and broadcast media in search of a company's or brand's name.

Closed-ended questioning – See Fixed-response questioning.

Closing – Asking for the order at the appropriate time in a sales presentation.

Closing cue – An indication that the buyer is ready to buy; can be expressed verbally or nonverbally.

Cluster – Ads grouped in a block of time during a break in a program or between programs, or in a section of a publication.

Clutter – The amount of advertising in a particular medium.

Cognitive dissonance – A feeling of doubt or regret in a consumer's mind once a buying decision has been made.

Cold canvass – The process of calling on people or organizations without appointments or advance knowledge of them.

Collateral materials – Visual aids used by sales representatives in sales presentations, such as price lists, sales brochures, and digital materials.

Communication – The transmission, receipt, and processing of information between a sender and a receiver.

Compiled list – A direct mail list prepared from government, census, telephone, warranty, or other publication information.

Consultative selling – A form of selling that stresses open, two-way communication between a buyer and seller.

Consumer behaviour – The combined acts carried out by individuals choosing and using goods and services, including the decision-making processes that determine these acts.

Consumer promotion – An incentive offered to consumers to stimulate purchases or encourage loyalty.

Consumer-generated content – Online content, often brand oriented, that is created by consumers for consumers.

Content marketing – A process of creating and distributing relevant content to attract, acquire, and engage a target audience.

Contest – A promotion that involves awarding cash or merchandise prizes to consumers when they purchase a specified product.

Contingency plan – The identification of alternative courses of action that can be used to modify an original plan if and when new circumstances arise.

Continuity – The length of time required in an advertising medium to generate the desired impact on the target audience.

Continuity discount (print) – A discount offered to advertisers that purchase space in consecutive issues of a publication.

Continuity discount (television/radio) – A discount for buying spots over an extended period.

Controlled circulation – The circulation of a publication that is distributed free to individuals in a specific demographic segment or geographic area.

Cookie – An electronic identification tag sent from a web server to a user's browser to track the user's browsing patterns.

Co-op allowance – See Cooperative advertising allowance.

Cooperative advertising allowance (co-op allowance) – The sharing of advertising costs by suppliers and retailers or by several retailers.

Cooperative direct mail – A mailing containing specific offers from non-competing products.

Core values – The primary attributes and benefits a brand delivers to the customer.

Corporate advertising – Advertising (paid for) designed to convey a favourable image of a company among its various publics.

Corporate culture – The values, beliefs, norms, and practices shared by all employees of an organization.

Corporate discount – A discount based on the total number of pages purchased by a single company (all product lines combined).

Corporate objective – A statement of a company's overall goal; used to evaluate the effectiveness or ineffectiveness of a company's strategic plan.

Corporate plan – A strategic plan formulated at the executive level of an organization to guide the development of functional plans in the organization.

Corporate strategy – See Strategic planning.

Cost-per-click – An Internet advertising pricing strategy where advertisers pay based on the number of ad clicks received.

Cost per thousand (CPM) – The cost of delivering an advertising message to 1000 people; calculated by dividing the cost of the ad by the circulation in thousands.

Cost per thousand (CPM) (online) – The price charged for displaying an ad 1000 times. The calculation for CPM is cost divided by impressions (number of impressions divided by 1000).

Coupon – A price-saving incentive offered to consumers to stimulate quick purchase of a specified product.

Creative brief – A document developed by a client organization that contains vital information about the advertising task at hand; it is a useful tool for discussions between the client and its advertising agency.

Creative concept – The basic sales message (a key idea) that an advertisement communicates through verbal and visual devices.

Creative execution – The stage of creative planning at which specific decisions are made regarding how to best present the message.

Creative objective – A statement that clearly indicates the information to be communicated to the target audience; usually involves a key benefit statement and a support claims statement.

Creative plan – A plan that outlines the nature of the message to be communicated to the target audience; involves the development of creative objectives, creative strategies, and creative execution.

Creative strategy – A plan of action for how the message will be communicated to the target audience, covering the tone and style of message, the central theme, and the appeal techniques.

Cross-coupon – See Cross-ruff.

Cross-ruff (cross-coupon) – A coupon packed in or with one product that is redeemable for another product. The product the coupon is packed with is the means of distributing the coupon.

Cross-tabulation – The comparison of answers to questions by various subgroups with the total number of responses.

Crowdsourcing – A technique that uses the collective intelligence of the public at large to complete business-related tasks a company would normally perform itself or outsource to a third-party provider.

Customer relationship management (CRM) – A process that enables an organization to develop an ongoing relationship with valued customers; the organization captures and uses information about its customers to its advantage in developing the relationship.

Data analysis – The evaluation of responses question by question; gives meaning to the data.

Data interpretation – The relating of accumulated data to the problem under review and to the objectives and hypotheses of the research study.

Data mining – The analysis of information to determine relationships among the data and enable more effective marketing strategies to be identified and implemented.

Data transfer – In marketing research, the transfer of answers from the questionnaire to the computer.

Database management system – A system that collects information about customers for analysis by managers to facilitate sound business decisions.

Day-after recall (DAR) test – Research conducted the day following the respondent's exposure to a message to determine the degree of recognition and recall of the advertisement, the brand, and the selling message.

Daypart – A broadcast time period or segment on radio or television.

Daypart targeting – The placement of online ads based on time of day.

Dealer display (point-of-purchase) material – Temporary display material placed in retail stores that advertises a product and encourages impulse purchasing.

Dealer premium – An incentive offered to a distributor to encourage the special purchase of a product or to secure additional merchandising support from the distributor.

Demographics – The characteristics of a population that include gender, age, education, income, occupation, and culture.

Demonstration – A sales technique that involves showing the product in action to portray its benefits to a buyer.

Diary system – A system to collect audience data where participants complete a seven-day log by recording the television viewing for all television sets in the household for each quarter hour of the day from 6 am to 2 am.

Digital (interactive) communications – The placement of an advertising message on a website, or an ad delivered by email or through mobile communications devices.

Digital video board – Outdoor advertising boards capable of displaying video content.

Dimensional mail – Direct mail that can take any form other than the typical flat piece of mail.

Direct competition – Competition from alternative products and services that satisfy the needs of a target market.

Direct mail – A printed form of direct response advertising distributed by Canada Post or independent delivery agents.

Direct marketing – A marketing system for developing products, sending messages directly to customers, and accepting orders through a variety of media, and then distributing the purchase directly to customers.

Direct response advertising – Advertising placed in a medium that generates an immediate and measurable response from the intended target.

Direct response communications – The delivery of a message to a target audience of one; the message can be distributed by direct mail, direct response television, or telemarketing.

Direct response print – A response-oriented ad delivered to prospects by magazines or newspaper advertisements.

Direct response television (DRTV) – Advertising that appears on television and encourages viewers to respond by telephoning a toll-free number, by mail, or online; often referred to as infomercials.

Directory database – A commercial database that provides information about a company (for example, size, sales, location, number of employees).

Divestment strategy – Selling off divisions or product lines that no longer fit the strategic direction an organization is taking.

Door card – A vertically oriented poster usually found beside the doors of subway cars and light rapid transit (LRT) commuter trains.

Double targeting – Market strategies that reach both genders effectively.

Editing stage – In marketing research, the review of questionnaires for consistency and completeness.

Elevator advertising – Advertising in display frames on elevator walls or on televisions mounted in the corner or above the door.

Encoding – The transformation of a message into a meaningful format, such as an advertisement, a mailing piece, or an article in a newspaper.

Endorsement – A situation where a celebrity speaks highly of an advertised product.

Engagement – The degree of involvement a person has with the media when using it.

Equivalent advertising value (AVE) – A mathematical calculation that considers the scale of coverage and positioning of a PR article and then estimates what a comparable amount of advertising space would cost.

Even schedule – The uniform schedule of media advertising over an extended period; also referred to as a continuous schedule.

Event marketing – The process, planned by a sponsoring organization, of integrating a variety of communications elements with a single event theme.

Event sponsorship – The financial support of an event in exchange for advertising privileges associated with that event.

Execution – See Tactics.

Expandable banner – A rich-media banner ad employing multiple panels that are launched when the banner is clicked on.

Experiential marketing – A form of marketing that creates an emotional connection with the consumer in personally relevant and memorable ways.

Experimental research – Research in which one or more factors are manipulated under controlled conditions while other elements remain constant so that the respondent's actions can be evaluated.

External publics – Those publics that are distant from an organization and are communicated with less frequently.

Eye movement–camera test – A test that uses a hidden camera to track eye movement to gauge the point of immediate contact in an advertisement, how the reader scans the ad, and the amount of time spent reading.

Feature – Tangible aspects of a product, such as durability, design, and economy of operation.

Field sales force – An organization's external sales representatives who regularly call on customers to pursue orders.

Fixed-response (closed-ended) questioning – Predetermined questions with set answers for the respondents to choose from.

Flight – A period of time in which advertising is scheduled.

Float – Money received by the issuer of a gift card without yet having offered any goods or services.

Floating ad – A rich-media ad that moves within a transparent layer over the page and plays with a specific area of the page.

Focus group – A small group of people with common characteristics brought together to discuss issues related to the marketing of a product or service.

Folder – A direct response sales message printed on heavy stock that can be mailed with or without an envelope; may be several pages in length.

Follow-up – Maintaining contact with customers to ensure that service has been satisfactory.

Format – The type and nature of the programming offered by a radio station.

Free sample – Free distribution of a product to potential users.

Free-standing insert (FSI) – A booklet featuring coupons, refunds, contests, or other promotional advertising distributed by direct mail or with newspapers, magazines, or other delivery vehicles.

Frequency – The average number of times an audience has been exposed to a message over a period of time, usually a week.

Frequency (online) – The number of times an ad is delivered to the same browser in a single session or time period. A site can use cookies to manage frequency.

Frequency discount (print) – A discounted page rate based on the number of times an advertisement runs.

Frequency discount (television/radio) – A discount based on the purchase of a minimum number of spots in a specified period.

Frequency distribution – The number of times each answer in a survey was chosen for a question.

Frequent buyer program – See Loyalty program.

Full wrap – An advertisement in the form of a vinyl covering that covers both sides and the back of the vehicle.

Game (instant-win promotion) – A promotional contest that includes a number of pre-seeded winning tickets; instant-win tickets can be redeemed immediately.

Gross rating points (GRPs) – An expression of the weight of advertising in a media schedule; calculated by multiplying reach by frequency.

Head-on positioning – A marketing strategy in which one product is presented as an equal or better alternative than a competing product.

Horizontal rotation – The placement of radio commercials based on the day of the week (same daypart on different days).

House list – An internal customer list.

Hypothesis – A statement of outcomes predicted in a marketing research investigation.

Image positioning – See Lifestyle positioning.

Impression (ad view) – An ad request that was successfully sent to a visitor. This is the standard way of determining exposure for an ad on the web.

Inbound telemarketing – The calls received by a company from consumers, whether to place an order, inquire about products or services, or in response to a toll-free telephone number promoted on a direct response television commercial.

Incentive – A free gift or offer included in a direct mail package.

Indirect competition – Competition from substitute products that offer the same benefit as another type of product.

Infomercial (long-form DRTV) – A long commercial (for example, 10 to 30 minutes) that presents in detail the benefits of a product or service; usually includes a call to action such as a 1-800 number. See also direct response television.

Innovation positioning – A marketing strategy that stresses newness (based on a commitment to research and development) as a means of differentiating a company or a brand from competing companies and brands.

In-pack self-coupon – A coupon for the next purchase of a product that is packed inside the package or under a label.

Insert – A preprinted, free-standing advertisement (for example, a leaflet, brochure, or flyer) specifically placed in a newspaper or magazine.

Inside sales force – An internal group of sellers, often referred to as order takers, who accept orders from customers by telephone or other means.

Instantly redeemable coupon – A removable coupon often located on the package or a store shelf that is redeemable on the current purchase of the product.

Instant-win promotion – See Game.

Integrated marketing communications – The coordination of all marketing communications in a unified program that maximizes the impact on the intended target audience.

Interactive communications – The placement of an advertising message on a website, or an ad delivered by email or through mobile communications devices.

Internal publics – The publics with which an organization communicates regularly; can include employees, distributors, suppliers, shareholders, and customers.

Internet radio – Listening to radio broadcasts via the Internet.

Key benefit statement – A statement of the basic selling idea, service, or benefit promised the consumer by the advertiser; appears in the creative plan section of an advertising plan.

King poster – An oversized poster attached to the side of a bus.

Leaderboard (Super banner) – An ad that stretches across the entire top of a webpage.

Leadership positioning – A marketing strategy in which a product presents itself as a preferred choice among customers.

Leaflet – A one-page flyer that offers relevant information about a direct mail offer.

Lifestyle (image) positioning – A marketing strategy based on intangible characteristics associated with a lifestyle instead of tangible characteristics.

Line rate – The rate charged by newspapers for one agate.

List broker – A company specializing in finding or developing lists for direct response purposes; finds prospect lists based on target market criteria established by marketing organizations.

Local spot – Advertising bought from a local station by a local advertiser.

Location-based targeting – An effort to integrate consumers' location information into a marketing communications strategy.

Long-form DRTV – See Infomercial.

Loyalty program (frequent buyer program) – A program that offers consumers a small bonus, such as points or play money, each time they make a purchase; the bonus accumulates and can be redeemed for merchandise or some other benefit.

Mail interview – In marketing research, the collection of information from a respondent by mail.

Mall poster – A form of advertising located inside shopping malls; relies on pedestrian traffic only.

Market share – The sales volume of one product or company expressed as a percentage of total sales volume in the market the company or brand is competing in.

Marketing communications plan – A plan that identifies how the various elements of marketing communications will be integrated into a cohesive and coordinated plan.

Marketing control – The process of measuring and evaluating the results of marketing strategies and plans, and of taking corrective action to ensure marketing objectives are achieved.

Marketing objective – A statement that identifies what a product will accomplish in a one-year period, usually expressed in terms of sales, market share, and profit.

Marketing plan – A short-term, specific plan of action that combines strategy and tactics.

Marketing planning – The analysis, planning, implementing, and controlling of marketing initiatives to satisfy target market needs and achieve organizational objectives.

Marketing research – A marketing function that links the consumer/customer/public to the marketer through information; the information is used to define marketing opportunities and problems, generate marketing strategies, evaluate marketing actions, and monitor performance.

Marketing strategy – A plan of action that shows how the various elements of the marketing mix will be used to satisfy a target market's needs.

Mass customization – The development, manufacture, and marketing of unique products to unique customers.

Media brief – A document that contains essential information for developing a media plan; used to stimulate discussion between a client and agency.

Media calendar (blocking chart) – A document that shows allocation of a brand's media budget according to time of year and type of medium; shows coordination of various media recommendations.

Media execution – The translation of media strategies into specific media action plans; involves recommending specific media to be used in the plan and negotiating the media buys.

Media kit – A package of relevant information associated with a product or organization that is distributed at a press conference.

Media objective – A statement that outlines what a media plan is to accomplish (who, what, when, where, or how).

Media plan – A document that outlines the relevant details about how a client's budget will be spent; it involves decisions about what media to use and how much money to invest in the media chosen to reach the target audience effectively and efficiently.

Media planning – Developing a plan of action for communicating messages to the right people (the target market), at the right time, and with the right frequency.

Media strategy – A plan for achieving the media objectives stated in the media plan; typically justifies the use of certain media.

Media-delivered coupon – Coupon packaged with another medium, such as newspapers, magazines, direct mail, in-store distribution, and the Internet.

Merge/purge – A process in which numerous mailing lists are combined and then stripped of duplicate names.

Microsite – An individual page or series of pages that is a supplement to a primary website.

Mid-roll ad – An ad placed during a video.

Mission statement – A statement of an organization's purpose and operating philosophy; provides guidance and direction for the operations of the company.

Modular advertising – Selling advertisements based on standardized sizes.

Monopolistic competition – A market in which there are many competitors, each offering a unique marketing mix; consumers can assess these choices prior to making a buying decision.

Motive – A condition that prompts an individual to take action to satisfy a need.

Mural advertisement – A hand-painted outdoor ad seen on the side of a building.

Native advertising – Paid advertising that matches the form and function of the user experience in the platform it appears in.

Need – The perception of the absence of something useful.

Negotiated rate – The rate ultimately paid by an advertiser as a result of negotiations between an ad agency and a particular medium.

Network advertising – Advertising from one central source broadcast across an entire network of stations.

New product development strategy – A marketing strategy that calls for significant investment in research and development to develop innovative products.

Newsletter – A document sent to a predetermined audience that contains news about an organization (for example, a newsletter sent to alumni of a school or to all employees of an organization).

Noise – Any potential form of disruption in the transmission of a message that could distort the impact of the message; competitive advertising or the clutter of advertising messages in a medium are forms of noise.

Non-probability sample – A sample of respondents who have an unknown chance of selection and are chosen because of factors such as convenience or the judgment of the researcher.

Non-verbal communication (body language) – The expression of thoughts, opinions, or information using non-verbal cues such as body movement, facial expressions, and eye contact.

Objection – An obstacle that a salesperson must confront during a sales presentation.

Objectives – Statements of what is to be accomplished in terms of sales, profit, market share, or other measures.

Observation research – A form of research in which the behaviour of the respondent is observed and recorded; may be by personal or electronic means.

Oligopoly – A market situation in which only a few brands control the market.

Online database – An information database accessible online to anyone with proper communications facilities.

Online selling – Using the Internet to conduct sales transactions.

Online sponsorship – A commitment to advertise on a third-party website for an extended period.

Online survey – In marketing research, using an online questionnaire to collect data from people.

On-pack self-coupon – A coupon that is printed on the outside of a package redeemable on the next purchase of the product.

Open-ended questioning – See Open-response questioning.

Open-response (open-ended) questioning – Space available at the end of a question where the respondents can add their comments.

Opinion-measure testing – A form of research yielding information about the effect of a commercial message on respondents' brand name recall, interest in the brand, and purchase intentions.

Opt-in list – A list of people who have agreed to receive messages via email.

Outbound telemarketing – Calls made by a company to customers to develop new accounts, generate sales leads, and even close a sale.

Overall goal – The objective of an advertising campaign.

Paid circulation – The circulation of a newspaper or magazine that is generated by subscription sales and newsstand sales.

Partnership selling – A strategically developed long-term relationship that involves selling products and providing comprehensive after-sales service and effective two-way communications to ensure complete customer satisfaction.

Pay-per-click advertising – See Search advertising.

Peer group – See Reference group.

Penetration strategy – A plan of action for aggressive marketing of a company's existing products.

Perception – The manner in which individuals receive and interpret messages.

Performance allowance – A discount offered by a manufacturer that encourages a distributor to perform a merchandising function on behalf of the manufacturer.

Permission-based email – Email sent to recipients who have agreed to accept email advertising messages.

Personal interview – The collection of information in a face-to-face interview.

Personal selling – Face-to-face communication involving the presentation of features and benefits of a product or service to a buyer; the objective is to make a sale.

Personality – A person's distinguishing psychological characteristics that lead to relatively consistent and enduring responses to the environment in which that person lives.

Podcasting – Audio programming that is downloadable to iPods and other portable digital media devices. Listeners listen when it is convenient for them to do so.

Point-of-purchase material – See Dealer display material.

Population (universe) – In marketing research, a group of people with certain age, gender, or other demographic characteristics.

Portable people meter (PPM) – A form of electronic observation in which household members carry electronic metering devices that register what is being watched on television every minute of every day.

Portal – A website that serves as a gateway to a variety of services such as searching, news, directories, email, online shopping, and links to other sites.

Position charge – The cost of requesting a preferred position in a newspaper.

Positioning – The selling concept that motivates purchase or the image that marketers desire a brand to have in the minds of consumers.

Positioning strategy statement – A summary of the character and personality of a brand and the benefits it offers customers.

Post-buy analysis – An evaluation of actual audience deliveries calculated after a specific spot or schedule of advertising has run.

Poster (billboard) – A common form of outdoor advertising; usually a picture-dominant advertisement with a minimum of copy.

Post-roll ad – An ad that appears after the video.

Post-testing – The evaluation and measurement of a message's effectiveness during or after the message has run.

Pre-approach – The gathering of information about customers before actually making sales contact.

Premium – An additional item given free, or greatly discounted, to induce purchase of the primary brand.

Pre-roll ad – An ad placed at the start of a video.

Presentation strategy – A plan of what to say to a customer in a sales presentation to identify customer needs, summarize benefits, and prepare for potential objections.

Press conference – A meeting called by an organization to present information to representatives of the media.

Press release – A document prepared by an organization containing public relations information that is sent to the media for publication or broadcast.

Pre-testing – The evaluation of commercial messages prior to final production to determine the strengths and weaknesses of the communications.

Price positioning – A marketing strategy based on the premise that consumers search for the best possible value given their economic circumstances.

Primary data – Data collected to resolve a problem and recorded for the first time.

Primary medium – A medium that receives the largest allocation of an advertiser's budget; the dominant medium in a media plan.

Primary research – The collection and recording of primary data.

Probability sample – A sample of respondents who are known to have an equal chance of selection and are randomly selected from the sampling frame.

Problem statement – A brief statement that summarizes a particular problem to resolve or an opportunity to pursue and serves as the focus of a marketing strategy.

Product advertising – Advertising that provides information about a branded product to help build its image in the minds of customers.

Product configuration – The bringing together of various products and services to form a solution for the customer.

Product differentiation strategy – A plan of action for communicating meaningful attributes and benefits of a product to a target market.

Product integration – See Branded content.

Product placement – The visible placement of brand name products in television shows, movies, radio, video games, and other programming.

Product seeding – Giving a product free to a group of trendsetters who promote the product to others by word of mouth.

Profile-matching strategy – A media tactic that involves matching the demographic profile of a product's target market with a specific medium that has a similar target profile.

Programmatic media buying – An automated media buying system that considers an advertiser's budget, objectives, and audience data. The system considers numerous variables in real time to determine the best media buy to produce the desired return on investment.

Promotional advertising – Advertising that communicates a specific offer to encourage an immediate response from the target audience.

Prospecting – A procedure for systematically developing sales leads.

Public relations – A form of communications designed to gain public understanding and acceptance.

Publicity – News about an organization, product, service, or person that appears in the media.

Publisher's statement – A statement published by the Alliance for Audited Media (AAM) twice a year that is the authority on which advertising rates are based.

Pull – Demand created by directing promotional activities at consumers or final users, who in turn pressure retailers to supply the product or service.

Pulse schedule – A scheduling of media advertising in flights of different weight and duration.

Pupilometer test – A device that measures pupil dilation (enlargement) of a person's eye when reading; it measures emotional responses to an advertisement.

Push – Demand created by directing promotional activities at intermediaries, who in turn promote the product or service among consumers.

Push down banner – A rich-media banner ad that slides advertising out of the way to reveal additional content rather than covering it up.

Qualifying (a customer) – Assessing if a prospect needs a product, has the authority to buy it, and has the ability to pay for it.

Qualitative data – Data collected from small samples in a controlled environment; the data describe feelings and opinions on issues.

Quantitative data – Measurable data collected from large samples using a structured research procedure.

Quick response (QR) code – A two-dimensional barcode that can be scanned and read by smartphones to allow sharing of text and data.

Rating – Television and radio audience estimates expressed as a percentage of a population in a defined geographic area.

Reach – The total unduplicated audience exposed one or more times to a commercial message during a specific period (usually a week).

Reach plan – Rotation of commercials in various dayparts on radio according to a predetermined frequency.

Real time bidding – An auction system in which advertisers bid against each other over ad impressions, in real time.

Rebate – A predetermined amount of money returned directly to customers by the manufacturer after the purchase has been made.

Recall test – A test that measures an ad's impact by asking respondents to recall specific elements (for example, the selling message) of the advertisement; can be aided (some information provided) or unaided.

Recognition test – A test that measures a target audience's awareness of a brand, copy, or the advertisement itself after the audience has been exposed to the message.

Rectangle ad – A large ad, slightly wider than it is tall, on a webpage.

Redemption rate – The number of coupons returned expressed as a percentage of the number of coupons that were distributed.

Reference group (peer group) – A group of people who share common interests that influence the attitudes and behaviour of its members.

Referral – A recommendation by a current customer of a potential new customer to a sales representative.

Relationship selling – A form of selling with the goal of developing a plan of action that establishes, builds, and maintains a long-term relationship with customers.

Reliability (of data) – Degree of similarity of results achieved if another research study were undertaken under similar circumstances.

Remnant time – Unsold television inventory available at lower cost to an advertiser.

Repositioning – Changing the place a product occupies in the customer's mind, relative to competing products.

Research objective – A statement that outlines what the marketing research is to accomplish.

Response card – A card filled in, usually at the time of purchase, that collects information about customers that can be added to the organization's database.

Response list – A list of direct mail buyers who have previously made purchases based on direct response offers.

Retail advertising – Advertising by a retail store; involves advertising the store name, image, location, and the re-advertising of branded merchandise carried by the store.

Rich media – A form of online communication that includes animation, sound, video, and interactivity.

Rifle strategy – A strategy that involves using a specific medium that effectively reaches a target market defined by a common characteristic.

Rotation plan – The placement of commercials in time slots purchased on radio; can be vertical according to the time of day or horizontal according to the day of the week.

Run sheet – A schedule of daily events that shows the various dates, times, and locations of activities at an event.

Sales presentation – A persuasive delivery and demonstration of a product's benefits; shows buyers how the product's benefits will satisfy their needs.

Sales promotion – An activity that provides incentives to bring about immediate response from customers, distributors, and an organization's sales force.

Sales promotion plan – An action plan for communicating incentives to appropriate target markets at the right time.

Sample – A representative portion of an entire population that is used to obtain information about that population.

Sampling frame – A list used to access a representative sample of a population; it is a means of accessing people for a research study.

Satellite radio – A radio service that offers commercial-free programming for a monthly fee.

Search advertising (pay-per-click advertising) – An advertiser's listing is placed within or alongside search results in exchange for paying a fee each time someone clicks on the listing.

Seasonal schedule – Scheduling media advertising according to seasonal sales trends; usually concentrated in the pre-season or the period just prior to when the bulk of the buying occurs.

Secondary media – Media alternatives used to complement the primary medium in an advertising campaign; typically less money is allocated to these media.

Secondary research – Data compiled and published by others for purposes other than resolving a specific problem. In advertising, secondary sources are frequently used to gain access to media information that benefits media analysis and planning.

Selective direct mail – See Solo direct mail.

Selective spot – Commercial time during a network show that is allocated back to regional and local stations to sell; advertisers buy spots on a station-by-station basis.

Self-image – One's own idea about oneself and one's relationship with others.

Setup – See Bump-in.

Seventy poster – A small poster usually affixed to the back of a bus.

Shopper marketing – Understanding how consumers behave as shoppers in all channels (retail, catalogue, and web) and then targeting these channels with appropriate marketing communications to enhance the sales of a brand.

Shotgun strategy – A tactic involving the use of mass media to reach a loosely defined target audience.

Short-form DRTV – 30- or 60-second commercials that run on cable channels.

Skip schedule – The scheduling of media advertising on an alternating basis, such as every other week or every other month.

Skyscraper – A vertical box-shaped ad that appears on a webpage.

Slippage – A situation in which a consumer collects labels in a promotion offer but fails to follow through and request the refund.

Slippage (breakage) – Gift cards that go unredeemed.

Slogan – A short phrase that captures the essence of an entire advertising campaign; it reflects the positioning strategy of the brand and is shown in all ads in all media.

Social media – Online tools that people use to share content, insights, experiences, and various media, thus facilitating conversations and interaction online between groups of people.

Social media network – A social website for example, Facebook and Twitter, that connects people with different interests together.

Socially responsible marketing – A form of marketing in which an organization conducts its operations in a manner beneficial to consumers and society.

Solo direct mail (selective direct mail) – A unique advertising offer mailed directly to a target audience by a marketing organization.

Spam – Unsolicited email.

Spectacular – See Superboard.

Spiff – An incentive offered to retail salespeople to encourage them to promote a specified brand of goods to customers.

Sponsored email – Email that includes a short message from a sponsor along with a link to the sponsor's website.

Sponsored post – A sponsored ad circulated by friends in a social network.

Sponsorship – The act of financially supporting an event in return for certain advertising rights and privileges.

Spot colour – The addition of one colour to an otherwise black-and-white newspaper or magazine ad.

Starch readership test – A post-test recognition procedure that measures readers' recall of an advertisement (noted), their ability to identify the sponsor (associated), and whether they read more than half of the written material (read most).

Statement stuffer (bounce back) – An ad or offer distributed in monthly statements or with the delivery of goods purchased by some form of direct response advertising.

Station domination – One advertiser purchases all advertising inventory available in a subway station.

Station poster – An advertisement located on the platform or at the entrance or exit of subways and light rail transit (LRT) systems.

Stickiness – A website's ability to keep people at the site for an extended period or to have them return to the site frequently.

Strategic alliance – A relationship between two companies where the resources of those companies are combined in a marketing venture for the purpose of satisfying the customers they share.

Strategic planning (corporate strategy) – The process of determining objectives (setting goals) and identifying strategies (ways to achieve the goals) and tactics (specific action plans) to help achieve objectives.

Strategic selling – A form of consultative selling that involves dealing with each customer as an individual, stressing that in the transfer of product information.

Strategies – Statements that outline how objectives will be achieved, such as the direction to be taken and the allocation of resources needed to proceed.

Streaming – Audio or video delivered online in small, compressed packets of data that are interpreted by a software player as they are received.

Street-level poster – A rear-illuminated unit consisting of two- or four-sided advertising faces, such as transit shelters and blocks or columns with advertising faces.

Subcultures – Subgroups within the larger cultural context that have distinctive lifestyles based on religious, racial, and geographical differences.

Super banner – See Leaderboard.

Superboard (spectacular) – Outdoor advertising that is larger than a normal poster and much more expensive to produce; can include extensions beyond borders and electronic messaging.

Support claims statement – A substantiation of the promise made in the key benefit statement; appears in the creative plan.

Survey research – The systematic collection of data by communicating with a representative sample by means of a questionnaire.

Sweepstakes – A chance promotion involving the giveaway of products or services of value to randomly selected participants.

SWOT analysis – An analysis procedure that involves an assessment of an organization's strengths, weaknesses, opportunities, and threats; strengths and weaknesses are internal variables, whereas opportunities and threats are external variables.

Tabloid – A smaller newspaper that is sold flat (not folded).

Tabulation – The process of counting various responses for each question in a survey.

Tactics (execution) – Action-oriented details that outline how a strategic plan will be implemented.

Tagline – A short phrase that captures the essence of an advertised message.

Target market – The group of persons for whom a firm creates and markets a product.

Targeting request – An ad placed to reach a specific target audience of a website, for which a premium is usually paid.

Teardown – See Bump-out.

Telemarketing – The use of telecommunications to promote the products and services of a business; involves outbound calls (company to customer) and inbound calls (customer to company).

Telephone interview – In marketing research, the collection of information from a respondent by telephone.

Test marketing – Placing a commercial, set of commercials, or print ad campaign in one or more limited markets that are representative of the whole to observe the impact of the ads on consumers.

Testimonial – An ad in which a typical user of the product presents the message.

Text messaging – The transmission of short text-only messages via cell phone.

Timeline Chart – A chart indicating when various planning activities start and finish.

Tip-in – An insert that is glued to a page in the publication using a removable adhesive.

Trade allowance – A temporary price reduction that encourages larger purchases by distributors.

Trade promotion – An incentive offered to channel members to encourage them to provide marketing and merchandising support for a particular product.

Trade show – An event that allows a company to show-case its products to a captive audience and generate leads.

Trademark – The part of a brand that is granted legal protection so that only the owner can use it.

Transient rate – A one-time rate, or base rate, that applies to casual advertisers.

Transit poster – A transit ad in the rack above the window or near the door of a bus or subway car.

Transmission – The sending of a message through a medium such as television, radio, newspapers, magazines, outdoor advertising, Internet, and so on.

Trial close – A failed attempt at closing a sale; the buyer said "no."

Unique selling point (USP) – The primary benefit of a product or service that distinguishes it from its competitors.

Unique visitor – The number of unduplicated visitors to a website during a specified period.

Universe – See Population.

Validity (of data) – A research procedure's ability to measure what it is intended to measure.

Venue marketing (venue sponsorship) – Linking a brand name or company name to a physical site, such as a stadium, arena, or theatre.

Venue sponsorship – See Venue marketing.

Verbal skills – Comfort and ability with speaking and listening.

Vertical rotation – The placement of radio commercials based on the time of day (within various dayparts).

Video strip – A rich-media banner ad that shows a strip of video in the banner space but, when clicked on, expands to reveal the video and audio in a full-sized panel.

Viewability – In online advertising when 50 percent of an ad is in view for at least one second.

Viral marketing – Online marketing that encourages the receiver of a message to pass it along to others to generate additional exposure.

Vision statement – A statement of what an organization would like to be.

Visit – A sequence of page requests made by one user at one website. A visit is also referred to as a session or browsing period.

Volume discount – A discount linked to the dollar volume purchased over an extended period; the greater the volume purchased, the higher the discount.

Volume discount (radio/television) – A discount based on the total number of spots bought in a specified period.

Wallpaper ad – A large image that replaces the web background.

Washroom advertising – A mini-poster ad located in a public or institutional washroom; usually placed above the urinal or on the back of the stall door.

Window ad – A rich-media ad that downloads itself immediately and plays instantly when a page is loading.

Word-of-mouth marketing – The transfer of a product message by people (often using technology) to other people.

Index